917.55 D263i
Davis
Intellectual life in Jefferson's Virginia

CHRISTIAN HERITAGE COLLEGE
2100 Greenfield Dr.
El Cajon, CA 92021

INTELLECTUAL LIFE IN JEFFERSON'S VIRGINIA

1790-1830

Publication of this book was sponsored by the American Association for State and Local History, Madison, Wisconsin, under its continuing program to promote a better understanding of our national heritage at a local level. It is the recipient of the Association's Manuscript Award for 1963.

Thomas Jefferson

Portrait by Rembrandt Peale. White House Collection.

917.55
D263i

#H101831 10/7/81

INTELLECTUAL LIFE IN JEFFERSON'S VIRGINIA

1790-1830

BY RICHARD BEALE DAVIS

Va--Intell life
Am lit--Va.

917.55

THE UNIVERSITY OF TENNESSEE PRESS: KNOXVILLE

55982

LIBRARY OF CONGRESS CATALOG CARD NUMBER 64-13548
INTERNATIONAL STANDARD BOOK NUMBER 0-87049-144-X

Second printing, 1972, by The University of Tennessee Press.

Reprinted by arrangement with The University of North Carolina Press. Copyright © 1964 by The University of North Carolina Press. All rights reserved. Manufactured in the United States of America.

In Memoriam

Henry Woodhouse Davis

Virginiensis

FOREWORD

This book is in large part an assemblage of evidence. It includes minutiae and details, many of them of little intrinsic separate value, which add up to what it is hoped is at least the broad outline of an image. The majority of the belletristic writers here discussed, for example, have left no great impression in the history of American literature. But they do offer through their work clues to an understanding of Virginia interests and tastes in a significant period, and a few of them deserve more attention generally than they have received. In some instances mere listing of titles, dates, and Virginia places of publication is indicative.

Admittedly the material of Chapter X, Politics and Economics, is in intellectual and general history the most appreciated and in many respects the most important. It has received relatively little space according to its importance, for it is the most familiar already, thanks to scores of published studies. Therefore the chapter, its political part especially, is more a summary and a recapitulation, really a reminder to the reader who has read the preceding nine chapters, than the fresh survey from largely primary or obscure secondary materials which the others attempt to be.

RICHARD BEALE DAVIS

The University of Tennessee
Knoxville, October, 1963

ACKNOWLEDGMENTS

A study of intellectual life in any age and clime should be indebted to many persons and institutions of varied character and interests. This is no exception. Individuals who have been most generous in supplying information and advice include Francis L. Berkeley, Jr., Irving Brant, Helen Duprey Bullock, Mrs. George P. Coleman, M. Boyd Coyner, Jr., George H. S. King, William M. E. Rachal, and Edward A. Wyatt, IV. Lynette Adcock, Research Archivist of Colonial Williamsburg; James A. Servies, Librarian of the College of William and Mary; John M. Jennings, Director of the Virginia Historical Society; Milton C. Russell, Chief of Reference of the Virginia State Library; and William A. Runge, Curator of Rare Books of the Alderman Library of the University of Virginia, also have been most helpful. As in several past instances, I am especially grateful for the assistance of Eleanor Goehring, Reference Librarian of the Hoskins Library of the University of Tennessee.

The cooperative staffs of the Library of Congress, the Virginia Historical Society, and the Virginia State Library made happy months spent in those institutions most fruitful. For lesser periods of time, the library personnel of several other institutions were equally helpful: the Universities of Duke, North Carolina, Virginia, and Yale; the Union Theological Seminary in Richmond; the New York Public Library; the Maryland and Pennsylvania Historical Societies; the American Philosophical Society; and the Henry E. Huntington Library.

A Huntington Library summer fellowship in 1950 and an American Philosophical Society grant in 1951-52 enabled me to work in San Marino, Philadelphia, and Washington during parts of those years. A research fellowship from the John Simon Guggenheim Memorial

Foundation in 1960-61 allowed me to complete the research and most of the first draft of the manuscript of this study. Without it I should probably have been many years longer in its composition. Finally, I must thank the University of Tennessee for subsidizing me in part during the Guggenheim year, and the English Department in particular for assistance in preparing the manuscript for publication.

TABLE OF CONTENTS

ILLUSTRATIONS

INTELLECTUAL LIFE IN JEFFERSON'S VIRGINIA

1790-1830

Immortal man! not only of thine own
The best and greatest, but of every age,
Thou whose meridian strength was prompt to wage
For liberty the war against a throne!
When thy gigantic mind had plac'd thee lone
And high, thou didst controul the wildest rage
of rival factions—scorning to assuage;
To thee all Nature's mysteries are known;
Oh! how shall we of less etherial mould
Address our souls to thine? Thy greatness weigh'd
Our love were too familiar and too bold;
Thy goodness, admiration were too cold;
But both united in men's hearts have made
A monument whose glory shall not fade.

"Sonnet to Mr. Jefferson," 1822,
by Dabney Carr Terrell
(Trist Papers, University of
North Carolina)

I

INTRODUCTION

Manners were not all their charm; for the Virginians at the close of the eighteenth century were inferior to no class of Americans in the sort of education then supposed to make refinement. . . . Those whom Liancourt called 'men of the first class' were equal to any standard of excellence known to history. Their range was narrow, but within it they were supreme. . . . Social position was a birthright, not merely of the well born, but of the highly gifted. . . . Law and politics were the only objects of Virginia thought; but within these bounds the Virginians achieved triumphs. . . .

Nowhere in America existed better human material than in the middle and lower classes of Virginia. As explorers, adventurers, fighters,—wherever courage, activity, and force were wanted,—they had no equals; but they had never known discipline, and were beyond measure jealous of restraint. . . . Among the common people, intellectual activity was confined to hereditary commonplaces of politics, resting on the axiom that Virginia was the typical society of a future Arcadian America.

—Henry Adams, *History of the United States,* I, 133-57

Between 1790 and 1830 Virginia assumed and developed a leadership in the affairs of the United States never held since by any single state. To be more precise, between her convention for ratification of the Federal Constitution in 1788 and her convention for the adoption of the new state constitution in 1829-30, the commonwealth held a political and intellectual primacy which was acknowledged and often envied by her sister states and indeed by much of the European world. Though she was the most populous and perhaps wealthiest state at the beginning of this period, Virginia's achievement was marked if not determined by the mental and moral character and political acumen of individual citizens. Four Virginians were Presidents for a total of thirty-two years; one was Chief Justice for thirty of these years; these men and others were secretaries of state, ambassadors, treaty-makers, explorers, soldiers, leaders in Congress, nationally known orators, and political theorists who shaped and expressed the mind of their time. The phrases "Virginia Dynasty" and "Virginia Breed" applied to them have been terms of approbation and opprobrium liberally employed by their contemporaries and later historians.

But the Virginians' intellectual and social origins, and even the nature of their minds and thinking, have never been thoroughly explored, much less elucidated. Many questions arise concerning them. Were they merely wealthy farmers in the most populous of the former colonies who seized the opportunity for power? Did they simply rationalize the rural way of life into an agrarian philosophy which they applied to society, economics, and politics? Did they lead such externally active lives that they lacked totally the introspection of the New England Puritan or his descendants?

What, other than agrarianism, shaped and conditioned their political theory? Were their minds purely political, relatively ignorant of or indifferent to the aesthetic and the belletristic? What did they read? Did they write anything other than political pamphlets and speeches?

How does one account for liberal and states' rights ideas of a Jefferson and the conservative-nationalistic ideas of a Marshall springing from the same environment? Did the Virginia mind really change on the slavery question?

Were only a handful of political leaders well educated? What did the Virginians believe and do about education?

Were they rationalists in religion who allowed or encouraged orthodox Christianity to be banished from their lives? Did they lack entirely the mechanical inventiveness of their New England contemporaries? Were they indifferent or hostile to the scientific trends of the time?

Were their greatest minds, men like Jefferson and Marshall, mere accidents of history, biological 'sports' radically differing from their fellows? Or putting it another way, was there a substratum of the same material beneath the surface leaders? If so, how far down the social scale did it go?

The discussions of these questions (certainly not final answers to them) in the chapters here following will bring the reader, it is hoped, to some understanding of intellectual life in Jefferson's Virginia. These discussions should illustrate the means of development and nature of the political mind through which Virginia made herself felt. They should demonstrate that this mind was not confined to one or two or three distinguished individuals but was evident in at least several hundred. And they should afford also conclusive evidence that the Virginia mind was not so narrowly political as some critics and historians have suggested, that it was broader in tastes and interests, wider in variety of reading, actually more fruitful in artistic and scientific accomplishment than has generally been recognized. And at least by implication these discussions will suggest that the *greatness* of the major minds among the Virginians who shaped the new nation was due at least partially to this breadth of general interest. Perhaps beyond any of their American contemporaries, they exemplified the best qualities of the Enlightenment which was just then disappearing in Europe, combining with it a sense of national destiny and necessity which turned occupationally many of them towards government and others as strongly toward religion, education, and even natural science.

Though they may have given the best years of their lives to one or more of these services, most of them felt that they were amateurs in all fields except one, farming. A few dozen others believed that the law was the most generally rewarding of livelihoods. From both groups came statesmen and politicians. The farmers usually entered government service with a traditional sense of *noblesse oblige,* the town lawyers from personal ambition, but there might be a mixture of motives in either, and genuine patriotism accompanied both the other motives. Some of the best minds, men like St. George Tucker of Williamsburg, John H. Cocke of Bremo, and John Holt Rice of Richmond, were not in any real sense politicians at all. They were concerned primarily with theoretical jurisprudence, general learning, social reform, evangelical religion, or belles-lettres. Each of these three was conscious, for example, that Virginia would not really become "a great nation" until its spiritual and aesthetic side measured up to its political, and they attempted in various ways to bring about the equilibrium.

Those Virginians of "the middle and lower classes" referred to by Henry Adams as fighters and explorers had their part in the Virginia mind and showed remarkable intellectual kinship with the Jeffersons and Randolphs. A Baptist frontier preacher, a Shenandoah Valley German-speaking printer, and a Scottish-born vituperative scandal-monger were among several score of those of humbler social station who wrote and were written about, who read and talked their way into the shaping of intellectual life.

A. *Colonial Heritage*

Though in the twentieth century a number of admirable studies in depth have increased our understanding of the New England colonial, in broad outline and even in most details he was depicted faithfully more than a century ago. Only within the last generation has the colonial Virginian been explored and interpreted by acute critical minds, and even now all the facets of his character and mind have not been satisfactorily presented. But the nineteenth century's concept of a swashbuckling cavalier, intent only on good living and material returns from his tobacco plantation, has been altered so as to be almost completely unrecognizable.

The seventeenth-century Virginian, freeman or redemptioner, usually came to the colony with the ambition of producing for himself and his heirs the rural life of England, not the atmosphere of London or a Calvinist utopia. His social background varied, but usually he came from middle-class origins, or was the younger-son-of-a-younger-son of the lesser gentry, as British settlers throughout the world so frequently have been. Blessed in his new home with a temperate climate and impelled by the economic necessity of outdoor life, he had neither the dreary days, nor the leisure if he had them, for the kind of introspection in which his neighbors to the north indulged. Though he put pen to paper in most instances to tally up his accounts or communicate with his London factors or friends, he was by no means without intellectual life or aesthetic enjoyment.

No matter what he had been born to, in his particular circumstances the English ideal of the country gentleman seemed the *summum bonum*. And he was close enough in memory to the mother country to comprehend fully the advantages and obligations of that ideal. Not all men completely realized the image they envisioned, for despite older historical conceptions, there was a strong small-farmer class, the majority of the white population, which in form corresponded roughly to the yeomanry of England. But those who did succeed in rising to their ideal, and there were many, became the principal instruments in perfecting a vital and significant society. The large-scale Virginia planter did achieve by and large what he set out to do and to be, but what he fashioned went far beyond the usual concept of the English squirearchy.

In external form Virginia plantation owners and English country gentlemen were the same. Born (in the colony sometimes after one generation) to privileges and responsibilities, they paid attention first to manners, to a code of conduct. Their virtues owed perhaps as much to Aristotle and Horace as to Christianity. They aimed to please. Grace in dancing, fencing, ability in conversation, personal perfection, proper proportion in everything, these were general requisites. Learning should be broad rather than necessarily profound, but a gentleman must know how to read Greek and Latin. Books like

Henry Peacham's *The Compleat Gentleman* (1622) and its successors for a century guided them in their reading and their manners.

As recent studies of the rebel Nathaniel Bacon have pointed out, it is still difficult to see the seeds of popular government or revolution in early colonial Virginia. What is obviously there is the intellectual heritage of training as gentlemen which comes straight from the seventeenth to the early nineteenth century and helps a great deal in explaining the early national Virginian.

The Virginia social classes and their intellectual habits were not precisely identical with their alleged parallels in Great Britain. The country squire had become a tobacco planter, the yeoman's opposite number was an adventurous small farmer tilling his soil on a wild frontier, and the peasant had been replaced by the African slave. Except for the slave, the New World society was definitely more fluid than that of the old. The planter's younger sons, unless they managed well their modest patrimonies in land, were likely to sink into the small farmer class. The church, the army, and the counting house were not open to them. The frontier yeoman-farmer, on the other hand, frequently in a generation or two, if he added lands and other property to his original tract, entered the ruling class. Or an Indian trader like William Byrd I might amass a fortune in business and move into the landed proprietor class. Although this landed aristocracy was thus relatively fluid, as a class it reigned supreme by the end of the seventeenth century.

No planter would think of shirking civic duties. County justice of the peace, member of the House of Burgesses or the Council, he assumed the sometimes onerous responsibilities as a matter of course. His fellow justices and burgesses were his kin or at least his neighbors. With them he could debate and resolve on equal terms. The long detailed journals and minutes of the House of Burgesses, for example, in which many speeches are given in full, afford little evidence of flowery language or learned rhetoric which might have been directed at a more general audience, but for almost two centuries they do show close reasoning and thoughtful consideration of theories of law and government, as well as a sharply conscious sense of history and even of American destiny. Quite clearly too, these legislative records indicate that the Virginia gentleman was not a citizen of the world and sometimes hardly conscious that he was a British subject

He was always aware of what he called the rights of Englishmen, and of Justinian's natural right, and towards the end of the era was applying the rights theory peculiarly to himself. Like other Americans, he preferred to start and stay with his own problems.

The graceful though modest frame and brick houses still surviving along the banks of the great rivers in Tidewater or perched on commanding hills in Piedmont indicate his good taste in architecture, and in their high windows and well-disposed rooms his sense of the useful. The house was usually equipped with articles straight from England—furniture, hangings, portraits of his friends and of his family. Except for his everyday homespun, even his clothes were English in fashion and material. Sometimes he had a servant who could copy furniture, make hinges and nails, and fashion doors and windows. Sometimes an itinerant painter limned his and his wife's features for posterity. The planter himself was likely to own a number of books on architecture and the simpler home manufactures.

"Better never be born than ill bred," wrote one planter to a friend in England as he sent his son abroad for an education. Contrary to certain older beliefs about him, almost every great Virginia landowner felt fiercely this desire for education. Surviving letters and account books are full of evidences of his endeavors to educate his children. Sometimes he imported a servant who could teach his and his neighbors' offspring in a school set up in one of his dependencies; sometimes the parish clergyman, or a Huguenot immigrant, would take the planter's children as boarders and instruct them in ancient and modern languages and some mathematics; towards the end of the period scattered throughout the colony were small privately owned schools roughly analogous to the English grammar schools, in which Greek and Latin, arithmetic and algebra, a little history and philosophy were drilled into young Jeffersons or Pages or Carrs. Just before the Revolution one finds Robert Carter of Nomini Hall preferring a tutor from an American university to one from a Scottish or English institution. Then, too, many were sent back to England to school, as a Lee to Yorkshire and a Fitzhugh to Bristol.

Higher education was not so universal among this ruling class, but there was a good deal of it. Figures gathered some decades ago show that there were less than three dozen Virginia matriculates at Oxford and Cambridge before the Revolution, though among them were representatives of most of the leading families. Many Virginians did have law training in the London Inns of Court, notably William Byrd II and some of the Revolutionary generation. And an appreciable number received medical or general education at Edinburgh, as they continued to do into the nineteenth century.

But the majority of university-trained Virginians received their education at the College of William and Mary, their own institution chartered late in the seventeenth century. From her first decade the colony had been conscious of the need for advanced training, and by the time of the 1622 Massacre "an university" at Henrico (near the present Richmond) was in operation, with an endowment in lands, a staff of servants, and an administrative official hard at work. When all the college personnel were murdered by the Indians, the colonial officials decided to wait for better times to begin anew.

William and Mary, which will be discussed in some detail later in this book, was consciously organized to train church and secular leaders for the colony. From its inception the sound classical and mathematical learning it offered was comparable to that of the British universities. Within a decade of its founding, the student orators of the graduation exercises of 1699 all implied or stated that their education and all colonial education was aimed at producing the leaders needed in their colony. They also spoke of the advantages of a Virginia education over one abroad (one should compare Jefferson on the same subject) and of what a well-rounded gentleman ought to be. There are other evidences too that social and political as well as spiritual and aesthetic concepts were woven into the education of the planter from the very beginning of his native college.

Since there was no public printing press in the colony until 17[illegible], most Virginians imported all their reading matter before that date from Europe. They continued to do so into the nineteenth century, for not until then were American presses producing in volume and variety what they wanted to read. New England printing never had much attraction for them, except among certain of the Presbyterians. Local and regional journals have in recent years afforded ample evidence of the presence of books in the plantation houses. Wills and inventories often give exact titles. Smaller planters might bequeath a bundle or a shelf of books. William Fitzhugh, who had started his career in Virginia in 1670 at nineteen, managed to leave a roomful to his two elder sons in 1701. And the Carters, Lees, Wormeleys, and Byrds collected distinguished libraries indicative of the breadth and versatility of their owners. John and Peyton Randolph, like William Byrd II, not only owned thousands of volumes in a dozen languages (which apparently they could read) but carefully gathered discarded official records of the colony, invaluable documents which eventually found their way through Jefferson's care into our Library of Congress.

Prevented from direct and daily communication with his peers by the exigencies of plantation life, the colonial found intellectual comfort in the books he ordered as regularly as he did his clothing and other necessities. Usually to be found in his library was Henry Peacham's *The Compleat Gentleman* or later books of the same stripe, or other general outlines of knowledge. There were some volumes of language and rhetoric, collections of aphorisms and eloquence, and handbooks of various kinds. From the early seventeenth to the nineteenth century he devoured histories, including Raleigh, Rushworth, Pufendorf, Boyer, and a number describing his own colony—John Smith, Henry Norwood, Robert Beverley, and William Stith. Frequently he owned treatises on ideal commonwealths (not to be forgotten as one reads the later John Taylor of Caroline), and usually, almost universally, devotional works such as *The Whole Duty of Man.* The Greek and Latin classics, philosophy, medicine, and light reading were represented usually in proportion to the overall size of his library, with due allowance for individual tastes. John Locke's great *Essay Concerning the Human Understanding,* destined to be influential in the Revolutionary generation, was already in Virginia libraries in the late seventeenth century. Indeed, there are many instances of the ordering of books before they were published in England. Despite the three thousand miles of ocean, there was little cultural lag in books and reading through the whole colonial period and actually down to 1830.

Most plantation owners included a number of legal volumes in their collections. Many, like William Byrd II, William Fitzhugh I, Robert Beverley I, and Ralph Wormeley II had been trained in the law, either at the Inns of Court or under some English or American barrister, in the latter case as later Virginians were to be trained until (and after) George Wythe's time. No man who owned lands, especially one who bought and sold and speculated in tracts on the frontier, could afford to live without legal knowledge. Property and laws and theory of property were all involved in his concepts of human rights long before even John Locke. And as a county justice and colonial legislator he needed theories of government of men and laws and nations: Filmer, Locke, Machiavelli, and Guicciardini he refers to in his letters. In the later colonial period Locke, Montesquieu, and Rousseau are frequently on his lips. He read these latter not so much to learn how to conduct his government as to receive approbation and confirmation in the political path already taken. The philosophers' vision of the heavenly city-country corroborated his reality.

The planter's library in the eighteenth as well as the seventeenth century contained many religious works. Whatever rationalism may have replaced his earlier orthodox Anglicanism by 1725, he continued to buy, acquire by inheritance, or at any rate to read, learned tomes of scriptural commentary, and above all sermons. From William Perkins through Tillotson to Hervey and Blair, the British divines were well represented. His letters tell us that he read them, Presbyterian or Anglican, Calvinistic or latitudinarian though they were. The devout treatises from the pens of his fellow Virginians, James Blair and Samuel Davies, he devoured in their multi-volumed form well into the nineteenth century. Even Jefferson's grandchildren at Monticello read and apparently enjoyed—they wrote with some excitement about them—several volumes of the eighteenth-century theologians. William Byrd's theological library bears comparison with Cotton Mather's, and so do many others with those of their New England contemporaries.

But there appears to have been some difference in the manner in which the saints of New England and the Virginia planters read and interpreted theology and ecclesiastical history. The Anglican Reverend Hugh Jones remarked somewhat drily in 1741 that in the Virginia church he found "enthusiasm, deism, and libertism" side by side. About the same time (1737) in remarkable prose Sir John Randolph's will indicates a beginning of Christian Deism in a Virginia mind. These men and others before and after show a religious tolerance which has a long and honorable history. Though it did not always extend to all sects and theories, it had been in active practice as early as the 1680's when the first Roman Catholic was admitted to the Virginia General Assembly. Whatever the shade of his orthodoxy or heterodoxy, the planter knew and exercised his responsibility as a parish vestryman, experiencing in that capacity, as Bishop Meade and Philip A. Bruce have suggested, the larger problems of taxation and representation in the smaller problems of election and support of the clergy.

The first settlers had been interested in American fauna and flora, in meteorology, and in the ways of the aborigine. For two centuries they sent specimens of plants and animals and Indian weapons, tools, and costumes to interested persons in the mother country. John Banister, John Mitchell, and John Clayton, respectively clergyman, physician, and lawyer as well as planters, made genuine contributions to botanical and zoological knowledge. Others assayed and shipped specimens of soil or ore. Mitchell and Byrd, among others, were members of the Royal Society. No major scientific treatise came from the colonials, unless one counts the Gronovius *Flora Virginica* (1739-43) based on Clayton's work, but the intelligent observations by Beverley, Byrd, and others were of considerable interest to English scientists.

From the time of William Parks until the Revolution, there was in the little capital at Williamsburg a newspaper which presented almost all the aspects of colonial intellectual life. The *Virginia Gazette* in its book and merchandise advertisements reflects reading, architectural, and decorative taste. Its news notes, copied from European journals or originating in the colonies, were almost all political. Letters signed with classical Greek or Roman pseudonyms are concerned usually with political matters, though some contain poetic and dramatic criticism. Many are really good informal essays modeled on *The Spectator* or *The Rambler.* Poems by the more popular English versifiers are printed frequently, from Pope to Stephen Duck. And there are dozens of rhymed pieces clearly originating among the Virginia newspaper subscribers, many of them worthy of modest comparison with the English verse.

The *Gazette* was not the first nor the only printed outlet for the mind eager to express itself. Before it existed a number of Virginians, compilers of laws, historians, occasional sermon writers, and a few belle-lettrists, had had their works printed in England. Some things continued to bear London imprints even after printer Parks set up shop. But the *Gazette* publisher himself turned out books and pamphlets on varied subjects and occasions. His list includes the first great political tracts heralding the Revolution and a volume of verse, William Dawson's *Poems on Several Occasions by a Gentleman of Virginia.* That a William Byrd or the anonymous author of "Bacon's Epitaph" should leave his work in manuscript may be due partly to the Renaissance gentlemanly tradition which discouraged publication of one's own effusions, but it was just as likely to have been the result of the practical difficulties of English publication. From the autograph poems, essays, sermons, even letters constantly being discovered and printed in our time, we know that the Virginia planter was not without his aesthetic yearnings and sometimes real abilities, that he who sat with pen in hand inditing a wistful letter to his London factor might have been in another age—or even in a colder or rockier clime—recognized as a thinker and man of letters.

The ruling class had not from the beginning ever been quite purely English in blood. A French soldier and author, Peter Arondelle, had been an honored member of the first generation of colonists. Throughout the seventeenth century, especially after the Edict of Nantes, the French Protestants flocked to Virginia. Their clergy often filled Anglican pulpits and all of them settled and intermarried with English planter families. One colonial congregation complained bitterly about their minister's French accent. But more often the parishioners eagerly sent their children to the schools conducted by the exiles. About 1690 William Fitzhugh could inform his English friend that his eleven-year-old son spoke and wrote French easily but had difficulty making himself understood in English! Perhaps this early French infiltration is to some extent responsible for the almost universal ability to read French, and frequently to speak it, among educated Virginians on through Jefferson's time. And concomitantly it may be partly responsible for their familiarity with French thought and fashions, as they were not familiar with those of Germany or Italy.

Scottish names are frequent in the colony from the mid-seventeenth century, especially among the Anglican clergy. But in the eighteenth century the several waves of Scotch-Irish and Scottish immigrants through Pennsylvania and Virginia seaports, immigrants moving into the Shenandoah Valley and southwest Virginia, came to form a recognized part of the Virginia religious and political mind. Establishing little centers of Presbyterian culture where they themselves were most thickly settled, in Lexington in the Valley or in Prince Edward county in the south-central region, they rose steadily to an influential place in the colony, in a few cases into the ruling class itself. Believing in education and possessing an educated clergy, they supplied tutors to Anglican families and persuaded several of the latter to send their sons to the Presbyterian grammar schools in Virginia or to the Presbyterian college at Princeton.

The Germans moved down the Valley of Virginia with the Scots. Not quite so insistent on learning and education as their Anglo-Celtic neighbors, probably because most of them were purely peasant in origin, they did establish at such places as New Market, Staunton, and Woodstock cultural centers later in the Jeffersonian period to blossom with schools and even one famous printing and publishing house.

These two sturdy ethnic groups, clinging generally to the orthodox Protestantism of Calvin and Luther but leaning at times toward the evangelical and pietistic, were to influence the Virginia mind of the first national period particularly in its religious aspects, indeed to turn its traditional latitudinarianism towards a narrower and less liberal attitude. Desiring governmental tolerance for themselves, they were wary of unorthodoxy (or rationalism) in the education of youth. Jefferson was to feel their power when he tried to gather the best minds regardless of religious belief for his first university faculty. And they, especially the Scots, were to have some part in familiarizing all Virginians with Scottish philosophy and critical theory. But this is anticipating.

Historians usually call the period of a generation and a half before the Revolution the golden age of the plantation aristocracy, for then they were wealthiest and most powerful. Within the form of a tolerant oligarchy, they ruled a generally happy and moderately prosperous people. Through their speculation in the vast tracts of undeveloped land along the frontier they saw an infinite continuation of their way of life. But mountain barriers, French and Indian opposition, the vast distances themselves, added to the weaknesses of their wasteful agricultural system and worn-out lands, were among a multitude of factors even then about to bring disaster upon them. In the first generation after the Revolution, as their political power and economic wealth crumbled, they actually had their finest hour. As they were being absorbed into the democracy which led to Jackson they were able to leave their permanent impression on the American mind. For it is not so much their manner of living, as the manner and content of their thinking, which has survived.

B. *The Revolutionary Generation*

Between 1763 and 1789, through the quarter century of local debate and united rebellion, open warfare, military losses and triumphs and postwar problems, to the adoption of the Constitution, the Virginia mind was concerned with many of the same problems which faced the rest of America. The ruling class in the commonwealth at last had a real opportunity to exercise leadership in the phase of human activity it knew best, politics. Outside their borders the agrarians found themselves allied with strange partners—New England clergy, New York merchants, and Pennsylvania Quakers. Within their own boundaries they discovered that the mountain frontiersmen and Scottish Presbyterians had become so strong in number and influence that they too had to be reckoned with. The aristocratic leaders were gratified when these latter groups became in the open-warfare phase of the period willing partners.

A long history of legislative insistence on the rights of Englishmen, of pondering various theories of natural right, of being taken advantage of by greedy English tobacco merchants, among the ponderables, had by 1763 made the Virginia planter ripe for protest and then for rebellion. As in other colonies, some leaders remained loyal to the Crown, sometimes men from the same families became the most active rebels. But in Virginia even the Anglican clergy as a whole supported the Revolution, far more than they did elsewhere, and Deists, Presbyterians, Baptists, Methodists, and orthodox Anglicans united behind Henry, Mason, Jefferson, Peyton Randolph, and a dozen others, all, with the half-exception of Henry, from the old ruling aristocracy. Conscious of the great republican examples of Greece and Rome, increasingly irked by the arbitrary dictation of a distant power and immediately by the taxation which seemed to violate their rights of every kind, accustomed to legislative argument and the composition of political essays for the *Virginia Gazette,* they became in the twelve or so years before independence gradually conscious of where they were heading, and they rejoiced in it.

After the Declaration, to be entirely consistent champions of an agrarian republic designed to give every man the rights England would have denied him, they had to give up certain things. One of these was the Established Church. Not without a fight, the more liberal among them proposed and finally had adopted a statute for religious freedom. Another sacrifice was primogeniture, fairly easily obliterated because it had never had too firm a hold. A third was private education exclusively for their own class. A full plan for a state educational system, fought over for many years, was not adopted until 1796. A fourth blot on the escutcheon (and an economic handicap), as almost every gentleman in the 1770's acknowledged, was slavery. Yet Jefferson was not allowed by other colonies to include a denunciation of it in the Declaration of Independence, and in the second ensuing generation the idea of emancipation became less and less popular in Virginia itself for reasons to be discussed in subsequent chapters.

As to the role the small farmer, frontier fighter, and artisan were to play in the new nation, these leaders were not all of one mind. Actually they ranged along a spectrum of opinion in this question all the way from total enfranchisement and total equality for "all men" to large property qualifications for any voice in affairs. "All men" even with the more liberal usually did not yet include the slaves. But one of the heartening episodes of human history, never satisfactorily explained otherwise by the scholarly or the sceptical, is the aristocratic championship of the common man by the Wythes, Masons, and Jeffersons of the Virginia of this quarter century. Children of the Enlightenment to be sure—certainly long thinkers on the relation of the individual to government—sharing with the small farmers occupational and economic problems alien to the merchant or industrialist and thus opposed to a government favoring business and "paper capital"—these men in debate and essay voiced, and undoubtedly felt, some of the greatest and noblest of social ideals. When they later came to power, they tried to put these ideals into practice.

Virginia liberalism, like all liberalism everywhere in all times, varied in form and object and degree from individual to individual. From the ungainly Patrick Henry to the polished Richard Henry Lee, there was remarkable unanimity in the cry for liberty and the determination to resist oppression. But a patriotic Pendleton held out for primogeniture, a dozen leaders for the Established Church, and many more for leaving education as it was. When they were faced with the question of ratification of a constitution for a stronger central government, they were almost evenly divided, and only the cogent reasoning and personal prestige of Madison, Edmund Randolph, and Washington won out over the misgivings of Patrick Henry, Richard Henry Lee, and William Grayson. In the years to follow, new alignments and alliances springing from new situations and old moved these same individuals and their younger followers toward positions labeled Federalist and Republican, conservative and liberal.

To the remarkable polemic writing of the period they contributed at least their share. And to political policy and theory they gave distinguished utterance. Perhaps in oral debate they were at their best, whether in the House of Burgesses and the subsequent state legislature or the Continental Congress and the Federal Constitutional Convention. But except in scattered instances such as Madison's notes on the national Convention of 1788, their persuasive arguments have not survived, or if surviving remain only in abbreviated and garbled form. It is in printed speeches and pamphlets alone that the reader today can gauge their persuasive powers and their political philosophy.

Between 1763 and 1775 committees of correspondence with the other colonies, legislative juntos concentrating on particular phases of stamp act or excise tax tyranny, or county resolves (such as that of Westmoreland) demonstrated to their contemporaries their alertness and the strong feelings which impelled their words. Writing in simple prose (one recalls the colonial's long practice in communications to his neighbors and fellow Burgesses), they did not fail to mention philosophic theories of right and the example of ancient republics and tyrannies. As individual writers the Virginians were even more effective, both in this period of prelude and later in the struggle over the Constitution.

Arthur Lee's *Monitor's Letters* (1768), printed originally in Rind's *Virginia Gazette,* were published in book form combined with John Dickinson's *Farmer's Letters,* to which they were a conscious sequel. Though not so probing or comprehensive as Dickinson's, they remain significant as a statement of the colonial position of the moment. Later in London in 1769 Lee addressed to the British press a series of letters signed "Junius Americanus." He did his best pamphleteering in *An Appeal to the Justice and Interests of Great Britain* in 1774 and in a *Second Appeal* in 1775.

Arthur's brother Richard Henry Lee, who as orator had performed distinguished service in the General Assembly and had moved the resolution for independence in the Continental Congress, in 1787 took the side opposed to the new Constitution, and in his *Letters of a Federal Farmer to a Republican* made the strongest printed statement of the case against adoption. As a recent historian has pointed out, if the Constitution had failed of ratification Lee's *Letters* might have the place among our political documents now accorded to *The Federalist.*

George Mason, best known for his Declaration of Rights, published his first state paper in 1773, *Extracts from the Virginia Charters, with Some Remarks upon Them,* a pamphlet which among other things convinced Virginians of the western extent of their sovereignty. Formulator of resolutions and writer of open letters to London merchants, he stated the constitutional position of the colonies for readers on both sides of the Atlantic. In 1776 he was the principal framer of the Virginia Constitution which included his own Declaration. Driven into retirement by his disgust at the state of affairs during the Confederation, he emerged again in 1787-88 as a member of the national Constitutional Convention. On the whole he was a constructive force in framing the Constitution, but in the final days he refused to sign because of certain excluded and included statements on which he felt strongly. His "Objections to the Federal Constitution" (1788), on the basis of which he conducted a campaign against ratification in the Virginia Convention, has proved to have been in many respects well founded. In at least two cases his objections have been written into the Constitution—in the Bill of Rights of the first ten amendments and the judiciary clause of the eleventh (1798). In a third instance, his principal reason for refusing to sign, he has been borne out by history. A consistent opponent of slavery all his life, he here objected to the compromise incorporated in the Constitution between New England and the extreme South on tariff and the slave trade.

As a youthful member of the House of Burgesses Thomas Jefferson proved his fitness for membership in the Continental Congress by his *Summary View of the Rights of British America* (Williamsburg, 1774), in which the denial of the authority of the British Parliament to legislate for the colonies was based upon "natural rights" rather than upon the more usual "rights of Englishmen." Within a year the pamphlet was republished in Philadelphia and London, the latter edition including a preface in the form of a letter "To the King" written by Arthur Lee. Basing American claims upon the right of expatriation and upon interpretation of early Saxon legal principles, it challenged the right of the King to make grants of land or set up governments in America of his own authority, and it advanced the proposition that a colonizing community had a right to the lands within the bounds it had set round itself.

When two years later the time came to compose the Declaration of Independence, Jefferson referred to "inalienable" rather than "natural" rights. His argument then was that the King had violated the law of nature by encroachment upon his colonial subjects' inalienable rights. Clearly Lockean in its argument, it is more than a mere statement of what was in the air, as the author modestly and somewhat querulously remembered years later. And surely its form and parliamentary logic would hardly have been what they were had it been written by one not brought up in Virginia legal and legislative debate from his early youth. "The Great Declaration" is an immortal expression of the American mind couched in terms long familiar to Virginia's ruling class.

From the battle over the Constitution emerged what the first historian of American literature, Samuel L. Knapp, called in 1829 the foremost American literary production,[1] whether considered from the point of view of form, style, or content, *The Federalist*. The joint work of Jay, Hamilton, and Madison, in eighty-five letters, it is naturally somewhat uneven and at times inconsistent, though remarkably effective as an expression of the case for the Constitution. Jay wrote only five numbers, Hamilton fifty-four, and Madison the remaining twenty-six, it is believed today. Madison's part in it, including the famous Tenth (on Faction), is now acknowledged as the ablest part in style, cogency of reasoning, and far-seeing statement of theory and principle. More of this in a later chapter. But one may note in passing regarding Madison's portion the familiar appeals to ancient and modern historical precedent, the use of Montesquieu as a point of departure in three essays, and the serious doubts as to the justice of numerical majorities, all characteristic of the earlier and later Virginia mind.

While he was Governor of Virginia during the Revolution Jefferson began gathering material for answers to a questionnaire sent him by the French diplomat, François Marbois. It had been sent to other persons in other states too, for it concerned the nature of the individual former colonies. The twenty-two queries, arriving in the midst of the vexations and perils of war, turned the recipient again to a natural interest of his, the history and resources of his native state. Immediately upon his retirement from office he concentrated on completing the answers. Virginia scientists, soldiers, and explorers sent him information on such things as fossils, Indians, and the Mississippi river. Peachy Gilmer once declared that Jefferson owed all the geographical section to his neighbor Dr. Thomas Walker.[2] It was thus in one sense a cooperative Virginia enterprise. At any rate, by December, 1781, he could notify Marbois that the task was done, though later he added and revised considerably.

Originally he seems to have had no idea of publishing his commentaries. By 1784 when the interest the manuscript excited among his friends brought a resolution to publish, he found Philadelphia printing costs too high. He took the enlarged and revised manuscript with him to France in that same year and by May, 1785, had a French-printed limited edition in circulation among a few friends. Alarmed that a French bookseller might publish a pirated edition in French, he agreed with the Abbé Morellet for an authorized edition in that language and soon made arrangements with the English printer Stockdale for a general edition of the original. During the author's lifetime *The Notes on the State of Virginia* was reprinted many times.

What Jefferson published remains in form primarily a handbook, not a unified development of a major thesis leading toward a climax or single impression. Beginning with a description of the boundaries of Virginia, still the largest state in the Confederation, the writer was led into a discussion of the great West. Then from consideration of natural resources he emerged in a contemplation of the problem of the physical characteristics of men and animals. From this he went on to "the nature of governments, the relation between the individual and society, and the enigma of man's being."[3] In one place or another he attacked the kind of vested interests in Virginia and the other colonies which he fought all his life. Slavery, the Indian, geography, mineralogy, meteorology, zoology, botany, population, the legal and constitutional history of the colony and state, education, religion, historiography, and bibliography are the subjects of chapters or groups of chapters which make this book the best single source of information about early Virginia, the best single-volume representation of Jefferson's individual liberal mind, and one of the major expressions of the American mind. How representative it is of contemporary Virginia ideas and nature and degree of knowledge, judged by what it includes and omits, may to some extent be determined by the discussions below, though they are primarily concerned with a slightly later period.

C. *Jeffersonian Virginia*

The forty-one years between the conventions of 1788 and 1829 in Virginia are peculiarly Jefferson's in that he was at once the representative and the dominant figure. Though the elderly Washington eclipsed the younger man in personal renown during the first decade of the era, Jefferson was just then coming to the maturity of his powers. Returning from a five-year period as Minister to France with a genuine longing to retire to his estate, Jefferson found public office once more thrust upon him. True to the Virginia tradition of *noblesse oblige,* he reluctantly accepted the Secretaryship of State in the first Cabinet. His prestige was enhanced rather than lessened when he resigned because of his disagreement with Hamilton on basic issues. Alarmed at what he and other radicals thought to be a thrust toward monarchy, he assisted in the crude beginnings of a liberal American political party, soon to be called Republican. Elected Vice-President and then President for two terms with the support of men of like political mind, in turn he and they elected for eight years each his friends Madison and Monroe. During his own tenure of office Louisiana was purchased, Lewis and Clark made their great trek across the continent, and the embargo as weapon in undeclared warfare startled the world. While Madison was President a war was begun and brought to satisfactory completion. During Monroe's terms the great Doctrine which bears his name established a new place for the United States in world affairs.

Within his own state the common man undoubtedly agreed with the majority of other Americans as to the greatness and goodness of the Sage of Monticello. But among some of the old ruling class, his name was anathema. To some of these groups the nationalist-centered Chief Justice John Marshall represented the ideal statesman; to others John Randolph of Roanoke, who by Jefferson's second administration had come to feel that the President had sacrificed the old Republican principles for expediency and executive power, was Virginia's true representative; and there were other dissident minorities and their idols.

But Jefferson was only the center stone in the Virginia diadem. Besides the other three Presidents and the conservative Chief Justice, Virginians were members of Cabinets (at least six were Secretaries of State), ministers to European and Latin American countries, negotiators of treaties, and majority leaders in both houses of Congress. Virginia-born William Henry Harrison and Winfield Scott became, except for Jackson, the best known soldiers of the decade after the War of 1812. To the very end of the period, on the surface of things, Virginia minds, liberal or conservative, shaped and ruled the nation.

But things were changing in Virginia even more than in the rest of the United States between 1788 and 1830. The sharply contrasting spirit and personnel of the two conventions are strongly symptomatic. In 1788 there were perhaps as deeply felt differences of opinion as in 1829, but the members of the state convention on ratification were old friends, neighbors, fellow legislators who felt that in fighting this family quarrel among themselves they also might be determining the fate of a nation. Giants they were on both sides with Madison, Edmund Randolph, the Nicholases, Marshall, Pendleton, and Wythe ranged against Henry, Mason, Harrison, Monroe, and Grayson. Washington and Richard Henry Lee watched from their homes, and the spirit of Jefferson (his body was in France) was invoked many times. All these men spoke with confidence and usually with hope.

In 1829-30 the names of those assembled were as distinguished as those of the earlier day. Feeble Madison and aged Monroe and Marshall were again present, as were the old Republican warriors William B. Giles and John Randolph of Roanoke. Somewhat younger Littleton

Waller Tazewell, Philip P. Barbour, Chapman Johnson, Abel P. Upshur, and Philip Doddridge had long since made names for themselves in the state and nation. But they were no longer a group of amicably differing neighbors. Doddridge, a leader of the agrarian western party, came from far off Brooke county and had little in common with Richmond lawyer Abel P. Upshur beyond the fact that both had distinguished themselves in the old Virginia way in debate. The fight this time was again between conservatives and liberals, but two kinds of conservatives and a new kind of liberal. The last, the reformers demanded legislative representation on a white population basis; they were largely the tramontane group, almost entirely non-slaveholders. They declared allegiance to the Declaration of Independence and the teachings of 1776 and based their plea on Locke and Milton. The older and more numerous conservatives, also devoted to the principles of 1776, were strict constructionists who admired the founding fathers and were fearful of the growing power of the West. The smaller group of conservatives, actually most significant of what was to come in Virginia and the South, accepted the doctrine of strict construction but cared little for the teachings of 1776. No longer thinking in national terms, they represented people who had become impoverished while neighboring states grew wealthy; they were concerned with minority rights and interests.

The coalition of conservatives won. But more important than this victory is the change in spirit of the political leadership of the commonwealth. Giles, now ill and on crutches, summed up much of the past and suggested the future when he said that, as an old Republican, he could not agree with Upshur that there never existed a state of nature and natural right, but that he would concur in the conclusion that in some situations simple majorities had no right to govern. Benjamin Watkins Leigh (of Tidewater) and Upshur argued that the Declaration of Rights was a conglomeration of metaphysical subtleties. And the now bitter and reactionary John Randolph declared that Thomas Jefferson could not be quoted as an authority on anything save the mechanism of a plow! Bitterness and obstructionism had replaced confidence and hope among the politicians, bitterness caused by the ever increasingly inferior position to which Virginia was being relegated by the westward expansion, the economic handicap of slavery, and a determination to obstruct any measure designed to alter the *status quo.*

This Convention was almost four years after Jefferson's death and about the same time at which the first collected edition of his works appeared. Looking back with reverence at the Revolutionary generation, Virginians like William Wirt in his *Old Bachelor* essays asked why the mental potential of the commonwealth had in the present generation never been realized. With all due allowance for nostalgic reverence for the good old days, thinking Virginians, even when their dynasty was at the height of its power, already pondered as to what was wrong. Slavery and the expanding West were harder to see as factors then than now, though some men saw both. That these Virginians did analyze themselves and record their misgivings is abundantly evident in scores of diaries and hundreds of letters surviving.

Yet visiting foreigners who left impressions did not see the Jeffersonians as a defeated or even a declining people. And more usually the Virginians themselves did not. Instead many of his fellow-citizens shared with Jefferson a confidence in their own future and sought ways to attain it. The Portuguese scientist and diplomat Correa remarked as late as 1820 that he should prefer to be a Virginian of all the North American people, for Virginia would become to America what France was to Europe, the haven of science and art. Morris Birkbeck admired the ordinary rural Virginian, seeing in him dress and manners superior to those of his counterpart in Europe. Fanny Wright voiced her esteem for the citizens of the state many times in her observations on America. Even the usually caustic and critical Francis Gilmer, looking at his fellow Virginians from a vantage point in England, found that in manners and mind they compared favorably with the noble and scholarly Britishers he had recently met.

Evidence that the Virginia temper as a whole was sanguine all through the Jeffersonian period is clear in its many and varied attempts to improve society in all its phases. One man urging another to write a play, a novel, or an essay reminded his correspondent that only thus—through the arts—was a great nation built, and more frequently than not the "nation" was Virginia rather than the whole United States. Others were as firmly convinced that realization of the state's high destiny must come through improvements in agriculture, education, and applied mechanics. The sense of shaping history, or of directing destiny, often a conscious sense among many people in great ages, was here sharply intense. What their fathers had begun in bodily sacrifice, in persuasive rhetoric and long vision, in laying firm foundations of government, the Jeffersonian Virginians felt it was their task to complete.

Viewed from the later twentieth century, their failure to achieve their end seems due more to factors beyond their control than to themselves, blind and obstinate and narrow as they sometimes were. But it is the failure of an old society which merges into the triumph of a new.

II

FORMAL EDUCATION

Learned institutions ought to be favorite objects with every free people. They throw that light over the public mind which is the best security against crafty and dangerous encroachments on the public liberty. They are the nurseries of skillful teachers for the schools distributed throughout the community. They are themselves schools for the particular talents required for some of the public trusts, on the able execution of which the welfare of the people depends. They multiply the educated individuals, from among whom the people may elect a due portion of their public agents of every description; more especially of those who are to frame the laws; by the perspicuity, the consistency, and the stability, as well as by the just and equal spirit of which the great social purposes are to be answered.

. . . The rich man, when contributing to a permanent plan for the education of the poor, ought to reflect that he is providing for that of his own descendants; and the poor man, who concurs in a provision for those who are not poor, that at no too distant day it may be enjoyed by descendants from himself.

—James Madison to W. T. Barry, August 4, 1822.

Like other Americans of the first national period, the Virginian found himself gradually altering his theories and practice in formal education. He began with the plantation tutorial system, a handful of free schools (some going back to the seventeenth century), several dozen more-or-less effective academies at the secondary level, and the College of William and Mary, already in a weak and declining state. He did not commit himself to a fairly complete system of public education until 1796, and then frequently with reservations as to its value and practicability. Although in a few instances the plantation tutorial continued, he did develop, somewhat under the influence of new European pedagogical theories, the old academies into a semi-public secondary-school-level system. Two of the earlier academies evolved, or developed, into recognizable colleges of considerable influence. And he planned and placed in operation a state university on an intellectual level which no institution of his region had before attained.

The politically oriented Virginia mind naturally stressed formal education as a major factor in building the new republic. In Fourth of July orations, gubernatorial or academic inaugural addresses, and newspaper or collected essays, the Jeffersonian had a great deal to say about the glorious future which would be realized through the new opportunities for education. He wrote and spoke of free schools and charity schools for the benefit of the indigent. In some instances, of which Jefferson's plan for education is a conspicuous example, he incorporated the elementary free-school idea into a more comprehensive structure through which every youth of marked ability might have the opportunity to proceed through all the stages including the university. This was but a more inclusive form of the traditional training for leadership. But he also recognized its value as background for professional training, and when he spoke of the *usefulness* of liberal education he meant the aesthetic as well as the practical.

But already his emphasis was more on the practical utility of the study of history, classical languages, French, and mathematics than it had been in earlier periods. Attainments in these subjects were not mere concomitants which graced social and political leadership, but basic groundwork on which the training in the professions of law, medicine, and religion rested.

Although some interesting departures from traditional curricula were made on secondary-school and college level in the Virginia of this period, the innovations were not nearly so striking as they were later (after 1830) to be. The stress among the Jeffersonians was on a *wider diffusion* of knowledge among those capable of assuming leadership and exercising the franchise, and on enlarging certain elements of the traditional curricula. The needs of both the potential planter-statesman and the intelligent yeoman-artisan voter were kept in mind, but the focus was on the former.

Certain individuals like John Randolph of Roanoke trained in the Revolutionary period were bitter about the inadequacies of their formal education, comparing it unfavorably with that possible earlier. The training of the new generation after 1790, however, was on the whole stronger in traditional subjects than that of the generation of Richard Henry Lee and George Washington. Whether it met the demands of the new age in science and politics may be another question. Certainly there was more attention to the physical and biological sciences, including agriculture. And the later eighteenth-century economic and general philosophies of Adam Smith, Hume, and the Scottish rhetorical and common sense school received attention in Virginia, as much as or more than in the rest of the United States.

One of the strongest influences on formal education in the period was the Presbyterian Church, which through a number of academies, two colleges, and several periodicals stressed the necessity for adequate training in politics as well as religion, and in the belletristic as well as the practical. Its educated clergy, opposed to William and Mary as a relic of the former established church, pointed out the religious 'tolerance' exercised in their own seminaries of learning and warmly advocated the establishment of a university supported by state funds—provided it did not employ atheists as professors. To the proponents of the University of Virginia the Presbyterians were allies of dubious value. But a glance at Virginia education generally in this period affords ample evidence that they were a significant factor in its development. Allied in some of their ways of thinking to the Scottish philosophers whose ideas were so congenial to the dominant Democratic Republicans, they were often felt when least suspected. Enlighten the people, both Presbyterians and Republicans insisted, and we shall have in Virginia a wise government and a moral creative populace.

A. *Elementary Education*

At the foot of the ladder by which the people were to climb to enlightenment was a system of elementary education. This Jefferson included in his 1779 *Bill for the More General Diffusion of Knowledge,* one of the noblest of all statements of the function of education in a republic. But the bill was not passed, and only a small portion of it remained in a later bill of 1796 for primary schools alone which left the organization at this level up to the officials of each county. What did come in the development of elementary education in Virginia in this period was largely a development of the older free and charity schools, with some of its origins in the colonial plantation tutorial system and grammar school or academy.

Jefferson's 1779 plan was well known in Virginia throughout his lifetime, however, and it was reintroduced in 1817-18 in a new bill aimed at the establishment of the University of Virginia. As early as 1803 the lawyer William Wirt (in his *Letters of the British Spy*) praised the "simple and beautiful scheme, whereby science . . . would have been carried to every man's door." Jefferson had proposed beginners' schools in each ward (a unit supporting one militia company) of each county, annually elected visitors (supervisors), teachers from the laboring classes (farmers and mechanics), choice of one able child in each twenty for further training at public expense, and support solely from county-levied taxes. The 1817-18 revision was a little less democratic in some proposed procedures and more complex in some, but in essence it remained the same. The original proposal had called for teaching of English, ancient, and American history in addition to the three R's. In the revision history was not mentioned but geography was included. In either case Jefferson intended these as the tools with which to equip the people generally for life and for citizenship.

When the 1818 Legislature passed a bill providing a state tax for elementary schools, Jefferson declared that it had made a mistake. For one thing, he hoped that the State Literary Fund (established in 1810) would be reserved for the completion of "the general system of education by colleges in every district for instruction in languages, and an university for the whole of the higher sciences." He was convinced that the large stake the counties would have in these elementary schools within their own borders would naturally compel strong support.

Not a great deal was done even after 1818 to develop the primary schools. The 1786 bill, leaving the establishment up to the counties, had resulted in nothing more than some state support for indigent students, a subsidization which itself became known as "the primary school system." After 1818 Jefferson perforce concentrated on higher education. But three of his younger friends and neighbors, Joseph C. Cabell, Andrew Stevenson, and William C. Rives, tried again and again during their long lives to improve elementary education. Cabell kept an eye on the lower schools in his home county of Nelson, and even proposed certain Pestalozzian methods for them. For a full generation after Jefferson's death he continued to support bills aimed at improving the situation. Rives once declared that the primary educational system was the great interest of his life, though his active national legislative and diplomatic career prevented his having much time to work for it. Stevenson, like Rives a diplomat and Congressman, had done what he could in Fredericksburg and Albemarle and in organizing a school in Richmond, as we shall see.

Although Jefferson's elementary schools were not intended for the poor alone, they were associated from the beginning in the public mind with the idea of charity schools. The pauper-school idea, never tolerated in the north, was a means employed by liberal Jeffersonians towards an end. For "benevolence" elicited support from conservatives as well as liberals, and through this entering wedge of the already existing individual charity or free schools might come a state system. Thomas Ritchie, editor of the Republican Richmond *Enquirer,* insisted in his own columns that "Society fulfill the claims of the poor" by the organized establishment of such schools. He had an essay on the subject in Wirt's collection *The Rainbow* in 1804. Ten years later, Wirt and his friends were continuing to discuss the needs in education in *The Old Bachelor* series. *The Old Bachelor* noted indignantly that despite strong efforts in some quarters, not a single school has been erected "where children may learn to read, to write, to worship God, to honor their parents, and to love their country."[1] The emphasis was not on its charitable aspects but on its function in a democracy.

Clearly through apathy a feeling that free education was somehow degrading to the Virginia yeoman who could pay for it if he really wanted it, and the eternal fear of local taxes, the state was not ready to undertake full-scale education for every man. In 1824 in a lecture at Hampden-Sydney College, even the patriotic and often liberal Presbyterian clergyman John H. Rice was sceptical as to the practicability of elementary schools. If they were established, he foresaw that adequately trained teachers (unlike Jefferson he insisted that primary teachers be college graduates) would and could not be available. As for "the primary school system" of help to the indigent, he felt that it demeaned the sturdy farmer by making him plead poverty in order to get free education. He thought that the "thousands every year squandered" on the system would be better spent on college preparatory schools, both male and female. Rice urged instead of the system then in force one that would make elementary education cheap, "so as to bring it within the reach of every honest industrious man."[2]

In 1826 another speaker at the same college, the Norfolk lawyer and Yale graduate William Maxwell, urged that the present state plan be replaced by real "Primary Schools (as they are called) all over our state."[3] Though he did not go into much detail, one may presume that he meant something of the kind planned by Jefferson or that he had seen in Connecticut.

At least as early as 1811 Virginians were reading and pondering the famous British Lancastrian system of public or free education. On October 14, 1815, Ritchie, Stevenson, and the lawyer-poet William Munford called a meeting at the Washington Tavern in Richmond to consider the establishment of a Lancastrian school. Evidently they were successful, for the first session began in May of the following year. The cornerstone of the building, which had been constructed from municipal and private funds, bore the inscription: "The Lancastrian school is dedicated to the elementary principle of education. . . ." Records of the school surviving for the 1822-32 period indicate that it was then a flourishing institution. It continued until 1851, long after a state system had been established.[4] Perhaps the visit to Richmond in 1819 of Joseph Lancaster himself, and his lecture in the Hall of the House of Delegates, gave it additional éclat. There is no evidence that any Lancastrian school ever served Virginia rural communities, though in Norfolk (1819), Alexandria (1812), and other towns and cities it was a connecting link between the old charity-and-private education and the modern elementary system.[5]

B. *The Secondary School*

The need for secondary schools was almost universally agreed upon, but they were rarely thought of as training for every man. Though Jefferson suggested that their curricula include some technical training which might be useful to those who would never go beyond them, they were primarily even in his mind aimed at preparation for higher education or teaching in the lower schools. He thought of them usually, as noted above, as language schools; but he also mentioned English grammar, geography, and higher arithmetic as necessities in their curricula. The one-poor-boy-in-twenty should have an opportunity in them, but the implication is that the schools would be filled principally with the children of those who could afford to send them. Other Virginians who supported Jefferson's plan of opportunity for the poor-but-able also seemed to assume that the greater number of students at the secondary and higher levels would be from the families who could afford to send them. His pyramid plan of education in practice is one of selection to give equal opportunity, not of rigid selection among all levels of society.

Actually these district schools he suggested were to differ but little in general curriculum and organization from those he and most other educated Virginians had attended before, during, or immediately after the Revolution. Men like Patrick Henry and William Wirt had never gone beyond such schools, though they spoke and wrote fluently with full-blown classical embellishments. Monroe studied at a small private school of this kind under the Reverend Alexander Campbell before he entered William and Mary, James Madison in a similar one under Donald Robertson before he entered Princeton. The latter is reported to have said of his teacher: "All that I have been in life I owe to that man."[6] John Taylor of Caroline, the elder John Tyler, and George Rogers Clark also studied under Robertson. John Page and Wilson Cary Nicholas attended the grammar school connected with the same college before they entered the higher branch. Almost at random one may note the academies attended by other prominent Virginians of the period before they matriculated at the Williamsburg college: Andrew Stevenson at Fredericksburg, John Taylor in King and Queen, Archibald Stuart in Augusta, and Littleton W. Tazewell under Walker Maury in Orange, to mention only a few. John Marshall and his great rival Spencer Roane received their secondary training under Scottish tutors at home. They, as well as the Virginians who went on to Princeton or Yale or Edinburgh, studied the same subjects in much the same way those previously mentioned did. These were the men who had reached their majority by the time of the adoption of the Constitution. Most of those educated during the next generation studied under similar circumstances similar subjects, though the number of academies available had increased a great deal and in several notable instances the masters employed new curricula and methodology.

Between 1790 and 1830 there were in existence in Virginia at least seventy well-known secondary schools for boys, usually called grammar schools, classical schools, or academies.[7] Each was at least nominally independent but actually represented entrenched interests of religious denominations, city or neighborhood pride (whether the schools were supported directly by municipal or community funds or not), and remarkable individuals who conducted them. Those who favored a state system of public education knew that these institutions would have to be incorporated into the system or forced out of existence. Jefferson certainly preferred the latter alternative, but he wisely suggested a method of organization which would have included many of them. His actual plan named several of their old locations as sites for his district secondary schools or "colleges." If his plan had been put into operation, only a few new institutions at additional key places would have been necessary to balance the organization.

During the forty years of the period the independent academies multiplied rapidly. Jefferson complained (July 5, 1814) to John Adams "of the petty *academies*, as they call themselves, which are starting up in every neighborhood, and where one or two men, possessing Latin, and sometimes Greek, a knowledge of the globes, and the first six books of Euclid, imagine and communicate this as the total of science. They commit their pupils to the theatre of the world with just taste enough of learning to be alienated from industrious pursuits, and not enough to do service in the ranks of science. We have some exceptions indeed."[8] When one notes that this was a preface to a statement of the necessity of establishing institutions of higher learning and remembers that the curriculum described is almost exactly what Jefferson himself had earlier prescribed for his district schools, it becomes evident that he is thinking of their deficiencies as terminal schools more than as preparatory schools. Most students in his time never went beyond them. He is suggesting that education for intellectual leadership must go further and for ordinary citizenship must be a little different, though in the latter respect he never specifically planned very far.

His proposed district schools were to employ a master and usher for twenty to twenty-five students, be housed in a brick or stone edifice, and follow the language, geography, and mathematics curriculum noted above. One third of the *selected* students were to be dropped at the end of the first year and all others save the one of greatest promise at the end of two years. In 1779 Jefferson had planned twenty school districts. In 1817, with the state reduced in size, he suggested only nine. Repeatedly he declared that there should be a "college" within a day's ride of every citizen. It is interesting that in the mid-twentieth century Virginia educators are attempting something of this plan in their system of junior colleges. It was not done in his time.

Tutors who sat enthroned among their pupils in a small "office" of a plantation taught the same subjects in much the same way as did the masters of academies. The early teachers, usually trained at the English or Scottish universities, were replaced in this period largely by graduates of Princeton or Yale or Harvard, though a few men from Edinburgh and Aberdeen still found their way to Virginia. Sometimes a tutor became head of a larger neighborhood academy. William Wirt, in recommending (February 7, 1799) a young teacher who had been tutor in the Gilmer family for a position as master of a proposed new academy in Lexington, Kentucky, declared that the man taught "the Greek, Latin, and French language with the greatest approbation; he also declares himself capable of teaching Spanish & Dutch & his assertion deserves credit. As far as can be collected from conversations with him he is a good mathematician, geographer, and [natural?] philosopher . . . we shall part from him with regret."[9]

Comments on other headmasters observe their abilities in Greek and Latin and often French, in arithmetic and simpler algebra or geometry, and occasionally in natural philosophy (the physical and biological sciences). Sobriety and discipline are also frequent subject for comment. One Albemarle Scot of unusual pedagogical ability was a too frequent tippler; a neighboring master of French descent employed the rod with cruel severity; the famous James Ogilvie, as everyone knew, was a user of laudanum when he was preparing his orations or even his class lectures. No one seems to have found such idiosyncrasies in Dr. Haller and L. H. Girardin, who operated the famous-for-the-moment Hallerian School in Richmond about 1807. In these cases the teacher-principals were conducting their own schools. The several Presbyterian and one or two Methodist and Baptist academies appear not to have employed men with personally reprehensible habits. Indeed most of the masters were men of strong character and some versatility.

The newspapers are full of notices of curricula, tuition prices, and the founding of new academies. The schools seem to have sprung up wherever there was a need, particularly in the older parts of the state. All the larger towns such as Richmond, Petersburg, Norfolk, Alexandria, Lynchburg, and Winchester had two or more. Even Staunton, Williamsburg, and Charlottesville had more than one, though not always simultaneously. Many Episcopal clergymen, as the Reverend Devereux Jarratt, conducted classical schools on their glebes, or what remained of them. Jefferson's nephew Peter Carr had a boarding school on his plantation in Albemarle. The great majority of those remembered today were at county seats or other small villages or in the country. When William and Mary's attached grammar school was discontinued, Walker Maury moved his academy from Orange to Williamsburg. Though Hampden-Sydney and Washington College evolved from grammar schools themselves, they maintained directly-connected secondary schools for some years after they assumed collegiate status.

Some schools had long and honorable histories. The Washington-Henry Academy of Hanover, for example, existed from the Revolution to 1878. Others lasted only a year or two. Sixty-four were individually chartered by the state, and at least forty of this number were in actual operation. They were almost entirely city-town located institutions.[10] But from Norfolk in the east to Abingdon and Shepherdstown in the west, a considerable number, chartered and unchartered, flourished during the period. There were undoubtedly a great many more than the seventy-odd for men and dozen for women whose records exist in manuscripts or extant newspapers.

Certainly almost all schools for boys offered the classical languages, basic mathematics, and some English composition. Usually French and some science accompanied these; a little of what we today call commercial subjects—simple accounting and shorthand—were sometimes offered. In 1797 the Reverend Hugh White, late of Princeton, notified the Richmond public (in the Virginia *Argus,* October 17) that he was opening a school in which, in addition to the usual languages and mathematics, he would offer geography, navigation, and surveying. In November 1801 the Reverend John D. Blair proposed (*Virginia Gazette and General Advertiser,* October 27) to open a grammar school where a liberal education or qualification for the learned professions might be obtained. He went into some detail as to why Greek and Latin should be studied (men like Jefferson and Gilmer doubted their *general* usefulness) and promised that every student would engage in English exercises and arithmetic for an hour each day. He wanted not more than twenty students, about the number most other schools desired. In the same newspaper in which Hugh White advertised his orthodox academy, Louis A. Dupuy "from Paris" notified the public that at his "French Academy" he continued to teach his native tongue. He makes no mention of other subjects. The Manchester Academy included Locke, Hutchinson, Paley, and Blair's rhetorical lectures among its textbooks, and there is evidence that these materials also used on the college level were frequently employed in many of the more advanced secondary institutions.

One of the more interesting of the rural academies was that conducted by John Lewis at Belle-Air and Llangollen in Spotsylvania county, from 1811-12 to 1833.[11] The owner and master was a novelist, poet, and philologist, who during the 1820's published two books on English grammar and etymology and (with two University of Virginia linguists) a third volume on comparative etymology, perhaps all intended as texts. In the earliest advertisement of his school the curriculum is divided into two parts, apparently with elementary as well as secondary instruction in mind. For one group he mentions the three R s; for the other English grammar, geography, use of terrestrial globes and maps, composition and criticism, the inferior branches of mathematics, and Latin, quite orthodox subjects. By 1825 he had added French. In 1830 he divided the school (perhaps the elementary group had long before been discarded) into one curriculum of languages (including Spanish and Italian), history, and philosophy; the other of geography, arithmetic, algebra, and geometry.

Lewis' miscellaneous accounts (surviving at least as recently as 1937) form the most complete chronicle of school life in this period. Persuasion instead of coercion was always employed. Girls as well as boys were in the later years admitted to classes. Outdoor sports, including fishing, hunting, and swimming were encouraged. Even traveling animal shows were brought in. The school menu included all the abundant vegetables and meats a plantation might produce. The 1811-12 charges were $25 for tuition and $75 per annum for board, washing, and fire. In later years the total cost rose to $125. In 1811-12 Lewis wanted fifteen or sixteen pupils from nine to fifteen years of age, of whom ten would board with the owner. Later he eliminated outside boarders.

Lewis apparently held high standards. In teaching Latin he attempted to follow the methods of the great English universities. His classes in Greek were conducted by the Reverend Mr. Boggs, an Episcopal clergyman of considerable erudition.

Equally as interesting as Lewis is John Davis, English-born traveler, poet, and novelist, who spent many years of his life in Virginia and wrote much about its scenery and legends. In 1801 he was a tutor in the family of a Mr. Ellicott, a Quaker residing on the banks of the Occoquan. In 1807-8 he was instructor in languages (and possibly headmaster) in the Petersburg Academy, one of the earliest Lancastrian schools in America. At one time he had an ambitious plan for a school in the country near Petersburg and wrote many letters to the newspapers describing it. A surviving brochure of another school he planned and may have placed in operation gives something of the flavor of the man and his pedagogical attitudes. Under "Regulations" he declares that no corporal punishment will ever be inflicted, "because beating the body debases the mind." The general advertisement[12] is interesting:

School
ON HIGH STREET, PETERSBURG,
IN THE HOUSE FORMERLY OCCUPIED BY DR. HOLMES.

Junior Department $8 per quarter. English from letters and spelling to the pungency of Junius and euphony of Gibbon.—Grammar, History, Writing and Arithmetic. Geography rendered pleasing as an Eastern Tale.—Senior Department $10 per quarter. English in its scrupulous purity, embracing Composition, Rhetoric and Declamation. Latin comprehending every writer of the Julian and Augustan Ages. The Poets read with an eye to their tropes, figures and fine turns. The structure of their verse examined as it depends on caesura. The verse scanned and proved. The Orators & Historians read with the application of prosody, and special attention paid to the crement [*sic*]. Composition according to the genius of the purest prose. Greek—The Greek Grammar rendered familiar as the Latin. The Greek parsed with critical exactness. Geography by extemporaneous Lectures. Astronomy and the Mathematics. (I studied these sciences in two voyages to the East-Indies.) Chemistry—The French language. (I learnt French in Paris.)

JOHN DAVIS

By far the most influential and widely known pedagogue of the era was the eccentric Scot James Ogilvie (1775-1820),[13] who spent some fourteen years in the state as a teacher. He arrived in Virginia about 1794 and almost at once opened a school somewhere in Essex county on the Rappahannock. In 1802 he was master of the Stevensburg Academy in Culpeper. In 1803 he conducted a school on Shockoe Hill in Richmond, in which city then or later the mathematician John Woodward and later editor Thomas Ritchie were his assistants. In 1805 he was established at Milton, two miles from Monticello. There he remained, a sort of protégé of Mr. Jefferson, through 1807. Then he moved back to Richmond, this time to Sixth and Grace Streets, from which place he began the oratorical-lecture tours from Massachusetts to Georgia he kept up until he returned to Great Britain in 1816 or 1817.

Described as a fairly significant "minor realist" among the philosophers, indebted to Hume and Locke, Ogilvie through his avowed devotion to Godwin and confessed opium-eating was looked upon by some parents with suspicion. This may partially account for his moving about. But his former students, including Winfield Scott, William Cabell Rives, and Francis Walker Gilmer testify that he was a most stimulating teacher. Other Americans like Washington Irving and George Ticknor admired his oratorical powers.

In an essay published in 1802 in Alexandria, *Cursory Reflexions on Government, Philosophy and Education,* Ogilvie states the two great objects of liberal education as he saw them, preparation for citizenship and for profession, and the prime duty of the instructor, "to excite in the breast of the pupil an ardent and decided thirst for knowledge" (p. 33). This latter can only be attained, he adds, "by painting in vivid colours and illustrating by striking instances, the benefits of knowledge and the mischiefs of ignorance and error. . . I have abjured every means of influencing the minds of my pupils, but reasoning, expostulation, and example." He confesses that Godwin's "sublime treatise" *Political Justice* has convinced him that "the extensive establishment of independent and philosophical schools is the only adequate means of diffusing knowledge" (p. 37). Later, in his *Philosophical Essays* (Philadelphia, 1816) Ogilvie describes his tremendously hard working day at the Milton school, where he lectured, heard recitations, and supervised composition and translation from dawn to sunset. Then he spent four or five hours in reading philosophy, partially in preparation for the Sunday morning "discourse" he delivered at the courthouse in Charlottesville (Jefferson attended). One Richmond student testified years later that "Ogilvie inspired in me new desires. He touched some sympathetic chord which instantly responded, and from that moment I felt that there was a divine spark in the human mind, at least in mine, which might be fanned into flame and which was infinitely of more value and of more enjoyment, than the mere pleasures of sense."[14]

Particularly did Ogilvie influence the practice and teaching of rhetoric and oratory in Virginia and the nation. All his students learned to speak on their feet, though by our tastes with somewhat ridiculous gestures and strained imagery. An announcement of July 4, 1804,[15] of an "Exhibition" to be given by seven of his senior students in the Hall of the Virginia House of Delegates illustrates the subject matter on which they were engaged in the classroom and, one may add, the interests of the teacher himself. Linn Banks was to deliver an oration on "an interesting principle in political economy"; William Pope, "on the comparative advantages of history and moral fiction"; William Roane, "on the connection between Chemistry & Agriculture"; Richard Ellis, "on the utility of periodical Essays"; Thomas Jones, "on Happiness"; and Edward Goodwin, "on Education." Though these topics would hardly have been startling from any college seniors of the period, they do indicate that Ogilvie went far beyond the conventional language-mathematics-geography curricula of most secondary schools.

Among Ogilvie's former students were several territorial governors and members of Congress from the deeper South and Southwest, and Senator William Cabell Rives, General Winfield Scott, Senator William S. Archer, and Judge John Robertson, to mention only a few prominent men from Virginia itself. His influence on thinking and ways of speaking cannot now be measured, but deep into the nineteenth century a number of significant Americans were asserting that it was considerable. Ogilvie urged and exemplified (except in his use of laudanum) the highest moral standards. His enthusiastic defense of Godwin was a liberal defense of liberal ideas, of course, and even his conservative students respected him for it. He was in some respects an impractical dreamer, in others a down-to-earth follower of the Scottish common sense school of philosophy. It is no wonder that his friend the artist C. R. Leslie, who always carefully sought models appropriate to the subject and character of his pictures, painted Ogilvie as Don Quixote![16]

Female education in this period was, like the charity school, the frequent subject of the periodical essayist. Wirt and his friends in their several guises came out strongly for wider training for the future mother of the republic and made flattering remarks about the superiority of women's minds. The essayists are usually rather vague as to exactly what the Virginia female should study, though occasionally some bold spirit suggested that she needed and could handle Latin and Greek as well as a male could. The orator and poet Daniel Bryan addressed a sympathetic audience "on Female Education" (later printed and rather widely distributed)[17] at the Female Academy at Harrisonburg, though he said nothing they did not already know. One Presbyterian clergyman offered religion as the proper basis for education for both sexes, but his *Mountaineer* (Harrisonburg, 1820) remains vague as to method and degree. Even John Randolph of Roanoke, who usually addressed himself to young male relatives and friends, took the trouble to give a letter of advice (January 19, 1822)[18] to a niece on what to read to secure a good education. The implication was of course that the young lady would educate herself

Some Virginia girls whose families were really in earnest about their education, social as well as mental, were sent to seminaries like Miss Lyman's in Philadelphia.[19] But others attended Virginia schools. With one exception the best-known seminaries were located in towns and cities. In 1801 (August 14) the Richmond *Gazette and General Advertiser* gave notice of a new boarding school for young ladies shortly to be opened by the wife of an Episcopal clergyman, Mrs. William Fenwick. She proposed to teach "Plain Work, Embroidery, Dresden and every fashionable accomplishment of this description," also French, reading, grammar, writing, and arithmetic. She would have some boarders and some day scholars. Immediately below her advertisement is a separate one of an adjacent dancing school.

A year later, on July 31, 1802, in the same newspaper "Miss Robbins, lately from London" announced the opening of a seminary offering similar courses but adding music and dancing, and the promise that "Particular care will be paid to their morals." The first entirely successful girls' school in Richmond appears to have been that founded in 1807 (see Virginia *Argus,* March 13) by Mrs. Anna Maria Byrd, in which the prominent clergyman John D. Blair was to teach moral philosophy, John Lataste dancing, and Auguste Peticolas drawing. Schools in Williamsburg, Lynchburg, and Winchester followed much the same pattern of polite accomplishments and language.

These subjects are in the main those assumed by Jefferson many years earlier when he recommended to his daughter Martha how she should divide her school day (November 28, 1783)[20] in the eight-in-the-morning to bedtime schedule he proposed. Little has come down to us of the details or effectiveness of such a curriculum. It is clear that Greek and Latin were rarely part of the bill of fare for young ladies but that French always was. Francis Gilmer, writing from Winchester on January 1, 1817,[21] spoke scornfully of the girl's school in that town in which Thomson's *Seasons* and Young's *Night Thoughts* were the chief things taught. That young ladies were steeped in the sentimental and lugubrious is indicated in a line of verse by the Virginia poetess Margaret Blennerhasset, when she writes (*The Widow of the Rock and Other Poems*)[22] of school girls reading "And at pathetic parts are made to sigh and cry by rule," adding the significant footnote that in a certain boarding school, the instructor "taught the young ladies in her charge, while reading, to hold their pocket handkerchiefs in readiness to be applied to the fountains of tears at such parts as her own delicate sensibility should dictate to be most pathetic." Yet in most respects these schools supplied what the parents wanted. On December 28, 1827[8?],[23] for example, Thomas Harrison and William Bolling sat through the long exercises from noon to seven P.M. at their daughters' school in Petersburg, listening with great satisfaction to the final recitations in the standard subjects.

By far the most thoughtful champion of education for women was James Mercer Garnett (1770-1843) of Elmwood in Essex county. After a fairly distinguished career as legislator, controversial essayist, and agricultural reformer he found himself, like many other Virginians in the early 1820's, impoverished. Thereupon he opened on his estate a school for young women in which he himself taught English composition and his wife and daughters other subjects. Once each quarter he delivered a formal discourse to the students. Later he gathered together and printed his remarks in *Seven Lectures on Female Education* (second ed., Richmond, 1824). In these essays Garnett demonstrated that his system of rewards and punishments was more efficacious than the rod, he pointed out obstacles to education in early home training, and he was most unusual in condemning the pedagogical methods which *drove* students to work and to a pernicious "envious rivalship." Naturally he advocated more education for women, emphasizing its usefulness as preparation for either marriage or career. These essays were good advertising. Garnett had students from all over Virginia and several neighboring states.

Although the activity on behalf of female education led to the establishment of no enduring seminary or college, it does afford evidence that a great many Virginians believed that the republic must have an educated womanhood as well as manhood. Among the plantation aristocracy at least they already had good examples. Martha Jefferson Randolph, who received part of her education in a French convent, was regarded as one of the learned Americans of her day.

As their letters testify, her daughters and the womenfolk of her neighbors were only slightly less learned in languages and world affairs.[24] One of the charming letters of the period, for example, written on April 25, 1829[25] by John M. Daniel to his young cousin Huldah Lewis (probably the daughter of John Lewis of Llangollen) on the values of the classics to a Virginia farmer, is significant for the tone of intellectual equality with which he defends Godwin, Byron, and Scott as preferable to the Latin poets and orators. Here was one young woman who did know Greek and Latin, and her male relative addressed her with real respect.

Dancing and music were a recognized and integral part of the training for young women. St. George Tucker's circle of ladies in Williamsburg and Jefferson's granddaughters at Monticello studied instrumental and vocal music. But the hundreds of surviving letters from plantation mistresses and daughters indicate that they studied most, formally and informally, literature and language. Above all they learned to spell, punctuate, and write in intelligible sentences!

The Virginia secondary school remained throughout Jefferson's lifetime a private or independent institution continuing traditions of classical and mathematical curricula. But in some respects it was adapting itself to its function in building a new republican society. Geography and history received new emphasis. Elementary science was introduced, though without real laboratory facilities. The political, economic, and aesthetic philosophies of the later eighteenth century were filtering down from the top, from the courses at Princeton, Yale, Edinburgh, and William and Mary. Letters from schoolboys indicate that they knew something of Godwin and Hume and Blair and Kames, though certainly they do not mention them in the same terms of familiarity or understanding as the collegians of Princeton or William and Mary display.[26]

The secondary school in its stronger manifestations was also preparing the way for future colleges and universities. Even one which never rose to recognized collegiate status, the famous academy at New London (founded 1795) in Bedford county, was held in such respect that Gilmer could refer to education there as at least comparable to that of Harvard or West Point, and a state lottery was held in its behalf in 1827. John Holt Rice and Conrad Speece were among its alumni. An early Prince Edward Academy grew into Hampden-Sydney and Liberty Hall Academy in Lexington became Washington College (now Washington and Lee University). Both of these were Presbyterian. In the generation after 1830 the Powhatan Baptist Academy (founded *ca.* 1813) was to evolve into Richmond College; and the Ebenezer Academy, founded by Edward Dromgoole and Bishop Asbury in 1793, fathered in 1830 the oldest American Methodist college, Randolph-Macon, though the Academy itself lived on until 1860.

C. *Higher Learning*

Nothing indicates more strongly the falsity of the conception that Virginians lacked breadth of interest than the history of the state's aims and achievements in collegiate education in the period from the Revolution to 1830. Law and politics were prominent in their minds, it is true, but so were science, religion, and philosophy. In at least two major projects were displayed a breadth and depth of vision rarely seen in intellectual history. That one of them was abortive was due to the world situation of the time. That the other was only partially realized may be blamed on national as well as state situations. Most leaders of Virginia, Episcopalians, deists, and Presbyterians alike, believed in collegiate training. Certain politicians obstructed, but a great deal was accomplished.

During the first generation of Virginia settlement a college had been founded at Henrico for whites and Indians. It perished in 1622 when its director and his staff were wiped out in the massacre. Despite sporadic attempts to establish another such institution, success did not come until 1693, when the College of William and Mary was chartered with royal allowances for endowment. All through the remainder of the colonial period this second oldest American college gave its students training comparable to that offered in the New England schools in languages, theology, philosophy, and science. During the earlier eighteenth century a considerable number of Virginians attended Edinburgh for medicine, the same institution and Oxford and Cambridge for the liberal arts, and the Inns of Court for Law, though most Virginia barristers studied with older distinguished lawyers in Williamsburg or in their native counties.

Of the Revolutionary generation a number continued to be trained at Edinburgh in medicine, men like George Gilmer and Arthur Lee. William Grayson, later to be one of Virginia's first Senators under the Constitution, was said to have attended Oxford and the Inns of Court. The rising generation after independence continued occasionally to go to Great Britain. Thomas Mann Randolph and two kinsmen in 1794 studied science and philosophy at Edinburgh, the latter under Dugald Stewart. While there Randolph persuaded the later eminent John Leslie to return to Virginia with him and tutor his younger brother at Tuckahoe. Three years before Jefferson had just referred to Edinburgh as the best university in the world. But other Virginians studied elsewhere: In 1787 Robert Beverley was at Trinity College, Cambridge; in 1794 Robert Scott of Dumfries worked at King's College, Aberdeen; and a little later John Augustine Smith, future noted research physician in New York and President of William and Mary, studied medicine at St. Thomas' Hospital in London.[27]

Well into the nineteenth century Virginia relations with the University of Edinburgh remained fairly close. Young Scottish tutors still came into the state, and young Virginians who could still afford it went to Edinburgh for medicine. Dr. George Watson of Louisa and Richmond, for example, after attending William and Mary went to Edinburgh in 1806, where he roomed with Charles Carter of Williamsburg and had a Dr. Parker of the Eastern Shore as a near neighbor.[28] Watson later went on to study in Paris. John Wharton, a poet as well as a physician of Culpeper county, also studied medicine at Edinburgh, where he became president of the Royal Physical Society.[29] The great influence of Edinburgh and Scotland on Virginia thinking came not through medicine, however, but through philosophy and theology. The rhetorical and philosophical writings of Blair, Brown, Stewart, and other Scottish university professors were standard texts in Virginia colleges, of which more later. And the contacts of the Presbyterians of Hampden-Sydney and Washington College with Edinburgh came partly through Princeton, partly through correspondence with Edinburgh's theological faculty, and occasionally through advanced training in the Scottish university.

A great many Virginians studied medicine in Philadelphia, in the period before the War of 1812 under Benjamin Rush, and often later under the Virginian Nathaniel Chapman. By 1830 Transylvania in

Kentucky and Jefferson Medical College in Philadelphia, as well as the University of Pennsylvania, were advertising their medical curricula in Richmond newspapers.[30] A few notably successful physicians studied under older men in their native state in very much the fashion the lawyers did, and for a period William and Mary offered medical courses under Dr. McClurg and his successors.

Here and there a Virginian sent his son to a northern school for academic training. David Ross, scholarly manager of the Oxford Iron Works in Bedford, wrote long letters of advice to his son at Carlisle College in Pennsylvania.[31] In the mid-eighteen-twenties a Tazewell, at least two Tayloes and a Rives attended Harvard, the former receiving many courtesies from George Ticknor. John Randolph and his kinsman Theodorick Bland were students at King's College (Columbia) in New York. Arthur Morson, Abel P. Upshur, Hugh Blair Grigsby, and William Maxwell, all men of distinction and three of them men of letters, took their academic work at Yale.[32] Despite the personal and family prominence of these alumni of the two great New England colleges, the influence of these institutions was negligible on Virginia thinking generally or on the pattern of higher education developing within the state.

Princeton is another matter. Virginia had early felt the influence of the New Jersey college; for John Todd, a Princeton graduate, had with Samuel Davies (later Princeton President) founded the first non-Episcopal academies in the state, and all but one of the six ministers founding the original Virginia Presbytery of Hanover were graduates. Liberty Hall (Washington College), which had close Princeton affiliations in all its early administrators and trustees, offered the same four-year course of study as the older institution, and like it was concerned largely with educating a ministry for a Scotch-Irish population. Hampden-Sydney had four Princeton graduates on its original board of trustees and many on its faculty. When President Samuel Stanhope Smith of Hampden-Sydney resigned in 1779 to accept a professorship at Princeton he took along with him a number of Virginians, including some of his own college students. Another Hampden-Sydney professor, John Holt Rice, declined the Presidency of Princeton after considerable heart-searching.[33]

Princeton had always invited young men of any Christian sect to be its students, and many of the early Virginia students there were

John Randolph

Portrait by Gilbert Stuart. Courtesy of the Mellon Collection, National Gallery of Art.

Judge John Marshall

Portrait by C. B. Fevret de St. Memin. In the Collection of The Corcoran Gallery of Art.

Isaac A. Coles

Portrait by C. B. Fevret de St. Memin. In the Collection of The Corcoran Gallery of Art.

St. George Tucker

Portrait by C. B. Fevret de St. Memin. In the Collection of The Corcoran Gallery of Art.

Littleton W. Tazewell

Portrait by C. B. Fevret de St. Memin. In the Collection of The Corcoran Gallery of Art.

William Clarke

Portrait by C. B. Fevret de St. Memin. In the Collection of The Corcoran Gallery of Art.

L. H. Girardin

Portrait by C. B. Fevret de St. Memin. In the Collection of The Corcoran Gallery of Art.

Meriwether Lewis

Portrait by C. B. Fevret de St. Memin. In the Collection of The Corcoran Gallery of Art.

William Wirt

Portrait by C. B. Fevret de St. Memin. In the Collection of The Corcoran Gallery of Art.

John Hartwell Cocke

Portrait by W. J. Hubard. Courtesy of the President and Visitors of the University of Virginia.

Episcopalians. James Madison and Light-Horse Harry Lee are cases in point. Slightly later William Branch Giles, John Randolph, George W. P. Custis, and Abel P. Upshur were others. In 1799 Samuel Wimbish of Pittsylvania county wrote his mother that on his arrival at Princeton he found all his Virginia friends well.[34] He spoke glowingly of regulations, situation, and faculty. His religious predilections are not evident.

Not always did Virginians get on well there. In the famous rebellion of 1802 for "student honor and justice," Edmund Pendleton, Joseph Cumming, Caleb and Robert Breckinridge, Charles Sneed, Andrew D. Holmes, and Upshur, all from the Old Dominion, were in the thick of the movement.[35] Upshur gave a fine display of eloquence before the trustees, but in vain, for several of the group were dismissed. A few years later, when the William and Mary alumnus William Cabell Rives visited the college, he compared it most unfavorably with his alma mater. He wrote[36] that there was too much puritanism and bigotry to offer the advantages of a free intellect, that the faculty was inferior, and that the student body seemed made up principally of indolent young men trying to escape honest toil at the plow by pretending to study for the ministry. The only good thing he could say for it was that in all four years the students were required to study languages. Early a Jeffersonian deist and later a devout Episcopalian, Rives represented a type of Virginian which could hardly be expected to view Old Nassau with sympathy.

No northern or European institutions were responsible for the training of most of the Virginians who did so much to achieve independence and then to carry the nation through its first great period of growth. The overwhelming majority of leaders of the Revolutionary generation, and a strong majority of those of the Jeffersonian period, received their training at home, at the College of William and Mary. Before the Sage of Monticello died his alma mater was in severe decline. But up to the War of 1812, despite war and poverty, she had a history of sound instruction, able faculty, and actually progressive ideas. In languages, law, and experimental science she was a pioneer. No one can hope to understand the Jeffersonian Virginia mind without knowing something of what went on at Williamsburg between 1760 and the 1820's.

Founded in 1693, by 1710 William and Mary had attained to real collegiate status. But though favored by Church, local legislature, and Crown-appointed governors, and possessing a fair endowment, during the seventy years before independence the college had an average of only sixty per year in its student body. Many of these sixty took advantage, however, of the unusual advantages it offered.

Its theological training must have been sound if not advanced. Bishop Meade states that almost all the weakness in morals and training among the clergy existed among the foreign men, not the alumni of the college. In preparation for politics its location was superb. After studying theory under his professor, the student could observe firsthand the House of Burgesses in session, the manipulations of committees, and the effect of the governor's veto powers and proclamations. In that school of politics in the generation before the Revolution were matured Jefferson and five other signers of the Declaration of Independence; Peyton Randolph, first president of the Continental Congress; Edmund Randolph, Attorney-General and Secretary of State under Washington; and the elder John Tyler, John Marshall, and James Monroe, among a dozen others of distinction.

One has almost to take for granted the sound instruction in the ancient languages and philosophies, for the destruction of the college records in a series of wars has left little direct evidence. Perhaps the best is the reading and writing habits of its alumni, matters to be discussed in later chapters. But there is piecemeal evidence that from the earlier eighteenth century William and Mary was unusually advanced in its attitudes toward scientific training. Established there in 1711, for example, was the first chair of science in America. By 1727 (published in 1736) it had adopted a wise statute regarding the teaching of all subjects but especially notable for the freedom it allowed the instructors in science and philosophy:

> Forasmuch as we see now dayly a further Progress in Philosophy, than could be made by Aristotle's Logick and Physicks, which reigned so long alone in the Schools, and shut out all other; therefore we leave it to the President and Masters, by the advice of the Chancellor, to teach what Systems of Logick, Physicks, Ethicks, and Mathematicks, they think fit in their Schools. Further we judge it requisite, that besides Disputations, the studious Youth be exercised in Declammations and Themes on various Subjects, but not any taken out of the Bible. Those we leave to the Divinity School.[37]

William and Mary continued to be the equal of Harvard and Yale in scientific training to the Revolution. In 1758 William Small, praised by Jefferson as one of the great formative influences in his life, became professor of natural philosophy and mathematics. His subjects became at once fashionable and exciting in their details, and there is evidence other than Jefferson's as to Small's contributions to the students' understanding of the expanding scientific world. In 1762 Small returned to England (where he had a place with Watt in the development of the steam engine), but he performed one more great service for William and Mary when in 1768 he purchased scientific apparatus for the college at least comparable to what Harvard then possessed. James Madison (1749-1812), graduate of 1771 who after theological and scientific study abroad assumed the professorship of natural philosophy he held until his death, was the chief user of the laboratory instruments. His own career as cartographer, topographer, and paleontologist indicates that he used them effectively. One of his students in 1797 wrote somewhat ruefully that "the study of [science] has opened to my View a World replete with discoveries not more Curious than Usefull; and not less explored by me than that Region in which I expect to be placed a thousand years hence."[38]

In 1779, when Jefferson's education bill was first proposed, William and Mary possessed six professorships: (1) Hebrew and Scriptures, (2) Theology and Apologetics, (3) Rhetoric, Logic, and Ethics, (4) Physics, Metaphysics, and Mathematics, (5) Latin and Greek, and (6) the School for Indian boys. Jefferson, as Governor a member of the college's governing board, preferred eight professorships but settled for the six he could reconstruct under existing statutes and charter. He actually was able to abolish 1, 2, and 6, and to substitute in their places Law and Police; Medicine, Astronomy, and Chemistry; and Modern Languages. He added other subjects to the already existing and continuing chairs. All this was with the idea that William and Mary would become the state university crowning his system of public education.

The chair of Medicine, occupied by his old friend Dr. James McClurg existed only a few years and is not really significant in the story of Virginia education. But Charles Bellini's professorship of Modern Languages was a pioneer, and the incumbent did some useful work.

It was the chair of Law, however, which attained real distinction as the first in an American college.

When Jefferson was in Williamsburg as a student, he and his friends had to study law under Wythe or other practicing attorneys in a sort of tutor-apprentice system after they had completed their formal academic work. Now first under Wythe, and later under his almost equally distinguished successor St. George Tucker, Law became a regular department in which scores of Virginians were trained during the period before 1830.

By 1779 President Madison (he had added the presidency to his professorship in 1777) could write to President Ezra Stiles of Yale that entrance requirements at William and Mary were flexible, especially in ancient languages and mathematics. But by 1792 the degree requirements would have seemed arduous and strange to a classically-oriented Yale or Harvard boy, for there was a striking insistence on specific attainments in advanced mathematics, physics, logic, and rhetoric, with only "a competent knowledge" of the ancient languages required.

Samuel Miller, in his 1803 *Brief Retrospect of the Eighteenth Century* (2 vols., New York), gives a good outline of the curriculum and general character of the college as they were in 1801. He points out that the works of Duncan, Reid, and Stewart were studied in the courses in Logic and Philosophy of the Human Mind; Paley in Moral Philosophy; Rutherford and Burlemaqui in Natural Law; Vattel and Martens in the Law of Nations; Locke, Montesquieu, Rousseau, and others in Politics; and Smith's *Wealth of Nations* in Political Economy. More about these writers and their place in the Virginia mind later. But Miller also mentions the scientific lectures and experiments, and the use made of the works of Rowning, Helsham, Martin, Desaguliers, Musschenbroek, Cavallo, Adams, Lavoisier, and Chaptal. The law professor, he states, gave a general survey of principles of government, commented extensively on Blackstone (Tucker edited Blackstone), and explained the structure and principles of American government, particularly the government of Virginia. Though students were not compelled to attend the ancient language courses (presumably the modern languages were required), they had to show competence in the classical tongues (as in 1792) before taking a degree. The reader may little doubt one concluding statement: "There is probably no college in the United States in which political science is studied with so much ardour, and in which it is considered so pre-eminently a favourite subject, as this."[39]

Miller gives other figures and facts. In 1801 William and Mary had only 53 students compared with Pennsylvania's 160, Princeton's 150, Yale's 217, and Harvard's 180 to 200. The "philosophical apparatus" was still tolerably complete but partially out of date. In library figures the college's relative position was better. Harvard was far in front with 13,000 volumes; but William and Mary's 3,000 compared favorably with Columbia's 3,000, Pennsylvania's 1,000, and Princeton's "small" (they would not commit themselves) number.

Though William and Mary retained some of its able professors like Bishop Madison and St. George Tucker a few years longer, in 1801-3 it was markedly in decline. Many factors contributed to this: the loss of British endowments after the Revolution, the Virginia cession of western lands, and above all the removal of the capital to Richmond, are chief among them. The *coup de grâce* was delivered by the establishment of the University of Virginia, which opened its doors in 1825. In 1827 Charles de la Pena, who in that year went to Williamsburg to teach languages, gave a pathetic picture of both town and college.[40] But for two generations the college had done much to direct the mind of the state toward the liberalism we today usually associate with American academe.

Bishop Madison, devoted churchman that he was, was also deistically inclined and a strong Republican. At one time his prayers in chapel are said to have referred to Heaven as a republic rather than a kingdom. But he did warn his students against going too far towards deism and especially towards unitarianism.

Students like David Watson, Joseph C. Cabell, and Garrett Minor could agree in 1798 on the college's "freedom of investigation and unfettered state of mind," expressing the reverse of Rives' opinion of Princeton a little later. The student learned much of "man's inalienable rights of life and liberty."[41] Cabell, back in Williamsburg in 1801 to study law, was impressed by its basic Republicanism. "You cannot imagine with what Paroxysms of Joy we received the news of Mr. Jefferson's election."[42] Religion, metaphysics, even Godwin's *Political Justice,* were not, Cabell felt, popular subjects for discussion then as in 1796-98, but Republicanism endured.

The sons of William and Mary under Bishop Madison were not merely good agrarian Republicans or politicians. A remarkable number of those best known through politics were as well-rounded gentlemen as their colonial ancestors had been, rich in reading, competent in ancient languages, and curious in science. William Short, a founder of Phi Beta Kappa, diplomat, and one of the early American millionaires, was a real scholar and avid book collector. He was not at all a politician. William Munford, George Tucker, and the first John Tyler, with their law professor St. George Tucker, were poets and essayists of local reputation as well as erudite lawyers. Bishop Madison, the same St. George Tucker, John Augustine Smith, and George Watson attained some national distinction in science. Winfield Scott as soldier, John H. Cocke and Isaac Coles as reformers in slavery and temperance, and Francis Gilmer as lawyer-essayist attained eminence outside politics. Bushrod Washington, John Blair, and John Marshall were all Justices of the United States Supreme Court, and Virginia Chief Justice Spencer Roane was in his own time acknowledged as at least their equal. As we survey in later chapters Virginia poets, novelists, essayists, economists, philosophers, rhetoricians, even architects, we shall again note several score William and Mary students of this period.

Outside Virginia the college's influence was also felt, though it is harder to measure. At least fourteen members of Congress born in Virginia before 1810 but representing other states attended William and Mary.[43] It is probable that there were many more. As late as the 1830's Joseph Glover Baldwin was impressed by the William and Mary men he met in Alabama and Mississippi, Virginians leading a variety of enterprises along the southern frontier.[44]

By the end of the Jeffersonian period in Virginia the influence of two Presbyterian colleges was a strong second to William and Mary's. The origins of Hampden-Sydney and Washington Colleges may be traced back to the Revolution, but they rose to college stature during the first national period. Their development symbolizes the growing influence and size of the Scotch-Irish population in the South.

Hampden-Sydney appears to have come into existence as an academy about 1774 when the clash between dissenters and Establishment was especially sharp. It was formed to supply the needs of the Presbyterians of Prince Edward, Hanover, and Cumberland counties, where they were thickly settled. It opened in 1776 as Prince Edward Academy, changing its name the next year to Hampden-Sydney. Among the original trustees were Patrick Henry and James Madison (the national President), both Anglicans, and its first rector or president was Samuel Stanhope Smith, later professor and president of Princeton. By act of 1783 the academy legally became a college, though its grammar school continued for many decades. From the beginning to 1820 the college was able to exist by having the local pastorate combined with the presidency. In 1821, under New Hampshire-born Jonathan P. Cushing, it took on new vigor.

At the outset Hampden-Sydney had taken Princeton as a model for organization and curriculum and had avowed its adherence to the ideals of the new republican government. Its announced policies were: (1) that sound learning be promoted, (2) that principles of liberty and patriotism be impressed on youth, and (3) that true religion be conserved and the kingdom of Christ advanced.

Associated with the college through the early years of the nineteenth century were a number of scholarly Presbyterian clergymen such as Moses Hoge, Conrad Speece, and John Holt Rice, whose names will appear again in later chapters. One of its professors in the early twenties was James Marsh, later president of the University of Vermont and a pioneer student of Coleridgean philosophy in this country. In 1807 the first Virginia Presbyterian theological seminary, with Dr Rice as its head, was founded in connection with the college.

Samuel Miller in his *Brief Retrospect* of 1803 dismissed Hampden-Sydney with few words, pointing out that it had scarcely any funds and only five hundred books in its library. But its sixty or seventy students were more than William and Mary had. And by 1819, when *The Virginia Literary and Evangelical Magazine* outlined (II, No. 5 [May, 1819], 237-38) Hampden-Sydney's curriculum, its offerings appear quite respectable. The grammar school still existed, but above it were four classes, each having two "studies" and one recitation every day. The freshman studied Cicero, Sallust, Xenophon, arithmetic and algebra, English grammar and rhetoric; the sophomores, geography, logic, Longinus, Euclid, Homeric and Greek prosody, and Livy; the juniors, chemistry with experiments and agriculture, trigonometry, surveying, conic sections, natural philosophy, astronomy,

Horace, and English composition; and the seniors, philosophy of the mind, rhetoric, moral philosophy, English dissertations (term papers?), law of nature and nations, and the elements of history and chronology. This seems a solid and varied curriculum, with far less emphasis on politics and political economy than William and Mary gave.

The institution's intellectual vitality is evident in the formation by certain faculty and alumni in 1824 of a "Literary and Philosophical Society." Cushing, Rice, and Marsh were among the eleven founders. There the problems of Virginia in the new age were to be the most frequent topics for discussion. The subject selected for the first lecture, to be followed by discussion, was "The Best Means of Exciting a Higher Literary Spirit in Virginia." The utility of language study, common schools for Virginia, influence of form of government on individual character, abolition of slavery, moral philosophy as a branch of liberal education, and the influence of the Christian religion in producing the American Revolution are among the subjects on which the earnest group read papers.

Later other persons, such as William Maxwell of Norfolk, were invited to speak before the Society. His paper of 1826 and that of Jesse Burton Harrison in 1827, both concerned with Virginia letters and education, were among the best given before the group disbanded in 1833 to merge into another college organization. These essay-speeches afford good evidence of the high quality of Presbyterian social and educational thinking at this period.[45]

Over in the Valley of Virginia, in Rockbridge and Augusta counties, the Scotch-Irish Presbyterians who had come down from the north also felt the need of educational facilities. The Augusta Academy begun in 1749 is said to have been the germ of the later collegiate institution, but is more clearly traceable in Liberty Hall Academy, chartered by the state legislature in 1782. In 1786, after some urging by General Andrew Moore of Rockbridge and General Francis Preston of Washington county, George Washington made a gift of his James River Canal stock as endowment to Liberty Hall. It was renamed Washington Academy (soon College). In 1803 the Cincinnati Society gave more funds, and in 1826 John Robinson of Rockbridge added to this endowment.

As suggested earlier, Washington College's early faculty and trustees were log-college or Princeton men, and they attempted to model their college on Princeton. The institution's collegiate status was so little recognized in 1803 that Samuel Miller ignores it in his *Brief Retrospect,* saying that the only Virginia colleges were William and Mary and Hampden-Sydney. Yet the course of study adopted at Washington College the next year, in 1804, was that generally followed at Princeton and was continued into the 1820's. It is strikingly different in organization from Hampden-Sydney's, despite both institutions' acknowledged indebtedness to Princeton. Washington College devoted the whole freshman year to study of the Greek and Latin classics, and the second year entirely to mathematics. The first five months of the third year were devoted to geography, and the second five to natural philosophy and astronomy. The senior or fourth year included work in Blair's *Lectures,* logic, Burlemaqui's natural law, with parts of Locke, Reid and Stewart "on the mind." President Henry Ruffner, who left notes on this curriculum, noted that after 1825 Stewart was usually omitted. The student might substitute French for the first year Greek and still get his degree. In practice many students doubled up and finished in three years. Dr. Ruffner himself graduated in eighteen months.[46]

Naturally the influence of the two Presbyterian colleges in Virginia in this period does not seriously rival William and Mary's. Yet it is by no means negligible. One may glance at politics alone. During the period up to 1825 eleven of Virginia's Senators had attended college, eight at William and Mary, one at Washington College, and one at both William and Mary and Hampden-Sydney. Of the sixty-nine Representatives who had attended college, 36.2 per cent attended William and Mary and 22.9 per cent Washington College or Hampden-Sydney, not at all an unfavorable proportion. Before 1826, the records indicate, at least thirty-six of Washington College's alumni became clergymen and forty-two more clergymen and teachers. The meager Hampden-Sydney records indicate at least twenty-four ministers became degree-holders between 1786 and 1820. Of this total of 102, all but eight were Presbyterians. Other types of alumni, by occupation, are more difficult to distinguish.[47]

Whatever their profession, these sons of Washington College and Hampden-Sydney carried with them through Virginia and the South, as I. Woodbridge Riley indicates in *American Philosophy: the Early Schools,* a combination of Scottish philosophy, "an intellectual glacier . . . of cold facts," combined with Calvinism.[48] As will be pointed out in later chapters, the Jeffersonian Virginian might get his Scottish philosophy by other means than the Presbyterian colleges. But there can be no doubt of the fact that the rising influence of the two institutions was a strong factor in bringing about the decline of deism among Virginia leaders toward the end of the 1820's.

The founding of a state university in Virginia, the capstone of the educational pyramid Jefferson insisted upon, has its actual origins in the College of William and Mary and the consciousness immediately after the Revolution of the need for a national university. The germinal idea present in several minds was fertilized and even altered by studies of European and British universities and the founding of the French academy in Richmond; in Jefferson's mind it was affected by the personal advice given him by scores of individuals. The plans went through several stages and forms, from the 1779 legislative bill aimed at secularizing William and Mary to the bill of 1819 which officially created the new institution. The idea has a history of grandiose visions, tremendous disappointments, compromises, and finally realization in a form superior to any other then existing in America but inferior to the original conception. It is above all the fulfillment of a great democrat's dream into which he incorporated the visions and the practical labors of his friends and neighbors. Jefferson could never have created the University of Virginia alone.

What he tried to do for William and Mary in 1779 has already been discussed. The new professorships were part of that plan of secularization, for he and his collaborators felt that religious freedom and education were mutually dependent. In the 1779 Bill No. 80, which was never passed, the statement was made that the college had not developed into the university expected, a significant remark in several ways. Yet at this time no one seems to have found any particular fault with its location in the capital city or in most features of its organization. In fact General Washington, for some years himself the college's chancellor, certainly had William and Mary in mind when during his Presidency he proposed a national university to be located in the nation's capital, with emphasis on political economy and government. Liberal arts would be but necessary concomitants in the institution he hoped might train for national leadership, though he emphasized the importance of a flourishing state of the arts and sciences to national reputation and prosperity.

While he was in France in the 1780's Jefferson continued to study higher education. He was so much impressed by the Swiss College of Geneva that when its representative later in 1794 proposed its removal to America he recommended it strongly to President Washington as a national university. The latter, with basic common sense, pointed out the difficulties which would attend an entirely French-speaking faculty, the probability that all the professors might not have the character of good citizens, the ill effect the aristocratic leanings of many of the group would have on a republican society, and the undesirability of thus shutting out all able professors from other countries.

The idea of a direct connection between European higher learning and the infant republic had considerable tangible popular support in at least one project, however. The Chevalier Quesnay de Beaurepaire, grandson of the French philosopher and economist and a former captain in the Revolutionary army in Virginia, was the father of this scheme. He himself said that the idea of founding an academy in America was first proposed to him by John Page of Rosewell, who urged him to secure professors from Europe, promising to secure their appointment. By 1783 Quesnay had the scheme well under way, soliciting funds in Europe and America, and planning to establish at Richmond, the new capital of Virginia, a kind of French academy of arts and sciences, with branches in Baltimore, Philadelphia, and New York. The institution was to be both national and international, and to be affiliated with the great learned societies of Europe. It was to have a president, vice-president, six counselors, a treasurer-general, French professors, artists-in-chief, twenty-five resident and one hundred and seventy-five non-resident associates selected from the ablest talent on both sides of the Atlantic. The academy was to have its own press and publications, museums and libraries, a system of furnishing the Old World with specimens of the fauna and flora of America, expert French teachers in every field for the instruction of American youth, and French mining experts to develop American natural resources. These were but a part of its proposed function.[49] The amazing thing is that the Academy got as far as it did. Scores of great names in France and the United States, and some famous liberal ones in England, were among its sponsors and more important, among the financial contributors. In Virginia citizens of Richmond, Williamsburg, Alexandria, Petersburg, Norfolk, and Fredericksburg, along with many planters, supported it. The six counselors, chosen by the subscribers to act with President Quesnay, were Jefferson, Colonel Thomas Randolph, Dr. James McClurg, Colonel Robert Goode, Dr. William Foushee, and Robert Boyd. The cornerstone of the principal Academy building was laid on July 1, 1786. Quesnay then returned to Paris to secure his faculty and raise more funds. He found support among the prominent Frenchmen of his time, including the King and Queen, the Royal Academy of Science, and the Royal Academy of Painting and Sculpture.[50]

Here was something concretely suggestive of what France had meant to the United States. In a sense, Quesnay's Academy represented the high watermark of French culture in the United States, at least in Virginia, where the common man as well as the leader was likely at this period to be strongly pro-French. Had the Academy succeeded, the coloring of our national mind, especially the southern mind, might have been quite different. Had it succeeded, there would have been no need for another University of Virginia.

But fate in the form of the French Revolution intervened, and the Frenchmen who might have got the institution in operation fought for their lives or their ideals without time or money for Quesnay's project. It remains among the fascinating things which might have been. But the great plan itself in its brochure form was probably before Jefferson as he tailored his own educational adornment for his state. The Academy building became a Richmond landmark: it served as the meeting place of the Convention which ratified the Federal Constitution in 1788, and fittingly enough as a center of the arts, it served as the city's theater until its destruction by fire in 1803. On its site stood the theater destroyed in the tragic fire of 1811.

By the time of his election to the Presidency in 1801 Jefferson was again considering a national university, perhaps simultaneously with one for his own state.[51] In his annual message to Congress of December 2, 1806, he spoke of a national university, though there is no evidence of his active movement in its behalf. Exactly when he conceived his plan for a new institution in a new place, for Virginia or the nation, it is now impossible to determine. As early as January 18, 1800, he did write to Joseph Priestley concerning his plan for an up-country university.[52] In the same year he was interested in Du Pont de Nemours' plan for a national university. Though he by no means agreed with it, it may have suggested some things he was to use. In 1806-7 he talked over with Joel Barlow that gentleman's plans for a national university.[53] But except for the Geneva episode and the paragraph in his annual message, he did little to foster such an institution, probably because of his growing anti-consolidationist attitudes toward government generally.[54]

By 1806-7 several of his friends were actively pushing the idea of a state institution. Governor William H. Cabell spoke out for it. And about the same time Isaac Coles was urging Joseph C. Cabell to enter the legislature so that he might work in its behalf.

The idea of a Piedmont-located university may not have been original with Jefferson. Anyone who had spent a year in the Williamsburg climate knew its drawbacks, especially the danger of malaria, and Tidewater Virginia and the old college seemed irrecoverable anyway to many Jeffersonian leaders. All his life one William and Mary professor and distinguished jurist, St. George Tucker, was interested in the establishment of a new university, which he did not want located in Williamsburg. By 1794 there are references in his papers to suggestions he had made to governor and legislature concerning such an institution. Two years later he suggested to President Washington plans for a national university. In 1804 Littleton W. Tazewell was reminding him of "the great fabric we talked of erecting somewhere near Charlottesville," and in the same year W. W. Hening urged that he draw up a bill proposing it. Perhaps it was as a result of Hening's request that Tucker drew up his "Sketch of a Plan for the Endowment and Establishment of a State-University, in Virginia," a remarkable document surviving among his papers in Williamsburg.[55]

Its preamble is worthy of Jefferson, and thoroughly republican. Tucker proposed the appropriation of $5000 per year for ten years beginning in 1805 to purchase sufficient land in some healthy part of the state "not more than twenty-five miles eastward of the blue ridge of mountains" and not nearer than three miles to any town. He made recommendations concerning modes of electing trustees, and he suggested ten-acre lots for the sites of colleges (clearly he had the Oxford-Cambridge organization in mind), the solicitation of farmlands as endowment, the building of staff-mechanics houses, even an official "Founders' Day" (to be the anniversary of May 15, 1776, when *Virginia's* Declaration of Independence was made). Like William and Mary, the new university should have both Chancellor and President, and Tucker outlined the duties of each. He proposed an ingenious use of one thousand Bank of Virginia shares as endowment for a system of junior and senior fellowships and for general purposes. The eight professorships he outlined were quite close to those Jefferson had suggested in 1779. And he further suggested that until more colleges than one be established, the president of the university should be professor of moral philosophy. Finally Tucker gave extensive figures of the proposed accumulated funds and their uses in various ways, including library and scholarships as well as fellowships. Altogether it is a plan worthy of comparison with Jefferson's later ones, and in many respects preferable to his earlier proposals for the rehabilitation of William and Mary.

James Madison during his Presidency of the United States more than once in his annual messages advocated a national university. From his brief outlines one may gather that he hoped it would act as a unifying agency for the national mind as well as a means of its development. Though there is no necessary conflict between this idea and that for a state institution, by 1816-17 Madison had with Jefferson concentrated his interest on a proposed university for their native commonwealth. Presumably he had found, as had Washington and Jefferson before him, that conflicting Congressional educational interests were impossible to reconcile.

The story of the struggle to establish the University of Virginia is too long and complex, and has been covered too thoroughly by Herbert B. Adams, Philip A. Bruce, and Roy J. Honeywell to warrant attempting it here. But in outline it should be traced, for it is the story of a cooperative intellectual enterprise to which many Virginians contributed. Father and founder was of course Thomas Jefferson, who had envisioned at least a quarter of a century earlier something quite like the institution that was opened in 1825. Some of its connections with schemes of elementary and secondary public education have already been mentioned It was to be the capstone of an educational pyramid. Finding that the total scheme would never be realized in his lifetime, Jefferson with his friends Cabell, Cocke, and Madison concentrated more and more on higher education, for they rightly felt that a comprehensive system must begin at the top. From the 1790's Jefferson read and pondered schemes of public education and of higher education. He talked and corresponded with English liberals like Thomas Cooper and Joseph Priestley, with the French philosopher Du Pont de Nemours with the Portuguese scientist Correa da Serra, and with scores of other Europeans and Americans.

But a concatenation of circumstances was necessary to bring the opportunity for action: the establishment of the Albemarle Academy, its elevation in 1816 into Central College, and the campaigns for endowment for the latter occurred from the end of the war in 1814 to the establishment of its successor the University of Virginia by law in 1819. The Jefferson group's strategy in the Legislature and in the Rockfish Gap meeting where the exact location for the institution was to be determined are significant phases of educational history. Often faced directly with almost certain failure, Cabell, Cocke, and Jefferson never gave up. They cut the size of proposed physical plant, faculty, and endowment, but they held firmly to the concept of a genuine university offering a variety of curricula under liberal auspices. It was inevitable that when the first Board of Visitors was appointed, Jefferson was named Rector, and Madison, Cabell, and Cocke were among the six others. Monroe was soon added.

The story of Jefferson's "academical village," today usually recognized as the handsomest in America and the world, is a story of architectural achievement, of the adaptation of classic and Palladian models to the American landscape and climate. The story of the search for a competent faculty is revealing of the appeal the whole idea of the University of Virginia had outside this country and of the excellent impression a Virginia private gentleman emissary could make on the British intellectual.

Unsuccessfully Jefferson tried to obtain Dr. Samuel Knox, George Ticknor, and Nathaniel Bowditch as original faculty members. Lesser northerners wanted the post, but Jefferson and his advisor Correa feared Harvard and Yale's "mediocrity." Earlier he had actually engaged Dr. Thomas Cooper, liberal theologian, chemist, and political economist. But strong opposition developed because of Cooper's alleged atheism or unitarianism from Dr. John Holt Rice and other Presbyterians who originally had welcomed the idea of a state university. Cooper felt compelled to resign. Jefferson wrote bitterly in 1820 that the larger-numbered dissenting sects, the Methodists and Baptists, supported him, but that the narrow and bigoted Presbyterians had stirred up the whole business. He never forgave them.

With the situation what it was, and always having liked the idea anyway, Jefferson determined to have a European-trained faculty. Though in some respects he and Madison preferred Frenchmen, they knew the language handicap, and sent their representative in the summer of 1824 to Great Britain. That representative, thirty-four year old William and Mary graduate Francis Walker Gilmer, visited Oxford and Cambridge, London and Edinburgh, in a search for suitable men. He also ordered thousands of books for the library from a list drawn up by Jefferson and Madison.

Gilmer made a fine impression in London, Cambridge, and Edinburgh (he didn't find many Oxonians at home). His Virginia manners, acute critical intelligence, and genuine learning made him something of a social lion in the Scottish capital. After some vicissitudes, he was able to return to Virginia at the end of 1824 with five professorships filled. The German George Blaetterman (Gilmer had talked with him in London) was to teach modern languages, including with them the Anglo-Saxon Jefferson insisted upon as a basis for understanding modern English. Cambridge Masters of Arts George Long and Thomas Hewett Key were to occupy the chairs of ancient languages and mathematics respectively; Charles Bonnycastle, son of a noted mathematician, the professorship of natural philosophy; and Robley Dunglison, a native of Cumberland, the chair of medicine and anatomy. Without exception these were able men. Bonnycastle, Long, and Key, still quite young, made names for themselves at Virginia and the two latter a few years later at the new University of London. Dunglison after many years at Charlottesville went on to Baltimore and Philadelphia and became one of the distinguished writers of his time on medical subjects.

Jefferson in 1824 as in 1779 preferred eight professorships and had so organized the curriculum. A sixth man, the Irish Thomas Addis Emmet, was found in New York for the chair of natural his-

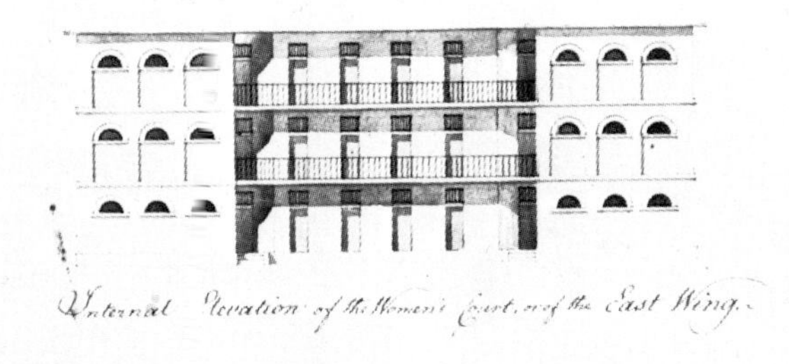

Virginia State Penitentiary

Drawing by Benjamin Latrobe. Courtesy of the Virginia State Library, Archives Division.

John Holt Rice

Attributed to W. S. Ford. Courtesy of the Union Theological Seminary.

Thomas Ritchie

Engraving by Adam B. Walter. Courtesy of The Virginia Historical Society.

Bremo

Courtesy of the Virginia Chamber of Commerce, photo by Flournoy.

Poplar Forest Near Lynchburg, Virginia

Courtesy of the Virginia Chamber of Commerce, photo by Flournoy.

tory. The other two professorships, Jefferson insisted, must be filled by Americans. For Moral Philosophy and Ethics (which included various forms of philosophy, psychology, and eventually in the Virginia system belles-lettres) and Law should be taught according to republican (he might have said Republican) principles. He would have no Federalist Richmond lawyer to corrupt the healthy agrarian democratic faith with which he believed they would enter the institution. After considerable negotiation the former Congressman and essayist George Tucker was engaged for the chair of Ethics, and Gilmer himself for that of Law (though the latter was in such desperate health that the chair was later filled by John Tayloe Lomax). Tucker will appear in several subsequent chapters, for he was an amazingly fertile thinker and versatile writer. Jefferson summed up the whole group of professors by writing contentedly to a friend that a better selection could not have been made.

The eight professorships represented the three major divisions of higher education, the disciplinary, the scientific, and the vocational. They also represented the new and the old, looking backward to Locke and forward to Spencer. Aside from this equilibrium, the general scheme was remarkable for three uncommon features, the division into schools, the ability of each school to expand of itself as its funds increased, and the unhampered right of election of subjects. Each professor was head of a school, and each school was confined to one comprehensive subject, though later this one was sometimes divided. A student might elect one or more schools. Edgar Allan Poe, for example, in 1826 elected only ancient and modern languages. Gessner Harrison, later professor of ancient languages, appears to have elected everything, and took a medical degree along with his liberal arts.

Jefferson believed in the right of unlimited inquiry, that is, in everything but the two chairs held by Americans only. The intolerance he condemned in the sectarians is manifest in the list of textbooks he had the Board of Visitors require for the courses in politics. They represent, when they are partisan, only the Republican, not the Federalist point of view. They were Sidney's *Discourses,* Locke's *Essay on Civil Government,* the Declaration of Independence, *The Federalist,* the *Virginia Document* [Resolutions of 1798] *of 1799,* and Washington's *Farewell Address.*

But men like George Tucker were anything but narrow even in their politics. Among the Rives Papers in the Library of Congress are one of his printed examinations in Moral Philosophy of about 1828, an answer to it or a similar examination, and a student notebook based on his lectures. The examination is a mixture of psychological, philosophical (especially ethical), and aesthetic questions, including a great deal on the Scottish associationists, Alison on taste and beauty, Brown on the sublime, and Mandeville's system of morals. It is by anybody's standards a stimulating exercise indicative of a stimulating teacher and material. One of the simpler queries would have pleased the late Rector: "Wherein do the love of liberty, and the love of power differ?" The answers include extended and thoughtful discussion of the Scottish philosophers like Brown, Blair, and Stewart, and something of Adam Smith, Burke, and Longinus. The notebook contains jottings under "Posthumous Fame" (with Jefferson as an example), "Desire for Power," and "Desire of Superiority," "Patriotism," etc.

Though similar questions might have been asked at William and Mary, the founders of the University of Virginia did have a clear perception of the difference between a college and a university. The whole concept of the Charlottesville institution was that of what we today call in America a graduate school, or what the Europeans still mean by university. It was not part of the original plan to do the work of a college. Soon it was realized that the plan must be modified, partly because of the inequalities of secondary training students brought with them, and some of the work was certainly on the ordinary college level. But it continued to aim at vocational training or the discovery of truth rather than at the simple conservation of truth usually aimed at in the college.

In his Rockfish Gap report of 1818, Jefferson defined the objects of higher education.[56] First of all, it was designed "To form the statesmen, legislators, and judges, on whom public prosperity and individual happiness so much depend." Then to expound laws, to harmonize the interests of agriculture and commerce by well-expounded courses in political economy, to develop the reasoning faculties and cultivate the morals, to enlighten with mathematics and physics and administer to the health and comforts of life, and finally to form the habits of reflection and virtuous conduct which lead to happiness. In other words, the aim of higher education had the same goal education had always had for the republican Virginian, to make leaders and citizens, in this case on an exalted intellectual scale. In the detailed plans for the university, Jefferson and his friends went beyond this. They were trying to prepare men in various specialized depths for their individual roles in a future more complex society. Law and politics were important but by no means everything.

A few words should be said about professional training outside the conventional college or university. Medical education has already been mentioned. And the foundation of the first Presbyterian theological seminary has also been referred to. It should also be pointed out that the first Episcopal theological school, the seminary at Alexandria, was also founded in this period in 1823 by Dr. William H. Wilmer. Both institutions are flourishing today, though the Presbyterian institution has detached itself from Hampden-Sydney and moved to Richmond.

Perhaps it should not be forgotten that Virginia President Washington at the same time he recommended a national university to Congress, suggested the establishment of what was to become the United States Military Academy at West Point. However pacific a nation might be, he declared, it must have a stock of military knowledge for emergencies. And a William and Mary graduate of this period who was later a University of Virginia professor was to conceive and found the Massachusetts Institute of Technology and thus inaugurate technological-research-training at the highest level.

Whether legal education in Virginia between 1790 and 1830 should be considered under "Formal Education" may be doubtful, for it was for the most part not carried on in institutions. Mention has already been made of the tutor-and-apprentice system followed by George Wythe before he became professor of law at William and Mary. Such was the prevalent mode of acquiring training for what was considered the most distinguished of professions, or rather the one in which the individual would have most opportunity to distinguish himself in a young republic.

The records of scores of such educational relationships between able lawyers and young aspirants survive. Usually the young man took up residence with his mentor's family and learned partly by acting as legal clerk for his tutor. Monroe and Rives were fortunate enough to study under Jefferson himself, the one before and the other after his major public career. John Randolph of Roanoke, as we have noted, studied under his relative Edmund Randolph. William F. Wickham, financially the most successful of Virginia lawyers, studied under Senator Henry Tazewell; Andrew Stevenson under Adam Craig; John Taylor of Caroline under Edmund Pendleton; and the elder John Tyler under Robert Carter Nicholas. William Wirt, as soon as he began to achieve fame as a courtroom lawyer, was besieged by young men. His ledger[57] indicates that many studied under him in Richmond, among them Francis Gilmer and Abel P. Upshur. After he became Attorney General of the United States, he ran what was almost a school for would-be lawyers. So many applicants had he that he drew up and caused to be printed in 1821 a set of regulations[58] for study which would frighten them off or at least warn them of what impended. He outlined the course of study (much that St. George Tucker had given earlier at William and Mary), described the required written opinion on one subject and several oral arguments on others each student must present, and listed some of the reading in history and belles-lettres to be done in the evenings. The hours of legal study were to be nine to three in the summer and ten to three in the winter, during which time they might also consult him on difficulties encountered. Wirt confessed this formal imposed schedule an experiment, but there are indications it may have been fairly typical of what many lawyers attempted to have their charges follow. That they were reasonably successful is evident in the tremendous reputations for legal erudition held by St. George Tucker, Jefferson, Gilmer, Roane, and several others, not to mention the Virginia lawyer's famed effectiveness in the courtroom.

Formal education was hardly designed to aid the farmer directly, though Virginia remained and expected to remain an agrarian state. The problems of erosion, fertilization of worn-out lands, improvement of livestock strains, and pomology, all vital concerns of most citizens, were only touched upon in minor segments of courses in natural history and philosophy, though there is evidence that they received more attention than they had in earlier periods. There were agricultural societies which grappled with these problems, but they were unconnected with formal education.

In Virginia, as in the rest of America, the Scottish common sense ideas were becoming the official philosophy of colleges and universities and as already indicated were finding their way into secondary school curricula and teaching. Their tendency to combine criticism and morality and their treatment of imagination and metaphysics are all evident in the four institutions of higher learning existing at the end of the period. As already suggested, and as will be discussed later, it was peculiarly agreeable to the liberal Republicans who dominated thinking and action in the period.

Yet contradictions and conflicts remained. Proficiency in Latin was required for graduation in the University of Virginia at the same time it encouraged free electives. The illimitable freedom of the human mind was stressed by Presbyterian and Jeffersonian educators alike, but in practice they imposed rigid restrictions. All educators encouraged national patriotism, but most of those in Virginia taught political and economic philosophies which led toward sectionalism.

And by no means all citizens wanted to pay the price of education or appreciated it at any price. Its proponents ran foul of many local interests. On February 7, 1826, just five months before his death, Jefferson observed somewhat grimly that "I have long been sensible that while I was endeavouring to render my country the greatest of all services, that of regenerating the public education, and placing the rising generation on the level of our sister states (which they have proudly held heretofore), I was discharging the odious function of a physician pouring medicine down the throat of a patient insensible of needing it."[59] Yet he clung firmly to the belief he had expressed ten years earlier that "the diffusion of knowledge among the people" will in the end cause "tyranny and oppression of body and mind [to] vanish like evil spirits at the dawn of day."[60]

III

READING AND LIBRARIES

The taste for reading is commoner [in Virginia] among men of the first class than in any other part of America.

—Duc de La Rochefoucauld-Liancourt, *Travels through the United States of North America,* 1799.

The Federalist *and other writings of Madison, the works of George Mason, Jefferson, . . . the Greek and especially the Roman historians, the Letters of Junius and the speeches of Burke, made up the bulk of his library, and fed his mind with thoughts of that deepest and saddest of all problems, human government.*

—Ellen M. Bagby, ed., *The Old Virginia Gentleman and Other Sketches by George W. Bagby,* 1948, p. 21.

You know the taste of the Virginian how passionately fond of handsome things, ergo let Guthrie be fresh *and* Nicely *bound.*

—Mason L. Weems to Mathew Carey, September 6, 1796.

The considerable number of Virginians educated in the rapidly expanding academies and colleges did not forsake their books when they matured. As farmers, lawyers, physicians, clergymen, and merchants of a still largely rural culture, they found much of their intellectual stimulus in reading. Sometimes as a solace in lonely hours, but more frequently as a means of understanding a changing world or keeping up with a demanding profession, they gathered around them quite respectable private libraries. Some organized library societies for their own and their neighbors' benefit. Some simply borrowed what they could.

These were the more serious. The multiplying English and American novels, popular poetry and drama, popular and semi-popular magazines, and newspapers representing factional or regional interest were also read by these men and women and by a new reading group, some of whom had never been educated beyond the "old-field" elementary schools. Religion, politics, geography, history, travel, and even some of the sciences, presented in simple terms, had a wide appeal in various printed forms.

Reading tastes can be determined in several ways for several different segments of the population. For the preferences of the common man who could read, we have little beyond a few inventories of wills and the contents of the newspapers, and even this latter means seems aimed at a more learned element of society. For the great middle group of fairly well educated men and women, we have the same sources plus a few diaries and letters, the testimony of one successful book agent, and the book and magazine advertisements in the newspapers. For "the first class," as foreigners liked to call the educated group of leading gentlemen in Virginia, we have all the above sources and some book order records, careful lists of the contents of certain libraries, and in some instances the actual surviving libraries. Before turning to general and specific tastes in books and the means of developing and satisfying these tastes among the upper and some of the middle group, we should look first at the two forms of the printed word most generally read, the newspapers and magazines.

A. *Newspapers and Magazines*

Everybody read newspapers. From the one journal of the earlier eighteenth century, the Williamsburg *Virginia Gazette,* had sprung weekly, semi-weekly, and daily sheets in every good-sized town. Alexandria, Fredericksburg, Petersburg, Lynchburg, Norfolk, and many smaller places published their own papers. Richmond by 1800 or soon thereafter had several.

Every man in the state who wanted to know what was going on within it subscribed to one of these newspapers of the capital city. The *Virginia Gazette* had moved from Williamsburg with the government and, published by several different men, continued for many years. Under Augustine Davis it was a Federalist journal, though most of its material was excerpted from foreign or eastern papers.[1] Later it became the *Virginia Patriot.* Junior to it but contemporary was the Virginia *Argus* (1793), Republican in politics and edited by the Quaker Samuel Pleasants, and like its rival showing dextrous use of the scissors. It is remembered chiefly as the vehicle for the first version of Wirt's *Letters of the British Spy.*

The *Examiner* (1798), edited by Meriwether Jones and his brother Skelton, was also Republican, perhaps more strongly so than the *Argus.* It was counter-balanced politically for a time by the Virginia *Federalist,* edited by Stewart and Rind.[2] Among other Richmond papers two are particularly notable. From the ashes of the *Examiner* emerged in 1804 the *Enquirer,* edited by the militant Republican Jeffersonian Thomas Ritchie. In 1824 appeared its rival the *Whig,* edited by John Hampden Pleasants. Both these papers endured beyond the limits of our period and had a great influence in the state. A man's political assertions were likely to be colored by the columns of the *Whig* or the *Enquirer.* Joseph Glover Baldwin, writing in 1856, remembered that in Alabama and Mississippi expatriate Virginians always continued to read one or the other of the two papers.[3]

Particularly did the *Enquirer* exert itself within and outside the state. Ritchie had as contributors some of the ablest writers of his time, the essayists of the William Wirt circle who first printed their *Rainbow* and *Old Bachelor* pieces there, and also famous jurists, brilliant young lawyers, teachers, and clergymen. The articles were completely anonymous, or more frequently, were signed with appropriate classical noms de plume, as "Agricola," "Cato," "Hortensius," or "Democritus." Even during John Quincy Adams' administration a cabinet meeting in Washington might consider seriously what some contributor to the *Enquirer* had said about some government policy. Wirt, who was then Attorney General would be asked to express his opinion as to the seriousness of the *Enquirer's* opposition.

In a day when any public man's reputation might be made or unmade by the frequently irresponsible comments in the journals, newspapers were devoured by a politically-minded state. Jefferson himself had so suffered in them from personal attacks, including those of the notorious James T. Callender, that in later years he canceled all his newspaper subscriptions—save one, the *Enquirer*. As he remarked on September 8, 1823, to the expatriate Virginian William Short, it is "the best that is published or ever has been published in America."

Like almost all other newspapers of the period, the *Enquirer* attempted to be a literary journal as well as dispenser of the news. Ritchie tried to keep it well-balanced, but actually it was about seven-eighths news and one-eighth literature, with some interesting advertising in addition. The first two pages contained verbatim records of Congress and world and national news taken from other papers. The third page also contained national news; and here too the Virginia contributors saw their essays published along with editorials, the two often indistinguishable. The fourth page, a miscellany, included scientific articles notices of "internal improvements," and a part of a column of poetry.

Earlier and contemporary papers such as the *Argus* also carried verse, original and excerpted. Simple effusions such as "To a Young Lady on Her Birthday" (*Argus,* May 19, 1804) were characteristic, as were old favorites like "Drink To Me Only With Thine Eyes" (*Argus,* September 4, 1805). Political, satiric, and sentimental "Lines" were frequent. In 1807 the *Argus* carried an "Ode" to Jamestown. Sometimes these papers printed excellent verse, as Shelley's "Hymn to Intellectual Beauty" (*Enquirer,* June 3, 1817, from the *London Examiner*). In 1825 the *Enquirer* printed "Byron's Last Poem." Actually the verse of Scott, Byron, and Moore made up about one-half the material published in the *Enquirer* poetry columns between 1815 and 1827. Wordsworth is occasionally referred to, but no mention of Keats has been discovered in the several years examined. Among Americans, Washington Allston, Richard Henry Wilde, and William Cullen Bryant appear, and Virginia poets like Richard Dabney and Daniel Bryan are represented or referred to in various papers.

The essays (see Chapters VIII and X) were largely political, but there was some literary and dramatic criticism and a number of pieces on oratory or eloquence. In the *Argus* (August 29, 1811), for example, appeared "The Character of Richard Brinsley Sheridan [as Orator]" and in the Fredericksburg *Political Arena* (April 8, 1828) "American Authors and English Critics." The latter journal, more avowedly literary than any of the Richmond papers, carried in 1827 a number of ghost tales, including one "old Virginian story" (August 31), and in one issue (June 6, 1828) had the whole front page devoted to a chapter from "a new Waverley novel."

While the newspapers thus offered political and general news, controversial essays, and belles-lettres, the contemporary periodical showed less variety, and it did not reach so wide a public. Though no figures are available, it would be safe to say that the literary-political periodical reached proportionately far more of the literate population than it does today.

Newspaper booksellers' advertisements, to be discussed further below, include titles of magazines ready for distribution. Individual numbers could be supplied to anyone wishing to purchase them or to regular subscribers. But dealers also had in stock complete sets of the earlier *Tatler* and *Spectator* (often in American editions), the *Edinburgh Review* (1802 on), the American Federalist *Port Folio* (1801-27), and the Navy-oriented *Analectic Magazine* (1813-20). The Baltimore news-periodical *Niles' Weekly Register* (1811 on) was also in demand.

The British Whig *Edinburgh Review* and its Tory rival the *Quarterly Review* (1809 on) were easily the most popular periodicals, native or foreign, in Virginia during the period before 1830. Library lists also reveal that Virginians read regularly British magazines like the *Analytical Review* (1788-99), which contained reviews of Jefferson's *Notes* and other American books; the *Annual Register* (1758 on), edited for thirty-one years by Edmund Burke; the *Anti-Jacobin Review* (1798-1821); *Blackwood's Edinburgh Magazine* (1817 on), famous for its caustic reviews; the *European Magazine* (1782-1826); the useful *Gentleman's Magazine* (1731 on); and a number of sporting journals. Virginians also in the early period subscribed to Mathew Carey's *American Museum* (1787-92), in which a number of Virginians published verses and political essays. Volume II, for example, had forty Virginia subscribers, including Dr. McClurg, John Marshall, James Madison, Jefferson, and George Washington. For the same volume Maryland had 145 subscribers (Philadelphia was close by), South Carolina 86, Georgia four, and Kentucky two. Later they read the *North American Review* (1815 on), the *American Quarterly Review* (1827-37), and the *Analectic Magazine* already mentioned. A fair number patronized the *Virginia Literary and Evangelical Magazine* (1818-28), and in the very last years of the period John Randolph and William C. Rives at least subscribed to the new Charleston, South Carolina, *Southern Review* (1828-32). There are long runs, often complete sets of several of these journals in the larger Virginia libraries.

B. *General Reading Tastes*

Perhaps the best indices to what most literate Virginians liked to read are the long advertisements of the booksellers. In the newspapers of every town these merchants listed by title and usually author hundreds of books. There were more than a score of such dealers in Richmond alone in the last twenty years of our period.[5] Many of them, like Samuel Pleasants, Peter Cottom, and Thomas Ritchie, were also publishers and printers. Others, like Frederick A. Mayo and the firm of Fitzwhylsonn and Potter, appear to have been primarily booksellers. Dozens of law, medical, and agricultural volumes, representing new editions of standard works and many really new things, formed one section of their lists. Dozens of editions of the Greek and Latin classics are also usually grouped together. Verse from Petrarch to Scott, and including American writers like Barlow, Trumbull, Freneau, and John Blair Linn, were especially popular. Native Virginia poets, however little they may be esteemed today, apparently sold well in Richmond. Bryan, Dabney, Branch, the Munfords (for whose verse see Chapter VIII) were all advertised frequently for some months, at times for years, after they first appeared.

Novels usually formed a major part of the list. Most of them were sentimental or Gothic tales by English authors long since forgotten but popular all over America at the time. But the better Gothic writers, Monk Lewis, Godwin, Maturin, and Mrs. Radcliffe were also favorites. Defoe, Richardson, Fielding, especially Smollett, and above all Sterne, were almost always present. Madame de Staël's *Corinne* (1807) was listed frequently from the time of its first appearance. Scott of course was present from the publication of his first long poem through the rest of the period. *Charlotte Temple, The Coquette,* all of C. B. Brown's works, and later Cooper were kept in stock.

Histories were apparently second only to fiction in the affection of the reading public, for they might both amuse and instruct. Besides the Greek and Roman histories, Rollin's *Ancient History* (1730-38)[6] in new editions and reprints, Hume, Gibbon, Voltaire, Goldsmith, Robertson, and a dozen more were among them. Closely allied and frequently advertised with them were the politico-economic studies such as Smith's *Wealth of Nations* (1776), Godwin's *Political Justice* (1793), Algernon Sidney's *Discourses Concerning Government* (Jefferson had a 1763 edition), Malthus' *Essay on the Principles of Population* (1798), Paine's works, Jefferson's *Notes on the State of Virginia, The Federalist,* and Curtius' [John Thomson's] *Letters* (1798). Lewis and Clark's *History of the Expedition . . . to the Sources of the Missouri* (1814), and Burk's *History of Virginia* (1804 etc.) were also with them. The considerable number of travel books indicates Virginians' curiosity about other lands or what foreigners had to say about America. The really remarkable number of advertised speeches, legal reports, histories and general essays, even in the 1820's novels, by Virginia authors suggests more than mere professional needs of the lawyer or politician.

Literary criticism and philosophy apparently sold proportionately much better than they do today. Samuel Johnson, Locke, Hume, Burke, all the Scottish common sense school, are among them. Sermons appeared frequently, ranging from the seventeenth-century English divines to contemporaries both English and American. Biography, particularly Marshall's, Ramsay's, and Weems' lives of Washington, were aimed at several different sorts of readers. Plays currently appearing in local theaters were also offered for sale, especially those written by Virginians like G. W. P. Custis or Gustavus A. Myers.

Rees' Encyclopaedia, number by number, was advertised as it appeared. The public could and did buy Alexander Wilson's *Ornithology* (1808-13); French, Spanish, Latin, and Greek grammars; and books on housekeeping, horse racing, and religion. The number of sizes and editions of Hugh Blair's famous *Lectures on Rhetoric* (1783) attest what we know from other sources, that every fairly well-read Virginian used this as a sort of textbook for English composition, oratory, and aesthetic theory while he was in school and long after he had completed his formal education.

The greatest individual book salesman of that day or any other in America then lived in Virginia and has left us some interesting comments on reading tastes. The Anglican clergyman Mason Locke Weems, himself a popular author, covered the Atlantic seaboard from New York to Savannah for the Philadelphia firm of the Careys. Making his headquarters in the little Virginia port of Dumfries near the Potomac, he traveled north and south taking orders and subscriptions and delivering the books published by the Careys or handled by them. His letters to Mathew Carey are sometimes full of pleas for more copies of a popular item, for publishing new material or reprinting old which he thinks will sell, or for payment for what he has sold. Bibles, almanacs, spelling books, elocution books, travels, novels, biographies, temperance tracts (or tracts against any sin), and hymnals are among them. Literally scores of these are his own compilations. He found Fredericksburg, Richmond, Alexandria, Petersburg, and Norfolk especially good markets, but he sold in many smaller places. Naturally he pushed the little volumes he himself had edited or authored. Among other English writers, Goldsmith seemed to please his customers. He sold seventy-five complete sets at one time in Richmond in 1796.[7] Norfolk people liked voyages and travels. Many everywhere bought Voltaire's histories and biographies, Tom Paine's works, and religious meditations. Weems might preach at a Methodist meetinghouse one evening and extol the virtues of a deistic or atheistic author the next morning. He sold to trinitarians, unitarians, and agnostics anything religious or anti-religious they wanted.

Though he protested against Carey's unloading on him many thousand "puritanicall books" which he could not sell in Virginia, he was enthusiastic about the sale of sermons of all kinds, especially those of the Hanover county Presbyterian Samuel Davies and the Scot Hugh Blair. Both were favorites over the years. He found that Jefferson's *Notes* was in demand, and he pushed John Taylor's *Inquiry into the Principles and Policy of the Government of the United States* (Fredericksburg, 1814) and St. George Tucker's *Dissertation on Slavery* (1796), the latter printed by Carey. It is perhaps significant that Weems warned Carey that books to be sold to Virginians must be attractively bound. To read Weems' letters and lists of books is to learn what most of the popular reading of Virginians was between 1796 and 1817.

Weems' Dumfries neighbor Timothy Brundige, postmaster and bookseller for Mathew Carey, bears out generally in his statements reporting sales in his one locality what Weems found true for the state, though the dates of his reports immediately precede rather than parallel Weems'.[8] Brundige in 1794-96 sold more fiction than anything else, with Smollett a strong first. Pope was the most popular poet except Shakespeare, and in other areas sales figures were relatively high for Chesterfield's *Letters,* Johnson's *Lives of the Poets,* Franklin's *Autobiography,* Rollin, Russell, Gibbon, Blackstone, Paine, Smith's *Wealth of Nations,* and Guthrie's and Moore's *Geographies.* A comparison of Brundige's figures and classifications with those of a Philadelphia bookseller at the same period reveals that they are quite similar except that in Philadelphia a greater proportion and variety of French works were sold. As in Philadelphia, Voltaire and Rousseau were favorites. But Rollin and Buffon sold much better at Dumfries than in the Quaker City. Brundige's sale of ninety volumes of French authors compared with 730 British appears to indicate that even in a small Virginia village the Gallic literary appeal was strong. But in Dumfries, Webster's *Spelling Book* outsold all else, and Bibles and Testaments were not far behind, a not unusual situation in any American community.

Diaries, letters, and biographies by contemporaries also give many details and titles representing reading tastes. One thus learns of Richard Henry Lee declaiming on *Don Quixote* at Edmund Randolph's, and of his methodical daily reading in the classic poets and in Shakespeare, Milton, histories, and government;[9] of editor Thomas Ritchie's love of Adam Smith, Ricardo, Malthus, Voltaire, Rousseau, and Paine; of Presbyterian clergyman Conrad Speece's poring over Wright's *Theology* and Knapp's *Lectures on Christian Theology* but also of his reading of Scott's novels as fast as they appeared; of John Randolph's feasting in 18[illegible]6 on "a delicious Quarterly Review" (xxvi).[10] Then one finds Jefferson's grandchildren at Monticello reading Scott and Cooper but also enjoying volumes of sermons.[11] Mrs. Mary Willing Byrd in 1814 after a child was killed found her solace in reading and "comitting [*sic*] to memory Young's Night thoughts" and portions of Milton.[12] Robert Lewis, secretary to Washington in 1789, devoted several mornings to perusing Lord Chesterfield's *Letters*.[13] R. N. Venable, southside lawyer, amused himself in 1791 on his lonely rides between courts with Milton, Goldsmith, Blair's *Sermons* and Soame Jenyns' "on internal evidence of the Christian religion."[14]

David Ross, manager of the Oxford Iron Works in Bedford county, wrote in 1812-13 to his son of his reading in Vergil, Cornelius Nepos, Homer, Cicero, and Horace, and referred casually to Brackenridge's *Modern Chivalry,* the Highland Erse language, *Don Quixote, Tristram Shandy,* Smollett and Chesterfield.[15] One lady not only read a surprisingly varied assortment of books but kept a record of what she read: fifty-four books in twelve months of 1806-7, including many eighteenth-century novels one hundred and two in 1807-10, including Lady Mary Wortley Montagu, Lady Morgan's *Wild Irish Girl,* and the *Arabian Nights*; six hundred and twenty-eight in the 1815-22 period, mostly contemporary novels (including Scott) but also Burke's *Origin of Our Ideas of the Sublime and Beautiful, Paul and Virginia,* Campbell's *Pleasures of Hope,* Plutarch, Boswell's *Tour of the Hebrides,* and the poetry of Moore.[16]

John Rogers Cooke, father of the poet Philip Pendleton and the novelist John Esten, was a Winchester lawyer who kept a detailed account of his book expenditures and a journal of his opinions of some of his purchases.[17] He too had read Lady Morgan, and charges her with stealing a line from Sterne in her *Wild Irish Girl.* He discusses "the Quarterly Reviewers" and the Koran. But his most interesting records show his expenditures for legal books, school books, literature, and magazines, compared with his expenses for tailor, horse, and brandy and whiskey. In 1825, for example, the books add up to $74.82, the other items to $204.75. Later both increase. He subscribed to the

North American Review and the *Museum,* among other magazines, but later he canceled most of them because the new Winchester Library was getting them. He noted in 1829 that he had spent since 1825 about $90.00 a year for political publications alone. They must have been useful, for he made a great name for himself in the 1829-30 Constitutional Convention. In 1827 he received one English, two Winchester, and two or three other newspapers, all adding up to $18.00. All this was with an income of from $4,600 to $6,000, derived largely from what he considered the best law practice outside Richmond.

In 1791 John Breckinridge, about to remove to Kentucky with all his family, ordered from the London firm of Donald and Burton one hundred and fifty volumes to carry with him.[18] His order is especially strong in history, poetry, and contemporary philosophy. Included are Blair's *Lectures* and *Sermons*; Rollin, Plutarch, Gibbon, Hume, Robertson, among the historians; Locke *On the Understanding* and *On Government*; Kames on philosophy, equity, and education; fifteen volumes of Rousseau, Smith's *Wealth of Nations,* Beccaria *On Crimes,* Reid *On the Mind,* Burke, Parliamentary Debates, Blair's *Ossian*; Malone's *Shakespeare,* Milton, Swift, Thomson, Cicero, and Johnson, among others. Although he was a lawyer, obviously his selection was not confined within the limits of his profession. Later he did try to fill some gaps in his legal library. United States Senator from Kentucky and Attorney General under Jefferson, Breckinridge was clearly a man after his chief's own heart.

One of the things every educated young man wanted to do—and had to do if he were lawyer, physician, or clergyman—was to start his own library, as Breckinridge seems to have been doing. There are in existence dozens of letters of advice from older to younger Virginians as to what they should include in that library or should read, letters which naturally are indicative of the writers' own minds and tastes. Though professional needs were kept in mind, it is evident that the colonial tradition of the well-rounded man was still alive, for the suggestions were never narrowly professional, except in the few cases when titles for a particular area of study were requested. Jefferson, Bishop Madison, President Madison, and St. George Tucker were among those who supplied actual lists. Jefferson's several letters on the subject, the first written when he was himself a young man in 1771, are well-known.

Equally interesting are some of the others; for example, that supplied to John H. Cocke by Bishop Madison on January 3, 1801.[19]

Madison warned that the books might cost £100, but that taken altogether they formed the requisites for a gentleman's library. He began with "Natural Philosophy" (perhaps his own favorite subject), listing Buffon's complete works, James Keir's *The First Part of a Dictionary of Chemistry* (1789), Richard Kirwan's *Elements of Mineralogy* (1784), and James Hutton's *Theory of the Earth* (*ca.* 1785, enlarged 1795-99). Under no circumstances should Cocke fail to procure Emanuel Mendes da Costa's *Elements of Conchology; or an Introduction to the Knowledge of Shells* (London, 1776) nor Keir's *Chemistry.* In poetry Shakespeare, Milton, Pope, Addison, Gray, Akenside, Thomson, Shenstone, and Mason should represent the earlier periods, and Burns, Ossian, Johnson, and Erasmus Darwin the later. Ariosto, Tasso, and Dante should be included, and Voltaire's tragedies. Under "Travels" eleven titles were named and the suggestions made that many others should be added. "History" had the longest list for any one subject, with titles familiar to most fair-sized Virginia libraries: Gillies' *History of Ancient Greece* (*ca.* 1786), a work with a strong Whig bias especially welcome to the Jeffersonian Republicans; Ferguson's *The History of the Progress and Termination of the Roman Republic* (1783); Gibbon's *Decline and Fall of the Roman Empire* (1776-88) with Watson's answer; Barthélmy's *Travels of Anarcharsis the Younger* (orig. Fr. ed., 1787), a popular fictional work giving a picture of Hellenistic civilization as the title character wanders through the Greek states; Hume's *History of England* (1754-61), others of France and Spain, and Coxe's *Life of Walpole* (1798-1800). About half the history list concern America, including a number on Virginia: John Smith, Sir William Keith, William Bullock, Robert Beverley, and William Stith on the colonial Old Dominion, and on other colonies or America as a whole Douglass, Oldmixon, Hutchinson, Belknap, Raynal, Robertson, Burke, and others. Only twelve books in all were listed under "Religion," including four favorites of the period, Bishop Joseph Butler's *Analogy of Religion* (1736) and William Paley's *View of the Evidences of Christianity* (1794), both gatherings of evidences, and Hugh Blair's and Bishop Porteus' *Sermons* (1777 and *ca.* 1772).

The miscellaneous portion of the list includes Franklin's *"Life,"* Priestley's *Lectures on History and* [*General*] *Police* [*i.e., Policy*] (1788), Lady Mary Wortley Montagu's *Letters* (1763), novels such as *Tom Jones* and *The Vicar of Wakefield,* Johnson's abridged *Dictionary,* Young's works on agriculture, a number of biographies, and Robertson's *Charles the Fifth* (1769). Finally, the good bishop listed under "Essays political and moral" Hume's *Essays* (1741 etc.); Locke's *Works*; Rousseau's *Social Compact* (orig. Fr. ed. 1762); Smith's *Wealth of Nations*; Ferguson's *Moral Philosophy* (probably *Principles of Moral and Political Science,* 1792); Paley's ditto (1785); John Horne Tooke's *Diversions of Purley* (1786, 1789), a philological work emphasizing among other things the importance of Gothic and Anglo-Saxon studies to an understanding of modern English, a book which was apparently a necessity in every Virginia library; Dugald Stewart's *Elements of the Philosophy of the Human Mind* (1792 etc.); Montesquieu's *Works* (orig. Fr. ed. 1767); Lord Kames' *Sketches of the History of Man* (1774, Am. ed. 1776); Mably's *Dialogues on History* (possibly *De la Maniere d'ecrire l'histoire,* 1783); Burke's *Orations* (perhaps any or all the editions of *Speeches,* 1777 etc.); Curran's ditto (various); Middleton's *Life of Cicero,* another book found everywhere; and Martin's *Law of Nations* (Georg F. von Martens' *Summary of the Law of Nations* transl. by Wm. Cobbett, 1795), and a half dozen more.

The Bishop's list was like Breckinridge's fairly representative of the nuclei of all Virginia libraries, though the former emphasizes science at the expense of the classics, poetry, and fiction. The fact that Cocke had already gathered some books may account for this. The fine library still surviving at Bremo on the James shows traces of the influence of Madison's letter. But more below of this larger library.

C. *Collectors and Collections*

The Virginia reader did not always purchase his books through itinerant salesmen like Weems (who supplied booksellers usually) or through local bookshops. Jefferson employed dealers in Richmond, it is true, but also in Alexandria, Philadelphia, and other places. So did Wirt and John Randolph and many others. Sometimes the reader who wanted out-of-print materials bought in part or in whole old libraries. Jefferson's collection owed much to the libraries of his Randolph relatives, parts of which he had bought with the cases in which they stood. William Wirt ordered dozens of volumes from the 1806 sale of the library of Ralph Wormeley in Middlesex county. John Randolph had some things from the Bland and other old libraries, and a few years later Grigsby enriched his library from the sale of Randolph's.

Whenever a Virginian went abroad, he was likely to buy for himself and his friends. Jefferson in 1814 said that his great collection was largely the result of his constant browsing while he lived in France. His protégés William Short and Joseph C. Cabell followed his example. Cabell, traveling in 1803-5, gathered scientific works, especially on botany and gardening, and a great many standard British and French authors. William Cabell Rives, Minister to France, spent his leisure profitably in enlarging his collection, as did Andrew Stevenson, Minister to England. Jefferson bought heavily for Madison in France, especially the historians and political economists. Ralph Wormeley listed in letters to his schoolboy son in England the books he wanted purchased. Littleton Waller Tazewell utilized ship captains coming into Norfolk to bring him books and British sporting magazines.

The libraries gathered by Virginians varied greatly in size, dependent naturally on personal interests, financial ability, and degree of education. The smallest library one might expect of literate people is represented in the June 10, 1799, inventory of the Estate of John Bernard of Buckingham county.[20] It includes a Prayer Book, two dictionaries, Butler's *Hudibras,* Buchan's *Family Physician,* a Bible, *Robinson Crusoe,* Watts' *Psalms,* Young's *Night Thoughts,* the "Economy of Human Life, Human Prudence & some old pamphlets." Bernard appears to have been a farmer of moderate means and education.

But there were scores, perhaps even hundreds, of much larger ones containing one or two hundred volumes. One finds, somewhat at random, that the Roslin estate near Petersburg, when inventoried in 1829 after the owner's death, showed two or three hundred books, including enough school readers in French and English for a class of twenty-five. This may have been a dealer's list, but the one copy each of the standard library items such as Blair's *Lectures,* Rollin's *Ancient History,* and Smith's *Wealth of Nations* would suggest that it was a private collection. It is particularly interesting for the large proportion of agricultural books, including Cobbett's *Cottage Economy* (*ca.* 1822?), *Farmers Magazine, Farmers Dictionary,* Twamley's *Essays on the Management of the Dairy* (*ca.* 1784), *Farmers Manual,* Taylor's *Arator,* and the *Farmers Journal* and *American Farmer* (1819 on) for several years.[21]

John F. Mercer, who annually inventoried everything he owned, showed in 1805 two hundred and fifty-four volumes valued at $494.75.[22] Mercer classified his books as folios, quartos, octavos, and duodecimos. He had approximately thirty-seven folios and octavos of Greek classics and sixteen of Latin. He owned nine French quartos or octavos, and twenty-two duodecimos. He also had twenty-two Italian quartos and duodecimos, including Machiavelli, Boccaccio, Davila, Ariosto, Guarini, Metastio, and Tasso. English Literature and history in all sizes make up most of the remainder, and include Robertson's histories, Paley, Thomson's verse, Smith's *Wealth of Nations,* Jefferson's *Notes,* and St. George Tucker's edition of Blackstone. When this inventory was made Mercer was living in Maryland, but he had been born and educated in Virginia and had been a Member of Congress from the Old Dominion.

Sometimes the record gives only the number of volumes, as the inventory of the estate of William Preston of March 6, 1790, which mentions simply "273 Vols. Books" worth $194.60.[23] In other instances we have only a learned man's word for what his library contained. Francis Walker Gilmer of Albemarle and Richmond mentioned somewhat casually in 1823 to Chancellor Dabney Carr that he possessed "the best library on general jurisprudence in Virginia—the best private one, I believe, in America."[24] This is quite an inclusive statement, but knowing Gilmer's inclination to moderation in everything and his enormous attainments in the law, we may well believe him. The library, dispersed among his many brothers and nephews after his early death in 1826, still turns up piecemeal here and there.

Another Albemarle library of excellence in a particular area was that of the Scottish schoolmaster John Robertson. Woods in his history of Albemarle points out that this was probably the finest private collection of Greek and Roman classics then in the state.[25] The inventory, in Will Book No. 7, p. 33, of the man of this name who died in 1818, does indeed show fine editions of the classics, such as a ten-volume Cicero valued at $100 and a seven-volume Plato at $50, but among 350-odd volumes are also many volumes of the historians, the Scottish philosophers, and the familiar essayists. It could best be summarized as a balanced small library with unusual emphasis on the classics.

Other libraries were large though we do not know exactly how large. John Tyler the elder left his considerable collection to his three sons to divide, George Mason his to five sons. The Reverend Conrad Speece, author and educator as well as preacher, left "a valuable library," according to one authority worthy of comparison with that of his colleague John Holt Rice.[26] Conrade Webb (1778-1842) of "Hampstead" had a large library, and some few titles are recorded.[27] James Mercer Garnett was probably the principal collector of the fine home library at "Elmwood" which in 1865 totaled twelve hundred volumes.[28] Most of it was bought through booksellers in Fredericksburg and Washington, how much of it before 1830 is hard to surmise. It stands today intact in a separate room in the Alderman Library of the University of Virginia.

About 1800 several communities, or the leaders of several communities, came to realize that most men could not own all the books they wished to read. As it was borrowing had been a bad habit among the gentry from the beginning. In 1790 Jefferson made a list of those who had borrowed from him. In 1805 the Librarian of Congress sent Madison a list of the books the latter had borrowed and not returned. In 1817 St. George Tucker suffered from borrowers. In 1812 Martha Jefferson Randolph offered to return a book she had kept for months and years but not finished, but the gallant representative of the owner suggested she keep it and return with the rest of the set when she had borrowed them! Whatever the combination of reasons, the library societies came into being. A notice of a meeting of the Richmond Library Society is carried in the *Virginia Gazette and General Advertiser* of January 1, 1801, as though its organization is a *fait accompli*, though W. A. Christian states that it was formed in 1809.[29] Incorporated under state law in 1806, it continued for more than twenty years and finally died (according to Mordecai, *Richmond in By-Gone Days*, 1860 ed., p. 239) because female readers of sentimental novels got the upper hand. In 1814 John D. Blair as president published in the *Enquirer* (January 6) a list of books missing at the library as long as sixteen months. It included a good deal of fiction but also enough of the standard works to have formed a good gentleman's library had they been returned. Adam Smith, Erasmus Darwin, Godwin, Malthus, Paley, Reid, Voltaire, Hume, Franklin, Curran, Junius, the *Quarterly Review* (three numbers), and Rabelais, are among them.

There was in 1812 a Christian Library Society, and in 1815 Peter Cottom advertised the forming of a circulating library in connection with his bookstore. A Juvenile Library Company was started in 1822, said to have been the first in the United States, "to consist of the elementary books in every branch of a liberal education" with a judicious selection of others.[30]

On February 4, 1806, at the same time as the Richmond Library, the Rockingham County Library Company was incorporated[31] On June 19, 1822, printer William F. Gray of Fredericksburg informed the public he would have a circulating library in connection with his bookstore and would carry all the standard English writers, the *Edinburgh, Quarterly,* and *North American* reviews, the new *Monthly, Analectic, Blackwood's,* the *Port Folio,* and *Christian Observer,* with "other popular periodicals."[32] The library would also include history, voyages, travels, poetry, novels, plays, general literature, reference works, newspapers, and maps. The subscription was to be $6.00 a year.

John Rogers Cooke had rejoiced when in 1825 the new Library Company of Winchester was formed because he could now cancel his heavily expensive magazine subscriptions. Though not everyone felt this way (if he could afford otherwise) both the public-cooperative and the private-enterprise circulating libraries helped to make all sorts of reading matter easily available. Their existence noticeably affected the gathering of really inclusive personal libraries more in the towns than on the plantations, but not until the twentieth century was the public library firmly established.

D. *Some Larger Libraries*

It is time to turn to the major libraries, those ranging in estimated size (in several instances the data are vague) from five hundred to sixty-five hundred volumes, in each case indicative of the intellectual habits and tastes of a leading Virginian. Partial or complete records of some fifteen of these survive for the period, ranging in time from

George Washington, whose inventory of 1799 suggests that many items were collected before 1790, to Hugh Blair Grigsby, who by 1830 had made only a beginning of his great library. Besides these two, the major collectors were Thomas Jefferson, James Madison, St. George Tucker, Ralph Wormeley, the Skipwiths of Prestwould, John H. Cocke, William Wirt, William Short, John H. Rice, John Randolph, William Cabell Rives, Andrew Stevenson, and William Munford. One can be reasonably sure that other men like George Tucker, Dabney Carr the younger, Joseph C. Cabell, James Mercer Garnett (who is mentioned above), William B. Giles, Louis Hue Girardin, Spencer Roane, John Taylor, Littleton W. Tazewell, Abel P. Upshur, and several of the Barbours, among others, collected libraries within the 500-3000 range, but the data is not available to prove it.

All these libraries, as far as one can now judge—with two exceptions, the Skipwith and Munford groups—were collected over a period of years from young manhood to old age by one individual who found in his books both personal profit and pleasure. Most of them were the collections of public men, statesmen, though the Skipwiths were not intimately concerned with public affairs in this era (except Fulwar in Paris), and Rice and Munford were public men in somewhat different senses. The generally acknowledged requisites for forming the mind of the complete gentleman and the representatives of individual taste were both present. In every case in which a complete or nearly complete list survives, Virginiana is a significant element, in several instances in manuscripts as well as printed books. The libraries will be considered in roughly chronological order, with the greatest of them in its proper second position. First is naturally that of the Father of his Country, who lived a decade in this era and was still gathering books during that time.

George Washington's library, after passing through two generations of his family, survives in great part today on the shelves of the Boston Athenaeum. When he died in 1799 the inventory listed some nine hundred titles. William C. Lane classifies[33] the titles as sixty-four in literature, thirty-six in periodicals, thirty-five in religious works, seventy-three in politics and political economy, forty-six in military works, fifty-seven in agriculture and other useful arts, fifty-three in history, twenty-four in science, more than twenty-five in legislation, and twenty-two in law, plus some smaller divisions. My own analysis by titles shows ninety sermons, by far the largest number in any classification, and thirty orations (probably gifts), with the rest roughly the same as Lane's. Washington subscribed to many English periodicals but also to several American, the latter represented among others by the *American Magazine* (Webster's 1787-88 or perhaps one of the earlier), the *American Museum,* the *American Remembrancer* (1795-6), and the *Massachusetts Magazine* (1789-96). He had only a few volumes of philosophy, and scarcely anything of the Scottish school, who were in most instances his considerably younger contemporaries. He had a large number of American books, many of them doubtless presentation copies, including several works of Thomas Paine (despite what the Federalists came to think of the author of *Common Sense*), David Humphreys, Morse, Noah Webster, and H. H. Brackenridge. His Virginiana includes titles by Beverley, Bland, John Taylor, St. George Tucker, Arthur, Charles, and Henry Lee, and William Dawson. He owned Edmund Randolph's *Vindication* (1795) of the charges before his resignation from Washington's cabinet and Jefferson's *Observations on the Whale-Fishery* (1788).

Though probably many of the pamphlet and collected sermons were presentation copies, the preponderance of these items in this category is perhaps indicative of the religious bent of mind of Washington, though it may represent too a taste not entirely synonymous with piety. The political and historical items he may as a statesman have found useful, though they are almost all standard works for any library of the time. His strong interest in agriculture and Virginia history is borne out by the titles. But the scores of miscellaneous and small-group items mark his library primarily as the well-balanced collection useful to the gentleman farmer.

Too much need not be said about Thomas Jefferson's library, for it has been described at length more than once in recent years.[34] But certain of its qualities should be emphasized. Jefferson gathered three libraries for himself and one for the University of Virginia. In 1770 the first, valued at £200, was destroyed by fire. From then until he sold it to the nation in 1814 to replace the Library of Congress destroyed by the British, he gathered patiently the 6,500 volumes of his greatest collection. From this time until his death he undertook to assemble a recreational library which finally numbered between nine hundred and a thousand volumes. In his last years he classified and listed the titles he had Francis Gilmer and others buy for the University, some three thousand titles in more than seven thousand volumes. The 1770-1814 collection, recently annotated and catalogued by Miss E. M. Sowerby in five large volumes, was one of the greatest American assemblages of all time, for it represented the fullest expression of the complete gentleman's library for which his colonial predecessors as well as some of his contemporaries were striving, and it illustrated concretely the varied interests and comprehensive sweep of one of the major minds in our history.

Though Jefferson said several times that he was assembling a library which would be useful to him as a lawyer and American statesman, what he actually planned and gathered represented all fields of knowledge. His famous cataloguing system, based on the divisions of learning made by Francis Bacon, was still employed in Washington until fairly recent times. He bought from dealers all over America and Western Europe, from Richmond, Philadelphia, London, Paris, Strasburg, Amsterdam, and wherever else he might find what he wanted. He also called upon friends to search for items on both continents. He himself did the major work during those hours he might snatch from official duties in Paris 1784-89, when he turned in his own hands thousands of offerings of the Paris bookshops. In addition, he had scores of volumes presented by friends and admirers.

Except in politics, science, and philology the 1770-1814 library might seem at first glance an amazingly representative and inclusive collection of some eighteenth-century planter or English squire. In the three areas excepted (and there are other individual exceptions) Jefferson kept up with the latest results of scholarship and experiment. In belles-lettres he was somewhat old-fashioned, though he admired Ossian and for perhaps other reasons praised Barlow's *Vision of Columbus* and *Columbiad.* Of the Greek and Roman classics he had several editions, with commentaries, including poetry, history, and political theory. There were 450 books concerned with government and political economy (his last library had 106, the University 170).[35] Concerning religion there were almost two hundred (compared with forty-seven in the last and 180 in the University). First of all Jefferson was a lawyer, and this greatest library contained 450 books of law, including Blackstone's *Commentaries,* Coke's *Reports,* Kames' *Principles of Equity,* and the Virginia titles of Purvis (*ca.* 1684) and Hening. The last library, less utilitarian, contained only sixty-four, the University 370, legal items.

Presentation copies and first editions alone made this 1770-1814 library a collector's dream. But it was especially rich in Virginiana. He wrote in 1823 that "it is the duty of every good citizen to use all the opportunities which occur to him, for preserving documents relating to the history of our country [i.e., Virginia]."[36] He lived up to this duty nobly. He emphasized all kinds of history, but especially that of Virginia. John Smith's *Generall Historie* (1632), Keith's *History of the British Plantations in America . . . Part I Containing the History of Virginia* (1738), William Stith's *History of the First Discovery and Settlement of Virginia* [1747], John Daly Burk's *History of Virginia* (1804-5), William Robertson's *History of America, Books IX and X* (1799), and Robert Beverley's *History of Virginia* (1705; he had the 1707 French edition) are today, except for the Robertson, quite valuable. He had also his cousin and enemy John Marshall's *Life of Washington* (1804, 1805, 1807), Wirt's *Life of Patrick Henry* (1817), Lee's *Memoirs of R. H. Lee* (1825), and Weems' and Ramsay's lives of Washington (1808 and 1807). The dozens of medical, agricultural, and general scientific treatises by Virginians were often presentation copies. Of the Virginia laws he owned at least a dozen besides the Purvis and Hening already mentioned, as well as long files of volumes of the Virginia legal *Reports.*

Destutt de Tracy's *Commentary and Review of Montesquieu's Spirit of the Laws* (1811), which he valued above Montesquieu proper, he had himself written a preface for. Madison, Monroe, his Italian-born neighbor Mazzei, St. George Tucker, Arthur Lee, Edmund Randolph, W. B. Giles, and John Taylor of Caroline are among the dozens of his fellow citizens whose political and economic essays and treatises were on his shelves.

Under the classification Geography he had a group of sixteenth- and seventeenth-century books which might have been included under History earlier. DeBry's *Voyages* (1590-1619), Hakluyt's *Principal Navigations* (1589, the copy from Richard Bland's earlier library), Edward Williams' *Virginia* (1650), Johnson's *Nova Britannia* (1609), and Bullock's *Virginia Impartially Examined* (1649) are today very rare. Lewis and Clark and William Tatham, among his contemporaries, are represented.

There are dozens of Virginia imprints from Richmond, Williamsburg, and Petersburg, and lesser numbers from Abingdon, Charlottesville, Fincastle, Fredericksburg, Martinsburg, Norfolk, Shepherdstown, and Staunton. These in themselves reveal a great deal about publishing activities in the state. Of newspapers there are eighteen titles from Virginia including long runs of the various *Virginia Gazettes*, the *Enquirer*, and the *Argus*, and also some files of Fredericksburg, Norfolk, and Staunton papers.

Certainly the most valuable portion of his library from the historian's point of view were the manuscripts relating to the earlier period of the colony. They came to him in a variety of ways, all these ways indicative of his awareness of the need of preservation. They consist of twenty-one items, seventeen or eighteen of which went to the Library of Congress in 1815 and the remainder in 1829. Only three are not legal, legislative, judicial, or miscellaneous official records of the colony.

The non-official manuscripts are "T.M.'s" account of Bacon's Rebellion, a description by an eye-witness; Sir John Randolph's commonplace-[legal] book; and "Extracts written by a gentleman who had explored Kentucky." Six of the official items are records of the Virginia Company of London (published in the twentieth century); the others are unique copies or contemporary transcripts of seventeenth century Court, Council, and Legislative records. Some he purchased from older Virginia libraries, as the autographs testify; one was given him by John Page and had belonged to that gentleman's grandfather; another Jefferson found ready to be used for wastepaper in Lorton's Tavern in Charles City county; and another was a gift of his father-in-law Mr. Wayles, to whom it had been presented by William Byrd III.

It was a *useful* collection in the broad eighteenth-century sense. To a government official, a practicing lawyer, a scholarly reviser of laws, a scientific farmer, a student of Anglo-Saxon, an architect, an anthropologist, an archaeologist, a musician, a reader in many languages, a political and moral philosopher, an engineer and inventor, a lover of Renaissance and classical verse and the eighteenth-century essay, among other sorts of people, it could have been and was useful, for Jefferson was all of these. For our purposes, one significant thing is that it is the traditional library of the Virginia gentleman which had been gathered a hundred years before Jefferson and was continued by other men all during his lifetime. The same belief in the usability of the past, the same interest in contemporary exploration and technical achievement, the same concern with the problems of man's government of himself in society, and the same laws of learning per se which William Fitzhugh and William Byrd and St. George Tucker and Andrew Stevenson displayed in gathering their libraries is here, merely in greater scale with proportionately greater means and vision.

St. George Tucker (1752-1827), nine years younger than Jefferson and his lifelong friend, was a city-dweller and had the library of William and Mary available to him most of his life. Yet he collected an admirable personal library of five hundred volumes, an inventory of which survives at his old college. Professor of law, jurist, inventor, poet, playwright, and essayist, he rivaled Jefferson in his versatility. His library reflects all his interests and as usual something of the traditional concept of the well-rounded gentleman.[37]

The five hundred volumes represent about 350 titles. Of these about ninety are law books, much like the list on politics and law he supplied to Joseph C. Cabell on December 1, 1800,[38] which contains the usual Beccaria *On Crimes,* Smith's *Wealth of Nations,* Locke, Rousseau, Godwin, Priestley, Paine, Vattel, Grotius, and Montesquieu, plus the Virginia law authorities. Tucker himself was author of a comprehensive edition of Blackstone designed for the American, especially Virginia, legal student.

There is some evidence that Tucker like Jefferson was interested in old documents pertaining to Virginia history, especially to laws. In 1826 and 1827 he corresponded with Madison about the loan of some of his "collection of old Documents," Journals of the General Assembly, which Joseph C. Cabell was to use.[39] These possibly may have been printed, for they were bound. But the whole correspondence suggests that they were rare, possibly unique.

Of a hundred historical works in Tucker's library, fifty-five are histories of ancient and modern countries or states, seventeen accounts of travel and exploration, eleven biographies, and twelve contemporary political and economic tracts.[40] The usual Robertson's and Ramsay's works on America (1777 and 1816-17), Raynal on the American Revolution (1781), and the Virginia John Smith's *True Relation* (1608), Beverley, and Stith, are among them. The travels include Lewis and Clark, Jonathan Carver's *Travels in the Interior Parts of America* (1778), and Sir Alexander Mackenzie's *Voyages from Montreal* (1801), as well as observations on Africa and Europe. The biographies include his close friend William Wirt's *Patrick Henry,* Ramsay's *Washington* (1802), and lives of Mahomet and Louis XIV.

Tucker's essays and tracts illustrated his belief in America's "manifest destiny." A violent anti-Federalist and ardent Republican, he indicated by the authors and titles he had selected where his convictions lay. He was another believer in the usability of the past, including the American, and was persuaded by Jeremy Belknap to join the Massachusetts Historical Society and thus obtain its *Collections.* He subscribed to *Niles' Register* (he had 28 vols.); Carey's *American Museum* (all 13 vols.), to which he had contributed verse and prose; Irving's *Analectic Magazine* (4 vols.); the *European Magazine* (43 vols.); the *Critical Review* (16 vols.); the *Annual Register* (4 vols.), as well as nine other periodicals of one or two volumes each. When he died in 1827 he had twenty-eight volumes of the Richmond *Enquirer,* the newspaper best expressing his political beliefs,

Among the classics were eleven volumes of Horace, and lesser representations of Herodotus, Ovid, Pliny, Juvenal, Tacitus, Livy, Cicero, Longinus, Lucian, Plutarch, and Marcus Aurelius. With them were Greek lexicons. His ten reference works include Johnson's *Dictionary.*

Of his forty titles of belles-lettres, about one-half are English or Scottish, the other half American or French. Most of them represent standard eighteenth-century taste—Savage, Thomson, Gay, Goldsmith, Akenside, Percy's *Reliques,* and Lady Mary Wortley Montagu's *Turkish Letters* (1763?). He also had Chaucer, Dryden, Butler, the *Faerie Queen,* and *Paradise Lost,* among older poets and poems. Though he owned Lord Kames' *Elements of Criticism* (1762), there is little evidence in his writings that he was affected by this or any other of the Scottish philosophers. Philosophically he had been educated in another school. La Fontaine, Marmontel, and the ubiquitous Barthélmy's *Voyage du Jeune Anarcharsis en Grece* are among the French works. Though he wrote hundreds of stanzas himself, he had only a few American contemporary poets on his shelves, chiefly among them being Trumbull, Freneau, and his fellow-Virginian Robert Munford.

He had Franklin's *Works* and his relative George Tucker's *Letters from Virginia* (1816).

Tucker's writings, to be discussed in later chapters, reveal that this library by no means represents all the poets and essayists, particularly, with whom he was acquainted. Pope, Shenstone, Young, Collins, Prior, and Gray among the English he did know, as he must have the Hartford Wits other than Trumbull, for his verses were published in some of the same journals as theirs. His younger Romantic contemporaries, Keats, Shelley, Byron, and even Cowper, Blake, Coleridge, and Wordsworth, he appears not to have known at all, though this is fairly characteristic of the Englishman as well as the American of his age. His poems are usually though not always modeled on eighteenth-century neo-classic verse. For his scientific experiments and inventions he probably consulted the volumes gathered by William Small and his colleague Bishop Madison at William and Mary.

The library of Ralph Wormeley (1744-1806) of Rosegill survives by reputation and by a list of books William Wirt bought from it. Hugh Blair Grigsby, who knew more about such matters than any other nineteenth-century Virginian, compared "the more modern" library of Wormeley with William Byrd's as two of the greatest of all Virginia collections, lamenting that both were now (1854) scattered to the winds.[41] William Wirt on November 20, 1806, ordered from the "printed catalogue" of Wormeley's library seventy-odd items of Law, History, Arts and Sciences, Plays Miscellaneous &c., Religion and Morality, and Classics (these probably being the classification headings in the Catalogue).[42] Besides these evidences, we have only Wormeley's letters of 1801-4 to his son Warner Lewis Wormeley at school in England in which the youth is asked to buy various books for his father.

The Wormeleys of Rosegill had possessed at the end of the seventeenth century the largest library in the colony.[43] Apparently they continued to add to it through the years. This Wormeley, educated at Eton and Trinity Hall, Cambridge, showed his own considerable erudition in his letters to his son,[44] advising the latter as to what English and French grammars to study, the value of reading "epistolary compositions" and Addison and Johnson to improve one's style, and what tracts on "Police and preservation of morals" the boy should procure. The youth was to read whenever he was not at his desk;

but he was also to fence and as a future Virginia militiaman learn the manual of arms, and above all French was not to be neglected. On June 4, 1804, just eighteen months before his death, Wormeley asked his son to have sent to him John Trusler's *Chronology; or the Historian's Vade-mecum* (1769?), Henry Kett's *Elements of General Knowledge* (1802), Rett's *History the Interpreter of Prophecy* (?), Robert Bissett's *History of the Reign of George the 3d* (1803), and Malthus' *Essay on Population* (1798). The reader will note how recent many of these were, one title having appeared just the year before.

Wirt, who in 1806 was beginning to build up his library, ordered twenty legal titles, including Coke's *Institutes,* an almost indispensable but expensive item for a young lawyer, and other standard legal-political items such as Swinburne on Wills (present in almost all legal libraries), Martens' *Law of Nations* (mentioned above), Burlamaqui, Grotius, and Puffendorf. He ordered seventeen from Wormeley's historical collection, again standard things such as Robertson's *Charles V, History of Scotland,* and *History of America,* Stewart's *History of Scotland,* Hume's *England,* Russell's "ancient & modern Europe," Machiavelli, and Barthélmy's *Anarcharsis.* Under the same classification Wirt wanted several biographies, among them Middleton's *Cicero,* lives of Leo X and Lorenzo de Medici, and Arthur Murphy's *Garrick* (1801).

Wormeley apparently kept up with philosophical trends better than Tucker or Jefferson, or perhaps he simply had different tastes. Wirt was able to order Stewart's and Ferguson's *Philosophies* for his list. Under "Plays Miscellaneous &c." Wirt wanted Temple's *Works,* the *Spectator,* Garrick's *Works,* Young's *Works,* the *Poetics* of Aristotle, Shaftesbury's *Characters,* and perhaps the very copy Wormeley's son had procured a year or two before of Malthus *On Population.* From "Religion and Morality" Wirt selected Blair's, Atterbury's, and Warburton's sermons, Tillotson's *Works* (Jefferson had the 1752 edition), and Hooker's *Ecclesiastical Polity,* among other things. From "Classics" he needed only Livy and Thomas Gordon's *Tacitus* (1737). As many of these as possible should be bought for the $300 he could allow, Wirt stated.

The library of the Skipwiths of Prestwould in Mecklenburg county was catalogued or at least listed in 1927 with dates of publication shown.[45] It goes back to 1700 and comes up to the twentieth century, but since about two-thirds or three-fourths were printed between 1776 and 1830 it should be considered among the collections of the Jeffersonians. The Skipwiths, who had a baronet, Sir Peyton, in the family even after the Revolution, were always prominent and allied by marriage to dozens of equally distinguished families. It is a real plantation home library, with less emphasis on public affairs than most.

Fiction—Gothic, historical, and sentimental—looms large. Titles such as *The Disinterested Nabob* (1787), *The Boarding School* (1798), *The Infidel Father* (1824) are frequent. But Mrs. Radcliffe, Clara Reeve, Maria Edgeworth, Scott, Sterne, Defoe, and Burney raise the quality level of the fiction. *Charlotte Temple* (1696, i.e., 1796) is among the American titles. Histories of India (1821), France (1800, another 1817), and Ireland (1757), English and French grammars, only a few periodicals, Blair's *Lectures* and someone else's *Elements of Rhetoric* (1805), two home medical books, a few other histories, eight or ten scientific works including Wilson's *Ornithology* and two agricultural works, maps, atlases, and dictionaries, are among the titles for this period. British poetry, law, and politics are present but scarce—they may have been thrown out long before the 1927 list was made. The library is significant primarily as an example of what a plantation family without marked professional or learned interests might accumulate.

Scholarly James Madison, fourth President of the United States, naturally gathered a considerable library. Unfortunately it was not preserved intact and as far as can be ascertained never catalogued. But portions of it survive today in the University of Virginia and other libraries, and we know from Madison's letters and book orders something of what his interests were. Irving Brant in *James Madison the Virginia Revolutionist, 1751-1780* (Indianapolis, 1941) aids us by going into considerable detail as to his subject's early reading. Madison studied the usual classics, mathematics, geography, and French with a Scotch accent under his tutor Donald Robertson. Also Montesquieu, Locke, Montaigne, and other political and general writers on Robertson's shelves were probably read by the boy. Later at Princeton, President Witherspoon proscribed the French philosophers like Diderot and Voltaire, the British Hume and even Adam Ferguson's studies of Civil government which Robertson had encouraged him to read. Though Madison did not give them up, he took full advantage of Witherspoon's great teaching of the principles of government. Then for a half year after graduation Madison returned to Princeton and studied Hebrew and theology.

All these experiences are reflected in his purchase of books. While Jefferson was in Paris he bought books for Madison. On April 27, 1785, Madison described[46] the kinds of titles he wanted—treatises on modern federal republics, on the law of nations, on the natural and political history of the New World, and the less-ordinary Greek and Roman classics. Of the last he gave some examples; then he wanted Blaise Pascal's *Provincial Letters* (orig. Fr. ed. 1656), Antonio de Ulloa's *Relacion Historica de Viage a la America Meridional* (1748) in the original, Linnaeus' best edition, and French tracts on the economics of different nations. He mentioned that he had Buffon's original work in thirty-one volumes and ten volumes of supplement and sixteen volumes on birds. He wanted whatever continuations might be published.

By January 22, 1786, he had received two boxes of the books and on March 18, expressed his satisfaction with them. Jefferson had, as ordered, added titles at his own discretion. The *Encyclopédie Méthodique* (37 vols.) and *Histoire Naturelle* he received in many volumes each. In 1787 Madison thanked Jefferson twice for book boxes received. Among other things, Jefferson had bought for him the *Dictionnaire de Trévoux,* Mariana's *History of Spain* (Latin 1592; Jefferson had the Spanish in 1737-39 ed.), Burlamaqui, Wulfius, Mably, Voltaire, Diderot, and a dozen more histories.[47] Altogether, almost two hundred volumes, with all of which the recipient was enormously pleased. Without them, as Brant points out,[48] the Publius of the *Federalist* would hardly have been able to employ so effectively the learned examples of ancient confederacies in comparison with modern in numbers 18, 19, and 20, nor in his earlier 1787 "Vices of the Political System of the United States."

Two other aspects or elements of Madison's library should be touched upon, his political tracts and his religio-theological works. In the Rare Book Division of the University of Virginia today is his remarkable collection of political and economic essays, mostly in pamphlet form and mostly American, which he bought himself or was sent by his friends and enemies. The collection numbers some

365, including a dozen or so on non-politico-economic subjects, individual items varying in date from the early eighteenth century to the year of Madison's death. The Library of Congress has more of his pamphlets.

One gets a good idea of what Madison's theological alcove contained from the list he sent in 1824 to Jefferson in this field for purchase for the University of Virginia.[49] As already mentioned, Jefferson had himself outlined the list of books for his projected university. But feeling he knew too little about theology, orthodox or otherwise (and perhaps also for strategic reasons), he asked Madison to supply that portion of his list. Madison's letter of September 10 includes his hastily-gathered titles. As he remarked, he had been proceeding at a leisurely pace when he received notice of urgency. Though shorter than John Holt Rice's theological list, it represents as many ancient authorities and church fathers as does even that clergyman's library (to be discussed below) and includes seventeenth as well as eighteenth-century editions. Ignatius' *Epistolae* (Amsterdam, 1607), Minutis Felix (Reeves' trans., Leyden, 1672), and Irenaeus (ed. by Grabe, 1702) are among the earlier editions. Josephus, Justin Martyr, Hermias, Athenagoras, Tertullian, Theophilus of Antioch, Celsus, and Lactantius, were suggested, among others, in eighteenth-century editions. Thomas Aquinas, Duns Scotus, Erasmus, Luther, Calvin, Socinus, Bellarmin, Chillingworth, Tillotson, Hooker, and Grotius were an assortment of divines intended as cultural background reading, for the University was to have no Professor of Theology. Bishop Butler's *Analogy,* beloved of Wirt and all other orthodox Christians, and present in most Virginia libraries orthodox or otherwise, was on the list, as were Paley, Priestley, Blair (*Sermons*), Clarke, Locke, and Sir Isaac Newton.

A frail man who lived somewhat more to himself than Jefferson was able to do, Madison could and did make good use of his library at Montpelier. Through the years when answering the letters of younger friends he consulted it as well as his memory. His essays contain everywhere modest evidence of his reading. And one should repeat that without the two hundred volumes from France the powerful *Federalist* papers would hardly contain the authority-and-history buttressed argument they do.

Another library assembled by a Virginian, though probably never in the state for any length of time if at all, was that of Jefferson's younger friend and sometime protégé William Short (1759-1849). Grandson of Sir William Skipwith, a founder of Phi Beta Kappa at William and Mary, Jefferson's secretary in Paris, negotiator of several treaties, minister to the Hague and Madrid, accepted as lover but rejected as husband by a famous French Duchess, and finally one of America's wealthiest businessmen, he is an interesting and romantic figure. Possessed of one of the acute critical minds of his generation, he left us in his letters some of the clearest commentaries on his contemporaries. It was natural that such a man, inspired by Jefferson's example and aided by his long residence in France (he did not settle in the United States permanently until 1810), should gather a good library. Undoubtedly Jefferson's example influenced him, for included in the Short Papers in the Library of Congress is a copy of Jefferson's catalogue for his own library in Short's hand.

In 1937 Samuel Ward, writing on the picturesque career of Short mentioned that at the moment Short's "delightful library" of more than three thousand volumes was being dispersed to eager collectors from a little bookshop in Washington, D.C.[50] Ward noted that the library was composed preponderantly of French works. Short's will of 1839, drawn up ten years before he died, bequeathed this library to the "Medical Establishment" in Louisville, Kentucky, where his nephew Charles W. Short was a professor. In a letter to Short of June 6, 1819, his friend Merit M. Robinson of Richmond chided him for taking comfort in things "without hearts to love and cherish us," his more than fifteen hundred volumes.[51] Two surviving lists,[52] one entitled "Catalogue without order" and the other "Catalogue des livres de la bibliotheque," together with purchase orders of September, 1791, and February, 1792, and several more of 1795-98 and 1810, indicate what more than half his three thousand were, and that in those years he was buying heavily in France. The "Catalogue without order" shows some 1330 volumes, the "Catalogue des livres" some 1500. The longer list was made later, with additions in 1816 and four later dates, one after 1833 (this contains some seventy items). The later list indicates incidentally that Short housed part of his overflowing collection at the American Philosophical Society in Philadelphia.

One may begin by pointing out some of the things these lists do not show, or show rarely. Only two English novels represent fiction. Buffon's multi-volumed work, Wilson's *Ornithology,* the *Memoirs* of the Philadelphia Agricultural Society, and *Transactions* of the American Philosophical Society represent science; and Bell's series of British poets, seventeen beginning with Chaucer and ending in the Akenside and the two Philipses, with Byron's *English Bards and Scotch Reviewers,* are his selections of English verse. The Law, in which Short had been trained by George Wythe, is not too strongly represented by Grotius, Blackstone, Hale, and a few French works.

But multi-volumed editions of the classics, including Cicero, Horace, and Cornelius Nepos, abound. French belles-lettres are represented by Boileau, Montaigne, La Fontaine, Voltaire, and a few others. French history and philosophy, politics and economics, predominate. The titles include seventy-three volumes of memoirs, many biographies, and Volney, Rousseau, Madame de Sévigné, Vattel, Montesquieu, Turgot, Boulanger, Mirabeau, and Barthélmy's *Anarcharsis.* Machiavelli, Petrarch, Ariosto, Tasso, Metastio, and Guarini appear in Italian editions; *Don Quixote,* Garcilaso de la Vega, Ustarez, Columbus, and De Solis in Spanish editions.

America is surprisingly well represented in the library of a man who assembled most of it abroad. Tudor's *Life* of Otis, Ramsay's histories, Adams' *Defense of the Constitutions of the United States* (1794); Ingersoll's *Inchiquin, The Jesuit's Letters* (1810) defending the United States from British aspersions; Franklin's *Works;* Barlow's *Vision of Columbus* and *Columbiad;* Walsh's *Appeal from the Judgment of Great Britain Respecting the United States* (1819), another work representing American nationalism; and a number of French travelers in America like Chastellux and Michaux, are among them.

Virginia he kept up with apparently almost all his life, for the last several added entries are lives of Jefferson by Linn (1834) and Tucker (1837), the younger Henry Lee's *Observations on the Writings of Thomas Jefferson* (1832), Edmund Ruffin's famous *Essay on Calcureous Manures* (1832), and William A. Caruthers' novel *The Cavaliers of Virginia* (1835). He even had Jefferson, Pendleton, and Wythe's *Report of the Committee of Revisors* (1784) of the Virginia laws. Ramsay's and Marshall's lives of Washington, Jefferson's

Notes, the four-volumes of Jefferson edited by T. J. Randolph, *Memoir of the Life and Correspondence* (1829), the *Federalist,* Taylor's *Arator* (1813), Lee on *Richard Henry Lee* (1825), and Henry Lee's *Memoirs of the War in the Southern Department of the United States* (1812), are other Virginia items published during his years in Philadelphia. Until 1814 he owned the "Indian Camp" property in Albemarle and often dallied with the idea of retiring to it. Until the mid-thirties when he was in his mid-seventies he made annual excursions back to his native state. Expatriate and urbanized Virginian though he became, Short in his library represented a tradition with which he had grown up. The accidents of time and place of acquisition gave his books a decided cosmopolitan caste, but they are essentially the library of a Virginian of the liberal school.

William Wirt, born in Maryland in 1772, is said to have arrived in Virginia as a youthful lawyer with three books in his saddlebags—Blackstone, *Don Quixote,* and *Tristram Shandy.* The three are representative indeed of his lifelong interests, but he could never have achieved his distinction as trial lawyer, orator, essayist, biographer and Attorney General of the United States with them alone. Marrying successively into two prominent Virginia families, the Gilmers and Gambles, he made his reputation within the state both as lawyer-orator and writer. All his life he bought books, as exemplified in the 1806 order for the volumes from the Wormeley library noted above, or the letter to a fellow lawyer in 1814 in which he jubilantly records picking up Verburgius' folio edition of all Cicero's works at a sale.[35]

How many books he owned we do not know. But his law library was large enough to have several students working with it at the same time he did, and his hundreds of letters indicate that he was familiar with, or had a speaking acquaintance with at least, a host of writers ancient and modern, from Chaucer to Poe (whom he befriended). The classical authors he could quote endlessly, at least in sententious tags, and he was master enough of one ancient language to compose extempore a Latin pun in a couplet that even the supercilious John Randolph thought worthy of quoting to his friend the New York Congressman Harmanus Bleecker. Horace supplied his ideal of the middle way, as he had to colonial Virginia gentlemen. Wirt has quotations from this favorite Roman as headings for dozens of his essays. Hooker, Boyle, Locke, Barrow, Bacon, Milton, Newton,

Chillingworth, Congreve, Algernon Sidney, and Baxter are among the seventeenth-century writers he refers to with familiarity. He was even better acquainted with Bolingbroke, Voltaire, Robertson, Burke, Soame Jenyns, Johnson, Hume, Gibbon, Addison, and Hervey. He attacked Godwin in the seventh essay of his *Letters of the British Spy* (1803). He read Paley and Butler's *Analogy* and approved highly of the latter, for he was in his later years a fairly devout Presbyterian. He knew eighteenth-century drama as no Virginia contemporary except St. George Tucker. Giovanni Paolo Marana's *Letters Written by a Turkish Spy, Who Lived Five and Forty Years at Paris* (1687) may have furnished him with the idea for his *British Spy*, as Poe alleged it did,[54] but more probably Montesquieu's *Lettres Persanes* (1721), Addison's use of the same device in the *Spectator*, George Lyttelton's *Letters from a Persian in England* (2nd ed., 1735), or Goldsmith's *Citizen of the World* (1762) was his point of departure. The tenth letter of the *Spy*, written in praise of the *Spectator*, certainly offers a key to the style Wirt attempted to develop.

Wirt's writing indicates wide rather than deep reading, enthusiasm more than contemplation of what he had read. His books were gathered in the eighteenth-century tradition, with little indication of understanding beyond it. He refers to Blair's lectures many times but gives no considerable evidence of knowing the Scottish philosophers, who pointed to the future. He had read some Byron and a good deal of Scott, but he confessed to young Poe that "Al Aaraaf" belonged to a new school of poetry beyond his comprehension.

John Hartwell Cocke (1780-1866), born in Tidewater but settling in Piedmont at Bremo on the upper James, was one of the more versatile of the versatile Jeffersonians. Brigadier general in the War of 1812, scientific agriculturalist, early temperance reformer and worker against slavery all his long life, architect who built a graceful mansion and assisted Jefferson in plans for the University and succeeded him as advisor on architectural matters there, youthful deist turned Southern puritan and Calvinist in later maturity and then promoter of Bible, Tract, and Sunday School societies, man of affairs who owned vast properties in Mississippi as well as in Virginia, he carried some aspects of the Jeffersonian age and the Enlightenment in its American form beyond the Civil War. Inordinately modest, he refused to hold public office and is therefore not as familiar a name as are those of most Virginia leaders of his generation.

Two years after he received the letter from Bishop Madison listing the essentials for a gentleman's library, he settled at Bremo in Fluvanna county. During the rest of his life he gathered books for the library still in large part on the shelves on which he placed them.[55] An incomplete typescript list[56] made in the 1920's contains titles printed after 1830 along with those before, but it is possible to sift out most of the items Cocke bought during Jefferson's lifetime. Even this partial list gives some idea of Cocke's interests. And the dates of publication for most items are shown. The dates here given are these, not the usual first edition dates.

The familiar histories are here: Robertson's *America* (1800), Gibbon's *Decline and Fall* (1804), Ferguson's *History . . . of the Roman Republic* (1799), Rollin's *Ancient History* (1815), Hume, and Burnet. The eighteenth-century poets, twenty-five or more editions strong, Spenser, Milton, Chaucer, and Dryden appear. Johnson's *Lives of the Poets* (1750), Erasmus Darwin's *Phytologia* (1800), Burke's *French Revolution*, Burlamaqui, Voltaire, Rousseau, Vattel, Godwin, are again typical. Sermons are frequent, including the popular Robert South's *Twelve Sermons* (1777), Blair's (1802), Jeremy Taylor's, Virginian James Blair's *Our Saviour's Divine Sermon on the Mount* (5 vols., 1724), a Richmond, Virginia, 1824 edition of John Flavel's sermons, *The Fountain of Life*, and Alison's (1815). Paley's *Evidences of Christianity* (1814) is bolstered by Virginian Archibald Alexander's *Brief Outline of the Evidences of the Christian Religion* (1825) and scores of other books on the Bible and theology generally.

Naturally agriculture is well represented. Charles Marshall's *Husbandry* (1799), probably the book Bishop Madison mentioned; a London 1818 *Treatment of Soils and Manures*; the *Encyclopaedia of Agriculture* (1821), S. W. Johnson's *Rural Economy* (1806), Stephen Switzer's *Iohnographia Rustica* (1742), and scores more on husbandry, horsemanship, horseshoeing, diseases of sheep, and fertilizers, are among them. Volumes on chemistry and electricity; Acts and Statutes and other law books; travel narratives of India, Italy, the West Indies, and the Rocky Mountains; military officers' guides; biographical dictionaries and encyclopaedias; some eighteenth-century novels of Fielding, Sterne, and Edgeworth are here. *Blackwood's Edinburgh Maga-*

zine and the *Edinburgh Review* are among the periodicals. Among the Scottish rhetoricians and philosophers are Blair, Brown, and Ferguson.

Books by Americans other than Virginians are present in more than usual quantity. Almost all of Irving's first editions, Silliman's *Tour* (1820), Fessenden's *The Register of Arts* (1808), Jonathan Edwards' *Life of Brainerd* in the American Tract Society edition, Brackenridge's *Modern Chivalry* (1807), "Hutchson's" *History of Massachusetts* (1760), and Ramsay's *History of South Carolina* (1809) are among the more interesting.

Cocke's Virginiana is varied and sometimes quite rare. James Blair's *Sermon on the Mount* referred to above is not a frequent title even in major Virginia libraries. Two works by the Presbyterian divine Archibald Alexander, also mentioned above, are again infrequently met with in the larger collections. First editions of Wirt's *British Spy* (1803) and *Patrick Henry* (1817) are to be expected. Other titles are Tucker's edition of Blackstone's *Commentaries* (1803); Weems' and Marshall's lives of Washington and Weems' *Life of Francis Marion* (1822); Hening's *Statutes at Large* (1809-23) and his *New Virginia Justice*; Henry Lee's *Memoirs of the War*; the Richmond 1819 edition of John Smith's *True Travels* and *Generall Historie* which Cocke's friends Gilmer and Rice had sponsored; John Daly Burk's *History of Virginia* (first vol. only), and Jefferson's *Notes* (1794). Rarer are Nathaniel Tucker's *The Bermudian* (1808), Beverley's *History,* and Stith's *History.*

Until a study of Cocke based on the enormous collection of his papers housed at the University of Virginia appears, one must be content to know him in glances and glimpses such as this brief survey of his library.[57] But one can see already that Cocke was the Southern-puritan version of the Virginia gentleman, neither prude nor prig (as the biographer in the *D.A.B.* puts it), a conscious Jeffersonian liberal in most things but withal a man of vigorous independence of mind. It is interesting to surmise what Bishop Madison would have thought of the collection of 1866 on which he had started the young Cocke in 1801.

One clergyman who possessed a good library in the Jeffersonian period is the Presbyterian editor, professor, and orator John Holt Rice (1777-1831). A native of Bedford county, educated at Liberty

Hall and Hampden-Sydney, tutor at Hampden-Sydney, Richmond pastor, the first professor in the theological seminary established at Hampden-Sydney, he declined the presidency of Princeton to remain with his denomination in Virginia. A voracious reader in belles-lettres, history, and the classics as well as in theology, and an antiquarian who anticipated the founding of the Virginia Historical Society, he gathered a library which is far more than a Calvinist clergyman's reference collection.

Rice bequeathed his books to the Union Theological Seminary he helped to found. Two years after his death that institution published a *Catalogue* of its library by Benjamin Mosby Smith, a list which contemporary and recent authorities (including the present librarian of the Seminary) assure us is made up almost entirely of Rice's books. The *Catalogue* (Richmond, 1833) lists some 3200 titles. Naturally the great majority are theological, but even these are by no means narrowly sectarian. And there are a great many interesting titles which have little to do with the Christian religion.

Rice owned the Latin and Greek church fathers in their own languages in scores of copies and editions. Renaissance and eighteenth-century churchmen of all attitudes, including Lutheran, Methodist, Anglican, and Unitarian, are present. Baxter, Bishop Burnet, Bishop Butler, Cudworth, Bunyan, Belsham, Grotius, South, Bishop Hall, Bishop Porteus, Archbishop Usher, and Archbishop Tillotson are among the more familiar. But Swiss, German, and Scottish professors of theology are present by the dozen. Sermons run into hundreds, including the great English and Scottish divines and New Englanders from Cotton Mather to W. E. Channing. Biblical commentaries, the secular Latin classics such as Horace, the philosophers from Aristotle and Plato through Locke, scientists like Cuvier, historians like Botta and Heckewelder, represent various sides of the collector's interests.

If one were looking for evidence that the Scottish common sense and associationist philosophies were spread in America, in part at least, by the Presbyterians, he would find useful material here. For this library contains Alison's *Essay on the Nature and Principles of Taste* (Boston, 1810) and his *Sermons* (1815), Blair's *Lectures,* Brown's *Inquiry into Cause and Effect* (1818) and *Philosophy of the Human Mind* (1822), George Campbell's *Philosophy of Rhetoric,* Ferguson's *Essay on the History of Civil Society,* Kames' *Elements of Criticism* in two editions (1778, 1819), Reid's *Works* in two editions (1813 and 1822), and three of Stewart's philosophical works and his lives of Reid and Robertson. Even Hume's *Essays* and former Hampden-Sydney professor James Marsh's *Preliminary Essay and Notes to Coleridge's Aids to Reflection* (1829) and Coleridge's *Friend* (Burlington, Vt., 1831) might be grouped with them, for there are associations.

Rice, a magazine editor himself, appears to have received at one time or another forty-four magazines, including the *Port Folio, Analectic, Analytical Review,* and dozens of Protestant and one Hebrew journal, but apparently not *Blackwood's,* the *Quarterly,* or the *Edinburgh.* Always interested in the state's past, Rice gathered Virginiana, secular and religious. He had the sermons by Virginians Archibald Alexander, Samuel Davies, John Leland, Conrad Speece, George Walker, and his own Richmond brother Presbyterian John D. Blair. He owned various Acts and Statutes, Campbell's and Stith's histories (1813 and 1747), a collection of tracts on the great Richmond Theatre fire of 1811, Robert Mayo's *New System of Mythology* (4 vols., Philadelphia, 1815) and his *Ancient Geography and History* (Phila., 1813), *Letter* to the Methodists (Staunton, 1828) and other sectarian *Letters,* two works on Government and moral character by John Augustine Smith (whilom President of William and Mary), and John Taylor's significant *Inquiry into the Principles and Policy of the Government of the United States* (Fredericksburg, 1814). Naturally he had the eleven volumes of one of the journals he edited, *The Virginia Literary and Evangelical Magazine,* now quite rare. He had Anglican Devereux Jarratt's *Life* (1806), his friend Wirt's *Patrick Henry,* the four volumes of Jefferson published in 1829, and Jefferson's *Manual of Parliamentary Practice* (1813), and he preserved pamphlets such as "Beccaria's" (this time an official of the Virginia penitentiary, not the Italian) "An Exposition of the Penitentiary System."

No catalogue was ever made of the library of John Randolph of Roanoke (1773-1833) before it was dispersed from the auction block in 1845. But thanks to Randolph's own garrulous letters, the diary and notes kept by Hugh Blair Grigsby, and the many volumes bearing the Randolph bookplate preserved in various libraries (most of them in the Virginia Historical Society), we know more of the character of the collection than of any other except the few for which complete catalogues were made. We know more about what Randolph read, almost day by day, than we do of anyone else of this period, for he insisted on discussing his books with his correspondents.

Actually Randolph collected two libraries, one before and one after the fire at his estate Bizarre in 1813. Soon after the library's destruction Randolph made a list of all he could remember of the titles, including a few he had saved.[58] In 1828 he made a memorandum of the books he imported from Van Tetroode of Amsterdam, most of them his remarkable collection of Elzevirs. Hugh Blair Grigsby, while living in the 1830's with his father-in-law in Charlotte county near the "Roanoke" estate, used to amuse himself by going over to the deserted Randolph house and spending the night so that he might browse in the library.[59] Later at the sale Grigsby bought most of the Elzevirs and other titles and even secured some book receipts, all now in the Virginia Historical Society.

Grigsby in his manuscript journals discusses many of the books, and in 1854 he published in the *Southern Literary Messenger* (XX, 76-79) a comprehensive description of the whole library. In many of the Randolph letters published in the William Cabell Bruce biography in 1922, in the *Letters to a Young Relative* (1834), in *Francis Walker Gilmer* (1939), and in the multitudinous unpublished correspondence with various persons, such as that between 1812 and the end of his life with Harmanus Bleecker of Albany,[60] are long disquisitions on what he was reading at the moment. There is therefore so much existing material on Randolph's books and reading tastes that it is difficult to summarize it in a few paragraphs.

A bachelor who spent most of his spare time when not attending the sessions of Congress in solitude on one of his estates, Randolph had more time than most planters to indulge his propensities. The books at Bizarre he remembered (naturally they are probably those he liked best) form a fairly standard Virginia gentleman's library except that the emphasis even then was on history and literature. Chaucer to Ossian and Burns are among the English poets; Rapin, Belsham, Voltaire, and Hume among the European historians; and Smollett, Sterne, Edgeworth (his favorite perhaps), and Godwin among the English novelists. Randolph remembered too that he had Sir Samuel Egerton Brydges' *Censura Literaria* (1805-9) in four volumes, a bibliographical and critical work most unusual for an American of the time to possess. He also lost in the fire his stepfather St. George Tucker's edition of Blackstone, Curtius' *Letters,* and Virginia *Debates* of various years.

Within the twenty years left to him Randolph gathered a new collection of what was surely several thousand volumes. Grigsby, a real bibliophile and student of Virginia history, judged that it nearly equaled in history and older English literature the library of William Byrd II and that it greatly surpassed in those areas any other contemporary private collection. Though Grigsby was probably not considering Jefferson's library in this comparison, what he describes of Randolph's is impressive. Whatever would illustrate Virginia colonial and state history Randolph owned in the original editions, Grigsby records, and in addition three vellum-bound manuscript volumes of Virginia Company and Court Records.[61] Though these last are not as valuable as Jefferson's comparable volumes, and are not, as Grigsby thought they were, Byrd's copies, they are of considerable historical interest. Other travel-histories also concern Virginia.

Barrow, Stillingfleet, Sherlock, Jeremy Taylor, South, and Tillotson were among the divines, and also the later Blair and Doddridge, Pascal, Bossuet, and Bordaloue. Grigsby noted the beautiful editions of Gibbon, Montaigne, Chaucer, Guicciardini, Machiavelli, and Bolingbroke. Near them were long runs of "the British Sporting Magazine and the British Stud Book" and others on horses, dogs, and sports.

Parliamentary *Debates, Journals* of the United States House of Representatives and Senate, and political pamphlets including several attributed to Randolph, represented another side of his mind and activity. And yet another facet of that mind appeared in the Latin and Greek classics in fine editions, good translations in prose and verse, modern Latin writers, dozens of Greek Testaments, the fifty little Elzevirs, and many dictionaries and grammars.

Randolph had complete sets of the original English (Grigsby emphasized his distrust of American reprints) editions of the *Edinburgh Review* and the *Quarterly Review,* and also the complete *Gentleman's Magazine* (through his time) and a bound volume of the *Anti-Jacobin Review.* His many volumes of older drama included a beautiful edition of Shakespeare. His volumes of verse of the Renaissance and eighteenth century represented on the whole the standard writers.

His printed orations included the work of the great British statesmen, Burke, Fox, Pitt, Chatham, and Wyndham.

Like many another Virginian, he liked to study the peerage and gentle families. He owned Collins', Debrett's, and Beatson's indices and genealogies. He had several English county histories, and a large number of "secret histories" in content much like the Memoirs collected by William Short. Medical writers in Greek and Latin folios are among the other books Grigsby notes.

Grigsby concludes his descriptive essay by asserting that Randolph's was "the most respectable library of pure literature made by any one of our eminent statesmen in Virginia since the Revolution." Collected all over Europe, it was a monument to good taste and genuine bibliophilia. The other information now available would indicate that Grigsby was too cautious. It was the best critical, bibliographical, and generally belletristic library collected by *any Virginian* since the Revolution.

Randolph's book receipts are from such firms as Samuel Pleasants in Richmond, Thomas Edgerton in London, William Duane in Philadelphia, Thompson and Howard in Washington, D.C., Longman's in London, and the Dutch firm of Van Tetroode already mentioned. We know he bought also in Paris, and there are receipts for binding at various places. Among items not already mentioned one notes receipts for four years of the *Westminster Review,* a subscription to the *Southern Review* of Charleston, the eternal Barthélmy's *Anarcharsis,* Kirwan's *Mineralogy,* Bage's *Hermsprong,* Smith's *Wealth of Nations, Don Quixote, Pilgrim's Progress* (Henry Adams was sure he had never seen the book), *Gil Blas,* the *Racing Calendar,* and St. Thomas Aquinas.

John Quincy Adams sneered at Randolph's affectation of erudition in debate by referring to his "scraps of Latin from the Dictionary of Quotations,"[62] but the annotated editions of the classics Grigsby saw, and a few which may be seen today, do not suggest that Randolph's Latin was small, though it may not have been large or profound. W. C. Bruce calls Randolph the greatest American letter writer, at least among public men.[63] Whether that be true or not, the letters are most useful to us here for the already mentioned allusions to his reading. In a letter to his young relative Theodore Dudley of February 16, 1817, Randolph listed his early reading, which he said began with Voltaire's *Charles XII* and went on to the *Spectator* and the English novel, *Don Quixote, Gil Blas* (he was buying new copies of these last in his old age), Plutarch, Swift, Tasso (in translation), and Thomson. Later like Wirt he read carefully such religious works as Butler's *Analogy,* but of all religious books he infinitely preferred his own Anglican *Book of Common Prayer.* In his *Letters to a Young Relative,* many written before the fire of 1813, he refers again and again to the histories of Rollin, Rapin, Robertson, Belsham, Hume, and Russell, and to Horne Tooke's *Diversions of Purley* for philological matters. Chaucer he thought the young man should read, along with the better-known poets, the *Arabian Nights,* Beaumont and Fletcher, Otway, Congreve, and Percy's *Reliques.* In science he seems to have been little interested.

Despite the pronounced classic and classical character of most of his books listed by Grigsby, during the last twenty years of his life Randolph did a great deal of reading in contemporary fiction and verse. Maria Edgeworth as his favorite novelist was succeeded by Scott, and in letter after letter from 1811 on he discusses the novels of the Great Unknown. In 1814 he informed Bleecker several times of his reading in Burke and especially Byron's poems, and in 1818 of Hazlitt's "character of Shakespeare" and Coleridge's "biographical work."[64] He tried to read the last but couldn't: "His mysticism is quite too deep for me, & his style seems purposely, as prolix & perplexed as possible. There are some interesting passages however." Though Coleridge was perplexing, Byron continued to be a delight. On October 10, 1818 he wrote that "Lord Byrons fourth Canto has been one of my travelling companions. . . . the fourth Canto is inferior to the first part . . . but yet very fine." A month later he was excerpting passages from that Fourth canto to send to Bleecker. In 1814 he had criticized favorably to James Mercer Garnett *The Bride of Abydos, English Bards and Scotch Reviewers,* and *The Giaour,* the last of which he thought much superior to the first.[65] On November 16, 1818 he read *The Heart of Midlothian* and decided that "Jeanie Deans is my heroine." In 1819 *The Bride of Lammermoor* was declared equal to any of its predecessors. He compared some of Scott's characters with Shakespeare's and Cervantes'. So on through the years the lonely lord of Roanoke amused himself with the work of the Laird of Abbotsford. But at the same time he was also reading

Madame de Staël on the French Revolution, the *Edinburgh* and other reviews, the British orators, Junius, Malthus, and Swift.

Randolph's brilliant and sometimes erratic mind was not quite characteristic of his state in this age (Henry Adams notwithstanding), but in reading tastes he was fairly representative of most of the readers of his time who kept up with new things anywhere in America. There existed in him, as in others, a taste for both neo-classical wit and sentimental romance, for savage satire and imaginative narrative and descriptive verse. He thought little more of Wordsworth than of Coleridge, and he almost ignored the younger Romantics; but here again he was characteristic of most Americans. His critical judgments, based on these tastes and other things, have proved in the long run to be unusually sound on both British and American contemporaries. At a moment when most of the country, for example, was acclaiming Wirt's *Patrick Henry,* Randolph called it "a wretched piece of fustian."[66] Always a little bitter about what he considered his irregular education, he tried through his books to entertain and to improve himself. His wide reading impressed even cynical British envoys.

One of Virginia's professed "literary men" of the period was William Munford (1775-1825), who earned his living as a lawyer and court reporter in Richmond. Son of an early Virginia poet and dramatist, Munford had studied classics and law under George Wythe at William and Mary and had brought out *Poems and Compositions in Prose on Several Occasions* in 1798. Published posthumously, his blank verse translation of Homer received considerable attention and some acclaim.

Because of an expensive and growing family, "the scholar and poet subsided into a domestic drudge,"[67] as one contemporary put it, when Munford became reporter for the Virginia Supreme Court of Appeals. The size of his library twenty-three years before his death, however, six hundred and thirty-five volumes, indicates that his literary interests were not then at any rate entirely submerged. His library list of October 10, 1802, is preserved among the Ellis-Munford Papers at Duke University.

Munford's own classification was Law 320 volumes, History 53, Novels 66, Poetry 75, Religion 34, Arts and Science 11, Politics 22, and Miscellanies 54. Only two magazines are named, *Scott's* and the *Uni-*

versal. He probably took the *Edinburgh* and quarterly reviews later, as did most Virginians. The classical materials, scattered through the lists, total thirty-nine, including a four-volume Latin Bible and an old Greek lexicon.[68]

He read apparently fairly widely. In French literature he had Montaigne, Voltaire, Lesage's *Gil Blas,* Fénélon's *Télémaque,* and Madame de Genlis' *Knights of the Swan.* English novels included three by Mrs. Radcliffe, Lewis' *The Monk,* and other Gothic and sentimental romances. The American C. B. Brown's *Arthur Mervyn* (1799) and *Wieland* (1798) were among them, and of course rather new in 1802.

The twenty-seven-year-old young man had only one American historical work in his library, Marshall's *Washington.* But he had Roman, English, Scottish, Irish, Portuguese, and French works within this genre, including Robertson's *History of Scotland.* He had the usual Swift, Addison, Milton, Parnell, Ramsay, Prior, Gray, Young, and Shaftesbury among the older writers and Ossian, Southern, and Thomas Campbell (*The Pleasures of Hope,* 1799) among the more recent. One significant omission is the Scottish philosophers, who apparently did not interest the young man bent on pursuing law and literature.

This is a remarkably good library, though partly old-fashioned one, for a man still in his twenties. Perhaps some of it came from his father, who died in 1784. That he added to it considerably during the twenty-three years remaining to him, despite the growing family, we may be fairly sure. But Munford's volume of verse published in 1798 including translations from Horace and Ossian and a five-act tragedy, some scattered sonnets, and the blank verse posthumously published Homer are in the spirit of the later eighteenth century, not the early nineteenth. The elaborate notes to the *Iliad* indicate that he was a good Greek scholar and knew some recent scholarship in Greek literature generally. But more on his writing later.

It was natural that William Cabell Rives (1793-1868), who married successively into the Cabell and Walker families, studied under Ogilvie and Jefferson and at Hampden-Sydney and William and Mary, served in the House of Representatives and Senate and was twice appointed Minister to France, and wrote of Madison and other people and things, should have been interested in books. Soon after his marriage to Judith Walker in 1819, "Castle Hill," the estate of the Walkers near Charlottesville, became his home. There he gathered his library. Among the Rives Papers in the Library of Congress are some of the shelf and purchase lists of the collection.[69]

Though it is not possible to ascertain the exact or even approximate size of the library, one gets some idea from the old manuscripts, all of the 1820-30 period, such as one marked "N. Western Shelves" with 118 titles in 292 volumes, and others listing 88, 127, and 188 volumes respectively. Then there are lists for six "cases." It is a fairly typical Virginia library if these lists are at all representative, with history and classics predominating, a good deal of Virginiana, novels, and political writings.

Priestley, Godwin, Adams' *Defense of the Constitution,* Junius Adam Smith, Hume, and Malthus are among the English political and economic writers; Rousseau, Turgot, Say, and Destutt de Tracy among the 118 French writers in the same fields. The legal items are such as Jefferson recommended to Cabell and others, and to Rives while the young man was his student. Locke, Stewart, Paley, Tooke, and Schlegel are among the representatives of philosophy, religion, and literary criticism. Collected political pamphlets abound on the "northeastern" shelves. Periodicals include the *Edinburgh Review* (55 vols.), Walsh's first *American Review* (1812?) and his later *American Quarterly Review* (9 vols.), the *Analectic Magazine,* the *Southern Review* of Charleston, the now-rare *Free-Trade Advocate* (2 vols.), and the *North American Review* (5 vols.). And like Cabell, Randolph, and others, he owned several volumes on the English peerage.

The Virginiana is strongly but not all political. Rives had John Taylor's *Construction Construed and Constitutions Vindicated* (1820), strongly anti-consolidationist (as Rives was not), and *Tyranny Unmasked* (1822), the anti-protective tariff pamphlet; Wirt's *British Spy, Rainbow,* and *Patrick Henry;* George Tucker's *Essays* (1822) and his satirical *Voyage to the Moon* (1827); Jefferson's writings (the 4 vol., 1829 ed.); Ogilvie's *Philosophical Essays* (1816), which Rives had reviewed in the *Port Folio*; St. George Tucker's multi-volumed Blackstone; Hening's thirteen volumes of *The Statutes at Large* and his *New Virginia Justice*; W. B. Giles' *Political Miscellanies* (1829); George Hay's "Hortensius" essays; Jefferson's *Notes*; many Virginia legal Reports, the "Debates of the Virginia Convention," collections of Virginia laws, and even the Catalogue of the United States Library, which was probably the Jefferson library list as printed by Watterston in 1815.

Rives bought some of his books from his relative Dr. Landon Cabell, ordered many while he was in France in 1829-30, and secured others from the usual American dealers. His library was apparently light on science and fiction, though now-missing sheets might show them. Though there are some titles published after 1830, the items just listed indicate that Rives probably began his collection as a young man. They are at least suggestive of the charming, scholarly, farseeing follower of Jefferson, Madison, and Jackson who could write on religion as well as politics, but was anything except a Puritan, a man who never followed the extreme states' righters into their irreconcilable position.

A neighbor and fellow-envoy of Rives was Andrew Stevenson (1785-1857), son of a Fredericksburg Episcopal clergyman, Congressman and Speaker of the House, and Minister to England in 1836. Educated at Fredericksburg Academy and William and Mary and in law under Adam Craig in Richmond, he married as his second wife Sarah Coles of "Enniscorthy," Albemarle county, sister of two prominent Jeffersonians. From the date of the marriage in 1816 he was for almost twenty years a close personal friend of Madison. With Rives he was a member of the Richmond Junto which supported Jackson. He was active in the Agricultural Society of Albemarle from its organization in 1817 and took a lively interest in the University of Virginia, finally becoming its Rector. At his death his library was numbered at 3,511 volumes valued at $1,808.50.[70] It was located in a separate building on his estate of "Blenheim" in Albemarle, where he settled after his marriage.

Though many of his books may have been collected after 1830, the library is essentially that of a Jeffersonian. Twenty volumes of Shakespeare, forty-one of Scott's novels and eleven of his verse, Gibbon's *Decline and Fall* in twelve volumes, and other works of European history were published before 1830. Buffon's *Natural History* in twenty volumes, Liancourt's *Travels,* Marshall's *Washington,* Pitt and Fox's speeches, Cobbett's *Parliamentary Debates* in twenty-five volumes, the *Journals* of the House and Senate of the United States were all characteristic of and from this period. So were the periodicals: *Niles' Register* (14 vols.), the *Edinburgh Review* (59 vols.), the *Critical Review* (112 vols.), the *Philosophical Magazine* (55 vols.), and the Richmond *Enquirer* (21 vols.). Like his friends, Stevenson bought his books in England and France as well as in America.

That the collecting of libraries did not die with these men born in the eighteenth century is made strikingly clear in the books of one who may be called the last of the Jeffersonians, Hugh Blair Grigsby (1806-81), and who in 1870 succeeded Rives as president of the Virginia Historical Society. Educated in private schools and at Yale, Grigsby was lawyer, historian, biographer, and orator. He published his first book in 1827, *Letters from a South-Carolinian,* a little volume containing sketches of major Virginia contemporaries somewhat in the *British Spy* tradition. His histories of the Virginia Constitutional Conventions of 1776 and 1829-30, the latter of which he was a member, and of the Virginia Federal Convention of 1788, are authoritative and entertaining.

Because of increasing deafness fairly early in his career, he removed from Norfolk to his wife's home at "Edgehill" in Charlotte county, living the life of a gentleman farmer, encouraging painters and sculptors, educators and would-be writers, everything that would bring his beloved state to its rightful pre-eminency. In his voluminous journal he calls himself a "poor boy" who gathered books without having the real capital to do so, but he admits in the same journal that his collection is better in most respects than John Randolph's ever was. It totaled some six thousand volumes, principally in literature, and was housed like Stevenson's in a separate building.[71] Like Randolph and the older generation, he bought scores of volumes from old libraries (as he did from Randolph's own) but also visited booksellers in various cities and ordered by mail when he could not. More of a scientific bibliographer and modern bibliophile than any of his predecessors, he knew bindings, editions, obscure authors, and above all, content. He was an ardent collector of Virginiana in anecdotal as well as book form, and his recorded memories in manuscript as well as his books in the Virginia Historical Society form perhaps the best record ever preserved by one man of the Old Dominion before 1860.

Like his ancestors and older contemporaries, Grigsby believed that a library should be useful. Usefulness of several kinds is suggested in a letter which he wrote to President Robert C. Winthrop of the Massachusetts Historical Society just a short time before he died. He mentions reading Paley to an invalid friend, and then concludes by saying "My employments for the past two weeks have been the reading of Justin, Suetonius, Tom Moore's Diary, and the building of a rail zigzag fence, nearly a mile long, to keep my neighbors' cattle off my premises."[72] The man at Monticello who left on his reading table when he died two French political pamphlets, Coray's edition of Aristotle's *Politics,* and the first volume of Seneca's works (Argentorati, Bipont., 1809)[73] would have agreed that the reading was as useful as the fence building to one who would ponder man's problem of his relation to his fellows.

These leaders among the Virginians who loved books represented almost every shade of religious, economic, and social opinion. In politics most of them exhibited some shade of Jeffersonian Republicanism. All read much the same books, even on religion. In every case opinions altered if not changed as the men grew older. Outside events clearly influenced these opinions, but it is equally clear that they read, pondered, and then drew their own conclusions. Burke should be read on the French Revolution, they said, but with replies at hand in print and in the head. Hume's *History of England* was indispensable, but it should not be perused without warning and understanding of its Tory bias. Blackstone and English law must be learned, but along with essential American differences, as Tucker tried to show in his edition. Though John Taylor spent years writing a reply to Adams' *Defense of the Constitutions of the United States* in a work which met with the full approval of most Virginia liberals, Adams' book was in all their libraries. Jefferson may have seemed and have been intolerant, in a sense, in the rigidly circumscribed list of reading he presented for the University students of politics, but everything he ever said would bear out his conviction that later in their maturity these young men should read and interpret for themselves. Books should liberate, but those who guided the reading of the young wanted to be sure that they really had the chance to do so.

IV

RELIGION, ORGANIZED AND INDIVIDUAL

. . . the two strains of thought, Calvinist and Jeffersonian, which entered into our original American heritage. On the problem of the resolution of potential conflicts of interest and passion in the community, the strain of thought most perfectly expressed by James Madison combined Christian realism in the interpretation of human motives and desires with Jefferson's passion for liberty.

—Reinhold Niebuhr, *The Irony of American History*, 1952, p. 96.

This was the spring tide of infidelity in many parts of Europe and America. At school and college, most bright boys, of that day, affected to regard religion as base superstition, or gross hypocrisy—such was the fashion. Bishop Madison, President of William and Mary College, contributed not a little, within his sphere, by injudicious management, to the prevalent evil. It was his pious care to denounce to the new comers certain writings of Hume, Voltaire, Godwin, Helvetius, etc., etc., then generally in the hands of seniors. These writings the good bishop represented as sirens, made perfectly seductive by the charms of rhetoric. Curiosity was thus excited. Each green youth became impatient to try his strength with so much fascination, to taste the forbidden fruit, and, if necessary to buy knowledge at whatever cost.

—Winfield Scott, *Memoirs of Lieut.-General Scott, LL.D., Written by Himself*, 1864, p. 10.

Not all the profound changes taking place in the religious life and ideas of Virginians between 1790 and 1830 are reflected in the political, social, belletristic, and theological records of the time. Much more evidence of these changes appears in the happenings of the decades immediately following, when the two majority denominations, the Baptist and Methodist, founded their colleges and made themselves strongly felt in political and social matters. But the forty years between the two Virginia constitutional conventions saw deism and scepticism at their height about 1800 and their subsequent gradual decline; the decay almost into dissolution of the Episcopal church and the beginning of its slow resurgence; the emergence and well-nigh dominance by the end of the period of Presbyterianism in intellectual circles and its corresponding rise in social recognition at the same time that it remained a vigorous evangelical organization; the continued rapid increase in numbers of the Methodists and Baptists, and the latter group's growing impress on politics; and the lessening of the small Quaker influence as the decades passed, the firm establishment of the Lutherans and other German sects in the Valley, and the growth into identifiable religious bodies of the Roman Catholics and Jews.

The period saw the publication of scores of sermons and addresses by Virginia clergymen, and for the first time many controversial pamphlets reflecting church doctrine, Calvinism *vs.* Arminianism, immersion *vs.* other forms of baptism, and the validity of apostolic succession. It saw a few written defenses of Godwin and Paine, but many more attacks upon them or what it was believed they stood for. It saw a continuation of earlier attacks on organized, especially established religion as the enemy of political freedom and equality, though most of these attacks came from those who had reached manhood during the Revolutionary period. It saw in its earlier decades the evangelical sects especially arrayed against slavery but in some instances becoming quiescent on this subject by 1830. It saw Reason as religion among the majority of its leaders replaced finally by orthodox Anglicanism, Presbyterian Calvinism, or a kind of sentimental primitivism which might be held by members of these two churches as well as by the Baptists and Methodists.

The political and social alliances and alignments among the religious groups crossed each other in several directions. It would not be safe to say that even among the social and political leaders liberalism went hand in hand with liberal politics or that orthodox Anglican or Calvinist Presbyterian conservatism was a natural partner of Federalism in politics. Deists and sceptics were, on the whole, Jeffersonian Republicans; but significant exceptions will be pointed out. Some devout Episcopalians, many militant Presbyterians, and most fundamentalist Baptists and Methodists were Jeffersonian Republicans for a variety of reasons, among the three latter groups partly because they believed the liberal political party championed their own recognition and independence. Like other men, these Virginians individually were combinations of diverse progressive and static and reactionary ideas and ideals.

As we have seen in a previous chapter, the Presbyterians were the strongest promoters and practicers of sound education at all levels among their communicants and others. They augmented the influence of their schools and colleges with tracts and periodicals, at times from their own presses. But though in the middle of this period they bade fair to become the largest and strongest religious body in Virginia and in America, by the end they had let the opportunity slip from them. The very demands they made of their clergy in education, and the philosophical complexity of their theology and organization, allowed the relatively uneducated, loosely or simply organized Baptists and Methodists to climb swiftly past them, especially along the frontier. Outnumbered already in 1790 by the two sects, by 1830 they were hopelessly behind in numbers and popular power. Yet so strong were their ecclesiastical and educational leaders in Piedmont Virginia and the Valley that they came in many respects to take the place of the colonial Anglicans as the state's intellectual leaders for at least another generation after 1830. They could and did prevent a professorial appointment at the new liberal University of Virginia, which most of them had supported in its foundation, because of the alleged atheism or philosophic materialism of the eminent scientist and scholar who was to occupy the position. Then and later they may have held or set back freedom of thought and speculation in the South. While New England Puritan intolerance decayed or ripened into Unitarian liberalism and stimulating intellectual and social inquiry, the Virginia puritan Presbyterianism helped by its theological intransigence and in some instances religious intolerance to turn the state along another road which led to Appomattox. Ironically, it was Reason—their own creed—advanced by able minds over this whole generation, that was able to do this. For the Presbyterian clergy and laity, as thinking churchmen, were superior to the members of all other churches in Virginia in this period. Only the older deistical-rationalistic minds were capable of combating them, and these minds were concerned primarily with other matters.

A. *Deism and Scepticism*

Deism and scepticism held strong positions in the Virginia thought of the Jeffersonian period, but the individuals who held such views usually did not parade them before the public in oral addresses or in print. There were a few men like the Southern Appalachian blacksmith who read and praised Tom Paine and Volney to his somewhat awed customers. He took delight in shocking the simple backwoodsmen, and he had a special antipathy to the Methodist circuit riders who had harsh things to say about him in their sermons. It was his habit to castigate bodily all of these preachers who journeyed through his pass. One especially agile and muscular brother was too much for the blacksmith, however, and "beat hell out of him."[1]

True or not, the story illustrates among other things the isolation of most sceptics in Virginia and elsewhere in the United States in this period. There were undoubtedly numbers of them who had read and pondered Paine and Voltaire and even Hume and had decided that their minds were their own churches or that they had no churches at all. The educated Virginian who was a speculative thinker on religion, however, was much more likely to be a deist than an atheist. As a child of the Enlightenment he had been nurtured on verse and prose which praised or explicated a benevolent deity in Nature.

But the orthodox churchman was likely to see little difference among atheist and deist and evil incarnate. Patrick Henry, writing a friend in 1796, was vehement: "The view which the rising greatness of our Country presents to my Eyes, is greatly tarnished by the general prevalence of Deism—which with me is but another name for vice & depravity."[2] John Randolph, who in his later years became a quite devout and orthodox Christian, was as bitter about the liberal atmosphere in which he grew up as he was about everything else. In 1813 he remembered that "The conduct and conversation of Mr. [St. George] Tucker [his stepfather] and his friends, as Col. Innes and Beverley Randolph . . . , had early in life led me to regard Religion as the imposture of priestcraft. I had become a deist and by consequence an atheist! (I shudder whilst I write it, altho. my intentions were pure and I was honestly seeking after truth.) I say 'by consequence,' because I am convinced that deism necessarily leads by the fairest induction to that conclusion."[3]

Virginia leaders of the Revolutionary generation had indeed in their thinking and reading often come to feel that established religion was designed to meet the needs of priestcraft. As usual, Randolph exaggerated. Tucker's letters and manuscript poems indicate his serene faith in Nature's God, a faith which is more Christian than pagan and not at all atheistic. Yet Randolph has put his finger on one reason why the enlightened liberal who wished to free mankind of all his shackles looked askance at intrenched Christianity: it aided in keeping the yokes about men's necks. Congressman John W. Eppes as late as 1819 expressed this position strongly in a letter to his son Francis: "I am glad you feel pleasure in the history you are reading—A correct history of the priests in all countries would perhaps place them much on a footing—In the formation of all the different sects meekness and humility has distinguished them—It is however a melancholy fact that all of them when armed with power have in turn become persecutors—The great value of history as far as respects Religion is that it carries irresistible conviction to the mind that it is unsafe for the Government of a country to give a preference to any. . . ."[4]

This is a fair introductory statement to Jefferson's personal ideas on religion, established and otherwise. He always insisted that no man but himself knew what he believed, but in various ways he revealed a great deal of it. Belief in the teachings of Christ had to be separated from priest-imposed glosses, he felt, and he included the neo-

Platonic doctrines of Paul and other writers of the New Testament with these latter. Jefferson made up his own Bible from Christ's actual quoted sayings. On one rare occasion he summarized his personal creed, as Franklin did, in a personal letter. It shows him a believer in one God, in Christian morality, and in a system of rewards and punishments in an after life. Once he confided to a Unitarian that his own creed was closer to Unitarianism than anything else. And as Carl Becker has pointed out in his *Heavenly City of the Eighteenth Century Philosophers*,[5] Jefferson and other *philosophes* of the Enlightenment were closer to orthodox Christianity than they themselves ever dreamed of in their philosophy.

But actually it was not Trinitarianism or Unitarianism, Calvinism or Arminianism, or any other shade of religious or theological doctrine per se which bothered Jefferson or most other Virginia deists. They were opposed to all ecclesiastical assumptions of the right to control mankind for its own good, to doctrines tending to relate church and government directly.

In an age when the established church in various European countries and most of America had ranged itself on the side of tyranny or despotism, the man who was already well read in the rationalists from John Locke on was likely to look for a substitute for orthodoxy as it was represented by the establishment. Rousseau, Voltaire, Hume, Godwin, then Paine himself, sceptics or deists or Unitarians, all encouraged independent thinking on the matter. Certainly John Locke, the great philosopher to the Revolutionary founding fathers, had suggested a line of reasoning for one's self. The Virginia deist arrived at his religious conclusions as he did at others, through his reasoning.

The paucity of writing on the subject of deism in this period in Virginia must be assigned more to a relative lack of interest in religion than to timidity or fear of public opinion. Jefferson was interested enough in a philosophy and morality of religion to formulate his own Bible mentioned above, but he rarely expressed himself on this matter of belief to anyone. Morality was related to religion, and both might be explained rationally. From here one went on to other things. Deism for Jefferson and his fellow-thinkers was not so much a religion as a step in the development of one's personal philosophy of life which had to be reached but from which one passed on to other vital matters. Most Virginia deists give us the impression that they were not religion-minded, the kind of men we meet in any age who feel that religion has its place but with whom it will never become an obsession. Some major minds, as John Taylor of Caroline, appear not to have been concerned at all with problems of faith and reason but were vitally interested in the relation of religious *institutions* to government. Taylor condemned atheism, but he insisted that in America religion must always be strictly laissez faire. These men employed the intellectual tools of their age, reason through observation of nature, and arrived at all they needed.

The Virginia founding fathers leave this impression strongly. George Washington, who agreed as to the necessity of religion and said that men would invent a God were there not one, was tactful with all religious bodies and shades of opinion. The reader of his papers feels that his was Nature's God. John Marshall, his heir in conservative Federalism, as a genuine friend of religion attended the Episcopal church but in beliefs was unitarian. Edmund Randolph like most of his relatives was from early life a deist, though a quiet one. So apparently was George Wythe. In the next generation men like Eppes and Thomas Mann Randolph were elected to Congress or to the governorship despite their alleged deism, some contemporaries observed, indication that they said little or nothing publicly on the subject. Even two presidents of William and Mary, Bishop Madison and John Augustine Smith, were accused of deism, though in at least the former case the accusation means nothing more than that he was too liberal a churchman and too much a natural scientist for some tastes. John Randolph in his later devout years, trying to make a case for his friend Littleton W. Tazewell's personal religion, could think of no better words than "manly and rational piety."

Joseph C. Cabell, through most of his life uninterested in religion, was persuaded in his last years by his anxious and orthodox friend John H. Cocke to read the Bible again. Nothing came of it. Andrew Stevenson, son of a devout and able Episcopal clergyman, became more liberal than his father, even deistic, and remained so all his life. The distinguished Virginia physician Thomas Ewell approached the problem of religion from a philosophical point of view in his *Essay on the Laws of Pleasure and Pain* (1819),[6] a speculative work ranging from conservative deism to extreme materialism. What he advocates is a Stoic doctrine of tranquillity similar to Jefferson's, and not incompatible with the latter's form of Christianity. President Madison, educated in theology and reading it all his life, leaves the impression that his interest is primarily historical and philosophical. George Ticknor recorded Madison's predilection for Unitarian doctrines and his wife's for the Quakers', to whom she once belonged.[7] Cabell and his old teacher James Ogilvie were often called Godwinians rather than deists or atheists. Undoubtedly they were interested in Godwin's theories as to the relation of man to institutions and laws, and undoubtedly they were mild rationalists in religion. In an early pamphlet and in his one book Ogilvie went out of his way to praise Godwin and thus defend himself, but the significant thing is the form of the praise. The tenor of his argument is that *Political Justice* is a book of ethics which would make an excellent volume of sermons teaching true Christian morality.

Orthodox Presbyterian and Methodist visitors to both William and Mary and the new University of Virginia wrote disapprovingly of the air of rationalism or Godwinism prevalent, observations which apparently indicate only that under Bishop Madison at the one institution and Mr. Jefferson and George Tucker at the other an atmosphere of free speculative enquiry on all subjects prevailed. That Godwin was a popular subject of discussion at William and Mary in the 1790-1830 period there can be no doubt. He was part of the curriculum, and those not considering him in class read him outside. Cabell observes that in the excitement of Jefferson's 1800-1801 election *even* Godwin was temporarily forgotten by the students.

As time went on many of the middle generation of Jeffersonians, those born in the 1770's or early 1780's, often turned from an early agnosticism or deism to affiliation with some orthodox church. Some instances of this change represented merely the natural growing conservatism of age. Some were partly the result of the active impact of evangelical religion, frequently sentimental and primitivistic, on a mind at least partially already naturally receptive. John Randolph's was one of these minds, as we have suggested. William Wirt's was another. Born and raised a Presbyterian, the latter became in the 1790's by his own admission "an infidel." Soon after the publication of the *British Spy* and the *Rainbow* in 1803 and 1804 he was definitely on the road back to religion. Compare the tone of the 1814 *Old Bachelor* essays with those of the *Rainbow* and one sees that in a decade Wirt and his group generally had turned from a mild deism to a sort of emotional fundamentalism.[8] Wirt's letter to Dabney Carr in 1804 shows that even as the earlier essays were being written the change had begun, though pantheism at least is still strongly suggested. Wirt remarks that he has been led from his earlier infidelity, and adds: "I cannot . . . look abroad on the landscapes of Spring, wander among blooming orchards and gardens and respire the fragrance which they exhale without feeling the existence of God. . . . I am happy in my present impressions—and had rather sit, alone, in Arabia Felix, than wander over the barren sands of the desert, in company with Bolingbroke & Voltaire. Reason, my dear friend, in its proper sphere, is the best and ought to be the only guide star of our actions —but let it keep within its proper sphere and confine its operation to its proper subjects. . . ."[9]

French and English rationalism of the Enlightenment did remain in Virginia, but it was combined with the more recent Scottish common sense and associationist philosophies which even the Presbyterians were inclined to accept and to use. And by 1830 rationalism was relegated to a place considerably removed from religion. Evangelical sentimentalism and emotionalism largely took its place. Clothed in its organized religious form, Unitarianism, rational deism began in the 1820's a moderate revival in the South, and in Richmond in 1830 there was a Universalist-Unitarian congregation. Though the group struggled along there and elsewhere, it made no real headway.

By 1854 one man observed that the only "Society" left in Virginia was at Wheeling.[10] The affiliation of the New England Unitarian leaders with abolition and the strong fundamentalism of Presbyterianism had caused bitter opposition to develop. The truth is probably that for Virginia Unitarianism came a little too late. If it had offered its doctrine and philosophy to the generation maturing in the 1790's it might have been moderately successful. Rationalistic argument has remained a recognizable quality of the Virginia and the Southern mind, but it has survived largely in the political and economic rather than the religious sphere.

B. *The Episcopalians*

The Episcopal church spent most of this period merely struggling to stay alive. Though never really opposed to the earlier evangelical moment known as the Great Awakening which had so vitalized the Methodists, Baptists, and Presbyterians, as a church it stood aside and watched and thus lost its chance to attract the common man. Disestablished after the Revolution and losing its Methodist communicants to a separate organization in 1784, it spent the years until 1802 in a fruitless attempt to retain control of its property, especially the glebe lands. Madison became the first Bishop of Virginia in 1780, but in order to live he had to remain as president of William and Mary and devote only two months of the year to his diocesan visitations.

The church had its friends in high places but not enough of them. Edmund Pendleton's last act as presiding judge of the Supreme Court of Appeals was an attempt to save the glebe lands, and Bushrod Washington as associate justice sided with him, but they were not enough.[11] Jefferson's friend Governor John Page, legislator Chapman Johnson, essayist and jurist Richard E. Parker, and James Mercer Garnett were among the devoted laymen who remained attached to the church all their lives. Garnett in 1828 even wrote two tracts defending the Episcopal position from certain accusations made by John Holt Rice, *A Defence of the Protestant Episcopal Church, Against the Charge of Enmity to the Civil Institutions of Our Country*[12] and *Correspondence between the Rev. John H. Rice, D.D. and James M Garnett, Esq. on the Subject of the Tendency of Episcopal Principles*,[13] both getting at the meat of the matter of the evangelical sects' continued fear of his denomination.

The Episcopal clergy did not include as many eloquent preachers or trenchant pamphleteers as the Methodists and Baptists, though several spoke out effectively. A man like the amiable Scot John Buchanan of Richmond contented himself with good preaching and brotherly democratic friendship with other sects, but a few were less serene. Dr. William Holland Wilmer for example, founder of the Protestant Episcopal Seminary in Alexandria and later president of William and Mary, engaged in written controversies with a Jesuit, defending in 1817-18 his church's position in sermons and letters to the newspapers, composing an *Episcopal Manual* (1815) explaining and vindicating church doctrine, and generally working for the revival of the church through his editorship of the *Theological Repertory* (1819). Dr. John S. Ravenscroft, rector in Mecklenburg and later Bishop of North

Carolina, published an extended "Vindication" of church doctrine from Dr. Rice's "Aspersions."

The two other clergymen best known were Mason Locke Weems and Devereux Jarratt. The former made most of his living, as we have seen, as a bookseller, and was so Low Church as to consort cordially with Methodists and other evangelical sects. Jarratt, the greatest of two or three evangelical Episcopal clergymen, was a friend of Methodists both before and after they were members of his church. At the time of their formal separation in 1784 he tried unsuccessfully to get their first regular minister to have himself ordained by an Episcopal bishop and thus remain within the older church. Never meddling in politics, Jarratt fought for a rebirth of spirituality and a renunciation of worldliness. His warm friend Methodist Bishop Asbury was convinced that more souls had been saved through the preaching of Jarrett than through that of any other man in Virginia.[14] Deeply attached to his own church, Jarratt was treated coolly by so many of its clergy that he rarely attended conventions. His printed sermons, tracts, and autobiography have in several instances been through a number of editions. He did as much as any other one man to encourage Methodism in Virginia, but his labors failed to arouse his own church. When he died in 1801 Episcopacy was at its lowest ebb in the state.

Though as a denomination the Episcopalians were notoriously unsuccessful along the frontier, in western Virginia they did have one tower of strength and activity, the Reverend Joseph Doddridge. Physician, historian, and playwright as well as clergyman, Doddridge tried to keep the church abreast of the western march. From his own parish in Wellsburg (now West Virginia) he rode on horseback over northwestern Virginia and Ohio and laid the foundations for the episcopate later attained in the latter state. A half dozen like him might have changed the history of his church in the West.

Bishop Madison's latitudinarianism and rationalism probably had little or nothing to do with the rapid decline of the church before his death in 1812. Certainly the defection to deism and hostility to the establishment of so many of its upper-class members who were political leaders had more to do with it. At any rate, so prostrate was the church in 1811 that a report to the General Convention expressed doubt that it could be revived. There had been no convention for seven years when in 1812, after Madison's death, Wilmer and another young minister, William Meade, took steps toward calling one. When it assembled in 1813 they and other younger clergy managed to get themselves elected members of the standing committee of the diocese and set to work. After some correspondence Dr. Richard Channing Moore of New York was elected Bishop at the convention of 1814. Wilmer was reelected chairman of the standing committee every year. These three men, Moore, Wilmer, and Meade (the last later Bishop himself) began the revival of the Episcopal church in Virginia which yet continues.

C. *The Presbyterians*

By 1790 the Presbyterians, as we have noticed, were the best organized and most influential in public affairs of all the denominations. Gewehr in his *Great Awakening in Virginia* calls them "the militant Presbyterians,"[15] and well had they deserved the adjective. There had been dissenters of the sect in the colony since 1683, though the number was small for sixty years.[16] They began to be felt as the Scotch-Irish descended into the Great Valley in the 1730's. Some of them spread across the mountains to Albemarle and then in a southeasterly direction to Prince Edward and Cumberland. And in the forties another group had settled in Hanover in the Piedmont, where they were soon aroused and organized under the preaching of the great Samuel Davies and other able men. From these three centers they spread.

The New Side Presbytery of Hanover, organized in 1755 just before the reunion of the Old and New Side factions in 1758, became the mother of all presbyteries in the South and West.[17] Led by forceful preachers and impelled by genuine zeal, the Presbyterians strengthened their numbers and organization through their active part in the revivals of the Great Awakening.[18] From this activity sprang their schools and colleges to train their own ministers, as their Log Colleges were already doing in the north. This same Hanover Presbytery was the first in the church to take action recognizing the Declaration of Independence when it sent a memorial to the Virginia legislature.[19] Thus from the birth of the nation the Virginia Presbyterians aligned themselves on the side of political liberty. They remained fighters against intrenched privilege and advocates of religious freedom—provided everybody practicing that freedom was Christian.

Equal to the Episcopalians in education and intelligence if not in wealth, they preserved a simplicity in their services which even Virginia Episcopalians, always Low Church, did not have. The Frenchman Bayard, traveling in the Shenandoah Valley in 1791, recorded sympathetically a Sunday he spent among them. He and other travelers worshiped with the inhabitants in a plain wooden building, its gallery filled with Negro men and women, the white mothers below nursing their infants publicly without shame. After singing several Psalms, a minister who was the grandson of a Frenchman preached "entirely upon the principles of the evangelical doctrines: he recommended the practice of those abstruse virtues, of general usefulness, and which society dispenses with less than those which make extraordinary men. He spoke with impressive simplicity; his voice became soft and sweet when he described the love of the creator for man." After listening in deep meditation, the congregation knelt for a long prayer which ended the service. When the minister descended from the pulpit, there was handshaking all around. After dinner the family with whom the traveler was staying withdrew to read chapters from the Old and New Testaments.[20]

These presumably were simple folk. But one may be sure that their procedures were much the same as those of a Fredericksburg congregation of 1816-18 whose minister in after years remembered with warmth and some pride the fine character and quality of his listeners. They included "Daniel Grinnan . . . , John Mundle . . . of the true Scottish mould . . . , Major Day . . . the very ideal of the old Virginia gentleman . . . , Seddon, from Falmouth . . . , Morson, of Hollywood . . . , a Scotchman's son . . . , majestic Patton, from the beautiful residence near the falls. And from the hills, above the falls, often came Thornton. . . . Near by Grinnan, when his profession admitted, sat Wellford the physician, of extensive reading, and wonderful memory, and great skill in the healing art. . . ." Other old Virginia names follow. These Presbyterians were leaders in this old community.[21]

Presbyterian attention to education was the denomination's strongest attribute, Baptist Elder John Leland thought. Not only did they establish schools and colleges; they insisted that their clergy be liberally educated, be able to write as well as to preach. The Minutes of the Hanover Presbytery indicate,[22] for example, that Moses

Waddel, a young minister, was required to write an "Essay upon the Freedom of the Will" and submit it to the next Presbytery before he could be fully qualified.

They were a missions-minded people. David Rice and Thomas Cleland were among the Virginia-born clergy who spent the greater part of their lives preaching and organizing in Kentucky. Though Presbyterianism became strong in that state, its slowness in organization generally along the frontier, as indicated above, prevented its rivaling the Methodists and Baptists. And on the whole, Virginia Presbyterians in this period were opposed to slavery. Certainly their clergy were, one of them, George Bourne, becoming so vehement an abolitionist orator and writer that he had to move north. And in 1827 layman William Maxwell of Norfolk barely escaped a coat of tar and feathers for publishing a temperate plea for emancipation.[23] But more of slavery in a later chapter.

The Presbyterian press was far ahead of that of any other denomination. They published a number of periodicals which reached many readers beyond their own church. For a time in Richmond Dr. John Holt Rice owned and controlled a printing press and publishing firm which was at least semiofficial. And more than a dozen of their clergy were writers on religious, moral, and social subjects, and in a few cases belletristic essayists.

The Valley Presbyterians had begun as early as 1804 at Lexington the Virginia *Religious Herald*, under the editorship of Archibald Alexander and others, to which Piedmont Presbyterians like John H. Rice contributed. It was entirely religious.[24] Rice's essays in this journal, for example, were on infidelity, Bible doctrines, and experimental religion.[25] In 1815 in Richmond Rice himself began to publish the *Christian Monitor* in pamphlet form, designed "to communicate religious intelligence." It was issued once in two weeks and was contributed to by the clergy from all over the state, but it lasted only until August, 1817.

In January, 1818, appeared the first number of the monthly *Virginia Evangelical and Literary Magazine*, also cited by Rice, so successful that it endured for eleven years. Wider in range, it had literary and scientific departments as well as religious. Its motto "For God and Our Country" pretty well expressed its purpose. Rice wrote many reviews, articles, and editorials. His brother clergyman Dr. Conrad Speece contributed, and so did able lay writers like William Wirt and William Maxwell. Reviews of Wirt's *Patrick Henry* and *Old Bachelor,* Paulding's *Letters from the South,* Dwight's *Theology,* and Speece's *The Mountaineer,* and essays on historical works, novels of character, and the theater were characteristic of the literary side of the periodical. Some sentimental verse was occasionally published. It also included essays on agriculture, inland navigation, the Fourth of July, road construction, public education, and "the classical part of a liberal education." It discussed slavery in moderate terms as "this greatest political evil ever entered into the United States." It took a nationalistic stand on American literature. Its religious essays were on such subjects as the immortality of the soul, death-bed scenes, a memoir of Samuel Davies, and Locke as "not a Socinian." In many respects it was a direct anticipation of the *Southern Literary Messenger,* which appeared six years after it ceased publication. Certainly it was the nearest thing to a critical journal published in Virginia during the Jeffersonian period.

Along with it, perhaps to satisfy his clerical brethren, Rice issued in 1819 and 1820 several numbers of *The Pamphleteer,* containing one essay to an issue, on subjects such as "Baptism" and "Irenicum the Peacemaker." In October 1822 he began also the *Family Visitor,* a strictly religious paper still continuing today in a union with other early religious periodicals as the *Christian Observer.*

In 1819 Rice purchased a printing press and announced a number of subscribers who would support his religious and literary publications. *Sermons Selected from the Manuscripts of the late Moses Hoge* (1821) and an edition of John Smith's *True Travels* and *Generall Historie* (1819) were the two most notable books brought forth by this "Franklin Press." The latter, one result of Rice's and Francis Gilmer's growing antiquarian interests, was a beautiful and costly book, the first edition in America of this original history of the Virginia colony. It brought Rice to the verge of bankruptcy, for despite the enthusiasm of Gilmer, Wirt, Dabney Carr, and John Randolph not nearly enough copies were sold to pay for the printing.[26]

The published sermons and tracts of the Presbyterian clergy, however, seemed to have greater appeal. They form one of the most imposing segments of American religious literature in the period. In this period, too, Weems and Carey brought out the sermons of

Samuel Davies in volumes which were best sellers. Archibald Alexander, John D. Blair, Stephen Bovell, Moses and John Blair Hoge, James Muir, Henry Ruffner, Conrad Speece, and William Claiborne Walton were among the ministers who published individual and collected sermons. In them they struck at Paine and *The Age of Reason*, Unitarianism, and slavery, or defended or explained predestination, the evidences of the authenticity of the Scriptures, and the covenant of works and grace.

Walton wrote a *Narrative of the Revival of Religion* (1825), an account of activities in his Baltimore church which defended revivalism in general. The work was reprinted in New York and New England several times. Rice himself gave (and later printed) earnest and moving discourses in Boston as well as in Virginia, usually breathing benevolence and brotherly love for all Christians, but in some instances bringing forth the ire of the Episcopalians. One printed pamphlet bears the title "High Church Principles Opposed to the Genius of our Republican Institutions" (Philadelphia, 1829), in which "High Church" did not have the meaning it does today; but the essay did induce Episcopalian rejoinders. Rice had sufficient reputation to be elected president of Princeton, but his devotion to Virginia Presbyterianism prevented his accepting the offer.

Conrad Speece, Rice's old schoolfellow at New London Academy, in *The Mountaineer* essays (1818) presented for younger members of the church a series of pleasantly sentimental moral discourses on "Beauties of the Morning Hour," "The Heroism of Idleness," "The Improvement of Manners in Our Valley," "Religion as the Basis of a Good Education" and a half dozen other subjects. The little volume went through at least three editions. Archibald Alexander as Philadelphia pastor and first Princeton Theological Seminary professor through his fervently pious and scholarly writings enhanced the prestige of Virginia Presbyterianism outside his native state.

Men like these gave the Presbyterians their place at the end of the period as the intellectuals of Virginia Protestantism. Others who came out in print less frequently if at all, men like William Hill of Winchester and Alexandria, Wirt's "Blind Preacher" James Waddel, and Cumberland Presbyterian organizer Finis Ewing, together with these same men gave the clergy a great reputation for pulpit oratory. Yet for all these positive qualities, perhaps partly because of them, they never reached all the people. Part of the reason lay, as we have suggested, in the complexities of Calvinism and church organization and in the kind of intolerance which caused them to fight Thomas Cooper's appointment to the University of Virginia. Though Rice was behind the opposition to Cooper, his own failure to identify himself with either progressives or conservatives within his church caused many of his brethren to look upon him as too tolerant, too undecided. Apparently the Presbyterians wanted a rigid intransigence, which never sat well with the sturdy yeoman. Also part of the reason lay in a sometimes unconscious desire on the part of their educated clergy to win leaders rather than people. A clue to this lies in a letter of John Holt Rice to Archibald Alexander in 1810 in which he boasts of the fact that John Randolph's "sister" Judith had made "a profession of religion," John Randolph himself attended the sacrament, William B. Giles regularly attended Presbyterian services, and the wife of John W. Eppes "is said to be under very serious religious impressions."[27]

At their best their clergy struck in their sermons the right note for their age, piety combined with patriotism. Here the theological doctrine of natural law combined with the political doctrine of natural right to place them on common ground with all their fellow countrymen. James Muir of Alexandria sounded it: "Do you love your country? Become righteous. . . . Has freedom a thousand charms? Be thankful you live in freedom. Be respectful to the laws. . . . Rest not however contented with civil liberty; the tyranny of sin is the worst of tyrannies. Throw it off. Seek the liberty wherewith Christ makes you free."[28]

D. *The Baptists*

Baptists were present in seventeenth-century Virginia, but they were even later than the Presbyterians in becoming numerous in the eighteenth century. In their development no particular racial stock seems to be involved. Their first organization, the Ketoctin Association, was formed in 1756, and in 1770 this group of General or Regular Baptists alone had ten churches with a total membership of 624.[29] In 1767 these Regular Baptists came into contact in Orange county with the Separate Baptists and in the end absorbed them. The Baptists increased rapidly between 1760 and 1776. By the latter date they claimed ten thousand, and by 1800 it is generally conceded that they stood first in the state in numerical strength, with the Methodists second.[30] After disestablishment they no longer suffered from persecution, jails, and fines. Their first general association, meeting in 1823 in Richmond, was composed of nineteen associations in Virginia and three partly in the state. This numerical supremacy seems to have been largely the result of their series of revivals between 1785 and 1800 led in Virginia by men like John Leland, and on the Kentucky frontier by fiery preachers like John Taylor (*not* of Caroline) and David Barrow.

Though most of their clergy were uneducated, the three just mentioned have left an extensive printed record of their ideas which may fairly represent most of their brethren. John Taylor (1752-1835), who came from an educated Episcopal family, married a Baptist wife in 1782 and the next year moved to Kentucky. There he became a large landowner as well as pastor of the Baptist church at Clear Creek and the organizer of many others. In 1823 he published *A History of Ten Baptist Churches,* in 1830 an attack on the Campbellites, and in 1820 curiously—in view of his own labors—an attack on missions. What he did in Kentucky was not missionary work, he felt, and he claimed that the missionary scheme was imposed on his church government to get money. Fearless, zealous, always cheerful, he influenced the western Virginia Baptists against missions as such.

John Leland (1754-1841), Massachusetts-born but a resident of Virginia from 1776 to 1791 and for years later a mighty influence, is remembered as politician as well as preacher.[31] He was a great force in the disestablishment of the Episcopal church and the move which led after his time to the confiscation of the glebe lands. His *Virginia Chronicle* (1790) is valuable secular as well as church history. An exponent of political and religious liberty, he was persuaded by Madison in 1787-88 to support the ratification of the new Constitution. He and most of his denomination remained loyal Republicans throughout the Jeffersonian era. He devoted the years after 1791 to overthrowing the established Congregational church in New England. Yet he was personally gentle and conciliatory, and above all tolerant of religious views not his own. The most amusing incident of his career is the presentation of the mammoth Cheshire cheese to Jefferson from his New England admirers in 1801.

A firm believer in the compact theory of government, Leland in his political essays always reflects Jefferson's ideas. That government is best which governs least, and universal peace will free the common man of religious tyranny, "the intrigues of lawyers," and "the frauds of priests." His ideal therefore included short sessions of the legislature, few laws, and a frugal treasury.

David Barrow, a Tidewater Baptist, left in his printed *Circular Letter* in 1798 just before he departed for Kentucky a statement of his political creed. Like Leland, he felt slavery to be iniquitous, and like his colleague he regarded government as a civil compact and a necessary evil.[32] He enumerated his views of government in twenty-eight points. He continued to write against slavery in Kentucky but devoted more time to sermons such as the "Testimony of Christ's Second Appearing" (second edition, 1810).

Other Baptist clergy handled their pens effectively. Henry Holcombe (D.D. of Brown University), a Captain in the Revolution and one of the most distinguished of pioneer Baptist divines, published in 1822 a series of *Lectures on Primitive Theology*. The later famous Andrew Broaddus brought out in 1795 *The Age of Reason and Revelation* against "Mr. Thomas Paine's late piece" and in the next decades other sermons and studies. "Edward Baptist, A.M." addressed *A Series of Letters* (1830) to the *Pamphleteer* disagreeing with Dr. Rice. Three preachers other than Leland left valuable historical accounts of their denomination, oft-persecuted Scot James Ireland in his *Life* of himself (1819), William Fristoe in *A Concise History of the Ketocton* [*sic*] *Baptist Association* (1808), and Robert B. Semple in *A History of the Rise and Progress of the Baptists in Virginia* (1810).

Conscious of their own and political history, most Baptists were like Leland, as we have said, Jeffersonian Republicans. In at least one instance, a Baptist congregation (the Mathews church) voted as to what political candidates it would support. But there was no absolute unanimity of opinion on politics or on slavery. Their part in the Great Awakening had brought within the Baptist fold men like Robert Carter of Nomini Hall, who gradually liberated all his slaves after he joined the church, but even some of their clergy owned a number. Concerned in their writings more with the proper form of baptism than with abstruse doctrines, they never bogged down in theology. Plain, zealous, and untiring, they reached the man the Presbyterians could not.

E. *The Methodists*

The Methodists were in education or lack of it, in plainness, in their appeal to the common man, much like the Baptists, and in Virginia and America the two denominations have contested the first position among Protestant churches in numbers and even political power. In doctrine and church organization the two were quite different, though in the latter respect the Methodist was as simple as the Baptist was loose. A part of the Episcopal church in America until 1784, the Methodists developed in England originally as a product of the Great Awakening. In the colonial period and later, their English leaders like Whitefield and Wesley came over to preach all along the Atlantic coast. Whitefield was Calvinist, Wesley Arminian, and in general church doctrine Wesley won. Both preached death and damnation as did certain other Episcopal clergy.

Norfolk had the first visiting Methodist clergyman in 1772, but the real beginning of the sect was made in Chesterfield, Dinwiddie, and Brunswick counties, encouraged in the former two by "flaming evangelical" Anglicans like Archibald McRoberts and Devereux Jarratt. Beginning in 1779 the Methodists held an annual conference in Virginia, and formed their separate organization, with other Methodists, at Christmas, 1784. Then three-fourths of the Methodists in America lived south of Pennsylvania. Originally using an abridged Episcopal prayer book and vestments encouraged by Wesley, they had by 1800 dropped liturgical form and adopted completely the emotional forms of preaching which had helped to produce them.[33]

The Methodist itinerant preaching system was more rugged in 1790 than it is today. Bishop Asbury, who himself rode on horseback some 200,000 miles in Virginia and the South and stayed at most a few weeks at any one place, well represented the ministers under him. In the beginning all the clergy were circuit riders, unmarried men, visiting in regular order each of the several churches within their charge. In the cities they were settling to stations, or single churches, but the majority throughout our period remained itinerants. An Elder presided over each district, and a Bishop over the assemblage of districts at the Annual Conference.

The Presbyterians had been strongest among the Scotch-Irish. The Methodists throve best where their mother church, the Episcopal, had decayed. Doctrine was similar but simpler, and the new emotional appeal struck fire in hearts long passive. The Methodists in Virginia did not increase as rapidly as the Baptists: in 1816, about the time of the death of Asbury, they had only 24,361 members, including 5,629 Negroes, and for the next fifteen years increased very little in the older part of the state.[34]

The Methodist preachers, like the Baptist, were rarely college-educated. When they were not reading their Bibles, they were studying their hymn books. Revivals were a marked characteristic from the beginning in Virginia, but they did not begin camp-meetings until 1803.[35] The psychological reactions of "the jerks," "the laughing exercise," and "the dancing exercise" were matters of grave concern to their ministers from their first general manifestations in 1804 in the camp meetings.[36] Yet the camp meetings were this church's great means: one in the Eastern Shore of five days and nights resulted in one thousand conversions. Members of other sects thoroughly and seriously enjoyed their meetings: Presbyterian R. N. Venable, the itinerant lawyer, mentions in his 1792 diary "coming upon" a Methodist gathering in the woods and being well pleased with the preacher's eloquent sermon.[37] Another Presbyterian, William Hill, preached at a Methodist meeting near Williamsburg and found the Methodists cordial personally but not at all pleased with his doctrine.[38] On the other hand Methodist itinerant Nathaniel Harris rejoiced when Stith Mead had in a Presbyterian stronghold "Broken up the very Bowels of Botetourt [county]. . . . O that the spreading flame might reach the Western Empire & finally consume Calvanistic [*sic*] Error."[39] The latter part of the good brother's wish is fair evidence, by the way, of the success of the Presbyterians in Kentucky at this early period.

Jesse Lee, who did as much to bring Methodism to the north and New England as Leland had to spread the Baptist faith in Virginia, had been a Virginia boy influenced by the preaching of Devereux Jarratt. The record of his life and work is very much the story of the development of the Methodist church along the Atlantic seaboard. His best known books are *A Short History of the Methodists in the United States of America* (1810) and his *Memoir* published in 1823 after his death. The identical folk story is told about Lee and Leland,[40] who preaching without notes were challenged contemptuously by clergymen of the Establishment (in one case Congregational in New England in the other Episcopal in Virginia) to preach extemporaneously from a text given after Lee/Leland entered the pulpit. The text was "And Balaam saddles his ass." Both men identified Balaam as false prophet with a hireling clergy, the saddle with their enormous salaries, and the dumb ass who bears the load with the people. The tale concludes that Lee/Leland was not asked to preach again.

The Methodists had other able men who could write as effectively as their Baptist or Presbyterian brethren. Virginia-born Peter Cartwright's famous *Autobiography,* showing the Methodist on the frontier, is one of the most entertaining and significant of all accounts of the region. English-born John Dickins, long a Virginia-North Carolina itinerant, from 1789 headed the Methodist book concern and was editor of the *Arminian Magazine* (1789-90) and the *Methodist Magazine* (1747-48). William Walters, the first Methodist itinerant, published in 1806 *A Short Account of the Christian Experience.* Stith Mead, one of the most effective camp-meeting organizers, born of Episcopal parents, kept a diary and wrote lively letters, often in doggerel verse, to his ministerial brethren.[41] He also composed and collected a volume, *Hymns and Spiritual Songs* (1805), containing Methodist pieces such as "Shout Old Satan's Kingdom Down" which eventually developed eighteen verses. Hymn No. 107 begins:

> The world, the devil, and Tom Paine
> Have done their best, but all in vain.

These are camp-meeting songs long since abandoned for the other Methodist tradition of most dignified hymns.

The Methodist preacher did occasionally touch the hem of politics with his pen. One sermon of 1814 against political slander by the Reverend Richard Ferguson has the picturesque title "The Fiery-Flying Serpent Slander, and the Brazen Serpent Charity, Delineated." Actually the Methodists of the Jeffersonian period appear not to have been nearly so politically active as the Baptists and Presbyterians. Jefferson spoke approvingly of the majority denominations of the Methodists and Baptists at the same time he denounced scathingly the Presbyterians for the interference in the Cooper case of the University of Virginia. The former two, he said, had made no objections. They still possessed a tolerance they have not always displayed in subsequent generations.

F. *Smaller Religious Bodies*

The German Protestant sects, largely confined in the Jeffersonian period to the Shenandoah Valley, have what one church historian calls "a confusing history" because they for a long time lacked organization.[42] They were primarily Lutheran, German Reformed, and Mennonite, though there were some Moravians. The first German Reformed group in Virginia were brought by Spotswood to work in his furnaces and mines. The Lutherans also had their beginnings among Spotswood's imported workers and by 1725 had formed the Hebron Congregation in what is today Madison County. In the next few decades more of them came down the Valley like the Scotch-Irish from Pennsylvania. The Mennonites in three groups first settled in Page county in the Massanutten Valley. These were much like the Quakers in their refusal to bear arms and insistence on a uniform plain garb. The Moravians had missionaries in the region as early as 1742.

The various sects, particularly the Lutherans, established some useful academies and taught usually both the German and English languages. From an intellectual point of view, the most noteworthy activity of the German sects was the establishment of German and English-language printing presses at Harrisonburg, New Market, and Staunton. They had German-language newspapers, too, but by the later Jeffersonian period the primary function of these presses seems to have been to publish educational books and religious tracts and sermons.[43]

What was probably the first German-language press south of Mason and Dixon's line and the oldest Lutheran publishing house in America was set up in 1806 by a member of the Henkel family at New Market. The founding father of the family, the Reverend Paul Henkel, had settled in the village in 1790. The greatest Lutheran home missionary of his generation, he traveled through much of Virginia, North Carolina, Kentucky, and Ohio and in his spare time wrote sermons, hymns, and catechisms in both German and English. Four of his brothers and five of his sons were trained by him for service in the church and did much to spread Lutheranism in the west and south. Ambrose (1786-1870), preacher and printer, first operated the press.

The first printing was the Minutes of a Special Conference held at an Evangelical Lutheran church in Rockingham county. It was printed in German. The next year the first of a series of "Virginia children's books" appeared. *Die Fromme Zwillinge* told a story of two Christian boys sold by a Jew into Turkey and their remarkable escape from death. In 1808 followed the first of many editions of an ABC book, with woodcuts of animals and poems about them illustrating each letter of the alphabet, and containing also the Ten Commandments and Lord's Prayer. In 1807 had begun the first German weekly of the South, edited by Ambrose Henkel, *Der Virginische Volksbarichter und Neu Marketer Wochenschrift*. It ran two years.

Ambrose then went to Philadelphia to learn more about his trade. Returning in 1810 with a new press, he published a German hymn book, and later in 1816 an English one. Solomon Henkel bought out his brother's business in 1814. Through 1830 the principal printings were of catechisms; church minutes for Tennessee, North Carolina, and Virginia; moral tracts and sermons, the latter including some of Luther's; and new editions in both languages of older Henkel writings. David Henkel published controversial sermons such as *An Answer to Mr. Moore, the Methodist; with a Few Fragments on the Doctrine of Justification* (1825) and *David Henkel Against the Unitarians* (1830).

At Harrisonburg the Mennonite Elder Peter Burkholder printed in 1816 his *Eine Verhandlung von der Äusserlichen Wasser-Taufe* and the Reverend John Brown in 1818 and later several sermons in German. Other clergy of the three major sects also occasionally committed their doctrines and convictions to print.

The Quakers, who had been in the colony at least from the 1650's, were in small numbers fairly active in Virginia from the 1690's.[44] They formed the Hopewell monthly meeting in 1735, but there are many records of earlier existence in the Richmond, Norfolk, and Winchester areas.[45] Numbers settled in the state in the decades just before the Revolution and several, like Captain Christopher Clark of Louisa, were quite wealthy. Lynchburg was especially a Quaker settlement, eight of its eleven original trustees having Quaker names. By 1798 the meeting there possessed a large stone church.[46] And the Quakers in the Valley were the first group to erect their own church buildings. Many of the records of the active Hanover county group survive.[47]

Since this church was unequivocally opposed to slavery, most planters among them in Virginia freed their slaves, and as a group they offered memorials to the legislature advocating emancipation.[48] Robert Pleasants of an estate on the James River in the 1780's liberated eighty slaves of his own at a cost of £3000 sterling. That the liberating of slaves was opposed by some is suggested in one compromise Quaker ruling that under certain conditions a few already owned might be retained. In 1814 the records of the Lynchburg Meeting show the complaint that though the members were "free from slavery [they are] reluctant to speak against it."[49] In 1831 the Quakers again pressed for emancipation in the Virginia legislature but frowned on national legislation, declaring it was a state affair, perhaps another indication of their neighbors' influence.[50]

Many prominent Jeffersonians came of what had been or still were Quaker families, as James (1769-1836) and John Hampden (1797-1846) Pleasants, cousins of Thomas Jefferson and descendants of a Quaker John Pleasants who had arrived in Virginia before the end of the seventeenth century. True to their heritage, James was a leading social reformer and John, who did not believe in dueling, died in a duel when he refused to defend himself. Samuel M. Janney (1801-80), poet, biographer, and Hicksite Quaker minister who published his first poems in the 1820's, came on both sides of Loudoun county Quaker families. Zealous abolitionist and philanthropist, he carried on Quaker reform ideas long after the Civil War.

The Roman Catholics were not numerous during this period, though a few of them too had been in the colony since the seventeenth century. By 1785 there were about two hundred in the state and by 1791-92 they were holding masses in the Virginia capital in a room across the hall from that used by the Presbyterians and Episcopalians.[51] The Abbé Dubois, the Richmond priest, had escaped from France during the Reign of Terror and was on cordial terms with Blair and Buchanan of the Presbyterian and Episcopal churches. He improved the French of young Virginians by teaching it in Harris' school.[52]

The history of Jeffersonian Virginia Jews is like that of the Lutherans hard to get at. From the seventeenth century there appears to have been a few in the colony. And in the earlier two-thirds of the eighteenth century, judging by names and a few court records, they were on cordial terms with other Virginians. Between 1790 and 1830 a number of them were prominent citizens of Richmond and Norfolk. They had rabbis and fairly thriving synagogues. But their story in Virginia up to at least the Civil War is that many of them intermarried with Christians and largely or entirely lost their racial and religious identity. As a group or as individual representatives of a group they did not enter into the major public discussions of the day. A family like the Mordecais in some individual cases intermarried and in others did not. The voluminous records of this family's activities in Virginia and North Carolina afford one of the more interesting pictures of Jeffersonian social and business life and bear few marks of the feeling of separateness the Jews of the north sometimes display when corresponding among themselves.[53] Gustavus Adolphus Myers (1801-69), Richmond lawyer and patron of the arts, City Councilman and member of the Executive Committee of the Virginia Historical Society, remained a member of the Beth Shalome congregation but married a daughter of William B. Giles. He has his place in our period largely through his 1821 adaptation of a French interlude, published as *Nature and Philosophy,* one of the popular American plays of the first quarter of the nineteenth century.

One of the most attractive religious figures of the time was unconnected with any church, though as he himself said he was variously labeled Baptist, Methodist, and Presbyterian. This was Elder Joseph Thomas (1791-1835), called "the white Pilgrim" from the gown he wore when preaching, a North Carolina born boy who grew up in southwest Virginia in Grayson and Giles counties. Having been converted under the preaching of Lorenzo Dow, he set up as an itinerant evangelist on his own, traveling through Virginia, Ohio, North Carolina, and other states, and baptizing by immersion.

Thomas left a number of printed works, including a hymn book, sermons, poems, and an autobiography, the last republished as late as 1861. In this *Life, Travels, and Gospel Labors of Eld. Joseph Thomas . . . , To Which Are Added His Poems: Religious Moral and*

Satirical (orig. ed. Winchester, 1817; with this title New York, 1861) he pretended to be nothing but the simple gospeler he was, saying that he spoke no language but his own. As for his poetry, he had courted the Muses in graveyards and along mossgrown streams, not in college libraries. As one might expect, his poems smack of Cowper and Goldsmith and the Graveyard School. But they are by no means primarily religious in tone or subject (see Chapter VIII below). Independent Christian that he was, he proposed union of all denominations. His fellow evangelical Protestants listened to his sermons and professed the faith he preached, but they usually affiliated themselves with one of the established sects.

By 1830 all religious groups not only had accepted the separation of church and state but took every opportunity to express their allegiance to the idea. Even the leading Episcopal clergy and laity joined in the chorus—read their Fourth of July orations. Two Virginians, Jefferson and Madison, had made before the period began the greatest American contributions to this separation and to religious freedom in their authorship and championing of legislation on the subject.[54] Their evangelical friends, especially the Baptists, made the completion of the task in this period easier with the strongest of all political pressures, a plurality of votes. Paradox or not, religious groups employed political means to insure their independence of politics. The tyranny of certain orthodoxies still lingered to embarrass and sometimes to hamper intellectual progress, as they continued to do for several generations.

V

AGRARIAN ECONOMY, THEORY AND PRACTICE

The capacity of agriculture for affording luxuries to the body, is no less conspicuous than its capacity for affording luxuries to the mind; it being a science singularly possessing the double qualities of feeding with unbounded liberality, both the moral appetites of the one, and the physical wants of the other. It can even feed a morbid love of money, whilst it is habituating us to the practice of virtue; and whilst it provides for the wants of the philosopher, it affords him ample room for the most curious and yet useful researches. In short, by the exercise it gives both to the body and to the mind, it secures health and vigour to both; and by combining a thorough knowledge of the real affairs of life, with a necessity for investigating the arcana of nature, and the strongest invitations to the practice of morality, it becomes the best architect of the complete man.

—John Taylor of Caroline, *Arator,* 1818 ed., p. 190

The greatest service which can be rendered any country is, to add a useful plant to its culture.

—Thomas Jefferson, note G. appended to *Autobiography,* L & B, I, 159.

The individual Virginian from the earliest settlement of the colony to the Civil War, whatever his occupation or profession, usually thought of himself as a farmer, living in a rural world. This is strikingly true for the 1790-1830 period. Possessing then no real cities comparable to those of the North and East or even to Charleston in South Carolina, the Virginian knew that his interests lay close to the soil, whether he was a great jurist, statesman, or the poorest plowman. One would expect Washington, Jefferson, and Madison, who lived on large estates, to be tremendously concerned with the plight of the farmer and with all the aspects of agriculture, but he may be surprised to learn that Chief Justice John Marshall, city dweller who stood with Federalism and capitalism in the formative years of the nation, always walked about with experimental seed in his pockets and was an organizer and first president of the earliest Virginia agricultural society. Active in studying and working with new methods of crop rotation and prevention of soil erosion, new plants and stock for breeding, and new machines which might put farming on a firmer economic basis were lawyers like Chapman Johnson and John Taylor, physicians like Drs. James Greenway and Benjamin Coleman, and educators like Louis H. Girardin and James M. Garnett.

A look at agrarianism in Virginia in the Jeffersonian period brings to mind many related things. Here is a major part of the explanation of the alliance between great landowner and small farmer in the democracy of the Republican party, an alliance Europeans and even many eastern Americans never understood. Here is the authentic continuation of the tradition of the colonial Virginia gentleman as the complete man, for over and over again men like Taylor, Madison, Jefferson, and Garnett announce that only the farmer can live the good life in all its fullness. Here at least lies a portion of the explanation of why even "pure Republican liberals" like John Taylor and the less liberal later Edmund Ruffin came to excuse and finally to defend slavery. And here in this agrarian way of life lies part of the explanation of the considerable scientific investigation and mechanical invention carried on by a large number of Virginians of the period.

Because there will be a later chapter on political thought, the political implications, impetuses, and alliances springing from agrarianism will be discussed here as little as possible. Slavery also will be considered more fully later with politics and political economy. And investigations in pure science and mechanical invention not directly related to agriculture will be looked at separately. Of course all these things have intimate, sometimes integral relationships with agrarianism, and some discussion of them cannot be avoided in the present chapter. But here agrarian economy, its theory and practice expressed in essays and recorded experiments and discussion groups by and among the Virginia farmers themselves in attempts to reason out and improve their condition, will occupy most of our attention. The glance at theory will include, as it must, some examination of their general social philosophies.

Paradoxes are everywhere in the economic agrarianism of this period. But the most striking is that a leisured Virginia class who had hitherto bestirred itself almost solely in politics, and then only for certain periods of individuals' lives, came to exert itself tremendously in thought and action, producing finally through men like John A. Binns, John Taylor, Edmund Ruffin, and Robert and Cyrus McCormick real improvements, really progressive measures leading to a prosperous agriculture in the south and southwest far surpassing any before experienced in America. And doing this largely under the impetus of their desire to preserve a way of life, the traditional gentleman's way. They would have said farmer's way, and by the farmer would have meant every citizen of the state. The freehold concept of land tenure, basic to their philosophy, included the propositions that every man has a natural right to land, that ownership brings status and self-fulfillment, and that a good political society must provide for the development of every farmer—all of which in the end led toward genuine democracy.[1] Though at this time Jefferson, Taylor, and Garnett meant to include their humbler brothers the yeoman farmers when they spoke of the tillers of the earth as the chosen people of God, most of the experiments they carried on in crop rotation, in artificial and natural fertilizers, and even in inventions were designed to improve large-estate farming more than anything else. The experiments themselves would have been impossible for small farmers to carry on, for a number of reasons, including necessary capital, labor, and fields. That in the end the gentlemen helped all kinds of farming and farmers seems in practice incidental even though in theory they always aimed so to do.

Yet these agriculturists were certainly not selfishly class conscious. For the sincerity of their belief in the corruption of urban and the virtue of rural living is unquestionable. They practiced as they preached. And as they looked about them, at the long line of Virginia leaders of the early republic and at their own modest pleasant way of life which some of them believed extended all the way down to their slaves, they felt that they had incontrovertible evidence of the rightness of their convictions. As their soil became depleted, the hold of their state on pre-eminence in everything was weakening, or so many of them thought. Restore the soil, and Virginia would be restored to her rightful pre-eminence. All things spring from the earth. Simple, primitive, noble, limited yet grand, thus went the conception. But anything except simplicity and primitive thinking or action were necessary to return the state and the citizen to its and his proper relation to the earth.

In one sense all this is a concomitant of the story of the American frontier. As it receded westward, so did fertile lands. Old lands exploited heedlessly were exhausted. Emigration from Virginia after 1800 alarmed many, and by the 1820-30 decade the rate of population increase had decreased alarmingly. Even those who viewed philosophically the trek of young Virginians westward, even those who in individual cases encouraged it (Madison, for example), were necessarily concerned for themselves and the region in which they remained.

Virginia's agricultural problems did not begin with the adoption of the Federal Constitution. Even in the colonial period individuals here and there had tried to do something about their exhausted lands, transportation of produce, and stock breeding. George Washington established a reputation as a progressive agriculturist fairly early in his career. When he returned to his estates after Yorktown he concentrated a great deal of his attention on farm problems. The number of books on agriculture in his library has been noted in a previous chapter. By 1786 he was in correspondence with the English agriculturist Arthur Young, whose writings were to be among the text books of the Virginia farmer for the next generation. Washington asked for advice and assistance, and Young gave it. Already the owner of Mount Vernon understood the importance of good plowing as a means of preserving fertility, and he now tried various experiments in erosion prevention, crop rotation, and Merino sheep-breeding. He began to work in the three main directions in which farmers were to move, toward (1) better plows and methods of soil preparation and prevention of erosion, (2) increased interest in manures and fertilizers, and (3) introduction of grass crops for feeding and green dressings as part of crop rotation systems.[2] He corresponded with Jefferson and Madison and other farmers about seed, fertilizers, plants, and stock almost up to the day of his death. His *Letters* to Young (London, 1801) and Sir John Sinclair (London, 1800), another eminent British agriculturist, discussed his personal methods, gave a map of his farm, included reports from neighboring farmers, and engaged in more general discussion of the rural economy of America.[3] Republished in 1803 in Alexandria and Fredericksburg, these *Letters* were read by his younger contemporaries on both sides of the Atlantic. They show that despite his and others' efforts old systems generally prevailed, though everywhere appeared the tendency to abandon tobacco in favor of wheat.

Dozens of travelers recorded their observations of Virginia farming. The Duc de la Rochefoucauld-Liancourt, for example, in 1799 reported unfavorably on conditions in the Piedmont and favorably on those in the Valley.[4] He was greatly impressed by Jefferson's attempts at reform. Actually scores of intelligent men, including those mentioned above and lesser figures like Israel Janney, John Minge, and Fielding Lewis were at the end of the eighteenth century working in various ways and recording, at least in manuscript, some of their findings. Plowing probably received the most attention early in the period. Men like Landon Carter, John Slaughter, John A. Binns, and Thomas Mann Randolph, with Jefferson, Madison, and Taylor, read the English Jethro Tull's *Horse-Hoeing Husbandry* (Jefferson had the fourth edition, London, 1762) and profited by the suggestions in this and other matters. Deep plowing for fertilization and erosion prevention developed especially in northern Virginia and Maryland. Between 1783 and 1820 the iron plow largely displaced the wooden variety, and the use of animal manure greatly increased on the farms of the men just mentioned and a number of others.

A. *The "Specialists"*

The experiments, inventions, and printed explanations of four or five men represent rather well the stages of thinking and acting on farm problems. For John Alexander Binns of Loudoun, John Taylor of Caroline, Edmund Ruffin of Prince George, and the two McCormicks of Augusta all have significant places in agrarian reform, though their results were not in every case of enduring value. In a relative sense when compared with the Jefferson circle, they are specialists. For they could and did devote major portions of their time and effort to experiment or invention.

John Alexander Binns (*ca.*, 1761-1813) was given 220 acres by his father in 1782 and at once began improving his land. From about 1784 he experimented particularly with the use of gypsum or plaster on clover, grass, and grains and had astonishingly successful results. It was not the first time gypsum had been used, and he probably received suggestions from his neighbor Israel Janney; but it was the first time that an ordinary farmer got wide practical results from it. At the request of his neighbors Binns published a summary of his findings in *A Treatise on Practical Farming* (Frederick-Town, Md., 1803), including chapters on the life-history of the Hessian Fly and other agricultural matters along with the discussion of gypsum as a fertilizer. "Not written in a scholastic stile," warned Binns, "Yet I hope my meaning may be plainly understood" (p. 39). Jefferson was so pleased with it that he sent copies to his son-in-law Francis W. Eppes and to his English friends Sir John Sinclair and William Strickland recommending the method and observing that "These facts speak more strongly . . . than . . . polished phrases." Binns' method became known as the "Loudoun system" and seems to have been widely used in Virginia and Maryland.[5]

John Taylor (1753-1824) of Caroline, United States Senator and successful lawyer and farmer, advanced theories from the same basic assumption as Binns—of worn-out lands—but both the theory and practice he advocated are much more complex than those of his neighbor to the north. Today he is receiving new attention as the philosopher of political agrarianism, the champion of "pure Jeffersonianism," the strict-constructionist. Vernon L. Parrington in *The Romantic Revolution in America* made much of Taylor's philosophical indebtedness to the French Physiocrats.[6] Though Taylor had much in common with them, their influence seems far less strong than his convictions from experience. Heir of the colonial Virginia tradition, he became the spokesman of both political and economic agrarianism.

In books and pamphlets Taylor spoke out over a thirty-year period. Only two of these writings are remembered today, however, his *Inquiry into the Principles and Policy of the Government of the United States* (Fredericksburg, 1814) and *Arator, Being a Series of Agricultural Essays* (Georgetown, D.C., 1813). As he stated in the Preface to the fourth edition of *Arator* (1818),[7] this book "is chiefly confined to agriculture, but it contains a few political observations; the *Inquiry*, to politics; but it labours to explain the true interest of the agricultural class." It was *Arator* which concerned the Virginia farmer to such an extent that it went through many editions during the author's lifetime and was reprinted by Edmund Ruffin in the 1830's. It had appeared originally as a series of essays in a Georgetown, D.C., newspaper.

Taylor held that the prosperity of his country depended upon its citizens' adequate knowledge of both agriculture and politics, the causes of our wealth and liberty. "If one is vitiated in practice, poverty, if the other, oppression ensues." "If agriculture is good and government bad, we may have wealth and slavery. If the government is good and agriculture bad, liberty and poverty." Agriculture was a guardian of liberty as well as the mother of wealth.

From here he proceeds to the real problem, the loss of fertility in lands. Beginning with a survey of the present condition of agriculture (he confesses he knew chiefly Virginia, Maryland, and North Carolina) in all its decay, he goes to the political state of agriculture and points out how bounties and protective tariffs for manufacturing have hurt the farmer. He devotes ten essays or chapters to these political evils. Then he turns to slavery, "a misfortune to agriculture"[8] which cannot be banished but must be coped with. He touches on the problem of free Negroes, and he takes issue with Jefferson's denunciation of slavery in *Notes on the State of Virginia,* for he feels that slavery incites more to benevolence than to the opposite passions. He insists that he does not approve of the institution but believes it must be faced realistically. Then he turns to specific practices which hurt agriculture and which might be reformed. The evils of the share-cropping overseer he denounces in a fashion anticipating later reforms aimed at sharecropping practices. He spends some time advocating "inclosing," by which he means shutting off arable fields from open cattle grazing so that by intelligent fertilization and crop rotation they may realize their full potentialities. So on to manuring. Contrary to many of his contemporaries, he felt that Indian corn was a most useful fertilizer as well as food crop and spent several chapters outlining his evidence. He cites Arthur Young and Jethro Tull in discussing the best plowing procedures. Succulent and leguminous crops, livestock (including sheep, hogs, cattle, and horses), live fences (hedges of cedar and other trees and shrubs) orchards, draining, and tobacco are the subjects of one or several chapters each. In the final section, 58 through 64 of the fourth (enlarged) edition, he returns to the philosophy of agriculture, entitling his chapters, "The Economy of Agriculture," "The Pleasures of Agriculture," "The Rights of Agriculture," and "The Present State of Agriculture," throwing in second thoughts on hay, fodders, and cotton. In a series of notes in an appendix he adds a few further thoughts, one of which is a summary of what he had in mind when he wrote the book, that "Society is unavoidably made up of two interests only . . . one subsisting by industry; the other by law. Government is instituted for the happiness of the first interest, but belonging itself to the second, it is perpetually drawn towards that by the strongest cords. . . . Agriculture is the most powerful member of the general interest, but if her sons are too ignorant to use this power with discretion,"[9] they will continue to suffer.

Taylor recommended Binns' practice of fertilizing with gypsum, the plowing methods followed by others who had written on the subject, and his own methods of such things as "inclosing," live fences, and of course Indian corn as fertilizer. He outlined a complete course of procedures for the farmer and at the same time attacked politico-economic measures which were hurting the markets for the crops the farmer did produce. Much of this latter evil came from consolidated government, of which Taylor was a lifelong enemy. A highly successful farmer himself as well as a revered elder statesman, he was listened to by many of his fellow farmers, especially in the South.

Taylor's *Arator* is part of his long series of expositions of the Southern agrarian point of view. Beyond any of his contemporaries, he saw clearly the significance of the economic factor in his ideal society of farmers—or country gentlemen.[10] Even in the democracy America was developing, he warned, farmers might become merely peasants. The complete man would never survive poverty.

In many respects Edmund Ruffin (1794-1865) took up where John Taylor left off. Certainly he marks the replacement of the Virginian of conservative instincts and liberal ideas and ideals with the out-and-out conservative whose strict-construction and states' rights convictions had assumed a definitely hardened complexion. Yet this man who wanted to fire the first gun at Fort Sumter was in one sense a genuine reformer—as scientific farmer.

Despite the intelligent experimentation and publicized report of men of the Binns-Taylor variety, by 1819 Virginia agriculture seemed to be in a worse way than before. Part of this was the result of the general depression affecting all America at this time. Part of it came from the apathy of those who decried "book farming" and obstinately continued in their old way. But much of it came because of the despair of many of those who had honestly tried the methods advocated by Binns and Taylor and found that on their own lands the procedure did not work. Surviving are a number of letters[11] in which gentleman farmers point out that most of Taylor's lands were unusually good to begin with in a section of the state quite different from theirs, or that gypsum-fertilization as Binns suggested it simply did not work for their lands. In other words, these two and other early reformers had found no universal panacea.

Ruffin, born and brought up in Prince George county in Tidewater Virginia, was among the large-scale farmers who read widely and intelligently and experimented in many directions. A kind master who was on affectionate terms with his slaves, he believed that the Negro was naturally inferior and that American slavery was the best possible condition for him. Unitarian in his religious beliefs, he was a regular communicant of the Episcopal church all his life, for he believed firmly in social conformity. Instinctively, his biographer suggests, he disliked Jefferson and all the abolitionist-egalitarian-democratic perfectionism the latter stood for.[12] Yet they held the common bond of love for the land and a desire for agrarian prosperity.

At nineteen Ruffin took over the responsibilities of farming at Coggin's Point in Prince George on land which was extremely poor. Enthusiastic and anxious to improve his estate, he first drained several swamps. These fields had three good years and no more. Then for four or five years he tried and was disappointed in Taylor's "enclosing" system and other methods. One day while reading Davy's *Agricultural Chemistry* he decided that he might have the remedy—that the lands about him in Virginia were acid and lacked calcareous earths. Without any published confirmations he concluded that vegetable acids produced the sterile soils and that the marl (common fossil shells) so abundant in his neighborhood might correct the situation. One February morning in 1818 his carts began to convey to his fields the marl dug from pits on his own lower lands. Two hundred bushels were spread over a field and corn planted. The new era had begun, for the yield was forty per cent better than that from his unmarled fields.

In October of that year Ruffin presented before the agricultural society of his own county an account of his findings and followed it in subsequent years with a series of valuable papers on this and other phases of agriculture. His enthusiasm and zeal mounted with his experimentation. In 1821 the 1818 paper was enlarged and revised and published as the lead article in a number of Volume III of John Skinner's Baltimore journal, the *American Farmer*. The editor called it the "first systematic attempt . . . wherein a plain, practical, unpretending farmer, has undertaken to examine into the real composition of the soils which he possesses and has to cultivate" (pp. 313-20). Skinner thought it so important that he published an extra edition of this issue and distributed it without charge to farmers all over the country.

In 1832 the original article, grown into a volume of 242 pages, appeared as *An Essay on Calcareous Manures*. It ran through five editions and continued to enlarge until it reached nearly five hundred pages. A government expert as late as 1895 in the *Year Book of the*

United States Department of Agriculture called it "the most thorough piece of work on a special agricultural subject ever published in the English language."[13] And Ruffin was not without honor in his own place and time, for contemporary writers hailed him as a deliverer worthy to rank with John Taylor of Caroline. President John Tyler was to hang his portrait beside Daniel Webster's and point them out to visitors as representing the greatest living agriculturist and the greatest living statesman.[14]

Ruffin's experiments have held up as Taylor's and Binn's have not, at least for a larger number of situations over a much larger territory. Avery O. Craven, his biographer, asserts that most of his basic assumptions and findings have never been challenged.[15] His theory bolstered by his experience as expressed in his first 1818 paper was enlarged but never substantially changed. Naturally poor soils differed from those naturally rich but reduced by cultivation in their power of retaining putrescent manures. Natural fertility, in turn, was dependent primarily on the presence of a proper proportion of calcareous earth, which neutralized vegetable acids and gave the power of combining with manures for productivity.[16] In Tidewater Virginia this element of calcareous matters was absent, and attempts to improve soil by animal and vegetable manures was useless until the soil had received enough calcareous matter to correct the defect. *After* this first step, Ruffin advocated the use of barnyard manures, rotation of crops, the growing of clover and cowpeas and other methods recommended by the Binnses and Taylors of his time. He occasionally took exception to earlier practices. For example, he advocated manure as a top-dressing as opposed to Taylor's practice that it be plowed under to prevent evaporation.

Authorities insist that Ruffin was far ahead of his time and are puzzled that an untrained man should approach and achieve in such a genuinely scientific manner the solution to a major agricultural problem. For Ruffin himself talks about his laboratory methods. In the 1830's he founded and edited the influential *Farmer's Register,* which published some of the best agricultural papers ever to appear in America. But his major accomplishment is the *Essay.* It is estimated that in Tidewater Virginia alone the application of marl to lands after 1820 increased their value by thirty million dollars.

The production of Ruffin's *Essay* is not difficult to understand if one remembers the character of the intellectual atmosphere in which the Virginia gentleman farmer lived. Ruffin was a wide reader for pleasure, from Shakespeare (by the time he was ten) and the British reviews to the four-volume English *Compleat Body of Husbandry,* which he had devoured by the time he was fifteen. He read Davy on chemistry, as we have seen, and later Lyell on geology. Smith's *Wealth of Nations,* Boswell's *Johnson,* and Scott's novels were favorites. As readers of previous chapters know, there was nothing unusual about this reading. Nor really is there anything strange about its result. Other country gentlemen experimented as he did, using the minds sharpened by familiarity with imaginative literature and disciplined by the classics and scientific writers.

A fourth major figure in the history of agriculture grew up in the Virginia of this period but made his great contribution a year after it was over. But Cyrus Hall McCormick's 1831 reaper grew out of, one might say evolved from, the experiments and inventions of Robert McCormick (1780-1846), his father, in the Valley of Virginia.[17] The elder McCormick, a substantial Scotch-Irish farmer who had in his youth access to an excellent library, was a reader of Skinner's *American Farmer* and an experimenter in grasses, deep plowing, and crop rotation as suggested in that journal. Robert McCormick also used the tools of his farm shops to make the machinery which he thought might help him. He invented a threshing machine, a hydraulic machine, a hemp-brake, blacksmith's bellows, and a grist-mill self-stopper, all aimed to be eminently practical but not always succeeding. The hydraulic machine was patented in 1830, but the threshing machine and the bellows were never patented, perhaps because he realized they were too much like those others were making at the time. He did build and sell five of the threshers before 1834.

Robert McCormick also built several reapers, one as early as 1809 or 1810, though probably never a really successful one. These early machines worked only for straight grain, though there is an accumulation of evidence on the part of two of Robert's grandsons to prove he was the actual inventor of the successful machine later patented by Cyrus.[18] Certainly, as a biographer of Cyrus observed,[19] the invention of the McCormick reaper in 1831 can only be explained in the light of the father Robert's experiments before 1830. The most influential mechanical factor in the development of American agriculture in the nineteenth century thus came from the imaginative and inventive genius of Virginia gentleman farmers.

B. *The Writing Farmers*

As we have pointed out, the men discussed above became in a sense specialists, devoting the greater part of their lives to farming and its problems alone. There were also great activity and some real contributions to agriculture from a number of Virginia planters who were so involved in politics or other professions that they simply never had the time for the laboratory experimentation and analysis of Taylor, Ruffin, or the McCormicks. Many of them did write, however, one or more essays, or published addresses, which formed small but occasionally significant contributions to the farmer's prosperity. Dr. Joseph Doddridge's *A Treatise on the Culture of Bees* (1813), Dr. James Greenway's *An Account of the Beneficial Effects of Cassia Chamæcrista in Recruiting Worn-out Lands* (*Transactions* American Philosophical Society, III [1793], 226-30), Jacquelin Ambler's *A Treatise on the Culture of Lucerne* [1808?], and G. W. P. Custis' *An Address* (1808) encouraging domestic manufacturers and descriptive of sheep-breeding at Arlington, are fairly typical. One Surry county gentleman, Richard Mason, published two widely used editions of a book on the care of horses, the first edition being entitled *The Gentleman's New Pocket Companion, Comprising a General Description of that Noble and Useful Animal the Horse* (1811). Others, like James M. Garnett, William Tatham, and Thomas Marshall printed the frequent addresses they gave on the condition or prosperity of the Virginia or American farmer. Garnett's frequent efforts in print made him a nationally known figure to such an extent that when the United States Agricultural Society was formed he was chosen its first president. Scores, perhaps hundreds, of specific and general essays or monographs on agriculture were published by Virginians between 1790 and 1830, with the great majority appearing after the War of 1812. Then there is the list published in 1913 (Virginia State Library, E. G. Swem, comp.) of agricultural manuscripts now in the Virginia State Library.[20] Between 1802 and 1830, this list drawn from one collection alone shows four or five dozen communications between individuals and individuals or individuals and societies concerning topics similar to those in the published essays.

There were several large-scale planters of the generation after Washington who devoted as much time as they could to agriculture and recorded in some instances what are perhaps more significant results than those just mentioned. This was the group centered in Albemarle but embracing the neighboring counties of Louisa, Orange, Nelson or Amherst, and Fluvanna, and including the close friends Joseph C. Cabell, John H. Cocke, James Madison, Thomas Mann Randolph, and Thomas Jefferson.

Joseph C. Cabell left little printed record of his work, but there is a good deal of manuscript evidence that when he was not active in the legislature and in education he was intent on agriculture. When he visited Europe in 1803-4 he studied botany at Montpellier and bought books on chemistry and mineralogy which might help him on his farms. He kept a notebook bearing the heading "Agriculture (Paris 1804)" which contains notes on grafting fruit trees, tree planting, beans and peas, grasses, orchards, and gardens.[21] Elsewhere his notebooks contain under "Agriculture Virginia" entries dated from Edgewood from 1809 on, including comments on fertilizers and plats of peach and apple orchards. His correspondence with Jefferson includes long discussions of live hedges.

James Madison was considered by Jefferson to be Virginia's best farmer. Though his public career prevented concentrated attention over a long period to his estates, the surviving letters and other manuscripts, as well as his activity in agricultural societies, afford evidence of his interest and activity in scientific farming. Near the beginning of the century he was a member of the Sandy Springs, Maryland, Farmers Society, and in 1803 he became the first president of the American Board of Agriculture, an association of farm groups initiated by the Quaker Isaac Briggs and organized in the Capitol at Washington at a meeting called by Madison. His correspondence with Briggs reveals that the two hoped to sponsor an agricultural experimental garden.

When Sir Augustus John Foster visited Montpelier a few years later his host talked freely about his farm problems, stating that he made absolutely no profit on his home place but something on two others nearby.[22] One gathers that the necessary overseer was the costly thing in Madison's farm operations. Madison gave his estimates of the annual cost of maintaining each of his slaves and other figures, all indicating businesslike methods. Foster also mentions his forge, turner's shop, carpentry shop, spinning rooms, and wheelright. The visitor was impressed by the "well constructed wagon" which had just been completed on the place.

Madison's letters to Jefferson, Cocke, the Abbé Correa, and others comment on seed, plant, soils, and other aspects of gardening and farming.[23] His activitity in the Albemarle Agricultural Society may not have been great, but his address as its president is among the better statements of the contemporary agrarian point of view.

Thomas Mann Randolph (1768-1828), Jefferson's son-in-law and kinsman, was an erudite gentleman interested equally in classical philosophy and modern natural science. On his estate Edgehill near Monticello he spent long days in the open fields superintending planting and harvesting, and occasionally taking an hour under a tree with a favorite Greek or Latin author. His best known contribution to agricultural reform is his theory and practice of contour plowing to prevent erosion.[24]

This he explained in papers and orally. By 1808 he had developed a hillside plow which he and his neighbors used with satisfaction. The contour plowing was not original with him, but he was the first to use it in his part of the country, and his demonstrations encouraged others. In 1818 and 1819 he read papers before his neighbors on the Hessian fly and the Bott fly of horses.

Long before, in the 1790's, he and his father-in-law had exchanged letters outlining their respective schemes of crop rotation, both based on the use of eight fields over eight years.[25] Number one field, for example, under Randolph's plan had corn and peas in the first year, and wheat, fallow, wheat, pasture, corn and potatoes, rye, and pasture in successive years. He noted that he differed from Jefferson principally in that the years of rest in his plan were not successive, that he substituted white clover for red, that one field would undergo a summer fallow, and above all that he gave two distinct systems for large and small fields while Jefferson used one system for all. The numerous letters which passed between the two men during the years following indicate that Jefferson had the greatest respect for Randolph's farming practices. That Piedmont Virginia appreciated him is evidenced by the silver plate presented by the Agricultural Society of

Albemarle for his "contribution to rural economy" and by its compliment of electing him its president.

One of the most thoughtful experimenters was that versatile gentleman Brigadier General John Hartwell Cocke, another of those whose library and reading tastes were noted in Chapter III above. Soldier, temperance and emancipation advocate, supporter of public education and the University, he declined public office because he preferred to live as a farmer at Bremo, his estate on the upper James. Jefferson once wrote that "there is no person in the U. S. in whose success [in certain vineyard experiments] I should have so much confidence. he is rich, liberal, patriotic, judicious & persevering."[26]

Over a long period to the very end of Jefferson's life he and Cocke exchanged agricultural news, seeds, and stock. Several times Cocke sent Jefferson carp and chub for his pond. Their servants went back and forth bearing lambs, pumpkin and asparagus seed, and broom plants for Cocke, and kale-seed, even a horse, for Jefferson. Cocke, like Cabell and Jefferson, seems to have kept a diary which was at least in part a farm journal.[27] Among the interesting entries are several of 1817 in which he records what Jefferson and Madison had to say about the introduction of the cedar into Albemarle and Orange counties and of the Lombardy poplar and weeping willow into America and Jefferson's story of the natural preservation (when wrapped in tow) of some Meriwether pears at Monticello. Cocke was an early user of marl and threshing machines and a pioneer in terracing, employment of new breeds of stock, crop rotation, and timber culture.[28]

Cocke was active in the Agricultural Society of Albemarle, becoming one of its vice-presidents when it was organized in 1817. He read several papers before it, most of them subsequently published. In the Richmond *Enquirer* of May 31, 1820, appeared an essay of his on peach trees, and in the *American Farmer* many comments which he hoped might be useful. In the latter journal in 1821 (III, 15[illegible]) his "Remarks on Hedges, Bene Plant, and Pisé Buildings" includes three aspects of farming which always interested him. The Pisé buildings for storage and livestock he demonstrated as durable and cheap. Living in good country for peaches, he wrote in 1823 (*American Farmer,* V, 118) again on the fruit, and in 1825 (*ibid.,* VII, 109) on the peach wasp. He also conveyed his observations on the Hessian fly (*ibid.,*

V, 241-44), on white flint wheat (VII, 109), and "On fallowing for wheat" (IV, 324-25), the last addressed to Edmund Ruffin, Esq., secretary of the United Agricultural Societies of Virginia. These are but scattered samples of his comments.

Cocke was even more determined than Jefferson that the new University of Virginia should have a professorship of agriculture. Though Jefferson had expressed an interest in agricultural education as early as 1803 and had incorporated a recommendation for a chair or course in agriculture in his Rockfish Gap report, when the legislature failed to support that phase of his proposals he consoled himself with the idea that the professor of natural history might give some agricultural instruction along with chemistry.[29] Cocke, not satisfied with this less-than-compromise, is said to have advocated the founding of the Agricultural Society in 1817 principally as a means of raising an endowment for the professorship. This seems doubtful, but there is no doubt of Cocke's proposal of October, 1822, that one thousand dollars of the Society's funds be donated for an agricultural professorship at the University, that the money be invested, and that an appeal be made through a letter to all other Virginia agricultural societies.[30] This was done, and a considerable sum was raised which was subsequently lost when the man to whom it was lent went into bankruptcy. In the 1830's Cocke and William C. Rives tried again to establish the professorship and again were not successful. Up to the time of the Civil War Cocke and his son St. George tried to get the chair established, the son offering in 1857 an endowment of $20,000 provided he should be allowed to name the incumbent. But this is another story.[31]

Thomas Jefferson's avid interest in every phase of agriculture is a well-known part of the saga which was his life. "No occupation is so delightful to me as the culture of the earth, and no culture comparable to that of the garden," he wrote,[32] adding that the infinite variety would always attract him. Agriculture had to be a part of every citizen's life, he knew. In suggesting to a young lawyer how he should employ his time, Jefferson told him to devote himself at the beginning of the day to physical studies, beginning with agriculture. Before eight in the morning the young man should read such books as Dickson's *Husbandry of The Ancients,* Tull's *Horse-hoeing Husbandry,* Kames' *Gentleman Farmer,* Young's *Rural Economy,* Hale's *Body of Husbandry,* and De Serres' *Théâtre d'Agriculture.*[33]

Agriculture for the American was of first importance, Jefferson urged again and again, as almost any other Virginian would have done. Near the end of his life he answered his own question, "Is my Country the Better for my Having Lived at All?"[34] Along with three politico-moral-social things he had done—the writing of the Declaration of Independence and his work for freedom of religion and abolishing entail—he included three others as of equal importance: (1) making the Rivanna navigable for produce, (2) bringing olive plants from France to South Carolina and Georgia, and (3) obtaining African rice and sending it to Charleston. He added, "The greatest service which can be rendered any country is, to add a useful plant to its culture."

From 1766 to 1824 he kept a Garden Book, in which he recorded his experiments with fruit trees, vegetables, flowers and flower beds, and other trees and shrubs. He recorded temperatures and other weather conditions, his crop rotation systems, the diagrams of his flower and vegetable beds the types of soil needed for each kind of plant, the time of seeding and harvest, and scores of other matters. In his Farm Book,[35] covering 1774 to 1826, he recorded the state of his various farms, some thirteen in all, the lists of slaves and the economics of clothing and feeding them, observations on various types of ground cover, grains, tobacco, rotation of crops, fertilizers, overseer problems, spinning, weaving, and cloth manufactures, the implements of husbandry, his stills and brewing practices.

From abroad he constantly introduced new agricultural machinery. His experiments in seed germination placed him far in advance of his neighbors in knowledge of planting. In 1795 he ran a one acre experiment which convinced him that poor land would produce as good wheat as rye.[36] He tried new methods of planting corn, various types of crop rotation including that he compared with Thomas Mann Randolph's noted above, and contour or horizontal plowing.

The Garden and Farm Books and other papers show his experiments with various kinds of nut trees, enormous cabbages and cucumbers, silk-nettle, upland rice, figs from France, peas from New York, vetch from England, grasses from various parts of Europe, strawberries and corn from Italy, the sugar maple, apricots, seeds and plants collected on the Pacific coast by Lewis and Clark, and scores of other plants. He experimented also with benne oil (note Cocke's interest in this plant also), vineyards, and agricultural implements. Like the McCormicks, he tinkered with, adapted, and improved farm machinery. By 1813 he had two spinning machines and by 1815 thirty-five spindles in operation. He operated a profitable nailery. Like the McCormicks, he had a hemp-brake. As early as 1793 he had imported the latest Scotch threshing machine, improving it himself. He wrote Washington that he was having a new machine made like the imported one, except that he had "put the whole works (except the horse wheel) into a single frame, movable from one field to another on the two axles of a wagon."[37]

He bought and tried a variety of European and American plows. His greatest tangible contribution to agriculture is the mouldboard plow "of least resistance" which he worked out by theoretical principles, discussed with friends, built models of and then working copies.[38] By 1790 he had sent a model to his son-in-law Randolph, and by 1794 seems to have tried the plow at Monticello. During his second term as President he found time to make some small improvements on it. With pardonable pride he referred to it as "the finest plow which has ever been constructed in America." He was right, for the plow received universal recognition, including the gold medal of the Agricultural Society of Paris and John Randolph's left-handed compliment at the 1829-30 Convention.

In his greatest library Jefferson listed under "Agriculture" some 134 items, American, English, French, and Italian. On his favorite subject he corresponded with Washington, Madison, Monroe, Giles, Mann Page, Archibald Stuart, and scores of other Americans; and Mazzei, Volney, Sir John Sinclair, William Strickland, Mme. Noailles de Tessé, De Meusnier, Du Pont de Nemours, and other Europeans. He was *a* founder if not *the* founder of the Agricultural Society of Albemarle in 1817.

Despite the years at the seat of government he would have preferred to spend on his acres, Jefferson as farmer accomplished a great deal for other people. That in the end weather conditions, an uncertain market, and an economic depression caused him personally to lose money and become at the end of his life almost bankrupt does not lessen the significance of his agricultural accomplishment.

For a number of reasons other than his practical farm work Jefferson is revered by agriculturists today. In 1943 M. L. Wilson in a paper[39] read before the American Philosophical Society outlined some of them, including his championship of the capabilities of the individual, the advocacy of soil conservation, the application of science to agriculture, and the recognition of agriculture as a learned profession. Most of these attitudes and ideas he shared with his neighbors, as we have seen, but his peculiar position of prominence and his energy and perseverance enabled him to have an influence far beyond anything they attained.

C. *The Inventive Farmers*

Besides major figures like the McCormicks of Augusta and the strictly amateur inventors who (like Jefferson and his son-in-law) did not care to sell their brain-children there were dozens of Virginians who did patent their devices to aid the farmer. In a list of patents secured by citizens of the state between 1790 and 1824, some 127 in all, at least thirty are directly applicable to farm use and half the rest are related.[40] Several plows and threshing machines are included, though the best-known one other than Jefferson's, that of Stephen McCormick of Loudoun, was not registered until 1828. John Balthrop of Loudoun's "Double Shovel" plow is among those that at least sound interesting. A rice huller, grain screen, wheat rubber, hemp and flax breaker, grinder for corn on the cob, grain elevator, corn weeder, beehive, corn sheller, several clover seed cleaners and gatherers, and various tobacco presses or processors were protected through the patent office, then under the Secretary of State. All are forgotten, but their very existence is indicative of the climate in which more successful inventors like Jefferson and McCormick worked.

The men who labored patiently to supply a need or improve an exciting facility were scattered over the state from the Eastern Shore to the banks of the Ohio. Many of them had more than one patent, indicative that they were at least inveterate tinkerers like their New England cousins. The brief descriptions of the items patented in no single instance suggests the fanciful or impossible. Farmers were genuinely down to earth.

D. *Agricultural Societies*

All farmers like Jefferson and his friends realized after the war of 1812 that Virginia agriculture was in such a plight that it could be best served through organized discussion and publication of individual findings from practical experience. The idea was not entirely new. As early as 1773 John Page and others had inaugurated at Williamsburg the Society for the Advancement of Useful Knowledge which included among other things discussion of agricultural affairs and which awarded the first gold medal for practical invention ever given by an American society, presented to John Hobday for his threshing machine.[41] In the 1780's the Philadelphia Agricultural Society had been founded by Jefferson's friend George Rogan. To this organization a number of Virginians belonged. Even before the war, in 1810, the Richmond Society for Promoting Agriculture was established with John Marshall as president, James Monroe vice-president, and Monroe's son-in-law, George Hay, secretary.[42] It was revived or reorganized in 1816 with John Taylor as president and attempted to be a clearing house for county and regional societies of the same kind. In 1811 the Augusta [county] Agricultural Society was founded with General Robert Porterfield as president and Chapman Johnson among its active members.[43] It seems to have expired before 1815. Between 1816 and 1830 a number of county and regional societies were formed: Fredericksburg some time before 1821, with James M. Garnett as president, a very active organization publishing papers and sponsoring an annual fair; Albemarle, in 1817, concerning which more below; Prince George, about 1818, to which Edmund Ruffin belonged, a society of several active and publishing members; and others of which we know less, including Sussex, Surry, Dinwiddie, Petersburg, Isle of Wight, and Nottoway. Then there were regional societies:[44] the Agricultural Society of the Valley, founded in 1822 and centered at Winchester, of which Jefferson's and Francis Gilmer's friend Hugh Holmes was president, composed of many active and publishing members; the Lower Virginia Agricultural Society, founded in the 1820's and meeting at Williamsburg with Andrew Hankins as president; and the Agricultural Society of Loudoun, Fauquier, Prince William, and Fairfax, founded in 1825-26, before which Cuthbert Powell and Thomas Marshall, among other prominent farmers, gave addresses. It is difficult to tell whether the United Agricultural Societies of Virginia included the whole state or simply eastern Virginia. It was founded about 1821, and at its 1822 meeting delegates were present from six Tidewater cities or counties only. Ruffin was active in this society and hoped that it would become the clearing house for information from all over the state as the Richmond Society had been, of which it may have been the direct heir. As we have noted, at least Cocke from the upper counties addressed communications to this group.

By far the most active, in publications at least, and equal to the Fredericksburg Society in sponsoring annual shows and prize-awarding competitions was that founded on May 5, 1817, in Charlottesville as the Agricultural Society of Albemarle.[45] Which of the thirty men from five counties present were the originators of the idea it is now impossible to ascertain; but almost surely Jefferson, Cocke, and Cabell were among them. Cocke was in the chair, and Peter Minor acted as secretary. The committee of five appointed to draw up rules and objectives was composed of Jefferson, James Barbour, John Patterson, Cocke, and Cabell. With his usual facility Jefferson penned a list of ten "Objects for the Attention and Enquiry of the Society" which probably represents the aims of all the other similar groups in Virginia. First, and principally, was the cultivation of the primary staples of wheat, tobacco, and hemp for market. Next came the subsidiary articles for the support of the farm, including food, clothing, and the comforts of the household. Grains, grapes, vegetables, cotton, flax, and Jerusalem artichokes were examples given. Third was the care and services of useful animals for saddle or draught, food, or clothing, and the destruction of noxious insects, reptiles, fowls, and quadrupeds. Then rotation of crops, implements of husbandry, calendars of work for laborers and animals, farm buildings and conveniences, manures and other dressings and fertilizers, reports on different practices of husbandry by individual members, and finally such other subjects "in husbandry and the arts" as might be considered pertinent. Clearly little could be added in the final "other subjects."

On October 7, these regulations were adopted and the society organized with James Madison as president, Thomas Mann Randolph first vice-president, John H. Cocke second vice-president, Peter Minor secretary, and Isaac A. Coles treasurer. The steering committee included Randolph, Cabell, Cocke, James Barbour, and David Watson. A sort of agricultural catechism which each member was to follow in reporting his own agricultural practices was drawn up. It included questions about rotation of crops, average produce of each crop per acre, number of acres under the course of cropping, the quantity of land cleared yearly, the number and description of labor-saving machines, and a half-dozen other matters. It was resolved that a committee should look at once into the establishment in the vicinity of Charlottesville of a nursery from which members might secure plants and trees. This first resolution was an interesting foreshadowing of agricultural collectivism. Along the same lines was the resolution at the meeting of March 2, 1818, that a manufactory of useful farm implements be established at Charlottesville, to serve as a machinery center for the society. One committee was appointed to look into the possibility of importing Spanish horses to improve the Virginia racing breed.

On March 12, 1818, Madison gave the presidential address in which he pointed out the nature and aims of the society. This was printed in pamphlet form and widely distributed. From this time on the membership increased greatly, drawing farmers from as far away as Fairfax county and the Shenandoah Valley. In 1819, with increased funds, the Society offered premiums for the best qualities of various grains, for recovering worn out lands, for the best animals of different kinds, for the best plows, etc. In 1822 Cocke's remarkable resolution as to an agricultural professorship was drawn up. By 1824 plans were made for annual exhibitions and prizes on a larger and more inclusive scale. Stephen McCormick of Loudoun, a distant relative of the Valley family, won a prize for his plow, so successful an implement that models were sent to France and an actual plow presented to Lafayette during his visit in Virginia. George Gilmer's man Richard won the premium as the best plowman for "having managed his plough and team with superior skill and gentleness." Prizes for wine went to Dr. Frank Carr and for the best complete suit of homespun to Colonel William Woods. The latter's finely-textured linen from home-grown flax was also commended. All this appears in the extant minute books of the Society in the 1817-28 period.[46] The later books are lost.

Many other interesting details occur in these carefully kept records: the election of honorary members from Europe and America, the representation among active members from more than fourteen counties, the titles and subjects of papers presented before the Society, and the titles of the addresses of the later presidents James Barbour and Thomas Mann Randolph. Little improvements on plows and threshers and little gadgets for use about the farm were made by men who at other times were legislators, physicians, lawyers, and schoolmasters. Perhaps no more distinguished group of men of equally small number ever assembled anywhere in behalf of agriculture.

E. *Virginians and the "American Farmer"*

Initially the Albemarle Society had designated the Richmond *Enquirer* as the medium for publication of the papers submitted by its members. When John Skinner in 1819 founded the *American Farmer* in Baltimore that journal became the printed repository of many of the Society's activities and records of experiments, as it became for other groups all over America.[47] That the Albemarle group was more active than most is indicated by the frequent appearance of its minutes or summaries of its deliberations and of papers by its members.

The *American Farmer* was the first genuinely successful farm paper, at least of the Southern states. Its editor traveled himself and observed farming practices. He wrote an interesting series, for example, on what was going on in the Valley of Virginia. And he gladly received and printed communications from individuals and from societies, the stylistic qualities of which, by the way, are generally good.

A sampling of one volume indicates how interested Virginia farmers were in their problems. Volume III, for the year beginning with April, 1821, includes several articles by Richard B. Buckner of Vint-Hill, Fauquier county, on Indian corn and wheat; an essay on agricultural schools by Richard K. Meade of Frederick county; one on hay stacking by Abel Seymour of Hardy county; another on the cut-worm by Dabney Minor of Albemarle or Louisa; and another on rotation of crops by Thomas Marshall of Oak Hill, Fauquier county. John Darby of Richmond county wrote on the curing of bacon, Dr. Benjamin Colman of Spotsylvania on a variety of subjects, Wilson Cary Nicholas on hemp (a reprinting from 1811), James M. Garnett on Indian corn and one of his Fredericksburg presidential addresses, and A[rchibald?] S[tuart?] of Staunton on the tobacco flea or fly. Ruffin, Hugh Holmes, Peter Minor, and others reported on the actual deliberations of various Virginia agricultural societies. And in this one volume appear John Taylor of Caroline's "Letter on the Necessity of Defending the Rights and interests of Agriculture, addressed to the Delegation of the United Agricultural Societies of Virginia," John H. Cocke's essay on "Hedges, Bene Plant, and Pisé Buildings" mentioned above, and Ruffin's most famous work, his *Essay on Calcareous Manures*.

Dozens of other Virginians appear in the volumes between 1821 and 1830, among them Dr. James Jones of Nottoway county, W. M. Barton of Springdale (in the Valley), Louis H. Girardin (on botany as aid to agriculture), James Barbour, and G. W. P. Custis. The last wrote several essays on earth banking and on sheep-raising. Governor Edward Coles of Illinois is represented by one address. And his name causes one to recall that he established the Illinois Agricultural Society along the lines of the Society of his native Albemarle and thus carried Virginia practice directly into the mid-West. Arthur Upshur of the Eastern Shore wrote two essays explaining the great fertility and fine climate of his native region. T. S. Pleasants of Beaverdam, probably one of the Quaker family, wrote of orchard grass suitable for a southern climate, and William H. Fitzhugh of northern Virginia estimated the profits possible from a farm devoted exclusively to sheep. These are by no means all. Through them and others like them Virginia agriculture during the subsequent three decades improved fairly steadily.

In all the volumes of the *American Farmer* to the end of the period (and beyond) Jefferson's spirit and word are deliberately invoked. Old letters of his reaching back to the end of the eighteenth century dealing with various phases of agriculture are reprinted. Even his "habits of living" are presented respectfully in an essay in 1824. In the years after his death in 1826 he continued to be quoted, always with admiration, and the implication that he was the agrarian oracle and champion.

Concerned for themselves individually these men certainly were, but there is probably no finer example of cooperative research and enterprise, of attempted pooling of information and abilities, in the history of a means of livelihood. Almost all of them agreed with Jefferson that this was the good life. Their diversified intellectual exercises dealing with the economics, the politics, the technology, and the general philosophy of agrarianism suggest that they agreed with him too that in agriculture a man might use all his mind as well as his body. To say with Henry Adams that law and politics were the Virginians' only subjects for thought is to ignore, among other things, a considerable and often distinguished body of writing and experimentation on agriculture.

VI

SCIENCE

Independent of the general utility which every branch of science may possess, by its natural affinity and probable benefit to the rest, they are all individually useful, by the exercise they afford to the intellects of those who pursue them. The mental discipline is nearly the same in every subject which may be denominated scientific. They all accustom the mind to comparing and discriminating—to generalization—and abstraction. They teach it to perceive analogies, and to invent illustrations. At one time, to resolve what is compound [sic] *into its constituent elements, and in another, to deduce remote and complex truths from simple and undeniable principles—above all, they form habits of patient and diligent inquiry, of method and arrangement. Though different sciences furnish different materials, the intellectual instruments and operations are, with little variation, the same.*

—George Tucker, "Scientific Pursuits," *Essays on Various Subjects of Taste, Morals, and National Policy,* 1822, p. 299.

I am not of the school that teaches us to look back for wisdom to our forefathers. from the wonderful advances in science and the arts which I have lived to see, I am sure we are wiser than our fathers & that our sons will be wiser than we are.

—Thomas Jefferson to [John Wayles] Eppes, February 6, 1818, HEH.

In a nostalgic look at what he called "the old Virginia gentleman" of Jefferson's day, George W. Bagby in the 1860's conceded his subject to have been almost perfect except for his neglect of science.[1] A generation earlier, in 1824, John Holt Rice lamented that Virginians had "no extensive philosophical apparatus . . . no great collections of subjects in natural history; no splendid cabinets of minerals; no botanical gardens; no anatomical preparations for the benefit of young citizens, for the excitement of their curiosity, and the aid of their researches."[2] Virginia was thus behind several other states in botany, mineralogy, and geology, he said, and he implied behind in science generally. Rice had been traveling in the northeast and had seen the respectable programs and collections at Harvard, Yale, Princeton, and Pennsylvania. Yet within Rice's lifetime Virginians had made significant contributions to medicine and geography (including exploration and cartography) and had demonstrated interest by activity in almost every other known area of science, especially including agriculture. In Europe a Virginian, Jefferson, was considered the greatest living American scientist. And the expeditions of Lewis and Clark to the Pacific had been a scientific achievement of the first magnitude.

Actually science had held an honored place in the Virginia mind since the seventeenth century, particularly in botany, zoology, and ethnology. From the beginnings of the colony educated men had sent back to eager English collectors flowers, trees, shrubs, birds, reptiles, and Indian costumes and artifacts. Writers beginning with John Smith and including Robert Beverley and William Byrd had spent some of their time carefully describing fauna, flora, aborigines and topography. And from the later seventeenth century there was a distinguished line of real botanists working in the colony.

The eighteenth-century planter as child of the Enlightenment had faith in science as a form of reason, and a belief in the doctrine of a mechanistic universe governed by immutable laws as promulgated by Newton, in the inductive method of arriving at conclusions, and in the efficacy of the scientific method as applied to human relations, including government. As his country developed from colony to state, he developed attitudes and principles regarding science from his own observation and practice, and from which he proceeded. These basic assumptions lie behind the casual work of a gifted amateur like John Page, the semi-professional experiments of Bishop Madison, the inventions of James Rumsey, and the enormously detailed labors of the Lewis and Clark expedition. They are perhaps most clearly articulated in the writings of Jefferson. Edwin T. Martin in *Thomas Jefferson Scientist* outlines them conveniently:[3] a firm belief in absolute freedom of inquiry and the basing of conclusions on observation and experiment, a conviction that science must be useful, that it must be taught in American schools and colleges, that it is a promoter of fraternal relations among all men, that America must benefit from scientific offerings from all over the world, and that government should be useful to science and science to government.

With all this went the optimism of the Enlightenment, the belief that progress might at least in part be achieved through science. With this in view the venerable botanist John Clayton and the young enthusiast John Page founded at Williamsburg in 1773 the Virginia Society for Promoting Useful Knowledge, a sort of colonial Royal Society.[4] As noted in Chapter V, this group had awarded the first gold medal for invention given by an American organization. Clayton was its first president, Page vice-president, the royal governor patron, Professor Samuel Henley of William and Mary secretary, St. George Tucker assistant secretary, and David Jameson treasurer. Clayton soon died and Page succeeded him as president.

For a time the Society flourished. One hundred Virginians became members, probably with the idea that their activity would be primarily in agriculture. But botanizing continued, and Page devoted himself to meteorology. Some papers, journals, and observations were collected during the first two years of the Society's existence, and some corresponding members, principally from among those already associated with the American Philosophical Society, were chosen. Though for some years Page wrote in the newspapers as though the group was still active, the coming of the Revolution apparently caused it to decline. Page later attempted to revive it several times, once in 1787 when the Alexandria Society for the Promotion of Useful Knowledge was formed; but few showed interest.[5] Men like Page and Tucker continued their observations and inventions the rest of their lives. Many scientifically minded Virginians gradually became members of the American Philosophical Society. And for a while in 1787-88 Virginians hoped the national academy proposed by Quesnay de Beaurepaire in Richmond would serve all their scientific needs.

This proposed Richmond academy of arts and sciences has been discussed in Chapter II above. One should recall here that one of its major goals was the advancement of science internationally as well as nationally, that French engineers and other scientists were to teach and advise in Virginia, that there would be official journals for scientific publication, and that a continuous exchange of ideas between the savants of Europe and America would be encouraged. It would have been a putting into large-scale operation all the basic principles and projects shared by the Virginia sons of the Enlightenment.

The only native development of the purely scientific organization in Virginia in the 1790-1830 period was the agricultural society, which did encourage experiment and invention on a rather wide scale and did find media for publication, as we have pointed out elsewhere. But almost from the beginning of the American Philosophical Society for Promoting Useful Knowledge, which had Benjamin Franklin as a founder, various Virginians had had some part in its development. Landon Carter was a member from 1769, Francis and Arthur Lee from the union of the two early societies to form the present organization, Dr. James McClurg from 1774, and George Washington, Thomas Jefferson, and one of the James Madisons (the other was elected in 1785) from 1780. Mann Page became a member in 1785, James Rumsey in 1789, John Beckley and Edmund Randolph in 1791, Richard P. Barton and Dr. John Rouelle in 1792, Dr. James Greenway in 1794, John Stewart in 1797, Meriwether Lewis in 1803, Bushrod Washington in 1805, Dr. Nathaniel Chapman in 1807, Dr. Joseph Hartshorne in 1819, and John Marshall in 1830, among others. Several Virginians active in the Jeffersonian period became members in the subsequent 1830-40 decade, including Edward Coles, William C. Rives, John Brockenbrough, Moncure Robinson, and the University of Virginia professors Dr. Robley Dunglison, Charles Bonnycastle,

William Barton Rogers, and George Tucker. Other Virginians as well as these, men like Francis W. Gilmer, contributed to the Society's *Transactions*. Jefferson was third president of the Society from 1797 to 1814 and Dr. Nathaniel Chapman its ninth president from 1846 to 1849.[6]

Following in spirit and theory the motivation behind the scientific organization was the Constitutional Society of Virginia "for writing about liberty," founded in 1784 with the idea of applying science to government.[7] Jefferson's neighbor Philip Mazzei was the moving force behind it. The Society first met on June 11, and on June 15 it was resolved that each member should prepare a paper every six months on some problem of politics or government. Thirty-four charter members, including both the James Madisons, William Short, five of the Lees, John Taylor, Monroe, Edmund Randolph, Mann and John Page, and W. C. Nicholas, signed its first roll. John Blair, later Associate Justice of the United States Supreme Court, was as president to receive the papers. Although it did not last long, this society's significance lies in its specifically articulated purpose of approaching government scientifically, a principle followed in the distinguished work of members like President Madison and John Taylor in the later Jeffersonian period.

Though Dr. Rice apparently did not know it, the city of Norfolk had erected a Museum Naturæ as early as 1808.[8] In 1807 Joseph C. Cabell was trying to establish one in Williamsburg.[9] And at the very time or slightly before the good clergyman was lamenting that there were no botanical gardens, the Abbé Correa and Jefferson had been planning them for the University of Virginia.[10] Even the Richmond Museum in Capitol Square in the years immediately after the War of 1812 had a small number of living and stuffed animals and birds.[11] Yet Rice was right in observing that Virginia was behind in these matters.

In matters that required more individual than cooperative scientific effort the state had shown creditable activity from the very beginning of the period. Virginia prophets of progress like John Page, St. George Tucker, the Reverend James Madison, and Thomas Jefferson encouraged scientific efforts in various directions and despite their busy official and occupational lives themselves set examples in investigation and invention from the years immediately following the American Revolution.

A. *Chemistry and Medicine*

Jefferson once wrote that the study of chemistry was really uncongenial for the country gentleman, that it was properly the pursuit of a city-dweller.[12] And several times he expressed adverse criticism of medicine as it was practiced in his time. Yet he encouraged the putting of chemistry to practical use, which had been little done, and he urged on a number of young men in their medical researches.

He was quite right about chemistry as primarily an urban employment. Except for a few privately conducted experiments by the teachers of the subject at Hampden-Sydney and William and Mary, almost nothing was done in Virginia. One young protégé of his, the son of a William and Mary classmate, did dedicate to him a popular book on the subject, and the correspondence ensuing included some of Jefferson's observations as to the kind of chemical treatises most needed. The title of the young man's book suggests a Jeffersonian point of view: *Plain Discourses on the Laws or Properties of Matter: Containing the Elements or Principles of Modern Chemistry; with More Particular Details of Those Practical Parts of the Science Most Interesting to Mankind, and Connected with Domestic Affairs. Addressed to All American Promoters of Useful Knowledge* (New York, 1806). The author, Dr. Thomas Ewell, had produced something useful, for it became a William and Mary textbook and sold rather well to the general public.

Medicine could not and did not suffer from neglect in Virginia, although until the last five years of the period there was no medical school in the state and during the whole period no medical journal. All through the earlier eighteenth century Virginians had studied the subject in Scotland and England. Dr. John Tennent's essay on pleurisy (Williamsburg, 1736) and Dr. James McClurg's on the bile and liver (London, 1772) are among the evidences of significant work. The pioneering Hospital for the Insane at Williamsburg sponsored by Governor Fauquier and the gentry just before the Governor's death, was opened in 1773. During the Revolution, Dr. William Brown, a Virginian who was an Edinburgh graduate, had published his *Pharmacopœia* (1778) based on the Edinburgh work of the same title but the first in the United States.[13] And Virginia physicians William Fleming, Thomas Walker, and Andrew Robertson, the last an extensive writer on medical subjects, performed distinguished professional service during the colonial wars. During the Revolution medical men like Hugh Mercer, Arthur Lee, Theodorick Bland, Jr., and Walter Jones were better known for their political, military, and diplomatic exploits than their professional, though all of them had good reputations as physicians. From the seventeenth century other physicians had frequently distinguished themselves as natural historians.

When the first issue of the first American journal, *The Medical Repository,* was published in New York in 1797 it contained two items from Virginia, one from Richmond and one from Norfolk.[14] In the six additional journals established in the first decade of the nineteenth century, Virginia physicians' observations appeared frequently. John Mitchell's 1744 account of yellow fever was published for the first time in the Philadelphia *Medical Museum* in 1805. Dr. Greenway's account of autumnal bilious fever written in 1794 appeared in the first issue of the *Philadelphia Medical and Physical Journal* (p. 8). Other physicians, including John Spangler, Robert Burton, Robert Dunbar, B. H. Ball, James Lyons, and Daniel Wilson sent papers published in the first decade of these journals.

Yet Virginia and American medicine generally remained in a confused state. The very application of Newtonian principles, by which physicians hoped to discover and work out precise quantitative methods, did not work in all too many aspects of this science.[15] Public hostility to anatomical experimentation, the woeful lack of reliable medical statistics and even a general theory, the frequent separation of surgery from physic retarded a clearly defined progress. The investigations of the period in basic medicine and the kindred fields of biology and chemistry did, however, do much to prepare for the real advances of the succeeding generation.

Virginia physicians were as well trained as any in the country. A few still pursued the courses in Edinburgh and London after 1793, but the majority studied at the University of Pennsylvania and later the Jefferson Medical College in Philadelphia and sometimes in New York or Baltimore.[16] Though no exact figures are available for the period before 1830, by 1860 the University of Pennsylvania, for example, had 5,501 medical graduates of whom 4,254 were from the South and 1,749 from Virginia alone.[17] In 1819 the College of Physicians and Surgeons in New York graduated nine from Virginia and only fifteen from New York. In 1826, to take a sample year, there were thirty-two Virginia-born graduates in medicine at the University of Pennsylvania. A few years later one graduate explained the popularity of Philadelphia by pointing out that for almost a full generation, the principal chairs of both the medical schools there were occupied by men from Virginia and Maryland.[18]

On December 30, 1825, an act was passed in the state legislature incorporating "the College of Physicians of the Valley of Virginia" at Winchester, with John Esten Cooke and Hugh Holmes McGuire as two of the senior professors. It lasted until 1829. Also in 1825 the University of Virginia Department of Medicine came into being, with North Britisher Robley Dunglison and Irish John P. Emmet occupying respectively the chair of anatomy and medicine and of natural history (including chemistry, botany, and comparative anatomy). In 1827 Emmet took over pharmacy and materia medica and relinquished most of the natural history, and in the same year an instructor in anatomy and surgery was added.

Jefferson had realized since his early attempts at medical education at William and Mary how badly the South needed a medical school. The University of Virginia department was his mature answer. The school developed slowly but soundly. The two original professors, both able men, made names for themselves in research. Jefferson was so taken with young Dunglison (1798-1869) on first acquaintance that he made him his personal physician. They developed a strong friendship, and Dunglison attended the old statesman on his deathbed. By the time he left Virginia in 1833 for teaching at Maryland and the Jefferson Medical College in Philadelphia, Dunglison had written two books, *Human Physiology* (1832, dedicated to President Madison, another of his patients) and *A New Dictionary of Medical Science and Literature* (1833), as well as shorter studies.[19] The *Dictionary* was extensively used up to 1874, when it was revised by Dunglison's son and published under the title *Medical Lexicon: A Dictionary of Medical Science,* reaching its twenty-third edition in 1897.[20] It brought to Dr. Dunglison a world-wide reputation. A recent writer points out that it was probably the innate scepticism and rejection of heroic treatment on the part of Jefferson that turned his young admirer from such therapy to milder forms. Dunglison's pioneer work in introducing physiology into the American medical curriculum in nineteenth-century Virginia was as significant to America as Albert Von Haller's great work in the field had been to eighteenth-century Europe, another medical scholar has recently pointed out.[21]

A number of medical dissertations from Philadelphia and Edinburgh by Virginians were presented to Jefferson and several were dedicated to him.[22] Two of his protégés, the distinguished James and Thomas Ewell, frequently consulted him on scientific matters. Thomas (1785-1826), a naval surgeon and philosopher whose popular work on chemistry has been mentioned, was also the author among other things of popular handbooks, one of medical advice to women, *The Ladies' Medical Companion* (1818), and the more general *American Family Physician* (1824). Ewell also brought out the *Statement of Improvements in the Theory and Practice of Medicine* (1819), which includes his own paper on the prevention of yellow fever. James Ewell (1773-1832) like his brother dedicated one of his books to Jefferson, the enormously popular *Planter's and Mariner's Medical Companion* (1807), a work which went through ten editions. A pleasant mixture of poetry, illustrative anecdotes, sentiment, and sound practical advice, it was a welcome addition to every isolated plantation household. James became a leading physician first in Washington, D.C., and later in New Orleans.

Men like the Ewells rightly felt the urgent need of dissemination of at least elementary medical knowledge among the laymen in sparsely populated rural areas. They also re-edited many European medical works for American professional use. Dr. Joseph Hartshorne (1779-1850), Alexandria native and Philadelphia practitioner, for example, edited with additional notes the *Lectures of Boyer on the Bones* (1805); John Augustine Smith (1782-1865), professor in the New York College of Physicians and Surgeons (later in 1814 president of William and Mary), performed the same function for John Bell's *Principles of Surgery* (1810); and Nathaniel Chapman (1780-1853) similarly for Richerand's *Elements of Physiology* (1821) and several other standard works.[23]

This was general groundwork. Many of these same men and others printed the results of their individual specialized investigations. James Ewell appears to have been the first man to use ice internally in dysentery cases. John Kearsley Mitchell (1793-1858), Virginia-born graduate of Edinburgh and Pennsylvania and from 1826 professor in various Philadelphia medical institutions, was the first to describe the spinal arthropathies.[24] In the *Philadelphia Medical and Physical Journal* he published essays on a curious case of monstrosity (1821-22), experiments on *corpora lutea* (1827), a new treatment for dysentery (1828), a new instrument for applying ligatures to fistula *in ano* (1828), and many later observations and experiments.

Perhaps the most distinguished Philadelphia Virginian was Nathaniel Chapman, popular speaker and professor of materia medica (1813) and theory and practice of medicine (1816) at the University of Pennsylvania and in 1847 first president of the American Medical Association at the same time that he was president of the American Philosophical Society.[25] In 1820 he established the *Philadelphia Journal of Medical and Physical Sciences* (which continued from 1827 as the *American Journal of the Medical Sciences*), dedicating the second number to Dr. James McClurg of Virginia. Chapman published studies of the canine state of fever (hydrophobia) as early as 1801 (his dissertation), of therapeutics and materia medica (1817), and many other volumes after 1830. He disregarded the theories of his predecessors Brown and Rush and based his own teaching on two essential doctrines: (1) "the association between the systems of the body in health and disease," probably from Cullen of Edinburgh and the French (he had studied several years abroad); and (2) the importance of the stomach in the causation of disease. The gastric origin of fever was one of his firm beliefs.

Virginia peopled the West as well as Philadelphia in medicine. Ephraim McDowell (1771-1830), father of ovariotomy and founder of abdominal surgery, made his fame in Kentucky, as did Samuel Brown (1769-1830), a pioneer vaccinator; and Bernard G. Farrar (1785-1849) went on from Kentucky to St. Louis. Brown was a contributor to the *Transactions* of the American Philosophical Society.[26]

These expatriates, usually located in centers of population near great hospitals, would naturally be expected to do more research than their brother rural or small-town practitioners back in Virginia. But

William Tazewell and George Watson of Richmond were active experimenters, though the former's *Vade-Mecum in duas Partes Divisum* . . . (1898)[27] is the only well-known published work by either of them. And a not unusual illustration of the attempts at health improvement in rural communities is the case in 1802-3 of Dr. John Gilmer of Albemarle, who was placed under bond for inoculating for smallpox. Virginia still had strict laws regarding the regulation of vaccine. Gilmer had become so much interested in the still far-from-safe modes of inoculation that he had established a hospital for the treatment of those who sought to escape the malady. The immediate cause of his court summons was of course the death of one patient. That the sympathies of the court were with him is evidenced in their light requirement that he give bond for "good behavior" for three months.[28]

Dr. Wyndham B. Blanton notes eleven articles describing surgical operations by Virginians before 1830, several articles on vaccination, and one on a bronchitis epidemic in Rockingham county in 1823, among others appearing in various medical journals. And one should not forget the contributions of laymen like Jefferson to the acceptance of inoculation and vaccination. The letters of Dr. Benjamin Rush, Jefferson, Madison, and others afford evidence that most Virginia physicians were highly respected individually. There were not enough of them, and many of the better minds among them became interested in politics or other affairs outside their profession. Jefferson was not alone in being sceptical of certain of their outworn practices which were not peculiar to Virginia medicine. What Virginia needed above all was medical training within its borders along the most modern and progressive lines. This in the last five years of the period the University of Virginia and the Winchester college attempted to supply.

B. *Botany*

Botany had been a popular pastime and occasionally a serious business in Virginia since the seventeenth century. The educated newcomer to the colony was often fascinated by the strange flora around him and turned to its investigation as a hobby. From the Indians and their own investigations the curious learned of the medicinal qualities of one plant, the nutritious qualities of another. Jefferson summarized the science's varied uses: "Botany I rank with the most valuable sciences, whether we consider it's subjects as furnishing the principal subsistence of life to man & beast, delicious varieties for our tables, refreshments from our orchards, the adornments of our flower-borders, shade and perfume of our groves, materials for our buildings, or medicaments for our bodies. . . . and to a country family it constitutes a great portion of their social enjoyment. no country gentleman should be without what amuses every step he takes into his fields."[29]

Virginia had a tradition of able botanists. John Banister (1650-92), who lived in the colony from 1678, engaged in extensive botanical investigation, corresponded with many of the major European scientists of his time, and published several studies of Virginia plants, some of them posthumously in the Royal Society's *Philosophical Transactions.* In the eighteenth century Dr. John Mitchell (d. 1768), who may have been a native of the colony, was sent from England specifically to study plant life.[30] His long lists of Virginia plants were published in Great Britain and Germany. He developed a sexual classification system differing from Linnæus' in that it made the method of reproduction a distinguishing factor. Fellow of the Royal Society and recognized natural historian in several areas, Mitchell made lasting contribution to botany.[31] The famous Mark Catesby (1682-1749), author of the *Natural History of Carolina,* did his first American field work in Virginia in 1712-19. Catesby's friend John Clayton (1685-1773), in his old age in 1773 first president of the Virginia Society for the Promotion of Useful Knowledge, collected the specimens from which the Dutch botanist Gronovius compiled the classic *Flora Virginica* (1739). Many Jeffersonian Virginians owned copies of this work, especially of the revised 1762 edition employing Linnaeus' binomial method of classification. The best early systematic treatment of American botany, the first two editions are now collectors' items. Before he died Clayton prepared two manuscript volumes accompanied by dried specimens and notes for the engraver, but all of it was lost by fire shortly after the Revolution and its contents remain unknown but not unguessed at.[32]

When the English natural historian Peter Collinson was asked to name the competent Linnæan botanists of America, Clayton and Mitchell were two of the three he cited. But there were a number of other planters who had gardens of rarities, men like William Byrd and John Custis, with the latter of whom Collinson carried on the long correspondence edited by Dr. E. G. Swem in the delightful *Brothers of the Spade*.[33] Straight down to and through Jefferson's time the Virginian was tremendously interested in botany as recreation and practical study. He knew that there was still a great deal to be done.

The major task was to collect and classify. Though no Virginian of the Jeffersonian period was a compiler or editor whose name is attached to a major work, many did contribute descriptions and specimens to the great collectors. Jefferson's listing in *Notes on the State of Virginia*[34] of trees, fruits, plants, etc., which were chiefly medicinal, esculent, ornamental, or useful for fabrication was brief and elementary, but it was referred to again and again. And his directions to the Lewis and Clark expedition as to what they should look for in the way of plants was to bring rich results.

Physicians were from the beginning some of America's most active botanists, partly because training in the discipline was a concomitant of medical education. Mitchell was a case in point. So was Dr. James Greenway of Dinwiddie, already mentioned in other scientific connections. His nationally known plant collection gathered in Virginia and North Carolina was examined with great interest by the traveler Castiglione when he visited Greenway in 1786.[35] Greenway left at his death a hortus siccus of some forty folio volumes. A regular correspondent of Jefferson and several Europeans, including Linnæus, Greenway published articles in Carey's *American Museum* in 1787 (II, 450) and in the *Transactions* of the American Philosophical Society in 1790 (III, No. xxix, 234-38) on cassia and a poisonous plant growing in southern Virginia. Dr. Richard Field (1767-1829), Edinburgh graduate and newspaper editor and publishing figure, was said by a contemporary to have known the botanical plants of Virginia as no one else except Gronovius. He was fully the equal of Dr. Greenway, it was declared.

Scholar and historian Louis Hue Girardin published several observations in the *American Farmer* having to do with the botanical aspects of agriculture. But the more typical botanical amateurs were the gentlemen planters or nonscientific professional men who collected and annotated specimens largely as a hobby. Joseph C. Cabell and Francis W. Gilmer, for example, kept throughout their lives, at least sporadically, botanical notebooks, apparently jottings primarily for their own amusement. Gilmer came under the invigorating influence of the old Portuguese scientist the Abbé Correa da Serra, who encouraged American amateurs everywhere to get into correspondence with European botanists and communicate their findings.[36] Gilmer himself corresponded with Augustine Pyrame de Candolle of Geneva and agreed to supply specimens with his own observations for a great *Systema* which De Candolle planned.[37] With Correa, Gilmer gathered and noted specimens on the sides of the Peaks of Otter in Virginia and in the Cherokee Country of Tennessee and Georgia. The two visited other botanical enthusiasts in Augusta, Georgia, and Charleston, South Carolina. Gilmer's now-published botanical notebook of this excursion contains interesting and in some instances significant early recordings of southern Appalachian flora.[38]

Gilmer, who confessed that some of his fellow lawyers laughed a little at his enthusiasm for botany, declared to his brother that it was exactly the kind of mental discipline "which we Virginians so often want [i.e., lack]."[39] Earlier he mentioned the plant *Gilmeria* named for him or his family, and moaned that he had not an independent fortune so that he might pursue his interests such as botany instead of being "condemned to the galley of the Common Law."[40] Since this comes from a brilliant and successful young barrister, it may be revelatory of the actual predilections of the gifted among a generation in which law and politics were held the surest intellectual paths to satisfaction and distinction

C. *Geology and Paleontology*

Mineralogy often accompanied botany among the intellectual interests of the Virginia planter, for specimens of the two could often be collected almost simultaneously. Again for practical purposes as well as satisfaction of curiosity the farmer wanted to know the nature of the soil and rock of his region. He knew that metals might lead to wealth. Jefferson devotes several pages of his *Notes on the State of Virginia* to the minerals of the area, including gold, copper, and iron, marble and limestone, coal and niter. He likewise describes the medicinal and other springs. And the Reverend James Madison conducted experiments at the Sweet Springs in Botetourt county, the results of which were published in the American Philosophical Society's *Transactions* (II, No. xxii).

Dr. Greenway secured from "a Continental Officer" living near the borders of North Carolina an account of a hill which seemed to be an extinct volcano. The account was read before the American Philosophical Society in 1790 and published in its *Transactions* in 1793 (III, No. xxviii). Jefferson and Correa, themselves much interested in the former's property the Natural Bridge of Virginia, persuaded Francis Gilmer to undertake a scientific explanation of its formation. Gilmer's paper, read in 1816, was published in the American Philosophical Society's *Transactions* in 1818 (n.s. I, No. xiii). It is still as far as it goes a sound basic explanation of the phenomenon. Benjamin H. Latrobe during his residence in Richmond in 1797-98 wrote a paper on the sand hills of Cape Henry which was published in the Society's *Transactions* (IV, 439-44).[41] Jefferson himself speculated on the formation of mountain ranges and rivers, on the origins of the Gulf of Mexico, and on the occurrence of sea shells in places removed from the ocean. He urged the American Philosophical Society to promote researches in the natural history of the earth.[42]

The most widespread interest in the area of geology, however, was in paleontology or fossil remains. This also goes back in America and Virginia to the very earliest days of the colony. In the later eighteenth century the study received particular stimulus from the French scientist Buffon's "attacks" on American climate, fauna, and flora, in which he declared that all were inferior to those of Europe, as proved partially by the inferior size of North American mammals. As anyone who has read Jefferson's *Notes* or his correspondence knows, the statesman in his middle age spent a great deal of time and money gathering materials to be used as refutations of Buffon. The discovery of mammoth (mastodon) bones in various places, particularly at the Big Bone Lick and later in New York state, seemed to provide evidence that America *had* possessed an animal superior in size even to the elephant, and for a long time Jefferson and others believed it and other huge animals were still alive somewhere in the West.

Jefferson became much excited when in 1796 John Stuart sent him the bones of a large animal heretofore unknown to American scientists. This was new ammunition to fire at Buffon. The parts of the skeleton had been found in a saltpeter cave in Greenbriar county. They belonged to a large cat-like animal with claws. Jefferson named it the megalonyx and described it in the A.P.S. *Transactions* (IV, No. xxx) of 1799 as a lion-like animal. But he found while his article was in press that it was actually the *megatherium,* identified a few years earlier in the British *Monthly Magazine* (1796) as having been found in South America. Had he thought to look back through his own correspondence of 1789, he would have seen a drawing of the bones by Juan Bautista Bru, sent to him by William Carmichael from Madrid. At least Jefferson had named and described an animal not before known in North America.[43]

A few years later in 1808 when Jefferson was President, the floors of certain unfinished rooms in the White House were piled with fossil bones from the great western plains. Jefferson had paid personally for the exploration which secured these, but General William Clark of the famous expedition had superintended the work.[44] This enterprise has fairly been called the beginning of American governmental work in paleontology.

In 1801, when Charles William Peale was engaged in excavating the mammoth bones in New York state, Jefferson agreed to supply him with government aid. Peale managed to get his skeleton out before the proffered help arrived and prepared it at once for his famous museum in Philadelphia. Jefferson believed so strongly in the educational value of Peale's institution that he sent his grandson Thomas Jefferson Randolph to study in Philadelphia while he lived in Peale's home.

Other Virginians were excited about the so-called mammoth. As early as 1795 Edward Graham of Liberty Hall Academy informed John Breckinridge in Kentucky that he had visited "your country" the spring before in hope of seeing some fossil bones but found that everything of a movable nature had disappeared. He urged that a complete skeleton of "that unknown animal called the mammoth should be obtained," for it would "enlarge the present bounds of science."[45] Later in 1805 Bishop Madison begged John Preston of Wythe county to secure for him the stomach of the mammoth recently discovered in that region. Madison wanted a peck or a bushel of the contents of the stomach, as many bones as could be gathered, and a careful description of the kinds of earth and rock in which they had been found.[46]

D. *Inventions*

Though the Jeffersonian Virginian probably never equalled his Yankee contemporary in useful inventions, he did create a number of new machines and gadgets, all designed to be eminently useful. As we have seen, a great many of those designed for agricultural use were never patented. The background of the McCormick reaper alone is a story of trial and experiment over many years in many forms now forgotten. But from letters, some surviving diagrams, and the official records of the Patent Office, there is evidence of scores of attempts by Virginians to improve man's lot through mechanical contrivances.

During most of our period the United States Patent Office was under the Secretary of State. Several times in the first decade of the nineteenth century Landon Carter of Cleve addressed Secretary Madison on the subject of patents and even tried to get Congress to sponsor his inventions for the benefit of the people. John Taylor on November 15, 1802, wrote the Secretary introducing Carter, who was coming to Washington with an unnamed invention. In 1807 Carter himself wrote Madison about "my new invention of a carriage," and in 1810 about his "new constructed lock" which was simple, cheap, and impossible to open without its key.[47]

A recent publication of the records kept from 1805 to 1824 in the Patent Office, presumably including patents going back to 1790, includes 127 known registrations by Virginians.[48] The earlier records do not show the places of residence of the inventors and therefore the list is incomplete even through 1824, and in this publication the last six years of our period are not included. This 127 includes some twenty-seven agricultural implements, most of them referred to in the chapter just above, three washing machines, two steam engines, nine items for increasing the production of water mills, five looms or spinners for textile manufacture, five devices for making or securing salt, four concerned with bricks or frames in building, and a host of miscellaneous machines including one for cutting screws and propellers, fireproof ceilings, a warm bathing vessel, many improvements for guns and rifles, improvements in river and canal boats, improvement in the universal compass, a mode of "knapping hats with rabbit's fur," and a mode of consuming smoke. One of the more interesting is the odometer of James Clarke of Powhatan which Jefferson bought and used before it was patented. Another is the mode of applying cottonseed oil to all uses of linseed oil. The canalboat patented by N. C. Dawson and A. Rucker of Amherst in 1821 was the type used on the James river for many years. And the device for "obtaining salt [from?] water" by David and Joseph Ruffin or Ruffner of Kanawha is said to have been useful.[49]

Four Virginians patented from three to five devices each. John Heavin of Montgomery county registered his device for propelling boats and his machine for cutting straw in 1805, his shingle dresser and loom in 1812, his rope and twine machine in 1813, and another loom in 1814. James Barron of Elizabeth City county, one of the famous naval family, patented a windmill improvement in 1816, a machine for making bottle corks and a pump for air or water in 1819, a washing machine in 1821 and an angle lever and stove in 1822 (and later in 1826 a carrying and lifting trunk dock). Andrew Glendining of Loudoun brought out in one year, 1824, an apple cutter, a fly killer, a washing machine, and a sausage machine. David Meade Randolph of Richmond, the city dweller among these more prolific inventors and onetime Federalist U. S. Marshal for Virginia, patented devices for making candles and for use in ship building in 1815 and an improvement for drawing liquor in 1821. A local historian claimed that Randolph's wife, a sister of Thomas Mann Randolph, invented the refrigerator for her own use, only to have the design copied and patented by a Yankee inmate of her household.[50]

Stephen McCormick's famous plow was not patented until 1826 and therefore does not appear on these lists. Nor does the 1826 cotton press of Charles Williams of Petersburg. And one should remember that just before the period begins, in 1787, James Rumsey of Berkeley county was trying out his steamboat on the Potomac near Shepherdstown.

The reader will note that very few of these contrivances were the inconsequential gadgets the complete gentlemen of the Enlightenment delighted in making. There were many useful small inventions, however, and others which reveal merely the active mind of the inventor. Even staid President Madison tried his hand, for he improved the cruet stand on a movable arm for use over the dining room table which his friend Jefferson had invented.[51] One has only to visit Monticello to see Jefferson's useful gadgets or his improvements on those made by others—his dumb-waiter, his simultaneous openers of double doors, his inside weather vane. He also made a swivel chair, a three-legged cane-stool, and an improved polygraph.

Besides his plow, Jefferson designed a gig, a carriage, and a light wagon for his own use, constructed a hemp brake, drew diagrams for dry docks anticipating more elaborate things along the same line fifty years later, and experimented with several steam engines.[52] Like another Virginian he designed fireproof ceilings. Even his proposals for decimal systems of weights and measures as well as coins (the latter was adopted) might be counted here. Other "improvements" he advocated run into the scores.

St. George Tucker, Jefferson's lifelong friend and correspondent, was almost as versatile and ingenious a man as the third President. Jurist, teacher, poet, essayist, musician, political economist, he found time to dabble in astronomy and construct several useful machines or articles. Fortunately for the curiosity of posterity, he diagrammed or described most of them in his commonplace books or letters. They include a bathhouse with copper bath and pipes from the well, an "earth closet" emptied from the outside, a steam engine for drawing water, and a code of signals. With others, he constructed and inflated a balloon. He left a manuscript explaining his plan for propelling a boat upstream without the aid of steam or other agent.[53]

His "telegraph," as he called his semaphore system by the use of flashing lights, he outlined several times in letters sent to friends for their criticism. His manuscripts show that he used the cupola of the old Capitol for his experiments. From that vantage point he flashed signals which Bishop Madison, with field glasses at the other end of Duke of Gloucester street, was able to read in whole sentences. He mentions the semaphore as early as 1795 in a letter to John Page, and in 1807 he tried to get Governor Cabell to use it to establish communication between Norfolk and Hampton.[54]

Admittedly very few of these Virginia inventions were practicable. Only a tiny fraction of those registered at the Patent Office ever have been, and that fraction more often than not only for a short time before being superseded. But that they were contrived at all is good evidence of intellectual activity and fertility. The few real triumphs such as Jefferson's and Stephen McCormick's plows and the Robert and Cyrus McCormick reaper are reason enough for the other experiments.

E. Astronomy and Meteorology

Virginians had few telescopes or other instruments to encourage an interest in astronomy, but men like John Page and Jefferson did give it some attention. John Page calculated an eclipse of the sun as early as 1769 and published his findings in the newspapers, earning for himself the sobriquet of "the John Partridge of Virginia," after a noted English almanac maker.[55] Page complained that the College of William and Mary failed to make use of its apparatus to observe such eclipses and the transit of Venus.[56]

An occasional essay such as Francis Gilmer's on the Lunar Bow and similar subjects by others of his circle was among the few evidences of active interest in this area in the 1790-1830 period.[57] Meteorology, or weather, was another matter. Its practical applications were almost endless. John Page spent countless hours studying it. Next to agriculture and gardening it was Jefferson's greatest scientific interest, and it probably stood first among Madison's in the scientific area.

John Page kept a meteorological diary over many years.[58] His comments on a meteor were published in the American Philosophical Society *Transactions* (II, 173-74). With his friend Jameson he made experiments in measuring the fall of rain and snow. In the spring of 1784 James Madison of Montpelier began keeping records of wind, rain, sunshine, and clouds, and as soon as he could get a thermometer, temperature. He carried on written conversations with Jefferson on the oblate form of the earth.[59]

Jefferson himself was for forty-six years a sort of unofficial weather bureau. His Weather Memorandum Book begun in 1774 was kept up in elaborate charts to 1820. Volney appealed to him for weather information to use in his book on America for the years 1779, 1789, 1793, 1796, and 1797.[60] He had various schemes for ascertaining the climate of the whole country. One of the instructions to Lewis and Clark was concerning careful weather observations. Jefferson compared temperatures at Monticello with those in Charlottesville or Williamsburg, of the mountain area with Tidewater. He supplied Dr. Nathaniel Chapman with data concerning Virginia snowfalls. Friends from

Mississippi to Quebec supplied him with temperature and barometric readings. From all this information he concluded that Monticello had the best climate in North America, perhaps in the world.

F. *Geography*

Exploring, mapmaking, and topographical analysis were among the forms of geographical investigation and explanation which came naturally to Virginians. Even Henry Adams acknowledged that they were superb explorers, though he probably did not have the intellectual qualities of men like Dr. Thomas Walker, Peter Jefferson, Joshua Fry, or Lewis and Clark in mind when he said it. From Captain John Smith's time Virginians had analyzed their topography, which was for them often an inclusive cultural as well as scientific term. From Smith's time too they had drawn maps of the colony which often included adjacent territories now divided into many states.

Samuel Miller in his *Brief Retrospect of the Eighteenth Century*[61] calls Dr. John Mitchell's *Map of North America* of 1755 the best extant for a considerable period. For the smaller region Thomas Jefferson's father Peter and his friend Joshua Fry produced in the *Map of the Inhabited Part of Virginia* in 1751 the best example of cartography done in or of the state up to the time of *Notes on the State of Virginia.*[62] Based on the authors' actual surveys and explorations, in its second edition it was reproduced in atlases for a generation or more. Patrick Henry's father John published a new map in 1770, but it was not based on original surveys and in no way superseded the Fry-Jefferson engraving except that it defined county boundaries.

It was Thomas Jefferson's own map prepared in 1786 for his *Notes* which was the next really good one. It is perhaps the least known of its author's accomplishments. This *Map of the Country between Albemarle Sound and Lake Erie Comprehending the Whole of Virginia, Maryland, Delaware and Pennsylvania, with Parts of Several Other of the United States of America* was prepared while Jefferson was in France, and of course was not based on the maker's original surveys. But he did use all cartographical works available from his father's up to his own time and supplemented them extensively with information he gathered from other sources, including his own latitudinal observations at Monticello and those of Bishop Madison at

Williamsburg. The data on the western limits of Pennsylvania was communicated to him by Rittenhouse, who had surveyed the area.

The map covered a territory from one degree east to eight degrees west of Philadelphia and from 36° to 42° north latitude. The Pennsylvania portion was based on a 1770 map of William Scull. The Fry-Jefferson map was naturally the basis for the Virginia portion. It was supplemented by the 1778 published surveys made by Thomas Hutchens in the same region Then the cartographer looked at other surveys and maps of part of the whole of the United States. The finished product was engraved in several hundred copies in addition to those used in the book and was often colored.

Though Jefferson had never made a map before, his experience as a lawyer drawing land plats and as architect outlining elevations and details was natural preparation for the task.[63] What he produced was a map which catches the tramontane advance at mid-point between his father's map and that of Bishop Madison.

The Virginia State Library in 1914 listed[64] some 230 maps in its collections showing Virginia in part or whole for the 1790-1830 period. As maps only those of Madison and Boye are really significant, however. The Reverend James Madison as a member of the 1779 commission to determine the Virginia-Pennsylvania boundary had useful early training for the map-making he carried on over a number of years. Later he made several surveys himself and published *A Map of Virginia from Actual Surveys and Latest Observations* in 1807. Commonly known as "Madison's Map," it remained standard for at least twenty years. During the 1807-27 period, Virginia map makers tended to concentrate on local areas, but in the latter year the state published Hermann Boye's nine-sheet *Map of the State of Virginia* which brought Virginia cartography into the modern era.[65] It was based on surveys and county maps executed by the able mathematician John Wood (Scottish master of a Petersburg school and a writer on various subjects) at a cost of about $70,000.

One Virginian, Robert Mayo (1784-1864) combined his classical and geographical interests in a series of books probably designed for school use. *A View of Ancient Geography and Ancient History* appeared in 1813, *Atlas of Ten Select Maps of Ancient Geography* in 1814 and 1815, *Atlas Classica, or Select Maps of Geography* in 1818, and *An Epitome of Ancient Geography* and *An Epitome of Profane*

Geography in 1818. Naturally derivative, they indicate some ingenuity and imagination as well as a wide if not deep knowledge of the classics.

Topographical surveys covered everything from a single county to multi-state studies including Virginia. Thomas Hutchens' *Topographical Description of Virginia, Pennsylvania, Maryland, and North Carolina,* accompanied by a map, had been published in London in 1778 and as we have noted had been used by Jefferson in his own cartography. The book included discussions of the fauna, flora, mineralogy, and meteorology of the region. Hutchens, in 1781 appointed "geographer of the United States," was a New Jersey man who knew the West as did no other man of his time. His book was to be useful to Virginians other than Jefferson.

In 1791 William Tatham (1752-1819), the picturesque and eccentric British-born engineer who was at the time geographer of Virginia, published in Richmond and Philadelphia in folio broadside *A Topographical Analysis of the Commonwealth of Virginia, Compiled for the Years 1790-1* and the next year in Richmond a continuation. These useful sheets give statistics on population, county lieutenants, representatives, courts, and the civil list of the commonwealth. A prolific writer and promoter of geographical and engineering projects, Tatham had in 1790 issued *Proposals for Publishing a Large and Comprehensive Map of the Southern Division of the United States* by subscription only, apparently too costly for materialization.[66] Quite different in format and intention was the scholarly topographical work of the Reverend J. J. Spooner, member of the Massachusetts Historical Society and the American Academy of Arts and Sciences and rector of Martin's Brandon. He published in the *Collections* of the Massachusetts Historical Society[67] "A Topographical Description of the County of Prince George, in Virginia, in 1793," a fairly detailed essay on the county in which Edmund Ruffin was later to make his agricultural experiments.

Tatham was best known among his contemporaries for his proposals regarding canal systems, in which he collaborated with Robert Fulton. Even before the Revolution, Philadelphia merchants were interested in a canal to the Chesapeake, and as the new nation got under way various surveys were made from South Carolina to Massachusetts of the possibilities of linking interior areas productive of raw materials with coastal harbors.[68] Tatham, who had surveyed English canals and written on the subject in England, was immensely interested in getting North Carolina produce to market by connecting the hinterland with the port city of Norfolk, Virginia. In the 1790's he and others formed a corporation with several canalization projects in mind. He explained their aims to his fellow stockholders in *An Address* (Richmond, 1794), and for many years corresponded with Jefferson, Madison, and other prominent citizens on this subject. In 1808 he reviewed the progress made up to that time in *A View of the Proposed Grand Canal . . .* and in *A Comparative View of the Four Projected Coastal Canals,* the latter discussing the relative merits of four routes between Norfolk and North Carolina. Jefferson and Madison were sent copies of at least the former. On October 24, 1808, Tatham wrote to Madison from Princess Anne, Virginia, discussing the four possible routes.[69] He also mentioned a national north-south canal, or chain of interlinking canals. Anyone who has taken a small boat from New York to Florida today knows that Tatham's vision and practical proposals have been realized in detail.

Colonel Claude Crozet (1790-1864), French-born former West Point professor who was chief engineer for Virginia from 1824, drew dozens of survey maps accompanied by recommendations for a "lock and dam" system on the upper James River.[70] In 1830 he proposed the "lock and dam" system instead of a canal from Richmond to Lynchburg to be linked with deep water on the Kanawha by a railroad. Had the railroad been then built Virginia ports might have remained in the competition with northern ones as outlets for western produce. As it is, Crozet anticipated the TVA river system and left in his official reports a wealth of information for the engineer and economist.

Virginians pushing west from colonial days sent back to the settlements diaries, detailed descriptions, and specimens of fauna, flora, and minerals. Jefferson, a prophet of manifest destiny who believed that the United States must span the continent if she was to preserve liberty and peace, long dreamed of a "literary expedition" to be sent through unexplored territory to the Pacific, gathering scientific data of many kinds on the way.[71] As early as his tenth year he had probably been familiar with the theory that the west coast might be reached by ascending the Missouri. About 1792-93 he had planned a smaller expedition. In 1803 he made his official proposal of a full-scale expedition to Congress, and soon after announced his choice of his young neighbor and secretary Meriwether Lewis as leader of the group. Lewis in turn chose William Clark, brother of the more famous George Rogers Clark, as his co-leader. Thus three Virginians planned and executed the great journey.

Jefferson's characterization of Lewis in the sketch prefixed to the official account of the expedition in 1814 reveals much of both men. Jefferson said that he had wanted and found a man "of courage undaunted . . . firmness . . . perseverance . . . careful as a father of those committed to his charge, yet sturdy in maintenance of order and discipline, intimate with Indian character . . . habituated to the hunting life . . . honest, disinterested, liberal, of sound understanding, and a fidelity to truth so scrupulous that whatever he should report would be as certain as if seen by ourselves. . . ."[72] In most of these qualities Jefferson was describing his ideal Virginia gentleman. He also added that Lewis already knew the fauna and flora of the settled portion of North America and would waste no time in redescribing the familiar. For training in scientific terms and astronomical observations, Lewis was sent to Philadelphia and Lancaster to study under the best men available.

Jefferson's orders to Lewis and Clark signed on June 20, 1803, are a model of scientific comprehensiveness. The explorers were first of all to find out all they could about the Indians: the names of their nations and the numbers in each; the extent and limits of their possessions; their relations with other tribes and nations; their language, traditions, and monuments; their ordinary occupations and implements for these; their food, clothing, and domestic accommodations; their diseases; the moral and physical circumstances which distinguished them from other unknown tribes; and the peculiarities of their laws and customs. Notes should be taken also on soils and the face of the country, growth and vegetable production, animals, race or extinct remains, minerals, volcanic appearances and rivers, lakes, and climate.

Much yet remains to be done in analyzing the expedition's "literary" (scientific) results, but the *History of the Expedition under the*

Command of Captains Lewis and Clark, to the Sources of the Missouri . . . (Philadelphia, 1814) includes almost enough for our comment here. The two officers and their men obeyed all the order-suggestions within their power and in some notable instances went beyond them. The Indian vocabularies alone, which were to have been printed in a continuation of the 1814 volumes, are of enormous interest to ethnologists and linguists. A detailed and comprehensive monograph has recently been written on Lewis and Clark as linguistic pioneers, pointing out their adoption and adaptation of names of many origins to the objects they came upon, the extensive word creation they undertook, and the Americanisms they popularized.[73]

Both Lewis and Clark kept journals, describing among other things thistles, ferns, rushes, liquorice, cattails, roots which might be eaten raw, and berries; trees from small shrubs to the great firs of Pacific northwest; horses, dogs, bears, wolves, foxes, antelopes, beavers, minks, seals, otters, and squirrels; rats, mice, panthers, hares, rabbits, skunks, and sewellels; pheasants, grouse, buzzards, hawks, bats, crows, magpies, piliated woodpeckers, geese, swans, and ducks; skate, flounder, salmon, and candlefish; clams and periwinkles; gartersnakes, rattlesnakes, lizards, and snails. In the appendices of the 1814 volumes are included an elaborate treatise on the western Indians and an impressive meteorological register. Lewis was moody, thoughtful, introspective. Clark, a native rather than a seeker of the wilderness, genial and untroubled by speculation, was Lewis' perfect complement.[74] Clark was the map maker and artist who meticulously drew birds, fish, and animals. Lewis possessed a restless, inquiring spirit and a faculty of command which made him the natural leader of the expedition. As he searched for new plants and animals or watched for hostile Indians or ferocious beasts he pondered the eternal problems of man's relation to the universe. It is no wonder that a recent study of western exploration declares these two leaders the most intelligent and generally able men who had ever ascended the Missouri.

Their conclusions from their experiences are as remarkable, in far-seeing anticipations, as the adventures themselves. The greatest fur country in the world would be opened to Americans and the trade would be in American hands. The lands themselves would one day become American soil, as Louisiana had. The results in the ethnological, botanical, zoological, mineralogical, and meteorological sciences have yet, as we have said, to be fully measured. Jefferson summed up the accomplishment with a masterpiece of understatement in his sixth annual message to Congress December 2, 1806: "The expedition of Messrs. Lewis and Clarke [*sic*], for exploring the river Missouri, and the best communication from that to the Pacific ocean, has had all the success which could have been expected. They have traced the Missouri nearly to its source, descended the Columbia to the Pacific ocean, ascertained with accuracy the geography of that interesting communication across our continent, learned the character of the country, its commerce, and inhabitants; and it is but justice to say that Messrs. Lewis and Clarke, and their brave companions, have by this arduous service deserved well of their country."[75]

The story does not end with the return of the expedition to St. Louis and Washington, nor with the death of Lewis, apparently by his own hand, in 1809. The findings had to reach as wide a public as possible. For years Jefferson with the help of others gathered the journals and miscellaneous papers of the leaders and tried to arrange for publication. Living plant and animal and mineral specimens collected were sent to the American Philosophical Society and to competent individuals for study or safekeeping. With the help of Nicholas Biddle, Paul Allen was secured as editor, and the authentic *History of the Expedition,* based on but not composed of the original journals, appeared in 1814. This did not end the matter, for during the years some manuscripts containing further valuable material had been lost or mislaid, and Jefferson again tried to have them collected so that in the future they might be available for detailed study.[76] He was quite aware that only a small fraction of the "vegetable and mineral" materials, Indian vocabularies, and meteorological tables had been printed. In the end most of the papers, though government property, were deposited with the American Philosophical Society, where Jefferson rightly felt they would be safe. That still more Clark original journals have been uncovered in the Midwest in the last few years would have rejoiced the old planner's heart, though their ownership was not in 1959 yet fully decided.[77]

Jefferson, interested in the Indians all his life, had during his Presidency done his best to protect them. Earlier in the *Notes* he first outlined the American idea of savagism, to which the key word is "circumstance," interpreting their moral character in terms of Scottish common sense philosophy.[78] Robertson and Kames both influenced him in his theories. Some of his researches regarding their language, government, and customs he published in the *Notes* but he continued to gather materials of all kinds concerning them. His excavations in a mound near Monticello have been called by present-day archaeologists startlingly modern in their technique.[79]

William Clark, from 1807-8 superintendent of Indian affairs at St. Louis, continued his earlier friendly relations with the western tribes and the collecting of information regarding them. From 1813 also governor of the Missouri territory, Clark attempted to conciliate his charges by a series of treaties as he made his collections of natural history and Indian artifacts. He encouraged others like his sub-agent Thomas Forsyth to make such reports as "An Account of the Manners and Customs of the Sauk Indians."[80]

George Rogers Clark, the older brother of the explorer, prepared in 1791 a lengthy statement on Indian mounds in the Ohio and Mississippi valleys not published until H. R. Schoolcraft included it in his *Archives of Aboriginal Knowledge* in 1860.[81] Here Clark developed the theory now generally accepted by archaeologists, that the builders of the mounds were the ancestors of Indians then occupying the region. Clark in 1798 supported Jefferson in a letter now regarded as proof of the authenticity of the speech attributed to the Indian chief Logan in the *Notes*.

Other Virginians wrote and many published letters or essays of observation regarding the Indians. Peyton Short, brother of William, left among his papers an 1816 essay entitled "Thoughts on the Civilization of the Aborigines of America."[82] Here he advocates intermarriage, interracial settlements to be set up in the west, and the assignment of agricultural implements and animals to the Indians. In other words, he proposed agrarianizing the red man and absorbing him gradually, a not unusual solution except that Short works out the specific details of land and equipment. The writer concludes by saying that his essay is addressed only to the liberal and philosophic: for only these people understood that a savage may be covered by a white as well as a red skin and that education and government are the sole factors which place one part of mankind higher in the scale of civilization than another.

Francis Gilmer, after the botanical excursion he made through Indian country with the Abbé Correa in 1815, wrote "Reflections on the Institution of the Cherokee Indians" and published it in the

Analectic Magazine.[83] Gilmer discusses the geographical conditions which made Indian tribes so much more alike than European nations are, describes the territory of the Cherokees, and comments on their legal code and several other customs. Constantly in drawing comparisons he uses the Roman historians, the Scottish economist Adam Smith, and the French Physiocrat Quesnay, but he never approaches Jefferson in insight or understanding, perhaps because the Scottish philosophy is so much less a constituent of his discussion. His answer to the Indian question is that they should be absorbed by the whites, very much Short's answer—or William Byrd's, for that matter. Though the essay does not present its author at his best stylistically or philosophically, it has some significance as a realistic approach from actual observation of conditions to one of the oldest American problems. Though some shared his view, others believed that the Indians should be exterminated or moved west, and yet others sentimentalized Rousseauistically about the noble aborigine without offering any solution. Few if any other than Jefferson applied the Scottish views of history and society, of moral absolutism but cultural relativism, to their red brothers.

In 1822 George Tucker in remarking on the great increase in interest during his life in "what may be *useful*" among the sciences regretted that studies of what was merely *curious,* as the higher branches of mathematics, were almost universally neglected.[84] He used the term *useful* more nearly in the modern narrow sense than in the inclusive Jeffersonian connotation. In other words, what we now call pure science was being neglected in America and in Virginia. Though he observed further that it is often difficult to ascertain where the *pure* ends and *useful* begins, he has put his finger on a weakness and strength of Jeffersonian science. Perhaps every man who worked in field or laboratory during the period at one time or another defended or proclaimed the *practical usefulness* of his interest. But undoubtedly many of the same people experimented at least partly if not largely out of pure curiosity. Yet this pleasure motivation, when it was held consciously, often produced a sort of guilt complex which impelled the writer of a scientific paper to explain why or how his accomplishment was useful before he explained the accomplishment itself. In doing so he was setting up psychological barriers to advanced research, though his feeling was natural in a society still laying its foundation.

VII

THE FINE ARTS

And I can tell you, the day is fast coming when there will not only be a liberal but a munificent patronage of the fine arts in America. The mania, I will not call it taste, is spreading. Ecce Trumbull! That vote of Congress (in which I rejoiced, for the paintings are of noble subjects admirably executed) will do much to diffuse the desire of possessing paintings, prints &c. If William or any of your children shew a genius for either, I should prefer seeing him such a Painter as Trumbull, Vanderlyn, or even as Sully, or Peale, to jogging through the woods of Patrick or Albemarle on a lean sorrel to a county court; or thrown in, cheek by joal [sic] *with Citizen Yancey in the Legislature to make significant nods, & drink whiskey with his constituents. . . . A new order of things is . . . rising in our country. . . . Letters, arms, the fine arts . . . are about to assume here the rank they have held ever since the revival of learning in Europe.*

—Francis W. Gilmer to Peachy R. Gilmer, February 9, 1817, Virginia Historical Society.

Jefferson's architectural achievements are second only to his political contributions to the history of the United States.

—William B. O'Neal, *Jefferson's Fine Arts Library for the University of Virginia,* Charlottesville, 1956, p. 44.

We . . . have contributed less to the advancement of the arts, ornamental and useful, in Virginia, than in any country on earth equally civilized," observed "A Subscriber" in the *Virginia Literary Museum* in 1829. The writer was looking back at his state's part in American affairs since the adoption of the Constitution and regretting that its energies had been channeled so largely into law, politics, and medical practice. His key word may be "contributed"; even so, it seems doubtful that he was right. As we have seen in the two preceding chapters, the Old Dominion's contributions to one useful art, agriculture, were major, and in the other sciences she had made at least modest specific contributions along with widespread if not concentrated activity. And if one includes in the definition of "contributed" the *encouragement* of the *fine* arts, Virginia since the revolution had done a great deal. In at least one of the arts, architecture, she had made what would be called contributions in any sense of the term.

Since the Revolution, Virginia had encouraged sculpture by ordering, planning, and paying for the Houdon Washington, to this day the major piece of historical statuary in the United States. She had produced one major American architect and encouraged by giving them training and commissions early in their careers two other major architects of the nineteenth century. Painters like the Sullys, Peticolases, Warrell, and some others considered Virginia their home for large parts of their lives and did some of their best work in the state. John Gadsby Chapman was born in Alexandria and did his first professional painting in Winchester. There were sacred and secular music societies in almost every town, musical instruments and group singing in most educated families, concerts and musical plays in the theaters and assembly halls. The theatrical audiences in five or six major centers supported the best companies of their time. One Virginia-authored farce ran on the New York stage intermittently for years, and the strongly national plays of George Washington Parke Custis were acted many times in the larger northern cities.

Though the art museum opened in Richmond by Warrell in 1817 never competed with those in the great centers of Philadelphia, Boston, and New York, as Virginians hoped that it might, it simply could not in a town with a population of 12,609 (1820), a considerable part of which was slave. Actually the houses of the Virginia gentlemen were the art centers displaying canvases and marbles from all over Europe. The fallacy in "A Subscriber's" thinking lay in what he was comparing with rural, agrarian Virginia. Certainly the eighteenth-century English squires in their country seats never did as much for the useful and ornamental arts as Virginia planters did in this period. What "A Subscriber" was actually doing was comparing his agrarian commonwealth with the city-states of Boston, Philadelphia, and New York in this country and with London, Edinburgh, and Paris in Europe, and even more perhaps comparing its indisputable contributions to politics and government with its relatively insignificant production of other things necessary to the well-rounded man.

A. *Architecture*

The numerous eighteenth-century Virginia country mansions and the buildings of Williamsburg today are solid evidence of the interest of the colonial in this useful and ornamental art. From the end of the seventeenth century, sometimes with the help of a professional architect or master-builder, the planters who lived on the banks of the great rivers were sheltering themselves behind graceful façades, in rectangular houses with wings or dependencies built usually in the later years of brick. Though a good deal of what is called the mediaeval style survived in these buildings, they were increasingly classical Georgian in outline and detail, as English country houses were.

Colonial libraries of any size contained books on architecture, among them usually one or more by the Italians Vitruvius and Palladio, who had adapted classical Roman styles to country villas, churches, city houses, and public buildings. William Byrd, who died in 1744, had twenty-seven architectural volumes in his library.[2] As the eighteenth century wore on these volumes of engraved plates of elevations, plans, and ornamental details, and smaller practical handbooks of building, appeared more and more in the inventories. After the

Revolution the classical ideals of form fused with ideals of modern convenience were greatly emphasized in building.[3] The manuals were widely used. One planter preparing to build in 1812, for example, asked the loan from a neighbor of Peter Nicholson's works on carpentry, the *Student's Guide to Architecture,* and the three-volume *Principles of Ancient Architecture.*[4]

This was in part a late flowering in brick and mortar of the neo-classic philosophies which were passing their climaxes. Jefferson's earlier designs are in one sense at least representative of the last major phase of the American Georgian. In another sense some of these designs mark the beginning of the Greek Revival, which was after all but a continuation of the Palladian with new emphases. The large-scale rectangular of the earlier structures was succeeded by a smaller-scale central block with a series of connecting units decreasing in size, in general like the lesser villas of Palladio. Octagonal or semi-octagonal rooms were widely used, as was the octagonal bow. The Palladian motif of the two-story classic portico employed by Jefferson and then by Latrobe and Mills and their disciples has become a symbol of the ante bellum Southern way of life.

Many planters advised their architects or master-builders personally, referring to the architectural manuals both owner and builder possessed. George Washington, who in 1798 was having twin houses built by Dr. William Thornton on North Capitol street in Washington (probably as an investment) did not accept all his architect's designs without murmur. A whole series of letters discuss the suitability of a parapet for either beauty or utility. "Rules of Architecture are calculated, I presume, to give symmetry, and just proportion to all the Orders, & parts of buildings, in order to please the eye," Washington begins[5] one of these discussions, following it with some technical detail which shows that he knew something about building for ornament.

Thornton, physician turned architect, did most of his work in the Federal City. His most famous domestic structure, the Octagon House, now the home of the American Institute of Architects, was designed for a Virginian, Colonel John Tayloe. Most of the large Virginia houses of the Jeffersonian period, however, were probably designed by master builders working closely with the owners. Fine houses like the Preston place (1810) in Abingdon or Conrade Webb's Hampstead

(1820) in New Kent were probably designed by the craftsmen who erected them. The Governor's Mansion (1813) in Richmond was apparently planned and supervised during construction by the local builder William McKim, concerning whom very little more is known.[6] In Palladian porticoes, details of pediments and cornices, steps and shapes of rooms, these houses clearly belong to the same family as those designed by the major architects about to be mentioned. That they lack certain qualities the "professionally designed" buildings possess may be argued. But then there is Bremo, the masterpiece without an architect.

The designs for private homes and public buildings as well as stylistic traditions of this period center, however, in the work of three men, Thomas Jefferson, Benjamin H. Latrobe, and Robert Mills. Next to his work in government, more than one critic has asserted, Jefferson's achievements in architecture constitute his most significant work. Certainly this son of a combination of rough frontier and Tidewater elegance is to this day a major influence in American architecture. Strictly an amateur as far as receiving remuneration for his work goes, and also in certain other respects, he built under his direct supervision and with gradually evolving plans his own Monticello and the academic village of the University of Virginia; he designed a lovely Episcopal church for Charlottesville; and he drew the plans for dozens of homes scattered over the Virginia hillsides and for courthouses, jails, and the state Capitol in Richmond.

Before 1814 Jefferson gathered at Monticello an extensive architectural library of some fifty titles in German, French, Italian, and English, including at least four editions of Palladio, and volumes by Morris, Gibbs, Inigo Jones, Rossi, Perrault, Scamozzi, and of course Vitruvius Pollio.[7] For style and detail he depended upon them and upon his own memories of classical buildings in France and Italy, combining with the traditional forms and ideas the vision of an inventor and the methodical precision of the first-rate mathematician. His work is fundamentally an adaptation of classical forms to local and modern needs. Like Lord Kames, he loved the simple and admired the functional. The white columns against the red brick walls, the details of moldings and cornices, all came from the authorities, but were employed with ingenuity and practicality which accompanied a sense of beauty.[8]

The Richmond Capitol was his adaptation of a Roman temple with which he fell in love at Nîmes, in France. In its original Jeffersonian form, of porch-portico without steps and only side and rear doors for entrance, it was severely criticized by George Tucker and others because it failed to fuse beauty of form with the practical.[9] Perhaps Jefferson learned from building and criticism. He never again allowed the exact form and dimensions of a model to tyrannize him to this extent, for his later edifices are notable for their functional application of the classical principles, though his stairways are still by some considered badly done. Monticello, begun long before the Capitol, is in its final form distinguished for its triumphant combining of the classical forms with utility. The little mountain as location and setting, the subordination and arrangement of dependencies, the plans for gardens and ponds, all unite with the building itself in one of the architectural harmonies of the world.

In his designs for the University of Virginia, Jefferson showed his insight into the human needs the buildings were to serve. Lewis Mumford calls it the embodiment of three great architectural essentials: (1) a well-conceived and well-translated program based upon new conceptions of the function of a university: a good building is the physical and symbolic setting for a scheme of life; (2) a realization that individual buildings should never be conceived as isolated units; (3) the ability to modify details to meet a special situation while holding to a rigorous and consistent plan. Jefferson certainly followed these principles always, but perhaps in a less conscious degree. This Palladian village of one-story white columns and colonnades and brick walls, of ten different "Pavilions" illustrating forms of classical architecture, of the Rotunda-Pantheon, puts "the work of his contemporaries and successors for the next fifty years distinctly into the third rank," thinks Mumford.[10]

The designs for the jails in Cumberland and Nelson counties, Christ Church in Charlottesville, the courthouses in Buckingham and Charlotte counties are essentially classically simple and functional. So are the pleasingly varied houses, but with more interior decorative detail, of Barbourville, Edgehill, Farmington, Frascati, Oak Hill, Ampthill, Edgemont, Morven, and Brandon, among others, planned for such personal friends as the Barbours, David Higginbotham, James Powell Cocke, and James Monroe. He designed in whole or in part the porticoes, wings, façades, of many other houses. He liked the suppressed passageway to outbuildings, the octagonal bow or room, the rotunda and dome, among the Palladian details. To execute his plans, he and a number of his friends employed the master builders James Dinsmore and John Neilson, both of whom he brought from Philadelphia. They worked for him between 1798 and 1808, then for Madison, then in Eastern Virginia, then for the University of Virginia, and also for Cocke while at Charlottesville. Some of the lesser buildings of the Albemarle country were done in the Jeffersonian manner by one or both of these men: Estouteville, for example, was designed in 1828 by Dinsmore for John Coles III.

Palladio, ingenuity, mathematical skill are evident in all these creations, but there is something more behind the Jeffersonian buildings. The ideal and idea of the classical agrarian republic which permeates the policies, belles-lettres, and education are here carried over into craftsmanship and art. These red-brick white-columned houses of the gentleman-liberals were the most striking symbols of the relationship between ancient and modern democratic aristocracy.

One who examines the buildings of Latrobe and Mills may not agree that Jefferson made them appear distinctly inferior. Benjamin Henry Latrobe (1764-1820), later to become the father of a style in architecture we call the Greek Revival, in his case expressed particularly in institutional buildings, entered the United States through the port of Norfolk in 1796. He had already enjoyed some success as an architect in England. He remained in Virginia for two and a half years. In addition to architectural work he wrote and produced a play *The Apology* (1797-98), composed some poor verses, consulted with others on several engineering projects including the proposed Dismal Swamp Canal, and wrote several scientific essays such as that on the sand hills of Cape Henry.[11] After his work in Virginia, Latrobe went on to Philadelphia and Washington, making a distinguished name for himself as architect of the great Philadelphia banks and of the rebuilding of the national Capitol in 1814. We might call Latrobe an architectural organicist, for to him integration of functional planning, construction, and beauty were essential and natural. Effect and plan to him could never be separate, as they sometimes were to Thornton, Hadfield, Hallet, and even Jefferson, of those who worked around him in the Washington area. Latrobe found architecture in America a polite accomplishment, says Fiske Kimball, and left it a profession.

In Virginia, Latrobe did some of his best work. His first American design was in 1796 for the Pennock house in Norfolk. For it he did a beautiful perspective of the stair hall which was the *raison d'être* of the whole design. The house itself is simple and graceful, with suggestion of the English Adam in some of its features. His strangest design is that for an enormous plantation house called Mill Hill, which may have been planned for one of the hills overlooking Richmond.[12] Among other works of this period is the formal house for Colonel John Harvie of Richmond, called later Gamble's Hill completed in 1799. A beautiful and brilliantly conceived design, it was planned to have a segmented projecting bay at the rear, elaborate wings, colonnaded porches, and Latrobe's usual simple exterior. Though the full design was never carried out, the completed house was one of Richmond's finest. Later, ten years after he had left Richmond, in 1808, the architect designed for Benjamin James Harris a deep house with a cupola-lighted central hall. This was Clifton, built on Council Chamber Hill. The front, like Mill Hill, has two semi-octagonal bays at the ends, collonnades, and end pavilions. In 1804 he had designed a residence for Dr. James McClurg, though one cannot be sure the house built at Grace and Sixth streets was according to Latrobe's design.

In 1811 he planned the country residence Long Branch for Robert Carter Burwell in Clarke county, a house still standing but retrimmed in 1845. Long Branch has two-story pedimented porticoes at front and rear, hipped roof with a central railed deck, a delicate glazed cupola, and brick arches which are characteristic of Latrobe's work.

One of the most interesting of Latrobe's drawings is his 1798 design for a theater-hotel-assembly hall for Richmond. It was to take the place of the old theater burned down that year and was drawn at the behest of the theater builder and promoter Thomas Wade West, of whom more later. The three parts are carefully differentiated on the exterior, with appropriate entrance doors, centrally located staircases, a superb ballroom fifty-two by twenty-six feet, and card and supper rooms. It would have been the outstanding exterior of its day in America the principal authority on Latrobe avows, but West's lack of sufficient funds prevented its realization. The theater section is apparently a completely original and effective design which in itself may afford some indication of the artistic tastes of the Virginians of the time.[13]

The last and perhaps greatest Virginia work of Latrobe during his residence was the penitentiary. Jefferson's and other Virginians' belief at the end of the eighteenth century that penology should be accompanied by humanity is reflected in its details and outline and even in the inscription composed by the architect for the cornerstone. Latrobe won a competition for its design in 1797, studied Philadelphia's famous vaulted prison in March, 1798, and returned to Richmond to devote most of his remaining time in Virginia to supervising its construction.

Though altered frequently and finally replaced, for almost a century the Richmond penitentiary was a landmark which shows in many existing views of the city. Latrobe's drawings still exist. French governmental visitors in 1835 recommended its plan for consideration by their own architects of such buildings, though with a few reservations. The scheme consists of a large semi-circular court, the vaulted three-story cells constituting the outer circumference. Every cell door was equally visible from one point in the center. The straight side of the semi-circle was enclosed by a wall with the keeper's residence at its center. In front of this was a forecourt, flanked by infirmaries and women's quarters, and a guardhouse. A semicircular arched entrance, heavy rough-stone lower walls, and long ranges of arcades, add up to an expression of the combination of humanity and severity the Jeffersonians envisaged.

Latrobe's schemes for ventilation, the cantilevered balconies around the semicircle, the dormitories for well-behaved inmates, are interesting and advanced concepts of prison construction. The things the French experts criticized about the penitentiary as they found it were largely alterations made after Latrobe's time, many of them diametrically opposed to his and the humanitarian concepts of his Virginia contemporaries. What Latrobe designed and supervised was America's first large prison conceived architecturally and embodying advanced penological ideas, a major evidence of his organic concept of his art. Yet he had an unpleasant time haggling with state officials about costs all during the building. Later he remarked sadly that his subsequent experience with "public bodies has not differed from that which I gained in Virginia."[16]

Latrobe left other memories of Virginia, too. Among his sketches are a "View of York River, Va.," "Colonel Blackburn's House, Virginia," "View of Appomattox River, Virginia," "Mount Vernon," and "Green Spring," the last a water color which gives us almost all our architectural knowledge of Governor Berkeley's seventeenth-century mansion. Richmond and Norfolk houses clearly not his show the influence of his designs in simply graceful exteriors, octagonal rooms and window bays, and other characteristic features. Jefferson had the greatest respect for him, seeking his advice on several occasions. One or more of the University Pavilions were according to Latrobe's design, and he suggested the kind of domed building at the head of the quadrangle which was finally adopted. Jefferson urged the youthful Robert Mills to study under Latrobe. Because there was no city in Virginia large enough to need and support an architect Latrobe had to go north to find the opportunities commensurate with his abilities.

Robert Mills (1781-1855), South Carolina born and married to the daughter of a Virginia planter, resolved as a young man to get regular training as an architect. In 1800 he went to Washington to work with Hoban, the designer of the White House, from whom he learned the rudiments of construction and craftsmanship. The young man came to Jefferson's attention and was in 1803 invited to Monticello. Here for two happy years Mills worked with Jefferson's books, watched the remodeling of Monticello, and drew elevations of that mansion and a plan for a new house at Shadwell. The drawing for the latter shows Jefferson's favorite *villa rotonda* with high central dome, oval salon, octagonal bows, and alcove bedrooms, some of them features Mills himself was to use. Jefferson sent him on to Latrobe for further training, and from 1803 to 1808 Mills worked as draftsman and clerk under the professional architect. From 1808 to 1817 Mills practiced his profession independently in Philadelphia. Long before this time he had been drawing plans independent of any of his three mentors.

After he won the competition for the design of "the Votive Church," or the Monumental Church, in Richmond, a number of commissions from that city came to Mills.[15] In 1814 he designed the Court House, destroyed many years ago. Documentary evidence of his relationship to a number of mansions is hard to come by, though his name is associated with at least six Richmond dwellings, in three cases perhaps indisputably, the Cunningham-Archer-Watson, Wickham-Valentine, and second Brockenbrough houses.[16]

In building the Wickham mansion, now the Valentine Museum, Mills had greater funds at his command than ever before in his experience. Rectangular and simple in its stuccoed-brick exterior walls, there is an "austere elegance" in its interior decorations.[17] The doors are solid mahogany with silver knobs, locks, and hinges, the floors of toughest heart pine, and on the first floor are the fine Florentine mantles Mills liked to import. The arched ceilings, curved corners, and rounded lines Mills generally preferred are also present in this house. Over the three parlor doors originally were painted scenes from the *Iliad* and *Odyssey*, and the center of the ceiling had a frescoed head of Homer and other Grecian designs, all evidence that Mills, like Latrobe, had preference for the Greek.

The Archer house at the corner of Fifth and Franklin had the characteristic stuccoed-brick exterior and an interior with Greek Ionic columns and pilasters in the vestibule. Much of the material for it was imported from England: a built-in drawing room fireplace of brass, for example, with British insignia wrought in relief. A third Richmond dwelling, that built for Dr. John Brockenbrough about 1813 and now known as the White House of the Confederacy, seems proved to be Mills' by a letter of Brockenbrough's to the architect of May 20, 1813.[18] There is also a letter of Dr. Brockenbrough of February 28, 1814, recommending Mills as successor to Latrobe as architect of the public buildings in Washington.[19] The physician states that he knows Mills to be an excellent man from having worked with him on the Monumental Church.

The house is rather unusual in its small Ionic-columned front porch and Doric-columned more-than-two-story grand portico at the rear. Again stucco on brick, it is heavier than Jefferson's designs and most of Latrobe's, though it has been made more so by an extra story added since Mills' time.

Other Richmond houses attributed to Mills are the Marx-Freeland house (1813-14, demolished 1891) and the Gray house (later Westmoreland Club, built in 1839, demolished 1937), though there is little evidence beyond stylistic resemblances in either case.[20] There is a letter of February 2, 1816, from Mills to Colonel John Ambler in which the architect expresses his own pleasure that Ambler likes the exterior of his house and that the marble mantles have arrived, evidence of another Virginia building apparently not noticed by students of Mills.[21]

The work of Mills, culminating in the Washington Monument may be seen today from Columbia, South Carolina, to Boston in public buildings, dwellings, and monuments. Externally the buildings have a sort of heaviness more nearly akin to the Greek-inspired work of Latrobe than the Roman-derived plans of Jefferson. In their interiors all three men are closer, with Mills showing perhaps more of Jefferson's kind of taste than of Latrobe's, but more of his own than of either.

Mills makes frequent reference to Jefferson's amazing knowledge of architecture.[22] Among the South Carolinian's unfinished manuscripts is the beginning of an essay on "The Progress of Architecture in Virginia." Jefferson, says Mills, was the founder of Virginia architecture, a native art, for he did not slavishly follow classic models but allowed nature to guide him. In other words, he adapted to time and terrain. Mills goes into an extended discussion of the superiority of the Houdon statue of Washington in the Virginia Capitol to all others because it is natural, representing the General in his uniform surrounded by the agricultural implements of his vocation, a combination of what he was in his time. "Study your country's tastes and requirements, and make classic ground *here* for your art"[23] a new classic ground, Mills added. The Richmond Capitol itself Mills also discusses and then begins an analysis of Latrobe as a Virginia architect. Here the manuscript breaks off.

Written in Mills' later years, this unfinished essay clearly reveals the impression Virginia architecture and architects had made on the mind of a man who was at the time he was writing at the head of the profession in America. The Virginians had created a native architecture, an American architecture, he implies, by the adaptation of the Roman and Greek to their New World situations. Mills was thinking of what Jefferson and Latrobe had done, but he might have illustrated by some examples of what the gentleman-farmer could do, almost casually, along the same lines.

George Washington Parke Custis, sheepbreeder, orator, and playwright, employed in the early 1820's the Washington architect George Hadfield (*ca.* 1764-1826) to design and build his new mansion at Arlington.[24] Trained in his native England and the darling of its aristocracy, brother of Jefferson's dear Maria Cosway, Hadfield had shown more promise than fulfillment in his Washington work on the public and other buildings. For Custis he designed a Doric portico modeled on the great temple at Paestum, and a house which is one of the landmarks of the Greek Revival. But Hadfield died several years before the house was completed, and Custis undertook the later construction and amplification of the plans himself in the end being partly responsible for many features of the house. The owner also was the painter of the murals which decorated its interior.

Even more of a part had John Hartwell Cocke in the construction and design of his house at Bremo in Fluvanna county on the James. In fact, the story of the building of this house is a classic example of what the Virginia gentleman of good taste could accomplish architecturally with good builders and a little advice from friends. Once it was thought that Bremo was designed by Jefferson, for many of its details resemble his. But from the Cocke manuscripts now assembled at the University of Virginia we know that the owner himself and various friends drew plans or parts of plans from 1803 for an early house; that when in 1815 Cocke decided on a building on an extensive scale at Upper Bremo he drew himself the excellent specifications for the monumental effect of the stone barn he built, the finest farm building in America; and that for the mansion he sought some advice from St. George Tucker, John Patterson, and perhaps Jefferson (who gave it orally if at all).[25] In January, 1816, his wife wrote that her husband had been amusing himself all winter in drawing plans for his new house. When the design was well under way Jefferson recommended two men to do the actual construction, the Dinsmore and Neilson mentioned above. Superior house-joiners, they were skilled in executing Jefferson's style. Currie, an Edinburgh native, was employed for four years for the stone-cutting, and the great mansion was begun. It seems to follow many of Jefferson's favorite fancies. It is built on the brow of a hill, employs depressed passageways to connect central block with the two temple-like dependencies, and has the customary Jefferson portico on the north front. The cubical mass is enriched altogether by four Tuscan porticoes.

The completed mansion was and is one of the finest in America. "Of all the houses in the Jeffersonian tradition," thought Fiske Kimball, who knew most about them, "not even excepting Monticello, it is Bremo, which makes the deepest impression of artistic perfection. . . . Bremo has the inevitability of a single ordered creation."[26] Serene and dignified, it suggests the character of the owner and builder who conceived and constructed it.

George Tucker in his essay "On Architecture" asks why the Greek style has persisted for two thousand years. His answer is that it always followed the principle of utility, even in columns, that it possessed intrinsic beauty, that the Greeks hit a happy mean between too little and too great variety in ornament, and that it had become habit. These same causes make it the model of imitation among moderns, he concludes. Tucker is of course equating or including Roman with Greek. He was thinking, as he suggests, of the buildings around him in Williamsburg, Richmond, Albemarle, and southside Virginia.

B. *Painting*

In painting Virginia produced no gentlemen amateurs of the stature of Jefferson or Cocke, and no professionals of the ability of Latrobe and Mills worked so long within her borders. But in Richmond several professional painters of some ability made their living over many years, many others appeared seasonally, and yet others occasionally. Norfolk, Alexandria, Winchester, and doubtless Petersburg and Fredericksburg had their portrait painters, and there was still at least one man who in an older tradition stayed for weeks or months in the country houses in which he drew or painted all the members of a family and many of their neighbors. Virginia supported miniaturists in oils and pastels, portrait painters, and at times depicters of landscapes or groups. Virginians owned some good portraits and animal pictures and water colors, and many indifferent landscapes or copies of the great masters. They showed their best taste in the engravings of great originals they could not own, especially of American historical scenes and events. Their tastes were consonant with their view of politics and morality. Painting to them was still largely a documentary art whose social function might be considered exhortation or portraiture. Though in the later years romantic subjects and treatments began to appear, the Jeffersonians usually still strongly favored the neoclassic, with a preference for the statuesque and commemorative.[27]

At least nine well-known miniaturists worked for varying periods in Virginia. Most of them were also painters of larger portraits. Three or four members of the Peticolas family, which came to Virginia via Pennsylvania from France about 1804-5, became substantial citizens.[28] The father, Philippe Abraham Peticolas (1760-1841), taught music and miniature painting and painted a number of Richmonders, including Philip Larus. One son, Theodore, was also a minor painter of miniatures. Another, Edward F. Peticolas (1793-*ca.* 1853), advertised as early as 1807 that he was taking likenesses in miniature. After study under Thomas Sully from 1805, in 1815 he went abroad and worked under Allston, West, and Leslie. He became a friend of Virginia travelers like William C. Preston in Italy and painted a number of water colors of scenes near Florence.[29] When he returned to Richmond in 1820 he became the city's own popular painter in oils. There William Dunlap visited him in 1821, praising the chastity and clear coloring of his work and declaring that he deserved his popularity.[30] Peticolas made two more trips to Europe and on the third, in 1830-33, was a considerable success in London. Sully commented that he was much beloved in Richmond but liked seclusion too much to get on.

The Sully family were as well known for their miniatures as for their larger work in oils. Matthew and Sarah Chester Sully, born in England, landed in Norfolk in 1792. They were actors, and their names appear frequently in notices of the West and Bignall performances, of which more later.[31] In the year they landed the Richmond *Virginia Gazette* carried their elder son Lawrence Sully's (1769-1804) advertisement as "a miniature painter and student of the Royal Academy, London." In 1801 Lawrence with his wife and children moved to Norfolk but returned to Richmond in 1803. Never a first-rate artist, he was soon surpassed by his younger brother Thomas. Among his portraits are those of Samuel Greenhow and (attributed) of John Marshall, and among his miniatures "A Lady."[32]

Thomas Sully (1783-1872), who was to become the foremost American portrait painter of his generation, after some years in New York and Charleston with some of his family, worked with his brother Lawrence in Richmond and Norfolk until the latter's death and a few years later married his widow. He studied miniature painting with Lawrence. Between 180[illegible] and 1806 he painted more than eighty oils and miniatures of local people, including a well-known miniature of "The Artist's Wife."[33]

In November, 1806, he moved to New York and continued his distinguished career by painting prominent people, including a number of actresses in the costumes of their roles. In 1809 he went to London and worked with West and Lawrence. Back in America in 1810, he settled in Philadelphia, where the commissions poured in. In 1818 he painted his famous picture of Washington crossing the Delaware, and in 1824 Lafayette. At the summit of his fame in 1837 he returned to England and painted the young Queen Victoria from life. During his career he produced more than twenty-six hundred works. At his best in painting lovely women, he also did some good studies of his male sitters.

All of his life he continued to be Richmond and Virginia's favorite portrait painter. His brother Matthew's family made Richmond their home, one of their sons, Robert, Poe's friend, becoming a fairly well-known painter. Thomas frequently came there to work. His register for the years after 1808 continues to list Virginia subjects. The Virginia State Library, the Virginia Historical Society, several Virginia museums, and a number of families own a considerable number of his works.

John Trumbull painted miniatures in Yorktown, Williamsburg, Richmond, and Fredericksburg in 1793.[34] A Mr. Henri advertised himself in the Virginia *Argus* of May 16, 1804, as a miniature painter working at the Eagle Tavern. Two months before, on March 14, W. Bache advertised "The last week the Physiognotrace will remain in Richmond," suggesting that he like his successor St. Mémin was using the mechanical aid in making miniatures, or at least silhouettes. He also mentioned his black and gold frames.

The most famous artist as miniaturist in Virginia during the period was the French aristocratic exile Charles Balthazar Julien Fevret de Saint-Mémin (1770-1852), who had arrived in America about 1796 and came to Richmond just before the Burr trial in 1807. He did work in oils and crayons, but he is remembered for the more than eight hundred profile miniature engravings he made of probably a majority of all the distinguished Americans of the first quarter of the nineteenth century.

Richmond he found surprisingly congenial. Chevallié the French consul, fellow noble exile Louis Hue Girardin, supervisor Jean Lataste of the balls given at the Hay Market Gardens, survivor Joseph Bonnardel of the old regime, and Philippe Peticolas were among his fellow countrymen settled in the city. Distinguished persons from all over the state and native sons now resident elsewhere were there to enjoy the spectacle. He painted then an interesting view of Richmond. But more important were his scores of miniature engravings of Virginia ladies and gentlemen which form the most interesting visual archive of the age.

St. Mémin's physionotrace or physiognotrace was invented in 1786 by Gilles-Louis Chrétien. With it St. Mémin secured an exact profile of his subject on red paper and then drew the hair, features, and clothing in black and white crayon. Later, by means of another machine, the pantograph, he reduced the large crayon to the size of a miniature about two inches in diameter and recorded it directly on a copper plate. By following freely directions in an encyclopedia, he made both machines and other tools himself.

It has been suggested that St. Mémin gives an entirely erroneous impression that the first Federal period in the United States was "gracefully neoclassic a la Française."[35] Certainly the hair fashions, costume, and even cast of feature have a Gallic tone, but except for perhaps the last he was faithfully recording the mode, especially in Virginia, for other paintings bear him out. The Virginia pictures show the queue and powdered horsehair wig of the gentlemen of middle age or more, the newfashioned windblown Parisian-style locks of the younger men, the neat caps of the dignified matrons and tighter-fitting caps and voluminous dresses of the older ladies, and the romantic curls of younger women. The combination of scale and skill enabled St. Mémin to secure great liveliness of detail.

A few years ago Mr. Fillmore Norfleet gathered the known original crayons and engravings of the Virginians the artist drew about 1807.[36] Most but not all of them were done in Richmond at the Burr trial.

It is an imposing array. Among about sixty surviving crayons, for example, are portraits of G. W. P. Custis, William Fitzhugh, John Marshall, Hugh Nelson, David Watson, George Washington, and John Wickham. The much more numerous extant engravings represent James Barbour, Theodorick Bland, James Breckinridge, William A. Burwell, Peter Carr, Bernard Moore Carter, Landon Carter, and Landon Carter II, John Augustus Chevallié, Isaac A. Coles, Sarah C. Conyers, Dr. Elisha Cullen Dick, John Wayles Eppes, Louis Hue Girardin, Robert Goodloe Harper, Wade Hampton, William Henry Harrison, David Holmes, three of Jefferson,[37] Mrs. David Meade Randolph, Thomas Bolling Robertson, Littleton Waller Tazewell, St. George Tucker, three of Washington, and William Wirt, among several score. Years later in France, St. Mémin disparaged this early work, and the brief stay in Richmond was but one of many memories. But he did record, with deft touch and a good deal of imagination, the Virginia Jeffersonians at the height of their power and prestige.

Including the Sullys and Peticolases, there were at least fifteen well-known painters in oils working in Virginia in the period. Between 1799 and 1806 Jacob Frymire was painting in Alexandria and Winchester.[38] Seven of his eleven recorded paintings are of citizens of Alexandria, among them the portraits of Colonel Philip Marsteller and Samuel A. Marsteller. Next to Thomas Sully, the most popular portrait painter among Virginians was Cephas Thompson (1775-1856), who worked in both Norfolk and Richmond from 1809 to 1812 during his tours from New York to New Orleans.[39] Apparently he traveled with canvases ready prepared except for faces, for three portraits of sisters in Norfolk are said to differ in costume only in a ribbon or band which draws the dress together in front.

Among Thompson's Norfolk sitters were doctors, mayors, wealthy merchants, and lawyers, including Mr. and Mrs. Samuel Moseley, Mr. and Mrs. John Nivison (he was a 1776 member of Phi Beta Kappa), Nimmos, Southgates, Tabbs, Walkes, and Norfolk's first citizen, Littleton Waller Tazewell. In Richmond, Thompson painted James Barbour, Bernard Moore Carter, William Fleming, John G. Gamble, Mr. and Mrs. George Hay, Fielding Lewis, Dr. McClurg, Chief Justice and Mrs. Marshall, Mr. and Mrs. Wirt, and many others.[40] Not a first-rate painter, he had a reputation for good likenesses.

Charles Bird King (1785-1862), Rhode Islander who at one time roomed with Thomas Sully in New York, painted in most of the southern cities including Richmond before he settled in Washington in 1816.[41] John B. Martin, who worked principally in stipple engravings after 1822, did at least two Virginia portraits, those of Major James Gibbon and "Parson" John Buchanan, both now in the Virginia Historical Society. English-born James Sharples (*ca.* 1751-1811)[42] painted George and Martha Washington in pastels, as he did other distinguished Americans, somewhat in the manner of St. Mémin. One of his two painter sons, Felix Thomas Sharples (*ca.* 1786-after 1824), worked for a long period in Mathews and Gloucester counties about 1814 and is said to have died and been buried in the latter county. He is the man who spent weeks and even months in the households in which he worked.[43]

George Cooke (1793-1849), Maryland-born but producing his first work in Virginia, married a sister of James E. Heath. By September, 1825, he was able to note that in the preceding twenty-eight months he had painted 130 portraits, forty in Richmond alone. He worked in that city until the summer of 1826, when he sailed to Europe. He was probably back by 1831, for his attractive view of Richmond was engraved in that year.[44]

John Wesley Jarvis (1781-1840), another English-born artist brought to America as a small child, spent some time in Richmond, one of his children being born there. In 1825 he painted among others Judge and Mrs. Cabell, Henry Clay, General and Mrs. William Clark, George Rogers Clark, John Marshall, John Randolph, Joseph Marx, and John Tyler. Chester Harding (1792-1866), Massachusetts-born artist whose reputation has increased with the years, had painted celebrities in London before he came to Richmond in 1829. He portrayed Wirt, Marshall, Mrs. George Watson, and John Randolph.[45]

That all portrait painting was not done in the larger towns is evidenced in the career of John Gadsby Chapman (1808-89), Alexandria-born Virginian who was painting professionally in Winchester in 1827. He had studied with George Cooke and C. B. King and was to mature into one of the distinguished painters of the century, though he came to feel that the best painting could never be done in portraits. His later "Baptism of Pocahontas," one of the eight large paintings in the rotunda of the Capitol in Washington, indicates his continued connection with things Virginian, as do his "Landing at Jamestown" and view of Madison's Montpelier. He is also known to have done a portrait of Madison. In the end he was remembered as he wished to be, more for his landscapes—many of them done in Italy—than for his historical scenes or portraits. But then times and fashions had changed.[46]

Early in his career George Catlin (1796-1872), later famous for his Indians on canvas, recorded the end of a Virginia era when he painted "The Constitutional Convention at Richmond (1829-30)" containing 115 figures. He also did a portrait of Dolly Madison.[47]

James Warrell (*ca.* 1780-1839) is in a number of respects the most significant figure as far as art history is concerned among the Virginia painters of the period.[48] His parents, actors and singers, had brought him with them from England in 1793. By 1799 James had a dancing school in Richmond and from 1806 a race track in Petersburg, apparently managing the two concurrently. He was also painting as early as 1806, and in 1810 was advertised in a Petersburg paper as a portrait painter. The *Port Folio* included favorable notices of the paintings of "J. Worrell of Virginia" exhibited in Philadelphia in 1812 and 1813. His work was shown with that of Stuart, Sully, Leslie, and the Peales. In 1813 his historical Virginia picture, "Peter Francisco's Encounter with the British," had attracted considerable attention, and the next year it was engraved. His "Bonaparte Crossing the Alps" was said to have been the largest oil painting ever shown in Virginia.

By the end of the War of 1812 Warrell was well established in Richmond, numbering among his artistic friends the Sullys and Peticolases, and having a wide acquaintance among the socially and politically prominent. He and others conceived the idea in 1815 of establishing an art and nature museum in Richmond. The moment was propitious, for there was considerable prosperity until the depression of 1819. On December 18, his patrons Ritchie, Mayo, Girardin, and John Marshall petitioned the Legislature to allow Warrell to use land on or about the Capitol Square for "a handsome edifice which would remain always a public repository of natural and artistic curiosities." The petition was granted, and by May 27, 1816, Warrell and a partner Richard Lorton had issued a prospectus soliciting subscriptions for the Virginia Museum at $200 and $100 per family. The patrons themselves contributed $10,000.

One of the prospectuses exists among the Madison Papers in the Library of Congress, and another is included with a letter from Warrell to the artist C. B. King.[49] The latter contains a light pen sketch by Warrell of the proposed building, a handsome edifice with cupola, double-curved stairs from the ground to the entrance way on the second floor, and wings. It was to be built on the southeastern corner of the Capitol Square itself, and Warrell was to go to Europe to secure portraits of distinguished characters, historical subjects, "and views of the sublime and beautiful in nature, together with casts from the finest models of antique sculpture."

The subscriptions were secured and the Museum opened in the summer of 1817. One apartment, perhaps a wing, was devoted to paintings, another to statuary, and yet others contained assortments of stuffed animals and birds, insects, minerals, Indian curiosities, coins, and a very "complete" collection of shells. A rattlesnake was the only living specimen. Once, frolicsome girls rigged out the nude statues in aprons, hats, and jackets.[50]

For several years the Museum was a great success, but as the novelty wore off and the economic crisis developed the owners found themselves in financial difficulties. Warrell increased his efforts with musical entertainments as additions to the painting exhibitions, advertising such attractions as "Mr. Stanhope on the Harmonical Glasses" and "Signor Pucci on the Pedal Harp." In 1820 he held a special exhibition of Sully's "Passage of the Delaware by the American Forces under the Command of General Washington." But by 1822 the financial situation was bad. In 1826 William Harris Jones advertised that he managed the Museum. Warrell was painting and exhibiting in New York.

By 1831 Warrell was back in Richmond with an exhibition of oil paintings from Europe, but the next year Lorton, who had a lien on the building, was forced to buy it in. Warrell was still on the scene in 1833, offering a display of old masters, but by 1836 Lorton had lost all hope and got the Legislature to convey building and lot to the Governor for $6,500. So ended the first Virginia venture at a museum of art. Mann S. Valentine bought the paintings left in the gallery, and many of them may still be seen at the Valentine Museum.

Warrell worked as a painter while he conducted the Museum and for some time afterwards. His "Sword-Swallowers from Madras" is now in the Valentine Museum, and his "John Taylor of Caroline" in the Virginia State Library. He made a copy of Sully's portrait of George Frederick Cooke and earlier had made one of Washington, the latter now in the Richmond City Hall. He painted John Tyler, Sr., and the Reverend Andrew Broaddus. The well-known portrait of Poe's Helen, Jane Stith Stanard, is attributed to him. This last and the Peter Francisco picture are the best known associated with his name.

Individuals as collectors also afford evidence of Virginia tastes. Families like the Randolphs, Moseleys, Fitzhughs, Byrds, Bollings, Lees, and Pages we know possessed from five to more than thirty paintings in single homes. Most of these, but not all, were portraits. Washington owned a landscape by Claude Lorrain and many portraits and engravings, the latter including "The Battle of Bunker Hill," "The Thunderstorm," and "The Death of the Fox." John H. Cocke had among his pictures two fine paintings of his horses "Roebuck" and "Lexington." William Carter among other things had Vanderlyn's sketch of Salvator Rosa's Roman Garden.[51]

Virginians abroad made extensive purchases. Andrew Stevenson gathered paintings and other works of art in Paris in 1833 as Jefferson had done more than a generation before. Between the two in time, Joseph C. Cabell in 1805 bought all sorts of *objets d'art* for himself and his friends, including views of Rome and Naples, several "heads" of Raphael, several of Paul, a copy of "The Chase of Diana by Dominican," many engravings, and a number of busts, in all 145 marbles and an indefinite number of pictures.[52] Visitors at Montpelier noticed Madison's portraits, including those of Jefferson and of himself and his wife, the busts of himself (by Ceracchi), John Paul Jones, Joel Barlow, George Erving, Homer, and Socrates, an engraving from Raphael, a bas-relief of Mrs. Madison, and other engravings such as "The Battle of Bunker Hill," this last apparently an American favorite, and a number of other pictures, principally landscapes, in the hall.[53]

Jefferson's interest in painting dates from 1766 when he visited Philadelphia and saw the Titian, Giorgione, Coreggio, and other great pictures there owned by wealthy citizens. Perhaps it was this experience that caused him to agree with Lord Kames that one of the things painting could do for man was to give a pleasing and innocent direction to the spending of the wealthy. Though he never considered himself one of these wealthy, for years he compiled lists of paintings from catalogues and building notebooks and when he was in Paris had copies made for himself of a Raphael, a Carlo Muratti, a Guido Reni, and a Simon Vouet, among others. Because he believed also that painting was valuable as a means of preserving the record of great men and events in representative and symbolic creations, he gathered portraits and historical scenes, from crude Indian pictures on buffalo skins to copies of great Spanish and Italian works.[54]

One list among Jefferson's papers suggests that he had at Monticello forty-six portraits in oil and eleven in crayon, fourteen pictures, prints, and engravings with frames of more than twelve inches, and thirty-nine pictures with frames less than twelve inches.[55] Visitors to Monticello almost always commented on the museum-like appearance of the hall, drawing room or parlor, and even dining room.[56] John Caldwell in 1808, George Ticknor in 1815, and a German prince in 1825 were impressed by the Indian statuary, maps, implements, and weapons, the library (at the two earlier dates), and above all by the classical and modern statuary, paintings, and engravings. The pictures of the Laughing and Weeping Philosophers; the copies of Florentine originals of the earliest navigators to America, Columbus, "Americus Vespuccius," and Magellan; portraits of Mr. Madison in the plain Quaker-like dress of his youth, Lafayette in his Revolutionary uniform, and Franklin in his customary dress; the copies of Raphael's "Transfiguration" and "Holy Family," Poussin's "Ascension," Rubens' "Scourging of Christ," and Guido's "Crucifixion"; the oil painting and engraving of the Natural Bridge; Vanderlyn's view of Niagara Falls, Trumbull's sketch for his "Surrender at York [town]," Benjamin West's drawing of Hector's Farewell (a gift of the artist to General Kosciusko); views of Monticello, Mt. Vernon, buildings in Washington, and Harper's Ferry; and the several portraits of Jefferson represent his aesthetic tastes as well as his more general activities and interests. Then there was the colossal bust of Jefferson by Ceracchi on a truncated and decorated column, a full-length reclining figure of Cleopatra after she had applied the asp, the plaster busts of

Voltaire and Turgot, and other busts of Napoleon and Alexander of Russia, of Washington, Franklin, Lafayette, and John Paul Jones.

Perhaps John Randolph of Roanoke has recorded the best artistic taste among the Jeffersonians according to modern standards. He seems rarely if ever to have purchased oil paintings or marbles, if one may judge by the absence of receipts for such things among the surviving records of purchases of many other kinds. Only one, for a half dozen British engravings, has been observed. But whenever he got a chance to see good pictures, he enjoyed them. In a letter of December 21, 1830, to a niece from London he speaks disparagingly of "West's daubs and Copeley's [*sic*] collection of wig blocks which he called the death of Chatham,"[57] things he would not look at after he had seen the old masters. He mentions his "favorite Murillo of a Spanish peasant boy so exquisite that I would freely give 100 guineas for it," pictures by Coreggio and Velasquez, "some glorious Claudes," "some divine Rembrants [*sic*]" and "some noble Van Dycks." Perhaps men like Cabell, Rives, Stevenson, and James Barbour who had also lived in Europe shared Randolph's enthusiasms or had their own differing ones among the masters, but record of such tastes is rare. The average educated Virginian during his whole life rarely got a chance to see anything better than a Copley or Stuart or Trumbull or Sully portrait or historical scene and a few plaster casts.

The tastes that are recorded are primarily, as we have indicated, neoclassic. Jefferson, for example, abhorred the Gothic in all its graphic and architectural forms as positively as did his friend Abigail Adams. Yet in his rhapsody on the Roman temple at Nimes or on the Potomac at Harper's Ferry he is more romantic than anything else. Some of these planters and many of the later painters of the period were certainly sentimental or romantic in their choice of pictures or in execution. Even the Bunker Hill and Yorktown kind of pictures became much romanticized as the period went on.

C. *Music*

At the end of the colonial period, a recent student of the subject declares, "the ground appeared to have been fertile [in Virginia] for the development of a musically erudite civilization whose taste and participation in art music would have been equal at least to that of many European countries."[58] There were in the colonial period group singing secular and sacred, in Williamsburg concerts of both types, and music teachers, music libraries, and a wide ownership of musical instruments by gentlemen throughout the colony. Instead of progressing, the interest in art music after the Revolution decreased at least relatively for a number of reasons, this observer notes. Financial difficulties, the concentration of interest on political and economic problems, the disestablishment of the church and the increased activity of the puritanical sects, and the deterioration in the quality of music from that of the great eighteenth-century composers to the sentimental banalities of the nineteenth were factors in this retrogression. With the westward movement the American musical center shifted to the Northern cities.

Yet there was a good deal of musical activity in Jeffersonian Virginia, in some respects superior to anything between it and the mid-twentieth century. It did not nearly equal the dramatic activity, nor possibly even the interest in painting. But gentlemen who had been young in the colonial period continued in some degree their activity and communicated their interest if not their skill to others. And with the continued interest in the theater, accelerated after 1819 in centers like Richmond, went an interest in musical drama, concerts, and oratorios.

Williamsburg had naturally been a center of musical as well as other activities in the 1760-80 period. During the golden age of Governor Fauquier there had been a weekly ensemble playing at the Palace in which the Governor, John Tyler Sr., and young Jefferson were performers. One might walk down a Williamsburg street and hear tooting and scraping of strings all the way. Spinets, harpsichords, violins, flutes, violincellos, trumpets, and French horns were everywhere. At Bruton Parish Church, Peter Pelham (1721-1805), organist from 1752 to 1802, gave concerts and directed the choir. At odd moments he ran the jail, instructed music pupils, and composed. His son-in-law, the Reverend Mr. Benjamin Blagrove, sang in a number of sacred concerts in which his wife, trained by her father, played the organ or harpsichord. Blagrove made a northern tour in 1790 and received rhapsodical praise. A singing school existed in Williamsburg as late as 1791.[59] In 1772 had been published there one of the earliest collections of American music, *The Storer, or the American*

Singer, Being a Collection of the Newest and Most Approved Songs, its title being in honor of Maria Storer, singing-actress.

Pelham was the single most important Virginia musician of the latter half of the eighteenth century. Brought from England to America at the age of five by his portrait-painter father, he first lived and studied in New England. From 1743 to 1750 Pelham was first organist at Trinity Church in Boston. Settling in Williamsburg in 1752, he assisted in installing the first Bruton Parish organ and was appointed to the position he held for half a century. He tuned, repaired, and even built musical instruments and played at all church services, including the funerals of Governor Botetourt and publisher William Rind. There is a record of Jefferson paying him 2/6 "for playing the organ," probably the price of admission to a concert.[60] In his recital he presented music from Handel, Vivaldi, and Felton, among others. He certainly composed for his sacred concerts and services, though as yet no manuscripts of this kind have been recovered. In a Virginia music notebook in the Southern Historical Collection of the University of North Carolina, among many marches, sonatas, and various works by Handel, including the "Water piece," there is a "Minuet by Mr Pelham Organist of the Church in Williamsburg."[61]

The St. George Tucker family in Williamsburg were all musicians. As we shall see, many of Tucker's own lyrics were designed to be sung and were inserted in his plays with musical directions. Found in a poem among his manuscripts, though not in Tucker's hand, is a "Musical Evening in the Family," in which Coalter (Tucker's son-in-law) played the drum, Fan (presumably Coalter's wife Frances) the welch-harp, Miss Blair the fiddle, "my dear Abby" the harpsichord, Jenny the flute, and one of the Nelsons (a nearby Yorktown family) the timbrels.[62]

Richmond included music among the other activities it inherited from the earlier capital. On social and public occasions, in the churches, in the theaters, in private soirees, music was a considerable part of the city's entertainment. There were many teachers, a few local composers, several local singers, and instrumentalists.[63]

In 1785 the Chevalier Quesnay de Beaurepaire himself was the first to advertise that he taught music in the city. Soon afterwards John Widewelt was teaching violin and flute, John Lataste the dancing master from 1808 to 1813 offered instruction on the viola, and at least half a dozen female academies offered all sorts of vocal and instrumental instruction. Prominent citizen Michael Benoît Poitiaux (1771-1854) offered musical instruction after he lost his fortune in 1819. Charles Southgate, possibly a native, sang, played, and taught during most of the period. P. A. and Auguste Peticolas offered instruction in piano and harpsichord. The list is long.[64]

Music could be bought usually at the bookstores, though Prichard and Davidson had a music store from 1795 to 1799. Fitzwhylsonn and Potter's from about 1800, and a little later Mayo and Frayser's bookstores, offered music, music books, and instruments of all kinds, from the smallest flageolet to the pianoforte.

The Episcopal St. John's and Monumental (the latter built after the fire of 1811) were the only churches possessing organs in this period. They, with the Episcopal congregation which met in the Capitol before 1812, were the prime encouragers and practitioners of sacred music. One Presbyterian congregation, the First Church, did not frown on instrumental music. There survives a whimsical letter of December 6, 1806, to the Presbyterian clergyman John D. Blair, President of the Society for Promoting Church Music, which indicates his approval. In 1824 a concert with instruments was given in the First Presbyterian Church. Already in 1818 an oratorio had been given at the Monumental Church, and another was given in 1825, to be followed a few days later by a concert of sacred music.[65] The musician Charles Southgate composed and compiled for use in the Episcopal Church the *Harmonia Sacra,* a volume containing a *Te Deum* and seven hymns by the editor-collector.

The Baptists and Methodists frowned on instrumental music in this period, but they did like to sing hymns. Many of their song books were published in Richmond. The Reverend Eleazer Clay's *Hymns and Spiritual Songs Selected from Several Approved authors . . . Recommended by the Baptist General Committee of Virginia* (Richmond, 1793) was a popular collection with the Baptists, as were Andrew and Richard Broaddus' *Collection of Sacred Ballads* (n.p., preface dated Caroline county, Virginia, 1790) and Andrew Broaddus' *A Selection of Hymns and Spiritual Songs from the Best Authors* (Richmond, 1798) and his *Dover Selection of Spiritual Songs* (Richmond [1829]), and John Courtney, Sr.'s, *The Christian Pocket*

Companion (Richmond, 1805, and perhaps an earlier edition of 1802). The Methodist circuit rider Stith Mead gathered a popular collection of camp meeting songs mentioned elsewhere, *A General Selection of the Newest and Most Admired Hymns and Spiritual Songs Now in Use* (Richmond, 1807, Lynchburg, 1811). There are no tunes indicated for any of these.

Most of the Richmond music of the period was connected in one way or another, however, with the theater. Small orchestras or individual instrumentalists often introduced the plays, filled the intermissions, or accompanied dramatic singers. The actors were frequently singers. Many of the orchestra members gave lessons.

The Hallam and Henry company gave the *Beggar's Opera* in 1787,[66] and West and Bignall gave several musical farces and comic operas, as well as songs in the plays, between 1790 and 1800. This tradition continued through the period. Versions of the opera *Rosina* by Mrs. Brooke or William Shield were performed many times in Richmond. Dibdin's *The Padlock* in 1791, Arnold's *Maid of the Mill* in 1792 and 1795, and the *Barber of Seville* in 1820. Musical farces and "musical entertainments" multiplied in the theater between 1800 and 1830.[67]

Closely connected with the theater were the concerts, sometimes given in the theater buildings or with theater personnel as performers. Concerts were also given by itinerant entertainers or amateurs and musician-teachers of the city. The first formal concert may have been given by Mrs. Sully, member of the theatrical company in 1792. She continued as a popular principal and accompanist for many years. At the Museum Southgate gave an instrumental concert with Richard Decker on the flute, Widemeyer on the violin, and Lacaste on the viola. Mr. and Mrs. West and Mr. and Mrs. Green of the theater sang on the stage and off, and Charles Gilfert, manager of the "New Theatre" opened in 1819, was a gifted musical performer. Mrs. Sully and Mrs. Pick formed a concert team which toured neighboring towns. Mrs. Matthew Sully the younger (Elizabeth Robertson of Richmond) had studied under Philippe Peticolas and performed on the grand piano and organ alternately, sometimes "assisted by several gentlemen amateurs" of Richmond.

Many of the concerts were given at the Museum, the Bell Tavern, or the Eagle Tavern and Hotel. Signor Pucci and L. Brucheri, touring musicians, played and sang in 1812 and Pucci alone gave a "Grand

Concert" four years later.[68] "The Lilliputian Songsters" (two midgets) were at the Eagle in 1821. The local organist at the Hay Market Gardens, Mr. Folly, gave a concert in 1804 and Richardson, orchestra leader at the circus, another at the Museum in 1819.

Mrs. French appeared in several concerts at the Eagle in 1818 and 1819 and later. On May 25, 1818, William Wirt wrote his friend William H. Fitzwhylsonn that he had recently heard Mrs. French of Baltimore, that he considered her superior to Catalani, and that his friend must hear her when she visited Richmond in a few days.[69] Samuel B. Mordecai heard her at two concerts and wrote on June 7, 1818, that at the second he was "so squeezed and stewed" he had not enjoyed her. But he added that later at Mr. Marx's he had heard her in two Italian songs and on the same occasion Signor Christiano on the piano in a marvelous performance.[70]

During all this time the Sully family were leaders in all kinds of music, private, church, and theatrical. Then there were the prominent citizens who patronized the arts, as Marx must have been doing when Mrs. French sang at his house. Gustavus Adolphus Myers, lawyer and playwright, Mann S. Valentine, himself an amateur performer on the violin, and William H. Fitzwhylsonn were among those who held some sort of soirees. Valentine especially was notably hospitable to local and visiting artists.

The amateurs too had a definite place in Richmond musical history. Harman Blennerhasset, in Richmond for the Burr Trial on September 17, 1807, mentions enjoying hearing Sally Conyers sing with the Harmonic Society. On October 8, he had another pleasant evening at the Musical Society, where he met Mrs. Wickham and Mrs. Chevallié.[71] By the next year at least there was a Philharmonic Society in the city, for its papers for a long period from that date survive.[72] These show that it owned tables, chairs, and stools, and that on one occasion it rented a room with sugar, lemons, tumblers, and poker and tongs. Some members thought the Society for the Promotion of Church Music should pay half the expense of this room, but the decision apparently went against them. Certain of the Philharmonic Society's bills are addressed to Charles Southgate, probably the treasurer. An 1812 list of members includes Mr. Blagrove (probably grandson of Pelham and son of the Reverend Mr. Blagrove), the musician Poitiaux, and Mr. Fitzwhylsonn. About 1820 there were eleven members. Whether the Harmonic Association of 1828, meeting every Monday evening in Mr. Guignon's Assembly Room for rehearsal, is the same organization as the Philharmonic or one or both the societies mentioned by Blennerhasset has not been determined.[73]

Richmond had at least two composers of some ability. One of the Peticolases' arrangement of dance music appeared in the early Richmond magazine *The Visitor* in 1810, and some other things by father and son are known.[74] The music editor of *The Visitor,* Charles Southgate, composed pieces other than the church music already mentioned. For the theater he did several things, including "President Madison's March," written for two cornos, two clarinets, and a basso, and "A New Song" for voice with piano. Both were published in the magazine. And apparently a number of the then popular "ballad songs" were composed by members of the theatrical companies or local musicians, often adapting or using popular tunes such as "Robin Adair" or "To Anacreon in Heaven."[75]

In Norfolk the records of music interest are much like those of Richmond, though perhaps not quite so frequent. *The Herald* and *Norfolk and Portsmouth Advertiser* of several dates in 1795 advertised all sorts of instruments for sale, including English and German flutes, clarinets, guitars, violins, and pianofortes, and sheet music. M. Thullier advertised at the same time his music school for ladies.[76] Several concerts are advertised as early as 1796 and 1797, one of them offering on its program several overtures, a violin solo, and part of Handel's *Messiah.* There were five vocal and seven instrumental performers.[77] Prominent Norfolk citizens like Captain William Maxwell and Donald Campbell in the later eighteenth century showed interest in music, and when Latrobe visited the city he found many doors open to him because of his knowledge of the art.[78] In the nineteenth century Norfolk was visited by many of the same theatrical companies and individual artists as Richmond.

There is record of a Harmonic Society in Fredericksburg by 1784 which gave concerts in the Market House on the third Wednesday of each month.[79] The *Virginia Herald* of May 6, 1790, announced a "Concert, Vocal and Instrumental," in Mr. Brownslow's Brick Building, with Mr. Kulin and Mr. Victor at the harpsichord, pianoforte, and violin. In 1797 a concert was given at Mrs. Gatewood's

Concert Room at which several gentlemen of Fredericksburg accompanied a five-year-old girl prodigy, who sang.

Petersburg like Norfolk and to some extent Fredericksburg and Alexandria shared with Richmond the theatrical companies and individual artists who brought music to the city. R. Shaw "of the Theatre" in 1796-1815 gave lessons in singing, harpsichord, and German flute. Mrs. Sully and Mrs. Pick had a benefit concert there on June 25, 1795, and they appeared in this neighboring city many times.

In John D. Burk's friend John M'Creery, Petersburg had a composer of its own. He published in the city in 1824 *A Selection from the Ancient Music of Ireland, Arranged for the Flute or Violin; Some of the Most Admired Melodies, Adapted to American Poetry, Chiefly Composed by John M'Creery. To Which Is Prefixed, Historical and Critical Observations on Ancient Irish Music.* On pages 112-13 is his "Nobody Coming To Marry Me" as "sang [*sic*] by Mrs. Poe, with unbounded applause, at the New—York Theatre." M'Creery's "The American Star" is said to have rivaled "The Star Spangled Banner" in popularity. A song or two by Burk are also included in the collection. Also an anonymous *Gospel Melodies, By The Author of the Several Fugitive Pieces* was published in Petersburg in 1821.[80] It contains 112 melodies and thirteen "original doxologies," the words without music.

Alexandria had concerts as early as May 4, 1793, when the audiences heard the harpsichord. Mrs. Sully and Mrs. Pick were there on July 16, 1795. And a "Sacred Harmony" concert of May 10, 1796, included works by "Haendel," Addison, Madan, Alcock, and Reed. *The Virginia Nightingale, Containing a Choice Selection of New Songs* was published in Alexandria in 1807. It is mainly a collection of Irish songs without music.

Even in a small town like Winchester there was considerable interest in singing. The Frugal Fare Club, a literary group in which Dabney Carr and Judge Holmes were leading lights, was often entertained by songs rendered by its members. "Give me, nymph, my heart again," and Burns' "Tam Glenn," were sung by Carr himself. Holmes had a wide range, from the pathos of "Highland Mary" and the sentimental humor of "John Anderson" to Irish witty pieces or ballads. One member, Singleton, rendered "You are welcome Paxton,

Robin Adair" as his sole accomplishment, but he did it with so much whimsicality that he was always encored.[81] In this town the independent evangelist Joseph Thomas published his *Pilgrim's Hymn Book* (1816) and *The Trump of Christian Union, Containing a Collection of Hymns Entirely Original* (1819).

Music had an important place in the lives of many Virginians prominent in other fields. William Wirt, convivial and sentimental, could be moved to tears by hearing his wife or daughter play. In a letter to Peachy Gilmer recalling old times Wirt wrote that his recent playing on the flute reminded him of the days at Pen Park, and he asked Gilmer what had become of his own flute and the book of old Scotch tunes the two had purloined from Dunlora. At Wirt's Washington home Josiah Quincy remembered to have heard a young Virginia lady play on the piano and harp and sing sweetly simple songs as the attraction of the party.[82]

Valley inventor Robert McCormick had among his other creations "an improvement in teaching the art of performing on the violin," indication at least of his interest in the subject. G. W. P. Custis played on the violin for the entertainment of his children. Industrialist David Ross, writing to his son at college in Pennsylvania, urged the young man to study music, for it would introduce "a stranger Gentleman into the higher grades of genteel society." He recommended the German flute as harmonious, and the violin and "Organized Guitar" as good relaxations.[83] Evidence that some Presbyterian churches still frowned on instrumental music lies in the case of Henry Easley of Halifax county, who was dismissed by the church elders from the fold because he refused to lay aside his violin, upon which instrument he was a locally famous performer.[84]

Probably the state's most accomplished amateur musician in the earlier part of our period was Thomas Jefferson. He himself said music was his first and lasting love. As we have noted, he had played the violin from his days at William and Mary. He had won a valuable instrument in a wager with a friend, John Randolph (not of Roanoke). He also had a Cremona. His former slave Isaac Jefferson said his master always kept three fiddles. Jefferson persuaded the Italian music teacher Alberti to come to Monticello and give him lessons. He played for a dozen years, he himself testifies, not less than three hours a day. Isaac remembered that he played in the "arternoons and sometimes arter supper," but that when he began to get old he didn't play.[85] The Randolph violin and the Cremona he had at the end of his life.

In Williamsburg he attended the theater on every possible occasion, partly because of a great interest in the ballad opera, of which he owned many scores. He had experienced good music in Paris, where he attended operas and concerts. His friend Maria Cosway was a composer and presented to him the copy of her *Songs and Duets* which bears his autograph.[86] And he was interested in the technical side of the art, as one might expect. He had correspondence with his Philadelphia friend Francis Hopkinson concerning improvements in the manner of quilling the harpsichord, and in the 1790's he helped by substantial encouragement John Isaac Hawkins in developing an upright piano. Hawkins in turn composed a number of marches and other pieces in honor of his friend and patron.

The master of Monticello owned a number of instruments other than the violin. He had a harpsichord built to his specifications in London in 1786, a matter in which he consulted the famous Dr. Burney.[87] M. Fauble, a Frenchman resident at his neighbor Walker's, frequently tuned his forte piano, Isaac remembered. He devised a unique scheme for assembling an orchestra on his estate. Since he could not afford full-time musicians, he attempted to find domestic servants who could play on "the French horn, clarinet, or hautboy, and bassoon." The music part of the library he sold to Congress contains only eight items. He must have retained most of his books in this art, for the catalogue made in 1782 has several pages of listings of books of instruction for the violin, harpsichord, and German flute.[88] Two pages are devoted to vocal and two to instrumental music. Handel, Purcell, Corelli, Vivaldi, and Boccherini are among the composers he enjoyed then. In Europe later he became acquainted with and enjoyed Haydn. Though he was a contemporary of Beethoven and Schubert, there is no evidence that he knew their work.[89]

Two extant music stands, one for violin and another for use in playing quartets, are solid evidence of his love of this art. Among the fragments remaining of his library, most interesting is the music copied in his own hand at an early period. There is also a small sheet listing the several compositions of Campioni he already owned and asking an agent to secure everything else the man composed. In his own hand too is a "Fingerboard for Spanish guitar" with notes on how to play the instrument, probably done for a granddaughter. In fact a letter from Hore B. Trist to his brother Nicholas may suggest that as late as 1819 Jefferson may have played the fiddle for his family to dance by, for Trist states that ever since Jefferson returned from Poplar Forest they had enjoyed most agreeable dances at Monticello.[90]

Isaac testified that Jefferson loved to sing when he was riding or walking: "Hardly see him anywhar out doors but what he was a-singin: had a fine clear voice, sung minnits [minuets] & sich." That he composed some pieces for voice or violin seems probable. But those studying the third President as musician have not yet given all their findings.

D. *Plays and the Theater*

Like the English country squire, the Virginia planter liked to attend the theater when he went to town. Some form of dramatic entertainment was probably almost as old as the colony, but the first recorded performance of English speaking America was "The Bare and the Cubb" in Accomack county in 1665.[91] By 1716 the Charles Staggs and their company were ready to open in Williamsburg, and that year the first theater in the little capital was built. This company had great success until Stagg's death in 1735/36. The more famous Lewis Hallam and his troupe made their first Williamsburg appearance in 1752 in *The Merchant of Venice.* From then until the Revolution, Williamsburg offered attractions almost every season.

Washington, a devotee of the theater, saw several plays presented by the Virginia Company of Comedians in Williamsburg in 1768. He remained a fairly regular attendant in New York, Philadelphia, and Washington almost up to the time of his death.[92] But in Virginia during those years theatrical activity, like political, shifted away from the old capital.

In the 1780's Richmond supported a theater. A 1782 city record refers to Dennis Ryan, manager of the theater, who was to pay taxes according to the number of plays produced. He is mentioned again in 1784.[93] In May, 1786, the "Hall" of Quesnay's Academy was used by the actors under the younger Lewis Hallam and John Henry, the best known company in eighteenth-century America. Their first play was *The School for Scandal,* and they continued with *Hamlet, Richard III, Jane Shore,* and other favorites. Though Quesnay felt compelled to explain in the newspapers why the Academy was used for such purposes, by 1787 this hall or another building of the Academy on Shockoe Hill had been named the "New Theatre" and another season begun. Thus in the 1780-90 decade it is evident that Richmond had at least three seasons.

In the nineties dramatic interest and enterprise in Virginia were immensely stimulated by the arrival of Thomas Wade West, who came to America as an actor-manager in 1790, organized the West-Bignall company, and remained the theatrical promoter in the state throughout the decade.[94] West and his wife were experienced actors, his daughter Anne West Bignall was to be called in 1805 the most distinguished ornament of the Virginia stage, and her husband John Bignall was the star of the company. Mrs. West sent for her brother Matthew Sully with his wife and seven children to join them, and in 1791 other actors were added. Such was the strength of the company that it was able to entice a promising young actress away from the best known American company in Philadelphia.

By October, 1790, the little company had an orchestra and a variety of scenery. The productions were too elaborate and costly for Richmond, with a population of only 3,761 (almost half Negro), and the answer seemed to be a theatrical circuit. Early in 1792 West bought property and built a theater in Norfolk, and late in the year did the same thing in Charleston, South Carolina. Norfolk became his headquarters while he built the Norfolk theater and another in Petersburg. By 1797 he had built a theater in Fredericksburg and was building another in Alexandria. The elaborate plan he had Latrobe draw up for the combination hotel-theater-assembly in Richmond was the graphic illustration of all his dreams. The six theaters already or about to be in operation probably tied up his funds so that he could not immediately undertake the ambitious enterprise. Then in 1799 he was killed in an accidental fall in his new theater in Alexandria.

Despite the loss by fire of one of his buildings and all of its equipment, West was successful during the whole decade. He knew how and where to employ musicians and actors. He maintained what was called unequivocally the best theatrical company in the United States and with it gave superior entertainment in scattered Southern towns.

He brought his wife's relatives the Sullys to America. He built five theaters in nine years, and with his productions Richmond became one of the eight or nine important theatrical centers on the Atlantic seaboard. The company he and Bignall had founded, which had absorbed his rival Placide's Charleston troupe, laid the foundation for twenty-two years of uninterrupted theater of fine quality.

The New Theatre burned about 1805, and for a time performances were held in the upper part of the old Market House. But the New Brick Theatre was soon built on the old academy site. It was in this building that Mrs. Poe (part of the time as Mrs. Hopkins) performed with Green's Virginia Company between 1802 and 1811, and it was here that the first great theatrical tragedy of American history occurred when the building burned on December 26, 1811, with enormous loss of life (seventy-two persons).[95] The catastrophe was described by onlookers dozens of times, sermons of warning or sympathy were preached as far away as Boston, and a number of lugubrious poems mourned the victims.

But before this happened twenty-four English plays had been acted in Richmond for the first time in America, five of them not known to have been acted at all elsewhere in this country. A number of these appeared in West and Bignall's time, but a great many were later. Thomas J. Dibdin's dramatization of *The Lady of the Lake,* for example, first performed in London and Edinburgh in 1810-11, was acted in Richmond on October 31, 1811, and repeated several times.[96] With these new things the repertory included the usual eighteenth-century comedies, tragedies, and Shakespeare. James Barker's *Indian Princess* was played on October 30, 1810. Mrs. Poe's benefit was announced for October 8 of that year.[97]

After the 1811 fire there was a long interval before professional productions were resumed in Richmond. The first to open was in "The Theatre" on June 11, 1819, with the excellent Gilfert company. There were thirty-three performances during the season, followed by sixty-four between October 4, 1819 and January 14, 1820. Then a summer season in 1820 included thirty-seven performances. The seventeenth season after the fire opened on October 2, 1830. Gilfert's company sometimes exchanged with the Petersburg company of Caldwell, as in 1820. Gilfert's last in Richmond was the eleventh season, Caldwell followed once, then the George P. Richardson company, then Flynn and Willis, and finally E. M. Willard's troupe.

The Theatre was a handsome stuccoed-brick building painted inside in light colors, with decorated boxes and a handsome curtain. The arms of Virginia were painted on a light ground above the proscenium. Both building and equipment were owned by the Proprietors, a stock company in which the principal men of the city owned shares. Among the stockholders were Joseph Marx, John Marshall, Richard E. Parker, Thomas Ritchie, Mann S. Valentine, Francis Gilmer, William Wirt, and James Warrell, who owned one share each. In payment for the lot on which the building was erected, Christopher Tompkins had forty-three shares. The whole investment was about $40,000. Each stockholder had a free pass to the performances but were not supposed to use it on benefit nights. This caused financial difficulties, and after 1823 the property deteriorated.

The audience represented a cross-section of the white population and there was a gallery for Negroes. In 1829-30 some of the notables attending the convention were present at every performance. On Saturday, October 31, 1829, for example, ex-Presidents Madison and Monroe, attended by the Richmond cavalry in full uniform, were present.

Junius Brutus Booth made his American debut here in 1821 and became a personal friend of many leading citizens. Among the seventy-three visiting stars in this period (1819-38) were Edwin Forrest, Edmund Kean, and Thomas Abthorpe Cooper, the last of whom acted frequently in Richmond and became the firm friend of William Wirt. Though many players were American, the British talent dominated the Richmond stage as it did the theater generally in America. Two local actors, George P. Richardson and Judah, did appear frequently.

The most popular play was probably *The School for Scandal.* Other favorite comedies were *The Belle's Strategm, The Honey-Moon, Merchant of Venice, The Soldier's Daughter,* and *The Spoiled Child.* Richmonders also liked historical plays such as *Charles XII, Joan of Arc,* and *William Tell,* the patriotic *Battle of New Orleans,* and the legendary *Rip Van Winkle.* The popular tragedies included *Hamlet, Othello, Pizarro,* and Moore's *The Gamester.* Sentimental plays remained popular and may have influenced the essays of the Wirt group. Fourteen of Shakespeare's plays were performed 114 times between

1819 and 1838. Eight plays of American authorship and more of English had their first American performances in Richmond between the same dates. Very popular was *The Indian Princess: or the first settlement of Virginia* (advertised in the Virginia *Argus* December 15, 1809). Many of the British pieces were produced within a few months of their London premières, indicative that the cultural lag hardly existed in the theater.

The student of American literature will see names of authors and titles of plays in Martin S. Shockley's study[98] of the Richmond theater which will remind him at once of the contents and even titles of Poe's early tales. Actually in the recorded productions of this theater is fresh material for a fresh approach to Poe's satiric intent in his fiction. In later years we know Poe was a regular attendant at the theater.[99] He must have formed the habit in Richmond.

Theatrical productions were given in Norfolk before the Revolution, but the first regular theater was a converted wooden warehouse on Main Street in 1793. Two years later a brick theater, presumably West's, was erected in Fenchurch Street. It was here that Booth appeared soon after his Richmond debut, in the year he arrived from England via Madeira. In his famous role as Richard III he delighted audiences several times. Here too Mrs. Poe appeared with Green's company in 1805 and with Placide's in 1811, in the latter instance just after the theater was sold at public auction. But the city gradually lost interest in the drama, or there was a series of bad managers, for the theater was sold in 1833 to the Methodists as a meeting house, and for some years there were no professional performances.[100]

Petersburg had the Old Street Theatre by 1773, for in that year the Methodists held a revival in a building with this name. The second building, the Back Street Theatre, was constructed at the cost of a thousand pounds by Thomas Wade West. This was burned in the great fire of 1815. And the third house, the Bollingbrook Street Theatre, was erected by subscription in 1818, probably in the same manner as the Richmond theater of 1818-19, under the sponsorship of James H. Caldwell, the English light comedian and manager. Said to have cost $20,000, it cleared half that amount in its first four months. Among the actors in the second building were the first great American tragedian, Thomas Abthorpe Cooper, the Wests, Warrells, Placides, Sullys, and Poes. In the Caldwell theater appeared Edwin Forrest, the Jeffersons, Booth and Tyrone Power.[101]

Several of the more interesting performances were given by amateurs. The Thespian Society was organized in 1806 by "a small number of our patriotic and enlightened citizens, who . . . seize every moment of leisure; resort to the drama, and exhibit in the public theatre—for what? not for their personal amusement or fame, but for the benefit of a public seminary" [actually for an orphanage and the Petersburg Academy]. Several plays were written especially for this group.

The Fredericksburg newspapers after 1789 carry frequent theatrical news and advertising, including information concerning the performances and actors in Richmond and Alexandria.[102] On October 22, 1789, *The Suspicious Husband* was advertised for local performance, and similar notices appear through the years of various plays identical with or at least much like those performed in neighboring cities. Wade's Alexandria theater seems to have been moderately successful. British diplomat Augustus John Foster, ordinarily supercilious concerning American art of all kinds, attended a performance in Alexandria in late summer 1807 and spoke of the "small but tolerably good theatre" in which the elder Joseph Jefferson, Mrs. Woodham, and Mrs. Melmoth had the leading roles in *The School for Friends*.[103] All three of them had already attracted favorable notice in northern cities.

All the theatrical activity was not confined to these larger towns. Amateurs and sometimes professionals produced plays even in the country. Some time before 1798 William Munford wrote a "Prologue to the Play of the Beaux Strategm, Spoken at a Theatre in Mecklenburg County, where a company of Gentlemen acted for the amusement of the public."[104] In February, 1796, Martha Bland Blodgett recorded in her diary that "a play [was] performed at City-Point; they did me the honor to send me a bill."[105] This City-Point production was probably by a professional company on its way to or from Petersburg.

Plays by at least a dozen Virginians of the period are known, some only by record of name and performance, but most of them in manuscript or printed text. Even during the Revolutionary period the country gentleman Colonel Robert Munford had written (and probably produced) two quite significant plays, *The Candidates* and *The Patriots,* concerned with contemporary politics, depicting indigenous American characters, and employing Virginia dialects or speech patterns.[106]

St. George Tucker in Williamsburg was probably writing plays almost as early, though his earliest surviving dramatic pieces date from about 1789. His papers include "Up and Ride, or the Borough of Brooklyne. A Farce. As acted in the Theatre of the United States. By the American Company of Comedians" (first version about 1789); "The Profligate: a Dramatic [ode?]; inspired by a rereading of *Gil Blas*"; "The Wheel of Fortune: a Comedy" (*ca.* 1796/97), set in Philadelphia and concerned with contemporary land problems, and including a number of songs of the author's own composition; "The Times: or the Patriot rous'd, a musical drama" (dated December 15, 1811), with nine of the author's patriotic poems inserted to be sung; and "The Patriot Cool'd" (after 1815?), performed at Tucker's own house.[107]

Tucker was at least willing to have his plays produced. A letter from John Page of March 30, 1797, regrets the writer's inability to carry Tucker's play to Philadelphia for reading, presumably by producers there.[108] This was probably "The Wheel of Fortune." On August 23, 1811, Tucker wrote Wirt of "The Times," intimating that he would be glad to present it to the Richmond theatrical company if they would produce it, keep his name secret, and donate one-tenth of the profits to the families of impressed seamen. It was deliberately a propaganda play "to rouse the public sentiment to support such measures as our national government might be of the opinion the Crisis should demand."[109]

Although Tucker's poems have been recently studied, only "The Wheel of Fortune" among his plays has been edited, and even it remains unpublished.[110] Most of Tucker's dramatic writing shows the satirical-propagandistic tendency suggested by his titles and is kin in spirit to his Probationary Odes to be discussed in another chapter. Tucker was an ardent Jeffersonian Republican. Most of his characters seem dramatic stereotypes or merely mouthpieces for political ideas. In a letter of June 3, 1789, probably to his brother Thomas Tudor Tucker, he referred to "Up and Ride" as a political farce, "the object of which is to ridicule the frivolity of the proceedings of the Senate, & to expose in its proper colours the Character of *their* President [John Adams], whom I consider the high priest of monarchy."[111] George Wheatsheaf, mayor of "Brooklyne," is of course George Washington, and Jonathan Goosequill is John Adams.

Some of Tucker's characters, especially the females, one feels who has gone through his papers, were partly modeled on women he knew. Yet they are not sufficiently individualized. Colonel Trueman or Truman of "The Times" is a fairly good depiction of a Virginia gentleman, whatever his affiliations within the play may be. Tucker had a good ear for the American vernacular, if not dialect, and he has several characters speak a blunt, ungrammatical English. The plays remain interesting primarily because of their themes and the detailed commentary on contemporary problems. One suspects that they were too controversial, too full of polemics for theater managers who had to please both Federalists and Republicans.

A more successful playwright than Tucker was Irish-born John Daly Burk (1770-1808), who had settled in Petersburg soon after 1798. He had come to Boston in 1796, conducted a newspaper, and by 1797 had written *Bunker Hill, or the Death of General Warren* (New York, 1797), one of the earliest plays to contain an American battle scene. It was produced in Boston on February 17, 1797, and made an enemy of John Adams, who disliked its strongly republican sentiments. The Boston engagement earned $2,000 for Burk and the play remained popular, especially for patriotic occasions, for fifty years, for all its inflated rhetoric and bombastic blank verse.[112] In 1798 his *Female Patriotism, or the Death of Joan of Arc* (New York, 1798) was presented at the Park Theatre in New York. Arthur Hobson Quinn calls it one of the best of the early American plays, with a credible heroine.[113]

In Petersburg, Burk gave up journalism for the law, delivered orations, captained a company of militia and assumed leadership among the Jeffersonian Republicans. In September, 1802, his play *Oberon, or the Siege of Mexico* was performed in the city. It was a historical drama in four acts, with songs and choruses. For the Thespian Club already mentioned he wrote *Bethlem Gabor, Lord of Transylvania, or the Man-hating Palatine* and played the title role himself. The published form of the play (Richmond, 1807) shows it was presented by a Richmond company, West's, for the title role was played by Green and Cornelia, the wife, by Mrs. West. Of course even then it may have been produced in Petersburg rather than the capital city.[114] Though Burk's earlier plays are in blank verse, this one is in prose, three acts, with something of a Wandering Jew motif and a great deal of Gothic claptrap.

From *Bunker-Hill* through *Bethlem Gabor* Burk wrote as a liberal republican, championing nationalism in *Joan of Arc,* liberty and the blessings of enlightenment in *Bunker-Hill,* and even in the melodramatic *Bethlem Gabor,* humanity and freedom. In the last the optimism of the earliest plays is gone, and he pleads for justice for humanity against the evils of war and the ambition of princes. The disillusion of the Napoleonic age had replaced the glow of confidence of the earlier age.[115]

Although William Dunlap assigns eight plays to Burk, two or three of them today usually are not believed to be his. But his *Innkeeper of Abbeville* was performed in Philadelphia as late as 1840, and his *Oberon: or the Siege of Mexico* was played in Norfolk in 1803. A most prolific and patriotic writer, he managed to finish three volumes of his *History of Virginia* (1804-5) and a number of lesser non-dramatic things before he was killed in a duel in 1808.

Tucker's friend William Wirt, a devotee of the theater, tried his hand at a play between 1813 and 1816. It was called "The Path of Pleasure," and Wirt says that he had actually begun it before December, 1811, for he had intended that the actor Green's daughter who perished in the fire should have the leading role.[116] Tucker, Dabney Carr, Francis Gilmer, and a few other friends read it, and Tucker wrote a prologue and epilogue for it. Wirt asked his friend the tragedian Cooper to criticize it. Though Cooper's verdict is not recorded, Wirt himself apparently decided that its production or publication would do his literary reputation more harm than good. The manuscript has disappeared from view, but Wirt's biographer Kennedy had seen it and agreed that the author's decision was wise.

William Munford, translator of Homer and Richmond attorney and court reporter, included a blank verse play in his 1798 *Poems and Compositions in Prose on Several Occasions.* It was entitled "Almoran and Hamet, a Tragedy founded on an Eastern Tale of that Name." Its chief subjects, the author informs the reader, were Morality and

Religion and the evils of arbitrary power. In five acts, it is full of crude Shakespearan echoes but in the end is no better or worse than other verse melodrama of the time.

There were several Virginians, besides Burk, who wrote plays which were produced on the stage. David Darling's *Beaux Without Belles, or Ladies We Can Do Without You, A Musical Farce* was published in Charlottesville in 1820. It had been produced at the Fredericksburg theater and was pronounced a very amusing piece. The characters are all men, though two are at times disguised as women.[117] In Act One very pronounced abolitionist sentiments are expressed. Everard Hall's *Nolens Volens, or the Biter Bit* is claimed by the author to have been the first play published in North Carolina (Newbern, 1809). Hall, son of a Blandford physician, wrote the play for the same Petersburg Thespians for whom Burk had written. It is a fairly effective comedy with a father and son motif.[118]

In the Richmond theater between 1819 and 1830 a number of plays by local authors were staged.[119] Albert M. Gilliam's "Virginia, or Love and Bravery," acted May 27 and June 6, 1829, seems to have been the second American play on the Pocahontas theme. Gilliam himself, co-editor of the short-lived *Virginia Souvenir and Ladies Literary Gazette,* played Nantaquas in both performances. Gilliam's editorial colleague, Bedford county native and lawyer Stephen T. Mitchell, had two of his plays produced and another published in Richmond before his early death in 1831. "The Maid of Missolonghi, a Tragedy," a Byronic affair, was acted to great applause on January 17, 1828, and repeated twice to overflowering audiences. Two months later it was given at the Bowery Theatre in New York. "The Heroine of the Highlands," a melodrama owing something to Scott, was acted first on November 12, 1828, and repeated four times within the month. Mitchell's *The Spirit of the Old Dominion* (Shepherd and Pollard) had been published in the city in 1827. First Farrel, a comedian, and then "Glascott" capitalized on Virginia interest in the novel by James Ewell Heath to adapt it for the stage as "Edge-Hill, or the Family of the Fitzroyals, a Melodrama." It was acted in Farrel's version June 2, and 10, 1829, and in Glascott's twice in 1831. The "republican sentiments" of the play, certainly taken from the novel, were highly applauded in the *Compiler* of February 25, 1831.

By far the most popular play by a local author was the adaptation from the French, *Nature and Philosophy*, "By a Citizen of Richmond," published in the city in 1821 and later in several editions in New York from 1830 to 1880.[120] Adapted from a comic opera by Auguste Duport of Paris, this one-act interlude has in recent years been assigned to Gustavus Adolphus Myers (1801-69), witty and charming lawyer who married the daughter of William B. Giles.[121] It was produced at the Park, Bowery, and Chatham theaters in New York and had a great run. Its sentimentality, lyrics, governess and poor-young heroine theme exactly suited the taste of the age. To the same author is assigned "Felix, a Drama in Three Acts," played only once, on July 24, 1822, when *Nature and Philosophy* was included in the same program.

The Episcopal pioneer clergyman Joseph Doddridge (1769-1826), best known for his historical work, *Notes on the Settlement and Indian Wars of the Western Parte of Virginia and Pennsylvania, from 1763 to 1783 Inclusive* (Wellsburgh, Va., 1824), presented the Indian chief as a noble red man in his one play, *Logan, the Last of the Race of Shikellemus* (Buffaloe Creek, Brooke County, Va., 1823). In the preface Doddridge states that he was gathering materials for his History when he came upon this story. Jefferson had already made Logan famous in his *Notes*, and a controversy had raged ever since they appeared as to the accuracy of Jefferson's account. Doddridge is definitely on the Jefferson side as far as sympathy for his subject is concerned. It is a four-act play, beginning with a discussion among a group of soldiers of the eternal frontier question, whether or not the Indians should be exterminated, and ending with the speech, "Who is there to mourn for Logan? Not one." The play is interesting as an early dramatic introduction of the boasting cockaroo of a backwoodsman, the half-horse, half-alligator tradition. It brought Doddridge considerable notice, though its primary importance is historical

George Washington Parke Custis (1781-1857), already mentioned in connection with agriculture, architecture, and music, is of considerable significance for his emphasis on nationalism in the plays he presented before the American public. His playwriting career began toward the end of our era, for his first, *The Indian Prophecy* (Georgetown, 1828), was produced as a new play at the Chestnut Street Theater in Philadelphia on July 3, 1827. Already a well-known writer, he, with others, was encouraged by the actors Edwin Forrest and James H. Hackett to cooperate in creating a genuinely American drama.

The Indian Prophecy was based on a little-known incident in his step-grandfather George Washington's career, and in it Custis took the opportunity to plead for and at the same time to prophesy a closer American union. "The Pawnee Chief," another Indian play, survives only by title. But in *Pocahontas,* (Philadelphia, 1830) he produced his best known work, combining nationalism, love of England and America, and sympathy for the plight of the red man.[122] It was performed for years thereafter in every city along the coast. Ignoring the anticlimaxes of one earlier play and several novels on the subject, he made his own climax the saving of Captain Smith by the Indian maiden, even though she and Rolfe were already in love. The minor character Barclay, a survivor of a previous English settlement with an Indian wife, is a curious and realistic bit of detail. The Indian chief opposed to the English, Matacoran, is also well drawn. The prose of the play is flowery but certainly no more so than the orations Custis and his contemporaries rendered in Washington. It remains one of the best of the forty Indian plays presented between 1830 and 1850.

Though Custis wrote many more plays, two others of interest fall within our period. The first was "The Rail Road" (apparently never printed), presented at the Walnut Street Theatre in Philadelphia on May 15, 1829, not long before his *Pocahontas.* The newspaper accounts describe a real locomotive introduced in the last act which moved off the stage to the music of the "Carrolton March" composed for the occasion! The rollicking song "The Steam Coach" also made a hit and was quoted in full in the papers. The second play, "The Eighth of January," was produced in New York in 1829 and in Washington, D.C., on March 15, 1830.[123] Concerned with Andrew Jackson and the Battle of New Orleans, it breathed nationalistic sentiment and patriotism—or so one gathers from the newspaper advertisements. It was popular enough to be performed several times during the decade.

Because of other responsibilities and the feeling that his peers frowned on the writing of plays as a gentleman's occupation or even as a literary attainment, Custis' dramatic output declined.[124] He did write several more pieces between 1830 and 1836, all but one strongly nationalistic in character but possessing little theatrical or artistic merit. The elaborate presentation of *Pocahontas* at the new National Theatre in Washington to the accompaniment of great applause and favorable newspaper notices, was probably the climax of his career as dramatist. Times were changing, and Southern romanticism was displacing the strong intellectual ferment of the Jeffersonians. Custis had expressed the pride in the youthful country of those who had made it.

Where the theater exists, criticism usually flourishes. In Richmond alone there were probably a hundred individuals who expressed in print their opinion of the local dramatic performances in the latter part of the period. In the *Compiler,* the *Mercantile Advertiser,* the Virginia *Argus,* the *Enquirer,* and other papers, and occasionally in collected essays they discussed the structure, theme, and characterization of individual plays, the merits of the actors, and the function of the theater in society. The American critic of this period thought of himself as the watchdog of society,[125] and the Virginia theatrical critic was not unusual. Frequent is the cry that the drama, or specific dramas, need to be purified.

These moral critics sometimes defended the theater as an institution "calculated to improve the mind, refine the manners and form the public taste" (*Compiler,* June 3, 1829). Here they were following the declarations of the Scottish critical philosophers on which they had been bred. *The Gamester,* for example, was a very moral play. *The School for Scandal* because it satirized scandal-mongering was morally instructive.[126]

Some critics discussed the theater's music, its scenery, its lighting effects. More often the actors were analyzed. A great future was predicted for Edwin Forrest in the *Compiler* of December 1, 1824. William Wirt (one of the very few definitely identified as a critic) gave an appreciative essay on Thomas A. Cooper in *Macbeth* in the *Old Bachelor* No. 31 and republished in the *Compiler.*[127] "Virginiensis" in the *Mercantile Advertiser* of July 9, 1821, gave the first American criticism of Junius Brutus Booth three days after that actor's American debut. It was a long disquisition on the relation of the American to the British stage, an analysis of Booth's acting, and a prediction of his great success.

These critics felt that only the actor who "represents Nature" can be great (*Compiler,* April 6, 1838). Some concerned themselves with analysis of the plays themselves, especially Shakespeare's. But it is difficult to find any even fairly rigid critical principles or standards. Two principles mentioned, the necessity of the actor's remaining true to nature and the theater itself as a moral influence on society, seem to underlie most discussions. The criticism is usually superficial and rarely more than mediocre, but it does show liveliness and familiarity with its subject and reflects Virginia society's involved interest in this one of the arts.

One of the fine arts, sculpture, has been touched upon only incidentally in this chapter, and landscape gardening and literature or belles-lettres not at all. The last is reserved for subsequent chapters. Much as sculpture touched Jefferson personally—it probably meant more to him than painting ever did—there is little indication of more than general interest in the subject among his contemporaries. In the generation after his death Virginians corporately and individually were responsible for commissioning major historical monuments and statuary, especially among Americans working in Italy.

Landscape gardening has not been considered at length because for this period relatively little material has been discovered. Through the active research groups now at Williamsburg, colonial gardens are being studied, and Edwin M. Betts in *Thomas Jefferson's Garden Book* (Philadelphia, 1944) and Fiske Kimball in various places did much to clarify Jefferson's interests and procedures in this art which gave him so much pleasure. But what Cocke, Madison, Cabell, Page, and a dozen or two others accomplished in this direction is largely to be guessed at from the remains of the grounds of their mansions once so lovingly laid out, a few references in their letters, and notations in their agricultural daybooks. Perhaps the most natural interest among all the fine arts to the gentleman farmer, its place in Jefferson's Virginia remains to be determined.

VIII

LITERATURE, PRINCIPALLY BELLETRISTIC

The study of Belles-Lettres, has not yet become a profession *in America; or if it has, it is only to a very* few, *not more distinguish'd in respect to Genius, than the great majority of those who for Centuries have filled the* Fellowships *of Oxford, & Cambridge, without producing one specimen of Genius, or Learning. Authorship is a trade . . . more or less, in every part of Europe. Considering how very few literary productions in this Country have appear'd in print, I think it no vain boast to say, that Britain has no right to reproach us with degeneracy, in respect to literature. Whatever faults a fastidious, or even a candid critic, must find in [what has been published] they must . . . be considered . . . as affording grounds for a happy presage of what future times may produce in America, where Genius shall have more opportunities for Exertion, and Taste, to improve itself.*

—St. George Tucker, "For the Old Batchellor," an unpublished manuscript essay signed "Candidus" (Archives Colonial Williamsburg).

The national and regional literary histories have very little to say about belletristic and other polite forms composed in Virginia between 1790 and 1830. Yet scores wrote in verse and published in newspapers and magazines, and some twenty-six persons produced thirty-six volumes of poetry, ranging in length and form from the sonnet or epigram to the epic. There were two important histories of the state, several of particular phases of the Revolution, the War of 1812, and border conflict, and one history of the world written and published within these years, as well as significant bio-historical works like Marshall's *Washington,* Wirt's *Henry,* or Weems' *Marion, Franklin, Penn,* and *Washington.* There were hundreds of newspaper essays—moral, aesthetic, and generally philosophical—and nine essay collections in book form, some of which ran through many editions. And seven or eight Virginia novelists wrote some ten works of fiction, at least five of them depicting the Virginia scene.

James K. Paulding in 1816 saw in Virginia writers an independence of literary fashions absent elsewhere in America.[1] Others have noted that neoclassicism appeared to linger longer in the South, including Virginia, than in the North, which may be what Paulding was saying in another way. Actually, Virginia writing in theory and practice ranges all the way from the pronounced neoclassicism of the early St. George Tucker to the new romanticism of Poe's *Al Aaraaf,* with a great many shades and variations between, including the moral aestheticism of Hartley and the Scottish metaphysicians and its concomitants and derivatives. In other words, their literary fashions were much the same as those of the rest of America. Virginians contributed to and, as we have already seen, read the same periodicals and popular fiction. If amidst the belletristic there is a stronger element of the utilitarian—economic and political—than perhaps in New England at the same time, it is primarily a matter of degree rather than of kind.

Poetry and fiction, as well as the critical essay and historical writing in Virginia, were largely in the hands of the professional classes. Lawyers, legislators, journalists, physicians, clergymen, and teachers, as in the rest of America, wrote in their spare time lyrics, tales, novels, and essays. In Virginia these men were joined in their endeavors by certain country gentlemen. And in Virginia it is perhaps significant that these writers from the professional classes were men with country backgrounds who thought in agrarian or rural terms—in motifs and sometimes in imagery. In writing as in other forms of the arts, the dominant classes in this period displayed an interest never before or perhaps afterwards equaled in our history.

Theory derived from their reading at home and at school determined their creation and their criticism. The earliest critics, it is true, relied more on their innate taste and experience than on the principles promulgated by the authorities. Jefferson and St. George Tucker, for example, were strikingly alike in their critical attitudes toward style. Tucker, when Wirt praised him as a critic, replied: "If the substance of what I read pleases me, I never stop to consider whether by an alteration of a sentence, or the substitution of one word for another, the Beauty of a passage might be improved. Though *Criticism* is defin'd by Critics (or by some of them) to be an humane Art, in my opinion it is altogether a captious one, as it is generally exercis'd." Jefferson, also writing to Wirt, remarked, "I have always very much dispised [*sic*] the artificial canons of criticism. When I have read a work in prose or poetry, or seen a painting, a statue, etc., I have only asked myself whether it gives me pleasure, whether it is animating, interesting, attaching? If it is, it is good for these reasons."[2]

Despite these remarks, neither was a thoroughgoing impressionist, either in criticism or creation. Elsewhere Jefferson many times emphasized the utilitarian moral quality of good literature. Tucker in his satires, plays, shorter poems and equally in practice emphasizes the moral element. In prose style both owed a good deal to the neo-classical models of their time—Bolingbroke, Hume and, in Tucker's case at least, Addison.

Francis Gilmer, of a much younger generation, in comments to Dabney Carr concerning a recent essay, admitted that he had always in his style been "obliged to sacrifice something to propriety, to the prevailing taste of our country, and the age in which we live. When

I become more firmly fixed in the stirrups, I shall ride my own gait." Addison, Burke, Caesar, Sallust, particularly Samuel Johnson—mentioned in this order—all had major weaknesses as stylists. Rousseau was better. "But in Virginia we must come more home to the business of life. The region of sentiment is too ethereal, for men fed on bacon & greens, and who always look at the nearest, not at the most beautiful objects."[3] The orthodox neoclassicism, Rousseauistic sentimentalism, and Scottish realism which were all floating in the air of the time are evident in Gilmer's one paragraph.

Neoclassicism was strong all through the period. Tucker in practice displayed the quality of "sound judgment" and held the attitude that imagination was a lighter faculty compared with reason and judgment. Wirt continued to evidence the same qualities in the *British Spy* and *Rainbow* and even in the *Old Bachelor* essays, and they are praised, and often practiced, by Edgar Poe.[4] Wirt urged the younger men to develop a style utilitarian, masculine, and reasoned. As models he offered Hamilton and Marshall.[5] George Tucker continued Goldsmithian and Swiftian satire in his Hickory Cornhill poem and in his *Voyage to the Moon* (1827). Nationalism for Wirt was a rational and neoclassical quality, not a romantic one, and in this he is followed by many others. Verse forms are as often Popean as Miltonic, though perhaps more frequently reminiscent of the Graveyard School and other pre-romantics than of either.

But in the first thirty years of the nineteenth century the writers of Jeffersonian Virginia were as much influenced as other Americans by the Scottish school of rhetoricians, aestheticians, and common sense philosophers. As we have observed in earlier chapters, by 1800 Blair's *Lectures on Rhetoric,* Lord Kames' *Elements of Criticism,* and Reid's works were widely used in schools and especially in colleges, along with Hartley, Adam Smith, and Hume. A little later Dugald Stewart's and Archibald Alison's philosophical writings were generally read.

Samuel Miller in his *Brief Retrospect of the Eighteenth Century* (1803)[6] defined common sense philosophy as a revolt from the sceptical conclusions which Berkeley and Hume had drawn from the old theory of perception as it had been taught from classical times to the mid-eighteenth century. Thomas Reid, the first of the new school, rejected the ideal system, or theory of perception, and maintained that the mind perceives not only the ideas or images of external objects but the objects themselves. These produce impressions, the impressions in turn sensations. The process is incomprehensible, but by the direct and necessary connection between the presence of such objects and our consequent perceptions we become persuaded that they exist. In other words, the appeal was to the common sense of mankind.

By no means all the Scots held precisely the same positions. But the divergences are minor, in the case of Alison, for example, being largely developments from the original positions. The common sense philosophy, introduced in America originally largely through John Witherspoon at Princeton, was a safe, conservative realism which left very little to the imagination. It made "rationalism, freedom, and individualism safe, even conservative," says Roy Harvey Pearce, and the Scots "had succeeded in making common sense out of Locke, revolution, Christianity and progress."[7] Originally, through its appeal to reason and the moral sense it was a means of freeing the American mind from dogmatism and of preparing it to receive the new science, but in the hands of Presbyterians it became for some a mere "moral sedative" used as an antidote to the powerful stimulants of the experimental sciences. In either case, it helped to make clear the need for social order in America.

Scottish realism had influenced Virginia founding fathers who were not Presbyterians.[8] All his mature life Jefferson held a high opinion of Lord Kames, pointing out to his young friends in his old age his agreement with Kames on the development of the moral sense from the "internal sense of right & wrong." He also pointed out to these young men how Kames was indebted to Locke for certain parts of his natural rights theory. But for Jefferson in his developing concepts of democracy Kames had always remained a guide. Even in his attitudes toward the Indian, one sees the effect of his study of Kames' *Principles of Morality and Natural Religion* (1751). Incidentally, Kames may be seen to some degree in the work of poets and other prose writers who discuss the red man. Jefferson also respected most highly Dugald Stewart's writings, kept up a lifelong personal correspondence with him, and asked his aid when he was seeking British professors for the University of Virginia.

As we shall see, George Tucker, William Wirt, and Richard Dabney are among the Virginia writers greatly indebted to one or another of the Scots. The critical principles held most commonly by the American writers of the period, springing primarily from this philosophy and its reconciliations of earlier concepts with common sense realism, were certainly shared by the majority of Virginia authors. Implicit or explicit in the work of the Virginia belletrist and historian alike is the idea that the writer is responsible for public morals, that he is the watchdog or the responsible representative of society.[9] Also that literature should not contain anything derogatory to religious ideals or morals, that it should be optimistic, that it should deal only with the intelligible, and that it should be social rather than individual in point of view. Another principle, that literature should not condone rebellion of any kind against the existing social order, widely evidenced in the largely Federalist magazines and critics of the rest of America, is by no means always evident in Virginia writing, simply because so many of the authors were liberals, extreme liberals like St. George Tucker and Jefferson and John D. Burk, or moderates like Francis Gilmer, the earlier George Tucker, and William Munford. But there were Virginia Federalists like Marshall and Henry Lee who were in full agreement with this principle, though at the same time they virulently attacked the Jeffersonian administrations in verse and the essay.

The empirical method, the appeal to common sense rather than to subtlety, the assumption of the existence of a benevolent God and benevolent principles in human nature, and the support of religious faith through confidence in intuitive convictions, were certainly natural and appealing to many early nineteenth-century Americans. In the aesthetic principles derived from the same Scottish philosophers, neither the philosophers themselves nor the American writers were always in agreement. Kames' idea that emotions of beauty always suggest sweetness and gaity and that grandeur and sublimity must produce agreeable emotions did not exactly fit what the Americans read in Edmund Burke, and more often than not they agreed with the Irishman rather than the Scot. Then the followers of Alison and the later "associational" system did not agree with the earlier Kames, who believed that beauty was absolute and intrinsic.

The romanticism of Byron and Walter Scott, in some of its aspects evolved from the Scottish realists but partaking of a good deal more, was also evident in Virginia by 1810 and grew stronger during the next two decades. The use of the past in themes and settings, the emotional noble savage and patriotic themes, the oriental, Gothic or sentimental materials in character and plot, the considerable diversity in verse forms, including a frequent use of the Byronic anapaestic tetrameter, are qualities which may be found in the work of many writers who are in some ways, at the same or at other times, strongly rational, disciplined, and social. Edgar Poe is the best known case of a reconciliation, or at least coexistence in one creative mind, of these allegedly conflicting elements.

Blair's *Lectures on Rhetoric and Belles-Lettres,* however, remained throughout the period the single great direct influence on literature. An elementary, down-to-earth textbook, on its bad side it encouraged artificial, impersonal, and unidiomatic precision in expression, encouraged Latinity of diction, and neglected emotion and sensibility. For the book is in general a summary of late neoclassical thinking by a long-time colleague of the common sense philosophers.[10] Blair's special interest was in the sublime, concerning which he agreed with Burke that it obtained its best effects from obscurity but disagreed in that he thought sublimity "a quality of things rather than an expression." In some respects Blair's principles are admirable and may be discerned in every textbook of composition and rhetoric since written. But his insistence that long words are more musical than short ones may have been, as Charvat points out, partially responsible for the continued Latinity of English style.

It may have been partially this Latinity which impelled both John Randolph and Francis Gilmer to urge that Blair be banished from the schools. In Randolph's case one suspects too that the Virginian was so partial to Burke that he could not forgive Blair's divergences.

Blair's constant conscious comparison of ancient and modern writing, especially in history, and his classifications of poetry, appear to be reflected scores of times by Virginia writers in familiar letters, formal essays, or organization to their own verse when published in book form. Blair preferred the style of Addison to that of Johnson, and in his analysis of the two gave Virginia essayists, especially William Wirt, their reasons for imitating the *Spectator* rather than the *Rambler.* Wirt, who again and again refers to Blair as authority, is indeed sometimes given credit for introducing through his *Letters of the British Spy* the new vogue of the Addisonian essay followed by such writers as Irving and the young Hawthorne.

In Virginia the close affiliation of politics, oratory, and the newspaper essay gave a rhetorician like Blair an especially strong appeal. Explicit in the Scottish textbook is the belief that literature and eloquence not only spring from the same origins but are in fact substantially the same art. Some of that fine hortatory-conversational quality usually associated with the Emersonian essay one meets frequently in Virginia prose of the period. Again Blair may be partially responsible for the wide variety of subjects for the Virginia essay, ranging from the almost formal aesthetic to the political, economic, and scientific, all of them often appearing in the same volume.

Finally, one should never forget that John Locke's philosophical ideas continued to be reflected in the literature of the period.[11] Though they are most strongly evident in political and economic theory, they are also present in Fourth of July speeches, academic addresses, familiar essays, even in verse. Locke is everywhere in Jefferson from the Declaration to the remarks to William C. Rives in his retirement.[12] Wirt reread the *Essay on the Human Understanding* many times, and always included it among the treatises in any list of reading he suggested to young men. George Tucker discussed the *Essay's* idea and analyzed its style for his students at the University of Virginia.[13] And at the end of the period, Poe was quoting Locke on the nature of personal identity as *raison d'être* for his series of tales concerned with the problem. "Morella," "The Fall of the House of Usher," "Ligeia," and "William Wilson" are in some sense but Gothicized versions of this one idea from the great philosopher.

The writer of belles-lettres in Virginia was sometimes a little ashamed that he devoted his time to such trifles, especially if he were a well-known public man or ever hoped to become one. Wirt had many heart searchings as to whether a lawyer who wished to be taken seriously by his colleagues and potential clientele should devote himself to essay writing or biography, and one reason for his not producing or publishing his play was his fear of the effect his interest in such a form might have on his professional reputation. George Tucker's reputation as a serious professor was actually hurt by the public's knowledge that he wrote fiction.[14] For these reasons and the older kindred one that the gentleman as writer always remain amateur and anonymous, almost all the essays, novels, and poems published as separate volumes or in newspapers or magazines appeared over or under pseudonyms, somewhat misleading initials such as "Z" (a favorite of George Tucker's), or without any indication at all of authorship. It should of course be remembered that political and other kinds of controversial essays were also published pseudonymously for somewhat different reasons. At least one fairly significant novel and one volume of verse, besides scores of poems and essays, remain to this day unidentified as to authorship. With serious history and biography appropriate activities for the men of affairs, the Virginia writers were less reluctant to identify themselves.

A. *Periodicals*

One reason, though probably rarely a major one, why so many Virginia poems and essays remained in manuscript was the difficulty of finding sufficiently dignified media of publication. The newspaper columns seem to have been open to almost any kind of short poem or essay, provided it did not offend the political principles of the editor. Though many fairly good original things appeared in the columns of such journals as the *Virginia Gazette,* the *Argus,* and the *Enquirer,* especially in the form of the familiar essay, many poets and fiction writers preferred some medium which had a literary reputation, or chose separate publication. If the prose or verse was too long for a magazine, it might be published at the author's personal expense or by subscription. Both methods were used in Virginia, and some interesting printed lists of subscribers' names are appended to certain volumes. Though very rarely did the publisher take the risk himself, occasionally he would print on his own the novel or historical work he felt sure would sell.

To the national periodicals of the time outside the state Virginians contributed fairly regularly, though infrequently to magazines published north of Philadelphia. At the beginning of our period, in 1790, several Virginia poets and a few prose writers were publishing in the most significant magazine in the nation, Mathew Carey's *American Museum* (1787-92). St. George Tucker, W[illiam?] Preston, Robert Bolling, and probably Margaret Lowther Page (wife of John) were among the contributors of anonymous or pseudonymous verse, and there were several essays, some of the scientific pieces having been mentioned in an earlier chapter. To the strongly Federalist *Port Folio* (1801-27) like the *American Museum* published in Philadelphia, citizens of the state were fairly regular contributors. "Arnold of Virginia," Dr. Nathaniel Chapman, and Dr. John Dunn of Norfolk, for example, in 1802 contributed verse. Dr. Chapman supplied a number of prose pieces between 1801 and 1809, Ogilvie an essay in 1813, and George Tucker a series entitled "Thoughts of a Hermit" in ten issues of 1814-15, pieces later collected in the 1822 edition of his essays.[15] In the Baltimore *Niles' Weekly Register's* poetry supplement for 1815 are a number of verses by Virginians, including John M'Creery of Petersburg. Samuel Janney's poem "The Country School House" won the *New York Mirror's* prize contest in 1824 and was published in 1825, and Mrs. Page's early elegy on the death of Hallyburton appeared in the *New-York Magazine, or Literary Repository* in 1790.[16]

Despite the state's tiny urban population, a number of attempts were made in the early nineteenth century to establish a literary periodical. James Lyon's *National Magazine; or, A Political, Historical, and Literary Repository* was issued in Richmond twice a quarter through 1799 and part of 1800. It printed government acts and other documents such as the United States Constitution. The nearest things to literary materials are the *Addresses* by John Page of Rosewell and John Thomson's "Character" of Albert Gallatin. It was followed in 1803 or 1805 by Louis Hue Girardin's *Amœnitates Graphicæ*, an ambitious undertaking appearing in just one quite interesting issue.[17] Its subtitle was "or instructing and amusing collection [*sic*] of Views, Animals, Plants, Flowers, Minerals, Antiquities, Customs, and other interesting objects. Selected and engraved from drawings after nature, with descriptive and explanatory sketches in English and French. The text, by L. H. Girardin, Professor of Modern Languages, History and Geography in William & Mary College. The engravings by Frederick Bosler." This number, containing six fine colored plates, was priced at two dollars (succeeding numbers at one dollar), perhaps too high for the public purse. Its pedagogical purpose made it a sort of early nineteenth-century *Book of Knowledge*.[18]

The American Gleaner; and Virginia Magazine was announced as having already published its first issue in the *Enquirer* of January 31, 1807.[19] It was to appear fortnightly, contain sixteen octavo pages, and sell for three dollars per annum. The first number contained the "Memoirs" of the late George Wythe, essays, and original and selected poetry. Each volume (of twenty-five numbers) was to be embellished by an engraved likeness of some distinguished American. The editors encouraged contributions from all over the state, reminding readers of the *Enquirer* that Virginia as "the Athens of America" must continue to merit that title, and that it was to be hoped that the *Gleaner* would do for Virginia what the *Mirror* had done for Scotland.

The surviving issues of the *American Gleane*r cover a period from January 24, 1807 (I, No. 1) to December 26 of the same year (I, No. 18). Its contents were a combination of excerpts from British books and periodicals and original pieces by Americans, most of them Virginians. Essays include discussions of manners, English poetry, atheism, Godwin's *Political Justice* (a defense), and in the last two issues excerpts from Irving and Paulding's *Salmagundi* published that year. Orations on patriotic or funeral occasions are by Skelton Jones, Thomas Marshall, and Armistead T. Mason, all of Virginia. The "Original Verse" page includes brief lyrics, sonnets, humorous pieces, elegies, patriotic odes (such as C. K. Blanchard's "Dythyrambic Ode" on Jamestown), and an epithalamium. A few are signed, as those by the Reverend J. Thornton of Fredericksburg and William Ray, but most bear pseudonyms or remain unsigned. "Ode to Melancholy, By a Carolinian" (p. 223) is more Miltonic than Keatsian in verse form and imagery. "Lapland Scene" (p. 191) is in couplets; and the versified "Letter from a Clergyman to a Young Lady," with an "Answer" in mere doggerel. We know from other sources that it was composed by the litterateur the Reverend John Buchanan and answered by his friend the Reverend John Blair.[20] Blanchard's Jamestown ode is probably the nearest thing to real poetry in the eighteen issues.

Perhaps because of lack of popular support, the printer-publisher Seaton Grantland apparently ceased publication at the end of the year. He soon moved to Georgia and made a name for himself in another field—as Congressman and Presidential Elector.[21]

On February 11, 1809, appeared the first number of *The Visitor,* to begin with a fortnightly magazine, printed and published by Lynch, an Irishman, and the musician Charles Southgate. It was a "brownish" quarto of eight pages, containing miscellaneous essays, the first installment of a Jane Porter-Walter Scott sort of novel, a humorous column, poetry, vital statistics, and in some issues both notes and words of music. It continued through August, 1810, the second volume appearing as a weekly of four pages.

Though contributions remain unsigned or bear pseudonyms, some owner of the Library of Congress copy has identified many of the authors, identifications corroborated in one example by a surviving manuscript of a published essay. "Senex" was the jovial Presbyterian clergyman John D. Blair, incorrigible rhymster and punster and defender of religious music. He contributed essays on practical joking, church music, and camp meetings (the manuscript is in the Huntington Library).[22] He also wrote as "Will Honeycomb" in good *Spectator* fashion. Poets include L. H. Girardin, whose Latin and English lines on dueling appearing through several issues were also published separately,[23] J[ames or Joseph?] Cabell, William Munford, James Heath, and even Southgate, who contributed a satire on Richmond musicians called "Ornithological Warfare." J. Bray "of the theatre," John Lataste, A. Peticolas, and Southgate himself supplied the notes or verses for the several musical pieces mentioned in the preceding chapter. Unidentified contributors with initials or pseudonyms include "S. G." [St. George Tucker?], "Carlo," and "Llabec."

The essays, including the several by Blair and R. S. Garrett's oration, are the best literary feature of the magazine. Stylistically they are sprightly and not overly ornate, and in context timely. Yet they do not measure up in quality to those written by the Wirt circle, who do not seem to have contributed. The verse includes the usual short elegies, love lyrics, a few sonnets, narratives, and nature lyrics on the seasons and snowstorms. "Henry Fitzowen, A Tale," with English setting and conventional plot, is characteristic of the prose fiction. The humorous anecdotes, though usually tame and trite, may be of some significance as indicative of American tastes of the period. Biographical sketches of Catherine the Great and the Princess Pocahontas are straightforward and unsentimental.

Rather unusual is the series of imaginative essays beginning in I, No. 6, entitled "Dreams." "Dream I. A Scene of Sorrow" is quite suggestive of Poe's "The Fall of the House of Usher" and of "The Haunted Palace," the poem embedded in the story. John Allan quite probably owned copies or a file of *The Visitor* which the boy Edgar may have read in the early 1820's, though there are other possible sources in similar essays to be found in the contemporary Scottish reviews.

The Visitor seems to have been almost entirely the work of a group permanently resident in Richmond. Its poetry, humor, and essays are about as good as one would find in the other periodicals of the time, except *The Monthly Anthology* and the *Port Folio.* Even the stiff and sentimental fiction is hardly worse than that in other journals. The failure of *The Visitor* to survive must be laid to the urban-rural imbalance in the Virginia of the period rather than to its inherent weaknesses.[24]

The religious journals which contained some literary material have been discussed in a previous chapter but perhaps should be mentioned again here in order to complete the picture. Archibald Alexander's *Virginia Religious Magazine* of 1804-7 published in Lexington was almost entirely religious, as was John Holt Rice's *The Family Visitor* of 1822 in Richmond. Rice's *Virginia Evangelical and Literary Magazine* (Richmond 1818-28) was, as we have seen, another matter. Its poetry was negligible, but the essays by Wirt, Rice, Speece, and probably Gilmer are significant in a number of ways and stylistically quite attractive. The efforts of the journal to interest Virginians in their own history was characteristic of its editor and his group of friends. "For God and Our Country," its motto, is quite indicative of its attitudes.

The last and best magazine from a purely literary point of view was the *Virginia Literary Museum and Journal of Belles Lettres, Arts, Sciences, &c.* founded by Robley Dunglison and George Tucker at the University of Virginia on June 17, 1829, and running through June 9, 1830. There were fifty-two weekly numbers, of sixteen pages each, in this one published volume. An editorial in the last issue states that it had been from the beginning a deliberate experiment and that it was being discontinued because contributors did not furnish enough material. Its pecuniary situation, curiously, appears to have been satisfactory, for the editors asserted that there would be no loss as soon as a few outstanding subscriptions were paid.[25]

The editors had intended a purely literary and scientific journal, but at the end of their year were convinced that to succeed in America a magazine must have the 'pungent seasoning of politics." The prospectus had promised that the *Museum* would begin publication when two hundred subscribers at $5.00 a year had been obtained, and presumably they obtained that number. The magazine contained Jeffersoniana, university news (its ostensible excuse for being), stories, reviews, studies, and poetry. Except for four or five short articles and the poetry, all the material was written by those "within the University," presumably faculty members. Professors Charles Bonnycastle and Robert Patterson contributed a few things. Dunglison, who edited every other issue, wrote many scientific, linguistic, historical, and other pieces. Tucker wrote on political and economic subjects, sometimes in fictional form, and several general tales. He also wrote aesthetic criticism. Many of his contributions suggest his earlier published novel but more of them seem derived from the materials of his classroom lectures.[26]

The *Virginia Literary Museum* contains some thirty-two pieces of verse, eighteen of them sonnets. All the sonnets and some of the other pieces were written by Dabney Carr Terrell, young Virginian of promise who had died of yellow fever in New Orleans in 1827.

No other Virginia magazine before the *Southern Literary Messenger* had editors or contributors of the ability of Tucker, Dunglison, and Terrell. The tales, including "A Country Belle," "Julia Moncrief," "The Gold Seeker," and "The Wilderness" are interesting for their Virginia locales. "The Maiden's Adventure" is an Indian-escape narrative based on an early James River incident. Pithy prefaces and Latin, Greek, and French quotations introduce all sorts of prose pieces. The faint smell of the academic lamp is on the whole attractive. But not until five years had passed, when a young alumnus of the University took his seat in a Richmond editorial chair, would there be a Virginia magazine of sufficient literary quality and variety to survive for a full generation.

B. *History, Biography, and Travel*

In this period John Marshall wrote biography as history, Wirt as romance, and Weems as myth, all three of them having taken Virginians as their subjects. John D. Burk wrote a history of Virginia partially to picture the triumph of democratic institutions, Henry Banks a history of contemporary France to prove Napoleon the man of the future, Nathaniel Claiborne a history of nineteenth-century "War in the South" partially to defend his brother the Louisiana governor, and the younger Henry Lee his *Campaign of 1781 in the Carolinas* to defend his father's military reputation. Residents of Virginia like John Davis described their experiences in their travels from Florida to Boston. Thomas Bolling Robertson devoted two books to his observations in Paris during Napoleon's last days. Anne Royall and Robert Bailey depicted the seamier side of American life in picaresque autobiographical travel sketches. And Joseph Doddridge and Charles Johnston told of Indian border warfare and captivity. And these were by no means all the historians.

Implicit or explicit in all these surveys is the cyclical theory of history and the belief that America was on the rising curve of a cycle. Implicit too is the belief that through the study of history would come a better understanding of the origins and even of the future of one's nation.[27] These writers were quite aware that at least in its segmented regions and periods the United States still remained a terra incognita. Biography, autobiography, and travel literatures are always tending to become history, and long before Carlyle writers like J. W. Campbell were implicitly interpreting Virginia history as the essence of innumerable biographies.

John Marshall's five-volume *Life of George Washington* (1804-7) is really a political history, and later Marshall recognized this fully by publishing the first volume as a separate work under the title *A History of the Colonies Planted by the English on the Continent of North America, from the Settlement, to the Commencement of That War Which Terminated in Their Independence* (1824). The fifth volume, which dealt with a period Marshall knew first hand, was strongly Federalist in its viewpoint and drew the fire of the Jeffersonian liberals. Madison once told Jared Sparks that while the first four volumes were acceptable, the fifth was inaccurate.[28] A staunch Federalist like Chancellor Kent naturally thought the fifth the best of all. Jefferson compared it unfavorably as far as sound research went with Wirt's *Patrick Henry,* and he infinitely preferred Burk's or Hening's historical interpretations of Virginia history to Marshall's.

Though Marshall had the sponsorship and advice of his subject's nephew Bushrod Washington, he depended entirely too much on secondary sources. Disproportionate in its presentation of events and qualities of character, it is also rather dull reading.[29] Yet it filled a distinct need and historians label it "a notable achievement," at least for the era in which it appeared.

Mason Locke Weems' imaginative brief lives of General Francis Marion, Benjamin Franklin, William Penn, and George Washington are in all respects except sympathetic treatment the antitheses of Marshall's biography.[30] Weems, who knew the tastes of his age as few men did, made each book a series of moral object lessons. *A History of the Life and Death, Virtues and Exploits of General George Washington* (1800), appearing in scores of editions with slightly varying titles throughout the nineteenth century, made its author famous and Washington the great figure of the American myth. Cherry trees and veracity, piety and patriotism, and dollars thrown across the Rappahannock were combined with a breezy, gossipy style in a book which has made an indelible impression on the American mind. A recent historian admits that all of modern scholarship has not been able to modify seriously the popular picture of our Revolutionary heroes created by Weems.[31]

Light-Horse Harry Lee (1756-1818) and his son Black-Horse Harry (1787-1837) had their part in bio-historical writing. Like Marshall, they were anti-Jeffersonian. The elder Lee's *Memoirs of the War in the Southern Department of the United States* (1809) is the major work of the Revolutionary cavalry officer, though his words as an orator have been longer remembered. Written in a clear, easy style, it contains neat biographical sketches of American officers and is documented frequently by letters. John Esten Cooke called it "an excellent military biography."[32] Certainly it is an important source book for any study of the period.

Perhaps more gifted as a writer was the son Major Henry Lee, whose personal reputation was ruined by a family scandal. John Quincy Adams, aware of Lee's bad "private morals" and unprincipled politics, admitted that he wrote "with great force and elegance," and added that Calhoun used him for political writing.[33] Later Lee went over to the Jacksonians. Believing that Jefferson had slighted his father's memory, he attacked the great man's character and veracity in

Observations on the Writings of Thomas Jefferson (1832). His *Campaign of 1781 in the Carolinas: with Remarks, Historical and Critical on Johnson's Life of Greene* (1824) is, as already noted, an earlier defense of his father's military reputation. Written in an easy style not unlike his father's, it contains an appendix of letters to bolster his claims. His other work of filial piety was a new corrected edition (1827) of his father's *Memoirs,* a book which includes many notes and additions by the editor. It is perhaps entirely in keeping with the character displayed in these works that later in France Major Lee came to admire Napoleon extravagantly. He completed and published the first volume of a projected biography of his idol before he died in 1837.

A third member of the family, Richard Henry Lee (1794-1865), representing liberal views unlike those of his cousins, wrote a biography of his grandfather of the same name, *Memoir of the Life of Richard Henry Lee, and His Correspondence with the Most Distinguished Men of Europe and America* (1825), a naturally useful but not entirely satisfactory monument of ancestor worship. The same man's *Life of Arthur Lee, LL.D.* (1829) is also eulogistic and inaccurate but useful. It should be observed that R. H. Lee's were no better and no worse than other biographies of Revolutionary heroes written in the period. Like Weems' work, they added more "evidence" to the myth of America's heroic struggle for independence.

In 1804, about a year after the appearance of his *Letters of the British Spy,* William Wirt informed his friend Dabney Carr that through reading Johnson's *Lives* of the poets and other famous men he had contracted an itch for biography: "do not be astonished, therefore, if you see me come out with a very *material* and splendid life of some departed Virginia worthy. . . . Virginia has lost some great men, whose names ought not to perish. If I were a Plutarch, I would collect their lives for the honour of the state and the advantage of posterity."[34] By 1805 he seems to have settled on Patrick Henry as his subject, for he then asked Judge St. George Tucker for detailed recollections of Henry's appearance, manner and actual speeches.[35] During the next twelve years, in what time he snatched from his legal duties and writing of essays for the *Rainbow* and *Old Bachelor* series, Wirt gathered his materials from those who had known the orator, including Jefferson, wrote draft after draft, and had various persons criticize individual portions of the work. When *Sketches of the Life and Character of Patrick Henry* appeared in 1817 it instantly attained a popular success that continued through half a century. The book was in its fifteenth edition in 1859. Reviews were generally favorable, including those in the *North American Review,* the *Analectic Magazine,* the *American Monthly Magazine,* and the *Virginia Evangelical and Literary Magazine.*[36] Even old John Adams, who argued with Wirt through a series of letters because of the priority given Virginia and Virginians in the Revolutionary causes and events, seemed to think it a major literary study. Yet both Wirt and his biographer Kennedy came to wish he had never written it, and from a critical point of view, in its effect on Wirt's ultimate literary reputation, most of us today would agree.

It has been observed that the *Sketches* is really a treatment of Henry's oratory and is not actually a biography and that it was a cooperative venture in which Wirt's friends had as much a part as he. Neither statement is quite accurate. Henry as orator is naturally the dominant theme, but the book is also a picture of a man in his time. The sketch of Richard Henry Lee, for example, in Chapter II, is a necessary part of the background for the backwoods orator and a significant historical criticism at the same time. As to cooperation, there was no more here than in many other and greater biographies. But John Taylor of Caroline put his finger on its weakness when he called it "a splendid novel." It was written in a sentimental tradition merging into the genuinely romantic and vitally affected by Wirt's congenital love for the fustian and flowery rhetoric he manifestly tried to overcome in his own speeches.

Though he meant it as a moral discourse and example for the young men of Virginia, his materials and treatment somehow did not fit. Conscientious as he was, and a great admirer of Jefferson, he was perhaps too much influenced by the latter's conception of Henry as a lazy backwoodsman possessed of one gift, oratory. Jefferson had presented his views in many letters to Wirt, for Jefferson was with Tucker foremost among those from whom the biographer solicited opinions and recollections of his subject. Through the book one may discern the constant struggle to be entirely accurate (as he felt the Jefferson view to be) and to present a model for future generations.

The "Give Me Liberty or Give me Death" speech has survived the rest of the book, though Wirt's summaries in indirect discourse of other speeches are also frequently alluded to. In recent years there has been considerable discussion among historians as to how much of the most famous speech is Henry's and how much Wirt's.[37] Wirt informed St. George Tucker that he had taken the speech almost entirely from the latter's remembrance of it, and that Tucker's account of its effect on delivery he had reproduced verbatim. Too often the whole condensed oration has been given as direct instead of indirect discourse. This creates a quite different effect from what Wirt intended.[38] Among them, at any rate, the three Virginians Henry, Tucker, and Wirt produced one of the stirring and most dramatic forensic passages of American history, a passage which has done much to make both the speaker and his surroundings a grand element of the American myth.

In lesser ways biography and autobiography engaged the attention of other Virginians. During the years when he was in and out of Virginia, John Davis composed, translated, or edited *The Original Letters of Ferdinand and Elisabeth* (1798), *The Life and Campaigns of Victor Moreau* (1806), and *The Life of Thomas Chatterton* (1806). Lewis Littlepage composed in Hamburg in 1795 a defensive and explanatory account of his own career as a European soldier of fortune, *Memoirs Politique et Particular,* printed as recently as 1957.[39] Jefferson himself set a model for brief biography when he wrote the life of Meriwether Lewis as a preface to the 1814 *History of the Expedition.*

Acting upon the conviction that knowledge of one's own territory made one a better citizen, two Virginians produced histories of their state. J. W. Campbell of Petersburg, father of the better known historian G. W. Campbell, published in his home town in 1813 his *History of Virginia, From Its Discovery Til the Year 1781. With Biographical Sketches.* This one-volume survey is notable chiefly for its brief and unsentimental account of the Pocahontas-John Smith story (pp. 39-40), its appendix of twenty-four biographical sketches of Virginia worthies, from Nathaniel Bacon to Peyton Randolph, and a "Sketch of the History of the Church in Virginia" (pp. 287-310) by the president of Hampden-Sydney.

The History of Virginia, From Its First Settlement to the Present Day (3 vols., 1804-5, 4th vol., 1816) by John Daly Burk was a more ambitious undertaking. Burk lived to finish the first three volumes, the fourth being completed by Skelton Jones and Louis Hue Girardin. Burk's portion is florid and bombastic; he has been accused of "making everything little to make everything great."[40] But Burk worked from original source materials, such as the newspapers and old laws lent him by Jefferson, and the older histories of Stith, Keith, Smith, and Beverley. He produced a political history with a liberal Republican bias which pleased Jefferson. The Richmond Federalists were inclined to sneer at it, partly because it was dedicated to Jefferson with the explanation "The History of Virginia, by a sort of national right, claims you as its guardian and patron. . . . I inscribe it to you because I conceive you to be the first and most useful citizen in the republic."

Henry Banks (b. 1761) of Stafford county in his *Sketches of the History of France, from the Earliest Historical Accounts, to the Present Time, 1806* (1806) became an apologist for Napoleon, especially defending his actions in 1797.[41] Though Banks' scholarship and literary ability were applauded in Virginia newspapers, few except Henry Lee agreed in his estimate of the Emperor. Thomas Bolling Robertson's *Journal of Events in Paris, from June 29, 1815 to July 13, 1815. By an American* (1815, 1816) and *Letters from Paris Written During the Period of the Late Accession and Abdication of Napoleon. By a Representative in the Congress of the United States* (1816), the latter appearing originally in Richmond and Washington newspapers, take the opposite point of view regarding Bonaparte. Letter I of the latter work, for example, describes Napoleon with contempt. Of interest in the *Letters* is the description (p. 190) of a visit to the House of Lords, when Robertson was accompanied by Taylor of Richmond, Ellis of Lynchburg, and Tabb of Gloucester. A third Virginian, William Clarke Somerville of Westmoreland, wrote on France in 182[illegible] in his *Letters from Paris on Causes and Consequences of the French Revolution,* a thoughtful and optimistic appraisal of the French character in its relationship to the Revolution and the Empire. Here the bias is in favor of the French nation as distinct from Napoleon or the regrettable excesses of the Revolution.

Nathaniel Herbert Claiborne of Franklin county published in Richmond in 1819 his *Notes on the War in the South; with Biographical Sketches of the Lives of Montgomery, Jackson, Sevier, the late Gov. Claiborne, and Others.* Written while the War of 1812 was going on, the defense and eulogy of W. C. C. Claiborne, Governor of Louisiana and the author's brother, was added later, it is claimed. Joseph Doddridge's Notes, on the *Settlement and Indian Wars, of the Western Part of Virginia & Pennsylvania, from the Year 1763 until the year 1783 inclusive. Together with a View, of the State of Society and Manners of the First Settlers of the Western Country,* published in Wellsburgh, Virginia, in 1824, remains a minor classic of the middle western border. The Episcopal clergyman author possessed imagination and curiosity, and caught the feeling of the wilderness also reflected in Cooper. Some of the chapter headings of Parts I and II are perhaps significant: "The Wilderness," "Antiquities," "Aborigines," "Weather," "Beasts and Birds," "Settlement of the Country," "Dress," "The Forest," "The House Warming," "Witchcraft," "Morals," and "Slavery." Part III deals with the Indian wars and contains several stirring captivity-escape narratives and a pleasant chapter explaining "The Indian Summer." Sentimental, liberal, pro-Indian and anti-slavery, Doddridge might have done more with his pen had he not worked so hard for his church.

The most exciting, and apparently quite accurate historically, of Indian captivity narratives was that of Charles Johnston of Botetourt county. In New York in 1827 appeared his *Narrative of the Incidents Attending the Capture, Detention, and Ransom of Charles Johnston . . . , who Was Made Prisoner by the Indians on the Ohio River, in the Year 1790; Together with an Interesting Account of the Fate of His Companions, Five in Number, One of whom Suffered at the Stake. To Which Is Added Sketches of Indian Character and Manners with Illustrative Anecdotes.* In his later years a businessman of Richmond and then manager of the Botetourt Springs resort on the present site of Hollins College, Johnston decided to write his own account because of the errors in the version published by the Duc de Liancourt. In his Introduction, Johnston states that he related his adventures to Liancourt while crossing the Atlantic in 1793 and received the promise that they would not be published without Johnston's being allowed to see the manuscript and correct errors. This promise had not been fulfilled.

Johnston writes easy, unlatinate English with straightforward narrative and convincingly realistic detail. Apparently a well-read man, he quotes from poets like Goldsmith and Moore, from Jefferson and Lewis and Clark, and from a number of other explorers and adventurers among the Indians. It is no unsophisticated account, for the writer spends a chapter contrasting the good and evil Indian in theory and fact, shrewdly sketches Indian character through illustrations, and devotes a chapter to Indian eloquence, including several examples.

His final chapter, on the practicability of civilizing the Indians, begins with the observation that the red men see no "just principle of nations" which allows the white man to come and populate unoccupied territory, but only the agency of force or fraud through which vast territories "once theirs, are now ours." Intercourse with superior whites, not the "worthless class" of the frontier which is the only one they have so far known, would improve relationships, he believes. As their game disappears, they may lend themselves to literature, science, and the useful arts. But in his last sentence Johnston observes that history contains no example of a black or red race ever rivaling whites in the attainment of genius and knowledge.

John Davis, novelist and poet who spent most of his fifteen American years as a schoolmaster, published in 1803 his *Travels of Four Years and a Half in the United States of America.* The book contains several descriptions of Virginia scenery, especially at Occoquan, a discussion of the slavery problem, and one of Davis' several versions of the Pocahontas-Smith story, to be discussed in greater detail below. The *Travels,* twice reprinted in recent times, is one of the better American travel accounts in style and content. Always on the move and recording with an eye for fresh materials, Davis produced an imaginative account in many respects comparable to the work of the Bartrams.

Anne Royall (1769-1854), who always spoke in her books of Virginia as her native state, was actually born in Maryland and wandered in her childhood in Pennsylvania before her family settled in the Great Valley. Widowed at forty-four and left penniless ten years later, she began in 1824 to earn her own living by published versions of her continuing travels through the United States. An ardent pro-Mason and anti-evangelical religionist, she suffered criticism and some persecution on both counts. Her two later newspapers *Paul Pry* (1831-36) and *The Huntress* (1836-54) were vigorously edited, with pronounced opinions on all subjects.[42]

But her "unenviable fame" came largely from the ten volumes of travels she published between 1826 and 1831. Probably the best are *Sketches of History, Life and Manners in United States, by a Traveller* (1826), and its sequel the three-volume *Black Book; or a Continuation of Travels in the United States* (1828, 1829). Her titles are sometimes misleading: *Letters from Alabama* (1830), for example, discusses Virginia Members of Congress and "my friend Wirt, the Attorney General." *Mrs. Royall's Southern Tour* (3 vols., 1830), a further sequel to the *Travels,* includes a discussion of the 1829-30 Richmond Convention, which she attended, and dozens of her sometimes left-handed compliments to its individual members.

Mrs. Royall's books are certainly not elegant literature, but she had a knack for picturing the men and manners of her age. She was basically an anti-reformer writing from profound convictions, but her wide-eyed curiosity, gift for the pungent phrase, and trenchant egotism-puncturing thumbnail sketches of politicians, resulted in books read primarily for amusement. She was too blunt to have been a best seller, but she did sell. Late in life, through Presbyterian machinations, it is said, she was convicted of being "a common scold," possibly because, as one of her biographers points out, she could always set the ungodly in a roar of laughter. A real "original," she anticipated and outdid twentieth-century newspaper columnists in gnarled anecdotes about people and institutions.

More in the eighteenth-century picaresque travel-account tradition is *The Life and Adventures of Major Robert Bailey, from His Infancy up to December 1821, interspersed with Anecdotes, and Religious and Moral Admonitions,* published in Richmond in 1822. Ostensibly a moral lesson from a misspent life, actually it is the memoir of an unrepentant sinner who boasts of his homicides, gambling, and dozens of paramours. Like Mrs. Royall, Bailey was an "original." Amazingly frank, full of real names and real rascals, his alleged autobiography-travel-account may be half fiction and half fact. It reads somewhat like *Moll Flanders* or some eighteenth-century highwayman's confessions, except that its scenes are largely Virginian and always American, and Bailey never swung from the gallows. Whether Bailey's political preference for the Republicans ever embarrassed Jefferson or Madison seems not to be recorded, though he ran for Congress several times on their ticket. He mentions (p. 172) his certificates of good behavior from the sheriffs of the counties in which he had been a candidate! He was once tried before St. George Tucker, once "whipped" Isaac A. Coles, and once called on President Madison—all three at least according to his own account. His final pages warn against gambling but insist that if one must do so, he should be sure to use Bailey's patented faro box, which will not cheat.

Nor should one forget in discussing the literature of travel and exploration that the classic American work in the field, *A History of the Expedition under the Command of Captains Lewis and Clark* (discussed in Chapter VI above), was but an editing of the journals of two Virginians. Clark's sententious simplicity and vigor of style, Lewis' more detailed and poetic and humorous forms, peer through the editor's frames and appear fully in the more recent editing of the original journals by R. G. Thwaites (8 vols., New York, 1904). Original or edited, the Lewis-Clark account is one of the great repositories of knowledge as well as a great adventure story of America by Americans.

Though it may be considered solely in its legal aspects, William Waller Hening's *The Statutes at Large; being a Collection of All the Laws of Virginia* (13 vols., 1809-23) is in a larger sense *legislative history*. In this larger sense too it is probably the most significant historical writing produced in Virginia in the period. The historian Bancroft remarked that "no other State in the Union possesses so excellent a work on its legislative history."[43] Hening, a lawyer who had been Jefferson's Albemarle neighbor for some years before he established himself in Richmond, resolved to collect and preserve the laws of Virginia from their earliest forms. Jefferson's manuscript and printed collections may have been his inspiration. At any rate, the master of Monticello had the utmost confidence in Hening's scholarship and general ability and lent him all his material, which the compiler supplemented from various other sources. As early as 1795 an act had been passed in the legislature sponsoring such a publication, and in 1796 Wythe and Jefferson corresponded on the subject. By 1806 Hening and Jefferson began a long exchange of letters concerning the latter's materials. In 1808 actual publication was authorized by the legislature.

Hening produced one of the major monuments of early American scholarship in his intelligently arranged and carefully transcribed collection of laws, which includes other historical documents such as charters relating to the commonwealth and the details of famous legal cases since the earlier seventeenth century. Equally important is his pointing out of the factual errors in the work of both John Marshall and John D. Burk, and the able survey of the rise and progress "of the most remarkable of our laws" which he wrote as a preface. On receipt of the first volume Jefferson summarized its double significance in his letter to Hening: "it sheds a new light on our early history, and furnished additional security to the tenure of our rights and property."[44]

There actually was in the colonial period a long line of vigorous Virginia historical writing from John Smith through Beverley, Jones, and Stith. The Jeffersonian historians were highly conscious that they were continuing a tradition, as Burk, Campbell, and Marshall show in their references. Edmund Randolph was even more conscious of writing "the history of my native country" in this tradition, but all he left us were some manuscript fragments.[45] Randolph, like Jefferson or Madison or St. George Tucker, was well qualified by education, background, and attitude for the task, but like them he had spent so much of his life making history he did not have time to write it. After his disgrace in Washington's cabinet, Randolph might have devoted his days to the kind of history he wanted to write. Instead he decided that he had to make a living. In this at least he was quite successful.

Neither Virginia nor the rest of the South in the decades after 1830 produced a Bancroft who could or would interpret the history of the nation from an implicitly sectional or regional point of view. Yet in 1854-58 the septuagenarian Jeffersonian George Tucker did write the four-volume *History of the United States from the Colonization to the End of the Twenty-Sixth Congress, in 1841* as an attempt to satisfy the need for a national history from the Southern point of view. It is only partially and perhaps incidentally a Southern-oriented history, though it does defend slavery. What Tucker actually wrote is a Congressional history of the United States which anticipates the later work of James Schouler. His work was generally ignored by the American public he tried to reach, who continued well into the twentieth century to read American history as New England saw it.

2. *The Essay*

From at least the time of William Byrd II the Virginia gentleman had not been averse to employing his pen in brief prose pieces. A few like Byrd might scribble their "characters" or moral observations for their own amusement or sometimes for the London papers, but many more could and did write their comments on economics, agriculture, politics, literature, and manners to the Williamsburg, Virginia, *Gazette*. Often in the form of letters, these comments are hardly extensive, dignified, or ambitious enough to be called formal essays. They were in form and purpose, especially those on literature and manners, more like the periodical prose of the *Spectator, Rambler,* and *Citizen of the World,* semi-formal familiar essays.

Later eighteenth-century Virginians did write some of what may be called formal essays, usually political or economic. The Revolutionary war papers of the Lee brothers, Madison's part of *The Federalist,* St. George Tucker's "Reflections" on the cession of the Louisiana Territory (1803) and his "Dissertation on Slavery" (1796) are among a number of more or less elaborate essay-treatises. These have already been discussed, or will be in later chapters, in connection with education, agriculture, science, politics, economics, and religion. They are rarely belletristic in intent.

But from the beginning of the nineteenth century there was in Virginia a considerable employment of the familiar essay. Modeled at times on the *Spectator* or Goldsmith or on both, and showing some influence of the British reviews, these essays usually appeared first in newspapers or magazines and in several instances were later gathered into volumes. They were composed most frequently by city dwellers, especially of Richmond, but an appreciable number, and some of the best, were written by men who lived on plantations or in small towns. They were strictly the work of amateurs—doctors, lawyers, teachers, farmers, newspaper editors. Though in other parts of the United States, notably in the Philadelphia of Joseph Dennie, this form of literature also flourished, the Virginia essayist by 1803-4 was as well known as any in the country. The playfully satiric portrayal of manners, the seriously moral or didactic, the philosophic or literary theory in layman's language, the half-sentimental commentaries on American antiquity and traditions—these are the elements of the Virginia essay.

The best-known writers of these prose exercises were William Wirt and his circle of friends who lived or gathered seasonally in Richmond. Wirt individually received credit for more than he actually wrote, but he was the prime mover and most frequent contributor among the group.

During August and September, 1803, he published anonymously in Samuel Pleasants' Virginia *Argus* ten miscellaneous essays purporting to be the observations of a British gentleman incognito in Virginia. They appeared in book form within a few months as *Letters of the British Spy*, still without the name of the author.[46] The tenth edition, with the author given, appeared in 1832, and there were many more thereafter. The book contained also two factually sound but not very attractive essays by George Tucker which answered or commented upon some of Wirt's superficial "scientific" observations on Buffon. In 1804-5 there was an imitation, "The British Spy in Boston," and in 1812 a British edition of Wirt's book.

The contemporary popularity of the *British Spy* outside Virginia may puzzle the twentieth-century reader, but its success within the Old Dominion in its own time should not be a surprise. Wirt dealt with subjects already dear to Virginia hearts or stimulated Virginians' pride by suggesting new things which might be accomplished. Though the theme or subject of the book has been said to be eloquence, or oratory, something dear to Wirt's and every other Virginian's heart, it could as easily be said to be an exhortation to Virginians to recover, or retain, the pre-eminence fast slipping from them, a theme frequent in other early nineteenth-century Virginia writing. If the exhortation is not quite so urgent as in later essays even of Wirt, it may be because Virginia still retained something of her eighteenth-century pre-eminence, for Jefferson was after all President of the United States.

Letter I is a mild criticism of the Virginia socio-economic system in observations of the inequality of land distribution. The not disapproving comment is made that in Virginia social rank comes from wealth and degree of intellectual refinement. Here and in several later essays Wirt discusses Virginia's past—the church at Jamestown, Pocahontas and John Smith, and Patrick Henry. In other essays he analyzes the characters and persons of James Monroe, John Marshall, Edmund Randolph, and John Wickham, all men he admired; but he does not fail to point out some of their genuine weaknesses as well as foibles. In letter III he elaborates upon what is wrong with eloquence in Virginia, and in VII he illustrates the combination of factors which made the Blind Preacher a great "natural" orator. Letter X, in praise of the *Spectator,* is the most interesting and significant of the group.

If he were sovereign of a nation, the author exclaims, he would supply every poor family with a copy of Addison's periodical and compel every wealthy family to buy it. In discussing its style, he mentions Blair's opinion that "the most sublime style is to be sought in a state of nature," remarking that if style thus progressed, civilization must decline. He goes on to comment generally on Bacon, Burke, and Robert Boyle as stylists, particularly in their use of ornament.

Wirt in these essays is clearly a transition figure attracted both to the sentiment and antiquarianism of the new romanticism and to Addisonian and Popean rationalism. In an essay such as that upon the Blind Preacher, he is overly rhetorical, overly sentimental, but in other discussions, particularly on oratory, he can be almost relentlessly logical and direct, even at the very moment when he praises emotionalism in public speaking. He had himself no very high opinion of the *British Spy,* remarking to Dabney Carr that it was too "frolicksome & sprightly" to be thoughtful or penetrating, and that the style was at times overloaded.

Nevertheless he and a group of friends, almost immediately after the *British Spy* appeared, began a cooperative venture in essay-writing. Under the guidance and enthusiasm of the schoolmaster and peripatetic philosopher James Ogilvie, ten men of Richmond formed the Rainbow Association, each of the members promising to contribute one or more essays to the Richmond *Enquirer.* Their work appeared in that newspaper between August 11 and October 20, 1804. Though the little city contained a strong element of Federalists, all the Rainbow group were Jeffersonian Republican liberals. Essayists like the Federalist clergyman John D. Blair, who wrote in *The Visitor* a few years later, were not among them.

Professor Jay B. Hubbell has identified most of the members of the Association and assigned to them the authorship of specific essays.[47] Only part of their work, a series of ten essays, was assembled in book form as *The Rainbow, First Series* (1804), but in the *Enquirer* a complete second series and the beginning of a third were published.

Ogilvie led off the original series with "On the Utility of Miscellaneous Essays" (signed "O"), pointing out the popularity of essays generally in his time, noting the literary and moral refinement they brought, and pleading for an enlargement of their subjects and aims.

Wirt himself seems to have written the second piece, "On the Condition of Women." Others on politeness, the French Revolution and Bonaparte, the American Genius, on building towns, on illusions of Fancy, another on the condition of women, and a final one on the establishment of charity schools were written by newspaper editors Meriwether and Skelton Jones, Lawyer Peyton Randolph, physician John Brockenbrough, George Tucker, lawyers George Hay and William Brockenbrough, and newspaper editor Thomas Ritchie. Series Two, uncollected, includes essays on luxury, forensic eloquence, celibacy, the American Genius; Part Two, the female sex, dueling, public schools, and education, all by the same group, though in slightly different order. Ogilvie began a third series with a second essay on luxury.

Thoughtful, restrained, and less rhetorical than the *British Spy* pieces, liberal in sentiment, basically rational and sometimes sceptical in the French sense, these essays deserve more attention than they have had. Wirt's "On the Condition of Women" is the most sentimental and superficial of the lot, yet it too makes its appeal to reason. Tucker's on Fancy is a significant step in the critical and philosophical theories he developed during his long life. Randolph's on American Genius is defensive and scholarly, using the old comparison with the Greek republic. John Brockenbrough in discussing the building of towns really comments upon architectural styles and patterns and their suitability in America, especially in Virginia.

Even better are the *Old Bachelor* essays, written by Wirt and perhaps a half dozen of his friends, this time including country gentlemen. Twenty-eight were published in the *Enquirer* from December 22, 1810, to December 1811, and five more in 1813. In 1814 the thirty-three were republished in book form in Richmond and in a so-called "third edition" in 1818 in Baltimore. Wirt always intended to add more to the last edition but never did. These are usually considered the best work of Wirt and his circle. The contributors have never been completely identified, though it is clear from Wirt's letters who many of them are.[48]

Wirt, who in later 1810 was publishing in the *Enquirer* a series he called *The Sylph*, abandoned it in December for what he believed would be a more naturally grouped and realistic series written by a group of friends. He had already discussed the possibility with Richard E. Parker and on December 24 wrote Dabney Carr about his projected plan. Kennedy thought most of the volume was written by Wirt, but of this we cannot be so sure. Certainly he wrote the opening numbers, probably 17, 18, 19, the first part of 9, possibly 13, 14, 20, and part of 12, and surely 30, 31, and 32.[49] The central figure is Dr. Robert Cecil, the Old Bachelor, a character vaguely reminiscent of Sir Roger de Coverley but more of an "enthusiast." "Alfred" is Richard E. Parker, later U. S. Senator and judge of the Virginia Supreme Court of Appeals. "Galen" was Dabney Carr's brother Dr. Frank Carr, a country physician. Dabney Carr may have written the letter from "Obadiah Squaretoes" in the ninth number[50] and helped Wirt manage Dr. Cecil and his niece Rosalie.

Kennedy suggests Louis Hue Girardin, French exile, farmer, and scholar as the contributor of the eleventh and twelfth numbers and part of the tenth. Major David Watson, a country gentleman of Louisa county, wrote the letter signed "John Truename" in the fifth number and the whole of final number thirty-three. The last the Philadelphia critic Robert Walsh singled out for special praise, and it may have been in Poe's mind as he wrote "William Wilson."[51] Incidentally Walsh considered that the *Old Bachelor* as a collection was superior to any earlier volume of American essays, and Wirt as "the finest genius that has yet ventured forth among us in the walk of literature."[52]

George Tucker contributed two letters to the fifteenth number as "Vamper" and "Peter Schryphel," and St. George Tucker and Francis Gilmer may have been among those contributing. Several essays which do not sound like Wirt have yet to be identified.

"Virtuously to instruct, or innocently to amuse" was an announced Addisonian aim of the series. The principal topic was to be education, though Wirt announced in the "Advertisement" that the original subject had been eloquence, on which only a few rough essays placed toward the end of the volume were ever written. Though the form is in some respects more clearly Addisonian than in the two earlier series, the tone is not at all so. The earlier melancholy expressions of regret at Virginia's past glory have here deepened into a sentimentalism not before evident, now with a more insistent urge that "the body of the people" be awakened to the need for education if the state is to return to her national leadership. Thus "Virginia in decline" is a major theme as it is in much of the verse and some of the fiction of the period. "Illustrious men! Immortal patriots! Where are ye now and your successors!!" (p. 121). They are gone, the essayist adds, because the youth no longer apply themselves to serious study—because they lack the "sublime enthusiasm" of the past. Therefore despite its nostalgic tone, the book is addressed to the rising generation.

Wirt and his friends grew tired of the theme of education, however, before they had treated it at all adequately. They went on to write of manners, gambling, avarice, and patriotism. Naturally the essays are extremely uneven, from the ability of the various authors and the degree of care they bestowed upon them. *The Old Bachelor* remains nevertheless the high watermark of the familiar essay in the early nineteenth century in Virginia and in some respects in the whole nation.

By 1818 Ogilvie was back in Great Britain, Wirt had become Attorney-General, St. George Tucker was growing old, and George Tucker had left Richmond and its social temptations behind for life in southside Virginia. The Carrs and Watson appear to have lost interest. Both the Joneses were dead. Francis Gilmer had published one small volume of essays in 1816 and written another, but ill-health and a growing law practice prevented his doing much more before his early death in 1826. Both Tuckers were to continue to write essays, and the newspapers were still full of prose disquisitions on political and timely popular subjects such as the theater and the problems of slavery and the American Indian. But much grace and lightness of touch departed with the moving spirits.

This Richmond group of amateur essayists forming a literary circle reminiscent of the coffee house coteries of Augustan England were paralleled in their own time in America by the men gathered about Robert Treat Paine in Boston, Dwight in Hartford and New Haven, Elihu Hubbard Smith and later the Irvings in New York, Joseph Dennie in Philadelphia, Hugh Swinton Legaré in Charleston, and the Delphian Club in Baltimore. Though the clergy of Connecticut may have surpassed these Virginians as poets, as writers of lightly satiric, lucid, seriously aimed prose they bowed to none.

There were a few other Virginia essays and essayists in this first third of the nineteenth century. Hugh Blair Grigsby, to establish his name as litterateur and scholar in the next era, published in 1827 when he was twenty-one *Letters by a South-Carolinian,* a volume of literary sketches of eminent fellow citizens very much in the vein of those of Marshall and Monroe in the *British Spy*. Littleton Waller Tazewell, John Randolph, William B. Giles, William Maxwell, and John Holt Rice were among Grigsby's representative men. Number XI, "On the Literature of Virginia," is perhaps more interesting today for what it omits than for what it contains. Grigsby divides the literature of the state into five groups. Under "History" he mentions the work of Marshall, Burk, Jones, and Girardin. Under "Politics," the *Letters of Curtius* (John Thomson of Petersburg) and John Taylor's works. Under "Polite Literature," the *British Spy, The Old Bachelor, The Mountaineer, Letters from Virginia, Notes on Virginia,* Garnett on Education, and George Tucker's *Essays.* Under "Poetry," only William Maxwell, Richard Dabney, and Daniel Bryan. And finally under "Biography," Wirt's *Henry* and Lee's *Memoirs.* He admits the list is imperfect, but these are all he can recall at the moment.

Robert Ruffin Collier's *Original and Miscellaneous Essays, By a Virginian* (1829) include some pieces approaching the familiar essay form, though the majority are scientific and political. The Reverend Conrad Speece, mentioned in Chapter IV above, in *The Mountaineer: or, a Series of Essays designed for the Improvement of the*

Minds of Young Ladies and Gentlemen (1818) is strongly pious and didactic. But in "Beauties of the Morning Hour," "The Eloquence of Patrick Henry," and "Improvement of Manners in Our Valley" he writes somewhat in the manner of the British Spy or the Old Bachelor. Simple, unpretending, and gentle, Speece's essays were read widely in several editions.

The most persistent and in certain respects most able, at the same time one of the least known, of the essayists was Bermuda-born George Tucker (1775-1861). A graduate of William and Mary and a kinsman of St. George Tucker, he married successively a granddaughter of William Byrd and a grandniece of George Washington. Establishing himself in Richmond about 1802 as a lawyer, he made friends among Federalists and Republicans alike, though he himself like his Tucker kinsman was a Republican. His contribution of two learned essays to the *British Spy,* the "Illusions of Fancy" and "Vindication of Duelling" pieces in the *Rainbow,* and the satirical letters in the *Old Bachelor* have already been noted. He probably was the author of *Letters from Virginia, Translated from the French* (1816) and certainly was of *Essays on Various Subjects of Taste, Morals, and National Policy, By a Citizen of Virginia* (1822) and *Essays, Moral and Metaphysical* (1860). In 1814-15 he had contributed the "Thoughts of a Hermit" series to the Philadelphia *Port Folio,* including discourses on "American Literature," "On Style," "On Beauty," "On Architecture," "On Rhyme," and "On Simplicity of Ornament," along with others on economics and political science.[53] These were all included in his 1822 volume. His thinking along the same lines is recorded, as his recent biographer has shown, in his University of Virginia lectures, the essay-editorials in the *Virginia Literary Museum,* his novels, and contributions to dozens of periodicals.

The great subject of his belletristic essays is aesthetics as related to literature—Taste, Beauty, Sublimity, and Style—and aesthetics in prose and poetry and in the development of American literature. As early as 1804, in the essay "On the Illusions of Fancy," Tucker had revealed considerable interest in psychological criticism. Here too are the germs of his later writings on Taste.[54] As in numerous later writings, he here showed his interest in the Scottish and English metaphysicians and critics of the generation just before his own or among his contemporaries. His use of Alison, Jeffrey, Kames, Stewart, Reid, Brown, Gerard, Hume, and Blair is extensive. In this early essay he relied particularly on Gerard's *Essay on Taste* (1759) in describing the nature of the Imagination in relation to literary criticism. The Fancy is "the mimic of the senses . . . substituting the pictures or images of its creation, for those of nature" and thus "only separates or combines those ideas which were imparted by the senses and reposited in the memory."[55] He goes on to develop his concept of a standard of taste based upon universal laws of association and nature.[56]

In the later essay "On Simplicity in Ornament" which appeared first in the *Port Folio* in 1815 and later in his 1822 *Essays* Tucker established as the principle underlying his aesthetic speculations "that the perfection of taste will consist in that middle point between extreme simplicity and extreme refinement,"[57] a principle congenial to his Scottish mentors and to the Virginians in the traditional ideal of moderation going back into the colonial period.

Perhaps his greatest aesthetic interest was in the nature of the Beautiful and the Sublime and the relationship of the two. From his 1815 "On Beauty" in the *Port Folio* and 1822 *Essays* to his final observations in the 1860 *Essays* and in his lectures, he discussed the matter, supporting himself with the conservative theories of Gerard, Kames, and Stewart against the newer concept of Alison. Tucker believed that it was against common sense to hold with Alison and Jeffrey that all aesthetic enjoyment takes place in the mind. The emotion of Beauty, he felt, is aroused by a direct organic pleasure which is affected in various ways by the association of ideas. Sublimity was for him a purely subjective emotion, though he had certainly not accepted extreme subjectivism anywhere else in his theories.

In the *Port Folio* in 1814 Tucker had begun his discussions of prose style, expressing his belief in the rise and ultimate decline of language as of cultures, but suggesting the possibility of arresting the decay. Undue innovations would ruin prose style if they were not curbed. The good taste already occasionally shown in the *Edinburgh* and *Quarterly* reviews might if developed be a salutary influence preventing the decline, he observed. In his lectures he always advocated delicacy, simplicity, and perspicuity. He outlined three styles of prose, the first addressing itself to the understanding, the second to the imagination (this includes all literary criticism), and the third to the imagination and the feelings.[58]

Employing a number of eighteenth-century critics and philosophers, Tucker also attempted to define the nature and function of poetry. Blair, Campbell, and Kames especially are cited in his lectures. Tucker summarized the characteristics of poetry as distinguished from prose in such things as inversion of word order, greater dignity of language, and more varied and copious imagery. He believed strongly in emotion as a basic effect of poetry, and differed from his Scottish mentors in calling its rhetorical aspects mere superficial ornaments. Great poetry, serving as a vehicle for the emotions, cannot be didactic. He thought highly of verse which evoked the emotion of sublimity.

It has recently been suggested that Tucker through these essays[59] may have influenced Poe, who was a student at the University of Virginia, in the latter's theories of poetry.[60] Certainly the two agree on many things, didacticism being perhaps the most obvious. But Poe as far as we know did not attend Tucker's lectures, and we have no evidence that he read the essays. Poe did know Blair, Kames, Alison, and others of the Scottish critics, and he knew the British reviews as did few contemporaries. Poe's general ideas seem more likely to have come straight from their common British sources than from or through Tucker.

Poe's earliest known critical writing is a sort of symbolic link between Tucker and the Jeffersonians and the writers of the American Flowering. Though Poe always expressed the greatest respect for Wirt individually and as a writer, it is with Tucker and the aestheticians rather than the new Addisonians that he is closely affiliated in his critical ideas and ideals and prose form. The 1831 "Letter to Mr. ——
——," forming the introduction to *Poems* (New York), can well be considered a product of Poe's Virginia heritage, as Robert D. Jacobs has recently pointed out.[61] In its emphasis on pleasure rather than truth as the "immediate object" of poetry, its anticipations of Poe's later theories even more clearly derived from the psychological critics of Kames' generation, and its attack on Wordsworth as a metaphysical poet of an un-Scottish kind, it derives, as Tucker's and other Virginians' theory did, from the Scottish rhetoricians and British reviewers.[62] Though space does not permit analyses or extensive evidence here, Jacobs has recently shown rather conclusively that from

Letters to Mr. ——— ———" through "The Poetic Principle" the most significant of Poe's critical essays all had their germs cultured in the intellectual climate of Jefferson's Virginia.

D. *Letters*

In no other form of written expression were the Jeffersonian Virginians more at home than in the epistolary, especially in the personal letter. "The letters of a person, especially of one whose business has been chiefly transacted by letters, form the only full and comprehensive journal of his life," wrote Jefferson to Robert Walsh in 1823.[63] As written by Jefferson and at least two dozen of his fellow citizens, they are a graceful, entertaining, and most valuable record of individual lives and intellect.

From the beginning the Virginian had taken pen in hand to address his absent friends. At Jamestown John Smith, Ralph Percy, John Pory, William Strachey, and many more had informed friends, relatives, or business associates in England of their triumphs and failures, joys and sorrows, in rounded rhetorical phrases, frequently suggestive of the secretaries' handbooks everywhere available. They wrote partly out of loneliness as isolated people always have, and partly to transact their business, as Jefferson suggested. As the seventeenth century wore on men like Francis Yeardley and William Fitzhugh reflect in their letters a more settled, agrarian society, and their own picturesque personalities.[64] In the earlier eighteenth century the two elder William Byrds, Governor Spotswood, several Carters, and several Randolphs were among the planters of the colonial golden age who left good reading in their letters on business, books, government, personal habits and inclinations and experiences, and travels and explorations.

From the 1730's the same men were addressing letters to the *Virginia Gazette*, letters which are really essays expressing their opinion on everything from the latest play in Williamsburg to the Crown's policy regarding taxes in the colony. These letters also have a strong literary quality, undoubtedly somewhat affected by the writer's habits in familiar and informal letter writing, but actually belonging more to the essay genre than to that gentlest art, the personal epistle. For their ancestry is more in the English periodical (also at times in letter form), and their descendants take distinguished places in American political literature during and after the Revolution.

The Virginia letter-writer of 1790-1830 shows that he was like his progenitors indebted still consciously and unconsciously to the rhetoricians of previous ages, and to the oratorical rhetoricians of his own time. For even at their best writers like Jefferson, Randolph, and Wirt employ the rounded phrase, the eloquent figure or image. Of the dozen ablest and most prolific letter writers, only George Washington strove to keep to a plain style, and even he, under stress in family or martial situations of the Revolutionary period, could pour forth strongly emotional and rhetorical paragraphs.

Naturally more of the letters of figures prominent for reasons other than their epistles have survived than those of more ordinary men, but there are remarkably constructed and intellectually provocative letters such as those of planter Ralph Wormeley and industrialist David Ross to their respective sons on reading and education, of John M. Daniel to Huldah Lewis on the value of a classical education, or of James Ogilvie on his experience as a peripatetic orator. In such letters we see the wit and deep piety of John Page, a facetious side of John Taylor hardly exhibited in his formal writings, Joseph C. Cabell concerned with reading and crops, the Methodist Stith Mead describing his evangelistic success to his brother clergy, and George Tucker, L. W. Tazewell, John H. Cocke, David Watson, Meriwether Lewis, and Peachy R. Gilmer communicating all sorts of information from petty gossip to the ascent of the Missouri, written with vivid figures, rhetorical questions, puns, or grim irony.

William Short measures himself in the role of romantic lover, shrewd business man, and sophisticated diplomat in the letters of his long life. They add up to a portrait of almost a great man, and fully a fascinating one. The Reverend John Holt Rice reveals the mixture of genuine political liberalism and sectarian and doctrinal intransigence, along with a conciliatory spirit and gentleness in his many letters to friends, brethren, and parishioners. St. George Tucker, wise and tender and intellectually energetic, poured out in scores of letters his ideas and his compassion. Nicholas P. Trist displays in his personal correspondence as he never could in official communications as diplomat the far-reaching transcendentally inclined mind and the philosophic bases of his friendships with men like the Owens of New

Harmony, Indiana. In his personal communications too is the key to the unconventional diplomat who disobeyed instructions and acquired for the United States a territory almost equal to the Louisiana purchase.

Half a dozen Virginians remind us that the Jeffersonian generations were born in the age of Chesterfield and Horace Walpole. Though the Americans' letters of advice suggest at least Chesterfieldian example in form, in most respects they are quite different. Like Walpole in the variety of their interests, they are entitled through the considerable body of their surviving correspondence to be called major letter writers of their age. These men were Jefferson, Madison, John Randolph, Wirt, Francis Gilmer, and Weems. As a major epistolarian Washington really belongs in an earlier period.

Perhaps no one who knows anything of American history and literature would deny Jefferson a place among our great letter writers. The monumental edition of his *Papers* under way since 1950 and the several less accurate and comprehensive collections printed previously alike attest the magnitude and clear artistry of his correspondence. Rounded phrase, urbane imagery, and classical allusion he never forsook in the style which yet transcends its elements in its obvious shaping for usefulness. Every facet of his comprehensive mind, including the religious convictions he said should not be enquired into by anyone, he revealed to one or more of his hundreds of correspondents. When he wrote to Madison, the Abbé Correa, Abigail and John Adams, and his family Jefferson was at his best. But he was equally revelatory, persuasive, showering the sparks of his mind, in individual letters addressed to scores of others.

Felicitous as his phrasing was, composition was not easy. He employed whatever mechanical aids he could, the polygraph and stylograph, for making copies.[65] He compiled a precise index, the "Epistolary Record," covering the years 1783 to 1826, an almost complete census of his letters for these years. Not only a prodigious letter writer, he is the only one of his generation to systematize his correspondence. This is one of the reasons why he is one of the most quoted of American epistolarians. The whole ideal of service to society which underlay the actions and thought of one of the great minds of his generation is chartered, line by line, in this great body of letters.

James Madison, never quite so systematic as his close friend, also never reveals himself quite so fully in his letters. The sly wit, the love of a shady story, the sense of humor Jefferson lacked—the qualities we know Madison possessed from the testimony of his contemporaries—we see almost nothing of in his surviving personal letters. Except for some family correspondence, these letters are most serious conveyances of political news, discussion of governmental problems, references to his reading, advice to young men, and references to architecture and building. The oratorical phrase and line, the general exhortatory quality of his formal communications, creep over into the style of his familiar letters, but they are never showy in the sense that Patrick Henry's or Richard Henry Lee's styles, written or oral, were. This must remain a preliminary estimate of Madison even more than Jefferson, for only the first volumes of the new comprehensive edition of Madison's papers have yet appeared.

As we have noted, Randolph was considered by Philip A. Bruce perhaps "the most brilliant letter-writer of whom the Old South can boast," and William C. Bruce broadens the statement to include the whole United States for the period.[66] It is significant that these statements came from two scholars who had access to a considerable part of the enormous unpublished corpus of Randolph's letters. Though in the generation since they made their observations a number of single and a few grouped letters of Randolph have appeared in print, anyone who wishes to become familiar with his mind and thought must turn to the fine manuscript collections. He who does must conclude that John Randolph was, with Jefferson, one of the major letter writers of our history.

Far more emotional than his early idol Jefferson, Randolph shows in his letters all his moody despondency and rarer crackling exuberance. Many series of his letters, to younger friends and relatives, are likely to be Chesterfieldian in form and tone but not in moral observation. The posthumously published *Letters . . . to a Young Relative* (1834) and the earlier letters to various other nieces and nephews and in some instances to Francis Gilmer are representative of the Chesterfieldian aspect of his correspondence. His political feelings and ideas are expressed everywhere, but especially when he addresses James Monroe (the earlier period only), John Taylor of Caroline, Tazewell,

B. W. Leigh, or his cronies William J. Barksdale and John Brockenbrough. Literary allusions are omnipresent, some favorite poetic and prose lines in Latin and English being frequently repeated. He is never better than when writing of books and art. The series to New York Congressman Harmanus Bleecker between 1814 and the end of his life, the occasional notes to Josiah Quincy of Boston, the Key brothers of Maryland and to Tazewell and Barksdale and Brockenbrough, and the later correspondence with Francis Gilmer reveal his limited Romanticism and keen but equally limited critical acumen (e.g., his remarks on Wirt's *Patrick Henry*). He understood and appreciated Scott and Moore and Byron, but he admitted his failure with Coleridge and Wordsworth.

Brilliant is perhaps the best adjective to describe Randolph's letters as it is his oratory. Both lack logic, organization, even at times solidity. Ideas, images, gloomy forebodings, dark and thunderous threatenings, genuine tenderness tread on each other's heels in a single letter, or trail one another like exploding rockets. Out-of-the-way erudition and startling criticism may be interspersed with rather trite observation and what becomes rather tiresome railing at fate and Jeffersonian democracy. Randolph certainly had no typical Virginia mind, Henry Adams to the contrary, but the stormy petrel of the Jeffersonian age summed up, in exaggerated or caricatured form, especially in his letters, most of the intellectual characteristics of the conservative planter.

William Wirt's letters are far more entertaining and attractive than any essay he ever wrote or oration he ever spoke. Though they display evidences of his legal and oratorically trained mind the flaming epithet, the cadenced period, the pathetic-bathetic aimed to impress a large public are muted or toned down into a pleasant, warm, yet frequently exuberant expression of ideas on his favorite subjects of belles-lettres, biography, oratory, family life, advice to youth, and in later years nostalgic reminiscence.

Wirt's letters, scattered and in most instances still unpublished in complete form, deserve a modern editor.[67] Kennedy published scores of them in garbled or bowdlerized form in his life of Wirt, frequently omitting what is most revealing or most entertaining from our point of view. In Wirt's letters can be traced the making of his peculiarly modest yet astonishingly popular character and career, his honest confession of his own limitations as scholar and orator, his generosity to young Americans seeking assistance in advice or training, his loyal friendships, and his lifelong ambition to assist in creating an American literature. To his contemporaries his achievement was the American success story, the American dream realized. Dimly conscious of all this, he tried in his letters to utilize his experience—negative as well as positive—in urging others on.

Though born in Maryland of Swiss-German immigrant stock, Wirt through his two marriages and legal career in Virginia developed consciously and unconsciously what may be called a fairly typical upper-class Virginia mind. His comments to Tazewell and Gilmer on eloquence, his observations to Benjamin Edwards on John Locke and Dugald Stewart, his several letters to Dabney Carr on religion *vs.* reason and his admiration for Butler's *Analogy* represent Virginia thinking in his age.

The information about contemporary men and events, from the campaigns of 1812 in Tidewater Virginia to musical performances and performers in Richmond or the hospitality of the Bostonians, is prodigious. But the most significant features of his correspondence are the gradually increasing lament for men of the caliber of Washington and Jefferson, in his letters as in his essays, the speculations with St. George Tucker as to how an American literature and a personal reputation might be built together, and the inside look at the creators and creations of the *Old Bachelor* and *Rainbow*. Wirt never outgrew his love for *Tristram Shandy,* and the whim-whams of Uncle Toby and Brother Shandy are behind the strong sensibility in all his communications with his friends.

The strongest critical mind, at least from a literary and social point of view, among the Jeffersonian epistolarians was Francis Walker Gilmer (1790-1826). From infancy surrounded by the fine scientific and and philosophical library of his father Dr. George Gilmer of Pen Park near Monticello, at an early age he browsed at will among the heavy tomes. His father died while he was still young and the youth was shunted from one school to another, getting his greatest stimulus if not knowledge under James Ogilvie at Milton. He read more under Jefferson's personal guidance at nearby Monticello. Then he attended

William and Mary under Bishop Madison, studied law under Wirt (whose first wife was his older sister), and collected the legal library in which he took some pride. Sent by Jefferson to Britain to collect the first faculty for the new University of Virginia, he continued to buy books. Jefferson declared him the best educated citizen Virginia had raised since the Revolution. But Gilmer never realized his own or his friends' high hopes, for he was dead at thirty-six as he was about to become first professor of law in the infant university.

Gilmer's letters to his brother Peachy from his school days at Milton indicate a precocious and shrewd mind.[68] He analyzed his master and his studies, commented on Albemarle politics of 1807, and poked fun at his good friend Mrs. Trist. In Richmond under Wirt he showed his absorption in the law and the genial and kindly influence of his tutor. His letter to Peachy of December 27, 1811, is one of the best of the dozens of accounts of the tragic theater fire. A few months later he compared discerningly the legislatures of Virginia and North Carolina and discoursed learnedly of Burke, Bacon, Boyle, and Burlamaqui, and a little later of Scott, Cicero, Demosthenes, and Patrick Henry.

Gilmer was frequently caustic. From the letters to his favorite older brother one gets stringent comments on the Philadelphia *Port Folio* or on George Hay as a political writer. Flattered and petted by Virginians who saw in him their shining hope in both politics and literature, he commented in 1813 somewhat bitterly:

> O that I had only a fortune to pursue the bent of my own wishes without being condemned to the galley of the Common Law. . . . as it is, we must satisfy ourselves with a little neighborhood reputation for good sense, a newspaper compliment for learning, & a tea table panegyric for wit—[I?] should be ashamed of the only kind of fame which genius, learning or eloquence would now give one in Virginia: We are such undiscerning puffers, such shameless flatters that . . . we rank Harrison with Hannibal, Wilkinson with Julius Caesar, Perry [with] Themistocles, Decatur with Nelson & so on. . . .[69]

In one of his several analyses of the Virginia mind and character he may have been hinting at his brother's (the recipient's) vacillations in the affairs of life:

> We Virginians seem to imagine ourselves an inspired and gifted people: that we are all born for lofty achievements, high exploits,

> & splendid renown. That we must all be lawyers, Physicians, writers, speakers, &c & c. I think we are a smart people—but I know we are inclined to be lazy, & in any of these paths to glory, all the genius in the world is good for nothing in this age at least, unless it be aided by patient and systematic industry.[70]

Later he included all Americans in a search for the causes of backwardness in the fine arts:

> [The imagination] is a faculty by the way which we Americans possess in a very small degree. . . . [Our fine arts are so far mediocre.]. This is not because we have by nature less genius, than others, but because we are purely people of business, our only idlers, are savages on the frontier, who possess nothing but a sort of Indian sagacity in tracking raccoons & oppossums. To make poets, there must be leisure, solitude, books, & a society occasionally to dip into of fancy and sentiment.[71]

Writing from Boston in Lincolnshire in 1824, he could be more chauvinistic:

> The tone of manners in the higher walks [of life in England] is exactly what I have seen in Virginia. Maclurg, John Walker, old Mr. Fleming & c were fully as elegant as Lord Teignmouth, or [the] Lord Bp. of Bristol & c.—but not more so, for the manners of all were unexceptionable.[72]

The sententiousness in these fraternal epistles is accentuated in the series of kindly letters of advice he addressed to his nephew Thomas Walker Gilmer, future governor and cabinet member under John Tyler. The series to the Abbé Correa between 1814 and 1820 reveal an insatiable scientific curiosity, and a considerable knowledge of botany, political and diplomatic problems, and human character. In his correspondence with his older friend John Randolph he displays a tact, a sensitiveness, he naturally did not always show when addressing his family. The two exchanged ideas on orators and eloquence, the classics, Virginia literature and Virginia speech patterns and pronunciations, and almost anything except politics, for Gilmer was an admirer and follower of Jefferson. To Wirt, to whom Gilmer felt closer than to anyone except his brother Peachy, he wrote with warmth and respect, of his studies and his career and of their friends and enemies. It is quite clear that he saw Wirt's limitations as well as his stronger qualities and fashioned his letters accordingly.

Though never the sentimentalist Wirt was at times, Gilmer had enjoyed and even translated Rousseau. *Sadness, misery, solitude, desolation, melancholy* are both terms and concepts in his letters, which in style and tone are a step removed from the written expression of Jefferson and Madison. Gilmer, like Wirt, frequently mentions Virginia's need for revival, but he was by no means so sure of how it should be done or whether it could be done. His abbreviated life and thwarted hopes, at times so poignantly expressed in his letters in some sense symbolize the last gasp, the ebbing will and energy of the age begun with Jefferson.

The Reverend Mason Locke Weems (1759-1825), bookseller extraordinary, is a letter-writer in a tradition all his own which reflects his unusual mind and character. The avalanches of letters he poured upon his publisher Mathew Carey are as whimsical, wheedling, irascible, and haggling as the man himself. The racy style too is all his own, as when he complains to Carey of "your ill treatment of me, your oppressing and crushing me to the earth by ten thousand puritannical books which as a good Catholic you know I did not request you to send, nay, was eternally remonstrating against your sending, representing them to you as unsaleable in this State as Fiddles at a Conventicle."[73] It is evident too in a protest against Carey's curb on advertising:

> O Vanitas Vanitatem That a Gentleman of your Craken character, & capable of plunging half way to the centre in bold search of the deepest truths, should leave that useful region & thus Dolphin like skim the surface in chace of a poor flying fish conceit ! ! You are a plain man & wont have y^r^ proposals stuck up in beer houses & grog pips? If our blessed Saviour who certainly was a very plain man, had been so fastidious as to leave the poor Beer house & grog pip Gentry to themselves whut w^d^ have become of those miserable grog blossom^d^ & carbuncled Devils[?][74]

Learned, witty, sincerely religious, the born salesman, Weems in these letters renders a lively portrait of himself as an "original" who was at the same time the forerunner of the modern sales manager. A shrewd analyst of the mind, temper, and taste of his fellow Americans, he records his observations in his own inimitable phraseology. There is no more amusing letter-writer in American history.

E. *Fiction*

During the twentieth century most critics of the novel have recognized a genre they refer to as the "Virginia novel." Though the term is used rather loosely, every casual reader of our national fiction is at least vaguely aware that a "Virginia novel" is a work set either amid the great scenes and events in the state's political and martial history or largely within the confines of a Virginia ante-bellum plantation. It need not have been written by a native; and mere setting within the Old Dominion's borders, in city, town, or small farm, does not make it a "Virginia novel" (from here on the quotation marks will be omitted). Ellen Glasgow's works may have been the social history of the state she insisted they were, but those novels she included in her unified group are not really Virginia novels in the traditional sense, for they present no great figures or events, and they are not set upon a great slave-operated plantation.

Some critics see the form as a minor branch of the American historical novel derived from Scott and Cooper. Others view it as the beginning of the "Plantation Novel," a term often embracing any and all fiction with an agrarian setting anywhere in the ante-bellum South. Almost all agree that it begins with Marylander John P. Kennedy's *Swallow Barn* (dedicated to Wirt) in 1832 or Virginian William A. Caruthers' *The Cavaliers of Virginia* in 1835, though at least one sees some of its elements in George Tucker's 1824 *The Valley of Shenandoah*. Clearly in the 1830's there had emerged a Virginia novel leaning toward the historical or plantation type or both. In both directions it was by and large romantic in general tone and often strangely realistic in detail, presenting stereotypes of a peculiar kind of lady and gentleman and young belle and beau, and including "originals" and slaves (the last often comic or minstrel-show types). Frequently it was realistic in the same sense Scott's novels were, its reality springing from a mass of detail and from a sort of Scottish common sense philosophical conception of idealized actuality. From Caruthers to the early Ellen Glasgow and Mary Johnston it celebrated various dramatic and significant moments in state history which were also national history. Its character stereotypes developed further into symbols of Virginia life and Southern life. Its heirs in local-color romance, in fictional common sense realism and ideality, and even in the social problem novel are still to be met with.

All this is necessary preface to the observation that there was a Virginia novel almost a full generation before *Swallow Barn,* or rather that there were some four or five really significant novels in the thirty years before Kennedy published his loosely-joined series of sketches of Virginia life. And these earlier novels, taken together, actually anticipate or at least adumbrate almost every quality the historical-event and plantation-setting variants of the genre ever developed. Although all the later Virginia novels were not written by Virginians, all these early examples were produced by natives or residents of Jefferson's Old Dominion.

Besides the five which best represented this genre, several other fictions by Virginians were well known and reasonably widely read. As early as 1797 Virginian Samuel Relf (b. 1776) had written a sentimental novel of Philadelphia family life, *Infidelity,* which has a definite place in the domestication of the type in America. Notorious-famous traveler and gossip Anne Royall, already mentioned in this chapter, had published in 1827 *The Tennessean,* a wretchedly contrived melodramatic tale of Southwestern life.

Also in 1827 George Tucker, whose earlier novel will be discussed below, brought out *A Voyage to the Moon,* half satire and half Utopian romance. On one side of the moon the inhabitants are distortions or caricatures of men of the earth, on the other they represent idealized humans in an ideal society.[75] On both sides are suggestions of the enlightened Virginian, the scientific gadgeteer, the pragmatic realist, the liberal philosopher—perhaps Jefferson himself. Details occasionally remind one of Poe's "Hans Pfaall," but there were other imaginary voyages which might have suggested these things to the younger satirist. Even the agricultural problems of the Virginia planter are suggested in the gentleman moon-farmer's breed of cattle and the discussion of the colonization society in Africa. But Tucker was more interested in oblique discussions of his associationist-philosophical, population-rent, and governmental theories. The book is a significant contribution to a then-popular form, but it does not fall within the genre to which the author had earlier contributed.

In 1828 the good Reverend Dr. Henry Ruffner published the first version of *Judith Bensaddi: A Tale Founded on Fact,* the first American novel concerned with the Jewish problem.[76] And in the same year the anonymous author (probably Miss A. M. Lorraine) dedicated *Donald Adair: A Novel by a Young Lady of Virginia* (2 vols., Richmond) "To the Young Ladies of Virginia." Covering a period from 1753 to the Revolution, it contains references to Patrick Henry and James Fenimore Cooper and includes George Washington as a character. But its setting is not clearly Virginian.

The earliest writer who presented a real Virginia setting in a novel is the English-born John Davis (1774-1854), already mentioned several times above in other connections, who spent many of the years between 1798 and 1817 in various places in Virginia as schoolmaster and private tutor, and perhaps as journalist. As a writer he is best remembered for his popularization of the Pocahontas-John Smith legend (see the section of this chapter just below). "It was in the tall forests of Virginia, before the door of my plantation log-hut, that, contemplating the moon, and listening to the mocking-bird, I first conceived of writing this story," Davis reveals in the preface of the 1817 edition of the tale. Picking up the germ of his tale in Robertson's *History,* Smith's own accounts, and perhaps other histories, he gives his first version in *The Farmer of New Jersey* (1800), a two-page story-within-a-story which depicts Smith's rescue as he was about to be burned at the stake. In his *Travels* (1803) Davis retells the story more effectively in much greater detail, this time getting straight the kind of execution to which Smith had been condemned. In 1805 appeared his novelette, *Captain Smith and Princess Pocahontas,* and later in that year a full-length novel on the same subject, *The First Settlers of Virginia.* Both novel and novelette were reprinted, the former in 1806 and the latter in 1817, 1818, and 1837. The shorter form is the more attractive, for *The First Settlers* is overloaded with historical detail inserted in all manner of awkward ways. As in other works of his, Davis in the Pocahontas accounts indicates his literary origins in Ossian and the sentimentalists generally, as well as in the Scottish ideas of Beauty, Sublimity, and Ideality.

Perhaps its celebration of a mythic-historical episode in Virginia history is alone enough to qualify *The First Settlers of Virginia* as the beginning of the Virginia novel genre. But this book includes also some other elements reappearing in later Virginia fiction. Though

Davis relies heavily on the historians and Smith's own account for his main facts and some details, he also presents in his scene-paintings and attempted mood-creations many aspects of life in the Chesapeake Bay area as he knew them. He was fascinated by Virginia birds. The mockingbird especially he sentimentally celebrates again and again, but the dove, red bird, cat bird, and whip-poor-will also with eerie or mournful calls help to form the Ossian-like moods of his characters. The Virginia cypress and oak, the pine and the laurel, the black snake and the squirrel, he employs as background for Rolfe's midnight vigil or the Indian maiden's lonely sighs for her lover. The conclusion is a primitivistic lament for the lost race of red men. All these some later novelist at one time or another has used.

More significant are the characterizations of Captain Smith and his red princess, characterizations far more suggestive of the later fictional Virginia gentleman and plantation belle than of the historical duo they purport to describe. Granted their debt to sentimental characters of the eighteenth-century English novel, they still suggest their American descendants as well as their British progenitors. The redoubtable Captain, for example, is thus epitomized as the practitioner of the Horatian mean that the "first gentlemen of Virginia" held as their ideal:

> The person of Smith was tall, graceful and manly. His visage was striking. He had an eye to commend, to threaten, or soothe. His aspect bespoke a man ready to face his man, yet capable of moderation; a character comprehending both firmness and refinement; blending taste with energy, and while ready to hit, yet able to forbear. It was a countenance that indicated a mind not easy to be deceived, and ever disposed more to suspicion than credulity. His vigorous, active figure qualified him eminently for the exercises of the field. It resembled more the graceful manliness of the Belvidere Apollo than the robust structure of the Farnese Hercules.[77]

Pocahontas is Virginia belle as well as sentimental female and noble savage:

> This tender girl was the daughter of the Indian monarch. She was of a delicate form, but admirably proportioned. Her fine dark eyes beamed forth that moral sense, which imparts a magic to every look, and constitutes expression. There was a dash of melancholy in her countenance more interesting than smiles. It denoted a vacancy of heart; the want of some object on which to fix her affec-

tions. There was a delicious redness in her cherub lips. . . . Her long black hair . . . flowed in luxuriant tresses down her comely back and neck, half concealing the polish and symmetry, the rise and fall, of the bosom just beginning to fill. . . .[78]

Another element of later Virginia and plantation fiction was introduced by Davis in his *Travels* and in novels which were not actually set in the state. This is the Negro servant or slave, often oppressed. Strongly anti-slavery in feeling, Davis tells lurid tales in several of his works of miscegenation and the mistreatment of slaves. But some years before Scott's Caleb Balderstone as faithful or resourceful servant or Cooper's varied Negro characters, Davis depicts the faithful Negro servant speaking in dialect. In *The Farmer of New Jersey* (1800) Orpheus and Old Dady speak of "Moser" and "Missee." In *Walter Kennedy, an American Tale* (1808), "Captain Jack, alias Quashee," anticipates the minstrel-show stereotype of the Negro of later Virginia romances. Like several other Davis Negroes, Quashee can sing to the accompaniment of his "banger" (banjo). One of the singer's favorites is his "Seditious Ode" voicing Davis' feeling about slavery, though the stanza quoted may seem an ironic attack on anti-slavery attitudes. It attempts fairly successfully the sort of dialect to be used frequently later:

Our massa Jefferson he say,
  Dat all mans free alike are born;
Den tell me, why should Quashee stay,
To tend de cow and hoe de corn?
  Huzza for massa Jefferson.

Thus several years before Scott's *Waverley*, and many more before Cooper's use of Virginia elements in *The Spy* (1821) and *The Two Admirals* (1842), John Davis had written two fictional versions of the most dramatic episode in Virginia's early history and in them had drawn a Virginia gentleman and Virginia belle. Elsewhere he had introduced the dialect-speaking Negro slave who was also a comic minstrel. Many of Scott's novels and some of Cooper's early work were to appear before the next Virginia novel in 1824, but Davis had between 1800 and 1806 already employed several of what were to be characteristic features of the form.

Two Virginia novels appeared in 1824. One of them, the anonymous *Tales of an American Landlord; Containing Sketches of Life*

South of the Potomac (2 vols.),[79] has been almost totally ignored in this century. Yet on its appearance it was hailed as a serious rival of Scott's work, and it includes several features of the later Virginia novel.

On August 27, 1824, Attorney General Wirt wrote to his friend Dabney Carr that he had just read that morning in the *National Intelligencer* "an extract from a Virginia novel, yet unpublished. I think it is excellent."[80] Wirt went on to inquire as to its authorship, and mentioned that he himself had for some time been contemplating just such "a historical novel, *flagrante bello,* of the revolution." The newspaper of the date mentioned includes under the caption "An American Novel, or Tale," an excerpt from *Tales of an American Landlord* concerned with Lafayette, "now [1824] the nation's guest," and pronounces this passage equal to anything of parallel length which had appeared from the British "Great Unknown."

Although the few literary historians who have commented at all on this book have dismissed it as a sort of Methodist tract, it is far more and far other than this. It does present an old Methodist preacher, John Fell, one Hell-fire sermon containing a "suspended over the pit of destruction by a single hair" phrase (I, 43-46) reminiscent of Jonathan Edwards, and a young aristocratic hero in disguise as a Methodist preacher. Though these elements are themselves historically indigenous to a Virginia setting, they by no means dominate the book. As its title suggests, *Tales of an American Landlord* owes something to Sir Walter Scott in structure, for it is a frame story encompassing three long tales and a number of shorter ones. The major characters—Colonel Berkley and his son the incognito hero, Mrs. Sparkle and her two daughters, and Mr. Percy the Byronic hero-villain—accompanied by literally dozens of lesser figures, move from one Virginia tavern to another (recall the title), making short stops at private houses in between. The novel is crowded with characters who go in and out and often do not return—innkeepers, robbers, Methodists, Quakers, Episcopal clergy, sentimental young females, etc. The author mentions (I, 43) the fictional qualities of Fanny Burney, Jane Porter, and Maria Regina (or Regina Maria) Roche. One may add too that the novel reminds us of a Fielding, among others.

The time of the frame-story action is the early 1790's, when Washington is President of the United States. Appropriate characters relate incidents of Indian captivity and torture and of Quaker patience and inner conflict during the Revolution. Three fairly long poems are quoted at proper moments: "Columbia's Farewell to General La Fayette On His Return to France at the Close of the Revolutionary War," "The Genius of America, Inscribed to His Excellency General Washington. On His Return to Mount Vernon, in December, 1783," and "Sonnet to General Washington, President of the United States of America." Although the old Methodist John Fell is presented most sympathetically, and Quakers are depicted as genuinely good people, it is perhaps significant that neither Methodist nor Quaker, but an Episcopal clergyman, Mr. Marmaduke Scott (a sort of Devereux Jarratt) converts old Ben Lock, the jailer, who afterwards lives an exemplary life. One should note that the local parish rector, often resembling the Reverend Mr. Scott, is to become from *Swallow Barn* on a familiar figure in the later Virginia novel.

The Washington newspaper by excerpting one brief dramatic scene presented the novel at its best. As already suggested, it contains too many characters and too many episodes; it also too frequently employs Gothic claptrap and sentimental disguise. On the other hand, the rhetoric is relatively restrained and the language generally, though stilted, is not actually stiff. Though the events of the main action might have happened in England as well as in America, such things as the plantation-settings of the Northern Neck and Piedmont, the Quakers in the Revolution in Virginia, the stockade and Indian massacre on the frontier of the state, the names of Colonel Berkley and Colonel Hopewell and the county estates Rosemount, Hopewell Hall, Norborne Lodge, Berkley Park, and Marlevale, are convincingly domesticated in the Old Dominion. The two colonels may be in a sense transplanted Squire Westerns, but they are also more than faint beginnings of fictional Virginia and Southern colonels. Even the Negro servant is here, though "good mammy Nellie" (II, 184-85) speaks more like the less-literate white than did Davis' Quashee. Old Sambo and Jenny (also in II) make only brief appearances and are not described in enough detail to recognize them as types or original characters. But they are present, and with names which are themselves to become stereotypes.

Altogether *Tales of an American Landlord* is a not uninteresting novel. Its depiction of mores and manners from several levels of Virginia society, its combination of historical and plantation scenes and settings, and its county colonels and faithful Negroes suggest that it anticipated *Swallow Barn* and even Cooke's *Surry of Eagle's Nest* (1866) in some specific as well as general features.

The second novel of the year 1824, George Tucker's *The Valley of Shenandoah; or Memoirs of the Graysons* (2 vols.),[81] has in recent years received a little more attention, though not all it deserves. Its author composed this best-known of his three novels (one is still in manuscript) between his years as a practicing attorney and Member of Congress and his appointment to the University of Virginia professorship. On January 1, 1825, Tucker wrote to Joseph C. Cabell, who had approached him on the subject of the professorship, that he wanted some time before deciding:

> I have for more than a year conceived the project & indulge in the hope that I might pursue the business of authorship as a profitable calling—I have (but this is a secret) actually essayed the public favor in a novel just published in New York and should I meet with any thing like the success which has attended Cooper, I should think my prospects of profit much greater than any professorship could hold out—He has made about $5000 by each of his novels—and the Valley of Shenandoah, my new work was written in two months—The situation to which you invite me would almost put a stop to my efforts as an author. . . .[82]

Thus Cooper's alleged financial successes in his very earliest novels impelled Tucker to try his hand. His book is a conscious attempt to portray real Virginia life in fiction. The plot, in which seduced heroine, avenging brother, and Lovelace-like seducer are disposed of in the best Richardsonian manner, is a tracing of the decline of a Virginia family because of inherent weaknesses of the society they represent. The father of the tragic heroine has been a bona fide Southern colonel, "Colonel Grayson, a meritorious officer of the 'continental line,' in the war of the revolution." (I, 1). His widow, forty years old, well read, a good housekeeper, is the beginning of a long line of gracious plantation mistresses. Her daughter Louisa, though more a Clarissa than a Scarlett O'Hara, shows in vivacity and grace some of the qualities of the later plantation belle. Her brother Edward, somewhat saturnine and "misanthropical," who dies in the attempts to avenge his sister's lost honor, is in pride, generosity, and nobility of heart the ancestor of all later young plantation heroes. James Gildon, the New Yorker-seducer, is more weak than dastardly, as are other figures of sentimental romance. He is not so highly individualized as the Graysons are.

Though the pages of *The Valley of Shenandoah* are not so cluttered with characters as were those of *Tales of an American Landlord,* there are a score of fairly significant minor dramatic personae, in a remarkable number of instances pretty clearly drawn from close personal observation. There are three plantation colonels who are convincingly individualized: Major (the rank didn't matter for some years yet) Fawkner, easy-going father of plantation-belle Matilda, and the two Tidewater officers, Colonel Mason and Colonel Barton. Colonel Grayson's attorney Barbawl and Dr. Cutaway, both Matilda's suitors, and the attorneys Trueheart and Worricourt, despite their eighteenth-century tag names, remind the reader at once of certain recognizable Virginia types drawn later by Kennedy in *Swallow Barn,* and earlier anticipated in William Wirt's three collections of essays. Equally localized are the amusingly drawn portraits (II, 149-50) of the rival Winchester physicians, one educated at Edinburgh, the other at Philadelphia, the one a disciple of Cullen, the other an admirer of Brown. These all belong more or less to the upper classes, most of them being Episcopalians or deists. For society here is feudalistic, as it was to remain in the later Virginia novel. But both Tucker and the anonymous author of *Tales of an American Landlord* are unorthodox in the Virginia novel tradition in their interest in and depiction of middle and lower-middle class persons. In *The Valley of Shenandoah* the middle class, often Presbyterian and Scottish, are as accurately drawn as the upper-class figures: e.g., Frederick Steenor, who went to "Lexington College" (now Washington and Lee), and his attractive but rather ironically presented love Susan Tidball, whose social status may be at least another half-step down the ladder. Jacob Scryder, the German wagoner, and M'Culloch, the free-spoken mountaineer, were types often to be met with in the Valley of Virginia. Primus, the faithful slave-servant, and Granny Mott, who has an aristocratic pride in her social position as an eighty-four year old slave, are quite realistic, for they have not yet become stereotypes.

Another side of Tucker's realistic presentation of slavery is the Grayson auction, at which dire necessity forced the family's disposal of their slaves (II, 203).

Local color is abundant: the Fredericksburg races; the lovely old college town of Williamsburg in 1796, including its literary circle, politics, and student love affairs; Richmond the new metropolis; the taverns of Colchester and Dumfries; Harper's Ferry much as it was in Jefferson's famous romantic description. Lesser details of deer hunting, morning mint juleps, pieced bed quilts, and fine old furniture give further touches of verisimilitude. The snapshot glance at a family in the act of moving from Westmoreland county near the Chesapeake to Kentucky, and the analysis of the "pioneer feeling" and other reasons for the move, are the work of a keen observer conscious of economic and psychological factors in the march of civilization.

Unlike most settings of the plantation novel then or later, the principal agrarian scene here is beyond the Blue Ridge in the Great Valley, though the author does follow his characters to Tidewater and contrasts the eastern and western forms of Virginia life. He points out the mixture of Scotch-Irish and "Dutch" in the Shenandoah Valley and describes and analyzes each group. The Germans are "the dray horses of society" (I, 49 ff.), the Scotch-Irish, their opposites, imaginative, bold, and daring (I, 54 ff.). Slavery is presented in most realistic fashion, as suggested above, and the tone of presentation is unfavorable. Tucker knows and distinguishes between Cohees and Tuckahoes (I, 40). East and west, it is a society in flux, and the author tries to make sure his reader is aware of the evolution which is going on.

The later-to-become-familiar description of the plantation mansion is for the first time here present. This first time it is a double-portrait, for Tucker described both a Valley and a Tidewater country house, though with not quite the detail Kennedy later lavishes upon the simple domicile of Swallow Barn. The Valley home of the Graysons in its materials suggests the region:

> The house itself was a modest mansion of rough blue limestone, in the form of a letter L, having three rooms on one floor. Below, were a passage, drawing-room, dining room, chamber, and a large closet which had been used as a dressing room, and was now the lodging room of Louisa—the three rooms above were bedchambers.

> A large kitchen garden was on the east of the house, containing a succession of falls as the ground sloped to a little rivulet, which was formed by a limestone spring, not half a mile from the house. But the most beautiful part of the view was the river, presenting always to the eye, except after a heavy rain, a smooth surface and a limpid stream when near, and a broad sheet of mirror when seen at a distance; in which the mountains with its woods all crimson and gold; its jutting cliffs and patches of cleared land, were doubled to the eye, and inverted in their position.[83]

The Stafford county house of Colonel Barton was quite different, yet typical, as the author suggests, of all the Northern Neck. Like the limestone house of the Valley, it gives the impression of simplicity:

> The house was of brick, and consisted of a wide passage through the middle, with two rooms on each side, both above and below stairs. There was, besides, a smaller building near the main one, in which there were two lodging rooms that were occasionally occupied by young gentlemen and other visitors.[84]

Tucker's personal ideas as to the weaknesses of the Virginia economic system he blends into his love plot. For the tragedy of Gildon and Louisa is the direct result of the involved financial position of her family, itself in turn the result of wasteful wearing out of arable lands and of reckless speculations, both matters very much in the minds of Virginians in the 1820's. Virginians too "have always been remarkable for spending their incomes before they made them, and for rating them very extravagantly" (I, 119), the author comments. Another theme to which space is devoted and which is close to Tucker's heart is the political opposition of "federalists" and "democrats" (e.g., I, 148), for Tucker, though he gradually became quite conservative, was at this time a strong Jeffersonian.

Tucker's novel then presents no great historical character or notable political or martial event. It has a manners-local-color setting suggestive of Scott's or Cooper's, of Virginia life as it was about 1796. It is much more realistic in problem if not in detail than anything Cooper had written up to that time, so realistic that it hurt Virginia pride (see M. M. Robinson to William Short, April 14, 1825, Short Papers, Library of Congress). It is a problem-and-thesis novel, yet it was written with the avowed intention of earning for its author a good income by faithful depiction of Virginia life. Though Professor Hubbell suggests that it "had no part in the building of the romantic plantation tradition,"[85] its careful and sympathetic descriptions of rural mansions, barbecues, and hunting, its strongly emphasized Virginia gentleman, as well as the fact that Virginians read it, would suggest that it marks a stage in the development of the Virginia plantation tradition, whether or not it specifically influenced later writing.

Almost as absolutely ignored in the twentieth century as *Tales of an American Landlord* is James Ewell Heath's *Edge-Hill, or, The Family of the Fitzroyals* (2 vols., 1828).[86] Much more romantic in tone than *Swallow Barn*, it combines stirring events with plantation setting and quite clearly anticipates Caruthers, Cooke, and Page. Avowedly indebted to Scott (II, 205) and obviously also to Cooper, it is individual in the details of setting, in some aspects of characterization, and in its presentation of the Negro and his dialect.

In outline it is a typical sentimental novel. It begins with the return to Edge-Hill of its master, Charles Fitzroyal, with his new second wife, formerly the Widow Dashwood. Old Fitzroyal, determined to marry his son Charles to his new stepdaughter, plays the heavy parental role tolerated only in this type of fiction. The son, in love with the beautiful but persecuted Ruth Elmore, joins the Continental Army against the wishes of his Tory father. Ruth is the near-victim of malicious plots, including an abduction and attempted seduction. After many vicissitudes, young Fitzroyal is forgiven, Ruth is rescued so that she may marry him, and the sweetmeats and sugarplums are distributed in lavish fashion to all except Monteagle and the former Widow Dashwood and her daughter Cornelia.

In style Heath's book is stumbling and uneven. Homely colloquialisms in dialogue, words like "swivet" and "racket" (noise), frequently lend an air of reality. But in other places the rhetoric is strained and overdone. For example, when the heroine Ruth is tending a favorite rosebush in the presence of Cornelia: "Mordecai at the King's gate was not more odious to the repining Haman, than the unoffending Ruth whilst rearing the blooming shrub, was to her resentful rival" (II, 5).

Harriet Wilton, Ruth's "sprightly friend," Albert Monteagle, Byronic hero-villain, and historical characters such as Benedict Arnold, Tarleton, and Lafayette are recognizable counterparts of characters in Richardson, Scott, or Cooper. But more original (though already suggested in *Tales of an American Landlord* and later developed in *Swallow Barn*) here is an American clergyman of a rural parish, in this case the Reverend Mr. Rubrick, who lives on the glebe near Edge-Hill. Rather caustically he is described as orthodox, moral, but really deficient in any "perception of divine truth" (I, 46). Here again also is a sympathetically drawn Southern plantation master, Harriet's father, Major Wilton (again not yet a colonel). Here is an anticipation of the middle-aged bachelor frequently met with in the later novel (cf. *Swallow Barn*), in this instance the lawyer-tutor Claude Kilwarden, who speaks a strong Scots dialect. And here are Negro gardeners and house servants and attempted dialect. The last is often ungrammatical English, but in such expressions as "a little arter dark" it represents sound and idiom rather accurately.

Perhaps the most dramatic character in the novel is a Negro version of Cooper's Harvey Birch in *The Spy*. James, young Fitzroyal's body servant, saves his master's life on the battlefield, plans and executes an unsuccessful stratagem to kill Benedict Arnold (now a British officer), and spies on the British successfully for Lafayette. In the last paragraph of the novel, when Lafayette in 1824 (on his return visit to America) recognizes his sable companion in arms and espionage, James' testimonial letter from the French general (cf. Harvey Birch's from Washington) as to hitherto unrecognized services is quoted in full. Thus James is the faithful Negro retainer raised to heroic proportions. He does not occupy enough space in the narrative, however, to become the memorable figure Birch is.

It is perhaps in its regional setting, the estate bordering on the James River in 1781, that *Edge-Hill* marks the greatest step forward toward the work of John Esten Cooke and Thomas Nelson Page. For the aura or halo these principal popularizers of the Virginia novel threw over mansion and garden, a sentimental light not evident in either the earlier *The Valley of Shenandoah* or slightly later *Swallow Barn*, is here considerably developed. Mellowed tradition, hallowed past, and Cavalier ancestors are all implied or expressed, for instance, in the description of Edge-Hill itself:

> The mansion was situated on the northern bank of the James, or more properly the Powhatan, the name of which, according to that romantic adventurer Captain Smith, 'this fair and delightful river' was first known. It was a large commodious brick building, con-

structed of materials principally brought from *home,* as England was familiarly called, and although it might have been inferior to more modern structures in elegance of design, it could hardly be surpassed for durability and convenience. Its front, or northern side, overlooked a spacious lawn, which was shadowed by some of the finest forest trees of lower Virginia; and in the rear, extending in terraces to the river bank lay the garden, which abounded in delicious fruit and beautiful shrubbery, and was accommodated with summer houses and pavilions, in various positions. The out-houses and edifices, disposed at convenient distances, occupied the flanks of the edifice, and beyond these the green clover paddocks, and fields of early wheat and corn, announced the owner's opulence, and presented a refreshing picture of rural beauty. The whole landscape, moreover, seemed mellowed by the hand of time, and amidst all the freshness of the vernal season, objects would here and there catch the attention, bearing a significant relation to long past days. The low gothic windows, and mouldered aspect of the walls—the high and thick-set hedges of box which bordered the walks, and the majestic height of the oak, elm and poplar, which threw their venerable boughs over the front lawn, referred to a distant period when the mansion of Edge-Hill . . . was first erected. More than a century had elapsed since Sir Rupert Fitzroyal, a loyal cavalier and gentleman of wealth and family, disheartened by the fate of the elder Charles, migrated to Virginia, and became proprietor of the estate. By him it was named in commemoration of the scene of one of those hard-fought battles between the English royalists and republicans, in which he himself bore arms, and was dangerously wounded; and from him, through three or four intermediate descendants, it was ultimately derived by the present occupant.[87]

Yet for all the halo cast over lost things in this and other descriptions in the novel, if the author had ever heard the term "idealized realism" applied to his work, he would certainly have insisted that of the two words, it was *realism,* as fidelity to fact, which should be emphasized. In 1835, in writing the ablest contemporary review of Caruthers' *The Cavaliers of Virginia,* Heath (in the *Southern Literary Messenger*) took the novelist sharply to task, and in painstaking detail, for Caruthers' carelessness with facts about historical characters, places and events. But Heath also remarked upon the lack of finish, or roundness, in Caruther's portraits. It is perhaps what he calls *roundness,* or finish, which brings the *idealization* to the *actuality* and forms the mellow light around it.

Heath, earlier a country gentleman and Virginia legislator and later editor of the *Southern Literary Messenger* and a playwright, was in 1841 called by Poe almost the only person of any literary distinction still residing in Richmond.[88] George Tucker ranked *Edge-Hill* with the novels of Cooper, Kennedy, and Robert Montgomery Bird. Yet because of its obvious weaknesses of plot and sentimental characterization, *Edge-Hill* has been forgotten even by those who read *Swallow Barn* or *The Cavaliers of Virginia.*

Thus there were novels between 1805 and 1828, set in Virginia and written by Virginians, which contained in one place or another every major quality or element embodied in the later conceptions of Kennedy, Caruthers, Cooke, Page, and Johnston. By 1828 the gallant gentleman who followed the Horatian mean already administered some broad-acred fictional plantation. His gracious wife, well read and pious and yet gay, presided over a country mansion. Young sons and daughters, fresher replicas of the master and mistress, carried on their affairs of honor and love and rescue and war. Local "originals," lawyers and clergy, added zest and humor in convivial and fireside conversation. Perhaps the most sympathetic and laudatory portrait ever drawn of the faithful Negro servant, James of Edge-Hill, had already been completed. And already painted in full colors was Virginia's greatest colonial hero, Captain John Smith, a figure mentioned again and again even in the Virginia novels in which he does not appear as a living character. Sketched into backgrounds and sometimes coming front and center were Washington and Lafayette. Accompanied by Jefferson and Stonewall Jackson and Robert E. Lee these three still live in fiction. Smith's story, for example, occupies forty-odd pages in the first edition of *Swallow Barn,* and whole novels by John Esten Cooke and George Eggleston, among many others, include his and/or his fair rescuer's name in the title.

One must grant that George Tucker's *The Valley of Shenandoah* is not quite a full-fledged Virginia novel, for the nostalgic atmosphere which usually accompanied glorious deeds or plantation life is not its main tone. Only in the twentieth century, when the critical spirit had again meshed with the creative, could novelists like Ellen Glasgow in *Barren Ground* or Willa Cather in *Sapphira and the Slave Girl* see Virginia life in its full irony and paradox as Tucker had, and one may argue that even they never quite overcame a certain sentimental myopia. Like them, Tucker probed and analyzed *con amore.*

John Davis and the author of *Tales of an American Landlord* also saw that all was not right in the Virginia world they depicted. Slavery and Indian brutality and white men's broken pledges marred this lovely Eden. James Ewell Heath, a little farther away in time from the eighteenth century and conscious of the South's growing need to defend its peculiar institutions, is in 1828 as nostalgic, as sentimental over a past Virginia heroic age as Thomas Nelson Page ever was to be.

In 1817, as he wrote his *Patrick Henry,* William Wirt had felt that the glory of Virginia was passing. By the 1820's most literate Virginians knew that the crest of their wave had passed. Here and there, in that decade before *Swallow Barn,* men attempted to preserve in fiction the memory of that high tide. For the rest of the century others followed their example. All of them together created a sort of American dream in reverse, or in retrospect.

F. *The Pocahontas-John Smith Theme*

On January 20, 1797, bookseller Weems informed publisher Carey that "If you coud get a copy of Smith's History of Virginia, you w[d] do well to reprint it, I could sell you many a thousand of that curious work. N B, it sh[d] have one or two Romantic Engravings in it. Bishop Madisson desir[d] me to reprint it. Many have express[d] a wish to have a copy of it."[89] As usual Weems was evidencing his salesman's eye for the profitable. When a complete American edition of Smith was published in Richmond twenty-two years later it did not sell well, however, perhaps because there were no romantic engravings to attract the curious or sentimental.

But Weems was right in sensing tremendous Virginia interest in Smith, particularly in one part of the story the redoubtable seventeenth-century captain had told. For Smith and his rescue by Pocahontas became in the first third of the nineteenth century the theme for plays, stories, poems, and essays and was even discussed in letters. Though it has in the hands of Hart Crane, Vachel Lindsay, Carl Sandburg, and Stephen Vincent Benet, among scores, become a great symbolic action representing American origins and tensions, the theme never touched a later people more widely or more frequently than it did the Jeffersonian Virginians.

The birth of the American nation and the beginnings of the triumph of Romanticism as an attitude toward life and art came almost simultaneously. Pride in liberty, nostalgic and sentimental glances at the past, and genuine antiquarianism existed side by side. Each state consciously and unconsciously was intent on finding at least some of its roots in an American rather than a European past. For Virginians, many of whom had known already that they bore the blood of Pocahontas in their veins, the story of her rescue of Captain Smith, their symbolic English ancestor, was a tradition exactly suited to arousing pride and fancy and sentiment. Though other Americans even in the Jeffersonian period wrote of and from the legend, a great majority of the poets and fictionists, even the principal dramatist, who employed it were Virginians.

The germ of the story of course appears in Smith's *Generall Historie* of the year 1624, where the writer tells of his own rescue by the King's dearest daughter: Beverley and other later colonial Virginia historians had repeated it, along with the account of her marriage to John Rolfe. Smith himself or one of his collaborators had recorded that Smith might have married the Indian maid had he wished and that she married Rolfe believing Smith was dead. By 1755 the anonymous writer of *A Short Account of the British Plantations in America*[90] went so far as to say that the success of the first settlement in America "was chiefly owing to the love this young girl had conceived for Capt. Smith." The Scottish historian Robertson in 1796 had repeated the story, perhaps the immediate basis for the interest Weems discovered among the Virginians.

In 1803 Wirt in the *British Spy* had devoted two essays to Jamestown and the Smith-Pocahontas story, wondering in Letter IV "that the Virginians, fond as they are of anniversaries, have instituted no festival or order in honour of [Pocahontas'] memory. . . . Pocahontas deserves to be considered the patron deity of the [Virginia] enterprise." He goes on to sentimentalize about the unfortunate princess who deserved a happier fate and perhaps as significantly to note that the most respectable families of Virginia pride themselves in their descent from her. Later in Letter VI Wirt asks, "Where is Smith, that pink of gallantry, that flower of chivalry?"

In the same year as the *British Spy*, John Davis' *Travels* was published and written within two or three more years were his more elaborate fictional versions of the story discussed above. In 1807 the Richmond *American Gleaner* after quoting Blanchard's "Jamestown Ode" remarked that the next "Virginiad" should be in honor of Pocahontas, and two years later *The Visitor* of the same city featured "A Sketch of the Life of the Princess Pocahontas," far less sentimental and more factual than Davis' accounts but including the detail that "the [pretended] grave of Smith [at Jamestown] was the favorite haunt of Pocahontas."[91] The Philadelphia *Port Folio* in 1812[92] contained a "Notice of Captain John Smith, the Father of American Colonization," which was probably written by one of the several Virginians who wrote for that magazine at the time. J. W. Campbell of Petersburg in his 1813 *History of Virginia*[93] included a brief factual account of Smith and the Indian princess.

The Richmond group of Wirt, Gilmer, and Dr. John Holt Rice were in this second decade of the century considerably interested in Virginia antiquities, as the *Old Bachelor* and Rice's *Virginia Evangelical and Literary Magazine* indicate. In 1819, with the encouragement of Wirt and John Randolph, Rice as financial sponsor and Francis Gilmer brought out in two volumes (without their names being attached to it) from the Franklin Press in Richmond the first American edition of Smith's *True Travels and Generall Historie* with beautifully engraved reproductions of original frontispieces and title pages and a faithful representation of the text.[94] The handsome volumes were dedicated "To the People of Virginia," for Smith's story was theirs by right. As we have observed, the book did not sell well. It was probably both too large and too costly for most Virginians. Dr. Rice sustained a crippling financial loss.

Later in 1824 in England, Gilmer had the manuscript Latin life of Smith by Henry Wharton meticulously copied. He intended to use it as the basis for a biography he might write himself, and perhaps to publish it. His correspondence with John Randolph frequently mentions the matter. But Gilmer was dead in less than a year after he received the copy of the manuscript in Virginia, and Wharton's *Life* did not appear in print until 1957.[95]

Though James Nelson Barker of Philadelphia in *The Indian Princess* in 1808 produced the first play by a native American on the theme—one based apparently on Davis' novelette—the best drama of the period on the subject is the *Pocahontas* (1830) of George W. P. Custis discussed in Chapter VII above. In the decades after Custis came many plays on the theme, so many that one man in 1846 called them a nuisance.

Virginia poets especially liked to employ the theme in short and long pieces for various effects and purposes. The first to use the fabled maid as subject was John Davis, who in the 1803 *Travels* included three poems on her. The first, in three octosyllabic quatrains, represents Rolfe addressing Pocahontas and urging that she forget her former "faithless lover" and favor his suit. The second, a twelve-line octosyllabic lyric, praises her lovely face and voice and kiss.[96] The third, "Sonnet to Pocahontas," has the requisite fourteen lines but in couplet form. Again Rolfe is represented as languishing for her love. It concludes:

> Here where the mocking-bird, the woods among,
> Warbles with rolling note her plaintive song,
> And the sad *Mucakawis'* ill-omen'd strain,
> Rings from the woods, and echoes to the plain,
> Here as I pensive wander through the glade,
> I sigh and call upon my *Indian* maid.[97]

"The Beauties of York," an anonymous poem in the 1814 *Port Folio*[98] probably written by a Virginian, contains one of the earlier poetic references:

> These are the walks, and this the bowery shade,
> The lov'd recess where Pocahontas stray'd;
> When Smith's dear image to her bosom stole,
> And love usurped the empire of her soul.
> For thee, heroic maid, no kind return,
> To him thou say'dst, no kindred fervours burn!

Two years earlier in 1812 Norfolk poet William Maxwell in lines "To William Wirt, esq." acknowledges his subject's interest in the Indian maid and his own romantic concept. He begins:

> See Pocahontas flies by night
> Tho' dark, alone, and late,

With beating heart, and step so light,
To avert her lover's fate.[99]

In *Letters from Virginia* (1816), as we have noted probably by George Tucker, the essayist in Letter XVII meditates upon "Smith and the Belle Sauvage, who, by the by, are almost the only poetical characters in the history of the state." Then he bursts into a bad "Ballad. The Indian Maid," beginning

Come all ye gay ladies draw near,
While I sing you a ballad of love;
'Twas writ for a delicate ear,
With the quill of Simplicity's dove.[100]

Though he relates the story of Pocahontas' night journey to Jamestown to warn Smith, he does not enhance her "poetical character" as far as moving verse is concerned.

Almost every Virginia poet of the 1820-30 decade had something to say about the Smith-Pocahontas matter. Bernard M. Carter includes his "Pocahontas" in both the 1820 and 1824 editions of his poems.[101] St. Leger Landon Carter in 1821 did more, for he published anonymously in that year in Baltimore *The Land of Powhatan, By a Virginian,* a work called by the reviewer in the *Virginia Evangelical and Literary Magazine* "a sort of epic ballad, or rhyming chronicle, of the first settlement of our state,"[102] with Powhatan, his daughter, Smith, and all the rest. Carter employs a variety of verse forms—among them octosyllabic couplets, ballad measures, and anapaestic tetrameter—in varying the tempo of his long verse tale. He begins in the late-eighteenth century pseudo-epic fashion.

Imperial Powhatan! thy day
In dark oblivion rolls away;
Thy warriors all in dust are laid,
And silent sleeps the Indian maid.

The poet admits he tampered a little with history by having Smith and the maiden united in marriage, but he was correct in feeling that his readers would not mind.[103]

Two Petersburg poets in 1825 devoted large parts of more ambitious poems to Smith and Pocahontas and the founding of Virginia. Hiram Haines (1805-1841) included the long "Virginiad" in his *Mountain Buds and Blossoms,* with an introduction and notes on the relation between the white soldier and red princess.[104] Written in twelve-line stanzas, it hails Virginia, whose cities, towns, and rivers each fill one or more stanzas. The Appomattox reminds him of

> Fair Pocahontas, of exalted mind.
> And race as noble as her heart was kind.

The Indian maid's song as she sighs under the moon is perhaps as good as anything in the poem. In the romantic tradition she concludes:

> I'll weave for my love a gay wampum belt shining
> With bright coral shells, so lovely and fair;
> And I'll bind him a crest together entwining
> The pelican's plumage with my waving hair.
> Oh! then to him quick I smiling will bear them,
> On his brow and his arms my hands shall them braid;
> Then when he's away the fair warrior may wear them,
> And look and remember his dark Indian maid.[105]

John Robertson (1787-1873) in *Virginia, or the Fatal Patent: A Metrical Romance. In Three Cantos*[106] rhymes at length on the separation of the colony from the British Crown, the patent being that conferred by James I on the London Company. Captain Smith is the hero of the romance, and naturally Pocahontas appears. The plebian name of his protagonist bothered the poet, however,

> John Smith, a name not deem'd, as I opine
> Fit to be measured in a Poet's song:
> What tho' it sounded low along the line,
> Yet does a hero's fame to it belong.

The romantic idea and ideal in the poem do not raise it above the mediocre, but it is interesting as an essay toward the Virginia epic.

Though the story may have been in "weak hands" all through the Jefferson period, from the end of the eighteenth century to 1830 it had developed from a footnote of history, at most a romantic anecdote, into a beautiful legend fit for the hand of later and better poets, playwrights, and novelists. By 1830 the sentimental John Davis and his fellow Virginians had in fiction and verse shaped the character of the Indian girl into something which would become a symbol of America, "Our Mother, Pocahontas" of Lindsay and Crane and humbler poets since. Biographies of Smith continue to appear, and the old question of his veracity is still threshed about. The ungifted Virginia writers of our first national period knew that such questions were all vain and beside the point. They knew a poetic subject when they saw one, and well before Cooper and Hawthorne and Melville they understood how to employ a symbol.

G. *Verse*

To say that literature of "a higher kind," especially verse, was written almost entirely north of the Susquehanna in the period between 1790 and 1830[107] is to ignore a vigorous poetic activity, if not tradition, in Virginia which began with St. George Tucker and continued through Edgar Poe. That it produced no remarkable result except in the work of the two named must be admitted at once. But in a period when only Freneau and Bryant were distinguished American practitioners of the art save for the aging Hartford Wits, it bears comparison with the endeavors in any other section. Perhaps more significantly, it affords ample evidence that dozens of Virginians were genuinely interested in making poems and in celebrating in rhyme the natural features and historic glories of their native soil.

Some fifty-five versifiers may be identified by name, several others published at least one volume anonymously, and scores more contributed occasional pieces without signature to the newspapers and magazines. As noted above, some two dozen persons produced thirty-six volumes of poetry. Though many Virginians like other Americans wrote poetic satire, especially in the period before the War of 1812, many more composed lyrics, *vers de société*, narrative and descriptive pieces, even a "metrical romance" and at least one attempt at an epic. Though heroic and octosyllabic couplets, ballad measures, Spenserian stanza, and quatrains popular at the end of the eighteenth century in England continued in Virginia throughout the period as the favored metrical forms, many verses show the growing influence of Scott, Byron, and Moore in experiments of various kinds, especially in the use of anapaestic tetrameter. Towards the end of the period there was at least one poet who could indite good sonnets. Imagery remained strongly Popean or Miltonic, but here too the three romantics had their effect, as perhaps even more did Blair through the *Rhetoric,* the graveyard poets, Ossian, Collins, Gray, and Cowper. In some circles Burns, in dialect and sentiment, was a favored model.

Philosophically their verse naturally has the same origins as their prose. At least three of the half dozen more prolific poets not only imply the sources of their ideas but include in their lines the names of Stewart, Reid, Locke, and Blair. Though much verse is consciously moral, the poets were aware of the potential conflict between aesthetic and didactic intention. Politically the versifiers range from the liberal Tucker to the conservative "Giles Julap" the satirist, with perhaps the majority of those who voice sentiments at all on the democratic side.

When they write of nature they are more nearly in the tradition of James Thomson than of Wordsworth or Shelley, but they celebrated Virginia seasons, birds, flowers, rivers, and mountains, sometimes with surprising freshness. Several record or interpret their dreams, many devote elegiac lines to their departed friends in much the tone of Kirke White or William Cullen Bryant, a number translate or paraphrase their favorite classical poets. A few translate from the Italian. Many devote lyrics to the ladies in what has become a Southern habit. America's future destiny provokes exultant tones in occasional poems for the Fourth of July, the Jamestown celebration of 1807, or Lafayette's visit in 1824. Virginia's great men are praised but her decline is mourned or denied. Sentimental humor, satiric humor, and the naughty tale also appear. Piety is often an element of the moral poem, but not always, and religious verse is rare except among the hymn writers mentioned in Chapter VII above.

The versifiers of the last decade of the eighteenth century were members of a group centering in St. George Tucker and Williamsburg.[108] Among them were Margaret Lowther Page and her husband Governor John Page, Robert Bolling, Mrs. Anna Byrd, Judge John Tyler, William Wirt, and William Munford. Tyler and the Pages lived on their estates near Williamsburg, Bolling was apparently one of the Petersburg family, and Munford, a former William and Mary student, lived in Mecklenburg county. Wirt did not live in Williamsburg until 1802, but he exchanged verses and other pieces with Tucker over a long period. Certainly most of their rhyming was for their own amusement, but at least three of them published volumes and contributed fairly regularly to the journals. By 1790 Tucker, the Pages, and Judge Tyler were veterans in the art. Tucker had already published a volume, and that year the Pages with Tucker and others had a book of verse printed. In the same year or soon thereafter Bolling, Tucker, and at least one of the Pages were represented in the poetry section of Mathew Carey's *American Museum.*

As the *Virginia Gazette* bears witness from the 1730's, the Tidewater Virginia gentry had early found verse-writing a pleasant indoor sport. Of the Jeffersonian practitioners of the exercise, John Tyler (1747-1813) seems to have been the earliest, for he began rhyming in his student days at William and Mary and from 1772 until his death kept a manuscript book containing his compositions. True to the gentlemanly tradition, he seems never to have published his verses. Not until his grandson published *The Letters and Times of the Tylers*[109] in 1884 did any of them appear in print.

Apparently Tyler wrote so purely for his own and his close neighbor's amusement that he did not feel any necessity of seeking comment on his verses from such a critic as Tucker, to whom so many others appealed. Tyler's verse is essentially lyric, much of it dedicated to young ladies under names like Delia, Celia, and Cynthia, in the stilted forms of the earlier eighteenth or seventeenth centuries. Octosyllabics, decasyllabics, quatrains and couplets are his favorite conventional forms. "To Cynthia" is typical, beginning

> Dear lovely maid, why thus so cruel grown?
> You fly for ever from my slightest touch;
> 'Tis naught but love pursues thee—love alone;
> Canst thou so soft a passion fear so much?

Some of his poems he composed while sitting on the bench, as "May 10, 1805, Fredericksburg District Court" or "Sitting on the bench at Brunswick." Besides the ladies, he celebrated the sickness which befell him on his journey or the hospitality of kind friends. True to his age, he found the sentimental clergy a convenient means of expressing his grief for the loss of his loved ones, as "On the Death of Mary Tyler . . . 1797" or "On the Death of Anne Contesse Semple. Written by her ever adored and adoring father." On his birthday, February 28, 1798, he indulged in the kind of moral meditation on mutability which his contemporary Freneau had expressed in "The Wild Honey Suckle."

> This day my years count fifty-one
> So swift my chequer'd time flies on:
> Too soon my pleasures have an end,

Too long my wayward care depend.
But time well managed, though severe,
May prove, in truth, my friend sincere;
And teach me how my latter days,
In peace may close as life decays.[110]

He loved acrostics containing the real name of his inamorata. And occasionally he wrote with humor in a rollicking mood, as "The Knight Errant" of 1800, which pokes fun at the two unwilling participants in a duel. Pedestrian or worse as his verses may be, he is among several dozen Jeffersonian Virginians who left manuscript evidence that they gave expression to their thoughts in poetic terms.

College youths have always been given to versifying, and those at William and Mary were not in this respect exceptional. Interesting especially are the precocious poems of Lewis Littlepage, later soldier of fortune and figure of romance, who at fifteen wrote "An Elegy on the Death of the Late Colonel Tarlton Fleming . . . 1778" and had even earlier written another commemorative poem on his friend Fleming.[111] About the same time he composed an "Ode to Death" including the line "Even Godlike Washington must die and fill the silent grave." His most impressive effusion, however, was his translation of the time-worn Ode XXII in the first book of Horace, a poem which has been reprinted more than once.[112]

The one example of verse preserved from the pen of William Short, nearly as romantic a figure as his college contemporary Littlepage, apparently also was done in his William and Mary days. It is copied in his hand into a copy of Horace's *Carminum* presented to him by his Professor in the Humanities, John Bracken. Four stanzas conclude with the familiar meditations upon mutability:

To Contemplations sober eye
    Such is the race of man:
And they that creep & they that fly
    Shall end where they began
Alike the busy & the gay
But flutter thru' life's little day,
    In Fortune's varying colours drest:
Brushed by the hand of rough mischance,
Or chilled by age, their airy dance
    They leave, in dust to rest.[113]

The resident early group at Williamsburg gave evidence of considerably more than these casual pieces. Tucker and the Pages exchanged poems and serious and facetious criticism of them, and Tucker himself consulted his brother Thomas Tudor Tucker about his verses. Mrs. Byrd, Colonel Byrd, Theodorick Bland, a Mrs. Dunbar, a Mrs. Skipwith, and Nancy Cocke were among those who from 1779 sent their verses to Tucker for criticism.[114] In the early nineteenth century William Munford, William Wirt, and Judith Lomax consulted him. Recognized throughout the state as a poetic critic of considerable ability and a practicing poet, Tucker took time from his multifarious activities and occupations to advise all these people. Perhaps it was on his advice that several Tidewater Virginians sent their verses to Carey's *American Museum* for publication. That Tucker was in regular correspondence with Carey is clear.[115]

Carey's journal in its "Select Poetry" section carried Virginia verse as early as Volume III, "A Poem," addressed to the people of Virginia, on New-Year's Day, 1788, [116] perhaps by a member of the Tucker coterie. In Volume VII (1790), there were a number of Virginia poems, including "On General Washington," "On General Arnold," and the elaborate "Liberty," all signed "T.," as near as Tucker ever came to publishing his name with his verse. Also, probably sent by Tucker, was "Rob. Bolling, jun." 's[117] "Time's Address to the ladies. In Imitation of Tasso: most humbly inscribed to Miss E. Randolph, on James river, in Virginia," a *carpe diem* poem of sixty-seven lines in quatrains. Also in Volume XII (1792), "Verses on the death of a beloved child. By a lady of Virginia, 1792," probably by Mrs. Page, and two of Tucker's best poems, "A Hymn to the Creator" and "The Belles of Williamsburg," to be discussed below.

Margaret Page Lowther, second wife of John Page of Rosewell and the mother of eight of his twenty children, was the daughter of a Scot and a practicing poet before she was married in 1790. There is evidence that during their courtship in New York the Pages addressed poems to each other and for each other on various occasions.[118] Some of these pieces are among those included in the volume they published in New York in 1790 about the time they were married. The book survives in one known copy and that without a title page, and the individual poems are unsigned except by initials, and most of these are added in the hand of someone who also copied verses into blank leaves. This was probably Mrs. Page herself, for the book seems to be her author's copy containing later inserted titles, the author's initials, and further autograph poems by her, principally.[119] Forty-one of the poems in the little book are signed "J. P.," twenty-eight by "M. L[owther]" or "M. L. P.," sixteen by Tucker (given as "X.T." and "S.G.T."), a few by ".N." [William Nelson?], "T.T.T." (Thomas Tudor Tucker), "Col. B–d" (Byrd), and "A.G.P." (Alice Grymes Page).

Mrs. Page's lines in this volume are poor stuff on the most conventional of sentimental and patriotic topics. Evidently she had a facile pen and was more highly respected for her powers than any of the group except Tucker. But her husband John's sprightly and humorous pieces are much better reading today. Page wrote on philosophic and religious and trivial topics as the mood suited him, on having read "[Jonathan] Edwards on Free Will," on Hume and the Deists, and on his scolding of his wife for over-indulgence in the snuff-box. He wrote on politics, canaries, sleep, a New York barber, Turgot and the Physiocrats, and "From the Italian of Metastasio." The mood is usually jovial, but the wit is sometimes slightly barbed, as in the political poems against demagogues and Federalists. Tucker's "Hymn to the Creator" and "The Belles of Williamsburg" are also here, in the latter a dagger denoting which verses were written by Dr. McClurg, and poems on the Pages' marriage, "To Genius," and others to be noted below. The verses by the minor contributors are unexceptional, Colonel B–d writing "An Anacreontic on Beauty" and W. N. an "Epithalamium," also for the Pages. The volume includes a selection from Nathaniel Tucker's *The Bermudian,* the only piece not really Virginian.[120]

In 1790 also Mrs. Page's lines on the "Lamented youth!" Hallyburton were sent by "Valentine" to be printed in the *New-York Magazine, &, Literary Repository,* where they appeared in the August issue. Many years later, in 1812, another friend sent her poem on the burning of the Richmond Theatre to the *Port Folio,* which published it with a note of praise and the usual comment that it was submitted without her knowledge. She began this "pathetic effusion" with lines from Young, followed by her own

Whence the wild wail of agonizing wo
That heaves each breast, and bids each eye o'erflow?[121]

About thirty-nine of her poems remain among the Tucker-Coleman Papers. Undoubtedly many others Tucker returned to her with comment. They cover many years, from the time of the lady's marriage until after the War of 1812. After her husband's death in 1808 she and two of her children moved to Williamsburg near the Tuckers. Here she could and did send almost daily notes and verses, seeking her friend's advice. Among her surviving pieces are some which indicate that she too could be witty, though more are elegiac and sentimental. Certainly she took verse writing seriously, though rather as a social than an individual accomplishment.

Her husband John thought his own verses inferior to those of his wife and of Tucker. Though he was right in regard to Tucker, we cannot be so sure when we compare his work with Margaret's. About twenty of his pieces survive among the Tucker papers, many not so good as those in the 1790 volume. That he wrote others, perhaps more ambitious and elaborate, is certain. More than half facetiously Page reminded Tucker in 1795 that the latter was to be his Warburton, the editor of his poems.[122] Perhaps Tucker judged all of them them correctly, for there is no edition.

After 1800 several of Tucker's poetic correspondents lived greater distances from him. William Wirt, whose surviving manuscript verses date from 1789 or earlier,[123] probably did not get to know Tucker until he moved to Williamsburg in 1802. But from then until Tucker's death, wherever he was Wirt consulted him on matters literary, sending him occasionally brief and usually jocular or witty verses, asking his advice on the biography of Henry, and sending him the play "The Path of Pleasure" for criticism. Tucker wrote a rhymed prologue for "The Path of Pleasure" which survives among the Tucker manuscripts, and later a number of essays for the *Old Bachelor,* as already mentioned.

Judith Lomax, who did not publish her volume of verse until 1812, was by 1800 seeking Tucker's advice. Her first request was enclosed in a letter of her lawyer father Thomas Lomax, who apologized for allowing his daughter to bother the eminent jurist with "these vanities of a girl."[124] Her father at least saw how bad her verse was.

William Munford (1775-1825) was a law student of Tucker's in Williamsburg in 1793-95. Son of the Revolutionary playwright and poet Colonel Robert Munford, William studied earlier Greek, Spanish, and Italian directly under the supervision of George Wythe. In 1793 Munford gave a much-praised Fourth of July oration in Williamsburg, and by then Tucker seems to have been reading his verses. A practicing lawyer and legislator in his native Mecklenburg and in Richmond from about 1795, he settled permanently in the latter place, where he married Sally Radford in 1806. From that time, because of the growing obligations of a large family, the potential artist degenerated into a legal drudge, at least according to one friend. Munford edited many volumes of Virginia legal reports, it is true, but he continued to write occasional verse and witty epigrams and to work on his translation from the classics. But the necessary absorption in mundane affairs is symptomatic of the condition which Francis Gilmer complained of so bitterly in his own career.

By 1798 Munford had published the only volume of his literary expression to appear during his life time, his *Poems and Compositions in Prose on Several Occasions,*[125] with his own name on the title page. Besides the play referred to in Chapter VII, his Fourth of July speech, and some political addresses, it includes some twenty poems. Three were translations of Horace, six or seven versified forms of Ossian, one an elegy, a few epigrams, one a poem on General St. Clair's Defeat in the ballad form of "Chevy Chase," a few other occasional pieces, some satiric, and the rather spirited "The Political Contest, A Dialogue." The last shows Munford in the role of a political moderate, though later evidence indicates he was a Jeffersonian Republican. The volume indicates tireless effort and a fair knowledge of eighteenth-century verse forms and fashions, but certainly not genius. Scores of manuscripts of later occasional pieces survive.[126] Though the 1798 volume shows the influence of the pre-romantics like Macpherson in *Ossian,* in his later poems Munford like Philip Freneau turned back to neoclassical models.

Perhaps the later poem which shows most thought and feeling is an exception, a translation of an Italian Ode on the deliverance of Italy from the Austrians and Russians by the victory of Napoleon. The mock-heroic "The Richmond Cavalcade" and "The Richmond Feast," anti-Federalist satires written in 1798 and 1799 are more characteristic, however. There are quantities of versified exchanges with the Reverend John D. Blair, and a few, as "The Friend to the

Fashionable Fair,"[127] a satire on women's fashions, which were published in Richmond newspapers.

When he was not taking notes as Reporter for the Virginia Supreme Court of Appeals or in the Legislature, Munford amused himself in his later years, at times even when he sat in court, by translating Homer's *Iliad.* Much of it he repeated aloud (probably not in court) to test the rhyme. A month or two after he completed the translation and wrote a preface he died. He had already been in communication with potential publishers, but for the time nothing came of it.

In his Preface[128] the translator states that he aimed to avoid Pope's mistake of clothing the Greek poet in the fashional garb of a modern gentleman, and Cowper's of clothing him in uncouth or savage dress. Since "the distinguishing traits of Homer's poetry are majestic simplicity of style, incomparable energy and fire of fancy and sentiment, with peculiar variety and harmony of modulation," he hoped in a modest way to recapture these qualities. The translator should, after preserving the spirit and fire of the original, however, write in the language now in use, "in words intelligible to his contemporaries." Miltonic blank verse he considered the most appropriate measure, making an attempt to combine "ease and smothness, with strength and variety." To amplify and interpret certain passages, he added copious notes, most of them new but some from Eustathius, Clarke, and other critics, as well as Pope and Cowper.

Through the efforts of his family Munford's translation finally appeared in Boston in 1846. Professor C. C. Felton of Harvard, the Greek scholar, had advised its publication and reviewed it in the *North American Review* in July of the same year. It also received extended notice in the *Southern Literary Messenger,* the *Southern Quarterly Review,* the *Christian Examiner,* the *American Whig Review,* and the *Literary World.*[129] Felton, aiming to be cordial, wrote in the somewhat condescending tone of the later New Englander looking at anything literary from the South. The translation did the state more honor than all her political dissertations, he thought, and was the best work of classical scholarship from Virginia since Sandys' Ovid. He considered the version "rich and rhythmical," more pleasing and effective in battle scenes and natural descriptions than in details of daily life. The Charleston *Southern Quarterly Review* adopted a bristlingly defensive Southern patriotic attitude. The *Southern Literary Messenger* in Munford's home town gave it a balanced, qualified analysis. The *American Whig Review,* proceeding apparently from a romantic frame of reference, asked why it had ever been allowed to be published.

All in all, it was treated in 1846 with as much respect as it then might expect. Twenty years earlier, in a literary world nearer to the neoclassic, it might have been received with greater warmth. Desire for clarity at times produced pedestrian prose where moving verse should have been. Notes and even translation tend too much toward the moral, like most eighteenth-century verse, and at times to a ridiculous attempt to reconcile the study of the classics with Christianity. The text itself is clear, moderate in imagery, and direct. If nothing else, Munford's Homer is good evidence that the Virginia gentleman amateur could still be, and in this case was, a sound classical scholar in a Southern tradition which runs from George Sandys to William Alexander Percy.

St. George Tucker was himself, however, a better and a more serious poet than any of those he advised. Though he observed to Mathew Carey in 1795 that his Muse "has never done anything but divert herself, having scarcely ever indulged a serious thought, and never for half an hour together,"[130] some of his poems strongly belie his modest statement, which may be after all but traditional gentlemanly disclaimer. He left behind well over two hundred separate poems in print or manuscript. Besides the 1790 volume mentioned above to which he contributed with his friends, he himself brought out as a separate work *The Knight and Friars* in New York in 1786 and *The Probationary Odes of Jonathan Pindar, Esq. A cousin of Peter's, and Candidate for the Post of Poet Laureat to the C.U.S.* in two parts in Philadelphia in 1796, both without the author's name. Besides the individual poems mentioned above as signed with his initial in the *American Museum,* others without signature were printed in Freneau's *National Gazette* in 1793 (part of *The Probationary Odes*), the *Alexandria Daily Gazette,* the Richmond *Enquirer,* the *Columbian Magazine, Niles' Weekly Register,* the London *Mirror of Literature, Amusement and Instruction,* and almost surely many other journals. Despite this publication, the majority of his surviving briefer pieces in manuscript are occasional lines struck off for the amusement of his friends or of himself.[131]

Surviving materials indicate that he was writing verse, along with considerable prose, from 1770 to 1825. His poems indicate that he shared the philosophical optimism of the liberals of his time. Man was self-perfectible, and religion was largely a sanction for morality he felt, as John Randolph so bitterly testified concerning this stepfather of his in later years.[132] The exercise of reason was man's best hope. Reason assured him that there was an omnipotent God who demanded virtuous living, and that there was a system of rewards and punishments. Tucker remained a deist of the stamp of Jefferson and Franklin all his life. "Written on Christmas Day, 1820" and "Lines, on the Murder of Doctor Hopkins" imply much of his religious philosophy.[133] Of secular philosophers, Locke appears to have influenced him most, the Scottish school scarcely at all.

Tucker's poems fall fairly easily, as William S. Prince has shown, into five or six categories, naturally sometimes overlapping. First are the verses to be passed around among his friends, usually *vers de société,* sometimes mourning the loss of a loved one or friend but more often frivolous and light. These make up a large part of his work. The long exchange with Mrs. Page and the poems to Mrs. Frances Randolph (whom he later married) are typical. The best remembered is "The Belles of Williamsburg," of which Tucker wrote eleven and Dr. McClurg nine of the original twenty stanzas. Another delightful piece is "Lines, supposed to have been found upon the palace green at Williamsburg on May Day."

Verses for public occasions were composed for a larger public. He celebrated the Richmond Theatre fire, the death of Edmund Pendleton, and the death of "Paulus" in elegies evidently intended to be published—two of them were. They are reminiscent of Gray and Edward Young and somewhat stilted in diction. His three prologues for plays are in conventional eighteenth-century couplets. His tales and anecdotes are better reading. To one familiar only with his edition of Blackstone or tracts on government, the dignified Tucker's strain of bawdy humor in his tales may come as a surprise. In *The Knight and Friars* he told in ballad measure an old story versified just the year before, in 1786, by R. P. Jodrell in London in octosyllabic couplets.[134] Sixteen poems are based on supposed Virginia incidents; for example, "Jerry Walker," an attack on evangelical preachers. Details of the daily routine of Virginia life are the most interesting feature of most of them. The character sketches in many tales are half Chaucerian and half personal observation. Though he employs several meters, including the ballad measure, Tucker in these pieces always remained within accepted eighteenth-century forms. Their bawdiness may account for the fact that most were never printed.

In his patriotic verses Tucker is always a thorough Republican. He is deeply conscious of the mission of America, as in his "Ode for the Fourth of July, 1794," which enumerates the great explorers and the statesmen who have made the nation. Here and in "Liberty" and "Ode to Union," as well as the verse plays mentioned in Chapter VII, he sought to inspire true union among the states. As the years passed he thought these poems his most significant. As late as 1823 he was corresponding with Carey regarding printing a volume of them. Their treatment of history suggests the development of the later American myth, but in all else they are conventional and stale.

In satire Tucker followed again a familiar literary tradition. But inspired by determination and indignation and a vital subject, he produced in this genre pieces well-nigh as effective and as memorable as those of his New England contemporaries Barlow and Trumbull. Tucker's barbs, usually aimed at the British or the Federalists, sometimes impale individuals or institutions regardless of affiliation. He began in 1776 with a doggerel attack on the British and followed with a parody of a proclamation of Cornwallis. He wrote against the Reverend Jacob Duché, Luther Martin (for his attack on Jefferson), Mad Anthony Wayne, and General Campbell. But his *Probationary Odes,* begun in 1793 in Freneau's *National Gazette,* is effective satire, and as good verse as usually occurs in the polemic form. It was aimed at wealthy Federalist security holders who were speculating with bought-up paper. Like many others, Tucker believed they had forced a bill through Congress for their own benefit. Most of them were from the North. The South was already bitter about the government's plan to assume state debts and to establish a national bank. The men who supported all these things became a natural target.

In the *National Gazette* odes Tucker hit men and enactments and parties. He attacked the Administration, Congress, and the Judiciary.

Hamilton is the arch-villain, but Jay and John Adams are ranged beside him. In the Fifth Ode "To a Truly Great Man," he even reminded Washington that he had no right to create a bank. Ode IX, "To Liberty," begins:

> O thou! what ever be thy doubtful name,
> Once dear to us, and still to Gallia dear,
> Whose boisterous accents, fill the trump of Fame
> Accents which we have grown too deaf to hear.

The later odes, composed in 1793-94 after the *National Gazette* ceased publication in October of the former year, are principally variations of earlier themes. Ode XVI, for instance, attacks Jay and his treaty.

Though it has numerous American ancestors and contemporaries, *The Probationary Odes* immediate model in stanzaic form and title was the verse of Peter Pindar (John Wolcot), the best of the British caricaturists of the period. Tucker's complete *Odes* was published in Philadelphia in 1796. For many years Freneau was thought to have been the author, but the Tucker-Coleman Papers at Williamsburg establish Tucker's authorship beyond any doubt. They are with *The Glosser* (to be discussed below) the only notable satire published by Southerners during the first national period. And they are among the very few in the whole country which dealt with significant national issues. They touch real issues as the *Anarchiad,* for example, does not. Their theme is the nature of the national government then being established, and they raise vital questions.

Tucker wrote about forty lyrics and personal poems, about half of them songs and odes. Several are Latin versions of English songs, and several more in English are paraphrased translations of the Latin. But Tucker had come to know Burns at least by 1789, and a number imitate the Scot's dialect and passionate libertarianism. "An Imitation of Burns" (1805) and "To Genius" (*ca.* 1811), a tribute to the poet, are indicative. Most of them are too rhetorical and sentimental, but at least one in the religious group is probably the finest expression of his personal feeling. It is dated January 13, 1790:

Hymn to the Creator

> O God! whose word spake into birth
> Whate'er existence boasts;
> The moon, the stars, the sun, the earth,
> The heavens, and all their hosts.

From world to world, from sun to sun
I turn my wondering eyes;
Their swiftest glance thy works outrun:
New suns and worlds arise!

Thy wonders still my soul pursues
Through each remoter world,
Till sight and thought their aid refuse,
To utter darkness hurled:

There lost—through endless time and space
I seek thy light divine:
O grant me Lord! to see thy face,
But—let thy mercy shine.[135]

"Resignation," the best known of his poems except "The Belles of Williamsburg," appealed to all his generation, including John Adams and Dolley Madison. The familiar line beginning

Days of my youth,
Ye have glided away

probably had appeared previously in some American journal before they were published in the British 1823 *Mirror of Literature, Amusement, and Instruction*.[136]

Tucker in all his verse emphasizes man in society, as the eighteenth-century English poets and many of his American contemporaries did. There is not a single nature poem among his writings. Universal qualities, moral truth, not his own imaginative experience, is the matter of his concern. The age of oratory is evident in his rhetoric, the neoclassic in his verse forms and artificial diction. He wrote no sonnets, little blank verse, no Spenserian stanza.

Yet he is less bookish, more natural than his New England contemporaries. Despite his disclaimer to Carey, he tried to be more than the gentlemanly dabbler, and he succeeded. Among his many interests he thought he might be best remembered for his semaphore. John Page disagreed and stood firm for the poems.[137] We must agree with his friend. Tucker deserves to be remembered as the Southern poet of the age of the Hartford wits, a poet who merits comparison and consideration with any of his American contemporaries.

In the first decade of the new century John Davis was writing verse on other subjects besides Pocahontas. His 1803 *Travels of Four*

Years and a Half in the United States of America contains eighteen poems, all on American subjects, eight of them labeled "Ode." Some of these odes are to a cricket, Ashley River, a mocking-bird, a young lady named Virginia, and morning and evening at Occoquan. Sonnets to a whip-poor-will and to Charlotte Smith are also among them. Reminiscent in diction of Shenstone, Gray, Cowper, and the Milton of the minor poems, they are worth noting for their celebration of Virginia and Southern nature and their anti-slavery sentiments.

The American Mariners, a long narrative poem of some quasi-epic intent published in 1822[138] after Davis returned to England, has a great deal to say about "the gay Virginians" (lines 108-9, 867-68) and slavery (lines 1616-2303) in the story of Yarrow "on Rappahannock's shore" as well as of John Smith and Pocahontas. One of his better shorter poems is also included in the same volume, "The Natural Bridge of Virginia. An Ode." Stanza four is indicative:

> And, here, perhaps, the Indian stood,
> With hands upheld, and eye amaz'd,
> As, sudden, from the devious wood,
> He first upon the fabric gaz'd.

Parson Mason Locke Weems was like Davis fond of interspersing his prose with verse. *Hymen's Recruiting Sergeant; or, the New Matrimonial Tattoo for the Old Bachelor* (1800) is a forty-page sermon including many songs, most of them calling upon bachelors and maidens to be patriotic and marry! The rhymes are as blithe and as lively as the same writer's biographies and letters. One begins:

> In the world's crooked path where I've been,
> There to share in life's gloom my poor part,
> The sunshine that softened the scene
> Was—*a smile from the wife of my heart.*

The bicentennial celebration at Jamestown in 1807 brought forth several patriotic songs and at least two odes. One of the latter by C. K. Blanchard was copied in many Virginia newspapers[139] and later in 1824 in a collection in honor of Lafayette's visit.[140] Another was the "Ode delivered by Leroy Anderson to a Select Company of Friends in the Old Church-Yard Amidst the Tombs," also reprinted in 1824. The patriotic poems are in the vein of those published by John M'Creery in *A Selection, from the Ancient Music of Ireland . . .*

(Petersburg, 1824), a volume which included at least sixteen songs by the editor-author's friend John Daly Burk. Burk and M'Creery had originally planned the volume together, with Burk in the role of lyricist. Many of Burk's lyrics are in the Moore-Byron-Burns vein on "Aileen Aroon," "Molly Macalpin," "Nancy of the Branching Tresses," and "The Flower of Virginia." Others specifically patriotic, set to old tunes, are "The American Star" and "Composed for the 4th July, 1818."

The decade which saw in other parts of America the publication of Thomas Green Fessenden's *Democracy Unveiled* (1805) and *Terrible Tractoration* and a number of lesser satires naturally elicited some such verse in Virginia. George Tucker, usually devoted to more serious things, composed one clumsy piece inspired by his wife's losses in a card game. "A Letter from Hickory Cornhill, Esq., to His Friend in the Country" survives in printed form in the *Enquirer* of January 9, 1806, and in a manuscript in the Virginia Historical Society. A backwoods bumpkin, "Being asked to a party of ladies at Loo," an ancestor of bridge, records his impressions. The light satire is on dress, inane conversation, and the wasting of time. This slight piece is said to have received as much attention as anything Tucker ever wrote. Certainly it elicited a number of responses.[141]

More ambitious satire had appeared in 1802 in *The Glosser; a Poem in Two Books, By Giles Julap, of Chotank, Virginia.*[142] It was one among the many American squibs against Jefferson which appeared during his two administrations. Dedicated to "Mrs. Minte G. Sling of James River, Virginia," it seems to have been written in a spirit of pique because the author had not received Jefferson's patronage. It ridicules the President's use of neologisms such as *belittle* and *looming* in *Notes on Virginia,* and refers to his red breeches. As the "great Montiklo" Jefferson is made to speak of his own scientific-political character.

> All science anthropologistic,
> I comprehend however mystic,
> And long have known with strict precision
> To weigh each bent, and give decision.
> In politics nice hydrostatic
> I know to cul the democratic
> From cast [*sic*] unorthodox, tho' lean they
> But half a hair's breadth from the clean way.

Often incoherent and unusually bad in meter, these verses indicate the author's devotion to the lady of his dedication. If all Jefferson's Virginia conservative opponents were no more organized than he, real rivalry within the state was negligible.

An English lady who lived in Virginia during some years of this decade paid her respects to the commonwealth in a rhyming and satiric *Poetical Picture of America, Being Observations Made, During a Residence of Several Years, at Alexandria, and Norfolk, in Virginia: Illustrative of the Manners and Customs of the Inhabitants; and Interspersed with Anecdotes Arising from a General Intercourse with Society in that Country, from the year 1799 to 1807. By a Lady of London* (1809). The lady, Mrs. Anne Ritson, listed among the subscribers to the book the Prince of Wales, Duke of York, and at least five Britishers resident in Norfolk. If they expected the curious or the genuinely devastating, they were disappointed. Mrs. Ritson had not the eye of the later Mrs. Trollope. Beginning with "A Voyage Across the Atlantic":

> To share an absent husband's woe
> And ease his grief, I wish'd to go

she describes a "Passage of the Potomak," "Alexandria," "Norfolk," and more of Virginia. Horse racing, ladies' gardening, Jefferson and the mammoth cheese, the Norfolk theater, where she saw "murder'd plays about a score," are among the things she ridicules. Soundly she concludes:

> Again I sought the raging main;
> With pleasure, words can ne'er describe,
> Left all the Pocahonta's tribe;
> Their trees, their negroes, and their fields,
> With all the sweets Virginia yields.

In 1812-13, just as the second war with Britain began, four Virginians published volumes of verse that received moderate contemporary notice. One, by Judith Lomax, the same young lady who sent Tucker her verses in 1800, was dedicated to her father's friend Thomas Jefferson and bore the title *The Notes of an American Lyre* (1813).[143] The Preface modestly describes it as a poetical notebook and the reader will agree that it should have remained a manuscript exercise. It contains a mixture of occasional and sentimental pieces characteristic of the verse by females just then beginning to become popular, or at least prevalent, all over America. Several poems were written at or about Monticello, one is on Mrs. Page and another to the memory of John Page. A few have some interest for their historical topics. Since Miss Lomax was from a prominent family, many subscribed for her little book. Jefferson himself gallantly ordered a dozen copies.

Not much better verse is to be found in the *Odes and Poems, by* [*a*] *Virginian*[144] published thus in 1812. The anonymous author includes verses to J[ohn] R[andolph] and Dr. Benjamin Rush, "A Scene on the Banks of Staunton," "The Virginia Cock Fight," "A Certain Spot in Virginia," and a number of reflective and sentimental pieces, most of them in couplets. The panegyric to Randolph assures the reader that the great man's fame shall endure.

Better verse than any in these two volumes was written by William Maxwell (1784-1857) and Richard Dabney (1787-1825), who in 1812 were publishing their first volumes. Maxwell, the Norfolk-born Yale graduate who was later to become a distinguished orator, lawyer, Presbyterian churchman, and educator, dedicated both his 1812 and 1816 volumes to his old teacher Timothy Dwight.[145] Two poems were written to William Wirt. And "The Widow of Ephesus," a delicate yet humorous handling in the 1812 edition of Boccaccio's old tale, also contains a reference to the Richmond lawyer:

> The soldier was no Wirt indeed
> But he could speak in time of need.

This poetic tale is in the same tradition as Tucker's "The Knight and Friars," though the bawdy element is toned down.

Elegiac verses to the beautiful Sarah C. Conyers who died in the theater fire also appeared in the 1812 volume. Perhaps the most lively piece in this book is the little poem on the Virginia topic "The Humming Bird." The bird gives a sprightly answer after the poet asks:

> Little Hummer, why so shy?
> Whither, whither would you fly?
> Let that little rose alone:
> Do you think it is your own?
> See yon Bee just coming by—
> Here! here! to my bosom fly.

Maxwell's 1816 edition contained fewer lyrics and more "serious," generally meaning sentimental, poems, on such topics as "The Natural Bridge," "The Missionary's Grave," and "The Bards of Columbia."[145] The last, with a subtitle "An Epistle to the Rev. Timothy Dwight," mentions Cliffon, Ladd, and Trumbull among other American poets. The poet regrets that he has not himself written more but praises the American poet and defines his function. He also discusses the difficulties of the American poet, including the preference of most of the American public for British verse. He pleads for the employment of native scenery as subject matter. A group of poems on the naval heroes of the War of 1812, mostly in couplets, are about the only other noteworthy pieces in this book.

Rice's *Virginia Evangelical and Literary Magazine* in 1818 reviewed this second edition most favorably, the writer concluding that "with this book in my hand, I will no more suffer the assertion to pass in silence, that Virginia has not yet produced a poet worthy of the title."[146] There was some promise here of things that never came. Variety in form, dignity, even an attempt at rendering his individual imaginative experience instead of the absolutes and morals of the older tradition, suggest that Maxwell might have been a poet had he not been so busy a public man, another example of a familiar story in the antebellum South.

Richard Dabney did devote most of his brief life to verse, but he was so afflicted with physical infirmities that he achieved little more than Maxwell. Born in Louisa county, a first cousin of explorer Meriwether Lewis and son of a wealthy farmer, Dabney was for a time a teacher in a Richmond school. He escaped from the theater fire with injuries which he bore the rest of his life. His first volume of verse was published in Richmond in 1812 and a second in Philadelphia, to which city he had moved, in 1815.[147] He is said to have been the author of Mathew Carey's *Olive Branch, or Faults on Both Sides* (1814). Carey issued the enlarged 1815 edition of Dabney's verse, but the poet soon returned to rural life in his native Louisa. Addicted to the opium he had begun using to alleviate his pain after the fire, he also became an habitual user of alcohol. Though he continued to read and may have written some verse, no more of it appeared in print. The obituary notice in the *Enquirer* (November 25, 1825) alludes to his verse but emphasizes more his thirst for knowledge, his extraordinary intellectual conversation, and his scholarship. With this verdict that he is more learned than creative even in his verse most readers would agree.

The "Preliminary Remarks" to the *Poems, Original and Translated* of 1815 reveal Dabney as critical theorist as well as practicing poet.[148] He calls the first poems of the volume "Gnomique—a character of poetic composition, when the expression is limited to prominent and concise associations, in the train of thought, consequent on any simple emotion of taste, so as, by the preservation of unity, to prevent the force of that emotion from being diminished." He proceeds to quote "Alison on *Taste*," " 'in all the fine arts, that composition is most excellent, in which the different parts most fully unite in the production of one unmingled emotion, and that taste the most perfect, where the perception of this relation of objects, in point of expression, is most delicate and precise.' " Dabney adds that the unified effect is lessened by multiplied associations and delicate perception blunted in the same way. He ventures to call his own work "the *moral* miniature painting of poetry; inasmuch, as the exertions of the graphic art are generally restricted to a single point, in relation to time, and to a paucity of objects in relation to experience." All this reminds us of Poe's theories of unified effect.

The poems themselves are not as impressive as this slight essay on theory. The translations from twenty Greek authors and half a dozen Italians show something of his wide range of reading, as do his quotations from Boileau as to the rules of the sonnet, and the references to Metastasio, Rolli, Manfredi, and many others.[149] The miscellaneous poems such as "The Charm," "The Bloody Wreath," and "The Relique" are not conventional in theme, but the forms are the usual mixture of romantic and neoclassical. His "Invocazione," which in idea somewhat anticipates Emerson's "The Enchanter," as Professor Hubbell has pointed out,[150] is characteristically late eighteenth century in its quatrains and diction and imagery of "torrent-beaten sides" and "bosomed vale."

Yet in several places Dabney is a genuine poet. In at least two he suggests Edgar Poe and is not unworthy of comparison. Certain lines in "Illustration I"[151] of "simple moral emotions" remind the reader of "Al Aaraaf" and "Tamerlane":

Another world unknown to THEE,
A world, from imperfection free,
Exists to HIM—what's wanting here.
Imagination fashions there—
All, that his early vision formed,
All, that his raptured vision warmed,
His memory and his hope combine,
And *consecrate* the scene divine.

And in another poem[152] Dabney suggests the first "To Helen" in imagery:

But, drive the alluring charms away,
That round thy form seductive play;
Quench the soft brilliance of thy eyes,
And stain thy cheeks' luxuriant dies;
Obscure thy neck, divinely fair,
And spoil the hyacinths of thy hair.[153]

His translations or adaptations possess a classical rather than a neoclassical tone, again suggestive of certain poems of the young Poe. "An Epigram, Imitated from Archias," has in its concluding stanza something of the Stoic quality his friends felt the poet possessed:

Death, kind and consoling, comes calmly and lightly,
The balm of all sorrow, the cure of all ill,
And after a pang, that but thrills o'er us slightly
All then becomes tranquil, and then becomes still.[154]

More ambitious than Dabney, at least in the years before he was forty, was Daniel Bryan (1790?-1866), chiefly remembered because Poe in 1841 referred to him in the "Autography" series as a man who had written some excellent poems of "'the good old Goldsmith school.'"[155] Yet Bryan's first work published in book form in 1813 is more romantic than neoclassic. He was Goldsmithean in his later poems published in the 1820's when Poe might have seen them as they appeared.

A native of the Great Valley, educated at Washington College, Bryan was even in his verse a good Presbyterian. An officer in the War of 1812 and a member of the state senate from 1818 to 1822, he became in 1826 postmaster in Alexandria and held the position for over a quarter of a century. Several surviving printed orations suggest that he was frequently a speaker on educational topics.[156] And in 1821 he made a much-discussed speech advocating gradual emancipation.

The year he became postmaster Bryan published two or three poems in form and diction typical of the eighteenth century. *The Appeal for Suffering Genius; a Poetical Address for the Benefit of the Boston Bard; and Triumph of Truth, a Poem* (1826),[157] in the first poem of the title ostensibly an appeal to help the needy Robert Coffin, is actually a call for a more generous recognition of the artist in America. "The Triumph of Truth" was impelled by the establishment of press censorship in France. *The Lay of Gratitude, consisting of poems occasioned by the recent visit of Lafayette to the United States* (1826)[158] is a hodge-podge of belated tributes to the Marquis in varying meters, parts of it labeled "Odes." In the same year he combined these with the earlier piece and published them as *The Lay of Gratitude and Suffering Genius*[159] in two volumes.

In 1828 Bryan even rendered his *Thoughts on Education in Its Connexion with Morals* into verse, read the poem before the Hampden-Sydney Literary and Philosophical Society, and in 1830 had T. W. White of Richmond publish it. Copies of this blank verse full of platitudes may still have been in White's shop when Poe became the editor of the *Southern Literary Messenger* there a few years later.

But Bryan's first work was his most ambitious and in some respects his best—his epic on Daniel Boone. The poet was doubly related to Boone by marriage. Apparently he labored on the poem for several years before he published it in Harrisburg in 1813 with another brief piece under the title *The Mountain Muse: Comprising the Adventures of Daniel Boone; and The Power of Virtuous and Refined Beauty*.

Clearly he felt that time and place were ripe for such a work. Ever since the Revolution one school of thought had believed that a new American literature must begin with a heroic poem celebrating a significant phase of national history. Timothy Dwight's *Conquest of Canaan* and Barlow's *Vision of Columbus* and *Columbiad* were the best known attempts of the New Englanders to fill the need, and there were efforts in the South a little later. Bryan's Preface mentions "how few there are in this section of the Republic, who have ventured to resound in Verse the praise of [America's] charms, or the honors of her distinguish'd Sons! A thousand times has the Author beheld in Fancy the genius of Columbian Poesy standing on the wildest cliffs of Allegany, tuning the tear-twinkling chords of her Lyre."

He found that the account of "Boone's Adventures" (John Filson's *Kentucke*) gave him a subject, and he resolved to interweave with it the story of the "Alleghany Robbers and the Lost Maid." Thus a decade before the first Leatherstocking Tale, Bryan resolved to treat the frontier, Indian warfare, and the westward expansion on an extensive scale. That he should choose the epic rather than the novel form may have been due to Blair's *Lectures on Rhetoric,* which emphasized the heroic poem rather than fiction.

The living hero of "The Adventures of Daniel Boone" was unusual, and the love story seems superfluous. Miltonic blank verse was not the happiest choice of meter, nor did the Miltonic figures and progressions seem appropriate in the western world. The "Divan, A Firmamental Hall" which the guardian spirits of the Western Wild were commanded to build in "the Alleganean Mountain-Heights" is ridiculous in the region of the pioneer. The speeches of four of the spirits are again too obviously Miltonic. Enterprise, one of them, suggests that Boone, brooding alone, be chosen for the great errand into the Wilderness, to prepare a home for the seekers of Liberty. Boone's exploits in conflict and escape are described with a vividness which might have been even more effective in less stilted language. The Indians are depicted sympathetically, though the poet gives the white man's argument for taking their lands:

> That NATURE'S common right demands of them,
> Partition with the Whites, of their wildlands;
> That Christian Domination there would shed
> Unknown delights upon their gloomy hearts.[160]

Book II begins the actual adventures, which with the love plot run on through Book VII. He concludes with tributes to historic heroes of the Kentucky "Dark and Bloody Ground" and an exhortation to the western states to remain true to their glorious heritage.

Locke, as one might expect, lies in the background of the poem. Upon Boone's "Fancy's pictured tablet" (II, l. 78) shone the visions of what the Future would bring. And Bryan, after mentioning Newton and Herschel, who had done so much to explore "Nature's deeps" (I, l. 45), pays tribute to two of his favorite philosophers in speaking of what the Winged Guardians of the World bestowed upon mankind:

> To Locke and Reid they gave th' ingenious skill
> T' unfold the labyrinthian web of mind;
> To teach us how the variegated west
> In *different* parts, peculiar tints assumes;
> How light runs into shade, and shade to light,
> Untill in mingled hues, the changefull whole
> A beauteous intellectual landscape forms.[161]

Highly rhetorical, Bryan's diction is full of his own coinages. Alison, Erasmus Darwin, Barlow's epic, perhaps some of the Indian captivity narratives, even Rousseau seem to lie in the poet's reading behind his scenes, imagery, and sentimental didacticism. He has succeeded in capturing in narrative episodes and occasionally in imagery the natural violence of the West and the civilized man's desire to create order in the wilderness. Scores of times he celebrates the beauty of the American forest. A new poetic language and a different form might have produced a good poem. A reviewer in the *Analectic* saw so many faults that the poem with a few more would have been mere caricature, but at the same time he felt "great respect for Mr. Bryan's poetical powers."[162] Had the extravagance of this 1813 effort been toned into moderation instead of turned back toward eighteenth-century sentimentalism Bryan's later works might have fulfilled the promise this critic saw. As it was, northern anthologists of the next generation ignored him while they recognized poets no better than he.

At least one other poet made an attempt at a sort of epic. This was the White Pilgrim Father Joseph Thomas, who published in Winchester in 1816 his *Poetical Descant on the Primeval and Present State of Mankind* in couplets, a pious poem concluding that peace and happiness are to be found in the practice of virtue and a religious devotion. But far more interesting to today's reader is "The Pilgrim, Contemplating the Winter Season," a poem included in *The Life* of the *Pilgrim Joseph Thomas* printed in Winchester a year after *The Poetical Descant.*

Born in North Carolina, Thomas went as a boy to Grayson county, Virginia. It is a snowstorm in the southwest Virginia area which he describes in the later poem. Again incomplete and reminiscent of Thomson, Cowper, and lesser writers of the eighteenth century, it looks forward to Whittier's "Snowbound" in some of the realism of its detail. Under the all-enveloping blanket of white

The grunting swine, now begs a meal of corn,
With looks of meaning, sullen and forlorn;
The poultry mute now scarcely leave the door;
Nor crow, nor cackle as they did before,
They shrug their wings, with cautious steps they go;
They tread the yard, and drop their heads with wo:
They look for food, they hop the dwelling's step
And scratch, and gather, where the e[y?]e [*sic?*] drops wept.[163]

Thomas describes indoor rural games, which he contrasts with gambling, theater-going, and acting in the city, "where vice is learned and dissipation spreads." True to a Virginia as well as a literary tradition, he saw the agrarian life as the happy and virtuous state

In the fifteen years after the War of 1812 Virginia women published at least four volumes of verse, in the main representative of the sentimental volumes American ladies were to submit to the public up to the Civil War. Martha Ann Davis (1790-1874),[164] a granddaughter of the great Presbyterian divine Samuel Davies, brought out in Petersburg in 1818 *Poems of Laura; An Original American Work.* Originality is not a marked characteristic of the collection, however, for it includes mainly "Lines" on the deaths of sister, husband, and children and conventional pieces on "Rural Felicity" and "On the Sun," most of them in couplets and quatrains. Somewhat more varied are the contents of *The Potomac Muse. By a Lady, a Native of Virginia* (Richmond, 1825), the author usually believed to be a Mrs. Alfred W. Elwes. She quotes Burns on the title page and indulges in anapaestic as well as more usual meters. She includes several poems on the Potomac River, and others on the Susquehanna and on the Richmond Theatre fire. Historically the most interesting is "Virginia," a poem in couplets long enough to occupy the first twenty-one pages. The poet celebrates the glories of her native land, for

There, first of eloquence the spirit rose,
There, genius still her ready smile bestows.[165]

Without party spirit or prejudice, she devotes sections to Washington, Wirt, Henry, Lee, Jefferson, Madison, Monroe, Randolph, Tazewell, Clay, Crawford, Brent, Giles, and Marshall. For good measure she adds Lafayette, who had so recently revisited this scene of his early glory. Virginia excels in everything. Does one ask for science? The answer is Jefferson:

Thou, who can'st every great endowment claim
Devoted all to one exalted aim.[166]

The Wreath; or Verses on Various Subjects, By a Lady of Richmond (Richmond, 1828) was the second edition[167] of a collection which had originally appeared in Lexington, Kentucky, in 1820. The authoress was apparently a Mrs. Littlefield. Though she too indulges in conventional occasional and sentimental pieces, she has a number on frontier life and battles. "The Backwoodsmen" seems to have sprung from her own experience in Kentucky:

O! who is he, with eager feet,
That treads the forest's tangled maze,
Wooes Freedom in her mountain seat,
And careless, wildly wandering strays.
Child of the Forest. . . .[168]

Perhaps she knew the white man who overcame the Indian and equaled the aborigine in savagery:

The tomahawk whizzed—his cheek it grazed.
He springs, he grapples, breath for breath:
His knife in his strong arm is raised,
He plunges—hark that groan—'tis death.
And must the muse record the rest?
She must—for true's the tale I tell;
Pity nor fear e'er crossed his breast,
Exulting rose a savage yell.
Exulting, too, he scalps his foe,
And home the blood-stained trophy bears;
Hung in his cabin for a show,
The hunter's tale, and jest, for years.[169]

In a different mood is the work of the wife of the star-crossed Blennerhasset who had lived on an island in the slave-holding Virginia territory of the Ohio river. Her beautiful house and its furnishings had long before been destroyed by militia, fire, and flood when she published in Montreal in 1824 *The Widow of the Rock and Other Poems. By a Lady.*[170] A lady of considerable ability Margaret Agnew Blennerhasset certainly was. She was her husband's niece, and they are said to have settled far from settlements and neighbors for this reason.

The poems, most of them written during her years in the States, display a variety of meter, including Byron's anapaestic tetrameter, and an equal variety of subject matter, from "The Mocking Bird" to "Sir Walter Raleigh's Advice to his son on the Subject of Matrimony." In two she is particularly bitter. "The Desert Isle" describes her lost mansion of Blennerhasset Island. In it she rails against the "Tyrants of Liberty," especially Jefferson, "self-dubb'd philosopher!—the mob's delight," who will, she mistakenly predicts, be remembered only as the "Confederate vile of Atheists and *Tom Paine*!" Several other pieces are satiric, reproducing conversations in phonetically spelled dialect between the slave Sambo and the hillbilly Jonathan. One especially aimed at Jefferson, "The Jackal King. To the Tune of 'Possum up dee Gum-Tree (with Classical Annotations by Sambo)," is an interesting mixture of the two dialects. It concludes:

> Nayow, I presume you've larn't enough—so, fear you'll
> think me reude;
> I guess, I b'lieve, I calculate,—I reckon I'll conclude—
> But first, should any critter think this is in ridicule,
> I'll tell him teu his face an' eyes, he is a *'tarnal fool!*
> *Den possum up dee gum-tree.—Raccoon in dee hollow,*
> *Let eb'ry varmin larn from dis—dee Jackal King to follow.*[74]

She had a good ear. At times acutely perceptive, naturally resentful of Jefferson, she is in some respects an earlier Mrs. Trollope, in others a female ancestress of Hosea Biglow.

Two gentlemen of the distinguished Carter family published their miscellaneous poems in the early 1820's. The ambitious *Land of Powhatan* (Baltimore, 1821) by St. Leger Landon Carter has been noticed above in connection with the Pocahontas-Smith story. His later volume of verse *Nugae, by Nugator* did not appear until 1844 and thus lies outside our period. He is represented in Volume I of the *Southern Literary Messenger* by some thirteen pieces of verse and prose. The other Carter, Bernard Moore, published four volumes of verse within five years, the first, *Miscellaneous Poems* in Philadelphia in 1820, the others in London (two) and Paris in 1823, 1824, and 1825. The 1820 and 1824 collections are much the same. Both contain the poem "Pocahontas," adaptations of Horace, and lyrics to various ladies. Several mention William Wirt, including one "To Mira, Accompanying Wirt's Life of Henry." Bernard Carter is notable chiefly for his avowed worship of Byron and thus departure in intent, at least, from older models. Neither his contemporaries nor moderns have found much of interest in his work, though "Ianthe" is distinctly suggestive of Poe, who also admired Byron.

Even closer to Poe, at least physically, was the Petersburg poet Hiram Haines (1803?-41), who entertained the author of "The Raven" at his home in 1836. Born in Culpeper county and receiving only an old field school education, he began rhyming at thirteen and at eighteen published his first poem, on the death of Bonaparte, in the Fauquier county *Palladium of Liberty*. He was printer and editor of the Petersburg *American Constellation,* a Republican newspaper, for many years.[172]

Haines' *Mountain Buds and Blossoms, Wove in a Rustic Garland. By the Stranger* was published in Petersburg in 1825. The usual odes, dreams, and poems to Lafayette, and tributes to Burns and Byron, make up most of the volume. "Roger Cloddy" suggests "Tam O'Shanter." Several poems concern Masonry, as do many others among his manuscript remains. "The Perishing Orphan" is set in "The month of December," when one may hear "the raven's croak." The most ambitious piece, "The Virginiad," occupies with its Introduction the first fifty pages of the book. The first of the twelve-line couplet stanzas begins:

> Virginia hail! thou loveliest land on Earth,
> Land of the Great!—of Beauty, and rare worth

and continues with descriptions of Pocahontas and tributes to Jefferson, Madison, Monroe, Randolph, Barbour, Scott, Harrison, and Tazewell. Among Virginia's glories he hailed her legal talent. But all this never gets the poem off the ground.

Samuel McPherson Janney (1801-80) of Loudon county, Quaker poet and clergyman, did most of his writing in the years after 1830; but his one volume of verse, *The Last of the Lenapi and Other Poems* (Philadelphia, 1839),includes a number of pieces written and published here and there in the 1820's.[173] In that decade he wrote "A Night Scene among the Mountains of Virginia," "Potomac," "Jefferson's Rock, at Harper's Ferry, Va.," "Lake George," and two to ladies. The 1822 "The Country School House" won the prize offered in 1824 by the *New York Mirror* for "the best poetic composition." In Gray-like quatrains he voices conventional sentiment. Calm and composed in all his lines, Janney well suggests the Quaker temperament. "Heavenly calm" filled him as he gazed at Harper's Ferry and at life. But as one contemporary observed, "His muse has no wings"—not even the wings of a dove.

Quite different from the work of all other contemporary Virginia poets is the one long composition of William Branch, Jr. (*ca.* 1790-1825), Prince Edward county attorney. Probably a friend of Dr. John Holt Rice, he had his book published by the Rice-sponsored Franklin Press of Richmond in 1819. Its long title is fairly indicative of its content: *Life, A Poem in Three Books; Descriptive of the various characters in life; the different passions, with their moral influence; the good and evil resulting from their sway; and of the perfect man. Dedicated to the Social and Political Welfare of the People of the United States.* Written in old-fashioned heroic couplets, this philosophical didactic autobiography suggests in content the outrageously long poems on aesthetic subjects such as Akenside and Brooke in England and John Blair Linn, Alsop, and Dwight in America had composed. Yet it also suggests Wordsworth's *Prelude,* for in one sense it is clearly autobiography. It is also an educational manual of advice to parents to follow the Pestalozzian methods in rearing their children, to become conscious of the roles of Reason, Fancy, Will, and Imagination in development toward the perfect man.

Branch's preface acknowledges that he will probably be attacked abroad because he is an American. But he affirms that he is content to submit "my words and diction to the *grammarian;* my *metaphysical reveries* to the *casuist;* and the *essence* of my sentiments to you, my fellow-citizens." He conceives that the function of New World verse is moral:

> The Muse in America is not a Laureat; she lives the disciple of *honest nature,* arrayed in the mantle of freedom, untarnished by the dear bought livery of a court. She warns of evil seen abroad; dreads its approach; and sings of happy things at home. She stoops not in heartless adoration of the tiara, surplice and diadem; but with rational zeal, in sweet devotion, yields up her soul to the author of nature.[174]

He also favors the moral when he discusses two kinds of critics:

> The philological critic, who preys on verbiage, is very beneficial to the literary world; for he sifts words; scrutinizes phrases, forms, and styles, and settles the exact standard weight and measure of language; but the moral critic is yet more useful; for he anatomizes the moral principle of every writing, and shows the *good* and *evil* which would result from their adoption and exercise.

Book I, "Infancy," the poet devotes to the mother's influence and the child's nature. Parental care

> Forms the Understanding to receive
> The numerous images, the senses give;
> *Reason* evolves, to note the hues and shades
> Of nice gradation, that over life pervades.[175]

He goes on to describe what Judgment, Reason, Will, Fancy, and Imagination are and how Parental Care may direct them. He warns of the dangers of allowing the child to be reared by slaves, for from them the infant "learns their jargon" and contracts their dishonest and flattering habits. Thus children are left susceptible to demagogues. Yet God

> *All equal made,* and of a kindred clay,
> *All free* to love, and him alone obey.[176]

In Book II, "Youth" the child is in school. His schoolmates, the dunce, the genius, the industrious boy, the mere learner of words, the learner of things, "the child of fancy, a sciolist, the son of reason, a philosopher" are described at length. As examples of genius, he cites Newton, Rittenhouse, and Franklin

> Nor let immortal Locke be left behind
> Who rais'd the value of the human mind[177]

and Chatham, Patrick Henry, and Shakespeare! As for the learning process, he hails "Pestalozzi of imperial pow'rs" and the inculcation of the knowledge of the past. He is hardly romantic when he observes:

> Some youthful minds too weak for reason's sway
> Are found to bask in fancy's vernal ray.[178]

Yet he admits:

> Let fancy wildly soar, the fact is this
> Her flight though wild, is still the road to bliss.[179]

And he concludes finally that Reason in common life "is man's best guide." In his opinion, this guide is well represented in "Lanc'ster's heart and Bentham's solid mind."[180]

Book III, "Manhood," presents lover, friend, family man," "the Pains and Pleasures of Retrospection," and death. Here there are curious and frequent references to the popular seduction novel *The Coquette,* which showed what the lover ought not to be. The allurements of female Beauty are sensuously if not sensually described. The poem concludes as it had begun, with the celebration of "Eternal reason; and eternal Truth"—the path of the golden mean. Thus a man of twenty-nine who was to die at thirty-four displayed his introspection—in social and moral rather than religious terms. What he derived from his poetic meditation was a Virginia gentleman's traditional philosophy of reason and moderation.

Another short-lived Virginia poet who was much more promising was Dabney Carr Terrell (*ca.* 1790?-1827) of Louisa county, friend of George Ticknor, N. P. Trist, and Francis Gilmer and sometime student at the University of Geneva.[181] His life saddened by participation in a fatal duel at seventeen, Terrell died in New Orleans of yellow fever. Someone in 1829 sent George Tucker and Robley Dunglison a sheaf of Terrell's unpublished poems for publication in the new *Virginia Literary Museum.* There some twenty-five of his pieces appeared, eighteen of them sonnets. Slight as they are, they are impressive. Again suggestive of Poe's early work, they are less Byronic.

Included are several translations from Metastio, and "On an Indian Mound," "Thoughts on Visiting the Grave of Jefferson," and "Washington's Dream." Terrell experimented successfully with several rhyme schemes in his sonnets. One of the better examples of this type, that to Jefferson printed at the beginning of this book, was not included in the *Virginia Literary Museum,* though there are two slightly differing versions of it in manuscript.[182]

There are several dozen more versifiers between 1790 and 1830 whose manuscript effusions properly repose in the archives of the Virginia Historical Society, the Virginia State Library, the Library of Congress, and at Duke University and the University of Virginia.

They are significant only as further indication of Jeffersonian Virginia's interest in Euterpe and Erato.

But one young Virginia poet had by 1831 published three little volumes of verse promising great things. At least two of them were written in Virginia and Maryland, and the three owe all but the genius behind them to the writer's heritage in the Old Dominion. In other words, *Tamerlane and Other Poems* (Boston, 1827), *Al Aaraaf, Tamerlane, and Minor Poems* (Baltimore, 1829), and *Poems* (New York, 1831) spring not from a mind haunted by morbid fancies suggested partially by exotic Gothic writings outside the experience of his boyhood friends, but straight from the intellectual climate of the Richmond and the Virginia of the first quarter of the nineteenth century.

Edgar Poe's conservative political and social attitudes may have come from the generation of Calhoun in the South generally. But as Robert D. Jacobs has recently demonstrated so amply,[183] and as we have pointed out above, his artistic and psychological goals, his scientific philosophy, all spring from the Jeffersonian Virginia forms of the Enlightenment and the Virginia interpretations of Scottish aestheticism. Wirt may not have understood Poe's *Al Aaraaf*; but Poe knew and understood Wirt's essays, he knew Virginia poets, and he shared much with them. One of his reasons for attacking Northern critics for their failure to recognize Southern poets was his recognition that this was also a failure to recognize his own characteristic qualities.

IX

LAW AND ORATORY

[In Virginia] the greater part study the theory or apply themselves to the practice of law, as an auxiliary to some other object, either of ambition or of immediate gain. The bar is the school of American statesmen—the arena where the prize of eloquence is awarded to the people—and the technicalities of law are very often employed only as foils to set off the dexterity and power of the logician. The profession of law is less unique in the United States than anywhere else. It approaches more nearly the ancient Roman than the modern European standard. Hence, perhaps, the number of aspirants in Virginia for forensic distinction.

—"Thoughts on the Choice of a Profession in Virginia," *Virginia Literary Museum,* I, No. 21 (November 4, 1829), 322.

Law and politics were the only objects of Virginian thought; but within these bounds the Virginians achieved triumphs.

—Henry Adams, *History of the United States . . . ,* I 134.

"Men of talents in this country . . . have been generally bred to the profession of law. . . . The bar, in America, is the road to honour" wrote William Wirt in *Letters of the British Spy*[1] in 1803. He added that a few years before the Supreme Court of the United States had pronounced the bar of Virginia "the most enlightened and able on the continent." One reason for composing the *British Spy* was to point out what the Old Dominion bar must do to remain pre-eminent and thus insure the state's pre-eminency in the Union.

Almost everyone in America agreed that the study of law was the road to distinction. Ferdinand-M. Bayard, who traveled in the new republic in 1791, regretted that all the sons of the wealthier classes were destined for the bar, for plantations were drained of the men who would best be able to manage them, and a sound agrarian economy was thus endangered.[2] Virginians accepted the fact without fully appreciating the alleged danger, perhaps because many good legal minds still continued to administer their farms. General Winfield Scott, looking back on the professions open in his youth, pointed out that the law was "the usual road to political advancement" and thus without question the path of the genuinely ambitious youth.[3] At the end of our period, in 1829, a writer in the *Virginia Literary Museum*[4] again saw study of legal theory or application to legal practice as equal auxiliaries to ambition or wealth. He noted that the bar was the school of statesmen, and that technicalities were less important than dexterous logic. More than in any other modern state, in America the profession of law was the means to eminence. Later in the century Henry Adams, who saw law and politics as the only objects of Virginia thought, admitted that in them Virginians achieved a great deal.[5]

It will be noted that the 1829 writer comments that some study theory and others practice but that both aim at "forensic distinction."

He was probably remembering legal theorists like Jefferson, John Taylor of Caroline, Spencer Roane, and John Marshall, whose active practice was largely forgotten, or others like George Mason, James Madison, and John Randolph of Roanoke who had never been barristers in any technical sense yet made at least a portion of their fame in discussion of public law. And "forensic distinction" implies the public speaking of the forum, the aptitude for eloquence which went hand in hand with jurisprudence. Among their contemporaries, even the speeches (as well as the written treatises) of Jefferson, Marshall, and Madison were studied as models.

A. *Lawyers and Jurists*

From the time of William Fitzhugh and William Byrd a considerable number of planters had studied and often practiced law.[6] By the period of the Revolution the proportion of Burgesses who were legally trained had increased enormously. Virginia signers of the Declaration of Independence were in most instances educated in the law, as were the larger number who were at various times members of the Continental Congress. As the state grew more populous and regional centers developed in the west, lawyers who might handle land cases as well as other civil and criminal matters came to be in yet greater demand. Virginians, like their legal and racial progenitors in Great Britain, were a litigious people. And then from 1789 through 1830 and indeed to the Civil War, it was the function of lawyers and jurists to interpret the Federal Constitution in its relation to the state.

The experienced trial lawyer or civil pleader and district judge alike were then natural candidates for election to Legislature or Congress, the State Supreme Court of Appeals, or the Federal Supreme Court. If one preferred active practice, he might move up the ladder from rural courts to city to state to Federal courts, acquiring fame and modest wealth as he did. Or if his forte was the written word, as it was for Madison, Jefferson, or John Taylor, his letters to newspapers or separate pamphlets on questions of public law would earn him equal distinction. In a land where society was pointed toward the future, the defender, attacker, and interpreter of law in relation to the individual and the state were indispensable.

Earlier chapters have indicated something of the factors which made the Virginian as much as or more than his fellow Americans especially capable of thinking in terms of the law. The leading classes in its agrarian society had acted as justices of the peace in county courts, and frequently as litigants in the same courts, from nearly the beginning of the colony. They had been compelled to think in terms of law and government, of the rights of the individual, or historical authority *vs.* New World situation, of the meaning of property and contract. In every library of any size were English legal volumes and American legal reports. When they came to form a new nation, they were therefore especially conscious of the part law must play in completing the new structure. It was the legal and political talent of its lawyers which placed Virginia at the forefront of the American colonies in 1776, one juridical historian has observed.[7]

As we have seen, the later eighteenth-century Virginia lawyer was trained at the Inns of Court and William and Mary or more frequently by older experienced lawyers.[8] In the first quarter of the nineteenth century he studied at William and Mary under St. George Tucker or his successor or in Richmond under men like William Wirt. A few attended the Litchfield, Connecticut, school of law under Tapping Reeve. Older lawyers throughout the period urged on the aspirants a well-balanced training in the arts and sciences as a necessary prerequisite to legal training and often suggested the books they deemed most useful. Usually the older men leaned to history, philosophy, and government, but grammar, the natural sciences, and mathematics were also recommended. Above all they urged the study and practice of oratory and rhetoric. And every lawyer cautioned the beginner to continue to read in all branches of knowledge as he grew older.[9]

In the professional area the first requisite was persistent and close study of Coke and other British authorities including Blackstone and Bacon, Virginia and other American codes, and chancery case reports. Jefferson and Wythe urged friends and pupils to broaden their reading to philosophical jurisprudence and government, including the classic authorities in Latin; manuals of the duties of the justice of the peace were among the books men like Gilmer, Wirt, Carr, Jefferson, and the Tuckers owned. Wirt, Tazewell, and Jefferson were among those interested in maritime law. All were concerned with law's twin brother, politics. But more of that in the next chapter.

Training by practice was new at the end of the eighteenth century in Virginia, but it existed. There were moot courts in Williamsburg then, and in Richmond in 1810 Judge Creed Taylor encouraged such exercise in a group of fledgling lawyers which included Abel P. Upshur, Francis Gilmer, John Tyler the younger, and William C. Preston. Taylor's laboratory was called a debating society or moot court, and may have been somewhat similar to the "Rhetorical Society" in which Henry Clay was a participant when he studied law in Richmond in 1796.[10] Besides this, all young students assisted in preparing briefs, acting as clerks for their mentors, and observing actual courtroom procedure and argument.

A number of Virginians were good legal scholars and more than competent editors of legal commentaries and reports. Jefferson's own major accomplishments in jurisprudence had been made before the beginning of our period in his Revisal of the Code of Laws of Virginia (with Pendleton and Wythe) in 1779 and in his analyses and statements of Virginia law in his *Notes on the State of Virginia.*[11] His attempts to revise the legal structure in accordance with "truly republican" principles, expressed in the "Report" of 1779, were never acted upon in their entirety, but more than fifty of the original 126 separate bills were made laws by 1786.

Good editions of Virginia *Reports* were compiled and edited during the Jeffersonian period by George Wythe,[12] W. W. Hening, Francis Gilmer, Peyton Randolph, William Munford, and Bushrod Washington, all able lawyers. B. W. Leigh, Hening, and Munford published a *Revised Code of Laws of Virginia* in 1819. St. George Tucker's edition of *Blackstone's Commentaries: with Notes of Reference, to the Constitution and Laws, of the Federal Government of the United States; and of the Commonwealth of Virginia*[13] in an appendix discussed the principles of government as related to the nature and interpretation of the Federal Constitution. These are the first legal commentaries on the Constitution to appear in this country.[14] Especially useful to Virginians, Tucker's volumes formed a text and reference work used widely throughout America. John Quincy Adams, for example, records its use. It earned for Tucker the sobriquet of "the

American Blackstone," and it remains as one of the significant law books of the period.[15]

William Waller Hening's *Statutes at Large* (1809-23), discussed in the preceding chapter as a distinguished contribution to legislative history, is also one of the monuments of legal scholarships in this country. Hening's first book, *The New Virginia Justice* (1795), a handbook of procedure for magistrates, was in its fourth edition by 1825. He edited American editions of Branch, Francis, and Noy's Maxims of the laws of England (1823 and 1824) and assisted Leigh in preparing the *Revised Code*.[16] With Munford he compiled the Virginia *Reports* of cases before the Supreme Court of Appeals for the years 1806-10 (publ. 1808-11).[17] He was also the author of several shorter essays on the law.

It is interesting and perhaps of some significance that Virginia-bred lawyers were active legal compilers and editors in other states. Benjamin James (b. Stafford county) published digests of South Carolina laws in 1814 and 1822. Augustine Smith Clayton (b. Fredericksburg) produced a Georgia version of Hening's *New Virginia Justice* in 1819 and other legal treatises. Henry Carlton Coxe translated from the Spanish and edited the old laws of Louisiana in 1818 and 1820. John Overton (b. Louisa county) edited the *Tennessee Reports* for 1813-17. And Edward Turner (b. Fairfax county) published *Statutes of the Mississippi Territory* in 1816. There were others.

Lawyers with considerable contemporary reputations for erudition might be learned in the general sense or in jurisprudence or in both. George Wythe, an acknowledged master of the law, often preferred to quote Horace or another classical author rather than Coke, Bracton, or Fleta in buttressing his argument. George and Thomson Mason and the latter's son Stevens Thomson Mason were all noted for their legal erudition, as were Edmund Pendleton and John Taylor. St. George Tucker and Jefferson had reputations for both kinds of learning, as did the elder John Tyler, but there is little evidence that they imposed their secular knowledge on courts either from the bench or the bar. All contemporaries acknowledge that Littleton Waller Tazewell and Francis Gilmer were learned in every way. How much they dazzled their opponents with out-of-the-way knowledge it is difficult to determine, though Wirt's repeated warnings to young Gilmer suggest that at least the latter was inclined to ornament his argument with historical, classical, and especially metaphorical allusions or comparisons. Edmund Randolph and Charles Lee, both Attorneys General of the United States under Washington, and John Wickham, polished and persuasive leader of the Federalists before the Richmond bar, all three gave thorough demonstrations of their legal skill and depth of knowledge as counsel for the defense in the Burr Trial. Scholarly and discriminating John Adams himself paid tribute to the learning and sound research of a third United States Attorney General of the period, William Wirt.

There is another segment of the legal profession which should be considered before turning to public speaking and a closer look at the lawyers best known as orators. This is the corps of exceptionally able judges produced in Virginia. In the law of the English-speaking world, as Roscoe Pound has pointed out, the common law, which is our law, is a law of judges, not of teachers or writers: "Its form is recorded judicial experience. Its oracles are judges. Its great names are judges."[18] The history of the profession in Jefferson's Virginia bears out every clause of this statement.

Every judge among these Virginia jurists was learned at least in the law, and each was known for the logic with which he reached his decisions. One of them was Francis T. Brooke (1753-1851), Revolutionary soldier, judge of the General Court of Virginia and then of the Supreme Court of Appeals, and finally president of the latter from 1824 to 1830. Another was Henry Tazewell, father of the more famous Littleton Waller Tazewell. He served as chief justice of the General Court and then as member of the Supreme Court of Appeals from 1785 to 1794, resigning to become United States Senator. Ten years younger than Jefferson, he is said to have been the most popular and one of the most gifted of Virginians when he died in 1799 at the age of forty-five. The elder John Tyler, after a distinguished legislative career and years as a member of the Admiralty Court in Virginia, became in 1788 a member of the General Court. Like others to be noted below, he early assisted in establishing the overruling power of the judiciary. From 1811 until his death in 1813 he was judge of the Federal Court for the District of Virginia. Liberal in politics and conservative in private life, he held a position very similar to that of Pendleton and others of the age of Jefferson.

Richard E. Parker (1783-1840), sometime member of Wirt's group of essayists, was United States Senator briefly, judge of the General Court from 1817 to 1837, and finally member of the Supreme Court of Appeals. Parker was noted as a steady and dependable jurist who united sound scholarship and humanitarianism. Wirt's friend Dabney Carr (1772-1837) developed into one of the most profound of Virginia judges after he assumed the Chancellorship of the Winchester District. In 1824 he became judge of the Supreme Court of Appeals. Humorous, kindly, well-read, he was according to his contemporaries a great jurist.[19] The *Reports* and his manuscript remains indicate that Carr gave his own opinions at length after searching investigation and close sifting of his detailed notes of the arguments at the bar. He is said to have been clear in perception, painstaking in his exactness.

George Wythe and St. George Tucker, the first two incumbents of the chair of law at William and Mary, also became respected jurists. Wythe as Chancellor and ex officio member of the Supreme Court of Appeals was compared to "Aristides the Just."[20] One of the earliest enunciations of the doctrine of judicial review came in a decision of his, rather ironically in view of his later adherence to Jefferson and his views and party. Tucker, member of the Supreme Court of Appeals 1803-11, judge of the United States district court for Virginia from 1813 until just before his death in 1827, made several notable decisions cited by later lawyers. Among them was his opinion in *Kamper* vs. *Hawkins* (*I Va. Reports*, 20) that the state Constitution in 1776 was a sovereign act of the people and therefore the supreme law, and that the Legislature might not go beyond it. This decision agrees with that of Wythe mentioned above but does not emphasize the judicial review aspect of the case. Other decisions of Tucker's support states' rights as authorized by the Federal Constitution and the constitutionality of the act of 1802 for sale of the glebes for the relief of the poor. In other words, the two former professors were liberal jurists, of the states' rights persuasion, and leaning more than their friend Jefferson to the doctrine of judicial review, the last perhaps an almost inevitable conclusion by any judge.

Another of this Revolutionary generation, Edmund Pendleton, went through a long and active legislative career before he became president of the Supreme Court of Appeals, a position he held from 1779 until his death in 1805. By nature a conservative and supporter of established institutions, Pendleton in opposing certain measures of the Washington administration placed himself among the liberal partisans of his old friend and colleague Jefferson. Jefferson testified that Pendleton was the ablest man he ever heard in debate. His biographer indicates the profundity of his research in every case and his frequent unearthing of the generally unknown old statutes and precedents.[21] As a judge Pendleton was conservative, cautious, and sound. His decisions were individual, never partisan. They have been rarely overruled even to this day.[22] The limitation of his fame to his native state was imposed by himself when he declined Federal appointment.

George Washington's nephew and heir Bushrod Washington, from 1798 until his death in 1829 associate justice of the United States Supreme Court, was not greatly overshadowed by his chief. His touring district included some of the eastern middle states. Here he showed in his individual decisions courage and perspicacious thinking. Not widely read in literature, he was a thorough student of the law. In after years one attorney who had pleaded before Washington in New Jersey and was himself later a Supreme Court justice of that state testified that of all the judges he had known, "taking into account integrity of character, learning, deportment, balance of mind, natural temper and disposition, and ability to ascertain and regard the true merits of a cause as determined by the law that he was called to administer,"[23] Bushrod Washington was the ideal. This more than offsets Josiah Quincy, Jr.'s, opinion that Washington was too small and took too much snuff to be a good judge![24] In constitutional matters Washington saw eye to eye with his friend Marshall. Here and in admiralty and commercial cases he expressed several opinions influential in the development of American law.[25]

The two giants among the judges, however, were the men who best expressed judicially the Federalist and Republican points of view. Spencer Roane (1762-1822), a member of the General Court from 1789 and from 1794 for twenty-seven years a member of the Supreme Court of Appeals, was deprived of the Chief Justiceship of the United States through Federalist resignations and the appointment of John Marshall just before Jefferson became President. There are good indications that he might have made as great a Federal jurist as Marshall, though certainly with very different interpretations. The Jeffersonian Republicans felt that he would have made a greater one.

Of Roane's service as jurist both *Reports* and individual contemporaries speak frequently. Widely read in all legal literature but strongest in contemporary law, he attacked each case with penetration and intensity. He wrote vigorous and clear-cut opinions, always insisting upon individual judgment and responsibility. He inclined, though not unfairly, to the side of liberty rather than property, always mindful of precedent but at the same time of public policy in his age. In 1793 he upheld the right of the General Court to declare void an unconstitutional act of the Legislature, thus ranging himself like several other jurists just discussed on the side of judicial review. He agreed with Tucker in the right of the Legislature to sell the glebe lands, and he approved the manumission of slaves. He was regarded as the ablest member of his court and its strongest defender against encroachment on its prerogatives by Legislature on United States Supreme Court. Gilmer and Wirt are among those who write with respect and approval of Roane's decisions and abilities. John Quincy Adams recorded that Wirt almost worshipped the man.[26]

Part of this approval naturally came from their general agreement with him in politics and after 1812 from his growing reputation as the principal champion of states' rights. Certainly many of his decisions reflect his and his state's developing position on the question. That of February 1, 1806 *Hunter* vs. *Martin*, for example, is said to mark the beginning of the record phase of states' rights agitation.[27] John Randolph Tucker, a later and able legal historian, thought that Roane deserved to rank as jurist and legal statesman with Chancellor Kent of New York.[28]

Better known today is John Marshall, called "the principal founder of judicial review and of the American system of constitutional law." After an able career as soldier, lawyer, member of Congress and of John Adams' cabinet, Marshall was appointed Chief Justice by Adams in the last days of his administration after Jay had declined the office. For the rest of his long life Marshall was a major figure in American government and is generally acknowledged as the greatest jurist our history has known. Opposed by executive and legislative branches of the government during most of his career, he stamped his strongly nationalistic interpretation of government and Constitution so indelibly on the minds of many Americans that a generation after his death the only recourse of his native region, when faced with intolerable pressures through the centralizing power he had been instrumental in forming, was through arms rather than law.

Though Marshall had been a student of Wythe, he had studied law for only a short time and never showed the breadth or profundity of legal erudition shared by many of his fellow Virginians just mentioned. In general literature, however, Marshall was widely read, and there is considerable indication that he studied law intensely during his years on the Supreme bench. That he rarely quoted legal precedent or authority was thus perhaps deliberate method, for he preferred the quiet, straightforward statements of his own reasoned decisions.[29] Wirt, who belonged to the opposite camp politically, expressed many times his admiration for this great jurist.

Wirt in 1803 observed that Marshall had "the faculty of developing a subject by a single glance of his mind."[30] The *Reports* of the 113 cases he argued before the Supreme Court of Appeals of Virginia between 1790 and 1799 indicate that this was true when Marshall was in active practice. He was called a common law lawyer in the best sense of that term, and he carried the qualities of profound yet simply outlined and convincing reasoning with him to the bench. His quiet sincerity and deep conviction as well as logic moved his hearers.

On the Supreme Court, gradually surrounded by Republican appointees, Marshall was able to develop and maintain his ascendancy, though there is no evidence of heavy-handedness. Convinced that the only future for America lay in a strong central government of the kind advocated by Washington and the elder Adams, in a series of notable decisions during more than thirty years he strengthened nationalism by his interpretations of the Constitution. He was not a judge noted for strict impartiality, as witness his almost outrageously partisan handling of the Burr Trial in 1807. But he presented his opinions with such incisive and overwhelming logic that he persuaded fellow justices or imperceptibly edged them toward his own position. He has been properly called a legal statesman rather than a great dispenser of impartial justice. Like his cousin Thomas Jefferson he was no mean hater—the two despised each other—and more than any legislative figure during the first third of the nineteenth century he represented the balance, the weight in the opposite scale, to Republican liberalism and states' rightism. This he accomplished through the methods and procedures of his profession.

In a sense, Marshall was the culmination of a conservative Virginia legal tradition which had begun two hundred years before, though his nationalist-centralization policy and problem had not really been faced in any way in the earlier history of his state. His genius was his own—and his ancestors'—but many of the characteristics with which John Quincy Adams endowed him in his journal at the time of Marshall's death are typical of the best Virginia judicial traditions. Marshall, said Adams, "by the ascendancy of his genius, by the amenity of his deportment, and by the imperturbable command of his temper, has given a permanent and systematic character to the decisions of the Court, and settled many great constitutional questions favorably to the continuance of the Union."[31] Among all American lawyers who have left their stamp on American institutions, said John C. Reed, "John Marshall, of Virginia, takes precedence."[32]

Though Benjamin Watkins Leigh, John Wickham, and a number of other Richmond lawyers were as conservative and sometimes as Federalistic as their fellow-townsman Marshall, they were not the lawyers who impressed their generation within the state most strongly. This was after all dominantly a liberal Jeffersonian age. A writer in the *Southern Literary Messenger* in 1838,[33] looking back at the state's great legal lights, mentioned none of them: "It is some solace to think that a century hence the learned will pore over the decrees of Chancellor Wythe, the expanded views of Edmund Pendleton, the vigorous opinions of Spencer Roane, and the profound investigations of Dabney Carr, as we look back to the judgments of old Hobart or the authoritative institutes of Sir Edward Coke." With all due allowance for his chauvinistic pride, he was not too far wrong. He simply should have added "the masterfully reasoned opinions of John Marshall" and he would have had the precedents from which constitutional and civil law may be argued today.

B. *Lawyers and Orators*

That law and oratory went hand in hand no American of the Jeffersonian period would have thought of denying. Every fledgling barrister felt that he must become an effective public speaker, though not quite all the public speakers were lawyers. No other kind of persuasion, literary or economic, was equal to that of eloquence—this the Jeffersonians knew from experience. In country or superior court in legislative halls, in popular assemblies, one must convince by the effectiveness of his oral argument. Eloquence was the road to wealth, to power, to distinction.

Though he had abundant examples in classical antiquity and in the history of the mother country, no Virginian needed them to be convinced that history and nations could be and were made by the orator. In House of Burgesses and Continental Congress, in significant court cases, he had seen and heard Patrick Henry, Richard Henry Lee, Edmund and Peyton Randolph, William Grayson, and a score of others debate the points and the issues which were to bring a people to revolution, to independence, and to organized and centralized government.

The Jeffersonian period had begun, as we have seen, with the mighty debates of the Virginia Federal Constitutional Convention and later the national Federal Constitutional Convention. Virginians had in both been divided on the question of a stronger centralized government. Those who were defeated like Henry and Lee returned to their constituents with increased reputation and found increased confidence in their abilities evidenced by their election to the principal state offices and to the national Congress. Those who won continued to devote their forensic powers to the great problems attending the new organization. For the next seventy years the principal legislative battleground was to be the Constitution, and victor and vanquished alike devoted their full powers to the individual engagements of the great conflict.

Less dramatic but hardly less significant were the smaller areas in which men had to demonstrate their abilities in oral persuasion. In the pulpit, in patriotic and other public assemblies, in the halls of academe, before local and county bars, they moved men by their words. Revival of religion, defense of the established church, freedom of religion were possible when men spoke for them. Reminders of the immediate glorious past political history and warnings or advice as to future courses came to the people in Fourth of July speeches, toasts, and other occasional orations. Most practicing lawyers' reputations derived from their speaking before the bar rather than in their technical case work beforehand. Even progress in education had to be urged orally in the collegiate communities.

When Virginia versifiers wrote of the great they usually mentioned Virginia's eminent orators, though the same men frequently had other qualities for distinction. When Wirt was choosing a subject for a biography of "some Virginia worthy now dead," it was as inevitable that he choose Patrick Henry as it was that Milton should have chosen Paradise Lost as the subject of his great Puritan epic, no matter how many divergent topics or subjects had originally appeared in either man's list. The newspaper columns are full of discussions or reportings of contemporary speeches. As we have seen, Wirt's ostensible survey of Virginia manners and mores in *Letters of the British Spy* is in reality a series of essays on the subject of eloquence, and one of his later essay series was begun with a similar topic in mind. When Francis Gilmer as a young man of twenty-six wished to send up a trial literary balloon, he decided that a series of sketches of American orators would have most interest for the public. Personal letters by the hundreds if not thousands during the era report reactions to speeches and speakers. Those of the Wirt group—Francis and Peachy Gilmer, Carr, Randolph, St. George Tucker, and others—recur again and again to the matter of what constitutes real eloquence and how it may be attained.

In all this Virginians were in agreement with other states. The Boston *Monthly Anthology* of 1806,[34] rejoicing that "Eloquence seems to flourish among us," urged "Let us therefore encourage its growth till it becomes the distinguishing feature of the American people." Likening America to the Greek and Roman republics, men saw the nation characterized by commerce and oratory. Even their estimates of poets were based largely on rhetorical criteria—thus their admiration for Pope. Perhaps accurately they saw their verse as strongly imitative of British models, their oratory as original and independent.

Yet Americans, Virginians especially, were fully aware of formal critiques of the art of eloquence from ancient Greece to their own time. During the latter half of the eighteenth century students in schools and colleges were taught rhetorical theory, including Aristotle's *Rhetoric* and *Poetics*, Cicero's *De Oratore,* and the critical epistles of Horace and Longinus.[35] Though too late to influence colonial speakers, Blair's *Lectures on Rhetoric and Belles-Lettres* was the most influential single book for potential orators as well as writers from soon after its appearance in 1783 through 1830, and even beyond. The British and Irish orators were read and frequently imitated, but the principles of public speaking to which critics always returned were those expressed in the classics or in Blair.

Of the classics, the Virginians paid most attention to Cicero and Quintilian. Though Wirt in the *British Spy* spoke slightingly of the *De Oratore* as "extremely light and insubstantial; and in truth little more than a tissue of rhapsodies,"[36] in later years he reread it and recanted, declaring it the greatest of all studies of his favorite art. Gilmer, Carr, Tazewell, and many an anonymous newspaper critic agreed earlier with his later verdict. It is not hard to see why. In detail and in broad outline, the *De Oratore* suggested their problems and their situation.

Cicero's insistence on the importance of oratory to society and to the state, his dialogues in which his characters argue whether or not oratory is a field useful only to law courts and parliament, his insistence that rhetoric is a "science" demanding both knowledge and style, they could agree with fully. Over and over Gilmer, Wirt, Randolph, and Jefferson, addressing the younger generation, echo Cicero in warning that every orator needs a wide education. All the Jeffersonians agreed with the Roman too that natural gifts were the first essential, and they liked to point out Patrick Henry as a modern example of Cicero's dogma that the natural orator could be the greatest. Cicero also directed his attention to legal oratory, its particular need for breadth and depth of knowledge though not necessarily of legal knowledge, which could be acquired by research. And he pointed out that there were different styles of speaking equally admirable. His four requisites for "style" in oratory—correct diction, lucidity, ornateness or embellishment, and appropriateness—[37] Jeffersonians followed perhaps too closely for our tastes, especially the third. They frequently warned each other as the Roman did his fellow countrymen against going too far in the adornments of expression. They approved Cicero's belief[38] that great oratory avoids narrow specialization, and finally that eloquence is one of the supreme virtues.

Quintilian, Cicero's great successor and disciple, they quote or refer to almost as frequently as to the master. Quintilian's outline of the stages of education necessary for the teacher and practitioner of rhetoric, from the cradle to the budding orator, they studied intently. Wirt and Gilmer, who wrote most about oratory, echo his ideas on invention, including arrangement, or eloquence, including memory and delivery, and his Ciceronian insistence that without natural gifts technical rules are useless. Quintilian's warning that oratory must be *proof,* that oratory is most powerful as instruction through emotional appeals, his insistence on the use of history as embellishment, they saw as practical in their time.

As we have noted, Blair's *Lectures* became the standard text and reference book for academy and college by the beginning of our period. Mature writers such as Wirt refer to it in various sorts of discussions. It was at once a guide to composition, a primer for aesthetics, and a manual of oratory, among other things. It differed from the earlier classical oratorical treatises in associating rhetoric with belles-lettres. Like Aristotle and Cicero, Blair largely ignored the matter of delivery. The book's popularity was concurrent with the tremendous upsurge of the democratic spirit in the form of Jeffersonian Republicanism, for it supplied what most felt they needed. Even in the generation after the Jeffersonians, it was to affect markedly the written and oral expression of the great New Englanders of the flowering through such a teacher of its principles as Ellery T. Channing.

Though Randolph and Gilmer agreed that Blair should be banished from the schools, both showed his influence. Randolph naturally preferred the classics: "Cicero, Quintilian, and Longinus should be the text books,"[39] he once wrote his younger friend. He was commenting that Gilmer had given "the frothy Fourth of July boys" good advice. Wirt also frequently warned against frothy sentences and general affectation. That Blair was any more to blame for the developing ornate style than the ancient writers is doubtful—there are yet other factors in the situation—except for the fact that he was so immediately popular.

After twenty-odd chapters of discussion of literature and of writing, including style, in Lecture XXV Blair began "Eloquence, or Public Speaking," with a running commentary on Grecian and Roman eloquence, including extracts from Cicero's and Demosthenes' orations. In subsequent chapters he discussed the eloquence of the pulpit, the conduct of discourse in all its parts, and pronunciation, concluding the specific consideration of the subject in XXXIV, "Means of Improving in Eloquence."

On most points Blair is in full agreement with Cicero and Quintilian, and at first glance it is difficult for the reader to understand why the more serious students of the art professed to despise the modern and revere the ancient.[40] Blair like Cicero speaks out against prettiness of style and affected ornaments, gives similar differing types of oratory, and emphasizes the need for persuasion and warm emotion, the necessity for profound knowledge of the legal profession by the lawyer, and that Nature is far more important than Art in the shaping of a great orator but that culture must bring the seed to perfection. Blair went out of his way to praise both Cicero and Quintilian, declaring the latter contained almost all the principles of good criticism.[41]

The Virginians liked Blair's reminder that great eloquence had never existed except where there was real freedom among men.[42] They may not have liked his assertion that French oratory was superior to British in both pleasing and persuading. And his *exempla* of model orations were sometimes as ornate as anything the frothy Fourth of July boys produced. Also, Gilmer in his *Sketches* alludes to the lawyer's following of Blair's "inadequate notions of metaphor and trope."[43]

In other words, though Blair paid lip service to moderation in figure and language generally, his insistence on the vital importance of moving the emotions, with his cited models and failure to define exactly the rhetorical figures, had a part in producing in the youthful and impressionable something of the spread-eagle style of oratory which was to remain characteristically American long after the Civil War. But one must repeat, whatever his distaste for Blair, he was far more admired and imitated than condemned.

Blair was not the only Scot who influenced Virginia and Southern oratory. The eccentric peripatetic philosopher and schoolmaster James Ogilvie, already mentioned several times, who was *au courant* with his age in believing that oratory was the most important subject to be taught the young, had from his first teaching in Virginia prepared his boys to be public speakers. His pupils studied Cicero, Quintilian, and Blair, but they also studied Ogilvie who, dressed in

Roman toga, demonstrated his model orations from a rostrum. Apparently his speeches were largely cemented-together extracts from famous orators from Demosthenes to Edmund Burke and Patrick Henry, but they made a great impression on the young and even on such discriminating adults as George Ticknor, Washington Irving and Francis Jeffrey (who heard him in New York). The latter and Ellery T. Channing, who reviewed Ogilvie's *Philosophical Essays*, felt that Ogilvie's work was better as elocution than as eloquence, though they never drew a distinct line themselves.[44]

In his last years in the United States, Ogilvie gave up teaching and made a tour of the seaboard states, proposing to establish schools of oratory in each which would be directed by a man trained by the master himself. Crowds heard him from Boston to Savannah, usually with great respect and approval, though occasionally with derision produced by his affected gestures and memorized recital. He was most successful in South Carolina, where he trained William C. Preston and a group of students who became the orators of Mississippi, Georgia, and Louisiana, as well as of South Carolina. Gilmer felt that in his later years Ogilvie was mad, but Gilmer himself, Winfield Scott, and William C. Rives, among two dozen other Virginians, were influenced all their lives by his style and insistence on appropriate subject matter. Wirt lamented that Ogilvie's enthusiasm had not been matched by his judgment.

The subjects on which Ogilvie had his students speak on July 5, 1804,[45] were representative of the sorts of things they would be concerned with, or should be concerned with, in law, government, and literature in later life. An interesting principle in political economy, the connection between chemistry and agriculture, education, the utility of periodical essays, were subjects like Blair's appropriate for either written or spoken expression. Later, in 1815, Ogilvie had his older students at the South Carolina College speak on a variety of literary topics and on the utility of public libraries, the character of Cicero, elocution, oratory, pulpit oratory, politeness, the press, envy and emulation, and the pleasures of literature and sense. He himself on his tour had spoken on the licentious press, the letters of Junius, national education, progress of civilization, usury, utility of public libraries, dueling, and beneficence, among other things, all subjects the budding or mature orator might use before academic or the generally more literate audiences of the time. During the War of 1812, Ogilvie gave two of his speeches before the assembled soldiers in Kentucky, with the full approval of their commanding officers. How the hardy woodsmen received his elaborate and erudite phrases is not recorded. We do know that Jefferson would journey from Monticello all the way to Charlottesville on Sunday to hear Mr. Ogilvie's weekly discourse.[46]

The newspapers and magazines, as we have seen, printed orations in full or quoted from them as they were given before Legislature, Congress, Fourth of July assemblies, or Inaugural crowds. The columns of these journals also contained essays on the art of eloquence. "The Character of Sheridan," for example, in the Virginia *Argus* of August 29, 1811, is a study of Sheridan as orator. Wirt's *British Spy* essays had originally appeared in the *Argus* too, most of them concerned in one way or another with oratory. The later *Rainbow* and *Old Bachelor* pieces, such as the several in the latter directly on the subject of American eloquence and an essay like "Truth and Eloquence: an Allegory," had originally appeared in the *Enquirer*.

Gilmer, George Tucker, and Wirt are the three ablest of the known or pseudonymous writers on the great subject. Wirt began his discussions of the art in his letters to his friends in the 1790's, and as we have seen first formalized and applied his ideas in the *Letters of the British Spy* in 1803.[47] That eloquence or oratory was *a* or *the* major subject is evident in the analyses of Marshall, Monroe, Wickham, and Edmund Randolph as orators, the demonstration of the the pulpit eloquence of the Blind Preacher James Waddell, and the essay on modern eloquence which assesses the reasons why oratory of the highest type was not present in Virginia. In the last Wirt refers to Blair and Cicero and Bacon, to his (unnamed) friend[48] who saturates himself in Bolingbroke before composing a speech, and to the need for cultivation of the art in Virginia. Implicit throughout is the idea that eloquence through learning and mental discipline may be Virginia's salvation, an idea he was to hold all the rest of his life. The *Rainbow* and *Old Bachelor* did not contain the completed discussion of eloquence Wirt planned but much on the subject appears in them. The latter includes his several later thoughts on the matter of Fourth of July orations, the quality of the oratory of the old bar and old Congress, and the importance of manner, voice, and earnestness in speaking.[49] These *Old Bachelor* papers he addresses, as we have pointed out, to a rising generation, and he continued his remaining twenty years to address youth in individual letters on the subject.

In the second series of the *Rainbow,* never collected from the *Enquirer,* Wirt wrote "On Forensic Eloquence."[50] In his *Patrick Henry* he analyzed the qualities that made Henry a great speaker, concluding that his subject was the Ciceronian orator *from Nature.* He perhaps overemphasizes this, for reasons suggested above. In two essays for his friend Rice's *Virginia Evangelical and Literary Magazine,*[51] "Hints to Preachers," he suggests to the clergy more complete preparation, more piety and sincerity in manner, and better models for their sermons. He cites Samuel Davies as an excellent model. He asserts bluntly that if lawyers prepared themselves no more earnestly or effectively than the clergy most of the profession would lose their employment. That Wirt did not always practice what he preached as to style, particularly restraint in imagery and figure, is evident in his speeches. But more of this later.

In *Letters from Virginia, Translated from the French* (1816) presumably by George Tucker, the author deplores the excessive Virginia attachment to oratory, and the readiness to select leaders on the basis of the ability to harangue an audience. Oratory is acknowledged as the only road to fame in Virginia. County court lawyers, Fourth of July orators, political spouters, slang whangers or stump-orators who are passionately fond of the word Republican, are satirized.[52] Tucker, a notoriously poor speaker, pays little attention elsewhere to the whole art of oratory, and his own inadequacy may in part account for his ridicule here. That some of this satire on popular oratory is justified is supported in dozens of contemporary writings, including H. H. Brackenridge's *Modern Chivalry.* A rhetorician and philosopher, Tucker studied Blair and the common sense school for their thinking on aesthetic questions more than for their ideas on oratory as rhetoric or the reverse.

Francis Gilmer's letters to his brother Peachy, Randolph, Wirt, and Carr and his little *Sketches of American Orators* (1816) indicate that he agreed fully with Wirt as to the importance of oratory in his age, its abuse by the ignorant or the lazy, its frequently excessive sentimentality, and the need for it to be taken more seriously by the younger generation. The early letters concern his own method of training himself in speaking. He memorized great passages from literature and recited "a la mode de Garrick."[53] He constantly combined legal with rhetorical study. And he came to analyze the qualities which made his contemporaries effective speakers.

The *Sketches of American Orators* begins with an assertion of the American need for discriminating criticism of its public speakers, the most influential men of the day. The author cites as authority La Bruyère, Cicero, and Hume. Then he plunges into his analyses of John Randolph, Marshall, Emmet of New York, Pinkney of Maryland, Tazewell, and Wirt, with many asides about Patrick Henry. In the revised and enlarged later edition of the work he added further discussions of Pinkney, changed his opinion of Randolph on many points, and added Henry Clay to his list. The analyses include some observations on Cicero's dictum of the necessity of depth of knowledge in the orator and of the difference between British and American oratory. He concludes by agreeing with Lord Bolingbroke that eloquence must flow from the depths of profound knowledge "and not spout forth a little frothy water on some gaudy day, and remain dry the rest of the year."[54]

Gilmer shows considerable knowledge of the great British contemporary or nearly contemporary orators such as Curran, Burke, Malone, and Grattan. His criteria for perfect oratory are clearly classical: one man is too deficient in matter, another has a richly stored and logical mind, a third always engaged his adversary on his own ground, a fourth has only lack of ambition and subtlety as faults, the best is a genuinely Ciceronian orator. That he takes for granted that most orators are lawyers is evident in the several suggestions he makes directly to members of his own profession, who ignore Cicero's warning that they must be thoroughly prepared in general education, who imitate Curran's tendency to false pathos, or who fail to study Demosthenes and Tully. Such a man as Henry, he noted in his revised edition, needed only a regular education to equal Cicero or Demosthenes, but that he lacked: "Let us not be told that education would have extinguished his fire."[55] In a letter to his brother Peachy of March 17, 1813, Gilmer states his firm belief that eloquence must adapt itself to the society and literature in which it is to flourish, though it must not yield to its environment as Henry did, who persisted in saying "yearth," etc.[56] In the later edition of the *Sketches* he exhibits Clay as an orator who, had he been disciplined by study of the accurate sciences, his imagination restrained by the taste of Virgil and Tully, and his style ennobled by Milton and Dryden, would have been the model par excellence for American orators.

Besides little studies of orators like this of Gilmer's, there were a number of anthologies of specimen orations designed for school, legal, and general professional use. Most of these, edited and published outside Virginia, indicate that America generally highly respected the Old Dominion brand of eloquence. S. C. Carpenter's *Select American Speeches, Forensic and Parliamentary, with Prefatory Remarks,* published in Philadelphia in 1815 in two volumes, includes four speeches by Patrick Henry, three by Edmund Randolph, two by Madison, one by Robert Goodloe Harper, and the speeches of Wickham and Wirt during the Burr Trial. *The American Orator; or Elegant Extracts in Prose and Poetry; Comprehending a Diversity of Oratorical Specimens, of the Eloquence of Popular Assemblies, of the Bar, of the Pulpet, &c. Principally intended for the use of Schools and Academies,* edited by Increase Cooke and published in New Haven and Charleston in 1819, includes samples from Cicero, and from Shakespeare, Sterne, Greville, Kames, Blair, and other British writers and speakers. Under "Pathetic Pieces" is included Wirt's "The Blind Preacher," and under the "Eloquence of the Barr" his "Burr and Blennerhasset" passage at the Burr Trial. Washington's "Farewell Address" appears under "Select Speeches." In a textbook devoted largely to European authors the two selections from Wirt indicate his popularity.

One of the most comprehensive and popular assemblages of the period, apparently designed for the use of professional speakers and the enjoyment of the general reader, was E. B. Williston's *Eloquence of the United States,* published at Middletown, Connecticut, in 1827 in five volumes. Here Virginia oratory is most generously represented. Volume I contains the 1788 speeches of Henry (three), Edmund Randolph, and Marshall; Washington's 1789 "Inaugural Address"; Nicholas' 1794 speech; Madison and Giles on the British Treaty; and Harper on France. Volume II includes another Harper oration, Jefferson's two Inaugurals, Stevens Thomson Mason's 1802 speech on the judiciary, two of Giles' speeches, Madison's first Inaugural, and a speech of John Randolph's. Volume III presents Monroe's two Inaugural addresses, and Clay's speeches in March, 1824, on the tariff. Volume IV includes 1824 addresses by James Barbour and Clay, and the speeches of Edmund Randolph, Wickham, and Wirt during the Burr Trial.

These three books are but random examples among dozens of such collections indicative of the popularity of oratory and the Virginia brand of it in the age. In some of them Fourth of July speeches and sermons are included, but the political material is overwhelmingly predominant in all.

Virginia actually had some notable speakers outside the areas of the law and politics. The only recent comprehensive study, W. N. Brigance's *A History and Criticism of American Public Address,* includes discussions of Samuel Davies and Devereux Jarratt among America's great pulpit orators, the latter being cited among the extemporaneous speakers.[57] Of those who lived well into or through the Jeffersonian period, a number of Presbyterians such as John Holt Rice, Moses Hoge, and Conrad Speece were known widely outside their own state as great preachers. Baptists John Leland and Andrew Broaddus, Methodists Peter Cartwright and Jesse Lee, and Episcopalians William H. Wilmer and Bishop Madison were effective preachers, as we have noted in Chapter IV above.

Academic oratory was a legitimate division of the art then as it is now. Though Virginia possessed few colleges and college-level students, the quality of the oratory surviving from William and Mary and Hampden-Sydney graduation exercises, and from literary societies, is quite high. When not rendered in Latin or Greek, its language is close kin to that of contemporary political eloquence, and many of the commencement addresses are on political subjects. But the series of addresses on education and literary culture of various kinds delivered before the Hampden-Sydney Literary and Philosophical Society in the 1820's by professors, lawyers, and clergy are strongly sincere, carefully reasoned compositions closer to the familiar essay than were most political speeches.[58] One of these orators, William Maxwell of Norfolk, was adept in both prepared and extempore speaking. Grigsby, who had spoken at Yale himself, declared that Maxwell was the only man he ever heard of who gave the Phi Beta

Kappa address at that institution without a single line of written preparation. And Maxwell was successful.[59]

Most other Americans and even many Europeans agreed that Virginians stood at the forefront of American political and popular oratory in this period, and that American oratory surpassed British after 1790.[60] This would make the Virginians as a group the most eloquent public men of the English-speaking world for this generation. Whether this is true or not, two or three dozen Virginians through their speaking did much to shape public opinion and the nation. The political ideas they had will be considered in the next chapter. The general methods and individual qualities of the more distinguished among them should be considered briefly here.

Richard Henry Lee and Patrick Henry, the great oratorical powers of the Continental Congress, lived to dispute in the Virginia Convention of 1788 and thereafter. Called the Cicero and Demosthenes of the age, they remained very much alive through their forensic reputations for two generations after their physical departures. Henry's name, methods, and actual (?) work were invoked by those who would offer models of popular style and later by those who argued for extreme states' rights. Lee, polished and urbane, learned and perceptive, Wirt characterizes as too smooth and too sweet. Yet in doing so the biographer of Henry was emphasizing the virtues of his own subject's more rough-and-tumble style.

Wirt, who never met Henry, fashioned his biography from the recollections of those who had—especially John Tyler, St. George Tucker, and Jefferson—and the embellishments of his own imagination and the romantic-sentimental fashion of his age. His emphasis, as we have noted, is on Henry as a speaker by nature, by natural gifts, as Cicero and Quintilian insisted the greatest orators must be. But Wirt also attempts, from the scattered and sometimes contradictory evidence available to him, to reconstruct Henry's speeches and analyze his personal oratorical qualities. Firm voice, distinct articulation, range from comedy to tragedy in emotional appeal, mild persuasion and yet sometimes vehement rousing of his listeners, gesture so appropriate many said his power depended upon it, these traits Wirt emphasizes. Finally the biographer asks, as though these were the traits one might expect in any orator, of what Henry's peculiar excellence consisted.[61] He wisely attempts no exact answer, but he does go back to the trait with which he started, natural ability, and explains it as a sort of *"strong natural sense"* of human nature and what was needed in particular situations. Gilmer in his *Sketches* agrees fully, comparing Henry's ability in these respects with Shakespeare's.[62] This figure of a "natural man" was aimed at the romantic taste of the new generation, not the taste of Jefferson or Randolph or John Taylor. But it was more than that, for Wirt was presenting the backwoods orator, the model for a new and popular democracy which was beginning its ascendance in America.[63] Henry's love of power is visible through Wirt's phrases, though it is soft-pedaled throughout the book.

Twentieth-century scholarship indicates that many of Henry's most famous sentences were actually what Wirt thought they should have been, especially in the "Give Me Liberty or Give Me Death" speech at the Virginia Convention of 1775. But Tucker, Tyler, and Jefferson were able to give him outlines and sometimes phrases, and there were stenographers' reports of Henry's later discourses. Some of the most striking language attributed to Henry seems to have been recorded by contemporaries as Richard Henry Lee's, but men like Tyler passed on to Wirt as verbatim quotations sentences such as "If this be treason, make the most of it." Modern scholars with access to materials not available to Wirt still agree with his general analysis.

A recent critic lists Henry's methods and techniques of persuasion.[64] His compliments to his opponents, his frequent use of unsupported general assertion, and his tremendous appeals to the feelings are first among them. His logic was never strong. He was a practical man and a realist who saw self-interest as the motivating force in human character and spoke accordingly.

In the lesser strokes of persuasive technique he was most skillful. Recognition of the rights of others to hold opinions differing from his own, simple but vivid language, images and figures drawn from common experiences, his use of the first person and the rhetorical question, were all parts of his method. As Cicero and Quintilian suggested, though perhaps without their help, he was careful to adapt his materials to his various audiences. He relied on the delivery Wirt describes. Emotional intensity, complete bodily expressiveness, and a clear, powerful, and flexible voice made him indeed an orator *ex natura*. If Wirt's cementing and amplification have made him a figure of legend and folklore, one must admit that the traditional figure was drawn from a historical reality to which modern research attests.

In qualities other than homely appearance John Marshall as orator seems to have been the complete antithesis of Henry. In fact, few remember him at all as an orator. Yet among his contemporaries he was placed in the front rank of American eloquence. In Virginia both Wirt and Gilmer, of the opposite political persuasion, admired his forensic as well as his legal abilities. In the *Letters of the British Spy*[65] in 1803, when memories of Marshall's appearance before the bar rather than on the bench were still fresh in the American mind, Wirt recorded the opinion that "This extraordinary man, without the aid of fancy, without the advantage of person, voice, attitude, gesture, or any of the ornaments of an orator, deserved to be considered as one of the most eloquent men in the world; if eloquence may be said to consist of seizing the attention with irresistible force, and never permitting it to elude the grasp, until the hearer has received the conviction the speaker intends."

Gilmer, whose analysis Beveridge feels is the best ever made of Marshall by a personal observer,[66] in his *Sketches of American Orators* (1816) expands Wirt's earlier summary. "The characteristic of his eloquence is an irresistible cogency, and a luminous simplicity in the order of his reasoning." He was all reasoning, Gilmer suggests, as John Randolph (see below) was all declamation.[67] This is good evidence, incidentally, that at least the discriminating Virginia listener did not admire only the ornate or emotional in oratory.

Though Jefferson and Madison are better known for qualities other than their oral eloquence, both are represented in contemporary and later textbooks and other anthologies of speeches. Both were eloquent with the pen, and both possessed voices of such pitch or volume that they were not effective in large assemblies. Yet from the two conventions of 1788-89 to his last years Madison had a reputation as a convincing and effective speaker—for those who could hear him. Grigsby, who gathered information concerning the giants of 1788 from those who had heard them, quotes John Marshall as observing that if eloquence is the art of persuasion, Madison was the most eloquent man he ever knew.[68] Gilmer speaks of "his consummate skill as a debater," offset by the fact that his lungs were too weak to permit him to be an orator. Grigsby summarizes various contemporaries on Madison's manner: he "always rose to speak as if with a view of expressing some thought that had casually occurred to him, with his hat in his hand, and with his notes in his hat; and the warmest excitement of debate was visible in him only by a more or less rapid and forward see-saw motion of his body. Yet such was the force of his genius that one of his warmest opponents . . . listened with more delight to his clear and cunning argumentation than to the eloquent and startling appeals of Henry." It was the intrinsic worth of an argument that won Madison's respect and on which he concentrated himself. It was largely in this Convention that Madison earned his solid reputation as effective thinker and able statesman which led eventually to the White House.

Another facet of Madison as orator should be noted here. Louis C. Shaedler, in a recent study of Madison as literary craftsman, notes the pervasive effect of his attention to oratory on the style of his writings.[69] In his "Address to the States" in 1783 and in *The Federalist* especially his papers are "basically oratorical in style." In fact, Madison's *Federalist* pieces are seen as imitative of neither the Addisonian periodical essay nor the English political pamphlet, but a new form evolved by adapting the techniques of oratory to the newspaper essay. This quality is also to be discerned in many of Madison's later essays.

The fireworks of the Virginia Federal Convention of 1788 which opened the Jeffersonian era included other Roman candles than Henry, Lee, Marshall, and Madison. Pendleton was "elegant if not eloquent" and most effective; Henry Lee gave promise of his later eulogy on Washington; William Grayson displayed his English learning and wide knowledge of political economy in convincing logical debate, "every speech a specimen in dialectics";[70] John Tyler, Sr., Archibald Stuart, Gabriel Jones, William McKee, William Fleming, Thomson and Stevens Thomson Mason, George and Wilson Cary Nicholas, all spoke effectively. Edmund Randolph, the Bolingbroke of Virginia, displayed the mixture of ornament, research, and persuasiveness which made him then and later a leader of the bar as well as a statesman.[71]

John Randolph and William Wirt represent the oratorical generation between these founding fathers and the last Jeffersonian generation of Gilmer, Upshur, and Rives. In the first quarter of the nineteenth century both the former achieved national reputations as speakers, and with Daniel Webster disputed first place in the eloquence of the nation. Wirt modestly said that Webster north of the Potomac, and Tazewell south, had the greatest reputations; but he was ignoring himself, he did not like Randolph and his style of oratory, and Tazewell was his admired friend.

Yet for general audiences, including the ladies, and for many members of Congress, Randolph was the orator of the age. Above all his contemporaries, asserted Grigsby, who had heard him, Randolph "was successful in fixing the attention of his audience of every class and degree throughout his longest speeches."[72] Whenever it was known he would speak, the galleries of the House or Senate were crowded. His speeches, like Henry's, have been reported inadequately, as any reader of the *Annals* and *Debates* of Congress will discover. Sometimes they are not reported at all, a speech of some length being noted only as "Mr. Randolph spoke for an hour" on such and such a question.[73]

John Randolph of Roanoke (1773-1833), stepson of St. George Tucker, scion of Virginia's prolific and distinguished family of his name, served in the House and Senate of the United States 1799-1813, 1815-17, 1819-25, 1825-29, as a member of the Virginia Convention of 1829-30, and as Minister to Russia in 1830. A conservative *ex nativitate,* he joined the Jeffersonian Republicans in opposition to what he considered tyranny, became estranged from them before Jefferson's first administration was over, led the *Tertium Quids,* and subsequently became an independent. A good hater of two early generations of the Adams family, he has been the model for or the object of one of the most vituperative portraits ever drawn of an American statesman by their descendant Henry Adams in a caricature of biography in the American Statesman Series.[74] W. C. Bruce's twentieth-century portrait may be too sympathetic, but it was necessary to balance the picture. And in the new age of conservatism since 1950 he has been the subject of a new critical study as champion of the conservative way of life, an example of the conservative mind, in the making of early America.[75] Whatever else Randolph may have been, he was the Jeffersonian example par excellence of the orator as political figure.

In replying to Henry Adams' statement that neither Randolph's wit nor his oratory would have been tolerated in a northern state, Bruce cites Josiah Quincy's fascination with Randolph's gifts as a talker and gives quotations from a northern newspaper's critique of Randolph's speeches which declare him "unquestionably the first [orator] in the country."[76] Certainly his discourse was charming or provoking according to the point of view of the listener.

The high clear voice, the absolute ease of delivery, the constant shifting in position, the witty thrusts and epigrams, the quotations from Latin and English poetry and constant references to the Homeric heroes, mixed with homely figures from everyday life, and indeed materials from almost every province of human learning, Gilmer, Josiah Quincy, Jr., the anonymous New York newspaper writer quoted above, and many others record. In his 1816 portrait of the orator, Gilmer emphasized his antithesis, beautiful conceits, jests, and parables, but concluded that he lacked certain requisites of greatness in the art. Randolph was deficient in matter, his discourse was not logically or even clearly constructed, and he was unable to move the emotions—these the young lawyer saw as real faults. Later, after knowing and hearing Randolph further, he altered his criticism markedly. That the speeches were desultory and unconnected might be a virtue rather than a fault, for Randolph was not a lawyer trying a case. And he found in Randolph considerable power to invoke the pathetic and the tragic. Quite clearly the writer had fallen under the spell of the orator.

Gilmer had touched on some of Randolph's major weaknesses in his original appraisal. Illogical and disconnected discourse with the notorious lack of preparation often referred to by other contemporaries cost the Jeffersonian party the impeachment of Judge Chase and a number of other important measures when Randolph was the Democratic Whip. His quarrelsome, sometimes insulting manner made enemies for life in all parties.

One has only to leaf through the *Annals* and *Debates* of Congress and read at random among the poorly reported speeches to realize why to his contemporaries he was a living legend, the embodiment of what oral communication might be as practiced by an individual genius. Single sentences have entered our historical and folk tradition:

Clay's eye is on the Presidency; and my eye is on him.
I am an aristocrat; I love liberty, I hate equality.

> Asking one of the states to surrender part of her sovereignty is like asking a lady to surrender part of her chastity.
> Life is not so important as the duties of life.[77]

Or in less sententious moods, and more at random, as in the debate on the Embargo:

> a partial repeal of an embargo! what is an embargo, sir?. . . . let us, for God's sake, sing a requiem to the ashes of the embargo; let not our successors have to take up the doleful ditty where we left off.[78]

Or in one of the peculiar "third person" reports of Randolph on the government of Louisiana:

> Mr. Randolph, in combatting the principle of universal suffrage, said it was impossible for the gentleman himself, (alluding to Mr. SMILIE,) or any piping-hot member from a Jacobin club—for any disciple of *Tom Paine* or the *Devil*—to carry this principle of equality to its full extent. . . . He also took occasion to pronounce a strong philippic against foreigners having any part in the government [and after Smilie had defended the name of Paine stating that]. . . . The heroes engaged in that great cause did not need the assistance of an English staymaker. . . .[79]

Or more directly:

> Sir, I am not going to discuss the abstract question of liberty or slavery, or any other abstract question. I go for matters of fact.[80]

One could go on and on picking the trenchant phrase, the apt simile or metaphor, the biting and palpable hit at causes and men. The Embargo was horse medicine, diplomats were privileged spies, his enemies represented backstairs influence. Randolph's apparently desultory procedure was partly deliberately misleading, for very often he did move his colleagues to action. Sometimes he used the text of a particular issue as a peg on which to hang a long exposition of his political convictions. The ghost of the emaciated figure, with shrill voice and gesticulating finger, haunted the minds of Americans long after the flesh and blood orator was gone. Modern conservatives see him as the warrior piercing beneath the mask of institutions to find in the morality of society the real flaw in politics, as the truly wise man of his generation. They like to cite his "Change is not reform."[81]

If eloquence was immediate persuasion, Randolph was only a moderately able orator. If eloquence was wit and genius showering sparks of truth and prejudice to stimulate the minds of men, he was among the great speakers of all time. Henry Adams says he was but an extreme caricature of all the characteristic Virginia qualities, good and bad. This one needs by no means to agree with to realize that the easy conversational tone in which brilliant talk was carried on, the matter of course assumption of superiority and leadership, the love of liberty and hatred of equality which marked his speech as well as his way of life, the congenital suspicion of change, were all possible derivatives of an upper-class Virginia rearing. The other side of the coin is seen in his democratic, genial, cooperative, more versatile and ingenious stepfather, St. George Tucker. Randolph is indeed the ominous foreshadower of the two following generations of gifted Virginia orators who would devote themselves to obstruction, would ignore extended logic as he did, and claim that they were realists when in truth they were only stubborn romanticists lost in shortsighted regional self-interest. In this respect he did represent what was to be much of the Virginia of the post-1829-Convention period, in its thwarted hopes and in its final tragedy.

Randolph, Wirt, and Gilmer joined in admiring the oratory of their mutual friend Littleton Waller Tazewell (1774-1860) of Norfolk, lawyer, senator, and governor who never quite achieved what he seemed in the first quarter of the nineteenth century to promise. Gilmer refers to him as Ciceronian, lacking only in ambition to make a great orator and statesman. In the debates of the 1820's, after he became a member of the United States Senate, Tazewell was recognized as an able leader of the group opposing President Adams. A supporter of Jackson, he was offered diplomatic and cabinet posts he declined, partly because as a life-long states' rightist he did not long find the old warrior congenial company. Most of the records of his court cases are lost, and the meager annals of his career in Congress offer little to explain the respect as forensic speaker in which his contemporaries held him. An individualist and an intellectual in the modern sense, and in the years when one might have expected him to become a great national figure an intransigent defender of a minority's cause, he had no real opportunity to achieve the stature his Jeffersonian contemporaries thought might one day be his.

With his good friend William Wirt things were quite different.

Self-educated, eager, genial, widely read but no intellectual, he made friends and worked diligently in his chosen profession the law. His biographer John Pendleton Kennedy felt that he deserved all he achieved, and he achieved a great deal in the way of public office and contemporary fame. Though his writings were known throughout the United States, his real fame was as a lawyer and orator, the two inextricably fused in his reputation.

Wirt reveals much of what lay behind his own oratory in his studies of Henry, the discussions of his contemporaries in the *British Spy*, the essays on eloquence in his later collections, and his "Hints to Preachers." The classical orators and their treatises as models or guides, the insistence on general reading and knowledge and solid preparation in the profession, the *sine qua non* of natural abilities, the study of manner, gesture, and voice, the danger of overdoing the emotional and the figurative, are among the things he suggests to his friends and pupils again and again.[82] He liked to study the "action of the mind" of great lawyers and speakers such as Burke and Marshall.

Successively young Albemarle lawyer, Richmond attorney, clerk of the House of Delegates, Chancellor for eastern Virginia, again Richmond attorney from 1806 until he became Attorney General of the United States under Monroe, a position he held from 1817 until Jackson came into office in 1829, Wirt was one of the best-known and best-liked lawyers of his day. He participated in the famous Callender libel trial of 1800 and the Aaron Burr trial of 1807, and in the Supreme Court cases of *McCulloch* vs. *Maryland,* Dartmouth College, and *Gibbons* vs. *Ogden,* in each of these and others increasing his twin reputations of orator and lawyer.

The texts of Wirt's legal and occasional arguments and addresses are scattered and in some instances fragmentary, but they survive in more complete condition than Henry's or Randolph's. The Burr Trial, the Steamboat Case (*Gibbons* vs. *Ogden*), the Dartmouth College Case, the Cherokee Case, the defense in the impeachment of Judge Peck, and the Jefferson-Adams eulogy in Congress are reported completely or in large part. They show Wirt's logical organization, his sound but not overwhelming logic, his proneness to literary, especially classical allusion, his sententiousness, and his tendency to the highflown or flowery. The last was a quality he was quite aware of and attempted to curb. He worked hard in preparing a legal case or in determining the facts behind his celebration of a great occasion.

Once questioned by Gilmer as to why he did not write out his arguments and speeches beforehand, he pleaded lack of time because of his legal practice. He observed that if Cicero and Demosthenes had been the kind of trial lawyer he was, they would not have written out their orations before delivery either.

Among great legal orators like Daniel Webster, Thomas Addis Emmet, and William Pinkney, Wirt acquitted himself with distinction. Sometimes paired with Webster and sometimes against him, Wirt held an admiration for his New England rival which seems to have been reciprocated. Both loved the long roll and thunder of rhetoric, somewhat on the Burkean model, and if Webster's is more to our taste today, we cannot say as much for their contemporaries.

The two together are among the fathers of spread-eagle oratory, for when lesser men imitated them, the bird screamed and clapped its wings with more abandon than they ever showed. Wirt's style is well represented in his peroration in the Steamboat Case. He begins with correcting his opponent Emmet's use of a situation and symbol from the *Aeneid,* quotes several lines of Latin himself, indicates the general application to war and peace for the nation in the decision in this case, concluding in a burst of spellbinding prophecy which predicts happiness and freedom or misery and mourning, his last words a Latin verse.

The Blennerhasset passage in the Burr Trial speech, with its figure of Burr as the serpent in Eden, is remembered because it is romantic American rhetoric at its most characteristic. Actually Wirt followed closely the reasoning of his opponents and replied point for point or advanced new points of his own, but this the general public then as now has forgotten. Perhaps Wirt's greatest recognition as an orator came when he was asked to address the Houses of Congress in joint session on Jefferson and Adams in the month after their deaths. Dozens of other men, including Webster, John Tyler, and Felix Grundy spoke on the same subject in various parts of the Union,[83] but it was Wirt who was asked to perform before the greatest audience. He had great themes, an embarrassment of them. In his address he followed a biographical structure, restraining his imaginative flights but soaring into rhetoric on the part the two had in the Declaration. Adams and Jefferson were not geniuses, but strong and steady minds sent to cheer and gladden a world. These were natural men. Providence clearly intended a moral in the time of their deaths. John Quincy Adams records that Wirt "chained attention" for two and a half hours "with apparent universal approval."[84] Adams thanked Wirt personally immediately afterwards.

Charged with lack of simplicity and strength, with indiscriminate praise of its two subjects, the speech could hardly, in the emotional state of the nation as it was at the time, have been other than the kind of thing it was.[85] Webster produced a more tightly organized discourse and a more intellectual peroration, in more restrained language, but Wirt's was the more satisfying popular oratory.

Certainly Wirt was in appearance the model orator. An aquiline nose and leonine head, an erect carriage and robust frame, a melodious voice and a courtly manner, twinkling eyes and whimsical mouth, were no negligible attributes. Gilmer thought his reasoning faultless, his pathos natural and impressive, conclusions John Randolph thought too partial. That Wirt did try to restrain his predilection for the ornate is borne out by a comparison of his Burr Trial discourse with the Jefferson-Adams and Peck Trial texts. The comparison indicates that he was in a measure successful.

Orator and man left their impress on the American world. For many years after Wirt's death in 1834 there were William Wirt Societies or "Literary Institutes" in a number of American cities before one of which, incidentally, the orator's young friend Edgar Poe spoke.[86] Few men who had never been members of Congress or the Supreme Court were so honored by those bodies as was Wirt when he died. The Court adjourned the day after and held an assembly in his honor at which Daniel Webster and John Marshall spoke in sober praise. On the day of his funeral, February 20, 1834, both the Houses of Congress adjourned, and in the procession were the President, Vice President, and Cabinet of the United States, the Bench and Bar of the Supreme Court, the members of the two houses of Congress, officers of the Army and Navy, and a large number of private citizens. Adams, Jackson, Calhoun, Van Buren, Marshall, Story, Clay, Webster, Taney, Everett, Cass, and Generals Scott and Macomb were among those who saw him laid to rest.[87] The next day John Quincy Adams addressed the House of Representatives in a eulogy on his departed friend. With Wirt was concluded much of the positive, liberal constructive side of Virginia thinking and expression after Jefferson.

Henry Clay, educated and trained in the law and in public speaking in his native Virginia, and another of the major orators of the nineteenth century, achieved his triumphs in Kentucky and in Washington rather than in the Old Dominion. The liberal attitudes of his mentors Wythe and Brooke shaped his mind and his oratory. Robert Goodloe Harper, expatriate Virginian, was a major figure in national politics and oratory. But in the generation after Wirt, Clay, and Harper there was still an abundance of forensic talent remaining in the state. One has only to look at the minutes or accounts of the 1829-30 state Constitutional Convention to be assured that eloquent speaking had by no means disappeared.

The older generations were represented by Madison, Monroe, Marshall, Giles, B. W. Leigh, and John Randolph; but it was the men of the future whose forensic powers made the strongest impression. The last of the mighty issues which had concerned Virginia speakers for a half century were before them. The matters of reform and manhood suffrage, the manner of representation, with overtones and undertones of the slavery and states' rights issues lay before them. It was in one sense a re-enactment of other scenes, for progressive West again stood against conservative East. But the Argonauts of other days, when still living, were content to ship their oars. Giles renounced his earlier liberalism and predicted separation or secession of Virginia from the Union. Randolph made and got away with scandalously unfair and vituperative remarks about Jefferson. Marshall remained consistent, supporting nationalism as he always had. Philip Doddridge and John Rogers Cooke, Abel P. Upshur and Philip Pendleton Barbour, Alexander Campbell and Chapman Johnson, and a dozen others were forceful speakers.[88] Abel P. Upshur, representative of the forensic qualities of the youngest generation, spoke in new and clear figures of speech and analogues, ridiculed the postulate that all men are by nature free and equal, and generally championed the cause of wealth and position. Graceful, terse, neither impassioned nor vehement, his early speech was considered one of the best in the Convention.[89]

It was an epic struggle with eloquence as the principal ostensible power on either side. That all this oratory determined the nature of the new Constitution may be doubted, but it is significant that for Jeffersonian Virginians the only approach to this gravest question of government and law lay through eloquence.

X

POLITICS AND ECONOMICS

The republic which Jefferson believed himself to be founding or securing in 1801 was an enlarged Virginia.

—Henry Adams, *History of the United States,* I, 239.

[*After congratulating Giles on his political stands.*] *Inflated with the spirit of French liberty, many of us about the year 1789 predicated our political principles upon the metaphysics of Locke, the sophistry of* Raynal, *& Sir Thomas More, blended, and amalgamated with all the extravagance,* political, *if it deserves the name, of modern illuminati in that science. Experience, however, and age, tho attended with some inconveniences, and afflictions, has also produced some advantages—and convinced us, that every innovation or change was not an improvement—that the pigeon hole constitutions of* Abbé Sieyes *were a flimsy shield against the sword of Buonaparte:—that the recipes of Paine & Godwin, aided by the arithmetical calculation of newfangled statesmen, could not govern the world— In short, that the millennium had not yet arrived.*

—William Halyburton to William Branch Giles, May 25, 1824, Virginia Historical Society.

For the forty-two years from the Constitutional Conventions of 1787 and 1788 to the end of our period, most of the best minds in all America devoted the greater part of their intellectual effort to the shaping of the new government. Pondering the lessons of the world's past, devising schemes suited to this republic of the New World, in the first years they fought and compromised their way into a constitution, then immediately amended it, and spent the next four decades interpreting it, or sometimes acting boldly and ingeniously in situations it did not appear to cover. There can be no doubt that the Jeffersonians agreed with Locke that "the pursuit of happiness," attained through wise government and clear understanding of the meaning of the phrase, was to be the major aim of their generation. Life, liberty and property were but necessary concomitants of this happiness.

In this period in which the government of the United States was formed, formulated, interpreted, and first experienced, several dozen Virginians, almost all of them mentioned in preceding chapters, were leading figures. They wrote and spoke, collaborated and dissented, originated and obstructed in every significant step of the process of genesis and experiment. What is more, individually and collectively they were easily the leading influence among the founding states. Except for Hamilton and Gallatin, no individuals seemed to have minds approaching theirs in political and even economic acumen. The Father of the Constitution, the Father of Democracy, the Father of Constitutional Law, the promulgator of the Monroe Doctrine, were all Jeffersonian Virginians, and the Father of His Country had just preceded them. Alongside these patriarchs men like George Mason, William Branch Giles, Thomas Ritchie, Spencer Roane, and John Taylor wrote and persuaded and shaped public opinion along the lines they believed government should develop. Beginning in the sympathetic role of builders and creators, many of them finally were cast, rightly or wrongly, as obstructionists. But the positive things they had accomplished they could not destroy, and in some instances their very demurrers became shaping traditions of government.

That Virginia was in 1788 the largest and wealthiest state of the new Union naturally accounts to some extent for the respect with which her representatives were heard on political and economic questions. But the almost all-pervasiveness of their opinions, plans, and philosophical concepts are really not thus explained. Half the preceding chapters of this book have discussed traits of these Virginians which do much more, it is hoped, to account for their political weight and leadership in the new nation. The nature of their education, itself frequently aimed directly at preparation for political careers; their reading in the classics, Locke, Montesquieu, Bolingbroke, the eighteenth-century economists, and the Scottish common sense school; their agrarian ideals growing out of their way of life; their training in law and oratory; their industrial sense of *noblesse oblige*—these were all means to political life and to some extent determinants in that life.

Two other distinctive qualities of early American political science and economy were also prominent in the Virginians. One is the strong legal sense, the feeling that government must develop within and through law, a conviction sometimes said to be a distinguishing mark of the Anglo-Saxon as opposed to the Latin world — a necessity for every well-educated Virginian, as has been shown in Chapter IX. His problems had always been taken before the courts—from the county to the Governor's Council or the later Supreme Court of his state or the nation. The other, the strong moral basis for forming or opposing, the belief that government itself must be moral, had been developed with the traditional sense of honor said to be the hallmark of the Virginia colonial. It was certainly a quality insisted upon by his favorite European and English authors. From his way of life, the agrarian, came many of the Virginians' ideas as to the nature of the governmental structure, slavery in relation to government and economics, tariffs, internal improvements, and army and navy. From his philosophical and religious reading he had decided that government was a necessary evil, perhaps caused by man's natural depravity, but certainly the less government the better. From Locke and others he acquired and clung tenaciously to the idea that government was a civil compact between the people and the organization they created. From the classical and Locke on ideas of national right, through political organization, came civil rights, often referred to in the more primitive term.

To say that the Virginia political mind began in liberalism and by 1830 reached conservatism is to oversimplify. *Liberal* and *conservative* are still hard to define. If they mean respectively *free progressivism* and *adherence to the status quo* it is still impossible to label the Virginia political mind of any one decade one or the other. Thomas Jefferson and St. George Tucker may appear to be at the left or liberal extreme, and Abel P. Upshur and John Randolph at the right or conservative opposite, with men like Mason, Taylor, Pendleton, Giles, Roane, the Tylers, George Tucker, and a dozen others between. Even the men at the two extremes were mixtures, albeit unequal ones. The alignments of individual Virginians in the Conventions of 1787 and 1788 are dubiously designated liberal or conservative. And though a conservative or stand-pat element apparently won in the 1829-30 state Convention, it had to make considerable concessions, indication that progressive strength was by no means destroyed in the state. That there was a trend must be admitted, and the reasons for it pointed out. Certainly much of the hard thinking on matters politic in the whole of the Jeffersonian period in the state was the result of this tension, or conflict, between relatively opposing theories and convictions.

Nationalistic, or *centralistic,* and *states' rightist* are perhaps more nearly applicable terms descriptive of the action or ideas of Virginians at any one time. Sometimes the lines are clearly drawn, but very frequently, in the most significant written expressions, neither descriptive adjective is easily or properly applied. Jefferson and Madison during their administrations, Randolph before 1805, or Giles before 1806, partook of both attitudes. States' rightism was for a time as strong in New England as in Virginia. Virginians had significant parts in the trend toward popular democracy, in the juridical strengthening of national ties, in the assumption by the Supreme Court of the function of interpretation of the Constitution, in attempting universal emancipation, in fighting protective tariff and in proposing it, in disestablishing and re-establishing a national banking system. Varying conditions and climates of opinion within and without the state naturally affected changes. The state's gradually weakening position among the states determined some of this. But whether the state was in national power or out, its citizens thought long and frequently effectively on the problems of government.

In the quarter of a century just preceding 1788 Virginians had shown their abilities in politics. The ordinances and resolutions of the House of Burgesses, the pamphlets of Jefferson and the Lees, the formulation of the Virginia Constitution of 1776 and the revised laws proposed by Jefferson, Wythe, and Pendleton, the work of the Randolphs, Lees, Madison, Henry, Jefferson, and a half dozen others in the Continental Congress, Jefferson's diplomatic career in France and his part in the forming of the French republic, not to mention the composition of the Declaration of Independence, were some of the things which informed the world of the political propensities of the Virginia gentlemen.

A. *First Major Theorists*

When the conventions which were to decide on a permanent Constitution met, Virginians were in the thick of things. In the national Convention, Washington, Madison, Edmund Randolph, George Mason, John Blair, George Wythe, and Dr. James McClurg supported "The Virginia Plan." It had been authored by Madison, generally acknowledged the most efficient and effective member of the Convention.[1] The motives of the delegates and specific interpretations of individual actions have been discussed many times, most notably by Beard and Brant.[2] In one sense it was a struggle between owners of two kinds of property, represented by the large manufacturing and mercantile interests opposed to the agricultural interests, and between the ambitions of states, groups, and individuals. Through the long days of proposal and counter-proposal, compromise and alteration, Madison and the other Virginians worked. During the last days George Mason, who had done much to shape the instrument of government, decided that in its finally revised form he could not conscientiously sign it. Edmund Randolph, with many reservations, also did not sign. Both the latter were to be significant figures in the Virginia Convention on ratification.

A little over a month after the Constitution had been referred to the states in September 1787 the first of the letters above the name "Publius" appeared in a New York newspaper.[3] In that state especially the proponents of the Constitution had found rough going. Alexander Hamilton, an ardent nationalist, began the series of essays now known as *The Federalist* as a calm and reasoned appeal for adoption. John Jay and James Madison were asked to collaborate and write some of the essays. The former wrote only five. Basically, *The Federalist* is a series of arguments that a government must be formulated so as to stand the inevitable strains from various directions.

Madison's part is today usually acknowledged as the most significant, especially his famous No. 10, on the sources of faction in government. Economic self-interest, observation told him, was by far the most compelling force. Political parties grew out of the struggle between rich and poor and the conflicting interests of agriculturists and financial, manufacturing, and trading groups. So far he and the later Marx agreed, but Madison saw democracy worth fighting for while Marx gave in to the dictatorship of the proletariat. The effect of this one essay has been to promote the economic interpretation of history and to induce reassessments all the way along our own history. Madison has been labeled therefrom everything from property-defending conservative to forerunner of socialism. He is more nearly "a pioneer advocate of controlled capitalism."[4]

Yet on the whole Madison's part of *The Federalist* is pure politics, not economic theory.[5] In Numbers 18, 19, and 20 he discussed the weaknesses of ancient and modern confederacies as our own weaknesses. Then he furnished all the materials for 37 through 58, in bulk more than a fourth of the whole, where with originality and close reasoning he discussed the legitimate powers of the Convention, the powers of Congress, elastic construction (to be compared with his later relatively strict construction), assurances that state sovereignty will be safe, the structure of the Federal government and the distribution of its powers, and protection of the right of suffrage, among other things. In two later essays, 62 and 63,[6] he presented the Senate as a balance and safeguard against the larger and more popular assemblies. As pointed out in Chapter I, the frequent dependence on Montesquieu as authority, the reservations as to the justice of numerical majorities and the appeals to historical precedent are characteristic of the Virginia mind before, then, and later in the period.

Almost as distinguished as *The Federalist* papers for the strength of their political thought and the grace of their rendering were a series written in 1787 opposing the Constitution, *Letters of a Federal Farmer to a Republican.* The author, Richard Henry Lee, called by contemporary William Maclay "the man who gave independence to America,"[7] produced a political treatise of real cogency, largely forgotten because it represents a lost cause. Lee opposed the Constitution on the legal grounds that the Convention had exceeded its powers, that it contained no bill of rights, that it was a consolidated rather than a federal government and therefore opened the way to despotism, and that the lower house was not sufficiently democratic. Later, as one of the first senators under the new government, his chief task was to see that a Bill of Rights was adopted in the first ten amendments. Lee's political and social thinking has yet to receive thorough study.

But it was in the Virginia Federal Convention of 1788, already mentioned so many times, that the active political mind of the state manifested itself. Jefferson was in France, Washington at Mount Vernon, and Richard Henry Lee at Chantilly, but the rest of the leaders were there.[8] The long and brilliant debates between pro and con forces show much of the temper and timbre of the Virginia mind. Ranged in opposition to the Constitution on a variety of grounds, including states' rights and the lack of a bill of rights to protect the individual, were Henry, Mason, Benjamin Harrison, John Tyler, Sr., Monroe, Grayson, others as prominent. Supporting were Edmund Randolph, who had reversed his earlier decision or had made up his mind, Madison, Henry Lee, Marshall, Pendleton, Wythe, and George and Wilson Cary Nicholas. The emotional oratory and appeal to prejudice by Patrick Henry was met by the legalistic reasoning of Madison, Marshall, and Pendleton. But every one of the others mentioned also voiced his own ideas of the function of government. The final count was 89 to 79 for the Constitution, with instructions to Virginia's first representatives that they immediately propose a bill of rights as an amendment to the new Constitution. Tidewater and north central delegates voted for the new charter, but it is difficult to see economic motivation behind their stand. The contest was obstinate, but even the cynical Henry Adams admits that "the majority by which the State Convention . . . adopted the Constitution, was influenced by pure patriotism as far as any political influence may be called pure."[9] The popular majority may have been hostile to or at least doubtful of the new Constitution, and developing events soon increased their numbers as far as opposition to many phases of national government were concerned.

One of the major constructive minds which made its final public expression in this assembly was that of George Mason. By conviction a private citizen, an aristocrat living a conservative life, he was a far-seeing statesman who adapted the theories Locke expressed in the second treatise on Civil Government to his own America. His earlier Declaration of Rights for Virginia was the design for a just commonwealth of equal rights among freemen—separation of the legislative and executive powers from the judicial, suffrage, the consent of the people, freedom of the press, a well regulated militia, and freedom of religion. Like other Virginians, he desired a government in which competence would be the prime requisite for office. The Constitution of 1776 in Virginia was primarily his. His *Objections to the Proposed [Federal] Constitution* was with Lee's *Letters of a Federal Farmer* the chief anti-Constitution literature of Virginia. Mason called attention to the need for a bill of rights, the small size of the House of Representatives, the over-extensive jurisdiction of the Federal judiciary, and the powers given to Congress in respect to trade and navigation laws but withheld with respect to the traffic in slaves. He won his point on the bill of rights, as we have seen, in the Virginia Convention.[10]

Mason's Declaration of Rights had substituted for Locke's "property" "the means of acquiring and possessing property and pursuing and obtaining happiness," a change Jefferson carried further in his Declaration of Independence. Both their concepts of property are more philosophical than legal, but Mason's other "rights" are strongly legalistic in expressed form, as in fact are all his political theories.

This meticulous aristocrat has been called the senior member of the Jeffersonian Republican party. He considered that Hamilton had done more harm to the United States than Great Britain and all her fleets and armies.[11] An ardent states' rightist, he saw eye to eye with the early Jefferson on the question. A lifelong crusader for suppression of the slave trade and for emancipation, he also said that slaves must be educated before being freed so that they might properly enjoy their liberty. His *Objections,* though largely negative, were to prove in the long run to be well-founded and to coincide with much of later Republican principle. His justification is written into the subsequent events of American history.[12]

Manumission must occur because no man should be at the mercy of another. At the same time property rights must be recognized, and termination should be gradual and not by confiscation. His conclusions here and elsewhere were thorough and objective, proceeding from conviction. In them Beard's economic interpretations are hard to see. Virginia heir of the Enlightenment, Mason was according to his friend Jefferson "of the first order of greatness."

Another natural conservative in personal life was Edmund Pendleton, who presided during most of the 1788 Virginia Convention. His position did not prevent his participation, and he frequently yielded the chair so that he might present from the floor his cogent arguments as to why the Constitution should be adopted. In the 1790's he saw the danger in the growing centralization under the Washington and Adams administration and became a thorough anti-Federalist. A few months after Jefferson's inauguration he published a celebrated article, "The Danger Not Yet Over," in the *Examiner,* setting forth the evils in government and the remedies for their removal.[13] Especially he urged that the legislative branch make the laws, the courts interpret them, and the executive enforce them. He feared the aristocratic tendency of the Senate and its attempt to control all three branches. He proposed eight points on which new amendments to the Constitution should be based, each of them aimed at confining one of the branches of government to its proper sphere or defining the precise and distinct power of the general and state governments. This became with Madison's *Report* of 1799-1800, the "Old and New Testaments" of the political faith of Thomas Ritchie, the Republican editor of the *Enquirer.*[14] Later, when Jackson was swept into office, "The Danger Not Over" was reprinted as a guide for the new President. But Pendleton died in 1803 without seeing his hopes or his fears realized.

One of the ablest practical organizers among the Jeffersonians was John J. Beckley (1765-1807), of Louisa county, a William and Mary graduate and Virginia state official, and not only first clerk of the United States House of Representatives but first Librarian of Congress.[15] Beckley acted as a political intelligence agent for Jefferson and other anti-Hamiltonians as early as 1789 and was one of the party organizers in the 1790's. Well versed in public affairs and political theory, he drew up and sent to Jefferson after the 1800 election a list of the principles he thought should guide the incoming Republican administration. His peculiar forte was the election campaign, as the party battler. In the 1790's he published essays in the *National Gazette, Aurora*, and *Gazette of the United States* signed with various pseudonyms.[16] *An Address to the People of the United States, with an Epitome of the Public Life and Character of Thomas Jefferson,* signed Americanus (Philadelphia, 1800) was widely circulated, extracts from it on Jefferson being the most frequently reprinted pieces in the Republican press.

His letter of suggestions to Jefferson of February 27, 1801, follows what was to become the Republican line—free trade, limitation of the Navy, avoidance of foreign entanglements, repeal of the Alien Laws, and promotion of agriculture by repeal of the Excises and Land Tax. He added that a reorganization of the Executive Departments be made so that all new appointments would "place the Executive Administrations in the hands of decided Republicans, distinguished for talents and integrity."[17] Thus the most practical of politicians also held firm theories of the principles of government.

Jefferson had long before 1800 worked out his basic theories of the relation between government and society. In his First Inaugural Address he outlined those theories as they were applicable to the American nation at that moment. All would work under "the will of the law" in common efforts for the common good. Majority will was sacred, but to be right it must be reasonable, and the minority possessed equal rights. All differences of opinion were not differences of principle. Even the would-be revolutionist must be heard. Men as individuals would support the government and the law, the Union and representative direction. Equal by birth, free in religion, adoring the Providence that delights in the happiness of man, the Americans must have one thing more, "a wise and frugal government."

Then he gave his conception of the general principles of good government: justice, peace, preservation of states' rights and vigorous national constitutional government at the same time, acquiescence to the decision of the majority, supremacy of civil over military authority, prompt payment of debts, encouragement of agriculture, economy in public expense, freedom of person under habeas corpus and trial by jury, "these principles form the bright constellation which has gone before us and guided our steps through the age of revolution and reformation."[18]

Thus his most distinguished statement of political theory is a reaffirmation of principles he believed had belonged to his fellow-citizens since before the Revolution itself. What Adrienne Koch calls his "political relativism," his belief that peoples are best governed by the government they are capable of bearing, though it may not adhere strictly to the ultimate good,[19] was not an issue on this occasion at least when he was addressing only Americans. That his system of republicanism was based on natural rights and natural law is perhaps more implicit than explicit here, but it is present. And formal law, as legislated morality, is emphasized more than has usually been noted. But this belief in majority rule, which follows Locke in being placed side by side with individual rights, a balance between state and national rights, and the sacredness of the individual are spelled out. Equality is equality before the law.

What he says here about agriculture is no more perhaps than even a Federalist President would have agreed to. But staunch agrarian that he was, the representative democracy of small farmers he envisaged all through his life was as much or more a concept of classical simplicity joined to "purified" Christianity than something developed from contemporary Physiocratic theory.[20]

The happiness principle, ultimately from Locke but coming also from Mason, as we have seen, had been in Jefferson's expressions at least since the Declaration. Perhaps the most significant feature of his theory of rights, it raises government above the merely negative function of resisting encroachment on individual rights. Jefferson's golden age is in the future, but his essential optimism assured him that it would come.[21] And thus his democracy is more a faith than a philosophy.

Widely and deeply read in the European economists of his time and earlier, Jefferson saw the Constitution in terms of economics, though it is often pointed out that he first evidences this after he had read *The Federalist*.[22] His reference to the Constitution as "an accommodation of interests" may have come from Madison's No. 10. He did not believe that it stood inviolable, and over and over asserted the danger of a static charter. His emphasis on checks and balances as the strongest feature of the Constitution probably reflects Montesquieu and Locke.[23] His purchase of Louisiana is the classic illustration of his repeated conviction that government may go beyond the Constitution in significant situations.

States' rights were for him primarily an extension of the rights of the individual. Sacred as both were, he held what we would call an organic conception of society in contrast to the individualistic idea of Locke. Education, for example, was a public rather than a private enterprise. In the end, too, he came to a belief in the equilibrium of commerce, manufacture, and agriculture.

All his life Jefferson's mind was both sanguine and elastic. The strict constructionists who had supported him when his party and policy were first formed in the late 1790's were in the early 1800's gradually left behind, though various events, and his fear of renewed strong centralizing tendencies, produced a sort of *rapprochement* with them towards the end of his life. But his faith in the ultimate rightness of an enlightened majority, his belief that all men must and should be free, never left him.

Yet Jefferson was after all a pragmatic son of the eighteenth century. That theory could become practice and that ideas and ideals might appeal to most men were among his convictions. Organizing his party, persuading men to his aims, he appealed as he knew he must to their self-interest in several different ways. He could and did compromise realistically, for even Americans, he knew, were not yet ready for some things. He left in broad outline and detail a great democratic theory, but he also left a political party which, under some difference in names and goals, has continued to adapt itself to men and conditions and has in the main held to his vision of the pursuit of happiness, to his faith that men are capable of governing themselves.

The sources of Jefferson's political theory have been somewhat suggested in previous chapters. There are a number of studies directed particularly to them.[24] They were in all the past, classical and Renaissance and eighteenth century, and in the European writers of his own time. But the theory sprang also from what a thoughtful Virginia son of the Enlightenment saw of conditions around him. His whole heritage of law and Christian morality, agrarian life and slave-operated plantation, monarchical pre-Revolutionary oppression, and experience with special-interest groups within the new nation entered into their formulation.

James Madison's political theory is as complex as Jefferson's, and as simple. It is equally difficult to summarize in brief space. In the twentieth century, under both the revived Jeffersonian liberalism of the Roosevelt era and the new conservatism of the next decade, Madison's reputation as solid and far-seeing thinker has grown. Like Jefferson a true child of the Enlightenment and eighteenth-century rationalism and champion of religious and intellectual freedom, he was in one great quality much more in the Virginia tradition than was his friend of Monticello. For Madison was always temperate, his way was the moderate way, and he saw human nature with a less sanguine eye than did Jefferson.[25]

Today Madison is universally acknowledged as the father of the Constitution, developed under the watch-mechanism system (checks and balances on power, multiple safeguards) of government concept he had discussed in No. 51 of *The Federalist*. Unlike Hamilton, he believed that man's depravity was not total depravity, and he somewhat reluctantly agreed with Jefferson that there was sufficient virtue in man for him to govern himself. As we have noted, his concept of society as a body of men divided along lines of special economic interests was probably the source of Jefferson's parallel belief.

Madison fought all his life for religious freedom, sometimes completing, sometimes anticipating Jefferson's work. He was much more interested than Jefferson in religion itself, as the latter's request that he prepare the theological book list for the University of Virginia Library would in some measure indicate. Like other Virginians, he warned that justice for the states must be observed, but over the years he was a consistent nationalist, denying the doctrines of nullification and peaceful secession, maintaining the constitutionality of the tariff, and insistent on the supremacy of the Federal judiciary in questions between the national and state governments.

B. *Other Theorists*

The expressed ideas of Jefferson, Madison, and Mason were paralleled, extended, or modified in the writings of other men. The Baptist clergymen David Barrow and John Leland, for example, were at one with the political leaders in declaring government a necessity because of man's depravity, that it was better than a state of nature. They insisted on a frugal government, which would naturally be one which governed little, with short sessions of the legislature and few taxes. With Patrick Henry and most other Virginians of the early period they liked to point out their agreement with Locke's compact theory of government.[26]

James Monroe's "Observations upon the Proposed Plan of Federal Government" (1788)[27] is a fairly strong point by point defense of the proposed Constitution, for Monroe had a certain grasp of political situations and peoples. Perhaps more significant was his *View of the Conduct of the Executive, in the Foreign Affairs of the United States* (1797), a vindication after his recall of his mission to France. Through the years he published pamphlets and addresses. An experienced diplomat, his success in foreign affairs was anything but brilliant, but the theory he made declaration in 1823-24 after consultation with his friends and legislative colleagues, the Monroe Doctrine, has preserved his name as a major figure in the history of our foreign affairs. Lacking the imagination and elasticity of either Jefferson or Madison, he possessed perseverance, strong ambition, and a capacity for solid thinking. His contemporaries, including the normally caustic John Quincy Adams, left favorable estimates of him as practicing statesman with ideals.

St. George Tucker made his contribution to political theory primarily in his appendix to his edition of Blackstone, in the essays "Of Several Forms of Government" and "Of Right of Conscience," which reveal strong Republican principles. They also indicate his sense of the moral obligation to serve one's country. "Remarks on the treaty of Amity . . . between Lord Grenville and Mr. Jay" (1796), "Cautionary Hints to Congress, Respecting the Sale of Western Lands" (1795), "How Far the Common Law of England Is the Law of the Federal Government of the United States" (1802), "Reflections on the Cession of Louisiana to the United States" (1803), and "The

Crisis" (1812) are among his consistently Jeffersonian, liberal, anti-Adamsian comments on aspects and situations of government over two decades. They deserve further study, particularly as to the extent of their influence on his friends Jefferson and Madison, for in some instances Tucker appears to have been the avant-garde.

Something of John Randolph's thinking has been indicated in several chapters above. As purely disinterested, at least personally, as any statesman America ever produced, he insisted on morality in government, condemned personal and plunder legislation, and fought corruption at all levels. Devoted to state sovereignty, hostile to all professional soldiers and excise-men, anti-slavery and defender of the slaveholder, he discussed all these topics in his widely reprinted speeches.

Randolph insisted that equality of opportunity did not mean equality of political privilege.[28] With Burke and Fisher Ames he agreed that constitutions were mere paper, that society is the substratum of government. He made speeches, all part of his frequent assertion that he was a realist, attacking the abstract doctrines of natural right and of natural equality. As the years passed he reflected Burke more and more, Locke less and less, and most of all his own stiffening intransigence. Yet to certain republican principles or theories he remained always true.[29] Wade Hampton and certain others were "cotton barons," not part of the ideal republic of small freeholders with a few large planters to lead and guide them. States' rights became more and more an obsession, for he always championed the rights of the individual and the minority. He and later Giles and certain others were referred to as Old Republicans, for they claimed that they always remained true to what their party had stood for in 1798 as expressed in the Virginia and Kentucky Resolutions. This was only half true, and one must also realize that the Resolutions expressed no more than half the Republican creed, and that Jefferson and Madison later insisted that the Revolution had consciously and necessarily overemphasized certain doctrines for their immediate effect. Randolph came to look upon innovation as decadence, not progress, another tenet in his finally evolved conservatism. In his own time he thought and fought largely in vain, but in the middle twentieth century the political leadership of his native state has reasserted the conservative values on which he insisted.

In the past forty years the stature of John Taylor of Caroline as political philosopher has grown steadily.[30] The books he wrote, little read north of the Potomac in his own lifetime but hailed as classics by New Yorker James K. Paulding as well as Randolph and Jefferson, have received more and more attention. From his pamphlets of the 1790's to his last book in the 1820's Taylor followed, and expounded, the principles of Jefferson and his party, especially as related to the Constitution, as they were in the nineties, or as Taylor saw them in that decade. His 1794 *A Definition of Parties, or the Political Effects of the Paper System Considered* exposed what he felt were corruptions and expressed his later frequently asserted idea that power was corrupting. *Tyranny Unmasked* (1822) and *New Views of the Constitution* (1823), his last published pieces and fourth and fifth books, were still concerned with the abuse of power by the national government and represent Taylor's constitutional logic in its most finished form.

In at least one sense Taylor is the central figure of the Virginia states' rights school: he was its champion in reasoned printed discourses. He was also the conscious philosopher-author who spelled out the Jeffersonian form of republican democracy. His expression of one phase of it, agrarianism, has already been examined in an earlier chapter. This pervasive agrarianism colors all his ideas on states' rights and anti-centralization and on the tariff and banking. His agrarian economic policy is based on moral principle, on the doctrine of natural law, and on his conception of human nature.[31] It is a defense of the Tidewater gentry and the security of the individual freeholder.

Taylor believed the distress of the United States, and he saw conditions for thirty years as distressing, was a result of the introduction of a selfish European economic system designed and executed by a selfish minority group,[32] the "patrons of privilege and paper . . . the mercenary capitalists" who utilized divergent sectional interest, the Federal judiciary, and the banking system for their own interest. The result was a tyranny best exemplified in the Hamiltonian fiscal policy.

Much of Taylor's writing is aimed at destroying the basis of demagoguery by a plan of government that will make human happiness less dependent in the fluctuations in the characters of individuals. It is lucidly Jeffersonian. A theory of history is implicit: despotism—

clerical, monarchial, aristocratic—may be measured by the kind and degree of greed found in the rulers. In a frugal, popular, laissez-faire government, individual self-interest works for the good of all. The perfectibility of man, however slow, is discernible through history, and man is able to judge the best means of promoting his own happiness.[33]

Taylor's arguments, like those of most Virginia political thinkers, are couched in legal terms and are legalistic in their direction. This does not mean he writes in an orderly or concise fashion. He launches into detailed discussion of particular phases of his theories when they occur to him, not as they suggest one another in a logical or coherent sequence. But he puts on record, with considerable repetition from book to book, what adds up to a clear, if somewhat one-sided (individualistic), conception of the function of and the dangers to government in America in his time.

In some respects he was far behind his time. His answer to John Adams' *A Defense of the Constitution* of 1787 came in Taylor's 1814 *An Inquiry into the Principles and Policy of the Government of the United States* almost thirty years later. But he was far ahead of his time in his early critique of Hamilton's fiscal policies when to most others they seemed good, in his attack on the tariff soon after it was enacted, and in his particular states' rights doctrine years before nullification and secession became grave concerns in his region. He anticipated Andrew Jackson on the constitutionality of the bank, Calhoun on tariff and his concurrent majority, and Douglas and others on the solution of slavery as the basis of popular sovereignty. He developed arguments used by Upshur and Calhoun against the supremacy of the Federal judiciary.[34]

The five books published during the last dozen years of his life are those on which Taylor's reputation mainly rests. *Arator* (1813), *An Inquiry* (1814), *Construction Construed and Constitutions Vindicated* (1820), *Tyranny Unmasked* (1822?), and *New Views of the Constitution* repeat, enlarge upon, and present various facets of his theory suggested by situations and problems at particular times engaging his mind. *Arator* has been discussed as an agricultural treatise in an earlier chapter. It is also a political treatise, for problems of government and the farmer are applied to each other all through the book. *An Inquiry* (not to be confused with his 1794 *An Enquiry into the*

Principles and Tendencies of Certain Public Measures) was noticed especially by Henry Adams and in Charles A. Beard's *Economic Origins of American Democracy* (1915) is called "the text-book of agrarian political science . . . among the two or three really historic contributions to political science which have been produced in the United States."[35] Roy F. Nichols in a new edition of *An Inquiry* says, "This plain Virginia farmer [here] made a significant contribution to the debate over the limits of liberty and authority."[36] Jefferson praised *Construction Construed* and, ignoring some past history, declared that he and Taylor had rarely if ever differed on any point.[37] Others like Spencer Roane thought *Tyranny Unmasked,* his attack on the protective tariff, his most significant book.[38]

The *Inquiry,* ostensibly written over many years as an answer to John Adams, reflects Taylor's basic disagreement with Adams in 1787, his fear of Hamilton in 1790-93, his opposition to the Federalists 1797-1801, and his disappointment in Jefferson 1806-9.[39] His extensive reading in history, ancient and modern, is reflected in his references to Godwin, Malthus, Tillotson, Samuel Johnson, Sterne, Walpole, ancient and medieval history, the Physiocrats, and English liberal writers like Price. But his whole approach was, or came to be typically American. He fought what he called the paper aristocracy, the natural enemy of agrarian economy, the only economy suited to the American world. Nichols calls him the first muckraker, the ancestor of the Populists, Progressives, and New Dealers of a later time.[40] His pleas for morality in big business, banking, and public office have been repeated in every reform movement since. That all this grew out of his own situation in life, the plantation world on the banks of the Rappahannock which was part of the larger world of a new republic, is evident in every point he makes. In other words, the practical experience of the enlightened Virginia farmer did much to shape the political theory of a dominant thinker of the first generation of our national existence. It is recognition of this environmental factor which will enable later generations to understand his weaknesses and shortsightedness on many questions, and to admire the vision and morality of his enunciations of major principles of government.

In summarizing the man his contemporary Thomas Hart Benton summarized that man's view of the individual in government:

> the ideal of a republican statesman . . . plain and solid, a wise counseller, a ready and vigorous debater, acute and comprehensive, ripe in all historical and political knowledge, innately republican—modest, courteous, benevolent, hospitable—a skillful, practical farmer, giving his time to his farm and his books when not called by an emergency to public service—and returning to his books and his farm when the emergency was over. . . .[41]

The men just mentioned are simply among the more prominent of the Virginians writing about government in the period. The question of liberty *vs.* authority had long been a passion. In an earlier chapter we have mentioned the "Society for writing about Liberty" formed in Richmond on June 11, 1784, in which thirty-four signers agreed to write an essay on some phase of the subject every six months.[42] The names of the signers include those of men who were later of all degrees of nationalism and states' rights, from Marshall to Madison, and including John Page, Henry, Edmund Randolph, Grayson, Roane, and five of the Lees. From that date to 1829, when the Constitutional Convention met and Thomas R. Dew published his *Lectures on the Restrictive System,* the Jeffersonians were busy with their pens. Anonymous essays on every subject of current significance, from liberty of the press to usury and the Florida and Missouri questions, but overwhelmingly directly on states' rights, occupied their attention, sometimes on a local situation alone but more often even on that situation's relation to national or diplomatic problems. William S. Archer, James and Philip Barbour, William B. Giles, George Hay, Henry Lee, the Nicholases, and scores of others are among the known authors who signed their names or have been identified since with separate pamphlets. John Thomson of Petersburg (1777-99), for example, in his *Letters of Curtius* (1798) published such a powerful attack on centralistic tendencies that he was for many of his fellow-citizens, including John Randolph throughout his life, the greatest writer of the age.

So many and varied are these newspaper essays, separate pamphlets, and even books, that it is impossible to survey all of them. Some of the more effective writing on the greatest questions—states' rights, slavery, the tariff, principles of political economy, and foreign policy—may, however, be considered briefly. Almost all overlap in theme one or more of the others, but they may be grouped roughly for convenience.

C. *States' Rights*

As one historian has recently pointed out, Americans north and south were vitally concerned with sectional and state interests long before the adoption of the Constitution.[43] As we have seen, in the 1787-88 Conventions it was a major issue. After adoption fears multiplied that rights were being subverted. The concern rose out of the natural rights philosophy so dear to most Americans and from the obvious dangers to the agricultural section from legislation tending to favor manufacturing and financial interests which the Hamiltonians were trying to push through. Virginians especially were alarmed. Many of them saw the social and political organization of their own state as almost-achieved near-ideal, and they were determined that no fiscal and commercial policies derived from decadent European monarchies should be thrust upon them to destroy what they thought should be carried out for the whole nation. As we have seen, they believed that the least government was the best, that land was the only true property, that financial manipulation made for dangerous aristocracies and for tyranny. New England, for somewhat different reasons, also developed a states' rights philosophy leading almost to secession in 1814-15 when that region saw itself as possibly engulfed by the triumph of Republican democracy. But no other region during the Jeffersonian period felt the danger so persistently or consistently as did the South, which saw in centralization and in new alliances between north and west more than a threat to its own supremacy in the councils of the nation. As Virginia slipped steadily down the scale in importance after 1800, its insistence on various aspects of states' rights which it believed might prevent and even turn back further deterioration in states became more vehement and assumed a somewhat different character, especially as slavery became a major issue.

Madison, writing to young Nicholas P. Trist on December 17, 1828, distinguished between the tendency toward nullification of recent South Carolina action and what had been done in 1798.

> You refer to the distinction noted between a usurpation & an abuse of power. There is another, too much overlooked, between the Exercise of power with, & against the will of the constituent body; and this distinguishes the course pursued by Virginia agst the Alien and Sedition Acts, from that of South Carolina agst the

> tariff: to say nothing of the difference between the cases on the point of Constitutionality. Virg.[a] viewing the Acts as forming a case between the federal Government and its constituents, appealed to her co-constituents, to unite in the regular means of reclaiming the Government from its unwarrantable career = with an abstract declaration, of the right of the former to recur to fundamental principles, when necessary in the last resort, as an alternative of passive obedience & non resistance. S. C. on the other hand, according to her popular orators, at least makes the tariff a case between a minority & majority of the Constituents, and declares her right to actual resistance; with the further declaration of an in compatibility of interests, not temporary even, which strikes at the utility of the Constitution, & saps the foundation of the Union itself.[44]

It is on these principles, of appealing within the Constitution and law, that most Virginia states' rights arguments were based until near the end of the period, and many of them to the very end. St. George Tucker, Spencer Roane, John Taylor, the later Andrew Stevenson, and even John Randolph so argued. The four latter were what came to be called strict constructionists, insisting on the rights expressed and implied in the Constitution and in its tenth amendment that all rights not specifically delegated to the central government were reserved to the states themselves. William Wirt had two real faults, his friend John Quincy Adams once observed—he believed too much in state supremacy and catered to "popular humors." These "faults" Adams might also have attributed to Jefferson or Madison.

As early as 1797 some men like Littleton Waller Tazewell saw the essential conflict between the interests of North and South and wished that separation might take place.[45] Since this was no longer possible, their only recourse seemed to be in appeal to the principle of states' rights as a Constitutional right. In 1804, at a patriotic dinner on July Fourth in Richmond, the toasts were all concerned with liberty and Union. Two of them were aimed especially at observance of the Constitution.

> 10. The Members of the Senate & H. of R. of the U.S.—May the happiness of the people always [inspire them?] & the Constitution always limit their measures.
>
> 12. The Judiciary of the U.S.—May they never forget, that the Constitution is, not only the source of their power, but 'the supreme law' of the land.[46]

Madison's philosophical emphasis was more on the rights of minorities, within the state or nation, than on those of the states as such. He had opposed the establishment of the United States Bank on Constitutional grounds, however, and his authorship of the Virginia and Kentucky Resolutions placed him early with the states' rights group.[47] But one must re-emphasize the fact that neither he nor Jefferson in 1798 stood for states' rights in any narrow sense. They were condemning the repression of public opinion in any form and thus provided a powerful precedent against any future attempts to destroy civil liberties. Later he gave even greater importance than Jefferson did to the right of people in the states, especially in real crises, to judge conflicts involving Federal versus state authority. He did not go so far as Jefferson as to believe that the Constitution might be remade in each generation, but he felt that the states in their sovereign capacity, or the people of the states, had the right to interpret the original compact. This was, of course, an implication of distinct limit to judicial power.

In the 1820's he thought the tariff constitutional and defended Jefferson from the extreme states' rights Republicans who quoted him out of context to support their position. He asserted in his last years that his attitude had remained unchanged since 1798 on all matters except the Bank (he had signed the law creating the Second Bank), explaining that on this point of interpretation he had been moved by the overwhelming force of public opinion. Despite his implications of limit on the power of the Federal judiciary, he asserted that from the beginning he had regarded its supremacy as essential for without supremacy by exposition and interpretation of the Constitution and laws, they would be futile. Thus he stood for rights, but only in the sense he had illustrated in his letter to Trist. Despite the terrific pressures of the 1820's and 1830's towards a states' rights interpretation of the Constitution, Madison's genuine nationalism at the time of the framing of the document remained his conviction.[48]

Jefferson's states' rights convictions grew out of his profound lifelong interest in individual rights. In later years looking back, he and Madison saw eye to eye on their purposes in the Virginia and Kentucky Resolutions. All during the national period he supported state prerogatives, though his Old Republican followers felt that in the Louisiana Purchase and certain subsequent legislation he had gone too far toward centralization. Like Madison, he felt that all differences between state and national governments should be settled peaceably, by the assembled representatives of the people. "It is a fatal heresy to suppose that either our state governments are superior to the federal or the federal to the states. . . . Each party should prudently shrink from all approach to the line of demarcation, instead of rashly overleaping it, or throwing grapples ahead to haul to hereafter," he wrote to Spencer Roane in 1821.[49]

Later, in 1825, expressing his alarm at the trend toward centralization, he could yet remark to the more extreme William B. Giles: "I see . . . with the deepest affliction the rapid strides with which the federal branch of our government is advancing towards . . . the consolidation in itself of all powers, foreign and domestic. . . . And what is our resource for the preservation of the Constitution? . . . Are we then *to stand to our arms*. . . ? No. That must be the last resource. . . . If every infraction of a compact of so many parties is to be resisted at once, as a dissolution of it, none can ever be formed which would last a year. We must have patience and endurance . . . and separate from our companions only when the sole alternatives left are the dissolution of the union with them or submission to a government without limitation of powers. Between these two evils, when we must make a choice, there can be no hesitation."[50] So spoke the voice of law, a voice which also placed the natural right to liberty as the highest law.

John Randolph, Giles, and the younger Abel P. Upshur were among those less patient and enduring who thought that the alternative choice was close upon them in 1829-30, and the two older men represented the Old Republican group who had taken the Virginia and Kentucky Resolutions literally as the only moral and genuinely self-preserving expression of their principles. More patient but equally militant was Thomas Ritchie, editor of the *Enquirer,* who has been called the states' rights "sentinel upon the watch-tower."[51] His life work was said to have been his attempt to preserve the ascendancy of Virginia. But Ritchie's and his cousin Spencer Roane's states' rights were more orthodox Jeffersonian than Randolphian. Ritchie was genuinely progressive. He ardently favored the 1829 state Convention in a hope of wider manhood suffrage and a constitution which might develop instead of obstruct. Jefferson near the end of his life could call Ritchie's newspaper the best in the Union, and long after 1830 western progressive Virginia backed him consistently. He was opposed to both Clay's and Calhoun's later policies, and frankly admired Van Buren and formed an alliance with him, ironically enough, because thus might be preserved the Virginia principles of '98.[52]

D. *Slavery*

With the more complete adoption of natural rights and other Lockean theories, the growth of deistic thought, and the decline in profitableness of their older slave-operated plantations in the later eighteenth century, Virginians began thinking and writing about slaves and slavery. That slavery was an evil was proclaimed from the beginning. Arthur Lee in 1764, in *An Essay in Vindication of the Continental Colonies of America from the Censure of Adam Smith, in His Theory of Moral Sentiments. With some reflections on slavery in general,* compared slave living conditions favorably with the miserable lot of peasants in Scotland and Ireland.[53] But still he spoke of slavery as "an irrepressible misery." Almost every great Virginian of the Revolutionary generation placed himself on record as favoring emancipation,[54] and Jefferson in his early draft of the Declaration and in his *Notes,* denounced the slave trade and spoke of slavery's pernicious effect on master and man, of its injustice, of its violation of natural right. By 1778 Virginia had passed an act prohibiting the slave trade, an act making the Old Dominion the first community in the civilized modern world to prohibit the traffic.[55]

In 1787 a committee of the Virginia General Assembly, including Carrington, Monroe, Edmund Randolph, and Grayson, brought forward the bill by which Virginia confirmed the ordinance for colonization of the Northwest Territory, recently its own, by freemen alone.

Over many strong Virginia protests, and through a coalition bargain between New England and the Deep South, the foreign slave trade was legalized in the Federal Constitutional Convention for twenty years more. George Mason spoke powerfully against 'this infernal traffic," with Madison and Edmund Randolph strongly supporting him.[56] In the first Congress of 1789, Josiah Parker of Virginia sought to amend the tariff bill by inserting a clause levying a heavy import tax on every slave, remarking that the importation ought to have been prohibited altogether. Again Madison, this time with Theodorick Bland, vocally supported the measure, though they were defeated. In 1806-7 President Jefferson, reminding Congress that under the Constitution the time was at hand when the African slave trade could be abolished, urged speedy enactment of a law to this effect. The act was passed.[57]

Long before this, at the beginning of our period in 1780, various Virginians had in public and in private correspondence voiced their feeling on various aspects of the problem. The clergy, the Quakers, planters, and politicians expressed their condemnation. Many of those who urged emancipation practiced it in their own households.

The evangelical preachers especially were most articulate, though not always confident they would accomplish a great deal. James Meacham, a Methodist circuit rider, was in 1790 reproving his congregations for slavery's existence.[58] The early Baptists David Barrow and John Leland, as we have mentioned good Republicans, never let slip an opportunity to illustrate the iniquities of the institution. Barrow's *Involuntary, Unmerited; Perpetual, Absolute, Hereditary, Slavery Examined on the Principles of Nature, Reason, Justice, Policy, and Scripture* was published in 1808.[59] Leland's 1790 *Virginia Chronicle* devotes a chapter to slavery, that institution "pregnant with enormous evils."[60] The early Virginia Methodist Peter Cartwright moved from Kentucky and Tennessee across Ohio into Illinois because of his hatred of slavery. Presbyterian George Bourne, in his *The Book and Slavery Irreconciliable* of 1816,[61] was one of the first to advocate immediate emancipation, though at this date he met with some bitter opposition. Perhaps nearer the norm among the Presbyterians was John Holt Rice, who in his will of the 1830's desired his wife to free their slaves (they were later sent to Liberia), but at the end of our era was "realistic" about what his church could do. In 1827 he wrote to Dr. Alexander: "It is physically impossible for any decision of the church to be carried into effect, because, taking the members generally, *three-fourths are women and minors,* persons not acknowledged by law. What could they do? Of the remaining fourth, three out of four men are in moderate circumstances, without political influence."[62] Rice believed that in the course of time, if outside influence did not ruin things, Virginia would throw off the system entirely.

Virginia Quakers like other American members of their sect had as early as 1722 opposed the slave trade. In 1757 they listened silently to John Woolman's protest that they had modified the Pennsylvania "Query" enough to permit the buying of slaves for their own use. In 1768 their Yearly Meeting condemned slavery, and in 1783 they categorically forbade the owning of slaves. As late as 183 , however, when they were still pressing the Virginia Legislature to pass an emancipation bill, they frowned on agitation on a national scale. In other words, as an organized group Virginia Quakers were consistent but moderate on the question, and in agreement with their neighbors that it was a state and not a national problem.[63]

As individuals they set notable examples. Robert Pleasants, of the family later prominent in Virginia politics, an upper James River planter, soon after 1783 liberated eighty slaves at a cost to himself of £3,000 sterling.[64] In 1791 Pleasants wrote to Madison, buttressing his argument with Biblical quotations: "And whilst I am mentioning the subject of the slave-trade, perhaps it may not be improper to intimate, a strong desire I have of seeing some plan for a gradual abolition of slavery promoted in this State, which appears to me such a moral and Political Evil, that loudy calls for redress. . . . liberty is allowed to be the unalienable right of all mankind. . . ."[65]

The most significant writing *contra* of the 1790's was St. George Tucker's *A Dissertation on Slavery: With a Proposal for the Gradual Abolition of It, in the State of Virginia* (1796)[66] Dedicated to the General Assembly, it was a part of a course of lectures on Law and Police given at William and Mary. Emancipation, its author asserts, is "an object of the first importance, not only to our moral character and domestic peace but even to our political salvation." Abolition of slavery in the whole United States was Tucker's dearest wish. His plan called for the freeing of every female born after its adoption and the transmission of freedom to all her male and female descendants, and as compensation to former owners, letting those freed serve until they are in their twenties, when they should receive $[illegible] and suitable clothing and bedding. Other points were registration of all Negro children born after the law with the clerk of each county, the placing of Negro servants on the same footing as white, their exclusion from public office, and encouragement of emigration to less settled portions of the United States. The last two points were designed to promote emigration, which Tucker felt would be a natural inclination anyway. He thought they might gravitate naturally to the unsettled areas of the southwest and establish all black societies. Tucker includes many statistics as to probable future slave population and concludes that when an effective remedy for slavery is discovered, "the golden age of our country will begin. . . ." Though Tucker undoubtedly voiced the sentiment if not the exact ideas of most leaders, his proposal was voted against before even being read by many members of the House of Delegates.[67]

Impressive lists of anti-slavery expressions from Richard Henry Lee and Patrick Henry in 1772-73 to Francis Gilmer, Marshall, Monroe, Leigh, and Madison have been assembled.[68] George Mason, from his first political paper to his final attack on the Constitution in the Virginia ratifying Convention opposed slavery, was but in full agreement with his friends Wythe and Jefferson.[69] More significant were the examples set by actual emancipation. Catterall and Munford have gathered a great many examples of wills and other documents of the freeing of slaves.[70] In the period from 1782 to 1806, there were no restrictions on owners. Between 1806 and 1833 anti-slavery sentiment showed strong growth, but so did the antipathy to the free Negro in the state, and restrictions were imposed.[71] In the records of wills of the former period 1782-1806, it is interesting to note that the emancipating families lived in all sections of the state, from Joseph Hill of Isle of Wight in 1783 and Robert Carter of Westmoreland in 1793 to Francis Preston of Washington County in 1793.[72] In the second period the distribution was equally wide. Among the emancipators were Charles Ewell of Prince William in 1823, John Smith of Sussex in 1825, and John Ward of Pittsylvania in 1826. George Smith of Powhatan's 1830 preamble summarizes most of the reasons for the enlightened Virginians' antagonism to the institution: "Whereas I, George Smith, . . . being fully convinced that slavery in all its forms, is contrary to good policy, that it is inconsistent with republican principles; that it is a violation of our bill of rights, which declares that *all men are by nature equally free*; and above all, that it is repugnant to the spirit of the gospel, which enjoins universal love and benevolence. . . ."[73]

John Randolph's will of 1819, probated in 1833, freed his 383 slaves, with an expression of regret that the conditions of his inheritance had not permitted him to do it earlier.[74] His will made provision for purchase of land in a free state, the removal of the former slaves, and the supplying of farming equipment to them. Augustus John Foster's assertion that Randolph assured him that possession of slaves was "necessary to the formation of a perfect gentleman" is perhaps contradictory to Foster's other expressions from Randolph and to Randolph's emancipation of his slaves.[75] Randolph's sister-in-law Nancy Randolph once taunted him for his avowals of anti-slavery sentiments in private and reticence on the subject in public as political expediency or cowardice.[76] She may have been partly right.

William H. Fitzhugh of Ravensworth, Fairfax county, dating his will in 1829, stated that after 1850 all his Negroes were to be unconditionally free. They would have the privilege of their expenses of moving to a free territory and encouragement of $50 in addition if they emigrated to Africa.

Despite all this condemnation and emancipation, the fear of severe property losses or of bankruptcy prevented the rank and file of Virginia owners from agreeing with these leaders or from setting examples. John Taylor probably came near to expressing the norm for his less distinguished brethren. He was extremely sceptical of the expediency of emancipation. He felt that Negro slavery was a misfortune to agriculture but incapable of removal and only within the reach of amelioration. Jefferson's censure in the *Notes,* in which the point was made that slavery corrupted and degraded the masters, Taylor felt was refuted by the profusion of splendid characters produced by the slave states.[77] He anticipated some of the arguments of later pro-slavery statesmen: the example of Greece and Rome, slavery as an incitement to benevolence, the viciousness of slaves increasing the virtue of the masters, chattel slavery as superior to industrial serfdom, slaves as morally inferior (the case for natural slavery), and the impossibility of legally abolishing slavery under the Constitution. Taylor did see African colonization as a partial solution.

Despite his convictions regarding the institution and his final emancipation of his own slaves, John Randolph on a states' rights basis was a firm and consistent defender of the slaveholder as property owner who was guaranteed his rights by the Constitution. Though the lower South even in the 1790-1830 period was developing a strong pro-slavery spirit and expression, most of the little Virginia expression and undercurrent of feeling in favor of slavery reasoned along the states' rights line, if reason entered at all into the compulsive clinging to property which caused legislation to fail or never to materialize.

For economic and political and other utilitarian reasons, sharpened by western Virginia opposition to slavery, the recent depression, and surviving consistent anti-slavery sentiment, the period from 1829 to 1833 has been called the high tide of the anti-slavery movement in Virginia.[78] Relations between master and slave between 1825 and 1830 had been perhaps better than at any other period since 1776. Few runaways occurred, and few criminal punishments were recorded. The rush to the southwest and the demand for Negroes had slackened, the price declining since 1818. In 1827-28 Governor Giles called for a change in the penal code to mitigate the harshness of punishment for trivial crimes by slaves. Other reforms were undertaken, though at the same time education for free Negroes was made more difficult. A combination of symbolic revolts such as the Nat Turner Southampton county insurrection and fear of northern dominance began to change the tide between 1831 and 1835. But in the debates of the General Assembly of 1831-32 on whether slavery should be abolished the arguments were far from one-sided. And actually this was almost the first time in state and national legislative history that slavery as such had been debated. Certainly it was a term appearing rarely in the legislative records from 1790 to the War of 1812. The Quakers and the other anti-slavery men, some of them of the liberal Jeffersonian persuasion but others like Marshall's own son, presented a strong case for public as well as moral sentiment against. Powerful too were the arguments of the economic harm slavery had done and would do, and warnings of dissolution of the Union. But the final vote, 65 to 58, gave slavery a new hold on Virginia it did not relinquish until 1865.[79]

Virginians were in the first third of the nineteenth century the most active agitators for and participants in the move toward colonization of freed Negroes. As early as 1777 in a plan submitted by Jefferson to the General Assembly the idea seems to have originated.[80] From that time Jefferson and most other would-be emancipators believed that black and white could not live harmoniously and profitably side by side. In 1804-5 Jefferson and his friend Governor John Page of Virginia collaborated in trying to get some of the new Louisiana Territory set aside for the colonization of emancipated persons of color. The number of free Negroes in Virginia was growing (and they committed thousands of petty thefts) the figures from 1783 to 1810 showing an increase from 3,000 to 30,000.[81] Sincere anti-slavery and pro-slavery men alike felt like Jefferson that the two races could not continue side by side, and the anti-slavery forces felt that colonization would be further inducement to emancipation.

There are several instances of slaveholding planters who tried individual experiments in colonization. The best known of these was undertaken by Edward Coles (1786-1868) of Albemarle, onetime private secretary to President Madison and emissary to Russia.[82] A sort of protégé of Jefferson as an "experimental philosopher," Coles determined to move to free soil and liberate his slaves. He set out in the spring of 1819 for Illinois, where he executed formal deeds of emancipation, settled his former slaves in their own homes near Edwardsville, and gave each head of a family 160 acres. Though he gained the ill will of the majority of the other inhabitants of the Territory by his actions, he had powerful backing. He was appointed Registrar of the Edwardsville Land Office in 1819 and in 1822 by a narrow margin was elected Governor. In a bitter struggle he successfully opposed the introduction of slavery into the state and lived to see the fulfillment of his lifelong hope of universal emancipation at the terrific cost of the Civil War. John Randolph's desire to settle his emancipated slaves in Ohio is another instance of the trend to colonization, as is the case of John Ward of Pennsylvania who in 1826 transported his emancipated slaves and settled them in Ohio in Lawrence county.[83]

The great experiment in colonization was undertaken by a group organized in Washington, D.C., in 1816 called the American Colonization Society.[84] It was essentially a movement of the moderate middle-state group of which Virginia was the most prominent member.[85] Its aim was to establish a home for freed slaves in an African environment. Among the Virginians taking part were Charles F. Mercer, John Randolph, John Taylor, Edmund I. Lee, Henry Clay, Bushrod Washington, Bishop William Meade, and the Reverend William H. Wilmer, both the latter Episcopalians. Bushrod Washington was the organization's president for thirteen years. Auxiliary societies were organized and in most cases were active in Richmond, Norfolk, Fredericksburg, Petersburg, Lynchburg, Wheeling, Charlestown, Shepherdstown, Hampton, and Harper's Ferry, and in some eighteen counties. John Marshall was president of the Richmond branch. Methodists, Baptists, Presbyterians, and Episcopalians were active in the various groups.

The Virginia societies collected money by private subscription. In 1826, a depression year, the Legislature appropriated $20,000 for the work. By 1828 the Virginia Society, with Marshall as president and Madison, Tyler, and other prominent citizens as vice-presidents, took over most of the work in the state. James Pleasants, William Maxwell, and Abel P. Upshur were among its strong supporters.[86]

The American Colonization Society and its Virginia branch did more than establish a few shiploads of freed slaves in Africa and found Liberia. It did much to promote national unity, for all sections were prominently represented in its membership before 1840. It was a powerful factor in the manumission of thousands of slaves, and but for the new thrust southwest in the thirties and consequent need for slave labor would have helped to free thousands more. Its influence in the suppression of the slave trade, Early Lee Fox points out, was long overlooked.[87] Fox estimates that at one period it saved an average of 20,000 native Africans a year from being sold into slavery. After 1839-40, when the Society was reorganized and came under the dominance of the Middle Atlantic and New England states, it was no longer a factor in the South.

William H. Fitzhugh, who as we have seen later freed his three hundred slaves and offered special inducements if they would consent to go to Liberia, believed that abolition would come only gradually, and that colonization in Africa was the best means of bringing about voluntary emancipation. He and others wrote pamphlets urging Congress to support the enterprise by national subsidy. Yet he would not have such subsidy if it were unconstitutional, or in other words, if it subverted states' rights. One debate between him and Judge J. W. Nash of Powhatan was published in 1827 as *Controversy between Caius and Opimius, in Reference to the American Society for Colonizing the Free People of Colour of the United States.*[88] Fitzhugh's was a strong yet moderate position, interesting and somewhat ironical in the light of his relative George Fitzhugh's later defenses of slavery such as *Cannibals All!* Madison and Marshall, by no means strict constructionists, were of course all-out advocates of national subsidization.

A national issue involving slavery and states' rights received the attention of many Virginia political writers—the Missouri Question. When the Territory of Missouri applied for admission to the Union as a state, a New York member of Congress proposed that the Territory should be required to abolish slavery before being admitted. Virginians argued that Congress under the Constitution could not demand that a territory should alter its proposed constitution as a condition of admission. If Congress could forbid slavery in a state, it could also forbid other rights.[89] Thus slavery was an open issue on a national scale. In January, 1820, the Virginia House of Delegates by an overwhelming majority resolved to denounce the alarming attempt of Congress "to manacle the soverign will of the people." Virginia's view in a sense won for the Missouri Compromise allowed the entrance of the new state without having to amend its constitution. But it also required that in all future states and territories from the remainder of the Louisiana Purchase north of 36° 30′ slavery should be forbidden. This line was the southern rather than the northern boundary of Missouri, a situation which made for unequal distribution. Virginians in both houses of Congress voted almost solidly against the Compromise. Jefferson remained uneasy during the whole struggle. "A fire bell in the night," it had filled him with premonitions of disaster. To him it was clearly a states' rights issue.[90]

The hundreds of essays and pamphlets produced by Virginians on the Missouri question were largely legalistic in tone, concerned with the fact that Missouri was within the area purchased from France in 1803, for opponents of the Compromise asserted that precedent had been established in the same territory when Louisiana was admitted as a slave state in 1812. But some arguments were moral in emphasis, for northern sectionalists now began to assert that slavery was wrong. Ritchie of the *Enquirer* defended slavery on the "moral" basis that it was not forbidden in the Scriptures, though he admitted that it was an evil.

Typical arguments are those by Francis Gilmer and George Tucker in the *Enquirer* of January 6, 1820. The former, as "Wilberforce," addressed himself to the "Missouri Debate."[91] Gilmer cited the treaty with France by which the Territory was ceded, the Louisiana precedent, and the "names of Philanthropy and Liberty." On the last two he argued that because slaves would live more abundantly and would multiply in less crowded Missouri, the northern critics had no right to deny them this breathing room; for in Missouri they would be no less free than in other slave states in which they would remain unless the new state were allowed its own wishes on the matter. His last and chief point is directly states' rights: the question of what the Federal government would or could do if Missouri were admitted with the anti-slavery qualification and *then* changed her constitution to allow slavery. Gilmer ends with the same solemn warning of revolution and dire disaster that his mentor Jefferson had uttered.

Tucker's "Missouri Question," signed "A Southron," which immediately follows Gilmer's piece, is a long legal argument entirely concerned with interpretation of powers of the Constitution. He writes of general principles and even particular clauses, warning against "false principles of construction" which would take liberty from the people. His is a far more convincing argument in both logic and law than Gilmer's. Tucker had as early as 1801 published in Baltimore and Richmond *Letter to a Member of the General Assembly of Virginia, on the Subject of the Late Conspiracy of Slaves with a Proposal for their Colonization.*[92] And on the Missouri question he spoke in Congress, publishing his remarks later as a separate pamphlet.[93] Though Tucker in his *History of the United States* in 1856-58 was to predict the eventful death of slavery, even there and then he presented the old stock arguments as to its benefits to whites and blacks, and in his manuscript Autobiography in 1858 doubted the wisdom of his manumission of his five household slaves before he moved north.[94] In the nineteenth century the black was better off, he seemed to feel, in the condition of servitude. But then Tucker had on this and certain other matters always been a Virginia conservative, though he voted the Jeffersonian Republican ticket. In his earlier years he seemed undecided. It was not until the 1840's that slavery appeared on the whole tolerable, when it had been a national issue for more than twenty years.

E. *The Tariff*

Tariffs had been clearly authorized by the Constitution, but whether for revenue or protection had not been stipulated. From the time of the adoption the Virginia and southern attitudes, apparently consistent agrarian points of view, had been in general to oppose protective tariffs which seemed to favor manufacture and hurt agriculture. Richard Henry Lee had tried in vain to persuade Congress not to enact import duties because they were "an oppressive though indirect" tax upon agriculture.[95] Yet Virginians and Virginia Republicans did not always feel this way on the subject.

In the early Jefferson administration, the President and his party stood generally for protective tariff, the Federalists for internal taxes. New England, at that time more interested in foreign trade than in manufacturing, opposed protective duties. Manufacturing, in the eastern and middle states, was at this time principally carried on by small shops and craftsmen, who with the agricultural interest made up the bulk of the Republican party.[96] The situation was entirely changed when the War of 1812 brought machine manufacturing on a large scale and capital invested in it instead of foreign trade, especially in New England. Since the protective policy now worked to the disadvantage of the southern states, Jefferson largely went back to an earlier advocacy of international free trade. But Madison, from consideration of national policy, particularly the feeling that the infant New England industries needed to be protected, favored in 1816 the modern protective tariff which was then adopted. But all during this time the Old Republicans, including John Taylor, had fought the protective duties.

The greatest amount of Virginia writing on taxes aimed at higher duties came in connection with the Tariff of 1820 and of 1824. Of the five principal opponents of protection in Congress three were Virginians—John Tyler, Philip B. Barbour, and William S. Archer.[97] They predicted that if the law permitting higher duties were passed, there would be increases in smuggling, population opportunity for prosperity would be distorted, and an endless spiral would be created. Chiefly of course they argued that farmers would thus be compelled to pay tribute to manufacturers. Southern newspapers, especially the Richmond *Compiler*, argued laissez faire.

The measure failed to pass the Senate in 1820, and substantially the same question came up in 1824. It was in the latter year that the constitutionality of the protective tariff was first seriously attacked.[98] Barbour said it violated the spirit if not the letter of the Constitution, and Clay replied. All but one Virginia Representative, a man from the western area, voted against the measure. But it was passed. From this time on the whole question of tariff came to be regarded as a sectional issue.[99]

In April, 1824, Madison had written Clay that he could not concur in the pending tariff bill, arguing that individual enterprise, not government enactment, should determine investment of labor and capital. Madison was, he said, "a friend to the *general* principle of 'free industry,' as a basis of a sound system of political economy. On the other hand, I am not less a friend to the legal patronage of domestic manufactures, as far as they come within particular reasons for exceptions to the general rule, not derogating from its generality. . . ."[100] Thus the veteran Virginian nationalist took his stand with free enterprise and agriculture as a natural combination, though he was to declare to J. C. Cabell that Congress had a constitutional right to lay duties with the idea of protecting manufactures.[101]

In the same month James Mercer Garnett, agrarian and educator, wrote to John Randolph[102] that he had been working hard against "the accursed Tariff" by writing three or four pieces for the *American Farmer,* one for the *Enquirer,* and one for the *Intelligencer*. Later repercussions in print were considerable and undoubtedly did much in Virginia to produce some sympathy for the later movement toward nullification.

Thomas R. Dew, in his 1829 *Lectures on the Restrictive System*[103] given originally before his senior class in politics at William and Mary, made probably the most extensive and logical survey of the whole situation from the free-trade point of view. Referring again and again to Quesnay and other Physiocrats, to Malthus, Smith, Destutt de Tracy, Locke, Sismondi, Hume, Say, and Stewart, and to Ricardo, he presented the pros and cons of free trade, the relative advantage of manufactures and agriculture as ways of living, and finally the reasons why the restrictive system had been established in most countries despite the fact that it is "contrary to the best established principles of our science." His strong conclusion, that the restrictive system is highly injurious to all classes except those protected, ran head-on against the protectionist propaganda of Mathew Carey and the Philadelphia manufacturers. Some historians have thought his work influenced a reduction in tariff.[104] Be that as it may, Dew's logic was in the tradition of the most convincing writing of Mason, Jefferson, Marshall, and Madison.

Today the essay carries additional interest for its vigorous defense of the intellectual. Knowing that he would be attacked as an impractical cloistered "philosopher," Dew declared: "If any men, then are likely to arrive at truth, they must be the philosophers who sit in the ship of state, and observe with calm but scrutinizing eye, all the movements on the deck. . . . And were I a leading statesman, upon whom the destinies of my country principally depended, I would rather hear the calm and dignified voice of approbation from such philosophers as Smith, Stewart, and Say, amid the shakes of retirement, than the plaudits of political expectants, who might hang upon my *skirts,* and sing hosannas to my merits."[105]

F. *Other Economic Issues and Ideas*

On various aspects of political economy or economics the Jeffersonians wrote almost as much as they did on relatively pure politics. George Hay and George Tucker composed pamphlets defending usury. Francis Gilmer attacked it—and Hay—in an essay which Jefferson, Carr, and Wirt thought unanswerable. Changing and divergent ideas on banking may be seen in pieces by Hay, W. C. Nicholas, Thomas Ritchie, and Henry St. George Tucker. J. M. Garnett opposed some of "Arator's reprehensible doctrines" on agricultural economics,[106] St. George Tucker in an *Old Bachelor* paper analyzed factors producing the bankruptcy of once wealthy planters,[107] Andrew Stevenson drew new ideas on agricultural economics from the British.[108] These writers and others printed hundreds of newspaper expressions of their problems. Most essays carry the coloration of agrarianism, though in certain shades and areas they differ considerably.

But out of the hundreds of writers four men of the period emerge today as significant economists for their own time and ours: Jefferson, Madison, Taylor, and George Tucker. As has been pointed out in earlier chapters, their reading and experience was in many respects quite similar. All four began as staunch believers in laissez faire in the relation between government and private enterprise. All had more than sympathy for the agrarian interest and opposed in varying degree the mercantile or industrial. All therefore, as we have seen, looked at economic problems largely from a states' rights point of view. To them all economy was political economy. Most of Taylor's ideas on the subject have been touched upon earlier, but the other three should be looked at again briefly as political economists.

In 1790 Jefferson thought Smith's *Wealth of Nations* "the best book extant."[109] Later he spoke favorably of Turgot and the Physiocrats, and with qualifications, of Montesquieu. Contrary to earlier opinion, the Physiocrats now appear to have little influenced him. In 1803 Say sent him a copy of his new *Traite d'economic politique,* while he was reading and approving Malthus. Say became "the best book" until the new *Treatise on Political Economy* by Destutt de Tracy was published in 1817.[110] Jefferson himself was responsible for the publication of Tracy's book and wrote a preface for it. Ricardo, Jefferson complained of in 1819 as full of "muddy reasoning" which would not stand up.[111]

Madison seems to have learned most from Smith, Hume, and Malthus, though he mentions six or seven others. Tucker knew them all but did his most effective writing in amendment or extenuation of Malthus and Ricardo.

Thoroughgoing agrarian, Jefferson believed until 1807 that the United States would be most prosperous if it made use of its superabundant asset, land. But with the Napoleonic wars and the springing up of manufactures, he adjusted to meet the new conditions. He felt that he was expanding, not altering his views, by advocating a balance among employments, though he still believed uneconomical city manufactures should not be developed. He never expressed himself on these matters in formal treatises, contenting himself with firm statements in his letters and in his messages to Congress.

Madison likewise did not write formally on the laws of production. He early declared himself a believer in laissez faire, on the ground that under it more goods would be produced. Americans stood to gain most by specialization in agriculture because of the cheapness of land. As conditions changed he came to believe that a balanced economy was a necessity. In the end he was more of an economic nationalist than Jefferson.

Both men were aware that as population grew, the relative rates of remuneration of land and labor might be altered; and they believed that when all land was occupied and the population was piled up in cities American corruption would begin. Madison did not predict, however, a fall in the wage level or control of numbers, as did Malthus.[112] Madison ascribed the relative poverty of Europe to the pressure of numbers on resources. He did not agree with Malthus that the ability to increase food supply was arithmetical, but pointed out that it varied from country to country, from zero in already highly cultivated China to an excess in thinly cultivated America. In several respects he anticipated Malthus by a dozen years.[113] Though he saw possible ultimate dire consequences, because America was thinly populated he advocated freedom of emigration in the interests of humanity. The westward movement, since it brought easier subsistence, was on the whole good in accelerating population increase. But he several times voiced a Malthusian pessimism in his conviction that population increase would continue despite its potentially evil effects.

Tucker, younger than his two fellow Republicans, was influenced by the new theories of Malthus earlier in his life than they were.[114] In 1815, in essays in the *Port Folio* which he later republished in his 1822 *Essays,* Tucker wrote what has been recently hailed as the first significant criticism of Malthus.[115] Here Tucker favored population growth on the grounds that it brought greater wealth, made for military security, encouraged the arts, brought internal improvements in roads and transportation, and developed healthy rivalry in industry.[116] A denser population might produce peculiar vices and sufferings but it was also favorable to peculiar virtues and enjoyments.[117] He suggested a middle point between excessive thinness and density. His criticism of Malthus' theory was primarily that it tended to reconcile man to wretchedness. He attempted to show that misery may be the result of other causes than overpopulation. Tucker predicted that within a century America would number one hundred and twenty millions with sixty persons per square mile.

Later, in 1837, Tucker was converted to the Malthusian doctrine, contending that the returns from land were limited and the supply of land fixed, therefore the quantity and quality of food would fall gradually to a mere subsistence level, a Ricardian theory, as we shall see. At this level population would be stationary.[118] This change was probably caused by his reflections on the slavery problems and his development of a rationale to defend slavery.[119] In the 1830's and 1840's also Malthus seemed a strong antidote for radical social theories. At any rate, he seems to have been the first writer to determine statistically that the rate of increase of the American stock of 1790 was declining.[120]

Tucker also seriously pondered the rent theory of David Ricardo, which began with the Malthusian assumption.[121] It supposed that as population increased there was a tendency to resort to poorer soils and more intensive cultivation. Rent arose from the productivity differential of marginal and richer soil and would rise with increasing population. Ricardo's "iron law" of wages supposed that as population grew wages tended to fall to the subsistence level but not below. Tucker dissented from Ricardo in believing that wages could fall below the minimum subsistence level, a belief inspired by his observations on slavery.[122] He argued that (1) the diversity of soil has no agency in creating rent; (2) the rise of raw produce is the cause rather than the consequence of the resort to inferior soils; and (3) a rise in raw produce means a fall in real wages. There are other facets of Tucker's theory of capital as value, or a productive agent such as land or tools, which enter into his ideas on the wage-rent-population theory. One economist argues that Tucker never really anticipated population pressure in the United States.[123] But most of those who have considered his work feel that he is the earliest American thinker on Ricardo.

To fiscal theory, money, and banking Jefferson and Madison devoted much of their time, Tucker was known to his students as "Old Money and Banks," and Taylor's favorite bêtes noirs, already discussed, were paper money and banks. Jefferson and Madison like Taylor opposed the use of paper money and rejected the arguments in favor of banks and discount.[124]

In 1791 Madison had opposed the establishment of the Bank of the United States because its disadvantages outweighed its advantages.[125] In 1815 he recommended the establishment of a second Bank and in 1816 signed the bill creating it, for the reasons we have cited above. He continued to condemn imprudent banking, which seduced people to live beyond their means.

Jefferson favored (as did John Randolph incidentally) a pay-as-you-go policy in meeting present expenditures and economy in their occurrence, both concomitants of the least-government-the-best theory of Republicanism. Debts were not to be shifted to the next generation, a view Madison did not entirely share. Madison did agree on frugality in operation, however, that economy should be the watchword of government.

Tucker, who wrote an essay in 1813 on "Banks of Circulation,"[126] did his most effective writing on legal matters in University of Virginia lectures, published as *Theory of Money and Banks Investigated* in 1839,[127] continuing to write on the subject to the end of his life. In the 1839 volume he analyzed the nature and function of money, the arguments for and against a double standard, and the nature and function of banks. He defended the credit bank "as an institution as much in advance of the deposit bank as the railroad was an advance on the turnpike."[128] He had earlier supported Madison's second Bank, writing articles in its favor in the *National Intelligencer* and one piece in the *American Quarterly Review* (IX [1831], 246-82).[129] He never became a fanatical supporter of the Bank, however, perhaps because of his early intellectual environment. When he was an open advocate before his classes at the University of Clay's American System and the desirability of an industrial economy, the Jeffersonian period was definitely past.

Jefferson, Madison, and Tucker all emphasized aspects of the class struggle, thus anticipating but not following Marx in his solution. Only Tucker seems to have anticipated the rise of corporations, of entrepreneurs and labor leaders who wished to freeze the American economy. Only Tucker among the four (including Taylor) was ever really concerned with the problems of economics as such, not merely with their relation to the classic problem of control of power. But Jefferson and Madison even more than Tucker saw that an ideal political system must have a proper economic milieu, and vice versa. They believed in economic as well as political education of all the people. Ironically, the only one of them actually to teach came after the others were gone to inculcate in his students the values of a kind of capitalistic system they did not fully anticipate. One cannot say that they would not have approved had they lived on another score of years.

As economist Tucker is read today as the example of an acute critical mind far ahead of its time, anticipating fiscal and population trends and endeavoring to cope with them. The twentieth-century economists who hail him as the foremost economic thinker of the first forty years of the nineteenth century also agree that he was in his own time little read. Yet Tucker's newspaper and magazine writing, his speeches in Congress, and his university lectures may have left their mark more than has been yet discovered. The problem remains to be investigated.

G. *Individual and Party Alignment*

The rise of Jeffersonian Republicanism, its quarter of a century of dominance, decline, and resurgence in differing form is one of the major themes of our national history. It has been discussed many times. In the present study we have already incidentally pointed out leaders thinking along divergent political lines. And there have been whole books, such as Charles M. Wiltse's *The Jeffersonian Tradition in American Democracy,* L. D. White's *The Jeffersonians,* and Noble E. Cunningham's *The Jeffersonian Republicans,* which discuss various aspects of the rise of the great party, its processes and ideas.[130]

Organization was certainly not, as we pointed out at the beginning of this chapter, clearly along lines of conservative or liberal, aristocrat or plebeian. For various reasons blue-bloods like John Page and Edmund Pendleton became active and devoted Republicans and supplied much of the party leadership in the state. As has been mentioned, the earliest Republican political boss or manager, and effective organizer, was the Louisa county gentleman John J. Beckley. Allied with these people were plain sons of the soil like the Baptist minister John Leland and sturdy middle-class Presbyterians of various intellectual backgrounds.

The Republican party in Virginia as in the nation seems to have developed from a genuine and general alarm of the agricultural interests over the centralizing tendencies favoring commerce and manufactures during the Washington and Adams administrations. In the first years of its triumph, the first administration of Jefferson, by and large, lived up to its ideals and campaign promises. But internal and external forces compelled nationalistic measures which a good minority of its members opposed. Thus came the *Tertium Quids,* or Old

Republicans, or Republicans of '98, represented by John Randolph and at times by Giles, John Taylor, and James M. Garnett, though in some situations all of them followed Jefferson and Madison. Always the regulars in the party included radicals like Jefferson and John Daly Burk and moderates like Pendleton, Edmund Randolph, and later Rives. The conservatives, like B. W. Leigh and the younger Upshur and Edmund Ruffin, could hardly ever be called real Republicans. Then there were the anti-Jeffersonians like George Hay and Dr. Charles Everett the former of whom was technically a party member and the latter hardly a real Federalist.

Opposed to these men in thinking were the recognized and avowed Federalists who faded with the advance of the nineteenth century. Beginning with George Washington and John Marshall, they included Associate Supreme Court Justices John Blair and Bushrod Washington, Presbyterian clergyman John D. Blair, Henry Lee, David Meade Randolph, and the able George Keith Taylor. Daniel Sheffey beyond the Blue Ridge was a leader of what were called the New Federalists. But it is quite clear that at least until after the War of 1812 a majority of Virginia's educated men were Republican, and relatively liberal, in their social and political sympathies.

The Whigs, who rose in Virginia after 1824 and absorbed most of the old Federalists, were of course an essentially conservative, commerce-favoring, protective-tariff-bank-sponsoring party.[131] Virginia's growing western industries, such as iron, required protection and a division of opinion and conviction about candidates for the presidency left an open invitation to new alignments. Though the Whigs were to be felt as a party in later Virginia politics, at the end of the Jeffersonian period their policies were still rather nebulous and the influence as a party little. John Hampden Pleasants (1797-1846) founded the Richmond *Whig* in 1824, a newspaper which quickly became the principal rival of the Republican *Enquirer* and the leading exponent of Whig doctrines in Virginia. It supported John Quincy Adams for the Presidency in both 1824 and 1828. In later years as a Southern and Virginia party the Whigs shifted positions on candidates and nullification and states' rights doctrines.

Directed toward and out from these party alignments were written and oral expressions of many kinds. It is significant, however, that the overwhelming majority of political essays and printed speeches do not mention party, and that many of them condemn party spirit. One of the ironies of Virginia and American history is that the symbols of party—Washington, Jefferson, and Madison—at one time or another condemned party spirit in government. It is likewise significant that Wirt could recommend a young Federalist to Madison or Monroe, pointing out his political affiliation, but saying he deserved appointment. Partly for practical reasons but more from moral convictions of the necessity of good government, the Virginia Republican Presidents never held to stiff party lines, nor did their major followers.

In the heat of the 1824 political campaign, a great deal was said in print about the "Virginia party" or "Richmond party" or "Richmond Junto," allegedly a small group who controlled politics, including appointments, in Virginia.[132] It was charged that they were all allied by marriage, a tight little group of self-interested men. They included Wilson Cary Nicholas, president of the Richmond branch of the Bank of the United States, the presidents of the two state banks with main offices in Richmond, and most of the members of the Governor's Council. Their power stemmed from an act of 1800 which provided that Virginia elect her Presidential Electors on a general ticket. This in turn required an electoral slate to be named by a caucus, which set up a corresponding committee to work with the counties in the matter. The power of this central committee came from its contact with county committees. Such was the "Richmond Junto."

The group was charged with running Virginia "for the purpose of consolidating and extending family interest, and promoting personal aggrandisement."[133] Individual "letters" concern Edmund Randolph, Nicholas, Robert Smith, Spencer Roane, and Ritchie. Others discuss Giles, Coalter, Fleming, and Pendleton. That the group formed a powerful party steering committee is obvious, and that the charge of personal profit is absurd is equally obvious.[134] Even the bitterest enemies of the Republicans would admit the latter. B. W. Leigh, replying to Henry Lee on November 29, 1824,[135] expressed his doubt that there was such a thing as a "Richmond party," but believed that there was a "Virginia party" which held irresistible sway at home.

> It has held its dominion, uninterrupted and absolute, for more than twenty years; and has fettered, and therefore enfeebled the public mind; for the genius of a commonwealth, any more than

of an individual, cannot act with vigor, unless it act with freedom. It is to this cause (I do most conscientiously believe) that the gradual and visible decline of talent for public affairs, in the old dominion, is to be imputed. I earnestly wish to see the curse removed. . . . But this Virginia party is (in the main) an honest party, and towards those who are content merely to maintain their own independency, and who forbear to offend against its peculiar tenets, tolerant and generous. One thing I have remarked, and with no little pride, that one can tell beforehand, with exact certainty, what Virginia will do on any occasion. She never disappoints expectation, in any case where third persons are concerned as well as herself. . .

This is a significant and interesting commentary on political thinking as well as action in Virginia then and a century and more later. Leigh took pride in something that was political consistency and also moral consistency, as he admits. Despite Leigh's assertion of long-held election power, facts do not bear him out, unless as individuals these men often supported candidates other than their party recommended. Politically Virginians remained strongly individualistic, within certain bounds, as the choice of John Randolph by his rural constituency over the objections of the party regulars would indicate.[136] Jefferson's control over his party's votes, even during his presidency, was more predictable for other states than for Virginia.

H. *Foreign Affairs*

One may add only a note about the Virginia mind in foreign affairs. It was certainly present, but in a capacity representing the nation, not the individual or the state. From Jefferson in France to Stevenson and Rives and Randolph in England, France, and Russia, from Washington to Monroe and Barbour, Virginia furnished diplomats and makers of foreign policy to the nation. In some instances, as in Jefferson's and Stevenson's as diplomats, they augmented already distinguished reputations and performed valuable service in representing American policies on trade, impressment, and other matters. As a treaty-maker Monroe was something less than distinguished; as the formulator or at least annunciator of a world-famous doctrine he is rightly better known.[137]

For tact, sophistication, and gracious manners Virginia diplomats were noted. They held innately or developed a breadth of view which stood them in good stead, and yet they remained throughout the period sturdy Americans.

A review of the contributions of Virginia Secretaries of State—including Jefferson, Edmund Randolph, Marshall, Madison, and Monroe—would be largely a restatement of American foreign policy from Washington through Madison. Though they made domestic as well as foreign enemies by remaining firm, Jefferson, Madison, and Monroe carried American prestige abroad to new heights by treaties, purchases, the Doctrine, and actual war. The Louisiana Purchase was perhaps as popular as the Embargo was unpopular, but both were evidences of Jefferson's determination to build a great nation on this continent with as little warfare as possible. American interests *and* the rights of man were determining factors in their decision in this sphere as in others. Thus came American sympathy for insurgent Spanish America and the negotiations-plus-force acquisitions in Florida and other territories.

Washington was pro-British, Jefferson and Madison largely pro-French, from conviction. Jefferson frequently voiced the opinion that all governments of the world could and should not be modeled on ours, but he and his two successors tended to favor those foreign governments which seemed to be attempting to establish civil liberty and democratic government. What he and his fellow Republicans of the stamp of St. George Tucker, Madison, Monroe, and Page wished to see for the future was a world enjoying the blessings of liberty as America enjoyed them, and they wanted to be sure foreign encroachment would not prevent America's continued enjoyment. Virginians composed the majority of the foreign policy makers or implementors in the first thirty-five years of national existence. They managed to lead a relatively weak infant through the forests of international pressures into a robust childhood.

I. *The Convention of 1829-30*

The Convention assembled in Richmond in late 1829 to decide on the question of a new state constitution may be considered the last act in the first national drama of Virginia's history or the first in the second exhibition on the subject, the new Jacksonian era. The significance of what was said and done there has already been touched upon in several of the preceding chapters.

It was an assemblage of planters, lawyers, career statesmen, western farmers, and editors. Included were two former Presidents of the United States, the Chief Justice, the Speaker of the House of Representatives, several present and former United States Senators and Representatives, several former ministers to foreign courts, and leaders of the bench and bar. The leadership was as far as eastern Virginia was concerned from the large planter and professional class, as we have seen, now gone overwhelmingly conservative. The tramontane leadership rested in the Valley lawyers like John Rogers Cooke and Chapman Johnson and Philip Doddridge, moderate farmers who owned few if any slaves.

The reformers, the western men, worked for white manhood suffrage as the basis of representation.[138] Interest in and attachment to one's country was the sole basis they admitted for the exercise of political power. The two conservative groups were strict constructionists and new anti-nationalists. The latter as we have seen were beginning to discredit the Lockean contract theory of government. They were the reformers' chief opponents, and on the white suffrage issue they won. But there were several compromises: the right to vote was extended to leaseholders and householders, and the western area received a somewhat larger share of representatives.

Slavery had not been an open issue, but with states' rights it lay behind much of the impassioned argument: Leigh and Upshur, intelligent and even intellectual, carried the conservative cause. Upshur, Wirt-trained lawyer and planter-philosopher of the Eastern Shore and Richmond, voiced the crystallizing resentment of his growing group among the large-scale farmers at the rising tide of leveling democracy, the *isms* of the free North, and even against certain tendencies of agrarianism. A decade later he would state pessimistically that the slaveholding states were the last stronghold of Liberty. He meant that majority rule had become tyranny. To this cul-de-sac had the Virginia political intellectual, the farmer-statesman class which had produced Marshall as well as Jefferson, arrived. Virginia would continue to produce great men and some great minds, but not again would those men carry their own state into a leadership in constructive national government.

The abiding impression left by the Jeffersonian mind is its reasoning quality, its morality, and its view of the ideal life for all mankind in terms of its own region. Jefferson saw the light of humanity as his cousin John Randolph saw the dark. The greatest minds—Jefferson, Madison, Marshall, Taylor, St. George Tucker—were in the end optimistic. For they believed that if man governed himself properly, he might actually pursue happiness. And they offered powerful reasons as to how and why he would do so.

Not the merest politician among the Jeffersonian Virginians ever believed that happiness would come from government alone. Their way of daily life, their encouragement of education and reading, their interest in science in all its forms, their moderate encouragement of the fine arts, their belief in a just but benevolent God, attest their knowledge that full happiness must come from engaging all the faculties. Good government merely assured that this engagement would be possible.

ABBREVIATIONS USED IN BIBLIOGRAPHY AND NOTES

AHR	*American Historical Record*
AL	*American Literature*
DAB	*Dictionary of American Biography,* eds. Allen Johnson and Dumas Malone (22 vols., includ. Supplement One, New York, 1928-44).
Duke	Manuscript Division, Duke University Library.
Ford	Paul L. Ford, ed., *The Writings of Thomas Jefferson* (10 vols., New York, 1892-99).
HEH	Henry E. Huntington Library
JSH	*Journal of Southern History*
L & B	A. A. Lipscomb and A. E. Bergh, eds., *The Writings of Thomas Jefferson* (20 vols., Washington, 1903).
LC	Library of Congress
Md HS	Maryland Historical Society
NYPL	New York Public Library
Papers	*The Papers of Thomas Jefferson,* eds. Julian P. Boyd, *et al* (Princeton, 1950——).
PAAS	*Proceedings of the American Antiquarian Society*
PMHB	*Pennsylvania Magazine of History and Biography*
SLM	*Southern Literary Messenger*
Tyler's Mag	*Tyler's Quarterly Historical and Genealogical Magazine*
UNC	University of North Carolina
U Va	University of Virginia
Va HS	Virginia Historical Society
Va St Lib	Virginia State Library

VMHB	*Virginia Magazine of History and Biography*
WMQ (1) (2) (3)	*William and Mary Quarterly*, first, second, and third series.

Note on periodical references: Where volumes and years correspond, only year is given with the volume number; where they overlap, month or number is added to year.

BIBLIOGRAPHY AND NOTES

INDEX

BIBLIOGRAPHY AND NOTES

General

The most significant sources for any study of Virginia life and history lie in the volumes covered in Earl G. Swem's *Virginia Historical Index* (2 vols., Roanoke, 1934-36) and in numerous manuscript collections in public repositories. The former covers all volumes through 1930 of *The Virginia Magazine of History and Biography* and the *William and Mary Quarterly,* through 1929 of *Tyler's Historical and Genealogical Register,* and all volumes of the *Lower Norfolk County Virginia Antiquary* (1895-1906), the *Virginia Historical Register* (1848-53), the *Calendar of Virginia State Papers* (1875-93), and W. W. Hening's *Statutes at Large* (1809-23). The files of the first two of these since 1930 and still current, and of *Tyler's Magazine* until it ceased publication in 1952, are also most useful. These are rich in primary documents, genealogical notes, and critical studies of many phases of Virginia history.

Fortunately most of the manuscript materials may be found within a relatively small geographical area, with Richmond, Charlottesville, Williamsburg, and Washington, D. C., as the principal points to be visited. In Charlottesville are the several million manuscripts of the Alderman Library of the University of Virginia, most of them representing some phase of Virginia life or the lives of her prominent sons. The Jefferson, Cocke, Cabell, Randolph, and Gilmer collections are perhaps the most valuable, but there are also many others. Nearby too are the Albemarle county court archives containing wills, book inventories, land grants, and other data concerning the Master of Monticello and his neighbors.

In Richmond are the rapidly growing collections of the Virginia Historical Society and the Virginia State Library. In the former are papers of many of the Lees, several Randolphs, Hugh Blair Grigsby, and perhaps a thousand other early Virginians. In the State Library are Wirt, Tazewell, and Bruce-Randolph papers, among hundreds of other groupings. And here too are microfilm or photostat copies of all Virginia county records. Also in Richmond are papers concerning early Presbyterians and Presbyterianism in the Union Theological Seminary Library, and a number of useful items, especially of art interest in the Valentine Museum.

At Williamsburg are the hundreds of records of early Virginia plantation and town life in the William and Mary Library. Also most useful are the Tucker-Coleman Papers, concerned with St. George Tucker and his family and friends, now on deposit in the Archives of Colonial Williamsburg. Equally valuable are the microfilm copies of many unpublished theses and dissertations on Virginia subjects as well as of scattered manuscript materials now being assembled by the Research Division of Colonial Williamsburg under Dr. Edward M. Riley.

In the nation's capital the Library of Congress has thousands of Virginia papers, including many of those of the first four Virginia Presidents, William Short, Nicholas P. Trist, William Wirt, John Tyler, and the Breckinridge family. Nearby in Baltimore the Maryland Historical Society has a large William Wirt collection from which little has been published since Kennedy's biography more than a century ago.

Next to these in the Virginia area, the collections of Duke University and the University of North Carolina are the most voluminous and most generally valuable. Those at Duke include a Munford-Ellis collection, Hiram Haines' notebook, and many miscellaneous items. The Southern Historical Collections at Chapel Hill include several hundred items of Virginiana, certain family letter-groups being especially useful. Among these are the Nicholas P. Trist Papers, which form a perfect complement to the collection with the same title at the Library of Congress.

The Brock Collection of the Henry E. Huntington Library in San Marino, California, is essentially a gathering of Virginiana and includes many items significant to the Jeffersonian period. In Philadelphia the American Philosophical Society and the Pennsylvania Historical Society are especially rich in Virginia material, and the Library Company of Philadelphia and the Academy of Natural Sciences also have pertinent manuscript holdings. There are scattered Virginia items at Yale, Harvard, the New York Public Library, and the South Caroliniana Library of the University of South Carolina. A few other repositories will be noticed in the chapter notes below.

Printed books and pamphlets written by or about, or owned by early Virginians are to be found in the same places in about the same ratio as the manuscripts. Especially noteworthy are the complete home library of the Garnetts of Elmwood and the Madison Pamphlet Collection of the University of Virginia, the large number of volumes from the libraries of John Randolph and Hugh Blair Grigsby at the Virginia Historical Society, the remains of Jefferson's great personal library in the Library of Congress, and many of the books of John Holt Rice in the Union Theological Seminary. At least parts of several notable Jeffersonian-period libraries still remain in private hands, as that of General Cocke at Bremo. All the Virginia-area institutional libraries mentioned above are rich in secondary materials.

Chapter One

A. *Bibliography in general* (more specific items in this and later chapters will appear only in the notes).

For the colonial period, incomparably the best political history is Richard L. Morton, *Colonial Virginia* (2 vols., Chapel Hill, 1960). Matthew Page Andrews' *Virginia: The Old Dominion* (New York, 1937) is also useful, as are Charles M. Andrews, *The Colonial Period in American History* (4 vols., New Haven, 1934-38); Daniel Boorstin, *The Americans: The Colonial Experience* (New York, 1958), especially Book I, Part 4; Philip A. Bruce, *Economic History of Virginia in the Seventeenth Century* (2 vols., New York, 1895) and *Institutional History of Virginia in the Seventeenth Century* (2 vols., New York, 1910); Wesley F. Craven, *The Southern Colonies in the Seventeenth Century* (Baton Rouge, 1949); Douglas S. Freeman, *George Washington: Young Washington*, Vol. I (New York, 1948); and Earl G. Swem, ed., *Jamestown 350th Anniversary Historical Booklets* (23 vols., Williamsburg, 1957).

For colonial cultural and scientific history see G. McL. Brydon, *Virginia's Mother Church and the Political Conditions under Which It Grew* (2 vols., Richmond, 1947; Philadelphia, 1952); Merle Curti, *The Growth of American Thought* (New York, 1943); Theodore Hornberger, *Scientific Thought in American Colleges and Universities*

1638-1800 (Austin, 1946); Bishop William Meade, *Old Churches, Ministers, and Families of Virginia* (2 vols., Philadelphia, 1861); W. W. Sweet, *Religion in Colonial America* (New York, 1942); Moses C. Tyler, *A History of American Literature, 1607-1765* (2 vols., New York, 1878); Harvey Wish, *Society and Thought in Early America* (New York, 1950); and Louis B. Wright, *The First Gentlemen of Virginia* (San Marino, 1940) and *The Cultural Life of the American Colonies* (New York, 1957). Also useful here are studies or editions of individual figures, such as Richard B. Davis, *George Sandys, Poet-Adventurer* (London and New York, 1955) and *William Fitzhugh and His Chesapeake World, 1676-1701* (Chapel Hill, 1963); H. J. Eckenrode, *The Randolphs* (Indianapolis, 1946); Burton J. Hendrick, *The Lees of Virginia* (Boston, 1935); Wilcomb E. Washburn, *The Governor and the Rebel* (Chapel Hill, 1957); and Thomas J. Wertenbaker, *Torchbearer of the Revolution: The Story of Bacon's Rebellion and Its Leader* (Princeton, 1940); and the editions of portions of William Byrd II's *Diary* by Louis B. Wright, Marion Tinling, and Maude Woodfin. Carl Becker's *The Heavenly City of the Eighteenth Century Philosophers* (New Haven, 1932) sheds considerable light on thinking in this and the succeeding period.

For the period of the Revolution the material is less abundant. Most important culturally and generally are John R. Alden, *The South in the Revolution, 1763-1789* (Baton Rouge, 1957); Evarts B. Greene, *The Revolutionary Generation, 1763-1790* (New York, 1943); Hugh B. Grigsby, *History of the Federal Convention of 1788,* ed., R. A. Brock (Richmond, 1890), which contains biographical sketches of all the prominent Virginians; John Marshall, *The Life of George Washington* (5 vols., new ed., New York, 1925), especially Vol. I; David J. Mays, *Edmund Pendleton, 1721-1803* (Cambridge, Mass., 1952); Russell B. Nye, *The Cultural Life of the New Nation, 1776-1830* (New York, 1960); William Peden, ed., *Notes on the State of Virginia, by Thomas Jefferson* (Chapel Hill, 1955); Charles S. Sydnor, *Gentlemen Freeholders: Political Practices in Washington's Virginia* (Chapel Hill, 1952); and Moses C. Tyler, *Literary History of the American Revolution* (2 vols., New York, 1897).

For the Jeffersonian period, Henry Adams' *History of the United States during the Administrations of Thomas Jefferson and James Madison* (9 vols., new ed., New York, 1921) is naturally indispensable, though one purpose of the present book is to correct some of its generalizations about individuals and Virginians as a whole. Hugh B. Grigsby's *The Virginia Convention of 1829-1830* (Richmond, 1854), though not so complete or useful as his later study of the 1788 Convention, is valuable. Philip A. Bruce's *History of the University of Virginia, 1819-1919* (5 vols., New York 1920-22) contains good material for this period on other matters as well as on education. Charles S. Sydnor, *The Development of Southern Sectionalism, 1819-1848* (Baton Rouge, 1948) and Thomas P. Abernethy, *The South in the New Nation, 1789-1819* (Baton Rouge, 1961), like the work of Wesley F. Craven and John R. Alden noted above, are volumes in the *History of South* series. They contain a large proportion of Virginia material. Several unpublished University of Virginia dissertations, to be noted in subsequent chapters, and certain printed studies of individuals, contain a good deal of material of general and especially cultural interest. Among books concerned with intellectual life are Mary H. Coleman, *St. George Tucker, Citizen of No Mean City* (Richmond, 1938); Richard B. Davis, *Francis Walker Gilmer: Life and Learning in Jefferson's Virginia* (Richmond, 1939), *The Abbé Correa in America, 1812-1820,* and (as editor) *Jeffersonian America: The Notes on the United States . . . of Sir Augustus John Foster* (San Marino, 1954); Robert C. McLean, *George Tucker: Moral Philosopher and Man of Letters* (Chapel Hill, 1961); and William P. Trent, *English Culture in Virginia* (Baltimore, 1889). The various biographies in process or recently completed such as those of Jefferson by Dumas Malone, Madison by Irving Brant, and Patrick Henry by Robert D. Meade are also useful for general materials and will be referred to at appropriate places.

B. Notes on Chapter One

1. *Lectures on American Literature* (New York, 1961), p. 112 (see the modern facsimile edition, eds. R. B. Davis and B. H. McClary, under the title *American Cultural History, 1607-1829* [Gainesville, Fla., 1961]).
2. Richard B. Davis, *Francis Walker Gilmer,* p. 373.
3. William Peden, ed., *Notes on the State of Virginia,* p. xxii.

Chapter Two

A. *Bibliography in general*

For ideas and curricula of American colleges in this period, these are especially useful: William A. Charvat, *Origins of American Critical Thought, 1810-1835* (Philadelphia, 1936); Merle Curti, "The Great Mr. Locke, America's Philosopher, 1783-1861," *Huntington Library Bulletin,* No. 11 (April, 1937), 107-51; Theodore Hornberger, *Scientific Thought in the American Colleges, 1638-1800* (Austin, 1945); Thomas C. Johnson, Jr., *Scientific Interests in the Old South* (New York, 1936); Samuel Miller, *A Brief Retrospect of the Eighteenth Century* (2 vols., New York, 1803).

For Virginia elementary and secondary education in this period, see A. J. Morrison, *The Beginnings of Public Education in Virginia: A Study of the Secondary Schools in Relation to the State Literary Fund* (Richmond, 1917) and Calvin H. Phippins "Legislation Affecting Secondary Education in Virginia from 1619 to 1845" (2 vols., unpub. U Va diss., 1932). Concerned with various levels of education are Herbert B. Adams, ed., *Contributions to American Educational History* (Washington, D.C., 1887-88), the first volume containing monographs by various hands on the University of Virginia and William and Mary, as well as discussions of secondary education; Cornelius J. Heatwole, *A History of Education in Virginia* (New York, 1916), and Roy J. Honeywell, *The Educational Work of Thomas Jefferson* (Cambridge, Mass., 1931).

For localities, institutions, and individuals concerned with education these are helpful: Agnes M. Bondurant, *Poe's Richmond* (Richmond, 1942); Mary H. Coleman, *St. George Tucker, Citizen of No Mean City* (Richmond, 1938); William Maxwell, *A Memoir of the Rev. John H. Rice, D.D., First Professor of Christian Theology in Union Theological Seminary, Virginia* (Philadelphia and Richmond, 1835). For the Academy at Richmond, Denis I. Duveen and Herbert Glickstein, "Alexandre-Marie Quesnay de Beaurepaire's *Mémoire* 1788," *VMHB,* LXIII (1955), 280-85; Quesnay de Beaurepaire, *Mémoire Statuts et Prospectus concernant L'Académie des Sciences et Beaus Arts des États de L'Amerique, Établie a Richmond, Capitale de la Virginie . . .* (Paris, 1788); and H. B. Adams, *Thomas Jefferson and the University of Virginia* (Washington, D.C., 1788, part of the

Contributions noted above). For Hampden-Sydney, William H. Foote, *Sketches of Virginia, Historical and Biographical* (1st and 2nd ser. Philadelphia, 1850 and 1855) and Adams, ed., *Contributions.* For the Union Theological Seminary, Walter W. Moore and Tilden Scherer, eds., *Centennial General Catalogue of Union Theological Seminary in Virginia, 1807-1907* (Richmond, [1907?]). For the University of Virginia, Philip A. Bruce, *The History of the University of Virginia, 1819-1919* (5 vols., New York, 1920-22); Richard B. Davis, *Francis Walker Gilmer: Life and Learning in Jefferson's Virginia* (Richmond, 1939) and [as editor] *Correspondence of Thomas Jefferson and Francis Walker Gilmer, 1814-1826* (Columbia, S.C., 1946) and "A Postscript on Thomas Jefferson and His University Professors," *JSH,* XII (1946), 422-32; John S. Patton, *Jefferson, Cabell, and the University of Virginia* (New York, 1906); William P. Trent, *English Culture in Virginia* (Baltimore, 1889). Also William B. Bean, "Mr. Jefferson's Influence on American Medical Education: Some Notes on the Medical School of the University of Virginia," *Virginia Medical Monthly, LXXXVII* (1960), 669-80 and Adams, *Jefferson and the University of Virginia.* For Washington College, William H. Ruffner, *The History of Washington College, Now Washington and Lee University, during the First Half of the Nineteenth Century* (Baltimore, 1893). For William and Mary, (anonymous), *The History of the College of William and Mary* (Baltimore, 1870), Adams, ed., *Contributions,* and various periodical essays (see Swem).

Unpublished University of Virginia dissertations, usually on individuals, which contain educational historical materials are William H. Dabney, "Jefferson's Albemarle: History of Albemarle County, 1727-1819," 1951; Raymond C. Dingledine, Jr., "The Political Career of William Cabell Rives," 1947; William H. Gaines, Jr., "Thomas Mann Randolph of Edgehill," 1950; Charles H. Hall, "Abel Parker Upshur," 1954; George G. Shackelford, "William Short, Jefferson's Adopted Son, 1758-1849," 1955; and Carol M. Tanner, "Joseph C. Cabell, 1778-1856," 1948.

B. Notes on Chapter Two

1. 1814 ed., p. 70.

2. A. J. Morrison, ed., *Six Addresses on the State of Letters and Science in Virginia . . . at Hampden-Sidney [sic] College . . . 1824-1835* (Roanoke, 1917), p. 12.

3. *Ibid.,* p. 17.

4. Bondurant, *Poe's Richmond,* pp. 73-74; W. A. Christian, *Richmond Her Past and Present* (Richmond, 1912), *passim.*

5. William B. McGroarty, "Alexandria's Lancastrian Schools," *WMQ* (2), XXI (1941), 111-18.

6. Quoted in Irving Brant, *James Madison, the Virginia Revolutionist* (Indianapolis, 1941), p. 60.

7. My own count, from records of individual schools and those discussed in Phippins, "Legislation Affecting Secondary Education."

8. L & B, XIV, 150.

9. Breckinridge Papers, LC.

10. Phippins, "Legislation Affecting Secondary Education," pp. 380-81, etc.

11. Matthew P. Andrews, *Virginia, the Old Dominion* (New York, 1937), pp. 362-64; Bruce, *History of the University of Virginia,* III, 229; Phippins, "Legislation Affecting Secondary Education," pp. 351-52. There is other scattered manuscript information on this school, and G. H. S. King has given the writer more in a letter.

12. Included in Davis' *Notationes in Virgilium* . . . (Petersburg, 1807), verso of title page.

13. There are accounts of Ogilvie in *DAB* and *DNB* and in Davis, *Francis Walker Gilmer.* He will be referred to several times below.

14. *SLM,* XIV (1848), 534-37.

15. Virginia *Argus.*

16. Richard B. Davis, "James Ogilvie and Washington Irving," *Americana,* XXV (1939), 435-58, and "James Ogilvie, an Early American Teacher of Rhetoric," *Quarterly Journal of Speech,* XXVIII (1942), 289-97.

17. Harrisonburg, 1816.

18. Va HS, typescript.

19. One was Hester Tabb of Matthews county, Duke MSS., 1816-22.

20. *Papers,* VI, 360.

21. Va HS, Gilmer Letterbook.

22. Montreal, 1822, p. 144.

23. Va HS, William Bolling Diary.

24. See N. P. Trist Papers, LC and UNC, and other letters in Va HS, Va St Lib, and Rives Papers, LC.

25. Va St Lib.

26. John Lewis' school certainly taught a great deal of the Scottish philosophers Reid, Brown, and Stewart. See Lewis' *Analytical Outline of the English Language* (Richmond, 1825), pp. 128-72. This was a textbook used in his school and others. Lewis even suggests (p. 176) that his readers see Jefferson's edition of Destutt de Tracey's *Elements of Ideology.*

27. See student notebook of Beverley, 1786-87, Va HS; letters from Scott at Aberdeen, 1781-94, Va HS; Smith's education in *DAB.*

28. Letters in Va HS.

29. See his *Virginia Wreath* (Winchester, 1814).

30. See the Richmond *Enquirer* for these years, and Wyndham B. Blanton, *Medicine in Virginia in the Eighteenth Century* and *Medicine in Virginia in the Nineteenth Century* (Richmond, 1931 and 1933), *passim.*

31. David Ross Letterbook, Va HS.

32. R. W. Hill, "A Virginian at Harvard, 1819-1823," *VMHB,* LII (1944), 262-66, for the Tayloes; letter of August 27, 1826, Rives to his sister, W. C. Rives Papers, LC, for Rives; Fitzgerald Flournoy, "Hugh Blair Grigsby at Yale," *VMHB,* LXII (1954), 166-80, for Grigsby.

33. Donald R. Comb, "Influence of Princeton on Higher Education in the South before 1825," *WMQ* (3), II (1945), 366-78.

34. July 1, 1799, Turpin Papers, Va HS

35. Hall, "Abel Parker Upshur," pp. 12-25.

36. Dingledine, "William Cabell Rives," pp. 22-23.

37. Given in Hornberger, *Scientific Thought*, p. 26, from *WMQ* (1), XXII (1914), 289; also pp. 61-62.

38. Benjamin Howard to John Breckinridge, February 24, 1797, Breckinridge Papers, Vol. 15, LC.

39. Miller, *Retrospect*, II, 503.

40. November 3, 1827, to John A. Smith, Valentine Museum, Richmond.

41. David C. Watson to J. C. Cabell, April 21, 1798, Cabell Papers, U Va, quoted in Tanner, "Cabell," p. 7.

42. Cabell to Watson, April 6, 1801, *VMHB*, XXIX (1921), 277-79.

43. Richard B. Davis, "The Jeffersonian Virginia Expatriate in the Building of the Nation," *VMHB*, LXX (1962), 56.

44. *Flush Times of Alabama and Mississippi* (2nd ed., New York, 1954), p. 7

45. Morrison, ed., *Six Addresses*.

46. Ruffner, *The History of Washington College . . . during the First Half of the Nineteenth Century*.

47. Comb, "Influence of Princeton," p. 377.

48. New York, [1907?], p. 8.

49. H. B. Adams, *Thomas Jefferson and the University of Virginia* (Washington, D.C., 1888), pp. 21-30.

50. Duveen and Glickstein, "Quesnay's *Memoire 1788*," pp. 280-85.

51. For Jefferson and the University of Virginia see Patton, Bruce, Honeywell, and Davis, *Gilmer*.

52. Honeywell, *Educational Work of Thomas Jefferson*, p. 64.

53. Ford, X, 232, 530.

54. Bruce, *History of the University of Virginia*, I, 64.

55. Mary H. Coleman, *St. George Tucker*, pp. 169-70. The manuscript plan is in Tucker-Coleman Papers, Archives, Colonial Williamsburg.

56. Adams, *Jefferson and the University of Virginia*, p. 89; Saul K. Padover, ed., *The Complete Jefferson* (New York, 1943), pp. 1097-98.

57. Md HS.

58. Va St Lib.

59. Honeywell, *Educational Work of Thomas Jefferson*, Appendix Q.

60. To Du Pont, April 24, 1816, L & B, XIV, 491-92.

Chapter Three

A. *Bibliography in general*

Almost all the material on reading and libraries for this period still remains in manuscript, as the notes below will indicate. Agnes Bondurant's *Poe's Richmond* (Richmond, 1942), Samuel Mordecai's *Richmond in By-Gone Days* (reprinted Richmond, 1946), and Emily E. F. Skeel, ed., *Mason Locke Weems His Works and Ways* (3 vols., New York, 1929), include information about book sales and reading tastes in general. The files of Virginia newspapers in the Henry E. Huntington Library, the Library of Congress, the Virginia Historical Society, and the Virginia State Library contain in the advertisements much useful information. The Richmond *Enquirer* and the Virginia *Argus* in the Huntington Library and the Virginia Historical Society were studied most intensively.

B. Notes on Chapter Three

1. Mordecai, *Richmond in By-Gone Days,* pp. 225 ff.
2. Bondurant, *Poe's Richmond,* and Mordecai, *passim.*
3. *Flush Times of Alabama and Mississippi* (New York, 1887 ed.), pp. 15-16.
4. L & B, XV, 468-69.
5. Bondurant, *Poe's Richmond,* p. 98.
6. The date of original publication of various titles is the only one given here and later unless otherwise indicated. Usually in manuscript book lists the date of a title is not shown.
7. Skeel, ed., *Mason Locke Weems,* II, 30-31. The date was 1796.
8. James Napier, ed., "Some Book Sales in Dumfries, Virginia, 1794-1796," *WMQ* (3), X (1953), 441-45.
9. William Wirt, *Sketches of the Life and Character of Patrick Henry* (2 vols., rev. ed. Philadelphia, 1841), p. 44 and Richard Henry Lee, *Memoir of the Life of Richard Henry Lee, and His Correspondence . . .* (Philadelphia, 1825), pp. 8-9.
10. March 2, to William J. Barksdale, Va St Lib.
11. N. P. Trist Papers, 1822-23, LC.
12. MS. sketch of Mrs. Byrd, p. 2, Brock Collection, HEH.
13. Diary, August 14, 1789, Va HS.
14. Diary, 1791, Va HS.
15. December 15, 1812; February 27, 1813; April 13, 1813. David Ross Letterbook, Va HS.
16. E. R. Lancaster, "Books Read in Early Nineteenth Century Virginia, 1806-1822," *VMHB,* XLII (1938), 56-59.
17. Diary, 1823-52, Va HS.
18. L. H. Harrison, "A Virginian Moves to Kentucky, 1793," *WMQ* (3), XV (1958), 209 ff.; also letter of Donald and Burton, February 17, 1791, Breckinridge Papers, Vol. 7, LC.
19. Cocke Collection, U Va.
20. Bernard Papers, Va HS.
21. Photostat, Va HS.
22. Inventory, Va HS.
23. Preston Papers, LC.
24. December 15, 1823, Va St Lib.
25. Edgar Woods, *Albemarle County in Virginia . . .* [Charlottesville, 1901], p. 86.
26. William H. Foote, *Sketches of Virginia, Historical and Biographical* (2nd ser., Philadelphia, 1855), pp. 484-85.
27. W. T. Hastings, *Conrade Webb of Hampstead* (Providence, R.I., 1958), pp. 42, 51-52.
28. Harry Clemons, *The Home Library of the Garnetts of Elmwood* (Charlottesville, 1957).
29. W. Asbury Christian, *Richmond, Her Past and Her Present* (Richmond, 1912), pp. 71-72.
30. Bondurant, *Poe's Richmond,* pp. 115-16.
31. *Enquirer.*
32. Notice in Grinnan Papers, Va HS.
33. "Inventory of Washington's Library," in A.P.C. Griffin, ed., *A Catalogue of the Washington Collection in the Boston Athenaeum* (Boston, 1897), pp. 479 ff.

34. E. M. Sowerby, Comp., *Catalogue of the Library of Thomas Jefferson* (5 vols., Washington, D.C., 1952-59); William H. Peden, "Thomas Jefferson: Book Collector" (unpub. diss. U Va, 1942), appendix; Richard B. Davis, "Jefferson as Collector of Virginiana," *Studies in Bibliography,* XIV (1961), 117-44.

35. William H. Peden, "Notes Concerning Thomas Jefferson's Libraries," *WMQ* (3), I (1944), 265-72.

36. October 4, to Hugh Taylor, L & B, XV, 473.

37. See William S. Prince, "St. George Tucker as a Poet of the Early Republic" (unpub. diss., Yale, 1954), pp. 12-21.

38. Cabell Collection, U Va.

39. Tucker to Madison, December 22, 1826; Madison to Tucker, January [illegible]5, 1827, both in Madison Papers, LC.

40. In addition to Prince, see an 1802 inventory of books apparently Tucker's in the Munford-Ellis Papers, Duke.

41. "The Randolph Library," *SLM,* XX (February, 1854), 76-79.

42. Letter to Staige Davis, Urbanna, Virginia. See Wirt Letterbook, Md HS.

43. Louis B. Wright, *The First Gentlemen of Virginia* (San Marino, 1940), pp. 197-211.

44. December 16, 1801; April 24, 1802; June 4, 1804, all Va HS.

45. Va HS.

46. Gaillard Hunt, ed., *The Writings of James Madison* (9 vols., New York, 1900-1910), II, 133.

47. Irving Brant, *James Madison, the Nationalist, 1780-1787* (Indianapolis, 1948), p. 410.

48. *Ibid.,* pp. 410-11.

49. Hunt, ed., *Writings,* IX, 203-7.

50. *Tyler's Mag,* XVIII (January, 1937), 132-40.

51. Short Family Papers, LC.

52. William Short Papers, LC.

53. John P. Kennedy, *Memoirs of the Life of William Wirt* (2 vols., rev. ed., Philadelphia, 1850), I, 332.

54. J. A. Harrison, ed., *The Complete Works of Edgar Allan Poe* (17 vols., New York, 1902), XIV, 41.

55. Letter of September 20, 1960, from Professor M. Boyd Coyner, Jr. to the writer. Coyner has recently completed "John Hartwell Cocke of Bremo. Agriculture and Slavery in the Ante-Bellum South" (unpub. diss. U Va, 1961).

56. U Va.

57. Coyner's dissertation (note 55) is a specialized study, as the title suggests.

58. Typescript, Bruce-Randolph Collection, Va HS.

59. Journal, Grigsby Collection, Va HS.

60. U Va.

61. Susan M. Kingsbury, ed., *Records of the Virginia Company of London* (4 vols., Washington, D.C., 1906, 1933, 1935), I, 50.

62. March 11, 1828, *Memoirs,* ed. C. F. Adams (12 vols., Philadelphia, 1874-77), VIII, 472.

63. William C. Bruce, *John Randolph of Roanoke* (2 vols., New York, 1922), II, 434.

64. Letters, U Va. The quotation is included in a letter of March 16, 1818. Other letters mentioned only by date are in the Randolph-Bleecker Collection, U Va.

65. March 29, 1814, Transcript, LC.

66. Bruce, *Randolph,* I, 86.

67. *SLM,* XII (July, 1846), 447.

68. Letter to writer May, 1961, from Virginia R. Gray, MSS. Dept., Duke.

69. In Box 102.

70. Francis Fry Wayland, *Andrew Stevenson, Democrat and Diplomat*, 1785-1857 (Philadelphia, 1949), p. 241.

71. R. A. Brock, ed., *The History of the Virginia Federal Convention of 1788, with Some Account of the Eminent Virginians of that Era Who Were Members of the Body,* by Hugh Blair Grigsby, Collections of the Virginia Historical Society, n.s., IX and X (Richmond, 1890), IX, xi.

72. Brock, ed., *The History of the Virginia Federal Convention of 1788,* IX, xxv.

73. 1826, N. P. Trist Papers, LC. Information on a single sheet apparently sent to a relative.

Chapter Four

A. *Bibliography in general*

Manuscript materials in the repositories already mentioned are quite extensive. The most useful general printed studies are Carl Becker, *The Heavenly City of the Eighteenth Century Philosophers* (New Haven, 1932); Agnes Bondurant, *Poe's Richmond* (Richmond, 1942); Clement Eaton, *Freedom of Thought in the Old South* (Durham, 1940); H. J. Eckenrode, *Separation of Church and State in Virginia: A Study of the Development of the Revolution* (Richmond, 1910); Wesley M. Gewehr, *The Great Awakening in Virginia, 1740-1790* (Durham, 1930), despite its inclusive dates pertinent for our period; William Meade, *Old Churches, Ministers, and Families in Virginia* (2 vols., Philadelphia, 1861), strongly but not entirely Episcopal in its viewpoint; Samuel Mordecai, *Richmond in By-Gone Days* (repr. Richmond, 1946); George W. Munford, *The Two Parsons* (Richmond, 1884); I. W. Riley, *American Philosophy: The Early Schools* (New York, 1907); Anson P. Stokes, *Church and State in the United States* (3 vols., New York, 1950); and William W. Sweet, *American Culture and Religion: Six Essays* (Dallas, 1951) and *Religion in the Development of American Culture, 1765-1840* (New York, 1952).

For the Episcopal church, G. M. Brydon's two volumes of *Virginia's Mother Church and the Political Conditions under Which It Grew* (Richmond, 1949 and Philadelphia, 1952) are indispensable. These are also useful for the history of other denominations. Basic material also lies in Francis L. Hawks, *Contributions to the Ecclesiastical History of the United States of America, Vol. I. A Narrative of Events Connected with the Rise and Progress of the Protestant Episcopal Church in Virginia* (New York, 1836) and William S. Perry, *The History of the American Episcopal Church* (2 vols., Boston, 1885).

For the Presbyterians, one should see William H. Foote, *Sketches of Virginia, Historical and Biographical* (1st and 2nd ser., Philadelphia, 1850 and 1855); W W. Moore and Tilden Scherer, eds., *Centennial General Catalogue of the Trustees, Professors, and Alumni of the Union Theological Seminary in Virginia, 1807-1907* (Richmond, [1907?]); John H. Rice, ed., *The Virginia Evangelical and Literary Magazine* (with varying title, Richmond, 1818-28); William W. Sweet, *Religion on the American Frontier, II. The Presbyterians, 1783-1840* (New York, 1936) with useful bibliographies; and Robert E. Thompson, *A History of the Presbyterian Churches in the United States* (New York, 1895).

For the Baptists, the most useful items are contemporary, including John Leland's sermons and essays and his *The Virginia Chronicle* (Fredericksburg, 1790); William Fristoe, *A Concise History of the Ketocton Baptist Association . . .* (Staunton, 1808); and Robert B. Semple, *A History of the Rise and Progress of the Baptists in Virginia* (Richmond, 1810, rev. ed. by George W. Beale, 1894). Also William W. Sweet, *Religion on the American Frontier, I. The Baptists* (Chicago, 1931), contains useful bibliographies.

For the Methodists the Reverend Jesse Lee's *Short History of the Methodists in the United States of America* (Petersburg, 1809) and *Memoir* (New York, 1823) are contemporary accounts. William W. Bennett, *Memorials of Methodism in Virginia from Its Introduction in the Year 1772, to the Year 1829* (Richmond, 1871) and William W. Sweet, *Virginia Methodism: A History* (Richmond, [1955]) and *Religion on the American Frontier, IV. The Methodists* (Chicago, 1946) contain much data and extensive bibliographies.

The Quakers in proportion to their numbers have perhaps been most written about. Some Virginia information is in Thomas E. Drake, *Quakers and Slavery in America* (New Haven, 1950); Samuel M. Janney, *History of the Religious Society of Friends* (4 vols., Philadelphia, 1860-67), written by a Virginia Quaker; Rufus M Jones, *The Later Periods of Quakerism* (2 vols., London, 1821); and Stephen B. Weeks, *Southern Quakers and Slavery: A Study in Institutional History* (Baltimore, 1896). Douglas S. Brown, *A History of Lynchburg's Pioneer Quakers and their Meeting House, 1754-1936* (Lynchburg, 1936) is concerned with one Virginia Quaker Community.

For the Catholics, the Reverend Peter Guilday's *The Catholic*

Church in Virginia (1815-1822), U. S. Catholic Historical Society Monographs, VIII (New York, 1924) supplies some useful information. For other groups, the scattered essays and manuscript items referred to in the notes have been the principal sources.

Many contemporary titles are mentioned in the text. In addition, there are scores of individual printed sermons and essays by Archibald Alexander, David Barrow, George Bourne, Andrew Broaddus, John Brown, Thomas Cleland, Joseph Doddridge, Adam Empie, Richard Ferguson, David Henkel, Paul Henkel, John Blair Hoge, Moses Hoge, Henry Holcombe, Devereux Jarratt, Jesse Lee, John Leland, Bishop James Madison, John Newton, John S. Ravenscroft, David Rice, John Holt Rice, Henry Ruffner, William Claiborne Walton, William Watters, William Wilmer, and others representing all the Protestant denominations except the Quakers. The Union Catalogue of the Library of Congress has cards on most titles by these men.

B. Notes on Chapter Four

1. Eaton, *Freedom of Thought in the Old South,* pp. 13-14 from M. L. Rutherford, *The South in History and Literature* (Athens, Ga., 1906), pp. 309-16. The story refers to an Appalachian Georgian rather than a Virginian.
2. August 20, 1796, Patrick Henry folder in W. W. Henry Papers, Va HS.
3. William C. Bruce, *John Randolph of Roanoke* (2 vols., New York, 1922), I, 75.
4. Duke MSS.
5. New Haven, 1932, p. 30.
6. Riley, *American Philosophy: The Early Schools,* p. 461.
7. G. S. Hillard, *Life, Letters, and Journals of George Ticknor* (2 vols., Boston, 1876), I, 30.
8. Frank P. Cauble, "William Wirt and His Friends, a Study in Southern Culture, 1772-1834" (unpub. diss., UNC, 1933), p. 298.
9. June 8, Va St Lib.
10. Clarence Gohdes, "Some Notes on the Unitarian Church in the Ante-Bellum South," *American Studies in Honor of William Kenneth Boyd* (Durham, 1940), p. 357.
11. David J. Mays, *Edmund Pendleton, 1721-1803: A Biography* (2 vols., Cambridge, Mass., 1952), II, 339-46.
12. T. W. White, publisher, Richmond.
13. Warrock, publisher, Richmond.
14. "Jarratt" in *DAB.*
15. Durham, 1930, title of Ch. III.
16. Eckenrode, *Separation of Church and State in Virginia,* p. 30.
17. Foote, *Sketches* (2nd ser.), p. 40.
18. Brydon, *Virginia's Mother Church,* II, 168.
19. Sweet, *Religion in the Development of American Culture,* p. 12.
20. Ben C. McCary, transl. and ed., *Travels of a Frenchman . . . in Maryland and Virginia . . . 1791* (Williamsburg, 1950), pp. 87-88.
21. Foote, *Sketches* (2nd ser.), pp. 588-90.
22. Union Theological Seminary, Richmond.

23. Thompson, *A History of the Presbyterian Churches in the United States*, p. 122.

24. For much of the discussion of these magazines, see A. J. Morrison, "Presbyterian Periodicals of Richmond 1815-1860," *Tyler's Mag*, I, No. 3 (1920), 174-7.

25. Foote, *Sketches* (2nd ser.) 329.

26. *SLM*, V (February, 1839), 115-16.

27. William Maxwell, *Memoir of the Rev. John H. Rice, D.D.* (Richmond, 1835), p. 54. See also P. B. Price *The Life of the Reverend John Holt Rice, D.D. Reprinted from the Central Presbyterian, 1886-1887* (Richmond, 1963), *passim*.

28. *Ten Sermons* (Alexandria 1812), p. 28.

29. Brydon, *Virginia's Mother Church*, II, 178 ff.

30. Statistical figures regarding communicants or members of the various churches are difficult to come by. With the kind help of Dr. Milton C. Russell of the Virginia State Library the following have been gathered:

1. *The Episcopalians:* the 1830 report of the committee on parishes gave the number of communicants in forty-three parishes as 2,102. The number in seventeen parishes in 1820 was 1,05[illegible]. Neither report is complete.

2. *The Presbyterians:* unascertained, for the Synod of Virginia established in 1788 was not set up on state lines; it excluded the Presbytery of Abingdon and included parts of Kentucky and Pennsylvania.

3. *The Methodists:* more complete than most church records, the *Minutes of the Annual Conferences in America* show in Virginia in 1790 a total of 17,778 (3,485 colored and 14,293 white) and in 1828 a total of 40,533 (6,400 colored and 34,133 white) within the borders of the state. There was progressive growth except for a drop between 1790 and 1800. Again since conferences did not fit state lines, overlapping North Carolina, Ohio, Maryland, and Pennsylvania, these figures are estimates. Virginia was a Methodist stronghold.

4. *The Baptists:* in Dr. Garnett Ryland's *The Baptists in Virginia, 1699-1926* (Richmond, 1955) membership in Virginia in 1791 is given as 20,443. Through the courtesy of Miss Blanche S. White of the Virginia Baptist Historical Society the following membership records are given: 1800—35,000 (approximate); 1820—40,000 (approximate); 1830—39,940 (accurate count).

5. *The Lutherans:* no consistent records of membership available.

6. *The Roman Catholics:* James Henry Bailey, *A History of the Diocese of Richmond* (Richmond, 1956), pp. 27, 79, says that in 1785 there were not more than 200 Catholics in the state but that in 1837 there were an estimated [illegible]000.

7. *The Quakers:* they were moving westward during all this period and there are not even approximate figures available.

8. *The Jews:* in 1790 in Richmond was a congregation with fifty-nine men on its rolls, there were some in Norfolk and a Sephardic group in western Virginia, but no figures are available

31. L. H. Butterfield, "John Leland, Jeffersonian Itinerant," *PAAS*, LXII (1952), 189.

32. Gewehr, *The Great Awakening in Virginia*, pp. 191-92. Barrow's *Circular Letter* has recently been reprinted with an introduction by Carlos R. Allen, Jr., in *WMQ* (3), XX (1963), 4[illegible]-51.

33. Brydon, *Virginia's Mother Church*, II, 236 ff.

34. Sweet, *Virginia Methodism*, pp. 155-73.

35. Bennett, *Memorials of Methodism*, p. 164, etc.

36. *Ibid.*, pp. 427-35.

37. Va St Lib.

38. Foote, *Sketches* (2nd ser.), p. 183.

39. Stith Mead Letterbook, Va HS.

40. Butterfield, "Leland," p. 169; Bennett, *Memorials*, pp. 199-201.

41. Va HS.
42. Brydon, *Virginia's Mother Church,* II, 79.
43. L. J. Cappon and Ira V. Brown, *New Market, Virginia, Imprints, 1806-1876* (Charlottesville, 1942); Willard E. Wight, "The Journals of the Reverend Robert J. Miller, Lutheran Missionary in Virginia, 1811 and 1813," *VMHB,* LXI (1953), 141-46.
44. Brown, *A History of Lynchburg's Pioneer Quakers and Their Meeting House, 1754-1936,* pp. 29-31.
45. Jones, *The Later Periods of Quakerism,* I, 403-80.
46. Brown, *A History of Lynchburg's Pioneer Quakers,* p. 50.
47. In HEH and Va HS.
48. Drake, *Quakers and Slavery in America,* p. 83.
49. Brown, *A History of Lynchburg's Pioneer Quakers,* p. 85.
50. Drake, *Quakers and Slavery,* p. 136.
51. Guilday, *The Catholic Church in Virginia,* p. xxi.
52. Mordecai, *Richmond in By-Gone Days,* p. 161.
53. Va HS and UNC.
54. Stokes, *Church and State in the United States,* II, frontispiece.

Chapter Five

A. *Bibliography in general*

Most of the items concerning agricultural activity and the literature on it are included in the items on individuals and societies in the notes for this chapter. A few other general titles should be noted: N. F. Cabell, The *Early History of Agriculture in Virginia* (Washington, D.C., n.d.), a forty-one page pamphlet dealing with earlier material, and "Some Fragments of an Intended Report on the Post Revolutionary History of Agriculture in Virginia . . . with Notes by Earl G. Swem," *WMQ* (1), XXVI (1918), 145-68; Avery O. Craven, *Soil Exhaustion as a Factor in the Agricultural History of Virginia and Maryland, 1606-1860* (University of Illinois, 1925); William Peden, ed., *Notes on the State of Virginia, by Thomas Jefferson* (Chapel Hill, 1955), for earlier material; John S. Skinner, ed., *The American Farmer, Containing Original Essays and Selections on Rural Economy and Internal Improvements, with Illustrative Engravings and the Prices Current of Country Produce . . .* (Baltimore, 1822-30), invaluable for the later years of our period; and Earl G. Swem, comp. *A List of Manuscripts Relating to the History of Agriculture in Virginia, Collected by N. F. Cabell, and Now in the Virginia State Library,* Virginia State Library, *Bulletin,* Vol. 6 (January, 1913), [1]-20, and *A Contribution to the Bibliography of Agriculture in Virginia . . . from the Manuscript of N. F. Cabell,* Virginia State Library, *Bulletin,* Vol. 11 (January, April, 1918), [1]-35.

In the addition to the several items on Jefferson included in the notes, see Everett E. Edwards, *Jefferson and Agriculture,* U. S. Dept. of Agriculture in Commemoration of the Two Hundredth Anniversary of the Birth of Thomas Jefferson, Agricultural History Series No. 7, 1943, and *Washington, Jefferson, Lincoln and Agriculture,* Bureau of Agricultural Economics, U. S. Dept. of Agriculture (November, 1937).

B. Notes on Chapter Five

1. C. E. Eisinger, "The Freehold Concept in Eighteenth Century American Letters," *WMQ* (3), IV (1947), 42-43.

2. A. O. Craven, *Soil Exhaustion as a Factor in the Agricultural History of Virginia and Maryland, 1606-1860,* p. 89.

3. *Ibid.,* p. 82.

4. *Travels in the United States of North America* (2 vols., London, 1799) II, 1-356 and Craven, *Soil Exhaustion,* p. 62.

5. For Binns, *DAB* and R. H. True, "John Binns of Loudoun," *WMQ* (2), II (1922), 20-39.

6. Pp. 10-15.

7. P. iv.

8. P. 48.

9. Pp. 200, 236.

10. A. O. Craven, "John Taylor and Southern Agriculture," *JSH,* IV (1938), 137-47; also Andrew N. Lytle, "John Taylor and the Political Economy of Agrarianism," *American Review,* III (September, October, 1934), 432-37, 631-43, IV (November, 1934), 84-99; E. T. Mudge, *The Social Philosophy of John Taylor of Caroline* (New York, 1939); and H. H. Simms, *John Taylor of Caroline: The Story of a Brilliant Leader of the States Rights School* (Richmond, 1932).

11. E.g., letter of n.d. in W. C. Nicholas papers, LC.

12. A. O. Craven, *Edmund Ruffin Southerner, a Study in Secession* (New York, 1932), p. 43; also J. C. Sitterson, ed., *An Essay on Calcareous Manures by Edmund Ruffin* (Cambridge, Mass., 1961), pp. vii-xxxiii.

13. P. 493.

14. Craven, *Edmund Ruffin,* pp. 55-56 and *Soil Exhaustion,* pp. 134-37; also Sitterson, ed., *An Essay,* p. xvi.

15. Craven, *Soil Exhaustion,* p. 139.

16. Craven, *Edmund Ruffin,* pp. 56-57.

17. W. T. Hutchinson *Cyrus Hall McCormick: Seed-Time, 1809-1856* (New York, [1930]), pp. 7-30.

18. R. H. McCormick and James H. Shields, *The Life and Works of Robert McCormick* (n.p., 1910).

19. Hutchinson, *Cyrus Hall McCormick,* pp. 75-76.

20. E. G. Swem, comp., *A List of Manuscripts Relating to the History of Agriculture in Virginia,* pp. [ ]-20.

21. Cabell Collection U Va.

22. Richard B. Davis, ed., *Jeffersonian America: Notes on the United States . . . by Sir Augustus John Foster* (San Marino, 1954), pp. 139-42.

23. E.g., letters in Richard B. Davis, *The Abbé Correa in America, 1812-1820* (Philadelphia, 1955), pp. 163 etc.; also Irving Brant, *James Madison, Secretary of State, 1800-1809* (Indianapolis, 1953), pp. 45-46.

24. W. H. Gaines, Jr., "Thomas Mann Randolph of Edgehill" (unpub. diss. U Va, 1950), *passim.*

25. Both schemes in diagram form are reproduced in Edwin M. Betts, ed., *Thomas Jefferson's Garden Book* (Philadelphia, 1944), pp. 195-97.

26. January 13, 1816, in Betts, ed., *Garden Book,* p. 554. For an extensive treatment of this phase of Cocke's work, see M. Boyd Coyner, "John Hartwell Cocke of Bremo. Agriculture and Slavery in the Ante-Bellum South" (unpub. diss. U Va, 1961).

27. Betts, ed., *Garden Book,* pp. 637-38.

28. Coyner, "Cocke of Bremo," *passim.*

29. P. A. Bruce, *History of the University of Virginia, 1819-1919* (5 vols., New York, 1920-22), II, 127.

30. R. H. True, "Early Days of the Albemarle Agricultural Society," *Annual Report American Historical Association (1918),* I, 253; see also Bruce, *History,* III 50-52.

31. Bruce, *History,* III, 50-52.

32. August 20, 1811, to C. W. Peale, in Betts, ed., *Garden Book,* p. xv.

33. Saul K. Padover, ed., *The Complete Jefferson* (New York, 1943), p. 1044.

34. Adrienne Koch, *The Philosophy of Thomas Jefferson* (New York, 1943), p. 189.

35. Edwin M. Betts, ed., *Thomas Jefferson's Farm Book* (Princeton, 1953).

36. See Betts, both *Farm* and *Garden* books, and Edwin T. Martin, *Thomas Jefferson, Scientist* (New York, 1952), p. 34.

37. Martin, *Thomas Jefferson, Scientist,* p. 102.

38. *Ibid.,* p. 104, and Betts, ed., *Garden Book,* pp. 649-54, *passim.*

39. *Proceedings of the American Philosophical Society,* LXVIII, 216-22.

40. A. J. Morrison, "Virginia Patents," *WMQ* (2), II (1922), 149-56.

41. Brooke Hindle, *The Pursuit of Science in Revolutionary America, 1735-1789* (Chapel Hill, 1956), p. 213.

42. D. R. Anderson, *William Branch Giles: A Study in the Politics of Virginia and the Nation from 1790 to 1830* (Menasha, Wisc., 1914), pp. 214-15.

43. J. L. Peyton, *History of Augusta County, Va.* (2nd ed., Bridgewater, 1953), p. 245.

44. See Vols. I-XII of the *American Farmer.*

45. R. H. True, "Early Days of the Albemarle Agricultural Society," pp. 241-59, and (as editor) "Minute Book of the Albemarle (Virginia) Agricultural Society," *Annual Report AHA (1918),* I, 261-349. The Manuscript Minute Book is in Va HS.

46. *Ibid.*

Chapter Six

A. *Bibliography in general*

There is no specialized study of science in Virginia in our period. For the years just before, most useful is Brooke Hindle, *The Pursuit of Science in Revolutionary America, 1735-1789* (Chapel Hill, 1956). Thomas C. Johnson, Jr., *Scientific Interests in the Old South* (New York, 1936) is concerned with Virginia in part of our period. Jefferson's *Notes,* already mentioned, in part the product of his and other scientists' observations before the mid-1780's, are enlightening. See also Gary S. Dunbar, "A Preliminary Checklist of Virginia's Scientific and Technical Societies, 1772-1959" (Typescript, Va HS) and Theodore Hornberger, *Scientific Thought in the American Colleges, 1638-1808* (Austin, 1945).

Studies of individuals are generally as well as specifically useful: Edwin T. Martin, *Thomas Jefferson, Scientist* (New York, 1952) is one of the most comprehensive of these. Also see Richard B. Davis, *The Abbé Correa in America, 1812-1820* (Philadelphia, 1955); *Francis Walker Gilmer: Life and Learning in Jefferson's Virginia* (Richmond, 1939); "Forgotten Scientists in Old Virginia," *VMHB*, XLVI (1938), 97-111; "Forgotten Scientists in Georgia and South Carolina," *Georgia Historical Quarterly,* XXVII (1943), 271-84; and "An Early Virginia Scientist's Botanical Observations in the South," *Virginia Journal of Science,* III (1942), 132-33.

For medicine, Wyndham B. Blanton's *Medicine in Virginia in the Eighteenth Century* (Richmond, 1931) and *Medicine in Virginia in the Nineteenth Century* (Richmond, 1933) are standard.

B. Notes on Chapter Six

1. Ellen M. Bagby, ed., *The Old Virginia Gentleman and Other Sketches by George W. Bagby* (5th ed., Richmond, 1948), p. 21.
2. A. J. Morrison, ed., *Six Addresses on the State of Letters and Science in Virginia . . . 1824-1835* (Roanoke, 1917), pp. 7-8.
3. New York, 1952, pp. 30-56.
4. Hindle, *Pursuit of Science in Revolutionary America,* pp. 213-15; "Williamsburg, the Old Colonial Capital," *WMQ* (1), XVI (1907), 37-38; Virginia *Gazette* (Purdie and Dixon), November 19, 1772 and June 16, 1774.
5. *American Museum,* VIII (1790), 95; December 7, 1780, Page to Jefferson, *Papers,* IV, 191-93, etc.
6. Data on members from *Transactions* and *Proceedings* of the American Philosophical Society.
7. Political Pamphlets, No. 95, LC; Hindle, *Pursuit of Science,* pp. 377-78; *AHR,* XXXII (1927), 550-52, 792-95.
8. H. W. Burton, *History of Norfolk, Virginia* (Norfolk, 1877).
9. February 17, 1807, J. C. Cabell to Isaac C. Coles, Cabell Collection, U Va.
10. April 27, 1826, Jefferson to J. P. Emmet, in Davis, *The Abbé Correa in America,* pp. 190-91. There are variant drafts of this letter in LC and U Va
11. Samuel Mordecai, *Richmond in By-Gone Days* (repr. Richmond, 1946), p. 347.
12. January 3, 1808, to T. J. Randolph, quoted in E. M. Sowerby, comp., *Catalogue of the Library of Thomas Jefferson* (5 vols., Washington, D.C., 1952-59) I, 374.
13. Hindle, *Pursuit of Science,* p. 237.
14. Blanton, *Medicine in Virginia in the Eighteenth Century,* pp. 114-15.
15. Russell B. Nye, *Cultural Life in the New Nation, 1776-1830* (New York, 1960), pp. 74-75.
16. Blanton, *Medicine in Virginia in the Eighteenth Century,* pp. 82-88.
17. Blanton, *Medicine in Virginia in the Nineteenth Century,* pp. 10-11.
18. John Davis, *The American Mariners: or, the Atlantic Voyage* (Salisbury,

Eng., [*ca.* 1805]), p. 103 gives the note: "Candidates for medical fame abound in the Southern States, and the wildest creature imaginable is a young Virginian doctor. There are generally a hundred or more, attending the lectures at Philadelphia; where the Quakers have named them the *Centaurs*; and when a riot takes place at the theatre, the city wags are sure to exclaim 'Turn out the Virginia doctors.'"

19. J. M. Dorsey, ed., *The Jefferson-Dunglison Correspondence* (Charlottesville, 1960), pp. 68-69. Dorsey states (p. 78) that Dunglison's *Elements of Hygiene* (535) and *Syllabus of Lectures on Medical Jurisprudence* were also written in Charlottesville.

20. Blanton, *Medicine in Virginia in the Nineteenth Century,* p. 20.

21. William B. Bean, "Mr. Jefferson's Influence on American Medical Education," *Virginia Medical Monthly,* LXXXVII (1960), 669-80.

22. E.g., William Stokes' *Testamen Medicum Inaugurale . . . Asphyxia* (1793), Sowerby, *Catalogue,* item 942. For William Tazewell's, see Sowerby, item 898.

23. Blanton, *Medicine in Virginia in the Nineteenth Century,* p. 376.

24. See *DAB.*

25. *DAB*; Blanton, *Medicine in Virginia in the Nineteenth Century,* pp. 374-75; Union Catalogue, LC.

26. *DAB*; Blanton, *Medicine in Virginia in the Nineteenth Century,* pp. 370 ff.

27. Sowerby, *Catalogue,* item 898.

28. Edgar Woods, *Albemarle County in Virginia* (Charlottesville, 1901), p. 76.

29. October 7, 1814, to Thomas Cooper, quoted in Sowerby, *Catalogue,* I, 479.

30. *DAB*; Samuel Miller, *A Brief Retrospect of the Eighteenth Century* (2 vols., New York, 1803), I, 141.

31. Hindle, *Pursuit of Science,* p. 56.

32. *Ibid.,* pp. 28-30.

33. *PAAS,* LVIII (1949), 17-190.

34. Query VI.

35. Blanton, *Medicine in Virginia in the Eighteenth Century,* pp. 149-51.

36. Davis, *The Abbé Correa in America, passim.*

37. June 26, 1820, Gilmer to P. R. Gilmer, Va HS.

38. Davis, "An Early Virginia Scientist's Botanical Observations in the South," pp. 132-39.

39. May 25, 1816, to P. R. Gilmer, Va HS.

40. December 21, 1813, to P. R. Gilmer, Va. HS.

41. Talbot Hamlin, *Benjamin Henry Latrobe* (New York, 1955), p. 80. Latrobe wrote other papers using Virginia materials for the *Transactions.*

42. Martin, *Thomas Jefferson, Scientist,* p. 21.

43. Julian P. Boyd, "The Megalonyx, the Megatherium, and Thomas Jefferson's Lapse of Memory," *Proceedings* of the American Philosophical Society, CII (1958), 420-35.

44. L & B, XIX, vi.

45. September 26, Breckinridge Papers, LC.

46. September 24, Preston Davie Papers, Va HS.

47. May 8, 1807; February 15, 1810. These and other pertinent papers are in Madison Papers, LC.

48. A. J. Morrison, "Virginia Patents," *WMQ* (2), II (1922), 149-56.

49. *Ibid.,* p. 149.

50. Mordecai, *Richmond in By-Gone Days,* p. 130.

51. Irving Brant, *James Madison, Father of the Constitution* (Indianapolis, 1950), p. 343.

52. Martin, *Thomas Jefferson, Scientist,* pp. 74-76.

53. Mary H. Coleman, *St. George Tucker, Citizen of No Mean City* (Richmond, 1938), *passim*; and Tucker-Coleman MSS., Colonial Williamsburg.

54. January 5, to Page, Col Wmsbg.; to Cabell, *Calendar of Virginia State Papers*, IX (1890), 520.
55. *WMQ* (1), XVI (1907), 37-38.
56. Hindle, *Pursuit of Science*, pp. 155, 163.
57. Davis, *Francis Walker Gilmer*, pp. 355-58.
58. Hindle, *Pursuit of Science*, p. 183.
59. Irving Brant, *James Madison, the Nationalist* (Indianapolis, 1948), pp. 308-9.
60. Martin, *Thomas Jefferson, Scientist*, pp. 55, 131-47.
61. I, 536.
62. Dumas Malone, *Jefferson the Virginian* (New York, 1948), p. 256.
63. Coolie Verner, "Mr. Jefferson Makes a Map," *Imago Mundi*, XIV (1957), 93-108.
64. Earl G. Swem, comp., *Maps Relating to Virginia in the Virginia State Library and Other Departments of the Commonwealth*, Virginia State Library, *Bulletin*, VII (April, July, 1914), [33]-263.
65. *Ibid.*, No. 529.
66. In the Va St Lib one 1790 manuscript map by Tatham of the Alexandria-Washington area survives (Swem, *Maps*, No. 328).
67. Vol. 2 for Year 1794, Vol. III, 85-92.
68. Hindle, *Pursuit of Science*, pp. 140, 210-11, 372-73.
69. Madison Papers, Vol. 35, LC.
70. Swem, *Maps*, pp. 95-97.
71. Bernard de Voto, *The Course of Empire* (Boston, 1952), p. 415, and *Lewis and Clark, Partners in Discovery* (New York, 1947), *passim.*
72. Elliott Cowes, ed., *History of the Expedition under the Command of Captains Lewis and Clark, to the Sources of the Missouri River* . . . (4 vols., New York, 1893), I, xxi.
73. I. H. Criswell, *Lewis and Clark, Linguistic Pioneers*, University of Missouri Studies, XV (1940).
74. De Voto, *Course of Empire*, p. 436.
75. Saul K. Padover, ed., *The Complete Jefferson* (New York, 1943), pp. [illegible]23-24.
76. For Jefferson's efforts, see Sowerby, Catalogue, IV, 347-50.
77. Julian P. Boyd, "'These Precious Monuments of . . . Our History,'" *American Archivist*, XXII (1959), 147-80.
78. Roy H. Pearce, *The Savages of America* (Baltimore, 1953), pp. 91-96.
79. Peden, ed., *Notes on the State of Virginia*, pp. 98-100; A. D. Fraser, "Thomas Jefferson, Field Archaeologist," *Four Arts, Dedicated to Artistic Virginia*, II (1935), pp. 3 ff; Karl Lehmann-Hartleleben, "Thomas Jefferson, Archaeologist," *American Journal of Archaeology*, XLVII (1943), 161-63.
80. Pearce, *The Savages of America*, p. 107n. Forsyth's work was published in Emma Blair, ed., *The Indian Tribes of the Upper Mississippi and Region of the Great Lakes* (2 vols., Cleveland, 1911), II, 183-245.
81. *DAB.*
82. Short Family Paper, LC.
83. XII (July, 1818).
84. *Essays on Various Subjects* (Georgetown, D. C.), p. 290.

Chapter Seven

A. *Bibliography in general*

Although there are no general studies of the fine arts for Virginia in this period, here as elsewhere Samuel Mordecai, *Richmond in By-*

Gone Days (repr., Richmond, 1946) and Agnes M. Bondurant, *Poe's Richmond* (Richmond, 1942) are useful. So are the two Jefferson items, William B. O'Neal, *Jefferson's Fine Arts Library for the University of Virginia* (Charlottesville, 1956) and E. M. Sowerby, comp., *Catalogue of the Library of Thomas Jefferson* (5 vols., Washington, D.C., 1952-59).

In architecture Fiske Kimball's studies, especially *Thomas Jefferson, Architect* (Cambridge, Mass., 1916) and *Domestic Architecture of the American Colonies and the Early Republic* (New York, 1922), contain general as well as Jefferson material. Robert A. Lancaster, *Historic Virginia Homes and Churches* (Philadelphia, 1915) and Mary Wingfield Scott, *Houses of Old Richmond* (Richmond, 1941) should also be examined.

In painting, several general studies contain a good proportion of Virginia material: William Dunlap, *History of the Rise and Progress of the Arts of Design in the United States* (2 vols., New York, 1834); Virgil Barker, *American Painting: History and Interpretation* (New York, 1950); Harry Wehle and Theodore Bolton, *American Miniatures, 1730-1850* (Garden City, N.Y., 1937); and *American Painters of the South,* Corcoran Gallery of Art (Washington, D.C., 1960). For Virginia, especially pertinent are *Richmond Portraits in an Exhibition of Makers of Richmond, 1737-1860,* Valentine Museum (Richmond, 1949) and Fillmore Norfleet, *St. Memin in Virginia, Portraits and Biographies* (Richmond, 1942).

In music, two recent studies are illuminating: John W. Molnar, "Art Music in Colonial Virginia," *Art and Music in the South,* ed. F. B. Simkins, Longwood College Institute of Southern Culture Lectures, 1960 (Farmville, 1961) and A. L. Stoutamire, "A History of Music in Richmond, Virginia, from 1742 to 1860" (unpub. diss., Florida State University, 1960). Many Virginia examples are to be found in O. G. T. Sonneck, *Early Concert Life in America (1731-1800)* (New York, 1949).

For drama, William Dunlap's *A History of the American Theatre* (New York, 1832) and Arthur H. Quinn, *History of the American Drama from the Beginnings to the Civil War* (New York, 1943) are basic. For playwriting and production in Virginia, see Frank P. Cauble, "William Wirt and His Friends," (unpub. diss., UNC, 1933) and Martin S. Shockley, "A History of the Theatre in Richmond,

Virginia, 1819-1838" (unpub. diss., UNC, 1938) and Dr. Shockley's several published essays listed in the notes.

Among the many Jefferson studies to some extent reflecting Virginia interest in fine arts, many of them listed in the notes, one discusses several phases of the subject: Eleanor D. Berman, *Thomas Jefferson among the Arts: An Essay in Early American Aesthetics* (New York, [1947]).

B. Notes on Chapter Seven

1. I, No. 21 (November 4, 1829), 322.
2. O'Neal, *Jefferson's Fine Arts Library for the University of Virginia,* p. 50; Louis B. Wright, *The First Gentlemen of Virginia* (San Marino, 1940), p. 335.
3. Kimball, *Domestic Architecture of the American Colonies and the Early Republic,* p. 145.
4. January 12, 1812, from William McKean, Va HS. There were editions of Nicholson's *Carpenter's New Guide* from 1792; Nicholson also wrote a three-volume *Principles of Architecture* (London, 1795-98) and *Student's Instructor* (London, 1804 etc.).
5. December 30, 1798, Thornton Papers, LC.
6. Scott, *Houses of Old Richmond,* p. 96.
7. Sowerby, *Catalogue of the Library of Thomas Jefferson,* items 4173-422[illegible].
8. I. T. Frary, *Thomas Jefferson, Architect and Builder* (Richmond, 1931); Fiske Kimball, *Thomas Jefferson, Architect*; and Berman, *Thomas Jefferson among the Arts,* pp. 113-48.
9. See his essay on "Architecture" in *Essays on Various Subjects* (Georgetown, 1822).
10. Lewis Mumford, *The South in Architecture* (New York, 1941), pp. 66-7[illegible].
11. Talbot Hamlin, *Benjamin Henry Latrobe* (New York, 1955), Chs. V and VI, pp. 67-126.
12. For plan, see Hamlin, *Latrobe,* p. 101.
13. See Hamlin, *Latrobe,* illustrations and engraved plates.
14. *Ibid.,* p. 126.
15. H. M. Pierce Gallagher, *Robert Mills, Architect of the Washington Monument, 1781-1853* (New York, 1935).
16. Scott, *Houses of Old Richmond,* pp. 102-46.
17. Gallagher, *Mills,* p. 39.
18. Kimball, *Domestic Architecture,* p. 291.
19. Madison Papers, LC.
20. Scott, *Houses of Old Richmond,* p. 113.
21. Ambler Papers, Va HS.
22. Gallagher, *Mills,* p. 86.
23. *Ibid.,* p. 156.
24. For Hadfield and Custis, *DAB.*
25. Fiske Kimball, "The Building of Bremo," *VMHB,* LXVII (1949), 5
26. *Ibid.,* p. 13.
27. Berman, *Thomas Jefferson among the Arts,* p. 91.
28. Wehle and Bolton, *American Miniatures,* p. 98, plate XIX; *Richmond Portraits,* pp. 150-57, 225-30.
29. Minnie C. Yarborough, ed., *Reminiscenses of William C. Preston* (Chapel Hill, 1933), *passim.*

30. Dunlap, *History of the Rise and Progress of the Arts of Design,* II, 321.
31. *Richmond Portraits,* pp. 232-33.
32. Wehle and Bolton, *American Miniatures,* plate XXXII.
33. *Ibid.*
34. *Ibid.,* p. 109.
35. Barker, *American Painting,* p. 259.
36. *St. Memin in Virginia, Portraits and Biographies.*
37. The Jefferson plate had several hundred new copies struck from it a few years ago.
38. *American Painters of the South,* p. 26.
39. *Enquirer,* November 10, 1809; November 9, 1810, etc.; Barker, *American Painting,* p. 381 ff.
40. "List of Sitters for Portraits in Norfolk and Vicinity and Richmond and Vicinity," typed, Va HS and Valentine Museum. Va HS owns six Thompson portraits: John D. Blair, John Rogers Cooke, Mary Lee Custis, William Maxwell, and John and Lucinda Mutter.
41. *American Painters of the South,* p. 29; Barker, *American Painting,* p. 276.
42. *DAB.*
43. *Richmond Portraits,* p. 231; *American Painters of the South,* p. 31.
44. *Richmond Portraits,* pp. 217-18.
45. *Ibid.,* pp. 220-21.
46. *DAB.*
47. *Ibid.*
48. *Richmond Portraits,* pp. 235-39.
49. July 5, 1816, Va HS. The LC prospectus is dated May 27, 1816.
50. Mordecai, *Richmond in By-Gone Days,* pp. 346-48.
51. Dunlap, *History . . . of the Arts of Design,* II, 35.
52. Cabell Collection, U Va.
53. L. G. Moffatt and J. M. Carriere, eds., "A Frenchman Visits Norfolk, Fredericksburg and Orange County, 1816," *VMHB,* LIII (1945), 197-214.
54. Berman, *Thomas Jefferson among the Arts,* pp. 75-78.
55. *Ibid.,* p. 78.
56. Francis H. Heller, transl. and ed., "Monticello and the University of Virginia in 1825: A German Prince's Travel Notes," *Papers Albemarle County Historical Society,* VII (1946-47), 34; G. S. Hillard, *Life, Letters, and Journals of George Ticknor* (2 vols., Boston, 1876), I, 34-35; W. M. E. Rachal, ed., *A Tour Through Part of Virginia in the Summer of 1808 . . . by John Edwards Caldwell* (Richmond, 1951), p. 39.
57. Va HS.
58. Molnar, "Art Music in Colonial Virginia," p. 91.
59. *Ibid.,* pp. 76, 83, 89-90; *WMQ* (2), IX (1929), 267.
60. Marie Kimball, *Jefferson: The Road to Glory, 1743 to 1776* (New York, 1943), p. 54; Molnar, "Art Music," p. 77.
61. No. 360, Vol. 21, 1790-1830 period, n.d.
62. William S. Prince, "St. George Tucker as Poet of the Early Republic" (unpub. diss., Yale, 1954), p. 29.
63. Stoutamire, "A History of Music in Richmond, Virginia from 1742 to 1860," pp. 48 ff.
64. *Ibid.,* pp. 83 ff.
65. *Enquirer,* May 24, 1825; *Whig,* May 11, 1824 (in Stoutamire, pp. 124-26); *Compiler,* November 24 and December 3, 1818 (in Stoutamire, p. 124).
66. Stoutamire, "A History of Music in Richmond," p. 57.
67. Bondurant, *Poe's Richmond,* p. 153.
68. Stoutamire, "A History of Music in Richmond," p. 117.

69. Brock Collection, HEH

70. Bondurant, *Poe's Richmond,* p. 141. For a long list of musical entertainments and their programs in full, 1790-1830, see Stoutamire, "A History of Music in Richmond," pp. 256 ff.

71. Norfleet, *St. Memin,* pp. 101, 157, 222, and William H. Safford, *The Blennerhasset Papers* (Cincinnati, 186[illegible]), pp. 331, 408, 448.

72. Brock Collection, HEH.

73. *Whig,* December 8, 18[illegible]8 (in Stoutamire, p. 167). Stoutamire says he located no other reference to this society.

74. Stoutamire, "A History of Music in Richmond," p. 91. *The Visitor* existed only in 1809-10.

75. Stoutamire, pp. 108-9; *The Visitor,* I, No. 12 (July, 1809), 96; I, No. 23 (December, 1809), 192.

76. May 9 (in Molnar, "Art Music," p. 105).

77. Sonneck, *Early Concert Life in America,* p. 59.

78. Molnar, "Art Music," pp. 82, 105.

79. Sonneck, *Early Concert Life,* p. 58.

80. Edwin A. Wyatt, IV, *Preliminary Checklist for Petersburg, 1786-1876* (Richmond, 1949), pp. 321-22, and item 132.

81. *SLM,* IV (February, 1838), 66-67.

82. Cauble, "William Wirt and His Friends," pp. 72-73; Josiah Quincy, *Figures of the Past* (Boston, 1926), p. 224.

83. February 27, 1813, Va HS.

84. Molnar, "Art Music," p. 108, note 321; W. J. Carrington, *History of Halifax County (Virginia)* (Richmond, 1824), p. 368.

85. *Memoirs of a Monticello Slave* (Charlottesville, 1951), p. 23; Marie Kimball, *Jefferson the Road to Glory,* pp. 55-59.

86. Helen D. Bullock, *My Head and My Heart: A Little History of Thomas Jefferson and Maria Cosway* (New York, [1955]), *passim.* I am indebted to Mrs. Bullock for her authoritative observations on Jefferson as musician.

87. A. B. Shepperson, "Thomas Jefferson Visits England and Buys a Harpsichord," *Humanistic Studies in Honor of John Calvin Metcalf* (Charlottesville, 1941), pp. 80-106.

88. Marie Kimball, *Jefferson: The Road to Glory,* pp. 57-58. See also Helen D. Bullock, "Program Notes," to the *University of Virginia . . . Founder's Day Concert . . . in Honor of the Two Hundredth Anniversary of the Birth of Thomas Jefferson,* April 13, 1943 [Charlottesville].

89. Berman, *Thomas Jefferson among the Arts,* p. 186.

90. September 24, 181[illegible], Charlottesville to West Point, N. P. Trist Papers, LC.

91. Robert H. Land, "The First Williamsburg Theatre," *WMQ* (3), V (1948), 359-74.

92. Paul L. Ford, *Washington and the Theatre* (New York, 1899), pp. 2-60 (Dunlap Society).

93. Martin S. Shockley "The Richmond Theatre, 1780-1790," *VMHB,* L[illegible] (1952), 421-36.

94. Susan K. Sherman "Thomas Wade West, Theatrical Impressario, 1790-1799," *WMQ* (3), IX (1952), 10-28.

95. Arthur H. Quinn, *Edgar Allan Poe: A Critical Biography* (New York, 1941), pp. 20-50.

96. Martin S. Shockley, "First American Performances of English Plays before 1819," *JSH,* XIII (1947), 91-105.

97. Cauble, "William Wirt and His Friends," pp. 251, 253.

98. Shockley, "A History of the Theatre in Richmond, Virginia, 1819-1838."

99. N. B. Fagin, *The Histrionic Mr. Poe* (Baltimore, 1949), *passim.*

100. Thomas B. Rowland, "Norfolk Theatres of the Olden Time," *Lower Norfolk County Antiquary,* II (1898), 102; T. J. Wertenbaker, *Norfolk, Historic Southern Port* (Durham, 1931), p. 129; Quinn, *Poe,* pp. 40-50.

101. Edwin A. Wyatt, IV, "Three Petersburg Theatres," *WMQ* (2), XXI (1941), (Petersburg, 1960), pp. 140-49.

102. *VMHB,* XIII (1906), 426-30.

103. Richard B. Davis, ed., *Jeffersonian America: Notes on the United States . . . by Sir Augustus John Foster* (San Marino, 1954), p. 133.

104. William Munford, *Poems and Compositions in Prose on Several Occasions* (Richmond, 1798).

105. Brock Collection, HEH.

106. Originally published in Col. Munford's *A Collection of Plays and Poems,* ed. William Munford (Petersburg, 1798), the two plays have been re-edited and printed in *WMQ* (3), V (1948), 217-27, 357-58; VI (1949), 437-503.

107. Tucker-Coleman Papers, Archives, Colonial Williamsburg.

108. Archives, Colonial Williamsburg.

109. Wirt Papers, Md HS.

110. By Hal Laughlin of William and Mary in 1960 as an M.A. thesis. Keith B. Berwick, of the Department of History of the University of California, Los Angeles, is now editing the plays for publication.

111. Archives, Colonial Williamsburg.

112. Edwin A. Wyatt, IV, *John Daly Burk, Playwright-Historian,* Southern Sketches No. 7 (Charlottesville, 1936), pp. 3-20.

113. Quinn, *A History of the American Drama from the Beginnings,* pp. 117-20.

114. The play was certainly performed in Richmond, Norfolk, and New York within the next few years. Burk also wrote four others plays, none of which has survived. See Joseph I. Shulim, "John Daly Burk, Playwright of Libertarianism," *NYPL Bulletin,* LXV (1961), 451-63.

115. Shulim, "Burk," p. 462-63.

116. J. P. Kennedy, *Memoirs of the Life of William Wirt* (2 vols., Philadelphia, 1850), I, 307; Cauble, "Wirt and His Friends," pp. 256-58; Wirt's letters to Tucker, October 10, 1813, and August 2 and 9, 1815, Colonial Williamsburg; to Dabney Carr, June 10, [1813?], Va St Lib; to T. A. Cooper, February 11, 1816, Md HS.

117. Quinn, *A History of the American Drama from the Beginnings,* p. 160.

118. Wyatt, *Burk,* p. 18; Quinn, *A History,* p. 119n.

119. Shockley, "A History of the Theatre in Richmond," pp. 77-79.

120. *Ibid.,* pp. 77-80.

121. *Richmond Portraits,* pp. 142-43.

122. Murray H. Nelligan, "American Nationalism on the Stage: The Plays of George Washington Parke Custis (1781-1857)," *VHMB,* LVIII (1950), 299-324.

123. *Ibid.,* pp. 316 ff.

124. *Ibid.,* p. 35.

125. William S. Charvat, *Origins of American Critical Thought, 1810-1835* (Philadelphia, 1936), p. 7.

126. Shockley, "A History of the Theatre in Richmond," pp. 195-236. The newspaper references are from Shockley.

127. It had been originally published in the *Enquirer.* See Jay B. Hubbell, "William Wirt and the Familiar Essay in Virginia," *WMQ* (2), XXIII (1943), 145-52.

Chapter Eight

A. *Bibliography in general*

As for other things, for literature in this period Agnes M. Bondurant's *Poe's Richmond* (Richmond, 1942) and Samuel Mordecai's *Richmond in By-Gone Days* (repr. Richmond, 1946) are generally helpful for more than the capital city. There is material of value in Russell B. Nye, *The Cultural Life of the New Nation* (New York, 1960) and in Vernon L. Parrington, *The Romantic Revolution in America, 1800-1860* (New York, 1927). For critical theory, most useful are William S. Charvat, *Origins of American Critical Thought, 1810-1835* (Philadelphia, 1936); Gordon E. Bigelow, *Rhetoric and Poetry of the Early National Period,* University of Florida Monographs, Humanities, No. 4, Spring, 1960 (Gainesville, Fla.); Terence Martin, *The Instructed Vision: Scottish Common Sense Philosophy and the Origins of American Fiction* (Bloomington, 1961); Samuel Miller, *A Brief Retrospect of the Eighteenth Century* (2 vols., New York, 1803); and Robert D. Jacobs, "Poe's Heritage from Jefferson's Virginia" (unpub. diss. Johns Hopkins, 1953).

On Virginia literature per se there is not a great deal, though Jay B. Hubbell, *The South in American Literature* (Durham, 1954) is a notable exception. Carol M. Newman, *Virginia Literature* (Pulaski, Va., 1903) is an early study. Useful is Ella M. Thomas, *Virginia Women in Literature: A Partial List* (Richmond, 1902).

The work of the individuals named in the titles and of their circles of friends is considered in Frank P. Cauble, "William Wirt and His Friends," (unpub. diss. UNC, 1933); John P. Kennedy *Memoirs of the Life of William Wirt* (2 vols., Philadelphia, 1850); Robert C. McLean, *George Tucker: Moral Philosopher and Man of Letters* (Chapel Hill, 1961); and Richard B. Davis, *Francis Walker Gilmer: Life and Learning in Jefferson's Virginia* (Richmond, 1939). For titles of works by Virginians, see E. M. Sowerby, comp., *Catalogue of the Library of Thomas Jefferson* (5 vols., Washington, D.C., 1952-59) and Richard B. Davis, "Jefferson as Collector of Virginiana," *Studies in Bibliography,* XIV (1961), 117-44.

For periodicals, F. L. Mott, *A History of American Magazines, 1741-1850* (Cambridge, Mass., repr. 1957) is most useful for the better known. Others as indicated in this chapter have not been treated but usually may be examined on microfilm from originals at LC, Va HS, or Va St Lib. Michael Kraus, *A History of American History* (New York, [1937]) comments on a number of Virginia historical writings of the period.

Jay B. Hubbell's "William Wirt and the Familiar Essay in Virginia," *WMQ* (2), XXIII (1943), 136-52 and *The South in American Literature* are the principal studies of the essay. See also Richard B. Davis, *Francis Walker Gilmer* and "Literary Tastes in Virginia before Poe," *WMQ* (2), XIX (1939), 55-68; and Robert C. McLean, *George Tucker*; J. P. Kennedy, *Memoirs of the Life of William Wirt*; and Frank P. Cauble, "William Wirt and His Friends." Most of these studies are also useful for examples of Virginia correspondence, as are the collected editions of the papers of many major figures given in the notes.

For Virginia fiction, see Francis P. Gaines, *The Southern Plantation* (New York, 1925); Jay B. Hubbell, *The South in American Literature* (Durham, 1954), *Virginia Life in Fiction* (Dallas, 1922), *Southern Life in Fiction* (Athens, 1960); J. G. Johnson, *Southern Fiction Prior to 1860: An Attempt at a First-Hand Bibliography* (Charlottesville, 1909). Much of the discussion of fiction in the present chapter has been published in "The 'Virginia Novel' before *Swallow Barn*," *VMHB*, LXXI (1963), 278-93. The Pocahontas-John Smith theme is discussed in a number of places, especially Jay B. Hubbell, "The Smith-Pocahontas Story in Literature," *VMHB*, LXV (1957), 275-300 and *Virginia Life in Fiction*; Loy Y. Bryant, "The Pocahontas Theme in American Literature" (unpub. M.A. thesis, UNC, 1935); and Richard B. Davis, "The Americanness of American Literature: Folk and Historical Materials in Formal Writing," *The Literary Criterion* (Mysore, India), III (Summer, 1959), 10-22.

Virginia verse is surveyed in F. V. N. Painter, *The Poets of Virginia* (Richmond, 1907) and criticized and anthologized in Armistead C. Gordon, Jr., *Virginian Writers of Fugitive Verse* (New York, 1923). Certain poets are discussed in Hubbell, *The South in American Literature* and in Edd W. Parks, *Southern Poets* (New York, 1936).

For selections from many Virginia belletristic writers, and brief biographical and critical sketches, see Edwin A. Alderman, *et al, The Library of Southern Literature* (16 vols., Atlanta, 1907-13).

B. Notes on Chapter Eight

1. J. K. Paulding, *Letters from the South* (2 vols., New York, 1835), I, 196-97.

2. Tucker's letter of August 8, 1811, Md HS. Tucker may be hitting at Blair's *Lectures,* three of which are devoted entirely to the structure of the sentence, and a number of others to imagery, vocabulary, etc. Jefferson's letter of November 2, 1816, is in Ford, XII, 35 (quoted in Hubbell, *The South in American Literature,* p. 128).

3. November 5, 1820, Va St Lib.

4. See H. H. Clark, "Changing Attitudes in American Literary Criticism," *The Development of American Literary Criticism,* ed. Floyd Stovall (Chapel Hill, 19_5), p. 25.

5. M. F. Heiser, "Decline of Neoclassicism," *Transitions in American Literary History,* ed. H. H. Clark (Durham, 1953), p. 111.

6. 2 vols., New York, II, 11

7. Roy H. Pearce, *The Savages of America* (Baltimore, 1953), pp. 88-89. For discussion of the Scottish philosophy in America, see Martin, *The Instructed Vision: Scottish Common Sense Philosophy and the Origins of American Fiction,* pp. 4-5, etc.

8. Notebooks of William C. Rives, Rives Papers, 1809 Folder, LC. Also Adrienne Koch, *The Philosophy of Thomas Jefferson* (New York, 1943); Charvat, *Origins of American Critical Thought, 1810-1835*; and Pearce, *The Savages of America.*

9. Charvat, *Origins of American Critical Thought,* pp. 7-26.

10. *Ibid.,* pp. 44-45.

11. Merle Curti, "The Great Mr. Locke, America's Philosopher, 1785-1861," *Huntington Library Bulletin,* No. 11 (April, 1937), pp. 107-51.

12. Rives Papers, 1809 Folder, LC.

13. *Virginia Literary Museum, passim*; and McLean, *George Tucker,* pp. 30, 156-64.

14. *Ibid.,* p. 99.

15. Randolph C. Randall, "Authors of the *Port Folio* Revealed in the Hall Files," *AL,* XI (January, 1940), 379-416.

16. Painter, *The Poets of Virginia,* p. 101.

17. I (August), 485.

18. Edith Philips, *Louis Hue Girardin and Nicholas Gouin Dufief and Their Relations with Thomas Jefferson . . .,* Johns Hopkins Studies in Romance Languages and Literatures, Extra Vol No. III (Baltimore, 1926), 4-5.

19. Va St Lib owns an incomplete file of this magazine which has been microfilmed in the Early American Periodical series. For a description of the journal, see Cauble, "William Wirt and His Friends," Appendix B; Mordecai, *Richmond,* p. 240; Mott, *A History of American Magazines,* p. 205n.

20. George W. Munford, *The Two Parsons* (Richmond, 1884), pp. 101-2.

21. *Biographical Directory of the American Congress, 1774-1949* (Washington, D.C., 1950).

22. MS. Box 45 dated October 24, 1806, Brock Collection. It is addressed to "Mr. Pleasants." Presumably it was intended originally for a Richmond newspaper or *The Visitor.*

23. *Lines, on Duelling . . . , Originally Published in The Visitor . . .* (Richmond, Lynch & Davis, 1810).

24. Another Virginia journal of short duration, *Virginia Souvenir and Ladies Literary Gazette,* ed. by Gilliam and Mitchell, has not been located.

25. J. W. Wayland, "The Virginia Literary Museum," *Publications of the Southern Historical Association,* VI, No. 1 (January, 1902), 1-14; McLean, *George Tucker,* pp. 95-96; and files of the magazine in U Va and VHS.

26. McLean, *George Tucker,* pp. 239-41, lists Tucker's contributions chronologically. Dunglison's may be traced by following his various pseudonyms or pseudonymous initials given in McLean, p. 96.

27. Nye, *Cultural Life of the New Nation,* pp. 42-44.

28. Kraus, *A History of American History,* pp. 156-58.

29. *Ibid.,* p. 158.

30. Hubbell, *The South in American Literature,* p. 233.

31. Kraus, *A History of American History,* p. 162.

32. J. E. Cooke, *Virginia, a History of the People* (Boston, 1892), p. 491.

33. November, 1821, *Memoir and Diary,* ed. C. F. Adams (12 vols., Philadelphia, 1876), VIII, 180.

34. Norfolk, June 8, 1804, in Kennedy, *Life of William Wirt,* I, 116.

35. Kennedy, *Wirt,* I, 122. Tucker in a letter to Wirt had strongly discouraged biographical writing with departed Virginians as subjects.

36. Hubbell, *The South in American Literature,* p. 973, gives a list of these reviews.

37. *Ibid.,* p. 240.

38. For further discussion of Patrick Henry and Wirt, see William R. Taylor, *Cavalier and Yankee: The Old South and National American Character* (New York, 1961), pp. 68-94.

39. Curtis C. Davis, ed., in *Proceedings* of the American Philosophical Society, CI (June 20, 1957), 255-69. Also C. C. Davis, *The King's Chevalier: A Biography of Lewis Littlepage* (Indianapolis, 1961), p. 398.

40. See Edward A. Wyatt, IV, *John Daly Burk, Playwright-Historian,* Southern Sketches No. 7 (Charlottesville, 1936), p. 31; *SLM,* III (1836), 235; Sowerby, *Catalogue of the Library of Thomas Jefferson,* I, 212 (Item 464).

41. Joseph I. Shulim, "Henry Banks: A Contemporary Napoleonic Apologist in the Old Dominion," *VMHB,* LVIII (1950), 336-37.

42. G. S. Jackson, *Uncommon Scold: The Story of Anne Royall* (Boston, [1937]); Sarah H. Porter, *The Life and Times of Anne Royall* (Cedar Rapids, 1909).

43. Quoted in *DAB* sketch of Hening.

44. Quoted in Sowerby, *Catalogue,* II, 260 (Item 1863).

45. Now in Va HS and HEH.

46. Hubbell, "William Wirt and the Familiar Essay in Virginia," pp. 136-52, and *The South in American Literature,* pp. 236-39.

47. Hubbell, "William Wirt and the Familiar Essay," pp. 142-44.

48. *Ibid.,* and Kennedy, *Life of William Wirt, passim.*

49. Hubbell, "Wirt and the Familiar Essay," p. 149n.

50. St. George Tucker in a letter to Wirt of August 8, 1811 (Md HS) indicates that he originated the name Obadiah Squaretoes and first used it.

51. Richard B. Davis, "Poe and William Wirt," *AL,* XVI (1944), 212-20.

52. *Analectic Review,* VII (1818), 265-94.

53. See bibliography in McLean, *George Tucker,* pp. 236-37.

54. McLean, *George Tucker,* pp. 117-19; *Old Bachelor,* pp. 49-54.

55. *Rainbow,* pp. 49-50.

56. McLean, *George Tucker,* p. 119.

57. *Essays* (Georgetown), p. 27.

58. McLean, *George Tucker,* pp. 121, 123-24, 129-30.

59. *Ibid.,* p. 138.

60. *Ibid.,* pp. 139 ff.

61. "Poe's Heritage from Jefferson's Virginia."

62. See Chapters II and III above, *passim.*

63. April 5, quoted in *Papers,* I, xi.

64. Richard B. Davis, "The Gentlest Art in Seventeenth Century Virginia," *Tennessee Studies in Literature,* II (1957), 51-63.

65. Boyd, *Papers,* I, xii.

66. Philip A. Bruce in *Library of Southern Literature,* X, 4334; William C. Bruce, *John Randolph of Roanoke* (2 vols., New York, 1922), II, 434. For a list of the letters, see W. E. Stokes and Francis L. Berkeley, Jr., *The Papers of John Randolph of Roanoke,* U Va Bibliographical Series No. 9, U Va Library ([Charlottesville], 1950).

67. There are large numbers of them in LC, Md HS, Va St Lib, U Va, etc.

68. For all his letters to Peachy R. Gilmer, see Peachy R. Gilmer Letterbook, Va HS. There are other Gilmer letters at LC, Va St Lib, and U Va.

69. December 21, 1813, Va HS.

70. February 9, 1817, Va HS.

71. January 19, 1824, Va HS.

72. July 2, 1824, Va HS and Davis, *Francis Walker Gilmer,* pp. 206-7.

73. March 10, 1798, in Emily E. F. Skeel, ed., *Macon Locke Weems His Works and Ways* (3 vols., New York, 1929), I, 9.

74. Skeel, *Weems,* III, 150.

75. For a more detailed but somewhat misleading account, see McLean, *George Tucker,* pp. 91-94.

76. Curtis C. Davis, "Judith Bensaddi and the Reverend Doctor Henry Ruffner," *Publications of the Jewish Historical Society,* XXXIX, Pt. 2 (1949), 115-42. A longer version of Ruffner's story was published in *SLM* in July, 1839.

77. P. 37, 1806 ed.

78. *Ibid.,* p. 38.

79. New York.

80. From Washington, D.C., Va HS.

81. New York. For a somewhat different and more detailed analysis of this novel, see McLean, *George Tucker,* pp. 75-89.

82. Letter misdated 1824, in Cabell Collection, U Va.

83. I, 17.

84. I, 21.

85. Hubbell, *The South in American Literature,* p. 252.

86. Richmond.

87. I, 6-7.

88. *Complete Works of Edgar Allan Poe,* ed. J. A. Harrison (17 vols., New York, 1902), XV, 241.

89. Skeel, ed., *Weems,* II, 70.

90. Published in the *London Magazine.* See Hubbell, "The Smith-Pocahontas Story in Literature," pp. 284 etc.

91. I, Nos. 10 and 12.

92. N.s. VIII, No. 3 (September), 218-33.

93. Petersburg, pp. 39-40.

94. Richard B. Davis, "The First American Edition of Captain John Smith's *True Travels and General Historie,*" *VMHB,* XLVIII (1939), 47-108.

95. See Richard B. Davis, "Early American Interest in Wharton's Manuscript," appendix in Laura P. Stryker, ed. and transl., *The Life of Captain John Smith English Soldier, by Henry Wharton* (Chapel Hill, 1957), pp. 93-96. Also F. W. Gilmer to P. R. Gilmer, November 20, 1824, Va HS.

96. *Travels of Four Years and a Half in the United States* (repr. ed., New York, 1909), pp. 309-10.

97. *Ibid.,* p. 311.

98. 3rd ser., III, No. 6 (June 1814), 594-97. The poem is inscribed to Thos. S. Pleasants. John Davis, "Jamestown, an Elegy," appeared in the *Port Folio,* n.s. VIII, No. 3 (August, 1812), 213-15.

99. *Poems* (Philadelphia, 1812), p. 59.

100. P. 190.

101. *Miscellaneous Poems* (Philadelphia, 1820); *Poems* (London, 1824).

102. IV (1821), 355-61.

103. *Ibid.*, pp. 360-61.

104. Petersburg, 1825, pp. 11, 13-57, 194-95. Also see Painter, *The Poets of Virginia,* 77.

105. See Painter, *Poets,* p. 79. There are two earlier stanzas.

106. Washington, D.C., 1825.

107. Henry Adams, *History of the United States during the Administrations of Jefferson and Madison* (9 vols., New York, 1921), I, 41-42.

108. There were other poets in other sections who left MS. verse in the period. E.g. "C. Pelham, of Greensville, Va." and Edward Dromgoole. See Dromgoole Papers, Sou. Hist. Coll. UNC.

109. Lyon G. Tyler, ed., 2 vols., Richmond. See also the small leather notebook containing some of his poems, in LC.

110. *Ibid.*, I, 196. There are fourteen more lines.

111. MS. Broadside, Va HS. Curtis C. Davis, *The King's Chevalier,* pp. 21-22, quotes a poem by Littlepage to Fleming which appeared in the *Virginia Gazette,* March 14, 1777.

112. E.g., *SLM,* II (January, 1836), 93; *Enquirer,* May 19, 1809; Gordon, *Virginian Writers of Fugitive Verse,* p. 183.

113. In Price Collection, College of William and Mary, quoted in George Shackelford, "William Short, Jefferson's Adopted Son" (unpub. diss. U Va, 1955), p. 36.

114. See Tucker-Coleman Papers, Archives, Colonial Williamsburg.

115. E.g., Tucker to Carey, October 5, 1795. Tucker-Coleman Papers.

116. Pp. 92-93. It is dated from Alexandria, Virginia, as some of Tucker's own later work is.

117. In LC is a 1764 "Pathetic Soliloquy" written by "Robert Bolling Esquire of Virginia."

118. See Page to Tucker, December 31, 1790, Tucker-Coleman Papers.

119. Mrs. Page's are hard to count, for there are many manuscript poems as well as the printed texts signed with the initials she used before or after marriage. Also see William S. Prince, "St. George Tucker as a Poet of the Early Republic" (unpub. diss., Yale, 1954), Ch. III, pp. 36-37. The William and Mary volume also contains twenty-six pages of "A Journey" (Journal form), a record of travel made by Margaret Lowther.

120. Lewis Leary, *The Literary Career of Nathaniel Tucker, 1750-1807* (Durham, 1951).

121. N.s. VIII, No. 2 (August, 1812), 206-10.

122. January 6, 1795. Tucker-Coleman Papers.

123. Md HS.

124. Both letters are dated October 27, 1800, Tucker-Coleman Papers.

125. Richmond, Samuel Pleasants, 1798.

126. Ellis-Munford Papers, Duke.

127. *Ibid.* One MS. states that this was published in the Virginia *Argus,* December 24, 1803.

128. William Munford, *Homer's Iliad* (2 vols., Boston, 1846), I, ix.

129. Hubbell, *The South in American Literature,* p. 951, and Richard B. Davis, "Homer in Homespun—A Southern Iliad," *SLM,* n.s. I (1939), 647-51.

130. October 8, 1795, Tucker-Coleman Papers.

131. The only thorough study of Tucker's verse is Prince, "St. George Tucker as a Poet of the Early Republic." I am greatly indebted to this work for bibliography, texts of poems, and some critical commentary, though I also personally

examined the Tucker-Coleman Papers of Colonial Williamsburg. There are a few poems by Tucker among the Wirt Papers of Md HS Mr. Prince did not see.

132. See Ch. IV above under A.

133. Prince, "St. George Tucker," pp. 88-89.

134. Tucker's presentation copy of his poem to Jodrell is now in the Yale library.

135. Tucker-Coleman Papers.

136. I, 468.

137. Page to Tucker, January 5, 1795, Tucker-Coleman Papers.

138. Salisbury, England.

139. E.g., Virginia *Argus*, June 15, 1807.

140. In *Half an Hour's Amusement at York and James-Town . . .* (Richmond, 1824).

141. McLean, *George Tucker*, pp. 55-57.

142. No place given.

143. Richmond.

144. Richmond.

145. W.H.T. Squires, "William Maxwell, A Virginian of Ante Bellum Days," *Union Theological Seminary Magazine*, XXX (October, 1918), 35-49, and *DAB*. Both editions of Maxwell's poems were printed in Philadelphia, though the Union Catalogue of LC lists a Baltimore, 1812 edition also.

146. I (October, 1818), 452-59, signed "Melancthon."

147. *Poems and Translations*, 1812; *Poems, Original and Translated*, 1815.

148. Pp. 13-14.

149. Pp. 156 ff. (also 1815 ed.).

150. Hubbell, *The South in American Literature*, p. 297.

151. P. 21.

152. P. 93.

153. In a note following an asterisk by "hair," Dabney quotes "The fragrant hyacinths of Azza's hair / Sir W. Jones."

154. Quoted in E. A. and G. L. Duyckinck, *Cyclopaedia of American Literature* (Philadelphia, 1881), pp. 794-95.

155. Harrison, ed., *Poe's Complete Works*, XV, 218 and *Graham's Magazine* (December, 1841).

156. Hubbell, *The South in American Literature*, pp. 287-93 and Elizabeth Binns, "Daniel Bryan, Poe's Poet of 'the good old Goldsmith School,'" *WMQ* (2), XXIII (1943), 465-73.

157. Washington, D.C.

158. Philadelphia.

159. Washington, D.C., 1826.

160. I, lines 767-70.

161. I, lines 87-93.

162. Hubbell, *The South in American Literature*, p. 289; Roy Harvey Pearce, *The Continuity of American Poetry* (Princeton, 1961), pp. 130-33.

163. Pp. 362-63.

164. For two obituary notes, see *Petersburg Index-Appeal*, June 30, 1874. In one copy of her poems someone has commented that she was Davies' granddaughter, a fact also noted in the obituaries.

165. P. 13.

166. P. 18.

167. The Lexington edition has 118 pages, the Richmond 132. Among the subscribers to the 1828 edition were Richmond's most prominent, including John Marshall and Thomas Ritchie; Haines of Petersburg; Thomas Walker Gilmer of Charlottesville and Wertenbaker of the University of Virginia, among others.

168. 1828 ed., p. 116.

169. *Ibid.*, p. 119, end of poem.

170. See *DAB,* under Herman Blennerhasset. The poems were published by E. V. Sparhawk.

171. P. 135.

172. In the bound MS. volume of Haines' poems in LC is a loose sheet, "To the Reader," a dialogue giving many facts of "The Stranger's" early life. In the Duke University Library is an "Original Manuscript Prose and Poetry, by Hiram Haines," dated November 29, 1820. The LC volume contains the poem on Bonaparte, a letter to Jefferson, essay-letters attacking J. Q. Adams as candidate for the Presidency, and many poems.

173. The Preface mentions that many of these were written in his youth, and a number of poems are dated. Only dated poems are here considered.

174. P. vii.

175. P. 16.

176. P. 44.

177. P. 96.

178. P. 121.

179. P. 123.

180. P. 142.

181. Davis, *Francis Walker Gilmer, passim*; and *Virginia Literary Museum,* I, No. 3 (July 1, 1829), 40.

182. Both are among the N. P. Trist Papers. The version here printed is that of the Sou. Hist. Coll., UNC. The second version, with a considerably different twelfth line, is in LC.

183. See his "Poe's Heritage from Jefferson's Virginia."

Chapter Nine

A. *Bibliography in general*

There is no comprehensive history of the legal profession in America. Useful are the essays included in *Law: A Century of Progress, 1835-1935* (3 vols., New York, 1937) and Charles Warren, *A History of the American Bar* (Boston, 1913).

For rhetoric, eloquence, and oratory, sometimes combined with law, there is much more. Most comprehensive is W. N. Brigance, ed., *History and Criticism of American Public Address* (2 vols., New York, 1943). A contemporary criticism and selection is Increase Cooke, *The American Orator: or Elegant Extracts in Prose and Poetry* (New Haven and Charleston, 1819) among others mentioned in the text of this chapter. T. E. Watson's Volume IX in *The South in the Building of the Nation* (12 vols., Richmond, 1909) on the history of Southern oratory, with chapters by Edward K. Graham and John C. Reed on eloquence in the Federal Period and on legal oratory, is enlightening. Gordon E. Bigelow, *Rhetoric and American Poetry in the Early National Period,* University of Florida Monographs, Humanities, No.

4, Spring, 1960 (Gainesville, Fla.), discusses the relation between the study of eloquence and literature. Contemporary studies especially useful are Francis W. Gilmer, *Sketches of American Orators* (Baltimore, 1816) and *Sketches, Essays, and Translations* (Baltimore, 1828), and William Wirt, *Sketches of the Life and Character of Patrick Henry* ([orig. ed. 1817] ed. of Philadelphia, 1841), the last including consideration of orators other than Henry. James Ogilvie's *Philosophical Essays* (Philadelphia, 1816) includes long and amusing accounts of the particular brand of oratory in practice.

Again F. P. Cauble, "William Wirt and His Friends" (unpub. diss. UNC, 1933), Jay B. Hubbell, *The South in American Literature* (Durham, 1954), J. P. Kennedy, *Memoirs of the Life of William Wirt* (2 vols., Philadelphia, 1850), and Richard B. Davis, *Francis Walker Gilmer* (Richmond, 1939) contain pertinent materials. Also see Richard B. Davis, "James Ogilvie, an Early American Teacher of Rhetoric," *Quarterly Journal of Speech,* XXVIII (April, 1942), 289-97.

B. Notes on Chapter Nine

1. Letter VII, tenth ed. (New York, 1832), p. 206.
2. B. C. McCary, ed. and transl., *Travels of a Frenchman . . . in Maryland and Virginia . . . 1791 . . .* (Williamsburg, [1950]), p. 56.
3. *Memoirs of Lieutenant-General Winfield Scott, LL.D.* (2 vols., New York, 1864), I, 9.
4. I, issue of November 4, 1829. See quotations introducing this chapter.
5. *History of the United States* (9 vols., New York, 1921), I, 134. See quotations introducing this chapter.
6. Richard B. Davis, ed., *William Fitzhugh and His Chesapeake World, 1676-1701* (Chapel Hill, 1963), *passim.*
7. Warren, *A History of the American Bar,* p. 46.
8. Ch. II.
9. Cf. Joseph C. Cabell to John Breckinridge, May 20, 1800, Breckinridge Papers, Vol. 19, LC.
10. Brigance, ed., *History and Criticism of American Public Address,* II, 105.
11. *Papers,* II, 305 ff; William H. Peden, ed., *Notes on the State of Virginia, by Thomas Jefferson* (Chapel Hill, 1955), pp. 120-49, 209, 222 and notes.
12. Three surviving copies of Wythe contain notes in Greek and Latin in the hand of Wythe's young law clerk, Henry Clay, notes dictated by Wythe. Warren, *A History of the American Bar,* p. 330.
13. 5 vols., Philadelphia, 1803.
14. Warren, *A History of the American Bar,* p. 336.
15. *Ibid.*
16. 2 vols.
17. 4 vols.
18. *Law: A Century of Progress, 1835-1935,* I, 8-9.
19. *SLM,* IV (February, 1838), 66-67.
20. *DAB.*

21. David J. Mays, *Edmund Pendleton, 1721-1803* (2 vols., Cambridge, Mass., 1952), I, 130.

22. *DAB* and Mays, *Edmund Pendleton,* II, 278.

23. L. Q. C. Elmer, *Constitution and Government . . . [in] New Jersey* (Newark, 1872), quoted in *Tyler's Magazine,* IV (1922), 32-35.

24. Josiah Quincy, Jr., *Figures of the Past* (Boston, 1926), p. 204.

25. *DAB.*

26. *Memoirs of John Quincy Adams,* ed. C. F. Adams (12 vols., Philadelphia (1874-77), V, 359 (October, 1821).

27. [W. E. Dodd, ed.,] "Spencer Roane, Reprints from the Richmond *Enquirer," John P. Branch Historical Papers of Randolph-Macon College,* IV, 325-73.

28. Edwin J. Smith, "Spencer Roane," *John P. Branch Historical Papers,* II, No. 1, p. 32. See also "Roane on the Constitution," *Branch Papers,* II, No. 1, pp. 47-122 and P. L. Ford, ed., *Essays on the Constitution of the United States Published During Its Discussion by the People, 1787-1788* (Brooklyn, N.Y., 1892), pp. 385-92.

29. Cf., e.g., A. C. McLaughlin, "Publicists and Orators," *Cambridge History of American Literature,* eds. W. P. Trent, *et al* (3 vols., New York, 1933), II, 73: Albert J. Beveridge, *The Life of John Marshall* (4 vols., Boston, 1916), II, 179-93.

30. *Letters of the British Spy* (10th ed., New York, 1832), Letter V, pp. 178 ff.

31. *Memoirs,* IX, 243-44.

32. Watson, in *The South in the Building of the Nation,* IX, 108.

33. IV (February), 66.

34. II (1806), 502-3, quoted in Bigelow, *Rhetoric and American Poetry of the Early National Period,* p. 27.

35. Brigance, ed., *History and Criticism of American Public Address,* I, 21, 201.

36. Letter III, p. 135.

37. III, xxiv, xxv.

38. III, xxxii, 132; xiv, 54-55.

39. To F. W. Gilmer, March 15, 1817, in Davis, *Francis Walker Gilmer,* p. 170.

40. Lecture XXV. Because of the many editions of Blair, references are to lectures rather than pages.

41. Lecture XXXIV.

42. Lecture XXVI.

43. P. 41.

44. *North American Review,* IV (March, 1817), 378-408.

45. See Virginia *Argus,* July 4, 1804, for announcement.

46. For Ogilvie, see Richard B. Davis, "James Ogilvie, an Early American Teacher of Rhetoric," pp. 289-97. For Jefferson and Ogilvie, Diary of Mrs. William Thornton, September 21, [1805? 6?], LC.

47. Kennedy, *William Wirt,* I, 106.

48. Probably Edmund Randolph.

49. Numbers XXII, XXXII, etc.

50. Jay B. Hubbell, "William Wirt and the Familiar Essay in Virginia," *WMQ* (2), XXIII (1943), 143-44.

51. IV, 455, 519-28.

52. See *Letters* and Robert C. McLean, *George Tucker: Moral Philosopher and Man of Letters* (Chapel Hill, 1961), pp. 61-62.

53. Wirt to Gilmer, November 16, 1812, Davis, *Francis Walker Gilmer,* p. 54.

54. *Sketches,* p. 47.

55. *Sketches, Essays, and Translations,* p. 44.

56. In a letter of February 7, 1813, F. W. Gilmer notes his brother's preference for the "rough-roll & tumble" style of Henry. Henry, he says, was the greatest orator who ever lived, though his fame will not live.

57. I, 23, 25, 26.

58. A. J. Morrison, ed., *Six Addresses on the State of Letters and Science in Virginia . . .* (Roanoke, 1917).

59. See W. H. T. Squires, "William Maxwell, a Virginian of Ante Bellum Days," *Union Theological Seminary Magazine,* XXX (October, 1918), 35-49.

60. Cf. e.g., George Tucker's *Essays* (Georgetown, 1822), p. 61.

61. *Sketches of the Life and Character of Patrick Henry,* pp. 386-94.

62. *Sketches, Essays, and Translations,* pp. 33-34.

63. See William R. Taylor, *Cavalier and Yankee: The Old South and the American National Character* (New York, 1961), pp. 78-89. Taylor discusses in some detail Wirt and his conception of Henry. Cf. also Robert D. Meade, *Patrick Henry: Patriot in the Making* (Philadelphia, 1957), the first volume of what will probably become the standard life.

64. Louis A. Mallory, "Patrick Henry," in *History and Criticism of American Public Address,* ed. Brigance, II, 580-602. See also Hubbell, *The South in American Literature,* pp. 240-41.

65. 1832 ed., pp. 178-79.

66. Beveridge, *Marshall,* II, 193-95.

67. This is Gilmer's 1816 opinion of Randolph.

68. *History of the Virginia Federal Convention of 1788* (2 vols., Richmond, 1890).

69. *WMQ* (3), III (1946), 520-33.

70. Grigsby, *The Virginia Federal Convention,* p. 200, etc.

71. Cf. *The British Spy* (1832 ed.), pp. 206-10.

72. William C. Bruce, *John Randolph of Roanoke* (2 vols., New York, 1922), II, 64.

73. See also Bruce, *Randolph,* II, 82, for excerpt from a printing of a Randolph speech in *Niles' Weekly Register* for 1826, with an accompanying statement that much of it was omitted in the *Senate* Record. *Niles' Register* is itself a better source than the official records for many speeches.

74. Published 1882.

75. Russell Kirk, *Randolph of Roanoke: A Study in Conservative Thought* (Chicago, 1951).

76. II, 61, 71. Bruce refers to the New York *Courier* article copied into the *National Intelligencer,* June 4, 1833. It was written about 1803.

77. Bruce, *Randolph,* II, 202. The Union Catalogue of LC lists some four dozen separately published pamphlets by Randolph, most of them full-length or complete texts of some of his speeches.

78. *Annals,* XIX (February, 1809), 1463, 1501.

79. *Annals,* XXIII (November, 1811), 358.

80. *Annals,* XLI (January, 1824), 1185.

81. Kirk, *Randolph,* p. 152 etc.

82. See too his letter to D. Carr, December 17, 1810, Kennedy, *William Wirt,* I, 261-62.

83. *A Selection of Eulogies Pronounced in the Several States in Honor of Those Illustrious Patriots and Statesmen, John Adams and Thomas Jefferson* (Hartford, 1826).

84. *Memoirs,* VII (October 19, 1826), 155-56.

85. For a study of Wirt's speech, see Taylor, *Cavalier and Yankee,* pp. 90-92.

86. Richard B. Davis, "Poe and William Wirt," *AL,* XVI (1944), 217-1 . There is evidence of their existence in at least western Pennsylvania, New Jersey, and Philadelphia.

87. Kennedy, *William Wirt,* II, 369-70.

88. H. B. Grigsby, *The Virginia Convention of 1829-1830* (Richmond, 1854), *passim.*

89. Claude H. Hall, "Abel Parker Upshur" (unpub. diss. U Va, 1954), pp. 120-30.

Chapter Ten

A. *Bibliography in general*

Among the political and economic histories Henry Adams, *History of the United States During the Administrations of Jefferson and Madison* (9 vols., New York, 1921), Thomas P. Abernethy, *The South in the New Nation, 1789-1819* (Baton Rouge, 1961), Charles S. Sydnor, *The Development of Southern Sectionalism, 1819-1848* (Baton Rouge, 1948), and W. Edwin Hemphill, *et al, Cavalier Commonwealth: History and Government of Virginia* (New York, 1957), are generally useful. John Alden, *The First South* (Baton Rouge, 1961), considers the origins and first manifestations of sectionalism, with much attention to Virginia. Indispensable are Charles A. Beard, *Economic Origins of American Democracy* (New York, 1915) and *An Economic Interpretation of the Constitution of the United States* (New York, 1913); George Bancroft, *History of the Formation of the Constitution of the United States of America* (2 vols., New York, 1882); Jonathan Elliot, ed., *The Debates of the Several States Conventions on the Adoption of the Federal Constitution together with the Journals of the Federal Convention* (5 vols., Washington, D.C., 1836-45); Max Farrand, ed., *Records of the Federal Convention of 1787* (4 vols., New Haven, 1911); Gaillard Hunt and James B. Scott, eds., *Debates in the Federal Convention of 1787, . . . Reported by James Madison* (New York, 1920); Charles Warren, *The Making of the Constitution* (Boston, 1928); and Gilman Ostrander, *The Rights of Man in America, 1606-1861* (Columbia, Missouri, 1960), in which bibliographies, pp. 327-31, are useful.

For Virginia, Jefferson, and Republican party matters see H. B. Grigsby, *The History of the Virginia Federal Convention of 1788* (2 vols., Richmond, 1890) and *The Virginia Convention of 1829-1830* (Richmond, 1854); C. M. Wiltse, *The Jeffersonian Tradition in American Democracy* (Chapel Hill, 1955); Leonard D. White, *The Jeffersonians: A Study in Administrative History* (New York, 1951); and Noble E. Cunningham, *The Jeffersonian Republicans, 1789-1801* (Chapel Hill, 1957). For growing Virginia divergences, C. H. Ambler,

Sectionalism in Virginia from 1776 to 1861 (Chicago, 1910) and H. H. Simms, *The Rise of the Whigs in Virginia, 1824-1840* (Richmond, 1929).

For Madison materials especially pertinent here, see Irving Brant's *James Madison*—all the volumes published in Indianapolis—*The Virginia Revolutionist, 1751-1780* (1941), *The Nationalist, 1780-1787* (1948), *Father of the Constitution, 1787-1800* (1950), *Secretary of State, 1800-1809* (1953), *The President, 1809-1812* (1956), and *Commander in Chief, 1809-1836* (1961); Benjamin F. Wright, ed., *The Federalist* (Cambridge, Mass., 1961); and Douglass Adair, "The Authorship of the Disputed Federalist Papers," *WMQ* (3), I (1944), 97-122, 235-64, and "The Tenth Federalist Revisited," *WMQ* (3), VIII (1951), 48-67.

For Jefferson materials, the *Papers,* L & B, and Ford, for editions of his writings. For his thinking, Adrienne Koch, *The Philosophy of Thomas Jefferson* (New York, 1943) and *Jefferson and Madison: The Great Collaboration* (New York, 1950); Gilbert Chinard, *Thomas Jefferson, Apostle of Americanism* (Boston, 1929); J. J. Spengler, "The Political Economy of Jefferson, Madison, and Adams," *American Studies in Honor of William Kenneth Boyd* (Durham, 1940), pp. 3-59; and E. M. Sowerby, *Catalogue of the Library of Thomas Jefferson* (5 vols., Washington, D.C., 1952-59). The first two published volumes of the biography by Dumas Malone, *Jefferson the Virginian* and *Jefferson and the Rights of Man* (Boston, 1948 and 1951) should be studied.

For John Taylor, Beard's *Economic Origins* and Wiltse's *Jeffersonian Tradition* are significant in placing him in the main stream. Other necessary books are Roy F. Nichols, ed., Introduction to Taylor's *An Inquiry into the Principles and Policy of the Government of the United States* (New Haven, 1950); H. H. Simms, *Life of John Taylor: The Story of a Brilliant Leader in the Early Virginia States-Rights School* (Richmond, 1932); E. T. Mudge, *The Social Philosophy of John Taylor of Caroline* (New York, 1939); and William E. Dodd, "John Taylor, Prophet of Secession," *John P. Branch Historical Papers of Randolph-Macon College,* II (1908), Nos. 3 & 4.

For Mason, John Randolph, Monroe, Ritchie, and others see the notes.

Of the many studies of slavery and anti-slavery the following have been most useful: A.H.H.T. Catterall, ed., *Judicial Cases Concerning American Slavery and the Negro* (5 vols., Washington, D.C.,

1926); Thomas E. Drake, *The Quakers and Slavery in America* (New Haven, 1950); Dwight L. Dumond, *Antislavery: The Crusade for Freedom in America* and *A Bibliography of Antislavery in America* (Ann Arbor, 1961); Clement Eaton, *Freedom of Thought in the Old South* (Durham, 1940); Early Lee Fox, *The American Colonization Society, 1817-1840* (Baltimore, 1919); William S. Jenkins, *Pro-Slavery Thought in the Old South* (Chapel Hill, 1935); Beverley B. Munford, *Virginia's Attitude toward Slavery and Secession* (New York, 1909); and Theodore M. Whitfield, *Slavery Agitation in Virginia, 1829-1832* (Baltimore, 1930).

Among studies of American economics and political economy, many have been mentioned in the first, third, fourth, and fifth paragraphs of this bibliography for Chapter X. Others are J. R. Turner, *Ricardian Rent Theory in Early American Economics* (New York, 1921) and J. J. Spengler, "Population Doctrines in the United States," *Journal of Political Economy*, XLI (1933), 433-67, 639-72, and "Population Theory in the Ante-Bellum South," *JSH*, II (1936), 360-89. For George Tucker's theories, L. C. Helderman, "A Social Scientist of the Old South," *JSH*, II (1936), 148-74; Jessie Bernard, "George Tucker: Liberal Southern Social Scientist," *Social Forces*, XXV (1946-47), 131-45, 406-16; George J. Cady, "The Early American Reaction to the Theory of Malthus," *Journal of Political Economy*, XXXIX (1931), 601-32; and Richard H. Popkin, "George Tucker, an Early American Critic of Hume," *Journal of the History of Ideas*, XIII (1952), 370-75; and of course Robert G. McLean, *George Tucker: Moral Philosopher and Man of Letters* (Chapel Hill, 1961), including the bibliographies, pp. 235-51.

B. Notes on Chapter Ten

1. Brant, *James Madison, Father of the Constitution*, pp. 27-30, 56.
2. Beard, *Economic Origins of American Democracy* and *An Economic Interpretation of the Constitution*, *passim*; Brant, *James Madison, Father of the Constitution*, Ch. V. See also Bancroft, Farrand, Hunt and Scott, and Warren listed in the bibliography above. For bibliography, Ostrander, *The Rights of Man in America*, pp. 327-31, is most useful.
3. Wright, ed., *The Federalist*, pp. 1-86; Adair, "The Authorship of the Disputed Federalist Papers" and "The Tenth Federalist Revisited"; Brant, *James Madison, Father of the Constitution*, Ch. XIV, pp. 172-84 and *James Madison, Commander in Chief*, pp. 426-28.
4. Brant, *James Madison, Father of the Constitution*, p. 174.
5. Wright, ed., *The Federalist*, p. 15.
6. Besides those already mentioned, he also wrote 14, 18, 19, and 20.

7. *Journal,* ed. Edgar S. Maclay (New York, 1896), p. 290. The entry is dated June 12, 1790. Maclay refers, of course, to Lee's motion for a declaration of independence in the Continental Congress. For Lee, see also Jackson Turner Main, *The Antifederalists: Critics of the Constitution, 1781-1788* (Chapel Hill, 1961), *passim,* esp. p. 177, where Lee is classified as a moderate.

8. Grigsby, *The History of the Virginia Federal Convention.* In the five volumes of Elliot, ed., *Debates in the Several State Conventions . . . Together with the Journal of the Federal Convention,* 663 pages of the third volume are concerned with "The Virginia Convention." Henry's speeches occupy about one-fourth of the whole.

9. Adams, *History of the United States,* I, 139.

10. Helen Hill, *George Mason, Constitutionalist* (Cambridge, Mass., 1838), pp. 215-16; Robert A. Rutland, *George Mason, Reluctant Statesman* (Williamsburg, 1961), pp. 81-110.

11. Hill, *George Mason,* pp. 253-55.

12. *DAB.*

13. David J. Mays, *Edmund Pendleton, 1721-1803* (2 vols., Cambridge, Mass., 1952), II, 333-36.

14. *Ibid.,* II, 334.

15. E. Griffith Dodson, *Speakers and Clerks of the Virginia House of Delegates, 1776-1955* (Richmond, 1956) pp. 19, 140; Noble E. Cunningham, "John Beckley, an Early American Party Manager," *WMQ* (3), XIII (1956), 40-52, and *The Jeffersonian Republicans, 1789-1801, passim*; Philip Marsh, "John Beckley, Mystery Man of the Early Jeffersonians," *PMHB,* LXXII (1948), 54-69; and Gloria Jahoda, "The Bickleys of Virginia," *VHMB,* LXVI (1958), 473-76.

16. Philip Marsh, "American Essays, 1770-1805" (Mimeographed, Austin, 1949), p. 3.

17. Cunningham, "John Beckley, Party Manager," pp. 44-45.

18. For convenient texts of this and other speeches, see Saul K. Padover, ed., *The Complete Jefferson* (New York, 1943). "The First Inaugural" appears on pp. 384-407.

19. Koch, *The Philosophy of Thomas Jefferson, passim.*

20. Chinard, *Thomas Jefferson, Apostle of Americanism, passim.*

21. Wiltse, *The Jeffersonian Tradition in American Democracy,* and White, *The Jeffersonians: A Study in Administrative History, passim.*

22. Cunningham, *The Jeffersonian Republicans,* and Koch, *The Philosophy of Thomas Jefferson, passim.*

23. Wiltse, *The Jeffersonian Tradition,* p. 88. See also Sowerby, *Catalogue of the Library of Thomas Jefferson,* for his reading in the political and economic thinkers.

24. E.g., Koch, *The Philosophy of Thomas Jefferson*; Wiltse, *The Jeffersonian Tradition,* and various biographies by Chinard, Malone, etc., and other studies by Chinard and others.

25. E.g., introduction to Saul K. Padover, ed., *The Complete Madison* (New York, 1953); Brant, the six volumes of his *James Madison,* especially the summaries in VI; and Koch, *Jefferson and Madison: The Great Collaboration.*

26. Lyman H. Butterfield, "Elder John Leland, Jeffersonian Itinerant," *PAAS,* LXII (1952), 155-242; and W. M. Gewehr, *The Great Awakening in Virginia, 1746-1790* (Durham, 1930), *passim.*

27. *Writings of James Monroe,* ed., S. M. Hamilton (7 vols., New York, 1898-1903), I, 347-97.

28. Russell Kirk, *Randolph of Roanoke: A Study in Conservative Thought* (Chicago, 1951), pp. 31-33, etc.

29. *Ibid.,* pp. 86, 156.

30. See Adams, *History,* IX, 194-95; Beard, *Economic Origins,* pp. 77-80, 165-97; Wiltse, *The Jeffersonian Tradition,* pp. 218-21; W. E. Dodd, "John Taylor, Prophet of Secession,"; Simms, *Life of John Taylor*; Mudge, *The Social Philosophy of John Taylor*; and Roy F. Nichols, ed., Introduction to *An Inquiry.*

31. Mudge, *The Social Philosophy of John Taylor,* p. 5.

32. *Ibid.,* p. 6.

33. *Ibid.,* p. 11.

34. *Ibid.,* pp. 4-5.

35. P. 322.

36. Nichols, ed., *An Inquiry,* p. 29.

37. Simms, *Life of John Taylor,* p. 179.

38. *Ibid.,* p. 191.

39. Nichols, ed., *An Inquiry,* p. 23.

40. *Ibid.,* p. 27.

41. Quoted in Simms, *Life of John Taylor,* p. 197 from *Thirty Years' View,* I, 45.

42. Political Pamphlets, No. 95, LC.

43. Alden, *The First South, passim.*

44. N. P. Trist Papers, LC. Cf. also Brant, *James Madison, Commander in Chief,* pp. 468-80.

45. See his letter to Henry Tazewell, January 5, 1797, Tazewell Papers, Va St Lib.

46. Letterbook "T", Va HS.

47. See Koch, *Jefferson and Madison, passim.*

48. Brant, *James Madison, Father of the Constitution,* p. 86, and *James Madison, Commander in Chief,* pp. 468-500.

49. June 27, 1821, quoted in Bernard Mayo, *Jefferson Himself* (Boston, 1942), p. 333.

50. December 26, 1825, *ibid.,* p. 339.

51. Charles H. Ambler, *Thomas Ritchie: A Study in Virginia Politics* (Richmond, 1913), p. 22.

52. DAB.

53. London, 1764. See Jenkins, *Pro-Slavery Thought in the Old South,* p. 40.

54. Eaton, *Freedom of Thought in the Old South,* p. 19.

55. Munford, *Virginia's Attitude toward Slavery and Secession.*

56. *Ibid.,* p. 30. See also Dumond, *Antislavery: The Crusade for Freedom in America,* pp. 27-40.

57. Munford, *Virginia Attitude,* pp. 30-34.

58. March, 1790, James Meacham Journals, Duke.

59. Lexington, [Ky?].

60. There are Fredericksburg and Norfolk editions of that year.

61. Published in Philadelphia. See W. H. Foote, *Sketches of Virginia, Historical and Biographical* (2nd ser., Philadelphia, 1855), pp. 360-63.

62. Foote, *Sketches,* pp. 446-48.

63. Drake, *The Quakers and Slavery in America,* pp. 48-83. See also the letters between London and Virginia Yearly Meetings for 1805, 1807, 1827, in Brock Collection, Society of Friends, Box 15, HEH.

64. Drake, *The Quakers and Slavery,* p. 83.

65. June 6, 1791, James Madison Papers, LC.

66. Philadelphia, Mathew Carey, publisher. For some discussion of this pamphlet, see Dumond, *Antislavery,* pp. 77-79.

67. So G. K. Taylor wrote Tucker, December 2, 1796. In Jenkins, *Pro-Slavery Thought,* p. 53.

68. Munford, *Virginia's Attitude,* pp. 82-85.

69. Hill, *George Mason,* pp. 216-17.

70. Munford, *Virginia's Attitude, passim*; Catterall, *Judicial Cases Concerning American Slavery and the Negro,* I, etc.

71. Munford, pp. 104 ff.

72. See Letters of Benjamin Dawson to Robert Carter, September 7, 1793 (Va HS) concerning lots to be laid out for the recently liberated slaves. They were to be given, with three persons to a lot.

73. Catteral, *Judicial Cases,* I, 317; quoted also in Eaton, *Freedom of Thought.*

74. William C. Bruce, *John Randolph of Roanoke* (2 vols., New York, 1922), II, 357.

75. Munford, *Virginia's Attitude,* pp. 110-13. For Randolph's warm affection for his slaves, see *Jeffersonian America: Notes on the United States . . . by Sir Augustus John Foster,* ed., Richard B. Davis (San Marino, 1954), pp. 165, 307, and Foster's "Journal," April 18 and May 22, 1812, Foster Papers, LC.

76. Bruce, *Randolph,* II, 244.

77. Mudge, *Social Philosophy of John Taylor,* pp. 205 ff.

78. Whitfield, *Slavery Agitation in Virginia, 1829-1832, passim.*

79. *Ibid.,* p. 94.

80. Munford, *Virginia's Attitude,* pp. 60-63.

81. Hemphill, *et al, Cavalier Commonwealth,* p. 221.

82. Munford, *Virginia's Attitude,* pp. 67-74, and *DAB.*

83. Munford, *Virginia's Attitude,* p. 68n.

84. *Ibid.,* pp. 60-68; Fox, *The American Colonization Society, 1817-1840.*

85. Fox, *Colonization Society,* pp. 50-51.

86. *Ibid.,* p. 61.

87. *Ibid.,* pp. 11-13.

88. Georgetown, originally published in the *Enquirer.*

89. Abernethy, *The South in the New Nation,* p. 308.

90. See Hemphill, *et al, Cavalier Commonwealth,* p. 206, and Sydnor, *The Development of Southern Sectionalism,* pp. 120-22.

91. See also Gilmer's letter to Dabney Carr, January 5, 1819 [i.e., 1820] (Va St Lib), in which he identifies himself and Tucker and refers to George Hay as "The American" who had also written on the subject.

92. Jay B. Hubbell, in *The South in American Literature* (Durham, 1954), p. 244n, says he saw the pamphlet in the Charleston Library Society.

93. *Niles' Weekly Register,* XVIII ([VI, n.s.,] March to September, 1820), 453-58; Speech of Mr. Tucker of Virginia on the Restriction of Slavery in Virginia (Washington, D.C., 1820).

94. McLean, *George Tucker: Moral Philosopher and Man of Letters,* pp. 42-44.

95. Hemphill, *et al, Cavalier Commonwealth,* pp. 193 ff.

96. Abernethy, *The South in the New Nation,* pp. 304-5.

97. Sydnor, *Development of Southern Sectionalism,* p. 142.

98. *Ibid.,* p. 146.

99. *Ibid.,* p. 148.

100. Padover, ed., *The Complete Madison,* pp. 272-73. In 1829 appeared Madison's *Letters on the Constitutionality and Policy of Duties for the Protection and Encouragement of Domestic Manufactures.*

101. Simms, *Rise of the Whigs in Virginia,* p. 39.

102. April 10, 1824, LC.

103. Richmond.

104. E.g., see *DAB.*

105. P. 195.

106. See his letter to John Randolph of Roanoke, September 30, 18[illegible], LC.

107. Unpublished, Archives, Colonial Williamsburg.

108. F. F. Wayland, *Andrew Stevenson, Democrat and Diplomat* (Philadelphia, 1949), pp. 173 ff.

109. This discussion of Jefferson and Madison is heavily indebted to Spengler, "The Political Economy of Jefferson, Madison, and Adams," pp. 3-59. See also Brant, *James Madison, Commander in Chief, passim.*

110. Georgetown. It was not published in France until 1823.

111. Spengler, "Political Economy of Jefferson, Madison, and Adams," p. 7.

112. *Ibid.*, p. 20-23.

113. *Ibid.*, p. 22.

114. For Tucker's theories, see Spengler, "Population Doctrines in the United States," pp. 433-67, 639-72; L. C. Helderman, "A Social Scientist of the Old South," pp. 148-74; Turner, *Ricardian Rent Theory*; and McLean, *George Tucker*, pp. 107-11; 152-53, etc.

115. "On Density of Population," *Port Folio*, 3rd. ser., VI (1815), 164-75 or "On the Theory of Malthus," *Essays* (Georgetown, 1822), pp. 305-36. Tucker also satirized Malthus in *A Voyage to the Moon* (1827).

116. *Essays*, p. 78.

117. *Essays*, p. 81-82. See also Helderman, "A Social Scientist of the Old South," p. 158.

118. *The Law of Wages, Profits, and Rent Investigated* (Philadelphia).

119. McLean, *George Tucker*, p. 210.

120. Spengler, "Population Doctrines," p. 650.

121. In 1837 in *The Law of Wages, Profits, and Rents* and earlier in 1829 in the *Virginia Literary Museum* (II, No. 18 [October 15, 1829], 273-76) essay on "Political Economy: Ricardo, Theory of Profits."

122. Turner, *Ricardian Rent Theory*, p. 102.

123. Spengler, "Population Doctrines," *passim.*

124. Spengler, "The Political Economy of Jefferson, Madison, and Adams," pp. 25-28.

125. *Ibid.*, p. 31.

126. Printed first in 1815 in the *Port Folio*, XIII, 416-28.

127. Boston.

128. Helderman, "A Social Scientist of the Old South," p. 164; McLean, *George Tucker*, p. 37.

129. McLean, *George Tucker*, p. 37.

130. See bibliography at beginning of this chapter for these and other titles.

131. Simms, *The Rise of the Whigs in Virginia, passim.*

132. Ambler, *Sectionalism in Virginia*, pp. 100-3; D. R. Anderson, *William Branch Giles* (Menasha, Wisc., 1914), pp. 201-13; Abernethy, *The South in the New Nation*, pp. 434-35; *Letters on the Richmond Party* (Richmond, 1823). The *Letters*, an attack on the group, was originally published in the *Washington Republican*. See also Simms, *Rise of the Whigs in Virginia*, p. 22.

133. *Letters*, p. 1.

134. Harry Ammon, "The Richmond Junto, 1800-1824," *VMHB*, LXI (1953), 395-418.

135. Va HS.

136. Simms, *Rise of the Whigs in Virginia*, p. 23.

137. Brant, *James Madison, Commander in Chief*, p. 441, points out that Jefferson and Madison long foreshadowed Monroe in proposing such a doctrine.

138. Ambler, *Sectionalism in Virginia*, pp. 149-50.

INDEX

This index is designed to indicate as far as space will permit, the diversity in kind and in location of the elements which characterized intellectual life in Jefferson's Virginia. Cities, towns, and counties have been included to indicate diversity in space within the territory, though subject entries under the headings have had to be kept to a minimum. Authors read or owned have been listed, though in most instances titles have had to be omitted. Classical authors, with the most notable as exceptions, have had to be included under the entry "Classics." The names of Virginians who contributed to one or more phases of intellectual life also appear, though except in the most significant instances without the details of their activities. Themes and factors have been analyzed in as much detail as seems feasible.

Italicized numbers in a series of page numbers indicate the most pertinent or comprehensive discussion of author, man, or theme.